A CHILD'S WORLD
INFANCY THROUGH ADOLESCENCE

Diane E. Papalia
UNIVERSITY OF WISCONSIN

Sally Wendkos Olds

McGraw-Hill Book Company

NEW YORK   ST. LOUIS   SAN FRANCISCO   AUCKLAND   DÜSSELDORF
JOHANNESBURG   KUALA LUMPUR   LONDON   MEXICO   MONTREAL   NEW DELHI
PANAMA   PARIS   SÃO PAULO   SINGAPORE   SYDNEY   TOKYO   TORONTO

To our parents,
Madeline and Edward Papalia
and
Leah and Samuel Wendkos,
for their unfailing love,
nurturance, and confidence in us,
and
for their abiding conviction
that childhood is a wondrous time of life.

A CHILD'S WORLD: INFANCY THROUGH ADOLESCENCE

This book was set in Palatino by Black Dot, Inc.
The editors were Robert A. Fry,
Robert Weber, and James R. Belser;
the designer was J. E. O'Connor;
the production supervisor was Leroy A. Young.
The photo editor was Inge King,
the drawings were done by Eric G. Hieber Associates Inc.
Cover illustration by Thomas Noonan.
Von Hoffmann Press, Inc., was printer and binder.

1 2 3 4 5 6 7 8 9 0 V H V H 7 9 8 7 6 5

A CHILD'S WORLD: INFANCY THROUGH ADOLESCENCE

Library of Congress Cataloging in Publication Data

Papalia, Diane E.
    A child's world.

    Bibliography: p.
    Includes index.
    1. Child study. 2. Children—Management. I. Olds,
Sally Wendkos, joint author. II. Title.
HQ772.P23   301.43'1   74-31496
ISBN 0-07-048450-3

CONTENTS

About
A CHILD'S WORLD

How children develop and why people turn out as they do should intrigue us more than any study we have turned to. We've all been there. We were all conceived the same way, and we all started to grow within a mother's body. We were all influenced by our early development. What more basic subject is there than ourselves? Furthermore, many of us will have an intimate, direct interest in children's development as we ourselves become parents, quite aside from the professional interest we may have in the children we teach, examine, interview, test, heal, or otherwise come to know.

And yet—despite our built-in interest—many books present child development as a dry and weighty topic, encumbered by reams of research, entangled in abstract theories, expounded in unintelligible jargon, remote from real people and real life. Too many teachers and writers have made a task of turning an exciting topic into one that is dull and dreary. We think children are exciting, and we hope that this book makes you feel the same.

In these pages we show how, as William Wordsworth said, "the child is father to the man" (or woman), and how our earliest years—and even the period before birth—determine what kind of adults we will be. Within the last fifty years or so, children have become fit subjects for scientific study. Research is beginning to catch up with our curiosity about why we are the way we are. But what does all the research really mean? How do surveys and measurements and laboratory experiments help us know ourselves? We try to translate empirical research findings and theoretical opinions into terms that are relevant to real children today.

Who are these real children? They are not "typical" children, who talk at one normal age, walk at another, and read at still another arbitrarily designated average point in time. Children, like people everywhere, have infinite variety. Real children exhibit a wide range of normality in everything they do, from learning how to control elimination to learning how to multiply 4 times 5. Furthermore, real children grow up in many different worlds—in middle-class suburban homes, in urban slums, on remote farms. They are raised by fathers alone or mothers alone or both together. They are raised on communes and kibbutzim, in wealth and in poverty, with mothers working at home, with mothers working at factories. They are children of love, of despair, of contentment, of loneliness. And whatever world they discover, however they are raised, their development is affected.

With this book, we hope to make you understand children better. We hope, too, that you will come to grasp both current and historical approaches to research and theory, normal prenatal development and the factors that influence it, and the sequence and timing of physical, mental, and personality development throughout the years of childhood. Finally, we hope you'll understand what, in your background, helped make you the person you are today, and how we can all work to improve every child's world, even those unborn.

Acknowledgments

We would like to express our gratitude to several friends and colleagues whose help with this book was inestimable. To Mark A. Stewart, M.D., Ida P. Haller Professor of Child Psychiatry at the University of Iowa College of Medicine, and to Dr. Lynn Ourth, Ph.D., Professor of Psychology at the University of Tennessee at Chattanooga, for the many valuable suggestions that they made after painstakingly reading an early draft of the manuscript. To Jonathan Finlay, M.B., Ch.B., pediatric house physician at Birmingham Children's Hospital in Birmingham, England, for his help on the sections on heredity and prenatal development. To Gene Cranston Anderson, Ph.D., Associate Professor of Nursing at the Chicago Circle Campus of the University of Illinois, for her help in the section on infancy. To Michael Warner, M.S.S.W., for his assistance in the enormous job of trying to keep up with the burgeoning research in child development. To Douglas Walker, M.S., for his help on the annotated bibliography. To Jane Weier for typing—and typing—and typing. We know the book is better for all their help, but we accept any shortcomings in it as ours alone.

Diane E. Papalia
Sally Wendkos Olds

INTRODUCTION
IN WHICH WE MEET VICKY AND DISCUSS
WHY AND HOW TO STUDY ALL CHILDREN

Development is not continuous like a hill; rather, it is episodic like a flight of stairs.
(Allport, 1964)

As a college student, you are far enough from childhood to view it with perspective. And yet you are close enough to it—as we all are throughout our lives—so that certain incidents and emotions of those years remain as clear today as they were when you first experienced them. What made you the kind of child you were—and the kind of adult you are now? The answer to this question is what we hope to find through the study of child development. When Alexander Pope said, "The proper study of mankind is man," he summed up the reasons for the increasing interest being paid to the study of human development.

By examining how children develop, from the moment of conception through the early adolescent years, we learn more about ourselves and about our fellow inhabitants on this planet. Only by knowing who we are and how we became this way can we hope to create a better world. Only by learning how children respond to influences around them can we offer them a better education, a better home environment, and a better start in life. They, then, will be better equipped to fulfill their individual potential, and to help society fulfill its potential.

What Is Development and Why Should We Study It?

The study of child development focuses on the *quantitative* and *qualitative* ways children change over time. *Quantitative* change is fairly straightforward and relatively easy to measure. A child's growth in height and weight is a quantitative change. So are the expansion of vocabulary, the proliferation of physical skills, the number of relationships with other people, and so forth. The study of *qualitative* change is more complex, involving, as it does, "leaps" in functioning—those changes in kind that distinguish an infant from a toddler or a talking child from a nonverbal baby, that trace the growth of intelligence, creativity, sociability, morality. But even these leaps result from a series of small steps. No child wakes up on his sixth birthday suddenly thinking and acting vastly differently from the day before. Quantitatively and qualitatively, development is a continuous, irreversible, and complex process.

The modern science of development is concerned primarily with behavioral changes—things we can see. We emphasize aspects of change that are readily observable in an effort to apply rigorous scientific criteria to our study of the growing child. Thus we measure and chart physical growth. We follow the progress of emotional expression. We study the development of language from the infant's artless babbling to more mature, grammatically correct speech. The field of child development has itself developed. Whereas its focus was once simply on recording observable behaviors and deriving age norms, developmentalists today try to explain *why* certain behaviors occur.

The study of child development has immediate and practical benefits, too. We learn how an average child behaves so that we can gauge how a particular child compares with the norm. Parents of a child who seems backward in development may be reassured that he falls within the limits of normality. Or they may be advised on how to help overcome any deficiencies. Parents of a perpetual truant may receive sound psychological advice that enables them to divert her from a path that leads to trouble. Educators can better plan classroom programs when they understand how children of any given age learn best. But aside from such practical applications of our knowledge of children, the study of childhood helps us understand all human beings.

Meet Vicky

This book is about all children, and it is also about each child. In our study of development, we are interested in patterns that govern the development of all individuals of the species *Homo sapiens*. But since each member of the species is unique, we want to know what factors make one person turn out differently from another.

To personalize some of the statements we will be making here, we have created *Vicky*. Vicky is Everychild. And she is no child. A creature drawn

(James R. Smith)

No child grows up in a vacuum: We must consider socioeconomic status, ethnic background, race, and sex.

from a composite of information culled from research papers and from the skilled observation of professionals, Vicky does not exist. On these pages, she is a typical, or an ideal, child at whatever stage of development we are discussing. But off these pages, there is no child exactly like her.

Although Vicky ideally represents all children—boys and girls, American and foreign, black and white, Jewish and gentile—in many cases she seems to represent the middle-class American child who has been raised in an intact home and been given good care, good nutrition, and a public education. By and large, these are the children who populate research studies. Yet even among this limited group of children, there is a wide range of differences.

No child grows up in a vacuum. When we talk about normal development for a child in favored circumstances, we cannot generalize our conclusions to a child who was born to a malnourished teenager, is raised in a rural shack, does not know his father, does not get enough to eat, fends for himself much of the time, is rarely spoken to at any length, and receives a deficient education. This child is growing up in a world light-years away from that of the "typical" child. What we say about one often does not apply to the other.

Many factors influence human growth and development. These elements are an integral part of the various subcultures all children belong to—their family's socioeconomic status, their ethnic background, their race, their sex. Not to know these facts about a child leaves large gaps in our understanding of that child and limits our means to help her. Unfortunately, the data on which many developmentalists base conclusions cannot always be so complete as is wanted. As a result, our information is not so precise as it should be. And our conclusions are not always so valid.

THE "GESTALT" OF VICKY

Vicky, as she stands before us, eyes unblinking, thumb in mouth, is a whole child. We cannot dissect her into a physical creature, an intellectual person, and an emotional self. Everything about her affects everything else about her, until it is virtually impossible to separate the various strands of the child Vicky.

Her physical self, for example, helps to determine both her personality and her intellect. If Vicky is in good health, of normal physical stature, and attractive in appearance (by the standards of her culture), her parents and other significant persons in her life will react to her in certain ways right from birth. The degree to which she is accepted, initially perhaps because of her physical characteristics, helps to determine the degree of her self-confidence and self-esteem. If her parents are disappointed in her looks or in the slowness of her physical development, their feelings may affect her personality adversely. As she grows taller and stronger, as she develops the skills that will enable her to master her environment, she will develop good feelings about herself, even though they may be tempered to some degree by the frustrations she experiences when on the threshold of some new ability. Thus the combination of her physical self and capabilities, plus the way others react to them, has strong effects on her personality. Abnormal physical development has many emotional ramifications.

Vicky the physical person also affects Vicky the intellectual person, since good physical health is often important for normal intellectual development. Malnutrition can impede brain development, and certain physical disabilities, like phenylketonuria (PKU) and Down's syndrome (mongolism), impede mental processes as much or more than they affect physical functioning.

Vicky's intellectual capabilities are closely related to both the motor and the emotional aspects of her being. In infancy, in fact, virtually the only way to measure an individual's intelligence is through motor development. If Vicky holds her head up, reaches for a toy, and pulls herself to a sitting position at certain ages, we can be assured that she is probably normal mentally as well as physically. Slowness in these activities is often the first sign of mental retardation.

And the social and emotional aspects of Vicky's personality affect both the physical and the intellectual aspects of her functioning. Emotional deprivation in infancy, for example, can have devastating effects on a child's mental and motor development, as well as on his personality.

Throughout our discussion of the ways children develop, we will be separately considering their physical, intellectual, and personality development. In our discussion of personality, we will actually be grouping together a variety of aspects involving *interpersonal interaction.* Our emotions affect our personalities, which in turn affect the way we act socially. Thus these interpersonal aspects of development tell us a great deal about how and why a certain child reacts a certain way in certain situations involving other people.

But while we carve Vicky into three beings for convenience and ease of discussion, we always have to bear in mind that these aspects of her life are all inextricably intertwined. We do not know any child until we know her or him in all spheres of functioning.

VICKY'S AGE STAGES

We have made another arbitrary division of Vicky. Her development, from birth till adulthood, is a gradual, continuous process. No sharp demarcations set her infancy off from her early childhood, or her childhood from her adolescence. Very often she is in one stage in one part of her development and in another stage in another part. For example, Vicky may have begun to menstruate (an activity which marks her physical transition from childhood to puberty) before she has outgrown many of her childish feelings and thoughts.

The individual differences among children are so great that they enter and leave these age stages at different times of life. Annie, at two, may have already achieved physical developmental milestones that Brian will not reach for another year. Yet Brian may be more advanced socially or intellectually. For example, a child who spends most of his days with loving, nurturant, stimulating parents and little time with children his own age is likely to have a fluent command of language, but little idea of how to approach, play with, and not be overwhelmed by another child. Vicky does not show these contradictory, individual tendencies. She is, by and large, a reflection of the average child as revealed by the scientific literature.

Vicky is an abstraction. But real children are not abstract. They are living, laughing, crawling, crying, shouting, shrieking, jumping, whining, skipping, reaching, thumb-sucking, nose-picking, diaper-wetting, tantrum-throwing, question-asking human beings. We have tried to help you see children more as they really are by relating the concepts we discuss to Vicky.

You can personalize these findings much more meaningfully if you look with new eyes at the children in your own life. Observe your little brothers and sisters, your cousins, your neighbors, even the youngster who sits across from you on the bus one afternoon. Talk to them. And really listen to what they have to say. Try to relate your firsthand observations to the more general points we make here, and you will know more about children than you could possibly absorb from reading alone.

Developmental Principles and Issues

Certain principles apply to the totality of developmental change and thus serve as useful guidelines for interpreting the raw information about development.

INDIVIDUAL DIFFERENCES IN DEVELOPMENT

Although all children go through developmental stages in the same sequence and according to the same general chronology, wide ranges in normal development allow for a great deal of individual difference. Throughout this book, we talk about *average* ages for the occurrence of certain behaviors: the first smile, the first word, the first step. In all cases, these ages are *only* averages. As we have said, Vicky as the average child is in reality *no* child, because no child hews to the average rate of development in every aspect of growth. The normal range of behavior includes a wide spectrum of individual differences—with respect to measures of height and weight, walking or talking, understanding various ideas, and so forth. Therefore, *all* the average ages we give should be regarded as flexible. Only when a child's deviation from these norms is extreme is there cause for considering her or him exceptionally advanced or retarded. The important

Although all children go through developmental stages in the same sequence and according to the same general chronology, wide ranges in normal development allow for a great deal of individual difference.

(Peter Arnold)

point to remember is that all children go through the same general sequence of events, even though the timing varies greatly among them.

CRITICAL PERIODS IN DEVELOPMENT

If a woman undergoes irradiation, ingests certain drugs, or contracts certain diseases at specific times during the first three months of pregnancy, her unborn baby will show specific effects. The amount and kind of damage to the fetus will vary according to the particular insult and to its timing. Experiments have shown that pregnant mice that have received x-rays 7 or 8 days after conception are likely to have pups with brain hernia, whereas those that are irradiated $9^{1}/_{2}$ days after conception are more likely to bear pups with spina bifida, a disease of the nervous system (Russell & Russell, 1952). Similar mechanisms operate in humans.

A *critical period* in development is a period of time when an event will have its greatest impact. The same event—such as radiation—would not have as much of an influence if it took place at a different time in development.

This theory of critical periods has been incorporated into a number of theories regarding various aspects of human behavior, including intelligence and emotional attachment between babies and their mothers.

The psychoanalysts, especially, have embraced the concept of critical periods. Sigmund Freud maintained that certain experiences undergone by the baby or young child in the *oral*, *anal*, and *phallic* periods could set an individual's personality for life (see Chapter 6). And Erik Erikson proposed eight ages, each of which constitutes a critical period for social and emotional development: infancy for trust, toddlerhood for autonomy, the preschool years for industry, adolescence for identity, and so forth.

Although some of the evidence for critical periods of development is incontrovertible (such as that involving the physical development of the fetus), some of the other theories, while persuasive, still need to be followed further, to be backed up by more research.

DEVELOPMENT IS ORDERLY, NOT RANDOM

There is nothing haphazard about development; it follows a well-defined path.

It always proceeds from the simple to the complex. In the development of language, for example, babies go from crying to babbling, then to words, and finally to more and more complicated sentences.

It proceeds from the general to the specific. Emotions begin as a global state of excitement in the newborn babe and gradually differentiate into a wide repertoire of feelings that include love, hate, fear, anger, jealousy, and so forth.

Physical development follows the rules of cephalocaudal (head-to-toe) *development*, by which the upper parts of the body develop earlier than the lower, and *proximodistal* (near-to-far) *development*, by which the central parts of the body develop before the extremities. (Cephalocaudal and proximodistal development will be discussed more fully in Chapter 4.)

Cognitive development also proceeds along orderly lines. Jean Piaget describes the stages of sensorimotor, preoperational, concrete operational, and formal levels of thought (see Chapter 5).

Although the precise timing of all these facets of development varies for each child, their sequence is invariant in conformity with the overall principles involved.

DIFFERENT TYPES OF DEVELOPMENT ARE IMPORTANT AT DIFFERENT TIMES IN LIFE

Motor and physical development is most rapid in infancy; language develops most quickly during the preschool years; the development of logical thinking and of sociability are most rapid during the elementary school years; and the reproductive system develops dramatically in adolescence. Children seem to concentrate intensely at any stage on those facets of development that are currently emerging. They may even seem to regress in earlier abilities.

The History of Childhood

Our culture is so child-oriented that it comes as somewhat of a shock to recognize that childhood as we know it is a very recent concept. For much of history, the child was considered a miniature adult, "merely a smaller, weaker, more stupid version of the adult human being. As the child grew older, he thereby became larger, stronger, and brighter, revealing adult characteristics which had really been there all the time [Looft, 1971, p. 7]." In the ancient societies of Greece and Rome, children were considered future citizens and, as such, were trained for their adult roles. Their own natures as children were not even thought of.

In the Bible, we see two conflicting views of children. The early sages who wrote the Old Testament saw children as deprived, wicked creatures, conceived in original sin. Such inherently evil beings needed strong controls to keep them from getting worse. The more optimistic writers of the New Testament took the view that children are inherently innocent and good and that they will grow up just fine if only the environment does not interfere with the normal course of growth.

In ancient times, attitudes toward children often bordered on the callous:

As late as the seventeenth century, in *Le Caquet de l'accouchée*, we have a neighbour, standing at the bedside of a woman who has just given birth, the mother of five "little brats," and calming her fears with these words: "Before they are old enough to bother you, you will have lost half of them, or perhaps all of them'' [Aries, 1962, p. 38].

While this seems heartless and, as Aries says, a "strange consolation," the neighbor's remark demonstrates the fragility of childhood up to the recent past. So many children died in infancy and childhood that it was unusual for the parents of a large family to raise all their children to adulthood. People expected to have a great number of children so that they could end up with a few. Since some were bound to die in childhood, parents tried—although they probably did not always succeed—to remain detached for a while, to spare themselves the great grief of a possible eventual loss. As a result, "[t]he infant who was too fragile as yet to take part in the life of adults simply 'did not count' [Aries, 1962, p. 128].''

Adults did not view children as qualitatively different from themselves, or as having any special needs, or as making any significant contributions to their own development. It was only natural, then, that adults should impose adult standards for children's behavior. This inability to see the child as a different kind of person from the adult is reflected in art through the ages. Children did not appear in artistic depictions until about the twelfth century. And even then, they were not so much children as shrunken adults. The

(The Metropolitan Museum of Art, Gift of J. P. Morgan, 1917)

Until about the seventeenth century, children were viewed as little adults.

only art work of the ancient world that depicted children at all realistically or even idealistically was that of the Greeks. Then childhood disappeared as an artistic theme and became apparently "a period of transition which passed quickly and which was just as quickly forgotten [Aries, 1962, p. 34]."

The failure to depict children as children persisted until the thirteenth century, when a few kinds of children appeared in art works who actually looked like real children. They are portrayed as pubescent angels, as the Infant Jesus, and as the *putto*, the naked child. These chubby little *putti* appeared at the end of the fourteenth century and soon became enormously popular as an ornamental motif. Says Aries (1962):

> The taste for child nudity was obviously linked with the general taste for classical nudity . . . but it lasted much longer and it affected the whole of ornamental art: witness Versailles or the ceiling of the Villa Borghese in Rome. The taste for the *putto* corresponded to something far deeper than the taste for classical nudity, something which can be ascribed only to a broad surge of interest in childhood [p. 44].

Nude babies have been popular throughout the twentieth century, too, as can be seen in a perusal of the old family album, which is sure to turn up some carefully posed pictures of naked infants lying on a bearskin rug, or in a glance at modern television and magazine advertisements, which sell a variety of products by showing a fetchingly bare-bottomed baby.

Even as the *putti* were peering out from one portrait or sculpture after another, they were never real children. In the fifteenth and sixteenth centuries, real children were very much a part of adult society.

> First, children mingled with adults in everyday life, and any gathering for the purpose of work, relaxation, or sport brought together both children and adults; secondly painters were particularly fond of depicting childhood for its graceful or picturesque qualities . . . and they delighted in stressing the presence of a child in a group or a crowd. Of these two ideas one now strikes us as out of date, for today, as also towards the end of the nineteenth century, we tend to separate the world of children from that of adults; the other foreshadows the modern idea of childhood [Aries, 1962, pp. 37–38].

In the seventeenth century a new concept of childhood appeared. Adults began to notice the sweet, simple, and amusing nature of children. Parents still dared not expect all their children to live because the rates of infant mortality continued to be high. But they did dare to love and appreciate them as individuals. They commissioned portraits of their children or gave them a place of honor in the family portrait. They began to dress them differently, instead of just cutting adult-styled garments in small sizes. And in their writings, they confessed to the joys they received from playing with little children. Some moralists and pedagogues began to accuse parents of "coddling" and spoiling their children.

This reaction against "coddling" showed, according to Aries (1962, p. 132), "the beginning of a serious and realistic concept of childhood." Not content to accept the levity of childhood, those who were more concerned with understanding the reasoning and behavior of children were the forerunners of present-day psychologists, educators, and physicians.

By the eighteenth century, the love of children, as expressed by "coddling," and the concern for their moral development were firmly ensconced within the family, as opposed to sources from outside the family, such as churchmen and moralists. From this point on, an interest in raising healthy, virtuous, and successful children was to be a prime concern of parents and a topic that would, through the years, cover enough pages of text to blanket the earth.

Methods for Studying Children

How do we know what children are like at various stages of development? Developmentalists draw on a variety of research approaches that allow us to

(The Metropolitan Museum of Art, Bequest of Maria DeWitt Jesup, from the collection of her husband, Morris K. Jesup, 1915)

In the seventeenth century a new concept of childhood appeared: Adults began to notice the sweet, simple, amusing nature of children.

observe children either as they go about their daily lives or as they act in planned experimental situations. Researchers are constantly coming up with new techniques for finding out about children and recording their findings.

NATURALISTIC STUDIES

These studies depend on observation, pure and simple. Researchers look at children in their natural habitats, making no effort to alter behavior through experimental manipulation. Naturalistic studies generally provide us with *normative* information, or information about the average times for various behavior to occur among normal children. These data may be based on averages of groups of people or may be derived from individual case histories.

Baby Biographies

Our earliest information about infant development comes from journals kept to record the progress of a single baby. The first such diary that we know about is that of Héroard, who in 1601 began to keep such a record on the heir of France, the child of Henry IV, who was born in that year. Almost

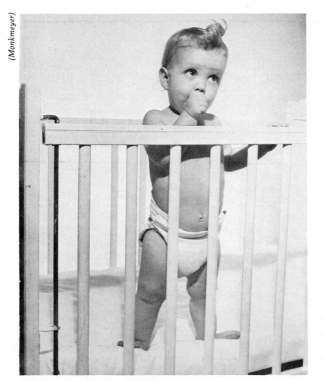

(Monkmeyer)

Our earliest information about infant development comes from journals kept to record the progress of a single baby.

two centuries later, in 1787 in Germany, Dietrich Tiedemann published his observations of the first 2½ years of his son's sensory, motor, language, and intellectual development. His work, laced with his own comments, included passages like this one:

> On the day after his birth, when the nurse placed her finger in the boy's mouth, he sucked at it, but not continuously, only in a smacking fashion. When, however, a sweet, tied in a cloth, was placed in his mouth, he sucked continuously; a proof, I think, that sucking is not instinctive, but acquired [Murchison & Langer, 1927, p. 206].

When the great teacher of evolution Charles Darwin saw fit in 1877 to publish his notes on his son's early development and to put forth the view that we could understand the descent of our species better by carefully studying infants and children, these baby biographies gained scientific respectability. About thirty were published over the next thirty years (Dennis, 1936). As recently as the twentieth century, Jean Piaget based his highly original theories about the ways children learn about space, time, and the permanence of objects on his meticulous, day-by-day observations of his own three children, Laurent, Jacqueline, and Lucienne (Piaget, 1952).

Baby biographies give us much useful, in-depth information, especially on normative development. They allow us to glimpse a single child's personality, as we could in no other way, as is shown by this excerpt from a contemporary journal:

> On Thanksgiving, [Debbie] spied the turkey all stuffed and ready for the oven, and somehow or other recognized this bald, headless, footless object lying on its back as "Bird, oh dear, *poor* birdie." At dinner she was so concerned for "Poor birdie, oh dear, oh dear," so insistent on patting and trying to reassure it that eating was of no importance whatsoever [Church, 1966].

But baby biographies have several shortcomings from a scientific point of view. They only record behavior; they don't explain it. Since they tend to be written by fond parents, they suffer from "observer bias," in which the recorder pays undue attention to the positive aspects of a child's development and gives short shrift to the negative. Furthermore, human beings are all so unique that isolated biographies tell us a great deal about an individual child, but much less about children in general.

Naturalistic Observations

In these studies researchers observe large numbers of children and record information about their growth and development at various ages to derive average ages for the appearance of various skills, behaviors, or growth measures. Bridges' studies on emotional development (1932), Shirley's on motor development (1933), and Gesell's on motor and behavioral development (1929) all fall into this category. In these studies, researchers neither make experimental manipulations nor attempt to explain behavior.

Time-sampling

This involves recording the occurrence of a certain type of behavior, such as aggression, babbling, or crying, during a given time period. Rebelsky and Hanks (1972), for example, went into ten homes on six different occasions to make twenty-four-hour tapes. They then analyzed the tapes to count the number of minutes in each twenty-four-hour period that a father spent talking to his baby. From studying these tapes, the investigators drew various conclusions about father-infant relationships.

Clinical Studies

Jean Piaget began his work with children by asking them all sorts of questions so that he could determine what questions children of various ages should be able to answer, for the purpose of standardizing an intelligence test. Piaget, however, became more interested in the wrong answers he heard from the children than in the right ones since he felt that in these wrong answers lay many clues to the ways children reason. Accordingly, when he decided to study the content of children's thought, Piaget developed a new type of examination called the *clinical method.*

In naturalistic studies, researchers look at children in natural habitats, making no effort to alter behavior through experimental manipulation.

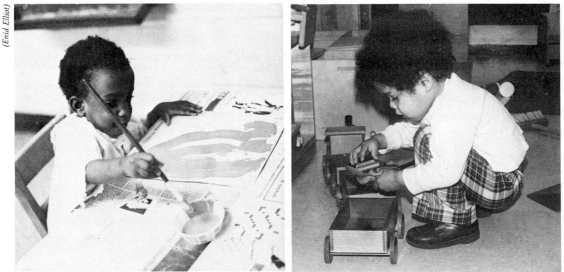

(Enid Elliot)

This method combines observation of a child with careful, individualized questioning. It is a flexible way of assessing childhood thought by tailor-making the test situation to the child being questioned so that no two children are questioned in exactly the same fashion. Its open-ended, individualized method is quite different from the standardized testing technique that aims to make the testing situation as similar as possible for all subjects. With the clinical method, the experimenter can probe further into responses that seem especially interesting, can use language that the particular child understands, and can even change to the language that a child is spontaneously using.

Although each child is asked the same basic questions, the experimenter remains flexible in the ways he or she responds to each child's unique answers. The child's responses determine the next question asked by the experimenter. In this way, the experimenter can probe for the underlying meaning behind what a child says. Examples of the clinical method can be found in Chapter 11.

There are drawbacks to this method of inquiry. Although it does enable an investigator to probe more deeply into children's thoughts than the standard method possibly could, its very flexibility means that we have to have a great deal of confidence in the interviewer's ability to ask the right questions and to draw the right conclusions. The only check on this method is to provide it to a great number of investigators who have varying points of view and then see whether their results corroborate each other. One thing, though, is certain. If Piaget had not used this method to explore children's thinking on a wide range of subjects, our knowledge about the ways thought processes develop would be far poorer. By his overwhelming curiosity and interest in children, Piaget has opened our eyes to their distinctive thought processes.

EXPERIMENTAL STUDIES

In an experimental study, we look at one factor in a child's life to determine its effect on another factor. For example, if we wanted to examine the influence of socioeconomic status on language development, we would compare two groups of children: a group of four-year-olds from homes that have been rated lower-class, based on a standardized rating system that assigns socioeconomic status on the basis of the parents' occupations, and another group of four-year-olds from middle-class homes. Then we would devise a way to measure the size of a child's vocabulary.

In such a study, we call the factor of socioeconomic status the *independent* variable and the factor of vocabulary size the *dependent* variable. We are assuming that socioeconomic status exerts some influence on vocabulary size or, in other words, that differences in vocabulary size *depend*, at least partially, on socioeconomic status. The reverse could not be true: A child's vocabulary size could not influence her socioeconomic status.

These two groups of children would have to be carefully chosen to ensure their similarity on every other independent variable. That is, they should be comparable in terms of age, of male-female ratios, of schooling, and so forth. We wouldn't compare a group of nursery school children with a group who do not attend school, boys with girls, or three-year-olds with four-year-olds unless these variables are the ones we want to test.

Another type of experimental study manipulates the independent variable even more. Suppose researchers want to study the value of an enrichment program for underprivileged preschool children. They will draw up two groups of children who are comparable in virtually every respect—age, sex, race, socioeconomic status, school attendance, IQ, and so forth. Then they offer the enrichment program to the children in only one group. After a certain time, the investigators will try to measure the effects of the enrichment program by giving both groups of children an IQ test.

If the group who has received the enrichment program, called the *experimental* group, has a higher average score than the group who did not receive it, called the *control* group, then the researchers may conclude that this particular program does seem to raise the IQ level of children such as the ones participating in the experiment. If there is no difference between the groups, it is possible that the enrichment program was not administered for a long enough time, was not begun at an early enough age, or for some other reason was ineffective, at least in raising IQ levels.

Experimental studies have several advantages over naturalistic ones. They are carefully standardized: their procedures are so highly regimented and carefully described that the study could be carried out again in exactly the same manner as before. We say that it could be *replicated.* By repeating a study with a different group of children, we can check the reliability of our results.

The one cautionary note we have to make about experimental studies is that they can look at only one or two facets of child development at a time. By zeroing in so narrowly, they sometimes miss some larger, more general knowledge about children's lives. We have to be careful not to miss the forest for the trees.

STANDARDIZED TESTING

After developing normative information from one large group of children, we can develop tests to be given to other children: tests of intelligence, of various aptitudes, of physical skills, of personality, and so forth. Test items are given to a representative group of children, known as the *standardization sample*. The standardization sample should be similar to the group for which the test is designed to be given. If the test will be given to poor black children living in an urban slum, for example, it should not be standardized on a group of middle-class white suburban children.

INTERVIEW STUDIES

By interviewing a large number of parents about their own child-rearing practices and about their children's activities and personalities, investigators get a broad picture of what parents say they believe about their own children and about children in general. Sears, Maccoby, and Levin (1957) interviewed about four hundred New England women—some from a residential middle-class neighborhood and others from an industrial working-class area. These mothers of five-year-old children were asked a broad range of questions, such as their reactions to having children, to weaning, to toilet training, and so forth.

Although interviews can give us in-depth information about child development and parent-child relationships, we have to remember that interviews frequently focus on past behaviors, thus making us dependent on the interviewee's memory and accuracy. Some subjects forget when and how certain behaviors actually took place, and others distort their replies to make them more acceptable—to themselves, as well as to the interviewers.

METHODS OF DATA COLLECTION

Information about children is usually obtained in one of two ways, either by a *longitudinal* or by a *cross-sectional* study.

Longitudinal studies measure the same children more than once to see the changes, with age, in their development.

(Erika Stone, Peter Arnold Agency)

John Locke (1632–1704), an English philosopher, originated the term tabula rasa to describe the idea that the newborn infant is a "blank slate," upon which parents and teachers can write to create the kind of person they want. He considered new babies to be at the mercy of their sensory impressions and to be born with no ideas, but rather with natural impulses, which their environment must teach them to curb.

Jean Jacques Rousseau (1712–1778), a French philosopher, believed that individuals go through a series of predestined, internally regulated, sequential stages. Like "noble savages," children are born good; they become warped only by repressive environments. If only the environment could avoid interfering with their growth, all children would develop optimally.

G. Stanley Hall (1844–1924), an American called the "father of the child study movement," invented the questionnaire method for studying children. Hall made popular the idea that "ontogeny recapitulates phylogeny," or the development of the individual human being parallels the development of the species Homo sapiens. He felt that in our early development we go through stages as a fish, an amphibian, and a monkey.

Sigmund Freud (1856–1939) was an Austrian physician with an interest in neurology, who originated the concept of psychoanalysis. While using it to treat troubled adults, he drew inferences on their early psychosexual development. His highly original theories emphasized the importance of the relationship between early experience and later personality development.

Alfred Binet (1857–1911) was a French psychologist who, in collaboration with T. Simon, developed the first individual intelligence test. The Binet-Simon scale was first published in 1905 and was the basis for the Stanford-Binet test, still widely used today.

Lewis M. Terman (1877–1956), an American psychologist, modified the Binet-Simon intelligence test in 1916 for use with American children, creating the Stanford-Binet test. Terman was convinced that intelligence was innate, and that the environment has so little influence that we can predict adult intelligence if we know the intelligence level of a young child. Absorbed in the study of genius, Terman conducted a major longitudinal study, following gifted children into middle adulthood.

John B. Watson (1878–1958), an American psychologist, has been termed the "father of modern behaviorism." He believed that human beings were illimitably trainable. He tried to prove this thesis by showing how people could be trained to respond in extraordinary ways to various stimuli. For example, he trained a baby to fear the furry animals that he had previously loved. Watson expressed his beliefs this way:

> Give me a dozen healthy infants, well formed, and my own special world to bring them up in, and I'll guarantee to take anyone at random and train him to become any type of specialist I might select—doctor, lawyer, artist, merchantchief, and yes, even beggar and thief, regardless of his talents, penchants, tendencies, abilities, vocations, and race of his ancestors. [*Watson, 1958, p. 104*]

Arnold Gesell (1880–1961) was an American psychologist who conducted with associates several normative studies, from which they concluded that normal children go through stages in development and that these stages are the same from child to child. Gesell, who wrote more than 400 articles and books, stressed the importance of maturation, a genetically determined timetable that enables abilities and skills to emerge. He laid very little stress on individual differences among children.

Jean Piaget (1896–   ) is a Swiss psychologist who formulated a major theory of cognitive development. Building upon his background in biology, Piaget originated his theory of progression in which children pass through a series of age-related stages and develop through their active encounters with the environment. A meticulous observer of children, Piaget developed the clinical method for studying them.

Erik H. Erikson (1902–   ) is a psychoanalyst who extended the Freudian concept of ego. Interested in society's influence on the developing personality, Erikson outlined psychosocial development in eight stages, from infancy through old age. Born in Germany, Erikson became an American citizen in 1939, and since 1961 has been at Harvard University.

(Horst Schafer, Photo Trends)

Cross-sectional studies compare children on a particular dependent variable by observing, at a single time of measurement, many children who differ in a known way with regard to one or more independent variables.

Longitudinal Design

By this method we measure the same children *more than once* to see the *changes*, with age, in their development. We may measure the stability or change with regard to one specific characteristic, like vocabulary size, IQ, height, or aggression. Or we may look at the children in toto, measuring every aspect of their lives as is feasible, with an eye to assessing the interrelationships between various factors. This design provides a more accurate picture of the process of development, rather than its status at any given time.

Cross-sectional Design

This method allows us to compare children on a particular dependent variable by observing, *at a single time of measurement, many* children who differ in a known way with regard to one or more independent variables. Suppose we want to measure the effect of various independent variables on one dependent variable, like vocabulary size. We can look at different children of various ages, of both sexes, of different socioeconomic status, of different IQ levels, and so forth. We may find that girls with high IQs from middle-class homes have the largest vocabularies. Or we can get a picture of the size of the average California two-year-old as compared with the average California three-year-old, or the average two-year-old in New York City as compared with the average two-year-old in Tanzania.

Comparing Longitudinal and Cross-sectional Designs

Longitudinal studies assess changes undergone by a single individual, and cross-sectional studies look at differences between different individuals. Each design has strengths and weaknesses of its own. Their shortcomings are different, and, consequently, developmental trends derived from the two different designs are sometimes contradictory.

Longitudinal studies are more sensitive to individual patterns of behavior and to the changes that individuals undergo. They're also much more difficult to run. It's hard to keep track of a large group of subjects over a period of twenty to thirty years, to keep records, and to keep the study unified despite inevitable changeovers in research personnel. Also, longitudinal studies have their methodological shortcomings. One is a probable inevitable bias in the sample. First, people who volunteer for such studies tend to be of higher-than-average socioeconomic status and intelligence. Also, there is the question of whether those who drop out or become lost to the study (through death, moving out of town, or loss of interest) are random members of the sample. If not, the sample is skewed in a different way. And what about the effects of repeated testing? We know that people tend to do better upon subsequent administration of certain tests simply due to the "practice effect" of learning how to take tests. In the Berkeley Growth Study, most of the subjects were tested at least thirty-eight times over a period of eighteen years (Bayley, 1949)!

Also, it is risky to generalize the results of a longitudinal study to members of a different culture or a different age group. We could not, for example, legitimately infer that a study begun twenty years ago in California would yield the same results if begun today in Russia. Bayley (1965) says:

> [O]ne cannot know whether certain changes are inherent in the subjects under study—or whether they are the result of certain environmental factors, all encountered by the subjects at about the same age. War, depression, changing cultures, and technological advances all make considerable impacts. What are the differential effects on two-year-olds of parents with depression-caused worries and insecurities, of T.V. or no T.V., of the shifting climate of the baby-experts' advice from strict-diet, let-him-cry, no pampering schedules to permissive, cuddling "enriching" loving care? On the other hand, as in some studies, one might eliminate this chronological problem by adding from five to ten newborn infants each year, and then making comparisons according to age of the child and not the calendar year. But then one must wait five years or so to get a large enough sample at any one age for statistical purposes [in Liebert et al., 1974, p. 189].

The cross-sectional method has its own set of built-in drawbacks. It masks individual differences by yielding average measures for the various subgroups in the study, and it also tends to give a misleading picture of the changes over time undergone by specific individuals. Another disadvantage is the generational influence that shows up when we measure people who were born at different times. Anastasi (1958) has said:

> Differences between 20- and 40-year-olds tested simultaneously (in 1940 or 1960) would reflect age changes plus cultural differentials, especially differences in the conditions under which the two age groups were reared [p. 220].

The problem in measuring children's growth this way, for example, involves the difficulty in separating out all the different factors that affect it, such as race, socioeconomic status, health, and so forth. Also, it is risky to assume that today's average two-year-old will, in a year, be the same size as today's average three-year-old. Children grow at different rates, environmental conditions may change, and other factors may also affect the rate of growth in a way to change the prediction markedly.

Ethical Issues in Studying Children

Four-year-old Vicky sits in a room with an unfamiliar adult. The adult asks her a question about some objects on the table. The adult does not expect the child to answer correctly, but Vicky does not know she is not "ready" to pass this test. All she knows is that she does not know the answer. The worried look on her face betrays the child's anxiety. *Should* she know this answer? Is she "dumb" because she doesn't? Should she take a chance on guessing? What will happen to her if she guesses wrong?

Vicky's experience as a subject in a respected psychological experiment illustrates one of the concerns that responsible scientists have voiced regarding the ethical considerations in the study of children. Since we are now convinced that children's early experiences often have long-term, unknown effects, how are we to know when the effects of participation in a research project might be harmful to an individual child?

We don't, always. But as this science itself matures, more and more researchers are raising these questions. With new awareness of the needs of children, many studies performed in the past probably could not be carried out today. But these issues are not always clear-cut. Many contemporary studies put children in the anxiety-producing condition experienced by Vicky. In such cases, the investigators have to ask themselves some hard questions. How much anxiety can children absorb and still keep their self-confidence? What is the long-term effect of failure? Is the experiment important enough to justify putting children under stress?

What are the rights of the child? This is the basic question. How can we balance the quest for knowledge about all children while retaining intact the intellectual and emotional integrity of individual children?

From bitter experience, we have learned the dangers of some kinds of experimentation. In the thirteenth century, for example, Frederick II wanted to find out whether there was a universal language that babies would speak if they did not hear the language of their own culture.

> So he bade foster mothers and nurses to suckle the children, to bathe and wash them, but in no way to prattle with them, or to speak to them, for he wanted to learn whether they would speak the Hebrew language, which was the oldest, or Greek, or Latin, or Arabic, or perhaps the language of their parents, of whom they had been born. But he laboured in vain because the children all died. For they could not live without the petting and joyful faces and loving words of their foster mothers [Ross & McLaughlin, 1949, p. 366].

Today we would not dream of depriving children of the loving care they need in infancy. Nor would we do to children so many of the things that scientists do in studying animals—isolate them from all contact with others of their species, administer experimental drugs, or modify their environments unusually in other respects.

In extreme cases like these, the decisions are easy to make. Any responsible scientist would be horrified at the notion of doing any of these things. The more difficult decisions crop up in experiments that seem more benign and yet may still produce unforeseen effects. One team of researchers, for example, found that eight- to ten-week-old infants could learn how to move their heads in such a way as to cause specially constructed mobiles to move (Watson & Ramey, 1969). Once they had made the mobiles move, the babies smiled and gurgled to the mobiles as they would to a person. The investigators warn:

> It should be . . . clear that providing infants with mechanically arranged contingency experiences must be pursued with caution. Until we more fully understand the social and intellective effects of providing response-contingent stimulation in early infancy, it would seem only reasonable to approach this form of early stimulation as an unknown quantity which might be either beneficial or harmful, depending on the amount and timing of its presentation [p. 226].

Elsewhere, Watson (1971) has expressed other fears related to the currently popular studies of infants' cognitive development. We know, for example, that infants pay more attention to their surroundings when something unexpected happens. What happens, then, if we consistently violate babies' expectations in order to study their attention spans? What would this do to their perception of their world and to their ease in living in an unpredictable place? Similarly, we know that babies pay attention to meaningful speech. If we present them with taped speech patterns to study their ability to attend, we are introducing meaningful speech into their environment outside its natural context. Would this confuse them? Would it weaken their ability to respond intelligently to real speech, because in the taped instances, their responses wouldn't bring the same kinds of counter-responses that they would if they were interacting with a live, present human being?

In sum, Watson (1971) concludes that child developmentalists must be extremely cautious and aware of the possible results of their investigations if they are not going to negatively affect the child in their studies.

> Until we understand the origins and the context of attentional development in infancy, we simply cannot proceed in a blind manipulation of that developmental context with vast numbers of infants [p. 146].

SOME BASIC ISSUES

Right to Privacy

A few years ago a doctor made the front pages of newspapers around the country when he recommended giving psychological tests to young underprivileged children, with the aim of predicting which ones showed signs of someday becoming delinquent. These children could be watched and given extra social help to try to forestall their criminal tendencies. The doctor's proposal was angrily attacked by many who felt that labeling children so early in life as potential delinquents would have detrimental effects rather than the beneficial ones the psychiatrist foresaw. The principle of the *self-fulfilling prophecy* might operate, so that children who were thought to have criminal tendencies would be treated differently from other children and might actually become delinquent *because* of the predictions.

This is an extreme example of the potentially harmful ways in which speculative information about children can be used. Similar concerns have also been voiced with regard to children's scores on intelligence tests. These scores follow them through school and often serve to influence their teachers in one direction or another.

One-way mirrors and hidden cameras and tape recorders enable psychologists to observe and record behavior without the subjects' awareness. Furthermore, much private information surfaces through parental and child interviews—information about income, education, child-rearing techniques, and parent-child relationships. What is the experimenter's obligation with regard to the collection and maintenance of such information? Smith (1967) answers this question as follows:

> Information collected from children for research should never be used to their disadvantage. When the nature of the research permits data to be collected and stored anonymously, the interests of the individual child can be readily protected.

When, on the other hand, identification of individual persons is essential to the research—as in "longitudinal" studies that follow the same persons over a period of time—elaborate precautions are essential to safeguard *confidentiality.* In such research, protecting the anonymity of the persons studied is an absolute about which there can be no compromise [p. 55].

Right to the Truth

Some experiments depend for their value on deception of the subjects. Children are told that they are testing out a new game, for example, when in reality they are being tested on their reactions to success or failure or on their ability to communicate the rules of the game to someone else. When is it legitimate to deceive children and/or parents regarding the real purpose of an experiment, and how can we safeguard their rights to the truth and to their own integrity?

Right to Informed Consent

Children do not give their consent to be part of scientific experiments, and even if they did, we could not accept their ability to make mature judgments. We have to rely on the parents' regard for the well-being of their children or on the school personnel's judgment in those cases when they permit students to participate in research projects. How is the child affected by all of this? Since the investigator does not have to justify his procedures to his subjects, the children, how can we be sure that his or her judgment takes into account the best interests of the individual child, as well as the best interests of the study of children in general?

Right to Self-Esteem

Many researchers try to discover at what point children become capable of certain skills or certain types of reasoning. They study children who are known to be too young to achieve the ability under study. Other investigators want to find out the limits of a child's abilities, and so they continue to pose problems to her until she is unable to answer. Built into the design of all these studies is the certainty of failure. How do these feelings of failure affect individual children? Even if the experimenter takes special pains to see that a child experiences a feeling of success by the end of the experimental session, does this make up for artificially induced failures? What are the long-term effects of such failures? Is the quest for scientific truth worth the possibility of damaging the self-concept of a single child?

Social Concerns

A problem that relates to the vast amount of research that has been carried out among children of minority groups and of socially disadvantaged groups involves a different kind of danger. If we consistently find that children from certain subcultures do not achieve intellectually as well as other children—and if this research is published—what is the ultimate result? One writer (Reinhold, 1973) has reported:

> It has been said that the cumulative, if unintentional effect of years of sociological research in the black community has been to damage the self-esteem of black youngsters [p. E13].

This damage may come about as a result of published findings showing middle-class white children to be academically superior to poor black youngsters. It may result from teachers' expectations. If they "know" from published reports that inner-city black children are not likely to do so well in school as suburban white children, they may gear their teaching to diminished expectations. By so doing, they ensure that their pupils will, indeed, live down to their expectations.

The question of possible social harm to a cultural subgroup is just as agonizing to answer as are the other questions considering the possibility of harm to individual children. At present, committees in the various social science disciplines are grappling with these issues in an effort to come up with solutions that will protect academic freedom and the quest for knowledge, and yet at the same time protect the rights of groups, as well as individuals.

COMPETING VALUES AFFECTING RESEARCH WITH CHILDREN

M. Brewster Smith has summarized some of the issues relating to research in child development as follows (1967):

> Humanitarian values require that we never harm the individual child and always strive to advance child welfare. Libertarian values require us to respect the integrity and privacy of the child and his parents. Scientific values prescribe the extension of knowledge for its own sake, usually with the faith that in the long run knowledge contributes to humanitarian ends. Legal values require us to respect the status of minors and the rights and obligations of parents, though legal rights in relation to behavioral research are still in the process of clarification [p. 55].

What happens when these different values conflict with one another—when Vicky's privacy is violated by her being observed without her knowledge or when she is tempted to cheat in a study of morality? Is this not entrapment, deliberately placing temptation in her path? And is this not an assault upon her integrity if she succumbs?

These questions and the others we have posed are very real ones for researchers. Developmentalists do not want to harm the children who help them learn, yet severe restrictions would put a halt to many current studies and would limit our understanding of children's needs. Where does the answer lie? In the integrity of each researcher, of course, in the imposition of professional standards that advance the cause of scientific truth and zealously protect the rights of each individual child, and in the awareness and sensitivity of every citizen and especially everyone who works with children. It is up to everyone in the field of child development to accept the responsibility to try to do good—and, at the very least, to do no harm.

A Word to the Student

Our final word in this introductory chapter is that this entire book is far from the final word. We are still learning about childhood and about children. Some of our research findings have put old ideas to rest forever. Others are still ambivalent and must be vigorously pursued. Some theories seem to make sense, but are hard to test scientifically.

As you read this book, you will no doubt consider many issues that will raise questions of value judgments in your mind. If you can pursue your questions, through research and carefully considered thought, it is quite possible that you, yourself, now just embarking upon the study of children, may in future years advance this study to the benefit of all humankind.

Summary

1   The study of development focuses on the quantitative and qualitative ways children change over time.

2   The study of development is primarily concerned with the examination of overt, observable behavioral changes.

3   Although we can look at different "types" of development (for example, physical, socioemotional, intellectual), we must remember that these do not develop in isolation. Each affects the others.

4   Certain principles of development apply to all children and are useful guidelines in interpreting behaviors. These include individual differences, critical periods, and orderly development. Different types of development are important at different times in life.

5   The concept of childhood is relatively recent. Attitudes toward children were quite different in the past.

6   There are many ways to obtain information about children, ranging from naturalistic studies to standardized experimental techniques. Each unique approach has strengths and weaknesses which should be considered in interpreting studies of children.

7   The two major data-collection techniques are the longitudinal and the cross-sectional. Each has its pros and cons which must be considered in interpreting data and in generalizing results to particular samples.

8   Work with children must reflect certain ethical considerations. A carefully designed study considers its effects on the subject as well as its potential benefits to the field of child development.

Suggested Readings

Adler, M. *A Parent's Manual: Answers to Questions on Child Development and Child Rearing.* Springfield, Ill. Charles C Thomas, 1971. *This parent's manual has chapters on the preschool years, the school years, intellectual and physical development, psychological development, behavior and discipline, the family's influence, and observations.*

Aries, P. *Centuries of Childhood.* Vintage, 1962. *This historical text presents the evolution of the modern family and the nature of modern children. It includes a well-presented discussion of the discovery of childhood as a distinct phase of life.*

Baldwin, A. L. *Theories of Child Development.* New York: Wiley, 1968. *A broad perspective of theory in child development that reviews the major concepts of each theory and assesses their possible usefulness for future child-development studies.*

DeMause, L. (ed.) *The History of Childhood.* Psychohistory Press, 1974. *This text is a collection of works by ten psychohistorians. They survey and discuss the history of childhood in Europe and America during the past 200 years.*

Dodson, F. *How to Parent.* New York: New American Library, 1971. *This is an approach to child rearing with discussion limited to the first five years of life.*

Erikson, E. H. *Childhood and Society.* New York: Norton, 1963. *This text is a collection of writings by Erik Erikson which includes "the eight ages of man," in* *which he outlines his theory of psychosocial development from infancy to old age.*

Gottlieb, D. (ed.) *Children's Liberation.* Englewood Cliffs, N.J.: Prentice-Hall, 1973. *A new and interesting study of American children as they are, in too many instances, victims of indifference, abuse, intimidation, and exploitation.*

Landau, E. D., Epstein, S. L., and **Stone, A.** (eds.) *Child Development through Literature.* Englewood Cliffs, N.J.: Prentice-Hall, 1972. *A collection of fictional pieces by major writers that dramatize important issues in child development. The editors provide brief discussions along with each excerpt relating the reading to pertinent research findings.*

Maier, H. *Three Theories of Child Development.* New York: Harper and Row, 1969. *This text presents a single-chapter discussion on each of the following: the psychoanalytical theory of Erik H. Erikson, the cognitive theory of Jean Piaget, and the learning theory of Robert R. Sears. Remaining chapters compare the three theories, discuss "the helping process," and note the implications of the three theories.*

Milgram, J. I., and **Sciarra, D. J.** *Childhood Revisited.* New York: Macmillan, 1974. *A fascinating selection of autobiographical excerpts by prominent people whose childhood recollections underscore the personal ways that issues in child development affect real people.*

Young L. *Life among the Giants: A Child's View of the Grown-Up World.* New York: McGraw-Hill, 1966. *Leontine Young explains and teaches what it's like to be a child and how to be one again. She shows the reader the lifestyles that are forced upon children and how they feel.*

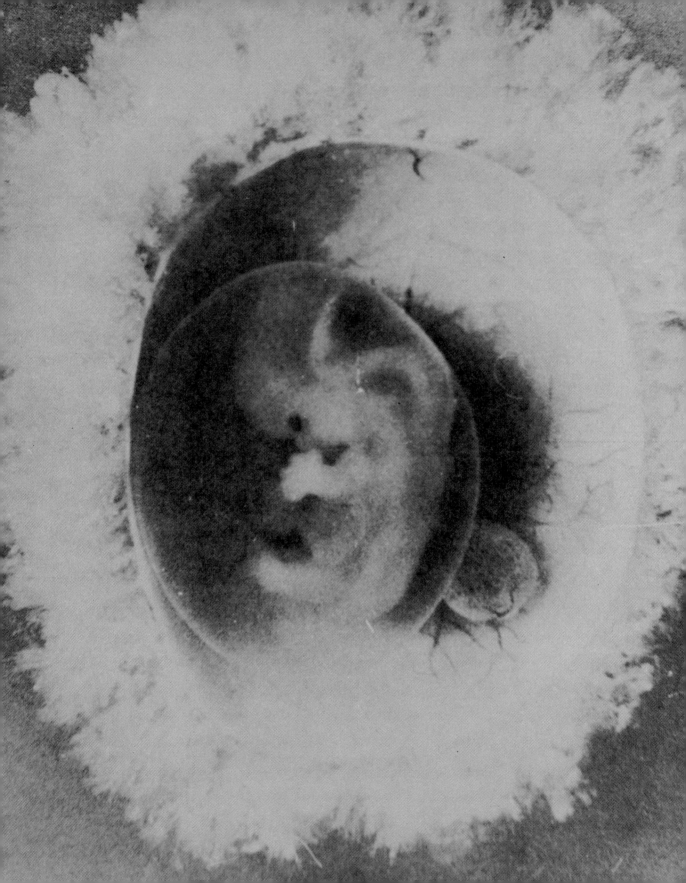

PART ONE
THE PRENATAL PERIOD

CHAPTER ONE
CONCEPTION AND BIRTH
IN WHICH VICKY IS CONCEIVED AND BORN

If I could have watched you grow
as a magical mother might,
if I could have seen through my magical transparent belly,
there would have been such ripening within; . . .
                                        (Anne Sexton, 1966*)

During the seventeenth and eighteenth centuries, a protracted debate raged between two opposing schools of biological thought about the origins of human life. The Ovists were convinced that a female's ovaries contained tiny embryos that were somehow activated by the male sperm. The Homunculists espoused an opposite, if equally incorrect, view—that preformed embryos were contained in the head of the sperm and were enabled to grow only when deposited in the nurturing environment of the womb.

Both these schools of thought were, of course, incorrect in their supposition that embryos exist preformed in either ovaries or sperm. Their erroneous thinking reflected the lack of appreciation and understanding of the fundamental scientific discoveries of two scientists from the Netherlands: Regnier de Graaf, who first viewed some embryonic cells removed from the reproductive tubes of a female rabbit, and Anton van Leeuwenhoek, the naturalist who, in 1677, noticed live sperm cells in a drop of semen viewed under the newly invented microscope. By the middle of the eighteenth century the work of the German-born anatomist, Kaspar Friedrich Wolff, had clearly demonstrated to the scientific world that both

*From "Little Girl, My String Bean, My Lovely Woman," in *Live or Die.* Boston: Houghton-Mifflin Co., 1966.

parents contribute equally to the beginning of a new life and that this new being is not preformed but grows from single cells, one male and one female in origin.

The beginning of life for all of us came long before that first lusty yell when, as newborn babies, we vacated our mother's womb. Instead, the beginning is a split-second event when a sperm (*spermatozoon*) joins an egg (*ovum*) in the female reproductive tract to start a new life. The question of which sperm joins which egg has tremendous implications for the kind of person that new being will become: what sex it will be, what it will look like, which diseases it will be susceptible to, even—to a hotly disputed extent— what kind of personality it will possess. Let us now see how this important union takes place and what then occurs during the nine months of life inside the womb.

Fertilization

Fertilization takes place when a sperm cell from the male unites with an egg from a female to form a single cell. This cell is called a *zygote* up until the time it begins to divide. The eggs and sperms are known as sex cells or *gametes.*

A newborn girl has about 400,000 immature eggs (*ova*) in her ovaries, each one encased in its own small sac, called a *follicle* (Ingelman-Sundberg & Wersen, 1965). The ovum, about one-fourth the size of the period that ends this sentence (Guttmacher, 1962), is the largest cell in the human body. It can, on occasion, be seen without a microscope. A sexually mature female ovulates about once every twenty-eight days, usually midway in her menstrual cycle. *Ovulation* is the process by which one mature follicle in one of the two ovaries ruptures, expelling an ovum, which then travels toward the *uterus* (the womb) by way of the Fallopian tube. The process of fertilization normally occurs during the ovum's journey along the Fallopian tube.

The tadpole-like spermatozoon, at 1/600 inch from the top of its head to the tip of its tail (Guttmacher, 1962), is one of the smallest cells in the body. It is much more active than the ovum. Spermatozoa are produced in the testicles (*testes*) of a mature healthy male at a rate of about several hundred million a day (Rugh & Shettles, 1971) and ejected in his semen at sexual climax. Although it takes only one sperm to fertilize one egg, the average ejaculation carries about 500 million sperm cells. Fertility studies have shown that a minimum of about 20 million must enter the woman's body at one time for fertilization to occur. The sperm enter the vagina and attempt to swim through the *cervix,* the opening to the uterus, and into the Fallopian tube, where one can fertilize the egg. Only a tiny fraction of those millions of sperm cells make it this far. More than one may penetrate the ovum, but only one can fertilize it to create a new human being.

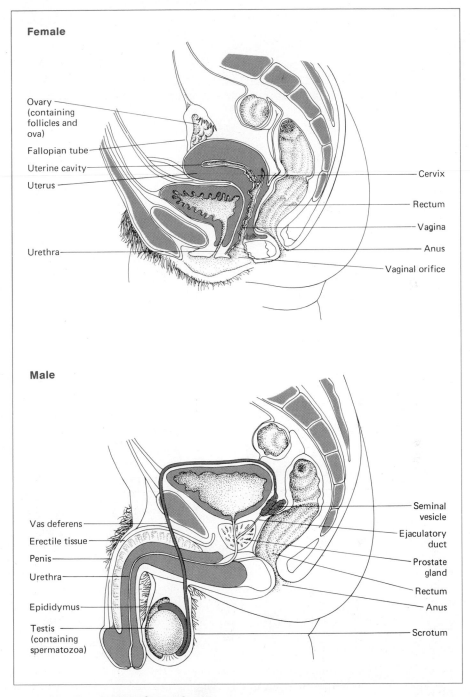

Figure 1-1   Human Reproductive Systems

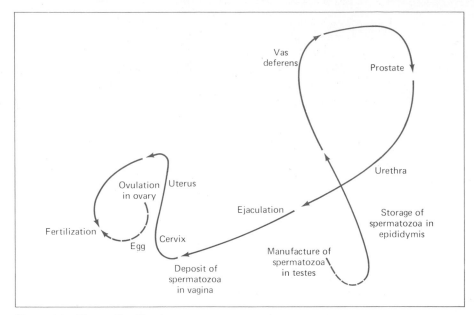

Figure 1-2   Human Fertilization

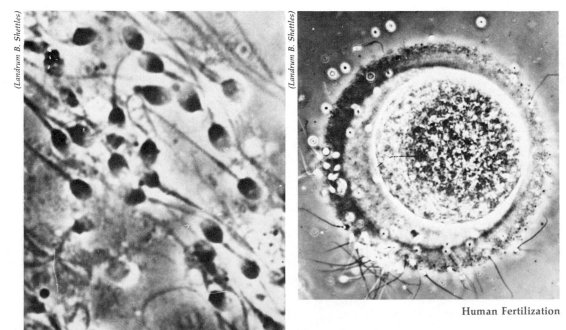

Human Spermatozoa

Human Fertilization

Spermatozoa can live for about forty-eight hours inside the woman's reproductive tract; unfertilized ova have a life span of about twelve hours. Thus there are about sixty hours during each menstrual cycle when conception can take place (Rugh & Shettles, 1971). If it does not, the sperm cells and the egg both die, the sperm to be devoured by white blood cells in the woman's body, the egg to pass through the uterus and exit through the vagina.

We'll look at what happens when fertilization occurs by tracing the life of Vicky, our Everychild.

Three Stages of Prenatal Development

Life in the womb is usually divided into three stages of development: the *germinal*, the *embryonic*, and the *fetal*. The *germinal* stage lasts about ten days to two weeks after the moment of fertilization. It is characterized by two main events: the rapid cell division and subsequent increasing complexity of the organism, and its implantation in the wall of the uterus. The *embryonic* stage, from two to eight weeks, sees the rapid growth and differentiation of major body systems and organs. And the *fetal* stage, which lasts from eight weeks until birth, is characterized by rapid growth and by the changes in body form caused by different rates of growth of different parts of the body.

Figure 1-3   Early Development of Human Egg and Embryo

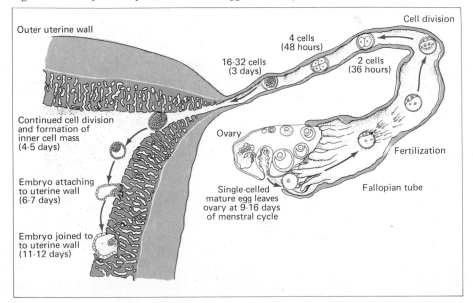

We will discuss these three stages in some detail, but we always have to remember that it is difficult at any particular time in any particular pregnancy to establish the exact age of the *conceptus*, the new life that has been conceived. Our uncertainty regarding precise prenatal age is due to the fact that no one knows the exact moment of fertilization. Physicians generally date a pregnancy from either the last menstrual period (menstrual age) or two weeks after the last menstrual period, which is assumed to be the period of ovulation and thus of fertilization (fertilization age). Because ovulation usually occurs midway in the menstrual cycle, its timing does vary somewhat from woman to woman, and even from cycle to cycle in the same woman. Thus, although the *sequence* of development as described below is true for all embryos, it is difficult to be precise in the actual *timing*.

GERMINAL STAGE (FERTILIZATION TO TWO WEEKS)

Within thirty-six hours after fertilization, the *zygote* (the cell which results from union of sperm and ovum) enters a period of rapid cell division. Seventy-two hours after fertilization, it has divided into thirty-two cells; a day later, it contains seventy cells. This division continues, until Vicky, who began life as a single cell, develops the eight hundred billion or more specialized cells each of us is made of. While the fertilized egg is dividing, it is also making its way down the Fallopian tube to the uterus, which it reaches in about three or four days. By the time it gets there, its form has changed into a fluid-filled sphere called a *blastocyst*, which then floats freely in the uterus for a day or two. Some of the cells around the edge of the blastocyst cluster on one side to form the *embryonic disk*, a thickened cell mass from which the baby will develop. This mass is already differentiating into two layers. The upper layer, the *ectoderm*, will eventually become Vicky's epidermis (outer layer of skin), the nails, hair, teeth, sensory organs, and nervous system, including the brain and spinal cord. The lower layer, the *endoderm*, will become her digestive system, liver, pancreas, salivary glands, and respiratory system. Later a middle layer, the *mesoderm*, will develop, which will differentiate into the dermis (inner layer of skin), muscles, skeleton, and excretory and circulatory systems.

The other parts of the blastocyst will develop into the organs that nurture and protect Vicky during her intrauterine life: the *placenta*, the *umbilical cord*, and the *amniotic sac*. The placenta, a miraculous multipurpose organ, is connected to the embryo by the umbilical cord. Through this cord it delivers both oxygen and nourishment from the mother's body and absorbs the embryo's body wastes. The placenta also helps to combat internal infection, and it confers on the unborn Vicky immunity to various diseases. It produces the hormones that support pregnancy, prepare the mother's breasts for lactation, and eventually stimulate the uterine contractions that will expel Vicky from her body.

The amniotic sac is a fluid-filled membrane that encases the developing baby, protecting it and giving it room to move. The outer layer of this protective "bag of waters" is called the chorion; the inner membrane, the amnion.

The *trophoblast*, the outer cell layer of the blastocyst, produces tiny thread-like structures called *villi*, which penetrate the lining of the uterine wall. With their help, the blastocyst burrows in vigorously, until it is implanted in a warm, nurturing, nesting place. It will continue to grow here for the next 8½ months. When ready for implantation, the blastocyst has about 150 cells with a hollow center. Once it is fully implanted in the uterus, the cell mass is called an *embryo*.

Multiple Births

We have discussed the usual situation following the union of one sperm with one ovum. Occasionally, however, two ova are released within a short time of each other; if both are fertilized, *fraternal* (also called *dizygotic*, or two-egg) twins will be born. Since they are created by different eggs and different sperm cells, they are no more alike in their genetic makeup than any other siblings. They may be of the same or different sex. If, on the other hand, the ovum divides in two after it has been fertilized, *identical* (*monozygotic*, or one-egg) twins will be born. They have exactly the same genetic heritage, and any differences they will later exhibit must be due to the influences of environment, either before or after birth. Identical twins are, of course, always of the same sex. Other multiple births—triplets, quadruplets, and so forth—result from either one or a combination of these two processes.

Multiple births have become more frequent in recent years due to the administration of certain fertility drugs that spur ovulation and often cause the release of more than one egg. The tendency to bear twins appears to be inherited and to be more common in some ethnic groups than in others. In Nigeria, for example, twins account for 1 birth in 22; in Britain, for 1 in 80; and in Japan, for only 1 in 160 (Gedda, 1961). More than half of all twins are of low birthweight, and they are thus at greater risk. In 1 out of 6 twin pregnancies, one or both of the twins die, with the second-born twin particularly vulnerable (Dunn, 1965).

EMBRYONIC STAGE (TWO TO EIGHT WEEKS)

During this period Vicky grows rapidly as her major body systems (respiratory, alimentary, nervous) and her organs develop. Due to this rapid growth and development, she is most vulnerable at this time to prenatal environmental influence. Virtually all developmental birth defects (such as cleft palate, incomplete or missing limbs, blindness, deafness, and so forth) occur during the critical first *trimester* (three-month period) of pregnancy. The most severely defective embryos usually do not survive beyond the first trimester, but spontaneously abort (Garn, 1960).

On the embryo one can see primitive structures that resemble a tail and gills. This observation has given rise to the saying, "Ontogeny recapitulates phylogeny," or "the development of an individual from conception to birth retraces the evolutionary history of the entire species [Rugh & Shettles, 1971, p. 39]." This is not really so, since the human fetus does not go through the stages of development of a fish, an amphibian, and a monkey on its route to becoming a human. All these species do share certain similarities in their development, because all derive from one-celled organisms and gradually assume a more complicated shape. But the primitive structures in the developing human are very different from those in the embryos of other forms of life. The structure that looks like a tail, for example, is the rudimentary spinal cord, which, at this stage of development, is longer than the rest of the body. The gill-like forms have a completely different function, eventually turning into the chin, cheek, jaw, and outer ear. From the time of fertilization, Vicky was all human, with the potential for developing into a fully formed human being—and nothing else.

For a month-by-month development of the embryo and the fetus, see Chart 1-1.

FETAL STAGE (EIGHT WEEKS TO BIRTH)
With the appearance of the first bone cells at about eight weeks, the embryo becomes a *fetus*. During the long period until birth, the finishing touches are put on Vicky's body parts, the form of her body changes because different parts of the body are growing at different rates, and she grows about twenty times in length.

Spontaneous Abortion
A miscarriage, known medically as a *spontaneous abortion*, is the expulsion from the uterus of a conceptus that is not yet viable, that is, one that could not survive outside the womb. Three-quarters of all known spontaneous abortions occur within the first three months of pregnancy. It has been estimated that at least three out of every ten conceptions do not go beyond the first trimester (Garn, 1960). The figure is probably quite a bit higher, since many women miscarry before they even know they are pregnant.

In ancient times, doctors believed a woman could be frightened into miscarrying by a clap of thunder or jostled into it if her chariot hit a rut in the street. But today we realize that the fetus is well protected from almost all jolts the mother may experience. As one obstetrician has said, "You cannot shake loose a good human egg, any more than you can shake a good unripe apple from the apple tree [Guttmacher, 1962]." The great majority of miscarriages result from abnormal pregnancies.

When we consider the awesome complexities of creating a new human

Chart 1-1   The Development of Embryo and Fetus

1 Month

During the first month, the new life has grown more quickly than it will at any other time during its lifetime, achieving a size 10,000 times greater than the zygote. It now measures from $^1/_4$ to $^1/_2$ inch in length.

Blood is flowing through its tiny veins and arteries. Its minuscule heart beats 65 times a minute. It already has the beginnings of a brain, kidney, liver, and digestive tract. The umbilical cord, its lifeline to its mother, is working. By looking very closely through a microscope, it is possible to see the swellings on the head that will eventually become its eyes, ears, mouth, and nose. Its sex cannot yet be distinguished.

2 Months

The embryo now looks like a well-proportioned, small-scale baby. It is less than 1 inch long and weighs only $^1/_{13}$ ounce. Its head is one-half its total body length, exemplifying the principle of *cephalocaudal development*, by which growth begins first in the head area and then progresses down the trunk.

Facial parts are clearly developed, with tongue and teeth buds. The arms

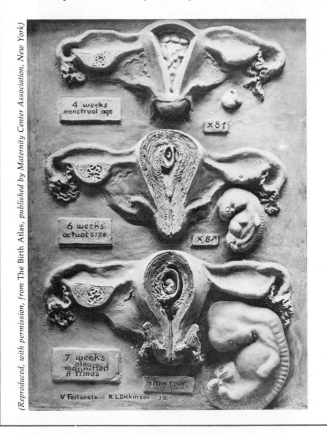

(Reproduced, with permission, from The Birth Atlas, published by Maternity Center Association, New York)

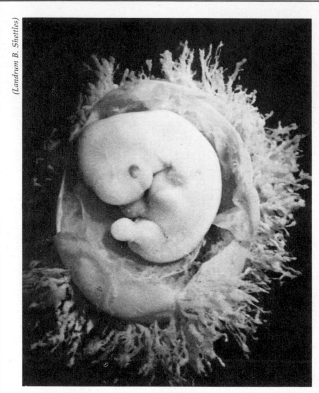

(Landrum B. Shettles)

Human Embryo at Six Weeks

have hands, fingers, and thumbs, and the legs have knees, ankles, and toes. It has a thin covering of skin and can even make hand and foot prints.

The embryo's brain impulses coordinate the function of its organ systems. Sex organs are developing; the heartbeat is steady. The stomach produces digestive juices; the liver, blood cells. The kidney removes uric acid from the blood. The skin is now sensitive enough to react to tactile stimulation. If an aborted 8-week-old embryo is stroked, it reacts by flexing its trunk, extending its head, and moving back its arms.

3 Months

Now a fetus, the developing person weighs 1 ounce and measures about 3 inches in length. It has fingernails, toenails, eyelids (still closed), vocal cords, lips, and a prominent nose. Its head is still large—about one-third its total length—and its forehead is high. Its sex can be easily determined.

The organ systems are functioning, so that the fetus may now breathe, swallow amniotic fluid in and out of the lungs, and occasionally urinate. Its ribs and vertebrae have turned to cartilage, and its internal reproductive organs have primitive egg or sperm cells.

The fetus can now make a variety of specialized responses: It can move its legs, feet, thumbs, and head; its mouth can open and close and swallow. If its eyelids are touched, it squints; if its palm is touched, it makes a partial fist; if its lip is touched, it will suck; and if the sole of the foot is stroked, the toes will fan out. These reflex behaviors will be present at birth but will disappear during the first months of life.

4 Months

The body is catching up to the head, which is now only one-fourth the total body length, the same proportion it will be at birth. The fetus now measures 8 to 10 inches and weighs about 6 ounces. The umbilical cord is as long as the fetus and will continue to grow with it. The placenta is now fully developed.

The mother may be able to feel the fetus kicking, a movement known as *quickening*, which some societies and religious groups consider the beginning of human life. The reflex activities that appeared in the third month are now brisker, because of increased muscular development.

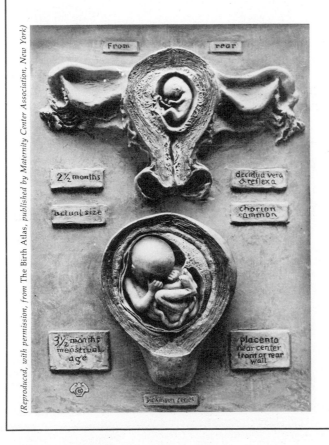

(Reproduced, with permission, from The Birth Atlas, published by Maternity Center Association, New York)

5 Months

Now weighing about 12 ounces to 1 pound and measuring about 1 foot, the fetus begins to show signs of an individual personality. It has definite sleep-wake patterns, has a favorite position in the uterus (called its *lie*), and becomes more active—kicking, stretching, squirming, and even hiccuping. By putting an ear to the mother's abdomen, it is possible to hear the fetal heartbeat. The sweat and sebaceous glands are functioning. The respiratory system is not yet adequate to sustain life outside the womb; a baby born at this time has no hope of survival.

Coarse hair has begun to grow on the eyebrows and eyelashes, fine hair is on the head, and a woolly hair called *lanugo* covers the body but will disappear at birth or soon thereafter.

6 Months

The rate of fetal growth has slowed down a little—the fetus is now about 14 inches long and 1¼ pounds. It is getting fat pads under the skin, the eyes are complete, opening and closing and looking in all directions. It can maintain regular breathing for 24 hours; it cries; and it can make a fist with a strong grip.

If the fetus were to be born now, it would have an extremely slim chance of survival because its breathing apparatus is still very immature. There have been instances, however, when a fetus of this age has survived outside the womb.

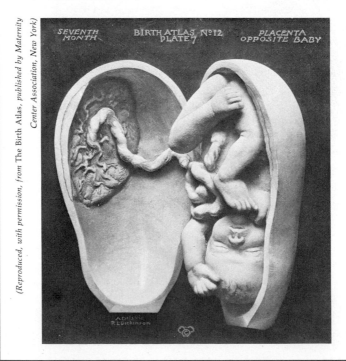

(Reproduced, with permission, from The Birth Atlas, published by Maternity Center Association, New York)

7 Months
The 16-inch fetus, weighing 3 to 5 pounds, now has fully developed reflex patterns. It cries, breathes, and swallows and may suck its thumb. The lanugo may disappear at about this time, or it may remain until shortly after birth. Head hair may continue to grow. Survival chances for a fetus weighing at least 3½ pounds are fairly good, provided it receives intensive medical attention. It will probably have to live in an incubator until a weight of 5 pounds is attained.

8 Months
The 18- to 20-inch fetus now weighs between 5 and 7 pounds and is fast outgrowing its living quarters. Its movements are curtailed because of cramped conditions. During this month and the next, a layer of fat is developing over the fetus's entire body, to enable it to adjust to varying temperatures outside the womb.

9 Months
About a week before birth, the baby stops growing, having reached an average weight of just over 7 pounds and a length of about 20 inches, with boys tending to be a little longer and heavier than girls. Fat pads continue to form, the organ system is operating more efficiently, the heart rate increases, and more wastes are expelled. The reddish color of the skin is fading. On its birthday, the fetus will have been in the womb for approximately 266 days, although gestation age is usually estimated at 280 days, since doctors date the pregnancy from the mother's last menstrual period.

being, it is not surprising that things do not always go smoothly. A defective ovum or sperm, an unfavorable location for implantation, a breakdown in supplies of oxygen or nourishment caused by abnormal development of the umbilical cord, or some physiological abnormality of the mother are all possible factors that may lead to a spontaneous abortion.

Determination of Sex

King Henry VIII divorced Catherine of Aragon because she bore him a daughter rather than the son he so desperately wanted. It's ironic that this basis for divorce has been valid in so many different societies, since we now know that it is the *father* who determines the sex of the child. At the moment of conception, every human being receives a total of forty-six tiny rod-shaped particles called *chromosomes*—twenty-three from the sperm and twenty-three from the egg. These chromosomes from the father and the mother align themselves in pairs. Twenty-two pairs are called *autosomes*; the twenty-third pair, called the *sex chromosomes*, determines the child's sex. The sex chromosome of every ovum is an X chromosome, but the sperm may carry either an X or a smaller-sized Y chromosome. When an ovum (X) meets an X-carrying sperm, called a *gynosperm*, the zygote is XX, a female. When an ovum is fertilized by a Y-carrying sperm, called an *androsperm*, the zygote is XY, a male.

Unexplained differences between the sexes appear at the moment of conception. An estimated 120 to 170 males are conceived for every 100 females (Shettles & Rugh, 1971). It's possible that there may be more androsperms than gynosperms, or the androsperms may be more successful in reaching or penetrating the ovum. This disproportionately high rate of male conception is probably a natural mechanism to offset the early biological inferiority of the male. Since males have a higher spontaneous abortion and stillborn rate, the proportion of male babies actually born drops to 105 for every 100 females (Baumgartner, Pessin, Wegman, & Parker, 1950).

Furthermore, the male develops more slowly in comparison with the female, from early fetal life into adulthood. At twenty weeks after conception, the male is two weeks behind the female; at forty weeks he is four weeks behind; and he continues to lag behind till maturity (Hutt, 1972). His higher vulnerability persists after birth, with more males than females dying during the first years of life (*Vital Statistics*, United States Department of Health, Education, and Welfare, 1967, 1969) and more males subject to postnatal behavior disorders associated with brain damage during pregnancy (Pasamanick, Rogers, & Lilienfeld, 1956). The disparate death rates of males and females account for the fact that there are now only 95 males for every 100 females in the United States (*1973 World Almanac*).

Prenatal Activities and Abilities

As we can see from Chart 1-1, Vicky—even as a fetus—is far from a passive passenger in her mother's womb. Apart from the basic body functions of breathing and taking in nutrition, she kicks, turns, flexes her body, turns somersaults, squints, swallows, makes a fist, hiccups, and sucks her thumb. Furthermore, she can respond to such sensory stimuli as sound and vibrations and may even show evidence of prenatal learning.

FETAL HEARING

Expectant mothers often relate incidents attesting to the sensory awareness of the unborn child. Vicky's mother, for example, noticed that her fetus increased its movement when she typed. Another woman had to stop going to symphony concerts because the audience applause caused such intense fetal activity that it was painful to her (Sontag, 1966). This anecdotal testimony has been corroborated by clinical experiments. One experimenter has reported that the fetus moves around in response to the sound of two boards being clapped together (Sontag & Wallace, 1936). And another found that, as early as the thirteenth week of pregnancy, a bell sounded near the mother's abdomen would cause convulsive fetal movements, similar to the Moro reflex, a startle reaction observed in infancy (Sontag & Richards, 1938). In one experiment, researchers used an apparatus that applied 120 double vibrations per second to the abdomens of pregnant women. Although in this experiment it is difficult to establish whether the fetuses were responding to the sound or the vibrations, it is clear that they did show a definite response to the stimulus. They reacted to the vibratory stimuli with increased heartbeats and with convulsive muscular activity. These responses developed at about the beginning of the twenty-ninth week and became more consistent and sharper with increasing fetal age (Sontag & Wallace, 1934, 1936).

Another experiment found that the fetus reacts differently to different tones, which seems to indicate that it can discriminate differences. Every week during the last 2^1/$_2$ months of pregnancy, various tones were sounded at a short distance from the expectant mother. Since there was no direct contact between the mother and the source of stimulation, any response had to be to something the fetus heard, rather than felt. The fetus responded differentially to a wide range of tones, with sharp body movements and increased heartbeat (Bernard & Sontag, 1947).

In still another experiment, thirty-two women in labor were presented with sounds of 70 to 90 decibels produced by either loudspeakers or intrauterine earphone, and with vibrations of 110 decibels created by mechanical vibrator or 120 decibels by clinical percussion. There were a total of 330 stimuli. The researchers found that 76 percent of the time the fetuses responded with a heartbeat change greater than 10 beats per minute within thirty seconds of the stimulus onset. The response rate increased with strong stimulation and decreased in those cases in which the mothers had received opiates during the preceding eight hours (Grimwade, Walker, & Wood, 1970).

FETAL SENSITIVITY TO MATERNAL STATES

In the New Testament we read that Zacharias's wife Elizabeth, in her sixth month of pregnancy, "heard the salutation of Mary, and the babe leaped in her womb" (Luke, 1:41). More recently, scientists at the Fels Research Institute in Ohio have reported eight cases over a period of ten years, in which they were able to observe an almost immediate marked increase in the number and violence of fetal movements in response to maternal grief, fear, and anxiety. The fetus of one pregnant woman who was terrified by the violent outbursts of her insane husband was reported to be "undergoing a series of convulsive movements, one or another of the small parts almost constantly causing sharp prominence of the maternal abdomen [Sontag & Wallace, 1934, p. 1053]." Such violent activity was in sharp contrast with that ordinarily observed by the researchers under less emotional situations.

Pregnant women also commonly report increased fetal activity at times when the mother is extremely fatigued. Although this has not been scientifically verified, possible explanations for such fetal response to either the mother's physical or emotional state might be attributable to changes in glandular secretions, in muscular tone or spasms, or other physiological manifestations within the mother's body.

INDIVIDUAL DIFFERENCES IN FETAL
ACTIVITY AND HEART RATE

The same clinical studies described above concerning fetal response to sound and vibration demonstrated a marked difference between various fetuses in both the degree of cardiac acceleration and body movement. These differences are borne out by other research, as well as by maternal testimony.

Fetal Activity

Many women who have borne more than one child have noticed differences in the amount and kind of fetal activity. One mother of a child who later turned out to be hyperactive has said, "I knew while Curt was still in the

Babies who were very active as fetuses turn out, at the age of six months after birth, to be more advanced on motor development than those who were less active in the womb.

(Magnum Photos)

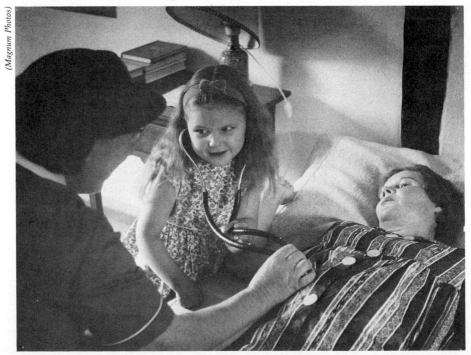

womb that he was going to be a pistol! He bounced around so much inside me that I would automatically put my hand over my abdomen to keep him from popping out! [Stewart & Olds, 1973, p. 253]." On the other hand, many mothers claim that their offspring were as placid prenatally as they are in childhood.

These individual differences among fetuses affect not only the total amount of fetal activity but also its kind. There are three different types of fetal movements: a sharp kicking or punching movement of the extremities, which increases steadily from six months till birth; a squirming or writhing slow movement, most observable during the third or fourth month before birth; and a sharp, convulsive movement that has been described as a fetal hiccup or spasm of the diaphragm (Sontag, 1966). Different fetuses seem to engage in different proportions of these three types of movement.

Differences in fetal activity appear to predict postnatal activity, restlessness, and resistance to handling during the first year (Sontag, 1966). Babies who were very active as fetuses, turn out, at the age of six months after birth, to be more advanced in motor development than those who were less active in the womb (Richards & Nelson, 1938). These differences in activity may represent inborn temperamental or developmental differences or represent reactions to different prenatal environments. As we'll see in Chapter 2, the effects of heredity and environment are not always clearly delineated.

Fetal Heart Rate

An individual of any age displays continuous variations in heart rate during rest, with the degree of fluctuation, or *lability*, apparently an individual characteristic. Although it is very difficult to determine the lability of fetuses, some preliminary reports indicate that some fetuses, known as *cardiac labiles*, have large fluctuations in heart rate, and others, *cardiac stables*, have minor fluctuations. Follow-up studies have found a tendency for fetuses designated as cardiac labiles in the eighth month of pregnancy to be cardiac labiles at twenty years of age (Lacey & Lacey, 1958). Further studies of this characteristic may shed some light on the possibility of predicting certain aspects of adult personality from factors that are measurable in the prenatal period (Sontag, 1966).

The normal fetal heartbeat pattern can be altered by sound and vibrations. It also reacts to other environmental stimuli, including, for example, the smoking behavior of the mother. The effects of these and other factors in the prenatal environment are described later in this chapter.

PRENATAL LEARNING

Can learning take place even before birth? Recent research points to the possibility that it can.

In a hospital nursery, 102 normal, newborn infants were exposed day and night, without interruption, to a sound that duplicated a normal heartbeat, with 72 paired beats per minute at a level of 85 decibels. The infants were in the nursery at all times, except for a brief period every four hours when they were taken to their mothers for feeding. A control group of 120 babies were in a different nursery, without the heartbeat sound. Initially the experiment called for another group of babies to be exposed to an abnormally fast, 128-per-minute heartbeat, and a "gallop" heartbeat with an irregular rhythm, but these babies responded immediately to these sounds with increased crying and restlessness. The experimenters, therefore, discontinued the use of these sounds "because of the critical influence of early infantile experience on later behavior [Salk, 1973, p. 29]."

After four days, 70 percent of the infants exposed to the heartbeat sound had gained weight, while only 33 percent of the control infants did so (Salk, 1973). The heartbeat babies showed a median gain of 40 grams; the control group showed a median loss of 20 grams (a usual weight loss in the first few days of life). The amount of crying in both nurseries was also measured. In the heartbeat group, one or more infants cried 38 percent of the time, while there was crying in the control group 60 percent of the time. Since there was no significant difference in food intake between the two groups, it appeared that the decrease in crying among the heartbeat babies helped them to gain weight. The experimenter (Salk, 1960) concluded:

> The data obtained indicate that newborn infants, when in the proximity of a stimulus that we can reasonably assume existed during its prenatal life, show relatively less anxiety than is otherwise the case. This reaction, under the conditions described, is consistent with the idea that sensory impressions from the maternal heartbeat are imprinted in the human during its prenatal life [p. 743].

However, as many critics have pointed out, there are many other possible explanations for these findings. It is possible, for example, that it is the *continuous* stimulation that quiets the baby.

An experiment of this type could have practical applications for the care of newborn infants. Assuming that a newborn baby has already been imprinted to the maternal heartbeat, we would expect those infants who remain in the same rooms with their mothers after birth, and who have increased body contact with the mothers, to cry less and gain weight faster than infants separated from their mothers. To encourage these aims, hospitals might then change the present policies that separate even normal, healthy mothers and babies immediately after birth and keep them apart for most of their hospital stay. These findings also carry important implications for the care of premature infants, who are especially vulnerable and must gain weight as soon as possible. A simulated heartbeat might help to quiet these infants, who must be separated from their mothers.

LONG-TERM EFFECTS OF PRENATAL LEARNING

An experiment with older children—twenty-six, from sixteen to fifty months of age—who were in a foundling hospital awaiting foster home placement, was based on their being divided into four groups. One group was put to bed in a room with the sound of a normal heartbeat of seventy two paired beats a minute, one to a metronome of seventy-two single beats per minute, one to recorded lullabies, and one to no sound at all. All the children were exposed to all four conditions for four nights each, and the experimenters recorded the amount of time it took each child to fall asleep.

Under the heartbeat condition, children fell asleep in about half the time as under any other conditions. The children in any of the three nonheartbeat conditions took about the same time to fall asleep, often an hour or more. Since the heartbeat sound has effects that are not obtainable with other sounds, it appears quite likely that some prenatal learning does, indeed, occur. The unborn infant, it seems, has already learned something about life before it emerges from the mother's womb.

The Prenatal Environment

Even before birth, Vicky is subjected to a myriad of environmental influences. What a mother does and what she undergoes can have profound influences on the baby she carries within her. The food she eats, the drugs she takes, the illnesses she suffers, the radiation she receives—even the emotions she feels—can all affect the new life to some degree or other.

Every year about 250,000 American babies, 7 percent of the more than 3 million born during the year, come into the world with some type of birth defect. Every year another 500,000 fetuses are spontaneously aborted or born dead (National Foundation/March of Dimes). Some of these birth defects are hereditary in nature and will be discussed in Chapter 2. But others are caused by environmental insults or by some interaction between heredity and environment. Following is a discussion of how disturbances in the uterine environment can affect the developing fetus.

MATERNAL NUTRITION

Earlier in this century, an unusually large number of *cretins* were being born in several Swiss cantons. These persons suffered from an underactive thyroid, a disorder that produces physical and mental deficiency. Government investigations revealed that the soil lacked iodine in the areas where cretinism was most common, and supplementary iodine was prescribed for all pregnant women living in these regions. The result has been described as "magical." "In the course of one generation, cretinism all but vanished [Montagu, 1964]."

This is an especially dramatic example of the relationship between maternal nutrition and both the physical and mental health of the child, a

(Michal Heron, Monkmeyer)

A mother provides the prenatal environment; her nutrition, general health, emotional states, and external factors can influence the unborn baby, too.

relationship that is corroborated by many animal and human studies. When an expectant mother eats well, her child will benefit; and when she eats poorly, her child will suffer. Some studies show that the fetus suffers more when the mother is malnourished early in pregnancy (Vore, 1971), while others find the effects of maternal malnutrition more extreme when it occurs in the last trimester of pregnancy (Naeye, Blanc, & Paul, 1973).

Many studies have found that mothers who eat well have fewer complications of pregnancy and childbirth and bear healthier babies, and that mothers with inadequate diets are more likely to bear premature or low-birthweight infants, or babies who are born dead or die soon after birth (Burke, Beal, Kirkwood, & Stuart, 1943; Read, Habicht, Lechtig, & Klein, 1973). Pregnant women whose diets are deficient in vitamins B, C, and D, and calcium and phosphorus are more likely to bear malformed infants than those who eat well, although the mother herself suffers less severely from malnutrition than the baby she carries (Murphy, 1947).

A study of poor Guatemalan women has demonstrated that nutritional supplements given to pregnant women increased their chances of having healthy babies. As the mothers consumed more calories, the babies' birthweights rose and their general health improved. Furthermore, the better nourished women breastfed their babies for a longer time, possibly because they were better able to produce high-protein milk (Read et al., 1973).

One team of researchers examined fetuses obtained from therapeutic abortions on malnourished women, and infants who had died accidentally or of severe malnutrition in the first year of life. Their data indicated that the number of cells in the human brain increases in a linear fashion until birth, and then more slowly until six months of age. After that, there is no increase in the number of brain cells, only in weight. Since the brains of the malnourished infants contained fewer cells than normal (at times only 60 percent of the expected number), it seemed that these infants had suffered malnutrition in utero.

Research with malnourished rats indicates that intrauterine malnutrition produces apparently permanent deficits in brain cell number (Winick, 1969; Winick & Noble, 1966). Rats are not people, of course, and it is not always possible to draw conclusions about human beings from animal work. But a number of investigators believe it is possible that the same irreversible results of poor prenatal nutrition may occur in humans.

The intellectual development of children has also been shown to be related to prenatal nutrition. In one study, one-half of a group of malnourished pregnant women were given dietary supplements, while the others received placebos. At three and four years of age, their children's IQs were measured, and the children whose mothers had received prenatal dietary supplements had a higher average score than those from the unsupplemented group (Harrell, Woodyard, & Gates, 1955).

Another study, however (Stein, Susser, Saenger, & Marolla, 1972), found no relationship between a mother's starvation during pregnancy and the child's mental performance at the age of nineteen. This study of 125,000 Dutch men compared those who had been conceived and/or were gestating during a severe famine with those who had not been exposed to famine conditions. All the men had been given IQ tests in connection with routine examinations for induction into the army. The study is especially noteworthy because it isolates the experience of malnutrition from other environmental factors, something which studies of poverty-stricken women are not able to do.

The authors of this study (Stein et al., 1972) drew three conclusions:

(i) Starvation during pregnancy had no detectable effects on the adult mental performance of surviving male offspring. (ii) Mental performance in surviving adult males from a total population had no clear association with changing levels of mean birth weight in a selected hospital sample of that population. (iii) The association of social class with mental performance was strong [p. 712].

It is possible, the authors add, for prenatal starvation to have an all-or-none effect. Possibly those fetuses that had been affected had died; those who survived were unaffected. In any case, the contradictory evidence points to a need for more research on this topic. Meanwhile, every effort should be made to improve the nutrition of pregnant and nursing women, especially in low-income neighborhoods where other environmental factors aggravate the effects of poor nutrition.

MATERNAL DRUG INTAKE

In 1960 they began to appear—babies born with *phocomelia.* These infants came into the world with no arms and legs, or with small, pitiful, useless limbs. Many had defects of sight and hearing; some lacked ears and eyes; others had fallen victim to a monstrous assortment of other abnormalities. Horror-struck investigators finally linked these infants' birth defects to an innocent-seeming tranquilizer, *thalidomide,* that had been taken by the children's mothers early in pregnancy (Lenz, 1966).

The hundreds of thalidomide babies who are now young adolescents bear tragic witness to the potent effects on the fetus of drugs taken by the pregnant mother. At one time it was believed that the placenta protected the developing baby from injurious elements in the mother's body. We now know that virtually everything the mother ingests makes its way in some form and to some degree to the new life in her uterus. Drugs may cross the placenta, just as oxygen, carbon dioxide, sodium chloride, water, and urea do. They have their strongest effects if taken early in pregnancy. As we have seen, the fetus develops most rapidly in its first few months. It is not surprising, then, that the fetus is especially vulnerable to disease and accident during this period.

Drugs can affect the fetus in three different ways. They can cross the placenta unchanged to affect the fetus the same way they affect the mother, as in the case of barbiturates, which slow down the breathing and heart rates of both. They can cause the formation of a drug metabolite in the mother, the placenta, or the fetus, as happens with synthetic sex steroids, which masculinize the fetus. Or they can alter the maternal physiology and, thus, the intrauterine environment. A spinal anesthetic given to a woman having a baby may lower her blood pressure so much that the supply of oxygen going to the infant is severely reduced (Bowes, 1970).

We know that certain drugs can be harmful. Besides thalidomide, they include the antibiotics streptomycin and tetracycline; the sulfanomides; excessive amounts of vitamins A, B6, C, D, and K; certain barbiturates, opiates, and other central nervous system depressants; and several hormones, including progestin, diethylstilbestrol, androgen, and synthetic estrogen. Furthermore, aspirin, phenobarbital, the tranquilizer chlorpromazine, and several antinausea drugs are known to cause fetal abnormalities in animals (Brody, 1973). Tetracyclines which are administered during pregnancy may cause retardation of bone growth in premature infants (Drage et al., 1966); when taken late in pregnancy, they can cause staining of the infant's teeth (Mull, 1966). And there are some very clear-cut relationships between several other types of drugs and effects on the fetus.

Despite current knowledge, however, much more work has to be done to determine the specific effects of these and other drugs. We also need information on the effects of drug intake by the father. Although his drug taking cannot affect the fetal environment, it is possible that drugs may affect genetic transmission by damaging his chromosomes, which are then passed on at fertilization to the babies he sires. This charge has been leveled at LSD, which is discussed later.

Hormones

Since some 8 million American women are now taking oral contraceptives, it is extremely important to discover whether taking the pill after a woman has unknowingly become pregnant might harm the developing fetus. Preliminary research indicates that it might. Of 34 fetuses that had been spontaneously aborted within six months after the mother stopped taking birth control pills (possibly having taken them early in pregnancy), 16, or 48 percent, had chromosomal abnormalities, compared with only 50, or 22 percent, of 227 spontaneously aborted fetuses whose mothers had not been taking oral contraceptives (Carr, 1970).

A delayed consequence of hormone ingestion during pregnancy can be seen in the cases of the ninety-one adolescent girls and young women who, as of December 1972, had developed either vaginal or cervical cancer, which had been fatal to some of them (Herbst, Kurman, Scully, & Poskanzer, 1972).

Doctors at Vincent Memorial Hospital in Massachusetts had previously found that seven out of the eight mothers of such patients treated there had received diethylstilbestrol (DES) during the first trimester of pregnancy, a drug that had at one time been thought to prevent miscarriage. In a control group of patients without vaginal cancer, no mother had taken DES. Since there was no significant difference between the two groups of mothers on such variables as maternal age at birth, smoking, intrauterine x-ray exposure, or breast feeding (Herbst, Ulfelder, & Poskanzer, 1971), the DES appeared to be implicated as the cause of these young women's vaginal cancers.

Another study of 528 women and girls, aged eleven to twenty-five, found that 90 percent of those whose mothers had taken DES while pregnant now had either gross or microscopic abnormalities of the vaginal tract, while the 41 unexposed controls exhibited no such abnormal conditions (*Medical World News*, 1973).

On the other hand, another study of 818 girls and women whose mothers had taken DES or similar synthetic hormones turned up no cases of vaginal or cervical cancer (Ref. needed: Mayo study).

It seems, then, that we cannot yet draw a clear-cut conclusion about the effects of synthetic hormones administered to a pregnant woman, but there appears to be a strong likelihood that they may have far-reaching effects on her fetus (Herbst et al., 1972).

Other hormones administered in cases of threatened abortion have been known to bring about partial sex reversal. *Progesterone*, for example, overmasculinizes male infants, causing hypertrophy (overdevelopment) of penis and scrotum, exceptional muscularity, accelerated neuromuscular development, hyperkinesis, gastrointestinal difficulties, tension, and irritability in the infant. Progesterone can also pseudomasculinize females, causing an enlarged clitoris and increased neuromuscular development (Russell, 1969; Ehrhardt & Baker, 1973). *Androgens* and *synthetic estrogens* can also masculinize the female fetus (Bongiovanni et al., 1959; Grumbach et al., 1960). Early surgery and/or cortisone treatment are often successful in helping to establish sexuality and helping such children to live a normal life.

Smoking

The pregnant woman enjoying her after-dinner cigarette may not think of herself as ingesting a potent drug. But the nicotine in her cigarette does go through her system, and the evidence is mounting that it does have some effects on the fetus, although the facts are not all in yet about the influence of smoking. There is some evidence that smokers tend to have more spontaneous abortions, more stillbirths, and more babies who die soon after birth (United States Department of Health, Education, and Welfare, 1973).

The clearest finding related to smoking is the tendency of pregnant smokers to bear smaller babies. On the average, the smoker is twice as likely to deliver a low-birthweight baby, a baby whose weight is low for its gestation age, as a nonsmoker (United States Department of Health, Education, and Welfare, 1973). Some researchers have postulated that these differences are not due to smoking per se, but that smoking behavior is a symptom of certain personality traits, such as anxiety, that themselves influence birthweight (Becker, King, & Little, 1968). New evidence, however, suggests that a woman who gives up smoking by her fourth month of pregnancy is similar to a nonsmoker in her risk of delivering a low-birthweight infant (Butler et al., 1972), which would implicate the smoking itself as the major factor.

Babies of smokers have been found to have an increased heart rate before birth. When the fetal heart rate was measured in relation to the mother's smoking, it was found that between eight and twelve minutes after smoking, the maximum effect was felt—sometimes up to 39.6 beats per minute faster than before the smoking incident. This cardiovascular response is more marked about the eighth month of pregnancy. Some fetuses show a deceleration in heart rate, with their hearts beating sometimes 16.8 beats per minute slower than before the mother's smoking (Sontag & Wallace, 1935).

Another effect of smoking is its influence upon the vascular system. By causing contractions of the uterine and placental vessels, smoking reduces the fetus's supply of oxygen and nutrition. On the other hand, since smoking decreases appetite, it may decrease the amount of protein the mother consumes, resulting in poor nutrition for her and her baby. Poorly nourished mothers are more likely to suffer complications of pregnancy and to have premature babies. In either case, smoking seems implicated, whether the poor nutrition of the fetus is caused by the mother's reduced food intake or by the cardiovascular effects that have reduced the ability of the food to reach the baby (Pasamanick & Knobloch, 1966).

Alcohol

About 1 million American women of childbearing age are alcoholics; that is, they cannot function without alcohol (National Foundation/March of Dimes, 1973a). Many more are "social drinkers." Doctors have long been concerned about the effects of alcohol on the human fetus, since animal research has shown that alcohol does cross the placenta and remains highly concentrated for long periods of time in the body of the unborn baby.

In 1973, a "fetal alcohol syndrome" was identified (Jones, Smith, Ulleland, & Streissguth), which apparently affects children of women who drank excessively during pregnancy. The effects of a pregnant woman's moderate drinking are still unknown. The "fetal alcohol syndrome" includes retardation in growth: the children are quite small at birth, and they don't catch up afterwards. It also includes subnormal intelligence and lagging motor development. Children suffering from the syndrome also have abnormally small heads, heart defects, facial abnormalities, and distortions of the joints.

It is not known exactly how the mother's alcoholism produces the birth defects. One possibility is that the ethyl alcohol, or a breakdown product, in whatever the mother is drinking, possibly reaches the fetus and poisons it. The mother's poor nutrition has also been considered, but this is probably not the whole story since the specific defects in the syndrome do not occur in children of nonalcoholic undernourished mothers. Further research may establish the precise mechanism of the defect. It may also determine how much alcohol is critical and at what time during pregnancy it has the greatest effect. Meanwhile, physicians can only try to keep alcoholic women "on the wagon" throughout pregnancy.

Marijuana

Investigation into the possible effects on the fetus of marijuana smoking by the mother has not yielded any relationship. But animal research has shown that fetal malformations can be produced experimentally. The 1972 report on marijuana by the National Institute of Mental Health recommended that women of childbearing age should not use marijuana, since its potential for producing birth defects is unknown.

Lysergic Acid Diethylamide (LSD)

This hallucinogenic compound has been implicated in several studies as a possible cause of chromosomal defects in the user, with an unknown effect on the next generation (Berlin, 1969; Jacobson & Berlin, 1972). One study showed that seventy-five pregnant LSD users had more spontaneous abortions, more major abnormalities in these aborted fetuses, and more chromosomal abnormalities in the mother and surviving infants than would be expected in such a group (Jacobson; cited in Brazelton, 1970). But these findings are complicated by the fact that many of these mothers used other drugs as well, suffered from various infectious diseases, and were marginally nourished, making it impossible to ascribe to LSD the source of their high rate of fetal complications. Another study of infants whose parents had used LSD before and during pregnancy found no statistically significant difference in the incidence of chromosomal breakage or rearrangement in forty-one out of forty-seven (Dumars, 1971).

One complication in the study of the effects of LSD is that street users of the drug usually use illicit forms of the compound, which may be impure and mixed with other drugs, as compared with the pure LSD used in laboratory and research studies. One study (Dishotsky, Longhman, Mogar, & Lipscomb, 1971) concluded:

> Early chromosomal studies implicated LSD as a potential cause of congenital malformations, fetal wastage, and germinal chromosome damage. A review of 15 rodent studies indicated a wide range of individual, strain, and species susceptibility to the affects of LSD. The applicability of such investigations to man is doubtful. In a study of human pregnancies, those exposed to *illicit* LSD had an elevated rate of spontaneous abortions. There is no reported instance of a malformed child born to a woman who ingested *pure* LSD. There are 6 cases of malformation associated with exposure to illicit LSD, four of which have similar limb defects. Given, however, the high frequency of unexplained "spontaneous" birth defects, the rare occurrence of malformed infants born to women who used illicit LSD may be coincidental. While there is no evidence that pure LSD is teratogenic in man, the use of any drug during pregnancy requires that its potential benefits significantly outweigh its potential hazards.
>
> From our own work and from a review of the literature, we believe that *pure* LSD ingested in moderate doses does not damage chromosomes *in vivo*, does not cause detectable genetic damage, and is not a teratogen or a carcinogen in man. Within these bounds, therefore, we suggest that, other than during pregnancy, there is no present contraindication to the continued controlled experimental use of pure LSD [p. 171].

Addictive Drugs

Women who are addicted to such drugs as morphine, heroin, and codeine are more likely to have premature babies. These babies become addicted to the drugs within the womb. When born, they show such withdrawal symptoms as restlessness, irritability, sleeplessness, yawning, sneezing, tremors, convulsions, fever, and vomiting. Sometimes the withdrawal symptoms are severe enough to cause death (Cobrinik, Hood, & Chused, 1959; Henly & Fitch, 1966). The child can be cured of its addiction by administering certain other drugs in gradually decreasing amounts, although it is often difficult.

MATERNAL ILLNESS

During the winter of 1964–1965, an epidemic of German measles swept the United States, causing 30,000 fetal and newborn deaths, and leaving in its wake 20,000 handicapped children. Although this disease, known scientifically as *rubella*, is very mild in the person who has it, when that person is a woman in the first four months of pregnancy, the disease has devastating effects on her unborn child. A woman who contracts rubella at this time has a 3 to 1 chance of having an infant with a birth defect (Swan, 1948). The child born to a rubella mother is likely to suffer vision and hearing defects, as well as mental retardation, central nervous system damage, heart defects, and growth retardation. A vaccine against rubella is now available to be given to girls before puberty, thus protecting them from the disease once they come of childbearing age. Once all women are protected, a very important cause of birth defects will have been conquered, since even in nonepidemic periods, rubella infection occurs in 1 delivery out of every 1,000.

A mild infection called *toxoplasmosis* is contracted by about one in every four people in the United States (National Foundation/March of Dimes, 1972). It usually passes unnoticed, since it produces either no symptoms or those resembling the common cold. When contracted by a pregnant woman, though, the disease can cause brain damage, blindness, or even death to the baby. Toxoplasmosis is generally contracted by eating raw or undercooked meat or by coming into contact with the feces of cats who have the disease. A pregnant woman, therefore, should avoid eating raw or very rare meat, should not get a new cat or handle those of friends, and should not dig in the garden if there is any possibility that cat feces are buried in the area. If she already has a cat, she should have a veterinarian check it for the disease, she should not feed it raw meat, and she should not empty the litterbox herself.

Other maternal illnesses seem to be implicated in the birth of handicapped children. For example, more mothers of children with birth defects have tuberculosis and infections of the urinary tract than do mothers of normal babies (Pasamanick & Knobloch, 1966). Nine out of ten of the children of 329 diabetic mothers required diet and insulin treatment at birth, and 20.9 percent of their children died in utero or in the first few days of life (Far, 1969). Also, offspring of diabetic mothers are more likely to be born with lower-limb phocomelia. Syphilis bacteria can enter the embryo and cause miscarriage, or the child of a syphilitic mother may be born with mental retardation or some deformity caused by congenital syphilis (Deppel, 1945). And the child born to a mother with gonorrhea may be attacked by the gonococci on its passage through the birth canal, ending up blind unless it is treated with silver nitrite eyedrops immediately after birth (Ziegel & Van Blarcom, 1964). Chicken pox, mumps, measles, smallpox, and scarlet fever bacteria are all transmissible from the mother to the fetus, occasionally resulting in babies' contracting these diseases in utero, often with fatal results (Goodpasture, 1942). And currently, viral infections are being investigated as a possible factor in chromosome breakage, and thus in the cause of Down's syndrome and other genetic irregularities (Nichols et al., 1962).

MATERNAL RADIATION

If there is any chance that a woman might be pregnant, she should not receive pelvic x-rays, because we now know that radiation can cause gene *mutations*, that is, minute changes that alter a gene to produce some new characteristic. Some mutations are beneficial, but the great majority appear to be harmful. X-rays can also cause chromosome breakage. Either of these effects can produce abnormalities in offspring exposed before birth to radiation. Radiation during the second to sixth week of human gestation is likely to produce such defects as microcephaly, mental deficiency, defects of coordination, Down's syndrome, spina bifida, skull malformations, ossifications, defects of the head, cleft palate, blindness, ear abnormalities, club feet, genital deformities, and general mental and physical subnormalities (Russell & Russell, 1952).

In one study conducted during the 1920s, seventy-four pregnancies in which expectant mothers received x-ray therapy for various conditions produced only thirty-six normal children. Of the others, twenty-three were severely retarded, and fifteen displayed such other abnormalities as very small size or blindness (Murphy, 1929). Another study reported gross deformities in infants whose mothers had been irradiated during the first two months of pregnancy (Goldstein & Wexler, 1931). Since the medical world learned of the relationship between maternal radiation and infant abnormalities, women who may be pregnant are given x-ray treatment only in life-threatening illness.

Most of our information on the effects of radiation on fetal development has come from research with animals. In one study, a group of pregnant mice were irradiated one time each, at different stages during the pregnancies, in an attempt to find *critical periods* for the development of particular anomalies. In other words, was there a specific time during pregnancy when mice were susceptible to particular defects? This experiment found that the gestation age when radiation occurred determined the specific defect that resulted. Thus a mouse that received x-rays 7 or 8 days after conception was likely to have a pup with brain hernia, whereas a mouse that had been irradiated $9^1/_2$ days after conception might give birth to a pup with spina bifida.

Similar critical periods seem to exist in humans, with most damage being done before the sixth week of conception, at the time of major organ development. Radiation at later times is also dangerous but does not produce such severe abnormalities. Later radiation is less likely, however, since most doctors will not radiate women whom they know to be pregnant. If there is any chance at all that a woman might be pregnant, she should not receive x-rays; since x-ray does not necessarily induce abortion, many irradiated fetuses do come to term, and many who do are born with serious birth defects (Russell & Russell, 1952).

MATERNAL EMOTIONS

The fetus who responded with increased movements to its mother's fear of her violently psychotic husband, mentioned earlier, is not so unusual. Other similar responses have also been reported. Because our physiological conditions are so closely allied to our emotional states, the fetus whose mother is calm and relaxed inhabits a much different world from the one whose mother is tense and anxious. The chemicals in the blood stream, the hormones coursing through the body, and the cell metabolism are all different, depending on the psychological climate. These physical responses to maternal emotional states may account for the observable differences between the fetuses and newborn infants of mothers with various emotional characteristics.

One study, for example, found that mothers who were very anxious about pregnancy were more likely to have problem deliveries and to bear abnormal children than were mothers who were not so anxious. And since the mothers were tested for their anxiety level on their first visit to the clinic, it did not appear likely that they were anxious because they knew of the possibility of complications (Davids, DeVault, & Talmadge, 1961). Another study found that mothers who had obstetric complications were more likely to exhibit psychopathology during pregnancy, as indicated by their performance on the Minnesota Multiphasic Personality Inventory (MMPI) than were women with normal pregnancies and deliveries (McDonald & Cristakos, 1963).

Why does one newborn infant cry incessantly, whereas another is the picture of contentment? Some researchers feel that the infant's behavior during the first days of life reflects its mother's prenatal attitudes. One team of investigators administered the anxiety scale of the International Personality Assessment Test to a number of expectant mothers during each trimester of pregnancy. The babies of nineteen women whose scores represented extremes of high or low anxiety were watched for differences. Observers found that the babies of the very anxious mothers cried more than the others on the second, third, and fourth days of life. Since the mother-baby contact in the hospital was typically minimal, they attributed the differences among the babies to the prenatal differences among their mothers (Ottinger & Simmons, 1964). (We cannot discount the possibility, however, that these babies were displaying inherited personality characteristics that had been genetically passed along by their mothers. In other words, perhaps general anxiety and nervousness are inheritable temperamental traits.)

It has even been suggested that maternal emotions during pregnancy might contribute to the development of such birth defects as cleft palate or hydrocephalus. The mothers of 232 children with *cleft palate* or *harelip* were questioned as to the degree and the timing of any stresses they may have undergone during their pregnancies. These two birth defects, which occur once in every 770 births, are closely related, often found together, and caused by the failure of the embryo's palate to fuse completely; when the cleft extends to the upper lip, the condition is known as harelip. Fusion of the maxillae (the bones of the upper jaw) normally takes place between the sixtieth and seventieth day of pregnancy.

Of these mothers, 68 percent reported emotional disturbance and 23 percent reported some physiological or traumatic stress during the first trimester of pregnancy. Of these women, 85 percent reported that they did not have similar stresses during other pregnancies, when normal children were born.

During times of stress, the adrenal cortex will secrete the hormone *hydrocortisone.* Larger-than-normal amounts of this hormone may have been secreted by these stressed women at crucial times in their pregnancies, preventing the fetal maxillae from fusing normally. Since 25 percent of the affected children had a relative with cleft palate or harelip, it seems that genetic influences also played a part, and that this defect illustrates an interaction between genetic and environmental factors. The authors of the above study say, "It is possible and perhaps probable, that two factors operate in the production of this congenital abnormality—genetic activity and stress. One operating without the other may be unable to produce cleft palate [Strean & Peer, 1956]."

MATERNAL-CHILD BLOOD INCOMPATIBILITY: THE Rh FACTOR

A compelling example of the ways in which genetics and environment are intertwined can be seen in those babies who suffer from *Rh hemolytic disease*, also known as *erythroblastosis fetalis.* The cause of this disease is ironic; in a sense a mother becomes allergic to her own fetus, and the system of immunity designed to protect her causes her body to attack the baby she carries.

About 85 percent of the population have a protein substance in their red blood cells known as the Rh factor (named for the rhesus monkeys in which it was first found). These persons are considered Rh positive; those without this factor are Rh negative. When an Rh-negative woman marries an Rh-positive man—as happens in one out of twelve marriages—their children may be either Rh positive or Rh negative.

The principle of dominant autosomal inheritance (see Chapter 2) determines the heritability of the Rh factor, since the gene that carries this factor is dominant. This means that the Rh-negative woman has recessive genes. If her Rh-positive mate is homozygous, all their children will be Rh positive; but if he is heterozygous, each of their children has an equal chance of being positive or negative for the Rh factor.

No problems will arise for the Rh-negative babies of this union. But all the Rh-positive babies (after the first, which is rarely affected) are subject to a severe anemia known as Rh hemolytic disease, because of an immune mechanism that causes the mother's body to reject her own fetus.

If, during labor or delivery, the unborn baby's blood penetrates the placenta and enters the mother's circulatory system, antibodies against the Rh factor may form in her blood. If this happens, her body becomes "sensitized" to the factor and reacts against it as against a foreign substance, in effect making her "allergic" to any future Rh-positive baby she may conceive. The mother is not affected, nor is her first Rh-positive baby (unless she has previously received a transfusion of Rh-positive blood). But if she becomes pregnant again with another Rh-positive baby, the antibodies in her system will enter the baby's blood stream, attack its red blood cells, and possibly bring about spontaneous abortion, stillbirth, jaundice, anemia, heart defects, mental retardation, spasticity, or death soon after birth. The risk and severity of the disease become greater with each succeeding Rh-positive pregnancy as the antibodies in the mother's system continue to multiply.

Thus we see how an inherited trait—the presence or absence of the Rh factor—provides the basis for an environmental force—the buildup of antibodies in the mother's system. The interaction of genetics and environment produces this illness of unborn and newborn babies.

Since April 1968, an Rh vaccine has been available to prevent this age-old disease, whose symptoms had been described by the ancient Greeks. Administered to a mother within seventy-two hours after she has given birth or aborted an Rh-positive child, it prevents her body from becoming sensitized. But many babies who develop Rh disease will continue to be saved by the same methods that have been in use over the past several years, usually a series of repeated blood transfusions. The new technique of amniocentesis can determine prenatally whether a baby has Rh disease. If so, it can receive a life-saving blood transfusion even before birth, or immediately after birth (Zimmerman, 1973).

Summary

1   The three stages in prenatal development are *germinal, embryonic,* and *fetal.* The germinal stage is characterized by rapid cell division and increasing complexity of the organism; the embryonic stage is characterized by rapid growth and differentiation of major body systems and organs; and the fetal stage is characterized by rapid growth and changes in body form.

2   Although the product of conception is usually a single birth, multiple births can occur. If two ova are fertilized, *fraternal* (dizygotic) twins will result, with different genetic make-ups. If a single fertilized ovum divides in two, *identical* (monozygotic) twins will result, with the same genetic make-up. Differences between identical twins results from prenatal or postnatal environments.

3   Virtually all birth defects occur during the critical first trimester of pregnancy. This includes three-fourths of all known *spontaneous abortions.*

4   At conception, each human being receives twenty-three *chromosomes* from the mother and twenty-three chromosomes from the father. These align into twenty-three pairs of chromosomes—twenty-two pairs are *autosomes,* and one pair are *sex* chromosomes. If the child receives an X chromosome from each parent, it will be female. If an X from the mother and a Y from the father join, a male will be born. The male organism seems to be more vulnerable than the female, both prenatally and postnatally.

5   Research indicates that a fetus hears and learns prenatally and that there are individual differences in fetal activity and heart rate.

6   Prenatal environment exerts an impact on the developing organism. We have considered the effects of maternal states, nutrition, drug intake, illness, radiation, emotions, and blood incompatability.

Suggested Readings

Flanagan, G. L. *The First Nine Months of Life.* New York: Simon & Schuster, 1962. *A lucidly written, well-illustrated, and scientific account of prenatal development.*

Newton, N. *Maternal Emotions.* New York: Harper & Row, 1955. *This text is an illuminating study of women's feelings toward menstruation, pregnancy, childbirth, breastfeeding, child care, sexuality, and relationships with men.*

Rugh, R., and Shettles, L. B. *From Conception to Birth.* New York: Harper & Row, 1971. *This text presents a complete and clear description of conception and prenatal development, with beautiful full-color photographs.*

Tanzer, D., and **Block, J. L.** *Why Natural Childbirth?* Garden City, N.Y.: Double-day, 1972. *This is an interesting and highly readable book explaining natural childbirth, setting it in a historical context. It reports on the results of a study that compared two groups of women—those who had given birth by conventional means and those who used natural childbirth.*

CHAPTER TWO

HEREDITY AND ENVIRONMENT

IN WHICH WE CONSIDER THE GENETIC
AND ENVIRONMENTAL INFLUENCES
AFFECTING VICKY IN THE WOMB

The greatness or smallness of a man is, in the most conclusive sense, determined for him at his birth, as strictly as it is determined for a fruit whether it is to be a currant or an apricot.

(John Ruskin, Modern Painters, IV, *1856*)

Place an infant in the heart of China, and but for the angle of the eye or the shade of the hair, the Caucasian would grow up as those around him, using the same speech, thinking the same thoughts, exhibiting the same tastes. Change Lady Vere de Vere in her cradle with an infant of the slums, and will the blood of a hundred earls give you a refined and cultured woman?

(Henry George, Progress & Poverty, X, *1879*)

Is our future laid out at birth by the many traits we inherit from our parents and forebears? Or is each of us a tabula rasa, a "clean slate," that awaits being written on by our parents, our teachers, and our life experiences to end up as their creation? The history of the science of child development is a history of the shifting views regarding the relative strengths of heredity and environment. The nature versus nurture controversy has raged for centuries, bouncing back and forth between those who felt that *nature*, or inborn hereditary factors, explained all development, and those who believed that *nurture*, or environment, was the sole determinant of the way we are. Both these theories imply that the individual child contributes little to the way he or she will eventually turn out, but is, instead, at the mercy of either heredity or environment. In the past, people tended to take one of these views or the other.

Interaction between "Nature" and "Nurture"

Today we recognize the importance of the interaction between heredity and environment. We also realize that we cannot separate the effects of these two major influences on our lives. And we know that individual children, by their own actions, exert great influence on their own lives. Is heredity responsible for 80 percent of Vicky's development and environment for 20 percent? Are they 50–50? It is impossible to break down their relative effects so specifically. For example, Vicky's intelligence may be determined partly by her heredity; but the kind of home she grows up in, the degree to which she is encouraged to pursue intellectual interests, her physical health, and the kind of education she receives will all have an effect on the eventual expression of her intelligence. Or a boy whose hereditary endowment predisposes him to shortness may never grow up to be a six-footer; but if he is well cared for, he will grow taller than he would have if he were kept in cramped quarters and got too little to eat, too little exercise, and too little love. Furthermore, the way these children respond to both their genes and their surroundings will affect their future development. Some behaviors seem to show more of the influence of one of these factors; others show more of the other.

Motor behaviors, such as creeping, crawling, walking, and running, unfold in a sequential order quite closely related to age, showing the importance of maturation, or a hereditary timetable. Environmental forces interfere with maturation only when they take very extreme forms. Hopi Indian babies, for example, who were kept for the first year of life on cradle boards that prevented them from freely moving their arms and legs still walked at about the same time as babies who had not been so restrained (Dennis & Dennis, 1940). But severe environmental deprivation over a long period of time does affect development. Infants in an Iranian orphanage who received little attention and no exercise sat up and walked quite late, compared with well-cared-for Iranian children (Dennis, 1960). Attempts to train children to walk or be toilet-trained early have generally been ineffective (Gesell, 1929; McGraw, 1940). Those behaviors that depend largely on maturation tend to appear then, whenever the organism is ready, but not before, and, except under extreme deprivation, not afterward.

When we begin to discuss intellect and personality, the mixture of the two influences becomes much more important. Let's consider talking, for example. Maturation is clearly a prerequisite to language development. Before Vicky can talk, she has to be at a certain level of neurological and muscular development. No matter how enriched her home life might be,

Today we realize that we cannot separate the effects of heredity and environment and that individual children, by their own actions, exert great influence on their own lives.

(UNICEF/David Mangurian)

Family of sixteen—soon to become seventeen—in a rural area of Paraguay.

(UNICEF/Ling)

Mother and grandmother tending children on a houseboat near Hong Kong

(George W. Gardner)

Family relaxing in New Hampshire

(UNICEF/Batya Weinbaum)

Father and son sharing a quiet midday lunch in Ecuador

she could not speak, read, or write this sentence at the age of a year. Speech cannot occur in the absence of maturation. But environment plays a much larger part in language development than it does in motor development. If Vicky's parents encourage her first efforts to make sounds by showing their approval and by babbling back and speaking to her, she will start to speak earlier than if they ignore her early vocalizing.

Thus we see that maturation lays the foundation, and the environment helps to build the structure. Once Vicky is ready for a skill, the timing of its appearance will reflect the stimulation in her environment.

HOW DO HEREDITY AND ENVIRONMENT INTERACT?

In a classic article in the "nature versus nurture" debate, Anastasi (1957) says, "The nature and extent of the influence of each type of factor depend upon the contribution of the other [p. 5]." Depending on circumstances, the relative proportions will vary.

Hereditary Influences

Anastasi (1957) arranges both hereditary and environmental influences on a continuum of their effects. At one extreme we find an inborn physical disorder that causes mental retardation; no matter how superior the environment, a baby so affected will be retarded. Next comes a physical defect like hereditary deafness. In itself this does not cause retardation, but it can interfere with a child's normal social relationships, her language development, and her education, with intellectual retardation the ultimate result. Third are the effects of long-term physical illness, which can prevent one child from developing his intellectual potential, while it leads another, like the author Robert Louis Stevenson, who was a very sickly child, to compensate for ill health by concentrating on intellectual pursuits. The fourth, and final, hereditary influence is the way in which inherited physical characteristics can lead to social stereotyping. Whether one is black or white, male or female, fat or thin is bound to affect myriad aspects of one's life, including one's self-esteem. Although skin pigmentation itself may have nothing to do with the amount of money one can earn in a lifetime, the prejudice against a black person may deny that individual the education needed for a high-level job or the opportunity to apply for the job itself. These effects of heredity are indirect; the genes involved do not determine the eventual outcome, but their influence is significant.

Environmental Influences

Anastasi (1957) divides these into two types: the *organic,* which produce physical effects that, in turn, may influence behavior (like inadequate food intake, which produces malnutrition, which in turn causes mental retardation); and *behavioral,* which directly cause psychological reactions (like a course in algebra that enables a person to perform complicated mathematical operations).

Organic influences may be arranged along a continuum with relation to the *directness* of their effects. At one extreme would be injury to the brain during birth, resulting in mental deficiency. Next might be a birth injury that would cause such severe motor deficiency as to make regular schooling impossible; the lack of environmental stimulation could bring about intellectual retardation. Finally, the altered physical appearance of a once-obese person who had lost weight would alter the opinions of others toward her and the more favorable reactions she received as a thin person would make her happier and more self-confident.

Behavioral factors can be arranged along a continuum of the *breadth* of influence. One particularly broad, all-pervading behavior influence is that of social class (Anastasi, 1957):

> Thus social level may determine the range and nature of intellectual stimulation provided by home and community through books, music, art, play activities, and the like. Even more far-reaching may be the effects upon interests and motivation, as illustrated by the desire to perform abstract intellectual tasks, to surpass others in competitive situations, to succeed in school, or to gain social approval. Emotional and social traits may likewise be influenced by the nature of interpersonal relations characterizing homes at different socioeconomic levels [p. 11].

Next comes the kind of education a person receives, the presence of a language handicap, and the accessibility to the specific information asked on standard intelligence tests.

Ways to Study the Relative Effects of Heredity and Environment

When we talk about eye color, blood type, or nose shape, we are fairly confident that we are talking about inherited characteristics. But when we study more complex traits, such as health, intelligence, and personality, which are subject to environmental influences as well, we want to find out the strength of the genetic components. We want to know for several reasons.

First of all, there is the quest for pure knowledge, to add to the sum total of what we know about our most absorbing topic of study, ourselves. Second, these findings have practical implications. If, for example, we discover that a trait we want to encourage—like high intelligence—can be influenced by environment, we can try to make the environment as favorable as possible. On the other hand, if we find that, say, a child's activity level is mostly inherited, we know what we have to accept and can be realistic in our efforts to raise this child. This knowledge helps us deal better with the problem of birth defects. If we find that a certain abnormality is hereditary, we can counsel prospective parents about their child's chances of being defective, and they can make their childbearing plans accordingly.

We can study the relative effects of heredity and environment in several ways. We can study *twins*, comparing twins reared together with those reared apart, and comparing identical twins and same-sex fraternal twins. When twins reared together are more alike on a certain characteristic than those reared apart, we attribute the effects to the influence of environment. When identical twins are more alike than fraternal twins, we attribute the effects to heredity. We can also study *adopted children* and relate their behavior to that of their adoptive parents and their natural parents. When the children are more like their adoptive parents, we see the influence of environment; when they are more like their biological parents, we see the influence of heredity. We can compare *full siblings* and *half siblings*. We can also conduct *consanguinity*, or blood-relationship, studies, examining as many members of a family as possible to discover whether certain characteristics are shared and whether the closeness of the relationship affects the degree of similarity for specific traits.

THE STUDY OF TWINS

Much of what we now believe about the relative effects of heredity and environment comes from the thousands of studies of twins that have gone

Differences between identical twins are assumed to reflect environmental influences.

(Roy Pinney, Monkmeyer)

on since 1875, when Francis Galton, an English scientist and a cousin of Charles Darwin, recognized the potential value of twin study (Scheinfeld, 1967). Many studies on inheritance compare behaviors of identical twins (who, both coming from a single fertilized egg that later divides, have the same hereditary makeup) with those of fraternal twins (who are the products of two separate fertilized eggs and are no more alike than any two siblings). It is assumed that if a particular characteristic is more likely to occur in both members of a pair of identical twins raised apart than in both fraternal twins raised together, that characteristic is largely inherited, rather than acquired. It is also assumed that any difference between identical twins must be due to environment, whereas differences between fraternal twins can be attributed to both environmental and hereditary factors.

Caution, however, must be observed in interpreting twin studies. Although identical twins receive the exact same hereditary endowment, their prenatal environment may be different almost from conception. One twin may lay claim to a more favorable position in the uterus, forcing the other to develop with less room, less air, and less food. The second to be born is often smaller and may, in addition, have suffered some injury or shock at birth. The mechanism of identical twinning, as described in Chapter 1,

Differences between fraternal twins can be attributed both to environment and to heredity.

(Hays, Monkmeyer)

seems to cause more complications of pregnancy and delivery, and hence more neurological and psychological difficulties for identical twins (Mittler, 1971). These difficulties may affect each twin disparately. At birth, then, these two babies who may have been equal at the moment of conception are no longer absolutely identical.

Then, after birth, it is not always easy to measure subtle differences in environment. The first-born and usually larger identical twin may, by his or her personality, elicit different responses from family and friends than does the smaller one. Yet identical twins probably have more similar environment than do fraternal twins, further complicating the task of separating out the effects of heredity versus environment.

There are many problems inherent in the basic design of twin studies. To get a clear picture of the influence of environment, we should be able to compare twins raised in widely diversified surroundings. Yet even when one or both members of a pair of twins are adopted, the adoptive homes usually tend to resemble the natural homes in a number of respects. If the environments are similar, even though different, how can we parcel out the effects of environment versus heredity?

Thus, although we can learn much from twin studies, we have to be careful in interpreting characteristics that are more similar in identical than in fraternal twins as being *completely* hereditary in origin. With these warnings in mind, we can learn a great deal from the study of twins, especially when there is consistency among twin studies and other kinds of studies with regard to specific characteristics.

OTHER BLOOD-RELATIONSHIP STUDIES

Just as we compare identical with fraternal twins, we can compare siblings with unrelated children reared together in foster or adoptive homes. We can compare full siblings and half-siblings. And we can conduct *pedigree* studies, examining as many members of a family as possible to discover how many share certain characteristics and whether the closeness of the relationship affects the degree of similarity in whatever trait we are studying.

SELECTIVE BREEDING

Through this method, which can, of course, be applied only to laboratory animals, researchers mate animals with certain characteristics in an attempt to bring about *strains,* or family lines, that will be particularly strong or weak in these traits. For example, by working with one strain of rats who were exceptionally good in running mazes and with another who were very poor, Seale (in Anastasi, 1949) showed that the two strains differed in a number of emotional and motivational factors, rather than in ability itself.

PRENATAL ENVIRONMENT

We have learned a great deal about the importance of the prenatal environment by investigating relationships between various conditions of children and their mothers' pregnancy experiences. It was medical detective work that linked the development of limbless babies with a seemingly harmless drug, *thalidomide,* taken by women during early pregnancy (Lenz, 1966). Similar probing has established the drastic effects a mother's mild case of German measles or a single exposure to radiation can have on the developing fetus. An experiment which we discussed in Chapter 1 established the value of good nutrition for the pregnant woman by providing dietary supplements to one group of low-income pregnant women and then, three and four years later, testing their children's intelligence. These children had higher IQs than did a comparable group of children whose mothers had not received any nutritional supplementation (Harrell, Woodyard, & Gates, 1955).

EARLY EXPERIENCES

A great deal of information has emerged from experiments with many kinds of young laboratory animals. Changing their diet, providing differential contacts with others of their own species, diminishing their opportunities for exercise, and instituting sensory deprivation have all affected various aspects of behavior. By comparing people with different life experiences, we draw inferences about the effects of these experiences on physical, intellectual, and emotional development. Theorists such as Freud and Erikson have stressed the effects of early experience on later development.

COMPARISON OF CHILD-REARING PRACTICES

A number of cross-cultural and intracultural studies contrasting parental practices have been carried out to determine the effects of various types of discipline, of parental encouragement of independence, of the intellectual climate in the home, and so forth. Many of these studies are discussed throughout this book. Some of the broad mass of data gleaned from them is ambiguous and contradictory, but some does provide us with relatively clear-cut findings. Generally, consistent discipline by parents who agree with each other on how to bring up their children produces the most beneficial results.

The Mechanisms of Heredity: Genetic Transmission

In Chapter 1 we saw that when sperm and egg unite to form the first one-celled organism (the zygote), they endow the new life with a rich hereditary legacy. Sperm and egg each contain twenty-three of those

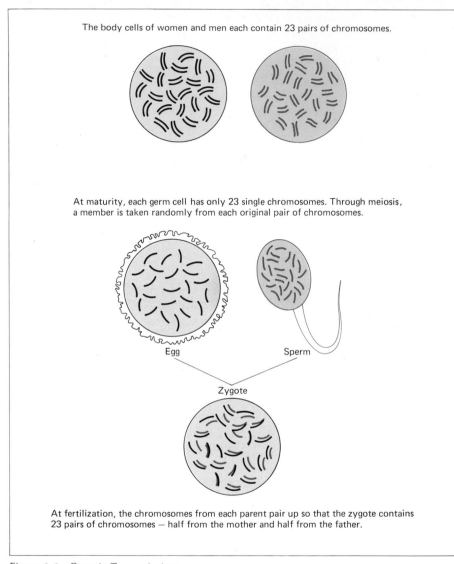

The body cells of women and men each contain 23 pairs of chromosomes.

At maturity, each germ cell has only 23 single chromosomes. Through meiosis, a member is taken randomly from each original pair of chromosomes.

Egg

Sperm

Zygote

At fertilization, the chromosomes from each parent pair up so that the zygote contains 23 pairs of chromosomes — half from the mother and half from the father.

Figure 2-1   Genetic Transmission

rod-shaped particles called chromosomes, so that the zygote will have forty-six chromosomes, like every other cell in the human body except the mature *gametes*, or sex cells, which (as a result of meiosis) contain only twenty-three each (see Figure 2-1). As the fertilized egg develops into a complex human being, it gradually differentiates into billions of cells specializing in hundreds of different functions. Every one of these cells has the same hereditary information. Every one has forty-six chromosomes, each of which contains about 20,000 segments strung out on it lengthwise like beads. These segments are the *genes*. Various genes appear to be located according to their functions in definite positions on particular chromosomes. These thousands of genes play a major role in determining all our hereditary characteristics—height, coloring, facial features, and, to a hotly debated extent, intelligence and personality.

Of the forty-six chromosomes, twenty-two pairs are called *autosomes*; the other pair is the *sex chromosomes* (sperm or egg). Genes on the autosomes can be transmitted equally to male and female. Those on the sex chromosomes are *sex-linked*; that is, they are transmitted differently to males and females (see Figure 2-7).

THE CHEMICAL BASIS OF HEREDITY

One of the most exciting scientific advances of the twentieth century was the discovery in the 1950s of the composition and structure of the genes and of how the information they bear determines the structure and function of our bodies (Watson, 1968).

In the late 1940s, O. T. Avery at the Rockefeller Institute, New York, demonstrated that hereditary traits could be transmitted, at least in bacteria, by purified molecules of a compound known as *DNA* (*deoxyribonucleic acid*). This chemical was known to occur in the chromosomes of *all cells*, and it was considered that all genes were probably composed of DNA. If one could describe the structure of this very complex molecule, DNA, one would have the key to understanding how the genes determine our inherited characteristics.

In 1951 Maurice Wilkins, a biophysicist from London, presented his x-ray pictures of the crystalline, regular formation of DNA; this stimulated the English biophysicist Francis Crick and the American biologist James D. Watson in their collaboration. In 1962, Watson, Crick, and Wilkins won the Nobel Prize for their formulation of the chemical structure of the DNA molecule.

The model they proposed showed the DNA molecule as an intertwined, double spiral chain with ladderlike rungs—often called the double helix. These DNA molecules possess the information that determines the makeup of every cell in our bodies—information that this cell is a human cell, that it will perform specific functions, and that it will perform these functions in a way unique to the individual. That such molecules can possess all the information relating to our hereditary functions and characteristics reflects the myriad permutations of basic structure that these DNA molecules can take. Further, the basis of the genetic role of the DNA molecule lies in its ability to duplicate itself during the production of new cells. The molecule does this by splitting and producing a new molecule.

HOW SPECIFIC TRAITS ARE TRANSMITTED

The science of genetics owes a large debt to Gregor Mendel, an Austrian monk, who, in the 1860s, conducted experiments on plants in his monastery. These experiments in genetic counseling laid the basis for modern theories of inheritance. For example, Mendel crossed one strain of purebred pea plants that produced only yellow seeds, with another strain of purebred plants that produced only green seeds. The first-generation offspring of these plants all had yellow seeds. The trait for yellow seeds is called the *dominant* trait, and the one for green seeds, which is suppressed in the first-generation offspring, is called the *recessive* trait.

When Mendel crossed the first-generation offspring with one another to produce a second generation, the recessive trait reappeared in 25 percent of the second generation, while the dominant trait was present in 75 percent. This 3:1 ratio of dominant to recessive was the same when he performed identical experiments with other traits (smooth or wrinkled seeds, tall or short plants). When Mendel crossed the recessive offspring of the green-seeded plants with one another, they continued throughout many generations to produce only green seeds. In further crossings of the yellow-seed offspring, one-third produced yellow seeds only, while the other produced, again, yellow-seeded plants and green-seeded plants in the ratio of 3:1.

Mendel interpreted the results to mean that various traits were controlled by *pairs* of "factors." One factor was derived from the "male" parent plant, said Mendel, and the other factor from the "female" parent plant. It took almost half a century for the scientific community to accept Mendel's "factors" and to resurrect his work from obscurity. Mendel's factors are now called *genes*. A pair of genes affecting the same trait are called *alleles*. In the experiment described above, the purebred, yellow-seeded plant contains a pair of genes for seed color (or *allelic pair*) which we represent by YY (capital letters signify dominance). The purebred, green-seeded plant contains an allelic pair which we represent by yy (lowercase letters for recessiveness). Such allelic pairs, in which both the maternal and paternal genes are identical (YY and yy), are called *homozygous*. Those allelic pairs in which both maternal and paternal genes are different (Yy) are called *heterozygous*. How we actually *observe* the expression of a particular genetic trait (yellow seed, green seed, tall plant, short plant) is called the *phenotype* of the trait. Figure 2-2 demonstrates the phenotypic makeup of the offsprings produced from one of Mendel's experiments. The *actual genetic* composition of these plants is called the *genotype* (see Figure 2-3). As can be seen, the phenotype and genotype of a trait are not always identical. Although 75 percent of the second generation *appear* (phenotypically) to be homozygous for yellow seeds, in fact a proportion of this 75 percent is genotypically heterozygous; only one-third of the 75 percent is homozygous.

The pattern of inheritance, demonstrated by Mendel's experiment, is

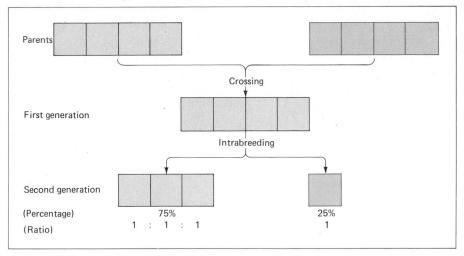

Figure 2-2   Phenotype: The Observed Expression of a Trait

applicable not only to other traits of pea plants, but also to all other species of animals and plants, including human beings.

Another of Mendel's studies helps us understand our unique genetic legacy. In this experiment, Mendel studied two traits at once. He crossed one seed in which yellow was dominant and green recessive with another in which a round shape was dominant and a wrinkled one recessive. He found that color and shape were transmitted *separately* to the next generation of

Figure 2-3   Genotype: The Genetic Composition of a Trait

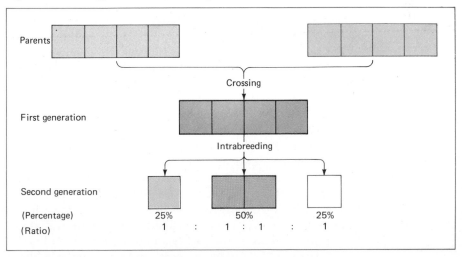

plants, with most being yellow and round, about the same number either yellow and wrinkled or green and round, and the smallest number green and wrinkled (Timiras, 1971).

This experiment showed that genes segregate independently. In other words, every hereditary trait is transmitted as a separate unit; only one of every two mated genes was carried by each parent to each child. Vicky, then, shows such different inherited traits as blue eyes, just like those of her paternal grandfather (via her father), frizzy hair like her mother's, a keen mathematical ability like her maternal grandmother's (via her mother), and so forth.

Characteristics Influenced by Heredity and Environment

PHYSIOLOGICAL TRAITS

On September 28, 1962, twenty-four-year-old Roger Brooks was drinking a cup of coffee in a Miami pancake house when he realized that he was being stared at by one of the busboys in the restaurant. The busboy finally walked over to ask Roger, "Aren't you Tony Milasi?" In this way, Roger Brooks and Tony Milasi, identical twins who had been separated at birth, found each other again (Lindeman, 1969).

The many instances of mistaken identity among identical twins attest to their carbon-copy physical appearance. But not only do they usually look exactly alike with respect to coloring, facial features, body build, and so forth, but identical twins also have a number of other physiological traits in common, supporting a belief that these characteristics are genetically determined. For example, identical twins are more concordant than fraternal twins in their rates of breathing, perspiration, and pulse, and in their blood pressure (Jost & Sontag, 1944).

When both identical and fraternal twins were measured with respect to galvanic skin response (GSR), which records the rate of electrical changes of the skin, identical twins showed greater concordance than did fraternals (Lehtovaara, Saarinin, & Jarvinen, 1965). Identical twin girls are likely to begin to menstruate within a couple of months of each other, while fraternal twin sisters show a mean difference of a year for the age of *menarche*, or first menstruation (Petri, 1934).

Although height and weight are two physical characteristics that can be environmentally influenced, it seems that both are determined primarily by heredity, since identical twins reared together or apart are more similar in both these measures than are fraternal twins reared together, even though the correlation is not quite so strong for weight as it is for height (Newman, Freeman, & Holzingen, 1937; Mittler, 1969). When various aspects of vision have been studied in twins, it has become apparent that visual sensory and perceptual functions are highly influenced by heredity (Mittler, 1971). It even seems as if our days on earth may be numbered by our genes, since senescence and death occur at more similar ages for identical twins than for fraternals (Jarvik, Kallmann, & Klaber, 1957).

INTELLIGENCE

In recent years, the whole nature-nurture controversy has reached its most fevered pitch in discussing the heritability of intelligence. For years, virtually all respected scientists publicly agreed that no racial or religious group was intellectually superior to any other. Great plans were made for a Great Society in which social action programs would do away with environmental inequities and allow all groups their chance in the sun.

In 1969 a California professor of education named Arthur Jensen published an article in which he referred to an impressive body of evidence that suggests that genetic factors determine most of the differences in measured intelligence among white Europeans and Americans. He then went on to say that the average 15-point difference in IQ scores between blacks and whites in our society also must be hereditary.

Jensen's argument, or "jensenism," as it has come to be called, impressed many in the educational and scientific community. It has given rise to a debate that is more political than academic. Furthermore, it has raised an urgent practical question. If intelligence is determined before birth by the genes we carry, programs of compensatory education are a waste of time, effort, and money—and a cruel hoax played on black children and their parents. If, on the other hand, environmental factors play a large role in determining intelligence, it is incumbent upon society to make ever greater efforts to overcome the disparities that do exist.

We will discuss intelligence in detail in Chapters 8 and 11. For the moment, though, we want to look at the classic evidence pointing to some degree of its heritability.

The classic studies of intelligence favor genetic components to the quality, if we define intelligence as an innate general cognitive factor, or a basic potential for learning. The actual learning that occurs, the educational attainments as evidenced in one's ability to read, spell, and calculate, are more subject to environmental influences of family and schooling.

Cyril Burt, a British psychologist, conducted a series of investigations to determine the relative effects of heredity and environment on intelligence and intellectual achievement. Burt studied two groups of children: unrelated youngsters who had been raised in orphanages and like institutions, and identical twins who had been separated soon after birth. He attempted to measure "pure" intelligence by administering an individual intelligence test (the London revision of the Terman-Binet test) and a group test, including both verbal and nonverbal items. He also gave tests of performance in reading, spelling, and arithmetic, and he took physical measures—height, weight, head length and breadth, and eye color. The findings from Burt's investigations are shown in Figure 2-4 and can be summarized briefly.

Unrelated pairs of children brought up together show very slight positive

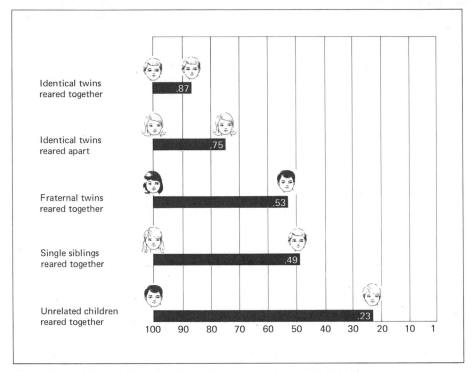

Figure 2-4   IQ Correlations for Twins, Siblings, and Unrelated Children

correlations of intelligence, while those from related pairs increase progressively according to the closeness of family relation. Monozygotic twins have a very high correlation; even when reared apart, their correlations are higher than for any two children reared together, pointing to a strong genetic component in intelligence.

On the other hand, educational attainments, as evinced by performance on reading, spelling, and math tests, seem to be more closely related to environmental circumstances than to genetic inheritance (Burt, 1966).

These findings duplicated those of an earlier report by another investigative team (Newman, Freeman, & Holzinger, 1937), which had studied mental and physical variables in identical twins who had been reared together, in identicals who had been reared apart, and in fraternal twins reared together. They found that physical traits of identical twins were very similar whether the twins had been reared together or apart, and that IQ scores were affected more than the physical variables when identical twins had been reared apart, but that they were still generally more closely related for identical twins reared apart than for fraternal twins reared together. However, achievement scores were more closely related for both identical and fraternal twins who had been reared together than for identical twins who had been reared apart. The more the home environments differed, the more they were likely to have affected any measures of intelligence or achievement.

A smaller number of studies (Vandeberg, 1966) have isolated specific cognitive skills and found genetic determinants for verbal, space, number, and word-frequency tasks.

Some aspect of intelligence does seem, then, to be based on heredity. But in evaluating these studies we must bear in mind several points.

First, we have to define what we mean by intelligence. Then we have to decide whether IQ tests measure this characteristic. And finally we have to evaluate the data we have. Also, we have to remember that most of those studies were done on people from relatively advantaged social environments. The differences among these individuals may result more from genes than from environment. In a disadvantaged community, though, the environment may become more important. We can see how this would operate in a comparison of stature. Under optimal conditions—of good nutrition and good health—genes determine most of the variations in height. But where illness and malnutrition are common, the effects of the environment often outweigh those of heredity. Then, the twin studies themselves were flawed in several ways (Daniels, 1973). The most prominent researchers—Burt and Shields—apparently tested both members of most of the twin pairs themselves. A certain amount of experimenter bias may, therefore, have crept into the testing situation. Also, the separated twins generally lived in very similar homes, and so their environment was not so drastically different as that between the typical white child in our society and the typical black child. Another problem with the twin tests was the lack of standardization of the tests for age and sex. The high correlations between the scores of twins may have had a great deal to do with the fact that both of a pair of twins were of the same age and sex.

Another major problem is that we may not be able to compare blacks with whites any more than we can add apples and oranges. Even if we do determine that differences within a subgroup are due to genetic differences, we do not know that differences between groups have the same basis— unless we can demonstrate without question that the biological and social environments of the two groups are identical. This is certainly not the case at the present time. Until it does become the case, it is essential for the well-being of our society that we try to equalize the environment as much as possible for all children. And until we can provide children from all racial and ethnic groups with the advantages of some children, we have to do our best to compensate for their lack.

It is most likely that what we generally describe as intelligence—how well someone performs in school and in life—is the product of the interaction of genetic and environmental factors, in proportions that are as yet unknown.

Intelligence is affected by maturation, and investigation shows that maturation is affected by heredity. The mental functions measurable in infancy change rapidly as new capabilities emerge and become fully developed, producing sharp spurts and lags in development. Every child seems to have his own rate of development. Billy, for example, may be precocious at six months of age, but may gain slowly for the next six months, and will have fallen behind the average child by the time he is one year old. Susie, on the other hand, may be a slow starter, but at two years of age she may be far ahead of the average baby.

For several years the Louisville (Kentucky) Twin Study has conducted a longitudinal study of growth and development of twins, testing them periodically up to the age of two with the research version of the Bayley scales of mental and motor development. On the degree of *developmental maturity* that persists across several ages, and also on the *spurt-lag factor* (the age-to-age changes in precocity), this study found more concordance between identical twins than between fraternals, indicating a significant genetic influence on both these aspects of infant mental development. Although differences between homes did affect the babies, these investigators found that it took an unusual disparity in environmental conditions to impose a major change in the normal course of infant development (Wilson, 1972).

PERSONALITY

If we define personality as "the pattern of collective character, behavioral, temperamental, emotional and mental traits of an individual [*American Heritage Dictionary*, 1971]," we realize that we are talking about something so complicated that it would be impossible to ascribe it all to one major influence, either hereditary or environmental. But if we separate out specific aspects of personality, we can find many grounds for ascribing some hereditary basis for individual factors that make us the kind of people we turn out to be. We have already, for example, looked at some of the evidence pointing to a genetic basis for the development of intelligence.

In 1956, two psychiatrists and a pediatrician (Thomas, Chess, & Birch, 1968) launched the New York Longitudinal Study to determine those aspects of personality that babies seem to be born with and that remain consistent through the years. By closely following 231 children from infancy through adolescence and examining them in regard to several traits, the researchers concluded that temperament, or the basic behavioral style of an individual, appears to be inborn.

They looked at such characteristics as a baby's activity level; regularity in biological functioning (for hunger, sleep, and bowel movements); readiness to accept new people and new situations; adaptability to changes in routine; sensitivity to noise, bright lights, and other sensory stimuli; whether a child's mood tended toward cheerfulness or unhappiness most of the time; intensity of responses; distractibility; and degree of persistence.

They found that babies varied enormously in all these characteristics, almost from birth, and that they tended to continue to behave according to this initial behavioral style. They also found, however, that many of the children showed some changes in behavioral style, apparently reacting to special experiences or to the nature of the parental handling they received. Again, then, we see interaction between apparently inherited characteristics, which respond in variable degrees to environmental influences.

Using the twin study method, other researchers have established closer concordance between identical twins than between fraternals on a wide range of personality traits, and, therefore, evidence for genetic causes of such characteristics as extroversion-introversion, emotionality, and activity (Vandenberg, 1967); depression, psychopathic behaviors, and social introversion (Gottesman, 1963, 1965); anxiety, depression, and obsession (Gottesman, 1962; Inouye, 1965); and neuroticism (Eysenck & Prell, 1951; Slater, 1953, 1958). And identical twins have been found to show more similar responses than fraternal twins to the Rorschach test, an inkblot test considered to be a measure of personality (Basit, 1972).

The *hyperactive child syndrome* appears to be a complex of behavioral characteristics, including impulsivity, restlessness, inability to concentrate, a high activity level, and emotional lability. Two recent studies, going two different routes, seem to point to some basis of genetic transmission of these traits. A twin study in which mothers were asked to rate their children on their activity level in a variety of situations found a much higher concordance in identical twins than in fraternals, pointing to the possibility of a genetic component (Willerman, 1973).

Another study compared a group of hyperactive children living with their biologic parents, a group of adopted hyperactives who had had no contact since birth with their natural parents, and a control group of children who had not been diagnosed as hyperactive. When the families of the three groups of children were compared, the researchers found a higher rate of alcoholism, sociopathy, and hysteria in the first group than in either the adopted or control groups. Also, more relatives of the biologic hyperactive group had been hyperactive themselves as children than was true for either of the other two groups. The authors suggest a multifactorial transmission of the syndrome, by which genetic, environmental, and hormonal elements interact. They also postulate a polygenetic transmission; that is, a number of genes, rather than one single gene, transmit various facets of the syndrome (Morrison & Stewart, 1973).

Behavior Traits

John walks in his sleep; David doesn't. Gina bites her nails; Dora doesn't. Both Stephen and Alan wet the bed practically every night. John and David, Gina and Dora, and Stephen and Alan are among 338 pairs of same-sex, school-age twins whose physical, mental, and behavioral attributes were measured in a twin study that sought genetic determinants for various aspects of children's behavior.

The pediatrician who conducted this study (himself the father of twin daughters) found that many behavior characteristics appear to have a genetic basis. In this study, identical twins were twice as likely as fraternal twins to be concordant for bed-wetting and nail-biting, $2^1/_2$ times for car sickness, 4 times for constipation, and 6 times as likely to be concordant for sleepwalking (Bakwin, 1970, 1971a,b,c,d).

Schizophrenia

Schizophrenia is a blanket term for a complex of mental disorders marked by an escape from reality and characterized by such symptoms as hallucinations, delusions, feelings of passivity, and other types of thought disorder. This form of psychosis appears in countries all over the world and has been the basis for many studies seeking to determine its causes. The findings point to some degree of genetic transmission.

One twin study found that 86.2 percent of identical co-twins of schizophrenic patients were schizophrenic or had once been, compared with only 14.5 percent of fraternal co-twins (Kallman, 1953). Another study found that the identical twin of a schizophrenic is at least forty-two times as likely to be schizophrenic as someone from the general population, and a fraternal twin of the same sex, nine times as likely (Gottesman & Shields, 1966).

Still another study compared a group of forty-seven adults born to schizophrenic mothers but separated from them by birth, with a control group of fifty adults who had no history of parental psychopathology. This study bore out the findings of the twin studies. Schizophrenia was diagnosed *only* in the offspring of schizophrenic mothers, and about one-half of the adults in this group exhibited major psychosocial disabilities, such as police records, neuroses, and so forth, as compared with only nine of the fifty in the control group. Although only one of the seventeen control males who had served in the military was discharged for psychiatric or behavioral reasons, eight out of twenty-one in the experimental group received such discharges (Heston, 1966).

Two other types of studies have given rise to the belief that schizophrenia has a hereditary component: consanguinity studies, which show that the risk of schizophrenia rises in direct proportion to the closeness of the genetic relationship with an affected relative, and the exploration of schizophrenia in different societies, which shows surprisingly small variations from society to society (Mittler, 1971).

Although there is, then, strong evidence of biological transmission of schizophrenia, we have to ask why all identical twins are not concordant for this trait. One answer may lie in the interaction between biological tendencies and environmental situations. In other words, what appears to be transmitted is not the illness itself, but the predisposition toward the illness. If certain environmental stresses occur in the life of someone who is so genetically predisposed, that individual may respond to these stresses with schizophrenia. At this time, we do not know either the actual genetic mechanisms involved in transmitting such a predilection or the precise stresses that act as its trigger.

Patterns for Transmitting Hereditary Characteristics, Including Birth Defects and Illnesses

In Chapter 1 we looked at some of the ways that a faulty prenatal environment can affect babies. Sometimes the prenatal environment is ideal, but a child is still born with a serious birth defect which has been passed on through the genes. Some inherited disorders are purely the result of defective genes; others result from the interaction of a faulty gene and some environmental factor. Phenylketonuria, for example, is a hereditary illness that is expressed only when a child is exposed to phenylalanine, an amino acid.

Hereditary defects are transmitted in a variety of ways, just as normal characteristics are.

AUTOSOMAL DOMINANT INHERITANCE

More than 900 illnesses or defects carried by dominant genes have been identified (National Foundation/March of Dimes, 1973). These disorders follow the pattern of inheritance that governed Mendel's yellow-seeded pea plants (review Figures 2-2 and 2-3).

When the defective gene is dominant and a person has one normal gene, he himself suffers or will suffer from the defect. A person cannot carry the trait without suffering from the disorder. With dominant inheritance, a person is either affected himself or completely normal. He cannot be a *carrier*; that is, he cannot be unaffected himself but capable of carrying the abnormal gene to pass on to his children. Thus the disease cannot "skip" generations in a family; it is either present in every generation, or it disappears. A disorder transmitted in this way is never one that kills the victim early in life, before he is of reproductive age. If it were, it could never be transmitted to another generation.

As is shown in Figure 2-5, when one parent has one abnormal gene, and the other parent has both normal genes and is free of the disorder, each of their children will have a 50 percent chance of suffering from the disorder. Each child has an equal chance of inheriting normal genes from each parent and being normal.

Among the diseases transmitted in this way are achondroplasia, a type of dwarfism; Huntington's chorea, a progressive degeneration of the nervous system; some forms of glaucoma, a major cause of blindness; and polydactyly, extra fingers or toes (National Foundation/March of Dimes, 1973).

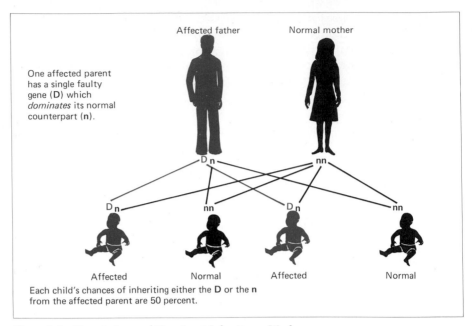

Figure 2-5   How Autosomal Dominant Inheritance Works

AUTOSOMAL RECESSIVE INHERITANCE

The 700 or so identified illnesses or defects carried by recessive genes are transmitted like Mendel's pea plants with green seeds (review Figure 2-3). They appear only when the child inherits two abnormal genes, one from each parent, as is shown in Figure 2-6. When one parent is normal and the other is heterozygotic, with one abnormal gene, each child has a 50 percent chance of inheriting two normal genes or of inheriting one normal and one abnormal gene. In either case, the person will be normal himself. In the latter instance, though, the heterozygote will be a carrier who is capable of passing on the abnormal gene to his own children. When both parents are heterozygotic, each child has a 50 percent chance of being heterozygotic also, unaffected, but a carrier. Each child has one chance in four of inheriting one normal gene from each parent, neither being affected by the condition nor capable of transmitting it. But each also has one chance in four of being homozygous for the trait by receiving two abnormal recessive genes, one from each parent, and thus displaying the symptoms of the condition.

Such diseases are often killers early in infancy because they can be transmitted genetically by people who are carriers of the disease trait but who do not actually suffer from the disease.

Recessive conditions are disproportionately common in marriages between cousins, since each of the mates may have inherited the same abnormal gene from the same common ancestor. This may be the basis for laws barring marriages between close relatives.

Some of the diseases transmitted in this manner are sickle-cell anemia, a crippling and often fatal illness suffered almost entirely by black persons; Tay-Sachs disease, a deteriorative disease of the central nervous system, particularly common among Jews of Eastern European ancestry; and phenylketonuria (PKU), a metabolic disorder caused by the absence of a liver enzyme, in which excessive amounts of phenylalanine, an amino acid, accumulate in the body with various effects, including mental retardation. If diagnosed right after birth, the untoward effects of PKU can be avoided by giving affected children a low-phenylalanine diet for their first four years (O'Grady, Berry, & Sutherland, 1970).

SEX-LINKED, OR X-LINKED, INHERITANCE

About 150 known conditions are transmitted by sex-linked recessive genes, which are carried on the X chromosome of an unaffected mother and expressed only in males (see Figure 2-7). If a woman with one abnormal gene mates with a normal man, their sons will have a 50 percent chance of

Figure 2-6   How Autosomal Recessive Inheritance Works

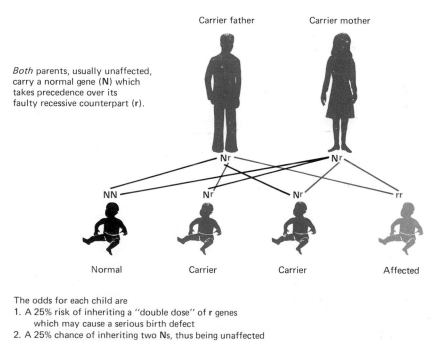

Both parents, usually unaffected, carry a normal gene (**N**) which takes precedence over its faulty recessive counterpart (**r**).

Carrier father

Carrier mother

Nr   Nr

NN   Nr   Nr   rr

Normal   Carrier   Carrier   Affected

The odds for each child are
1. A 25% risk of inheriting a "double dose" of **r** genes
   which may cause a serious birth defect
2. A 25% chance of inheriting two **N**s, thus being unaffected
3. A 50% chance of being a carrier as both parents are

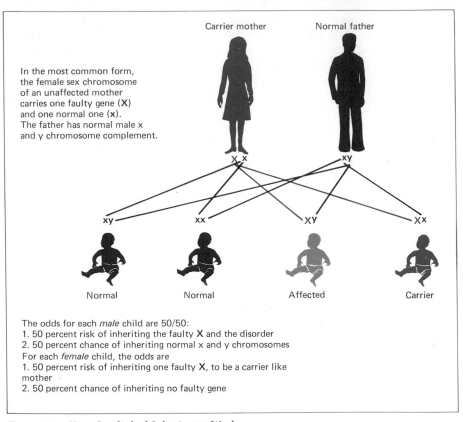

In the most common form, the female sex chromosome of an unaffected mother carries one faulty gene (**X**) and one normal one (**x**). The father has normal male x and y chromosome complement.

Carrier mother   Normal father

Normal   Normal   Affected   Carrier

The odds for each *male* child are 50/50:
1. 50 percent risk of inheriting the faulty **X** and the disorder
2. 50 percent chance of inheriting normal x and y chromosomes
For each *female* child, the odds are
1. 50 percent risk of inheriting one faulty **X**, to be a carrier like mother
2. 50 percent chance of inheriting no faulty gene

Figure 2-7   How Sex-linked Inheritance Works

inheriting the abnormal X chromosome and the disorder, or of inheriting the mother's normal X chromosome and being unaffected. Their daughters will have a 50 percent chance of inheriting the abnormal X chromosome and being a carrier like their mother, or of inheriting two normal X chromosomes and being incapable of transmitting the condition. An affected father can never pass on such a gene to his sons since he contributes a Y chromosome to them. He can, though, pass it on to his daughters, who then become carriers for the disease.

Hemophilia, a blood-clotting disorder that is severely disabling and often fatal, is transmitted in this way. Sometimes called the "royal disease" because some members of Queen Victoria's family were afflicted with it, it affects about 1 male in 10,000. Other sex-linked recessive diseases are some forms of muscular dystrophy, a progressive wasting of muscles, and some forms of spinal ataxia, a degenerative disease of the spinal cord. Red-green color blindness also follows this pattern of inheritance.

MULTIFACTORIAL INHERITANCE

Many normal traits and a number of defects and illnesses appear to be inherited in a much more complicated way, either through certain combinations of genes, or through the interaction of environmental factors with genetic predispositions. Height, weight, the hereditary components of intelligence, and other general traits are probably determined by many genes, rather than one or two. Less is known about the numbers of the disorders so transmitted, their probability of inheritance, and the specific modes of inheritance. Some defects thought to be passed on through the interaction of various factors are spina bifida, a disorder in which there is an opening of the spine; hydrocephalus, or water on the brain; pyloric stenosis, in which the opening from the stomach to the small intestine is obstructed; and cleft palate, a condition caused by the failure of the embryo's palate, and sometimes the lip, to fuse completely. The mental illness, schizophrenia, and the behavior disorder, hyperactivity, may also be passed on to children multifactorially.

CHROMOSOMAL ABNORMALITIES

Some chromosomal errors that cause genetic defects are due to isolated accidents that occur during the development of an individual organism and are not likely to recur in the same family. More often, however, chromosome defects are passed on from parent to child.

Down's Syndrome

Down's syndrome is the most common chromosomal birth defect and is caused by an extra chromosome. It is also called *mongolism* because one of its physical manifestations is an Oriental-looking skin fold at the inner corners of the eyes. Other signs are a small head; flat nose; protruding tongue; peculiarities in the palms of the hands and the soles of the feet; defective heart, eyes, and ears; and a variable degree of mental retardation, with IQs averaging between 25 and 50 and occasionally going higher. Down's syndrome people used to have an average life expectancy of ten years, but now with increasing care and intensive education, they are living in increasing numbers into their thirties and forties (Smith & Wilson, 1973).

Instead of the normal forty-six chromosomes, a mongoloid child has forty-seven. The extra chromosome is number twenty-one. Or the child may have forty-six chromosomes, with an extra number twenty-one chromosome grafted to another chromosome. The mistake in chromosome distribution may occur in the development of the egg, the sperm, or the fertilized egg itself when it first divides (Smith & Wilson, 1973). In only about 3 percent of the cases is this disorder hereditary; in these cases, one parent is found to have one normal twenty-one chromosome, but the other half of pair twenty-one is grafted to half of pair fifteen.

(Ursula Mahoney, Monkmeyer)

The most common chromosomal birth defect, Down's syndrome, results from an extra number twenty-one chromosome; the defect can be hereditary or accidental.

The mothers of children with Down's syndrome tend to be older than the average mother, and it has been postulated that if women over the age of thirty-five stopped having babies, the mongolism rate would be reduced by half. When a younger woman has a mongoloid baby, the likelihood is greater that the defect is hereditary; with the older woman, it is more likely to be a chromosomal accident. Since the syndrome is preponderant among older mothers and since we know that a female has all her ova at birth, the possibility arises that the eggs of some women may deteriorate with advancing age.

Although Down's syndrome children have a limited potential for development, within their limitations they can be happy, pleasant companions. They tend to be cheerful, friendly, and sociable, with a gift for mimicry and an enjoyment of music. They do have a stubborn streak but respond to firm management. They usually enjoy their day-to-day life, either at home with an understanding family or in a well-run institution. Many learn simple skills and, as teenagers and adults, can help to support themselves.

Klinefelter's Syndrome
Affecting males only, this syndrome occurs in 1 in 800 live male births, more frequently in sons of older women (Kennedy, 1971). In 1949, Dr. M.

L. Barr discovered the presence of sex chromatin, called the *Barr body*, in the nucleus of the female cell but not of the male. Instead of the normal male chromosome arrangement (XY), Klinefelter males have an extra X chromosome (XXY), and they show the Barr body in their cells. This syndrome includes mental retardation, small testes (Timiras, 1971), pubertal development of female secondary sex characteristics, such as breast enlargement, and the possibility of effeminacy, homosexuality, transvestism, and transexualism (Money & Pollett, 1964). The administration of the male sex hormone *testosterone* to Klinefelter adolescent males gives them more masculine body contours and sexual characteristics, makes them more assertive, and heightens their sexual drive (Johnson et al., 1970).

Turner's Syndrome

This syndrome affects females only. It occurs in 1 of every 3,000 female births (Kennedy, 1971) and results in a female's having only forty-five chromosomes—twenty-two pairs of autosomes and one X. One X is missing, and the Barr body is lacking or minimized. The chromosome picture is XO. An affected individual is dwarfed with webbing of the neck. She is often mentally retarded (especially in spatial ability), and sexually underdeveloped, with the ovary almost entirely atrophied. Estrogen therapy at puberty induces sexual maturation (Timiras, 1972).

XYY Syndrome

The XYY syndrome, in which a male has an extra Y chromosome, is often found in tall men in prison. The incidence of XYY in the general population of men 5 feet 11 inches or taller is one in eighty. But one in eleven tall men found in a criminal population had marked chromosomal abnormalities (Telfer et al., 1968), Such men tend to have low intelligence, and it is believed that the extra Y may influence aggressive violent behavior. They may be sterile and bisexual (Money & Ehrhardt, 1972).

XXX Syndrome

Characterized by three X chromosomes and two Barr bodies, this syndrome occurs three times as often as Turner's. Even though the individual appears normal, the sexual characteristics are often poorly developed and the incidence of mental disturbances and psychotic behaviors is higher than in the general population (Timiras, 1972).

Genetic Counseling

Five years after their marriage, Bill and Mary Brown decided that they were ready to start their family. Mary became pregnant right away; the couple turned their study into a nursery; and they eagerly looked forward to bringing the baby home. But Bill and Mary's first baby never set foot in that brightly decorated nursery. She was born dead, a victim of *anencephaly*, a birth defect in which the baby's skull is missing and some of the internal organs are malformed.

The young couple were heartbroken over the loss of the baby they had both wanted. More than that, they were afraid to try again. They were afraid that they might not be able to conceive a normal child. They still wanted to have a baby but felt they could not go through another crushing disappointment.

It is to help couples like Bill and Mary that a new service called genetic counseling has been developed. People who have already given life to one handicapped child, who have a family history of hereditary illness, or who suffer from a condition known or suspected to be inherited can get information that will help them determine their chances for producing future afflicted children. Genetic counseling aims to discover the cause of a specific defect in a specific child, to establish a pattern for inheritance of a certain defect, and to determine the chances of an individual couple's producing normal children.

The genetic counselor may be a pediatrician, an obstetrician, a family doctor, or a genetic specialist. He or she takes a thorough family history, including information relating to diseases and causes of death of siblings, parents, blood-related aunts and uncles, and grandparents; any marriages between relatives; previous abortions or stillbirths; and other relevant material. Then each parent and any children in the family receive a physical examination, since a person's physical appearance often gives a clue to the presence of certain genetic abnormalities.

Sophisticated laboratory investigations of a patient's blood, skin, urine, or fingerprints may also be indicated. Chromosomes prepared from a patient's tissue are analyzed, then photographed. The photographs of the chromosomes will then be cut out and arranged according to size and structure on a chart called a *karyotype* to demonstrate any chromosomal abnormalities that may exist. Improved techniques for examining karyotypes make it possible to determine whether an individual who appears normal could possibly transmit genetic defects to his or her children.

Based on all these tests, the counselor determines the mathematical odds for this couple's having an afflicted child. If a couple feels that the risks are too high, the husband or wife may choose to be sterilized or the couple may consider artificial donor insemination or adoption.

The availability of the new procedure of *amniocentesis*, which can determine the presence of certain birth defects in the second or third trimester, encourages some couples to take a chance on pregnancy. Should they then discover that their baby is likely to be born with some defect, they may choose a therapeutic abortion in those states where this is a legal option. Amniocentesis also alerts doctors to the need for special treatment, either in utero (as in Rh disease), or immediately after birth (as in PKU).

Through amniocentesis, fetal chromosomes may be sampled before birth. A large, hollow needle is inserted into the abdomen of a pregnant woman, penetrating the uterus, to withdraw a small amount of fluid surrounding the fetus. The amniotic fluid is spun in a centrifuge, where the liquid and cells separate. The liquid is discarded and the remaining cells cultured on a nutritive medium. It takes from three to six weeks to get the culture and make the karyotype. By running certain laboratory tests on cells in this amniotic fluid, the presence or absence of a number of birth disorders can be definitely ascertained (Valenti, 1968). Although amniocentesis poses virtually no danger to the mother and only a very small one to the fetus, it is indicated only in certain high-risk pregnancies. It is rarely effective before the fourteenth week of pregnancy.

Another prenatal procedure involves scanning the womb with *ultrasound*, a method that uses sound waves originally developed by the United States Navy. Through this technique it is possible to see the outline of the fetus. After Bill and Mary had gone to a regional genetic counseling center, they had been told that anencephaly was probably due to an interaction between genetic and environmental factors. There was, then, a fairly strong possibility that they might have another anencephalic child, but the ultrasound monitoring could detect the condition before birth; and if the child turned out to be anencephalic, Mary would be able to have a therapeutic abortion. They decided to take the chance. When Mary went in for the ultrasound monitoring, she learned that her baby's skull development was normal. She also learned that there was more than one baby. Both twins were normal at birth.

A genetic counselor does not give a couple advice on whether to take the risks indicated for the condition in question. Rather, the counselor can only try to find out and help a couple understand the mathematical risks and the implications of particular diseases and to make them aware of alternative courses of action.

Some people think that a 25 percent risk of inheriting a recessive disease, for example, means that if the first child is affected, then the next three children will not be similarly affected. But the saying, "chance has no memory" applies here. A 25 percent risk means that the odds are one out of four for every child born of the union to inherit the disease. If a disorder is not particularly disabling or is amenable to treatment, a couple may choose to take a chance. In other cases, counseling will enable a couple to realize that the risk they feared so much is actually quite slight or even nonexistent. In the future, geneticists hope to be able to do much more to help parents; they even hope to be able to modify abnormal genetic structure to cure inherited genetic defects.

The *1974 International Directory of Genetic Services*, published by the National Foundation/March of Dimes, lists 272 places in the United States that offer genetic counseling. Individuals can get information on the centers near them by writing to the Medical Department, The National Foundation/March of Dimes, 1275 Mamaroneck Ave., White Plains, New York 10605.

Summary

1   In determining various types of development, it is difficult to disentangle the relative contributions of heredity and environment. Certain aspects of our development are more heavily influenced by our heredity, others by the environment in which we are raised and live. Our genetic endowment sets the parameters for our development, while our environment determines the extent to which this potential is fulfilled.

2   The method most frequently used to study the relative effects of heredity and environment is *twin studies.*

3   Characteristics influenced by heredity include physiological traits, intelligence, personality, and mental illnesses such as schizophrenia. Not all scientists agree about the extent of the contribution of heredity to these characteristics.

4   Patterns for transmitting hereditary birth defects and illnesses include
autosomal dominant inheritance: achondroplasia, Huntington's chorea, forms of glaucoma, and polydactyl
autosomal recessive inheritance: sickle-cell anemia, Tay-Sachs disease, and phenylketonuria (PKU)
sex-linked inheritance: hemophelia, some forms of muscular dystrophy and spinal ataxia, and red-green color blindness
multifactorial inheritance: spina bifida, hydrocephalus, and cleft palate
chromosomal abnormalities: Down's syndrome, Klinefelter's syndrome, Turner's syndrome, XYY syndrome, and XXX syndrome

5   *Genetic counseling* is a relatively new service through which potential parents can obtain information about the mathematical odds of having children with specific birth defects. *Amniocentesis* is a procedure by which fetal chromosomes can be sampled before birth to determine if the fetus is afflicted with certain conditions, such as RH disease or PKU.

Suggested Readings

Apgar, V., & Beck, J. *Is My Baby All Right?* New York: Trident, 1973. *An explanation, for the lay reader, of birth defects—what they are, how they are caused, how they may be prevented, and when to seek genetic counseling. It includes many good illustrations.*

Hutt, C. *Males and Females.* Baltimore: Penguin, 1972. *Corinne Hutt discusses human sex differences, beginning with chromosomal and hormonal determinants of sexual characteristics. She discusses sex-typical patterns of behavior, normal* *and abnormal sexual development, human sex differences that affect intellectual skills and aptitudes, and the implications of male and female roles in society.*

Levine, L. *Biology of the Gene.* St. Louis: Mosby, 1969. *This undergraduate text provides a very clear explanation of molecular and molar genetics. It includes excellent diagrams, illustrations, and tables, with questions and problems following each chapter.*

Money, J., & Ehrhardt, A. A. *Man and Woman, Boy and Girl.* Baltimore: Johns Hopkins, 1972. *Drawing on many disciplines, Money and Ehrhardt focus on the interaction of hereditary endowment and environmental influence on sexual differentiation. Their findings reveal a new model of sexual differentiation, indicating that the social roles of men and women should not be fixed, but rather should be related to individual biography, achievement, and incentives.*

Scheinfeld, A. *Twins and Supertwins.* New York: Lippincott, 1967. *A well-written compendium of facts about twins and the results of many twin studies.*

Scheinfeld, A. *Your Heredity and Environment.* New York: Lippincott, 1965. *A clear, very readable discussion of "nature and nurture." It is well-illustrated with photographs, drawings, and charts, and is replete with lively examples.*

Tanzer, D., & Block, J. L. *Why Natural Childbirth?* Garden City, N.Y.: Doubleday, 1972. *An interesting, readable book explaining natural childbirth in a historical context. It reports the results of a study that compared two groups of women— those who gave birth by conventional means and those who used natural childbirth.*

Watson, J. D. *The Double Helix.* New York: Signet, New American Library, 1968. *A scientist's account of the events that led to the solution of the structure of DNA, the fundamental genetic material.*

PART TWO
BIRTH TO AGE THREE

In many ways, Vicky is an enigma to us, especially in the first three years of life. We know less about her physical and mental capabilities during these early years, less about her as a social and emotional being, and less about the relative effects of various influences in her life than we will know about her as she grows older. The child from one week of age to three years has traditionally been understudied and, as a result, underestimated. Only in recent years has psychology begun to catch up with the child at this critical time, when physical, intellectual, and emotional components are all in basic developmental stages.

Why do we know so little about the very young child? First, because he's harder to get under the psychological microscope. From the time the neonate leaves the hospital till that day, some three years later, when he pops up in nursery school, he is relatively inaccessible to researchers. He is usually in the cozy and comfortable isolation of his own home, instead of where the researcher would like him to be—in a group setting with a lot of other children the same age, all of whom can be put through their paces under the watchful eyes of the research team.

Even when children under three are recruited for research through newspaper advertising, university bulletin boards, or other sources, they still pose a challenge to investigators. The verbal techniques used in dealing with older children just won't work with babies who neither understand nor speak the language.

But research seems to be catching up with this elusive group of children. More and more efforts are being made to recruit these small subjects, more and more ingenuity is being applied to devise ways of testing nonverbal children, and, as a result, more and more information is being accumulated about children in this crucial, impressionable age range.

Early infant research was essentially *normative.* That is, its emphasis was on determining the ages at which normal children first creeped, walked, talked, and achieved other developmental milestones. These studies were, and continue to be, valuable, because they help us to understand the normal course of development and to identify at an early age many children who are not developing normally.

Recently, more precise information about many aspects of children's lives have been uncovered by the use of behavioral studies. These utilize artificial situations, set up to explore various hypotheses about the ways children will behave. Through these experimental techniques, we learn more exactly what physical and mental processes children are capable of, in what ways their personalities appear to them.

In Part Two, as in the following sections about older children, we will be discussing the young child's development from three different points of view: the physical, the intellectual, and the socioemotional. As we pointed out in the introduction, however, we must always bear in mind the interrelatedness of all these threads in a child's life and the way our knowledge of one thread helps us to understand the others.

CHAPTER THREE

BIRTH

IN WHICH VICKY FIRST CONFRONTS HER WORLD

Young fathers with your infants in your arms,
you'll prosper on what honor you can save
from youth's remorseless charge and questioning,
and find this also bears the name of love.
                              (Barry Sparks, 1972*)

As a newborn infant, Vicky is the ultimate emigrant to an unknown land. She struggles through a difficult passage, only to be faced with the overwhelming mission of learning the language and customs. The very core of her being has to learn to breathe, eat, adapt to the climate, and absorb and respond to confusing surroundings. By all criteria, this is a mighty challenge for a creature weighing but a few pounds. Let's see how Vicky faces such Herculean tasks.

The Birth Process

Vicky's mother woke up feeling rather strange. She felt some unfamiliar sensations in her belly, heavy with child. According to the doctor, the baby wasn't due for another couple of weeks. But these certainly felt like the birth contractions she had heard and read so much about. Was she in labor?

No one knows exactly why this specific woman's uterus began to contract at that precise moment with the express purpose of expelling from her

*From "Young Fathers," by Barry Sparks, in *Something Human*. New York: Harper & Row, 1972.

womb the life that had been there for some 266 days. It is possible that in normal births the maturational level of the fetus itself may signal its readiness to begin life in the outside world. One physiologist (Timiras, 1972) has suggested that the maturation of the fetal *hypophysis*, a small endocrine gland upon whose development infant survival depends, may contain the key factor that signals labor to start. Other factors have been suggested as possible triggers for the onset of labor. The placenta may be genetically programmed. Changes in fetal and uterine size are probably a factor to some degree since twin births are usually about three weeks early and more multiple births are almost always even earlier. Changes in hormonal levels, possibly produced at a certain point in development by the placenta, may set off labor. And outside physiological and psychological influences on the mother may also play a part.

The process of childbirth, once started, takes place in three overlapping phases of labor. The first stage is the longest, generally lasting about twelve hours in the woman having her first child. During this initial stage, uterine contractions cause the *cervix*, the lower part of the uterus, to dilate, or widen. The uterine opening thus becomes large enough so that the baby's head can pass through it. During the second stage of labor, which typically lasts about 1½ hours, the baby descends from the uterus, travels through

The ultimate emigrant to an unknown land

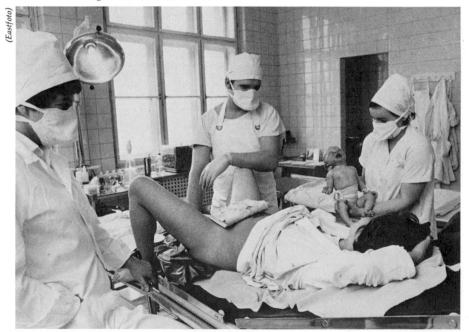

(Eastfoto)

the cervix and the vaginal canal, and emerges from the mother's body. During the third stage, which lasts only a few minutes, the umbilical cord and the placenta (the "afterbirth") are expelled.

The tiny, wrinkled creature who first forsakes the womb for the unknown excitements of the larger world hardly looks like the adorable, dimpled infants we see smiling at us from the pages of magazines. It will take several months before Vicky will look like the baby of our dreams.

Who Is the Neonate?

The first two weeks of Vicky's life—from the moment the umbilical cord is cut, about fifteen to thirty minutes after birth, until the dried stump of the cord falls off, about two weeks later—mark the *neonatal* period. These two weeks provide the transition from Vicky's intrauterine life, when, as a fetus, she was supported entirely by her mother, to an extrauterine existence. Still enormously dependent on adults, the *neonate* is nevertheless embarked on her own unique existence.

As an average-sized newborn baby, Vicky is about 20 inches long and weighs in at about 7 pounds—less than an average rib roast. Males tend to be a little longer and heavier than females, and there is an increase in birth weight with increasing birth order (Pineau, 1970). In other words, a first-born child is likely to weigh less at birth than will later-born brothers and sisters in the same family. Size at birth roughly predicts size in later life, as shown in one study (Pineau, 1970) which found that thirteen-year-old children who had weighed more at birth were now taller and heavier, with larger waist and chest circumferences, than their lighter counterparts. Black babies are typically smaller than white babies at birth. This may be attributed to socioeconomic factors such as diet rather than genetic factors.

During her first few days of life, Vicky loses as much as 10 percent of her body weight, primarily because of a loss of fluids. On about the fifth day, she begins to gain, and somewhere between the tenth and the fourteenth day is back to her original weight. Light, full-term infants lose less weight in this period than heavy ones, and first-borns lose less than later-borns (Timiras, 1972).

Since newborn babies have very little skin pigmentation, Vicky is quite pale. (This is true even of black babies, who will later become very dark complexioned.) She does have a pinkish cast, caused by the thinness of her skin, which barely covers the blood flowing through her tiny capillaries. Like some other new babies, Vicky is also very hairy, since some of the *lanugo*, that fuzzy prenatal body hair, has not yet dropped off. It will, within the next few days. Like all new babies, she is covered with the *vernix caseosa* (the name means "cheesy varnish"), an oily covering that protects her against infection. Instead of being wiped off at birth, it is allowed to dry naturally over a few days' time.

During the Middle Ages, people attributed special healing properties to "witch's milk," a secretion that sometimes issues from the swollen breasts of newborn boys and girls. Now we know that this common phenomenon, like the blood-tinged vaginal discharge of some baby girls, is due to the high levels of estrogen secreted by the placenta just before birth.

At one-fourth of Vicky's body length, her head is big, compared with what it will be in later life. It is also elongated and misshapen because of the gradual "molding" that facilitated its passage through the pelvis. This temporary molding was possible because Vicky's skull bones are not yet fused together; they will not do so completely for another eighteen months. As a newborn, she has six places on the head where the bones have not yet grown together; these *fontanels*, or soft spots, are covered by a membrane as tough as canvas. Because the cartilage in her nose is also malleable, the trip through the birth canal leaves that protuberance looking squashed for a few days.

Medical Assessment of the Newborn

The baby boy was only one minute old—but doctors had already learned that he was in grave trouble and needed immediate emergency care to survive intact. The physicians had diagnosed his danger with the help of the Apgar Scale.

In 1953, Dr. Virginia Apgar, an anesthesiologist at Columbia University, devised a series of tests to measure the degree to which a newborn infant

Chart 3-1   The Apgar Scale

Apgar score Sign	0	1	2
Heart rate	absent	slow (below 100)	rapid (over 100)
Respiratory effort	absent	irregular, slow	good, crying
Muscle tone	flaccid, limp	weak, inactive	strong, active
Color	blue, pale	body pink, extremities blue	entirely pink
Reflex irritability	no response	grimace	coughing, sneezing, crying

Each sign is rated in terms of absence or presence from 0 to 2; highest overall score is 10.

seemed capable of making the adjustments from intrauterine to extrauterine life (Apgar, 1953). Now the Apgar Scale is used in virtually all American hospitals. One minute after delivery, and then again five minutes after delivery, the scale's five subtests are administered to every infant. The Apgar score yields measures of *Appearance* (color), *Pulse* (heart rate), *Grimace* (reflex irritability), *Activity* (muscle tone), and *Respiration* (breathing). The infant receives a rating of 0, 1, or 2 on each of these five measures for a maximum total score of 10 (see Chart 3-1). Ninety percent of normal infants like Vicky receive a score of 7 or better; but an infant who receives 4 or less needs immediate treatment to survive.

The Apgar scores provide an immediate means of determining which infants need life-saving measures. They have also been shown to bear a relationship to fetal life, and then also to later development. Normal fetal heart rate patterns are accurate predictors of high Apgar scores, and abnormal fetal heart rate patterns sometimes predict low Apgar scores (Schifrin & Dame, 1972).

Adjusting to Life outside the Womb

As a fetus, Vicky was far from a passive resident of the womb, but the mechanisms for her vital functions did lie in abeyance till they were fully developed and needed for extrauterine life. Until then, existence was relatively effortless. At birth, she begins to actively initiate interactions with her environment, and all her senses operate to some degree. (Table 3-1 compares several characteristics of prenatal and postnatal life.)

Table 3-1   A Comparison of Prenatal and Postnatal Life

Characteristic	Prenatal Life	Postnatal Life
Environment	amniotic fluid	air
Temperature	relatively constant	flutuates with atmosphere
Stimulation	minimal	all senses stimulated by various stimuli
Nutrition	dependent on mother's blood	dependent on external food and functioning of digestive system
Oxygen supply	passed from maternal bloodstream via placenta	passed from neonate's lungs to pulmonary blood vessels
Metabolic elimination	passed into maternal bloodstream via placenta	discharged by skin, kidneys, lungs, and gastrointestinal tract

THE HEART AND THE CIRCULATORY SYSTEM

Although Vicky and her mother had independent circulatory systems before birth, with separate heartbeats, Vicky's blood was not cleaned by circulating throughout her own body, but rather through the umbilical cord. Through this, used blood was carried to the placenta and clean blood carried back to Vicky. Now her own circulatory system must take over. Like the fetal heartbeat, the neonatal one is accelerated and irregular, and blood pressure does not stabilize till about the tenth day.

THE RESPIRATORY SYSTEM

Vicky's umbilical cord also brought her the relatively small amounts of oxygen she needed and carried back carbon dioxide. After birth, she needs much greater quantities of this essential gas, and must now get it all alone. As she draws that first momentous breath, umbilical activity slows down and then stops. It is time for Vicky's own respiratory system to take over.

Mere exposure to air is often the only stimulus needed to make a baby start to breathe; otherwise, a slap on the buttocks will usually do the trick. A baby who has not started to breathe within a minute or two is undoubtedly having trouble. If breathing has not begun within five minutes after birth, the child is bound to suffer the results of permanent brain injury caused by *anoxia*, or a lack of oxygen.

Vicky's early fast and shallow breathing is a noisy symphony of snuffling, gurgling, sneezing, snorting, and coughing as she works hard to clear her lungs of amniotic fluid and mucus. With a great surge of effort, most babies get the hang of this new rhythmic activity. But more infants die from respiratory problems than from any other single cause.

THE GASTROINTESTINAL SYSTEM

Back in the uterus, eating and eliminating were as easy as breathing for Vicky, whose umbilical cord brought food from her mother and carried body wastes away. With birth, her own body takes over these functions, too. As a healthy, full-term infant, she is born with a strong sucking reflex to take in milk and with the gastrointestinal secretions necessary to digest it.

Meconium, a stringy, greenish-black waste matter formed in the fetal intestinal tract, is still present at birth. Vicky excretes this during her first couple of days of extrauterine life. When the bowels and bladder are full, her sphincter muscles open automatically, permitting elimination. Many months will pass before she can exert control over these muscles. (Presumably some parents don't know this and persist in putting four-week-old infants on tiny "potty seats.")

Three or four days after birth, about half of all babies develop physiologic jaundice: their skin and eyeballs look yellow. This kind of normal jaundice is caused by immaturity of the infant's liver function. It is not serious, has no long-term repercussions, and occurs most often in premature babies.

TEMPERATURE REGULATION

The weather was dully predictable for Vicky in the uterus. But once she reaches the outside atmosphere, she has to be able to keep her body temperature constant despite the fluctuations in the air. This ability is crucial for her survival. Fortunately, the layers of fat developed during the last couple of months of fetal life enable the healthy, full-term infant to regulate temperature. Lack of this additional fat is one of the biggest dangers for premature babies and the reason why so many succumb. This system is still sufficiently immature to make temperature regulation more difficult in neonate than in older infants.

THE NERVOUS SYSTEM

Since the cerebral cortex—that part of the brain that controls perception, thought, and memory—is not fully mature at birth, the infant seems to operate on a subcortical rather than a cortical level. Behavior is controlled by the spinal cord and lower brain centers at first. With increased cortical maturation, many reflexes present at birth (see next section) gradually cease to operate. Although some sensory abilities are astonishingly keen at birth, others do not mature for some time.

In Vicky's journey through life, her first day is the most important for survival. As each day passes, her chances for a healthy life grow stronger and stronger. The healthy, full-term neonate generally adjusts to postnatal life within these first two weeks, but the premature baby almost always needs more time to make these crucial adjustments.

Reflex Behaviors

When we blink at a bright light or kick out a foot after being tapped lightly on the knee, we are not acting in a deliberate, planned, voluntary way. We are reacting *involuntarily*, through *reflex behaviors*. Human beings have an arsenal of reflexes, many of which are present even before birth (see Chart 3-2). Some, like the eye-blink, help us to survive. Although we are not sure of the functional value of many of the others, their presence or absence is a guide to evaluating neurological development, since the study of normal individuals reveals a definite timetable for the development and dropping out of many reflexes. We are not yet sure just what an abnormal finding means, nor what implications it has for the individual's future development, since, according to some neurologists, "We are . . . still at the stage of finding out what is normal and what the normal variation is [Andre-Thomas, Chesni, & Saint-Anne Dargassies, 1960, p. 7]."

Chart 3-2   Infant Reflex Behaviors

Rooting reflex

When Vicky's cheek is stroked with a finger or a nipple, her head turns, her mouth opens, and sucking movements begin. This important reflex enables the baby to find and take in food; it has been observed in an awake infant only thirty minutes old. An infant in a heavy sleep, however, does not exhibit the rooting reflex.

Darwinian (grasping) reflex

When the palm of Vicky's hand is stroked, she makes such a strong fist that she may be raised to a standing position if both little fists are closed around a stick. This may be a phylogenetic carry-over from the primates, which, as infants, grasp and hang onto their mothers' furry bodies. This reflex, which is present in a nine-week-old fetus, drops out by the time a baby reaches the first birthday. It is often used as a measure of neurological maturation.

Moro (startle) reflex

The Moro reflex is a total body movement that can best be seen when Vicky is lying on her back. A sudden stimulus, like a gun shot, the onset of different tones, or being dropped in the crib, will spur this reflex. Her arms are thrown out in full extension, her fingers out, her back is extended or arched, her head is drawn back, and her legs are extended. This reflex, which may also be a phylogenetic representation of an infant animal's ability to reach for and hang onto its mother, drops out sometime between the third and the fifth month of life.

Swimming reflex

If Vicky is put in water stomach-down before she is six months old, she will show well-coordinated, involuntary swimming movements. After six months of age, if she is put in water this way, she will struggle and flounder. Not until eight months of age are babies able to make voluntary swimming movements.

Tonic neck reflex

When Vicky is placed on her back, her head will turn to one side or the other and she will assume a fencer-like position, extending the arm and leg on the preferred side and flexing the opposite limbs. The preferred side seems to predict later handedness. This reflex is found as early as the twenty-eighth prenatal week.

Babinski reflex

When the sole of Vicky's foot is stroked, her toes fan out and her foot twists in. By six months of age, this reflex no longer operates. After this time, Vicky's toes respond to such stroking by curling in.

Babkin reflex
When one or both of Vicky's palms are pressed, she turns her head and opens her mouth. She may yawn shortly after the pressure to her palms is released.

Walking reflex
When Vicky is held under the arms, with her bare feet touching a flat surface, she will make step-like motions that look remarkably like well-coordinated walking. This reflex drops out at about eight weeks.

Placing reflex
When the backs of Vicky's feet are drawn against the edge of a flat surface, she will make placing movements similar to those a kitten makes. This reflex also drops out at about eight weeks.

Ocular-Neck reflex
When a light is flashed in front of Vicky's eyes, she will bend her neck back in an apparent effort to avoid it.

Since we share some of our more primitive reflexes with the lower animals, some observers feel that our reflexes tell us something about the phylogenetic evolution of humans, that is, our evolution from a simpler form, of life. The more primitive reflexes, described in Chart 3-2, appear very early and then drop out during the first year of life. Their brief appearance reflects the subcortical control of the infant nervous system, since the maturation of the cerebral cortex inhibits their expression. Those reflexes that clearly protect the human organism—such as the pupillary (in which the pupils of the eye contract when exposed to bright light), the eye-blink, yawning, coughing, gagging, and sneezing—do not drop out.

By examining an infant's reflex behaviors, we can judge his or her degree of cortical functioning and tell whether or not neurological development is proceeding normally. The relationship between reflex behaviors and normal development during childhood is a fruitful area for research.

Sensory Capacities of the Infant in the First Few Weeks

In 1890, the psychologist William James lyrically expressed a fallacy that was considered a fact for many years: "The baby, assailed by eyes, ears, nose, skin, and entrails at once, feels that all is one great blooming, buzzing confusion." We now know that this is far from true.

Many researchers have, by both traditional and ingenious methods, sought ways to assess the abilities of tiny infants. Most investigators have traveled along four principal avenues of research. These avenues involve observing infants closely and noting what they do; recognizing that they

(Shelly Rusten)

By examining an infant's reflex behaviors, we can judge his or her degree of cortical functioning and tell whether or not neurological development is proceeding normally.

have different moods, or *states* (see "State of the Newborn," in this chapter), in which they behave in a predictable, not a chaotic way; observing their responses to specific stimuli, by which we can see that they do exhibit sensory and perceptual capabilities; and seeing how they use their motor responses appropriately, indicating their ability to learn (Stone, Smith, & Murphy, 1973).

Researchers have also used their imagination to devise new ways of studying infants. And they have made use of new technology, like videotape, infrared photography, and computers, to open windows in the world of the baby. From a wealth of recent research, we know that—even as a neonate—Vicky is a competent human being.

VISION: THE SENSE OF SIGHT

Even though Vicky's eyes differ from those of adults in several ways— smaller size, incomplete retinal structures, and an underdeveloped optic nerve—she is capable of certain visual activities right at birth. She blinks at sudden increases in light intensity (Peiper, 1963), her pupils constrict when the light intensity changes, and the stronger the intensity is, the faster is her pupillary response (Sherman, Sherman, & Flory, 1936). During the first two months of life, she becomes increasingly sensitive to contrasts in brightness (Doris, Cooper, & Poresky, 1967).

Although Vicky, as a newborn infant, cannot move both her eyes together to focus sharply on an object, she does shift gaze in response to a moving light (Wickelgren, 1969), and she can follow a moving target (Gesell, 1941; Graham, Matarazzo, & Caldwell, 1956; Rosenblith, 1961). Because the ciliary muscles of the newborn's eye are too immature to accommodate images at all distances, new babies see best at a distance of about $7^1/_2$ inches (Haynes, 1965).

Depth Perception

Very young babies seem to have some idea of depth. The perception of depth may be an innate mechanism that protects the young of the species from falling, or it may be learned during the first few months of life. In an ingeniously clever experiment, Walk and Gibson (1961) constructed a "visual cliff." The "cliff" consisted of a flat, glass-covered board. A checkerboard pattern on the board was set up in such a way that on one side of the visual cliff an illusion of depth was created. On the other side there was no such illusion.

The babies in this experiment crawled readily on the nondepth side, but they refused to crawl on the side that looked deep, even to reach their mothers who were on this side and beckoning them to come over. These infants were six months old or older. Although the authors felt that depth perception was innate, it is possible that the babies might have learned about depth during their first six months.

In an effort to find out whether younger babies can also perceive depth, Campos, Langer, and Krowitz (1970) investigated two- to three-month-old infants. Since these babies could not yet crawl, the researchers recorded the differential heart rates of babies on the deep and shallow sides of the "visual cliff." They found that babies placed on their stomachs on the "deep" side had slower heart rates than those on the shallow side. The slower heart rates of the deep-side babies may be a sign that these babies were distinguishing and responding to the deep side as a novel stimulus. If so, this indicates that depth perception occurs quite early in life.

Visual Preference

How do we know what babies prefer to look at? Usually by finding out how much time an infant looks at certain patterns. When Vicky spends a longer time looking at one item rather than another, we conclude that she can tell the difference between the two, and for some reason likes one of them better. R. L. Fantz (1971) performed an extensive series of experiments to study what infants can see and what they like to look at. Dr. Fantz designed a special apparatus that contains a chamber in which an infant can lie and look at a specific visual stimulus chosen by the experimenter. While the infant is lying in this chamber, an observer can peek through a tiny hole in the chamber ceiling to see a minute corneal reflection of the visual stimulus over the pupil of the infant's eye. As soon as this corneal reflection is seen on one or both of the baby's eyes, the observer starts to time the baby's visual fixation, stopping only when the baby closes or turns away her eyes.

From experiments performed with the Fantz apparatus, we have learned a great deal about infant vision. Babies are apparently born with some preference for looking at a human face. Infants as young as ten hours who are presented with pictures of normal faces and also with pictures of "scrambled" faces (in which the facial features are rearranged in grotesquely unnatural patterns) spend more time looking at the normal faces. Young infants also spend more time looking at such complex stimuli as a bull's-eye or a checkerboard than at simple stimuli like plain circles and triangles (Fantz, 1963). They can obviously discriminate differences between patterns, and they show preferences for certain ones. These preferences seem to have significance in human development. By studying them we can draw certain conclusions about the chronological development of sensory abilities. For example, twenty-week-old infants prefer more complex patterns than do thirteen-week-olds (Karmel, 1969), and full-term infants develop a reliable preference for looking at new images by the age of ten or eleven weeks, whereas premature babies do not develop these preferences until fourteen or fifteen weeks of age (Fagen & Fantz, 1971).

Visual preferences among infants tell us that the neonate's world is far from chaotic, that certain innate mechanisms predispose us from a few hours after birth to prefer to look at others of our kind, and that these mechanisms help us to become socially responsive.

We also know that even very young infants prefer to see clear images over blurred ones and that they can direct their behavior in accordance with this preference (Kalnins & Bruner, 1974). A group of thirty babies, from five to twelve weeks old, were shown a silent film depicting Eskimo family life. The movie interested the babies because it was in color, it showed close-ups of expressive human faces, and it had continuous movement. The babies were able to change the picture from blurred to clear by sucking on a specially rigged pacifier.

These young infants learned to keep the picture clear by regulating the length of their pauses between bursts of sucking. They also learned to look at the film when it was clear and to avert their gaze when it was blurred. Thus we see that the infant's visual perception is more sophisticated than anyone ever dreamed. It also seems that we have grossly underestimated infants' voluntarily controlled, problem-solving abilities. New babies are not as helpless and passive as they seem to the naive observer.

AUDITION: THE SENSE OF HEARING

When Wilhelm Preyer wrote *The Mind of the Child* in 1881, he was convinced that newborn infants were deaf. We now know better. Within the first few hours after birth, Vicky is sensitive to some aspects of sound.

In one experiment, neonates were presented with a high-intensity sound of 100 decibels and with lower-intensity sounds of 85, 70, and 55 decibels. The greater the sound intensity, the greater the babies' increase in heart rate and movement (Lipton, Steinschneider, & Richmond, 1963).

The phenomenon of *habituation* has also been used to determine how well a baby can hear. Habituation is the process of "getting used to" certain stimuli. We are, for example, aware of the way our wristwatch feels when we first put it on, but within seconds we are no longer conscious of it. We have adapted to or habituated to that sensory stimulus. Russian psychologists have studied habituation in some depth, especially in regard to hearing, and have made important discoveries about its value for the newborn child.

As a new baby, Vicky reacts in two ways to an unusual sound. First, she orients physically toward the source of the sound by turning her head toward it, displaying the orienting reflex (OR). She also *inhibits*, or stops, any other ongoing activities. It is often difficult or impossible to observe the orienting reflex because a newborn baby's muscular control of voluntary skeletal and eye movements is still so rudimentary. But since inhibition regularly accompanies orienting, the extent to which she inhibits some other activity, like sucking, can provide some idea of the degree to which she is orienting.

In one study (Bronstein & Petrova, 1952), forty-three infants—thirty-three aged from two hours to eight days, and ten from one to five months of age—were presented with a variety of sounds. They heard the playing of organ pipes and harmonica, the blowing of a whistle, and the tapping of a pencil. The first time the infants heard a particular sound, they usually stopped sucking and did not begin again until the sound stopped. After the same sound had been presented again and again, however, it lost its novelty and had no further effect on sucking activities. Under these conditions, the OR may be said to have been extinguished—or the infants may be described as having habituated or adapted to the stimulus. Changing the pitch of the sound or presenting some new sound will, however, immediately reinstate the OR. Thus we see that even the very young infant can discriminate differences between sounds, even differences in pitch. This indicates the auditory system is operating and is developed well enough to detect differences between sounds.

From such experiments we can also conclude that the cortex functions to some degree from the first day of life. Although the OR and *external* inhibition (the cessation of sucking) are brought about by subcortical activity, the habituation is apparently due to the process of *internal*, or active, inhibition, which is a cortical activity.

OLFACTION: THE SENSE OF SMELL
Newborn babies may not be able to hold their noses when they don't like the way something smells, but they can, indeed, discriminate among

various odors. Neonates who smell an asafoetida solution—which smells like onion—breathe faster and move around more than they do when presented with a solution that has no smell (Lipsitt, Engen, & Kaye, 1963). In another study, a group of neonates was presented in turn with two distinct odors—asafoetida, and anise oil, which smells like licorice. Half the infants smelled the asafoetida first for ten trials, and the other half smelled the anise first. After twenty trials with the two odors, the first odor was reintroduced for two more trials.

The experimenters measured the babies' body activity and respiration and found that repeated exposure to an odor brought about a lower level of response. After the babies had smelled one odor for ten trials, they were not so sensitive to the second stimulus. But when the new stimulus was presented, the infants did respond more intensely than to the subsequent preparations of the initial odor. Thus habituation had apparently occurred, since presentation of the new odor, which the babies obviously recognized as different from the first odor, caused a resumption of response (Engen, Lipsitt, & Kaye, 1963). We see, then, that the olfactory system operates and is sophisticated enough to distinguish different odors.

GUSTATION: THE SENSE OF TASTE

Little research on the infant's sensitivity to taste is available. Some early students of infant behavior felt, though, that this is the most highly developed sense at birth and speculated that an early developed sense of taste may have a survival value in that it protects the infant from eating harmful substances. A few different experimenters have given infants sweet, salt, sour, and bitter solutions and have observed their reactions. In one such study (Pratt, Nelson, & Sun, 1930), twenty-eight neonates, whose age ranged from the first to the fifteenth day of life, were "treated to" 858 tastes of solutions of sugar, salt, quinine, water, and citric acid, all at room temperature. Reactions varied according to the strengths of the solutions, with the infants most likely, however, to respond to the sugar with sucking movements and to the quinine with a grimace. But when the taste solutions were of about equal strength and not too strong, the infants showed very few specific reactions. This would indicate that the new infant is not much of a gourmet and has a relatively insensitive palate.

One interesting fact brought out by this experiment was that infants seem to respond differently to taste than do adults. One solution of citric acid elicited strong reactions from the babies, although the adult experimenters who also tasted it thought it was quite weak. On the other hand, the adults reacted strongly to a quinine solution that brought hardly any response from the babies. We don't know why this should be so.

SENSITIVITY TO TEMPERATURE

The ability to regulate body temperature is vital to the survival of the newborn infant, as it is to all of us. The full-term, healthy neonate can usually maintain normal body temperature in the face of a slight drop in room temperature. The premature baby, though, lacks this ability and is thus likely to succumb. Babies apparently maintain their body temperature by increasing their body activity in response to a drop in the temperature of the air (Mestyan & Varga, 1960; Pratt, Nelson, & Sun, 1930).

SENSITIVITY TO PAIN

Can babies feel pain? Yes, and they can feel it more and more with each day of life. In one experiment (Lipsett & Levy, 1959), researchers gave a series of two-second electric shocks to one-day-old babies, continuing to administer the shocks each day for four days. They increased the voltage in 5-volt increments until the baby immediately pulled back the affected leg in response to the shock. On the first day of life, the infants usually did not pull back their legs until they had received 85 to 90 volts. They were obviously more sensitive to pain on the fourth day than they had been on the first.

Discussing an infant's sensitivity to pain brings to mind some ethical issues that were raised in the Introduction. There *are* useful, practical applications to knowing just when an infant reacts most strongly to pain—for example, in setting the date for such operations as circumcision, and in weighing the dangers of anesthesia against the infant's degree of discomfort. But since an infant's life experiences may well influence his future emotional development, few experimenters are willing to risk subjecting young children to repeated painful experiences. We don't know what such a child's initial view of the world would be—or what far-reaching effects such painful experiences might have. It is quite possible that a succession of unpleasant events in early infancy can stay with a person throughout life.

INDIVIDUAL DIFFERENCES AMONG NEONATES

Infants behave quite differently from one another right from birth. Vicky likes to stick her tongue in and out of her mouth; another baby makes rhythmic sucking movements; a third baby never does either. Some infant boys have frequent erections; others never do. Some show frequent smiles; others don't. Korner (1969) reports:

> Study of individual records revealed interesting, and often self-consistent, sequences in spontaneous behaviors. For example, some infants during regular sleep startled several times in rapid succession; others showed long intervals between startles. One infant's startles regularly alternated with episodes of rhythmical mouthing; another invariably startled immediately following bursts of rhythmical mouthing [p. 1048].

Such findings have important implications for babies' futures. The way a particular baby responds to stimulation is bound to have some bearing on this child's interactions with his or her parents. Parents respond very differently to a placid baby than they do to an excitable one, to a baby who is quieted by something the parents do than to one who is inconsolable, to a baby who seems aware of his or her environment than to one "in a world of her own." Neonatal responsivity may hold important clues for an individual's later psychological functioning. Also, if a particular baby responds very differently to one modality than he does to another, this may be a clue to an atypical form of development.

State of the Newborn

One day seems very much like the next in Vicky's life. But within the day, she undergoes cycles of wakefulness, sleepiness, and varying degrees of activity. She sleeps soundly for a while, when she is completely oblivious of her surroundings. She sleeps lightly, when the slightest noise will wake her. She spends a fair amount of time looking around. And she keeps herself busy for a while with crying and kicking.

To describe the periodic variations in the newborn's day, the term *state* has been coined. This is a relatively new concept used to describe "a behavioral condition that (1) is stable over a period of time, (2) occurs repeatedly in an individual infant, and (3) is encountered in very similar forms in other individuals [Hutt, Lenard, & Prechtl, 1969, p. 132]." Vicky's state gives us clues to the way she is responding to the environment; it influences many physiological characteristics; and it determines how she will respond to stimulation.

CLASSIFICATIONS OF STATE

Since all babies show variations in state throughout the day, and since the abilities they show are influenced by their state at any one time, it is important to differentiate one state from another. The following states, typical for newborn babies, combine two separate but similar classification systems (Wolff, 1966; Prechtl & Beintema, 1964).

Regular Sleep

Vicky's eyes are closed, her breathing is regular, and she makes no movements except for sudden generalized startles. Strong stimulation, either internal or external, is absent or minimal. This is the low point on the arousal continuum since the infant in this state cannot be aroused by mild stimuli.

Irregular Sleep

Vicky's eyes are closed, her breathing is irregular, her muscles twitch slightly from time to time, but she still makes no major movements. The

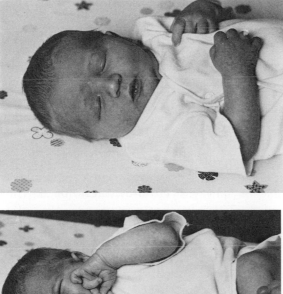

(Erika Stone, from Peter Arnold)

"State" describes a behavioral condition that (1) is stable over a period of time, (2) occurs repeatedly in an individual infant, and (3) is encountered in very similar forms in other individuals.

sounds or light flashes that were subliminal during regular sleep now bring smiles, sneers, or pouts—in her sleep.

Drowsiness

Before and after sleep, Vicky's eyes may be open, and her body is more active than in regular sleep. Her breathing is irregular. Yet an infant is sensitive to such external stimuli as the sound of the radio or the sight of the mother. The incidence of spontaneous discharges—reflex smiles or startles, sucking movements, or erections—is high at certain times, low at others.

Alert Inactivity

After Vicky has been fed, diapered, and burped, and is free from distressing internal and external stimuli, she may be awake for a short time with her eyes open. She may move her head, limbs, and trunk while looking at the immediate environment or at a particular "interesting spectacle," like a mobile swaying over her head, her two-year-old cousin building with blocks, or her mother varnishing a table. An interesting environment can initiate or maintain a quiet, alert state.

Waking Activity and Crying

This state makes the strongest impression on anyone who spends much time with babies. It can be set in motion by intense internal stimulation, like hunger, cold, or pain, or by intense external stimulation, like restraining the baby, putting her down in the crib, or removing a pacifier from her mouth. The state may begin with soft whimpering and gentle movements and turn into a rhythmic crescendo of crying or kicking. Or it may begin and remain as uncoordinated thrashing and spasmodic screeching. Infants in this state may be too "busy" to respond to stimuli which might have elicited a reaction during sleep, drowsiness, or alert inactivity (see next section).

HOW STATES OPERATE

Our bodies are governed to a great degree by inner "clocks" that control our cycles of eating, sleeping, elimination, and, possibly, even mood. These biological clocks seem inborn, since they appear to contribute to the various states in infancy. This inner timing mechanism, in combination with visceral or external stimulations, takes the infant from a state of regular sleep to that of irregular sleep.

When Vicky is sleeping lightly, she may become aware of such stimuli as the sound of her father's voice, the sunlight streaming in through the nursery window, or a slight breeze—none of which would have penetrated her awareness during deep, regular sleep. Depending on the intensity of the stimuli, she may continue to sleep lightly and eventually fall back into a deep sleep, or she may reach the next, more alert state. When Vicky drowsily blinks open her eyes, her attention may be drawn to the objects and activities in the environment; and the very act of paying attention makes her even more wide awake. Eventually, hunger or the need to eliminate or the discomfort from soiled diapers will take her from the pleasant state of alert inactivity to the more assertive one of crying (Wolff, 1966).

Let us look at a typical day in a newborn baby's life, according to one team of researchers (Hutt, Lenard, & Prechtl, 1969). Of the seventeen to twenty hours a day that Vicky sleeps, 75 percent is spent in the state of irregular sleep. She is awake and quiet for two to three hours every day, awake and active for one to two hours, and she cries and fusses the rest of her waking time—anywhere from one to four hours. Her sleep cycles range from forty-five minutes to two hours, divided into ten- to twenty-minute periods of regular sleep and twenty- to forty-five-minute periods of irregular sleep. Vicky's schedule may be typical, but other perfectly normal babies have very different schedules, due partly to individual differences among the babies and also to differences in their environments.

ENVIRONMENTAL CONDITIONS THAT INFLUENCE STATE

Parents have been influencing states from time immemorial. The state they most want to change is, of course, the last one, in which the baby is squalling unhappily. Aside from saving the sanity of harried parents, determining ways to quiet an unhappy baby has particularly important implications for the premature. The more quiet Vicky is, the better she will be able to maintain body weight and the better equipped the infant will be in the struggle for survival.

Feeding is one way to quiet a baby. Not unexpectedly, we learn from research that an awake baby shows more motor activity before than after feeding (Wolff, 1966). We also learn scientifically what Whistler's mother knew—that rocking a fussy infant soothes him (Van den Daele, 1970). Research has also shown that *swaddling* a baby, or wrapping him or her snugly in a blanket, is also soothing. Swaddling, which is a very common

A number of studies flatly contradict "common sense" by indicating that constant stimulation actually quiets babies.

(Amy Stromsten, Photo Trends)

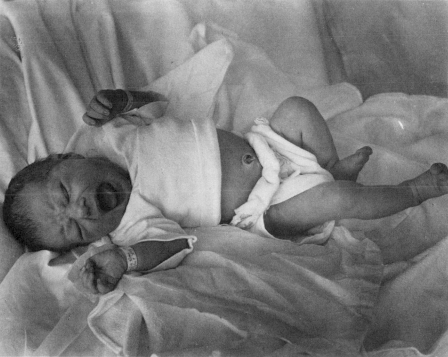

practice in Russia, leads to less muscular activity and lower heart and respiratory rates (Lipton et al., 1965).

A number of studies have yielded the finding that continuous stimulation quiets restless babies. Irritable infants have been presented with such constant stimulation as continuous rhythmic sound, a sweetened pacifier, rocking, immersing a foot in warm water, being put in a warmer place, being clothed rather than unclothed, and being swaddled from neck to toes. In general, the babies' crying stopped, their heart rates slowed down, their breathing became more regular, they moved around less, and they slept more in response to all these stimuli (Birns & Blank, 1965; Irwin & Weiss, 1934a; Salk, 1960; Irwin, 1941; Brackbill et al., 1966; Irwin & Weiss, 1934b; Brackbill, 1971). Findings such as these have practical value for parents and child-care professionals, especially since they flatly contradict "common sense," with the paradox that continuous stimulation actually quiets babies.

PHYSIOLOGICAL VARIABLES THAT ARE INFLUENCED BY STATE

When we go into Vicky's room, the state she is in at the moment will probably influence our actions. If she is sleeping lightly, we may tiptoe around so that we don't awaken her. If she is sleeping heavily, we can feel fairly confident that normal household sounds will not disturb her sleep, and so we'll go about our business. And if we see that she is awake, we may be likely to stop what we are doing and go over to try to coax a smile from her.

Vicky's states also determine the way she will respond to us—or to anyone or anything—at any particular time. Thus, if we want to understand how the body of the newborn baby works, we always have to be conscious of the particular state the baby is in. A baby in a state of deep sleep will obviously respond quite differently from either an alert baby or a drowsy one. Vicky's state is an important determinant of the way she functions at any given time—in the way she behaves, the way she responds to various stimuli, and the reflex behaviors she displays.

Breathing, for example, is extremely responsive to an individual's state. Respiration is slow and regular during regular sleep, irregular and faster during irregular sleep, more regular but no faster during quiet wakefulness, and fastest and most irregular during active wakefulness. Heart rate also varies according to state. During regular sleep it is stable and slow; during irregular sleep it is faster, with more fluctuation; during quiet wakefulness, the heart beats slightly faster but more regularly; and during active wakefulness and crying, it beats fastest and most irregularly (Hutt et al., 1969).

We have to know the individual's state when we study reflexes, since some reflexes are more responsive to one state, others to another. The *patellar*, or knee-jerk reflex, in which the leg jerks out in response to a tap on the knee, is strong during regular sleep and wakefulness, but weak during irregular sleep. The grasp and the Babkin reflexes, on the other hand, are almost totally absent during regular sleep, weak in irregular sleep, and strongest in wakefulness. And the Babinski reflex is elicited easily in all states (Lenard, von Vernuth, & Prechtl, 1968).

The effects of auditory stimulation on the heart rates of premature babies appear to be a function of state and may possibly be a predictor of central nervous system damage. Thirty-one infants weighing 1,800 grams (almost 4 pounds) or more were divided into a low-risk group of sixteen infants and a high-risk group of fifteen. An 80-decibel, low-frequency buzzer was sounded in their incubators on ten different occasions for three seconds each time. While they slept, the heart rates of both groups were faster; but when they were awake, the high-risk babies showed a faster heart rate, while the low-risk babies' rates slowed down (Schulman, 1969).

Another study also found that infants' hearing of certain sounds was affected by state, but that cold and touch were "compelling stimuli" that were strong enough to override the influence of state (Lamper & Eisdorfer, 1971).

The usual state of a particular infant can have a great effect on the way that child is treated by his or her parents, which itself has major consequences for the kind of person the baby will turn out to be, as we will see in Chapter 6. Just as parents react differently to babies who respond differently to stimulation, they are influenced in their parental attitudes by state—by whether a baby is awake and crying much of the time, or is spending a great deal of time in a state of interested, quiet wakefulness, or is almost always drowsy or asleep. The differences in state that may differentiate newborn boys and girls guarantee a certain difference in treatment right from birth, a phenomenon that will be discussed later in this chapter.

Birth Complications

PREMATURITY

One of the most difficult things for new parents to do is to go home from the hospital leaving the new baby behind. This is often necessary when the baby has come into the world too soon. The premature, low-birthweight baby—that infant born after a gestation period of less than thirty-seven weeks and weighing less than 2,500 grams (5½ pounds)—is vulnerable to infection and has difficulty maintaining body temperature. Thus the "premie" usually has to stay in an incubator for days or even weeks. A "small-for-date" baby is also at considerable risk. This is an infant who weighs less than 5½ pounds, although the gestational age is more than thirty-eight weeks, indicating some prenatal developmental lag or nutritional deficiency.

Since it is rarely possible to determine an infant's precise gestational age, prematurity is most often reckoned in terms of weight. A baby who weighs less than 2 pounds at birth has virtually no chance for life. The more the newborn weighs, the better are his or her chances (see Table 3–2). Today, with constantly improving methods of caring for low-birthweight babies, a premie weighing more than 4 pounds 6 ounces has better than a 96 percent chance for survival (Guttmacher, 1962).

Causes of Prematurity

The woman most likely to bear a premature baby is a poor, poorly nourished, nonwhite teenager who has received little or no prenatal care (Birch & Gussow, 1970; Wortis, 1963). A woman who suffered toxemia or certain other illnesses during pregnancy also has a higher-than-average chance of having a premature baby (Guttmacher, 1962). Twins are usually premature, and with more than two babies in the womb, prematurity is virtually a certainty, since the uterus can stretch only so far.

Effects of Prematurity

Because the intrauterine development of premature babies has not gone its full course, their body systems do not work so well as those of the full-term infant. When these tiny babies do die, they usually succumb from respiratory system malfunctioning in their first month of postnatal life (Davis & Tizard, 1961; Timiras, 1972). Even those premature babies who do survive are often at some disadvantage; and the more severely premature they are, the more marked will be their long-term deficits.

Among children and adolescents who had *very* low birthweights, intelligence appears to be significantly impaired, possibly as a result of brain damage. The closer the newborn was to $5\frac{1}{2}$ pounds, the more minimal the impairment, if, indeed, there is any at all (Caputo & Mandell, 1970; Pasamanick & Lilienfeld, 1955). A relatively high proportion of mentally retarded persons, individuals institutionalized for a variety of reasons, and high school dropouts seem to have had low birthweights (Caputo & Mendell, 1970; Pasamanick, Rogers, & Lilienfeld, 1956). Other problems

Table 3-2   Birthweight and Infant Mortality Rate

Birthweight (grams)	Birthweight (pounds)	Mortality Rate (per 1,000 live births)
1,000 or less	2 lb, 3 oz or less	919
1,001–1,500	2 lb, 4 oz–3 lb, 4 oz	548
1,501–2,000	3 lb, 5 oz–4 lb, 6 oz	207
2,001–2,500	4 lb, 7 oz–5 lb, 8 oz	58
2,501–3,000	5 lb, 9 oz–6 lb, 9 oz	19
3,001–4,500	6 lb, 10 oz–9 lb, 14 oz	9
4,501 or more	9 lb, 15 oz or more	13

Source: U. S. Department of Health, Education, and Welfare, Health Services and Mental Health Administration, National Center for Health Statistics.

(Lew Merrim, Monkmeyer)

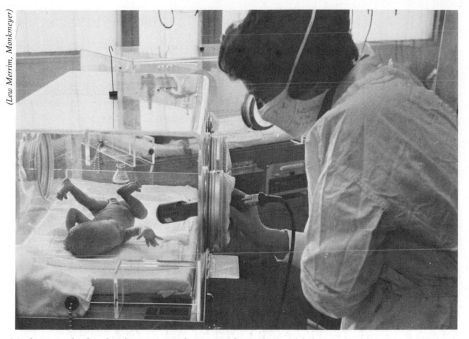

Modern methods of infant care and increased awareness of the needs of premature babies have made the prognosis brighter.

that seem to afflict severely premature infants disproportionately are epilepsy; cerebral palsy; autism; difficulties in language development and academic achievement; deficits in physical growth, motor development, and neurological functioning; accident-proneness, and possibly hyperactivity (Caputo & Mandell, 1970; Kawi & Pasamanick, 1958; Lilienfeld & Pasamanick, 1954, 1955). In one longitudinal study of infants born at 1,000 grams (2.2 pounds) or less, a higher-than-normal incidence of low IQ, eye defects, and delays in attaining normal height were noted during childhood (Dann, Levine, & New, 1958). And another study found that over 60 percent of very low-birthweight infants showed intellectual, physical, or behavioral deficits (Drillien, 1961).

In one recent study (Braine et al., 1966), 406 poor, black babies who weighed 2,100 grams (4.6 pounds) or less were followed for fifteen months and compared with a control group of fifty full-term infants from the same community. A significant linear relationship existed between the degree of prematurity and the extent of impairment. The more premature a baby was, the worse off he or she was likely to be. The authors also felt that "poor nutrition, lack of prenatal care, and other factors associated with extreme poverty and poor education may have led to making the infant more vulnerable to the hazards of extreme prematurity [Braine et al., 1966]."

Today, with modern methods of infant care and an increased awareness of the needs of premature, low-birthweight babies, their prognosis is much happier. When sixty-eight infants who had weighed 3 pounds 4 ounces or less at birth were followed up from nine months to four years later, 86.7 percent of the children seemed quite normal (Rawlings, Stewart, Reynolds, & Strang, 1971). The authors of this study believe "that much of the handicap found in surviving children by previous workers would have been avoidable with modern methods of care [p. 518]."

Because of premature infants' vulnerability to infection and inability to maintain body temperature, they usually spend their first weeks of life in an antiseptic, temperature-controlled incubator. Although this environment has saved many babies' lives, it has also deprived them of normal contact with other people and of the almost constant sensory stimulation received by other babies from the moment they emerge from the womb. Until recently, the dominant philosophy regarding premature infants was a "hands-off" policy in the belief that the less these fragile little beings were disturbed, the better their chances for the future would be. But now we have some basis for belief that this very isolation and subsequent sensory impoverishment may contribute to some of the premature baby's difficulties later in life.

Recent research shows that enriching the neonatal environment of premature babies will be beneficial for their future development. In one group of ten premies, five were handled only when being fed, burped, or diapered. The other five received round-the-clock touching. Every hour a nurse or an aide rubbed the infant gently about the back, neck, and arms for five minutes. After ten days, the caressed infants were more active and had regained their birthweights, as opposed to fifteen days for the controls. Seven to eight months after birth, a pediatrician who examined all the babies (without knowing their experimental status) found all the experimental babies active and physically healthy, compared with only one of the babies who had not been fondled (Solkoff, Yaffe, & Weintraub, 1967).

In another study (Scarr-Salapatek & Williams, 1973), thirty infants who weighed between 1,300 and 1,800 grams (from less than 3 pounds to almost 4) were divided into two equal groups. The control babies received standard care in incubators, but the babies in the experimental group lived in a much more exciting world. Nursery birds detached from a mobile hung in their incubators, and practical nurses took them out of these incubators for feeding, fondling, rocking, and conversation. While the babies were fed they could see the nurses' faces, and when they were burped they were held upright so they could look around the room. When the babies were big enough to leave the incubators, the same differences in care persisted for the four to six weeks they remained in the hospital. After they went home, social workers visited the experimental babies' homes every week until the infants' first birthdays, bringing a variety of stimulating toys and instructing the mothers in child care.

The control group—the babies who were not handled—tested slightly better at birth and at one week of age on the Brazelton Cambridge Newborn Scales, a test that assesses babies on their behavioral and neurological development. But by four weeks, their superiority had disappeared. By this time, the experimental babies scored significantly better and had gained more weight. By one year, the experimental babies had reached nearly normal levels of behavioral development, unlike any comparable group of premature babies that had ever been tested at the same hospital. Apparently, professional intervention and new ways of caring for premature babies can reap rich rewards for the babies and their families.

There seems to be some possibility that some parents of premature babies who have to stay in the hospital for several weeks may have more trouble later on in being effective parents. In one study of sixty-eight new mothers (Leifer, Leiderman, Barnett, & Williams, 1972), it was found that the mothers of full-term infants (who had had many opportunities to hold their babies during the hospital stay) smiled at their babies more and held them close more often than did the mothers of premature babies, even though some of the latter had visited their babies regularly and had even handled them through the portholes of the incubator. These differences in maternal behavior held true just before discharge from the hospital, and also one and four weeks later.

There could be several explanations for this difference. The mothers of the prematures could have been frightened by the fragility of their infants, even though they had been assured they were out of danger. Or there could be a deeper, underlying disruption of the parent-infant bond, caused by the baby's frail condition. When babies are sick and weak at birth, their parents often stay aloof from them deliberately, trying to protect their emotional vulnerability if the baby should die. Sometimes they put off naming the baby for more than a month. Said one mother (Barnett, Leiderman, Grobstein, & Klaus, 1970):

> I don't want to get that close. I don't want to touch her. . . . She isn't really a part of our family, but she will be when she comes home [p. 202].

When the babies do survive, the parents have to overcome this distance and try to take up where they left off. It is not always easy. Evidence that it may be even harder for white mothers than for black mothers comes from some statistics on child abuse. Although only about 7 percent of white babies are premature, 39 percent of those abused by their parents are premies. This compares with a 16 percent rate of prematurity among black battered babies, the same as their incidence in the general black population (Elmer & Gregg, 1967).

These findings indicate that while we are seeking new and better ways to save the lives and health of premature babies, we also have to pay attention to improving their emotional environments once they get home.

BIRTH TRAUMA

Vicky, like almost all infants, sailed through labor and delivery like a breeze. For a small minority of babies (1 to 3 percent of those born in modern hospitals, according to Graham, Matarazzo, & Caldwell, 1956), their passage through the birth canal is the most difficult journey of their lives and may leave lasting marks in the form of brain injury. Infants who have suffered oxygen deprivation at birth, mechanical birth injury, or neonatal diseases and infections are likely to display abnormal scores in their first few days of life on pain threshold, maturation scale, vision scale, irritability, and muscle tension. The more severe the trauma, the more abnormal the test results (Graham et al., 1956).

Some of these infants are left with permanent brain injury, causing mental retardation or behavior problems. Relationships have been found between birth trauma and childhood reading retardation (Lyle, 1970); impairment in verbal abstract ability, perceptual skills, and social competence (Corah, Anthony, Parnter, Stern, & Thurston, 1965); and a variety of neurological and psychological problems (Bishop, Israel, & Briscol, 1965).

More recent investigations, however, have found that birth trauma is not always so debilitating. To determine the results of such birth stresses as prematurity, difficulties in delivery, and neonatal illness, 866 children born on the island of Kauai, Hawaii, in 1955 and 1956 were examined ten years later (Werner, Bierman, French, Simonian, Connor, Smith, & Campbell, 1968). A small group of children had survived severe complications and still bore the scars. They had major physical handicaps and/or were moderately to severely retarded. But most of the children who had experienced severe *perinatal stress*, or stress around the time of birth, were, at the age of ten, doing well in school and at home. They were no more likely to get poor grades or to have language, perceptual, or emotional problems than were the other children—unless they had been so severely affected that they had had to be institutionalized.

The kinds of homes these children lived in after birth had a much greater effect. Most of the ten-year-olds with problems had had no problems at birth, but had grown up in poor homes where they received little educational stimulation or emotional support.

> More than 10 times as many children were affected by deprived environment than by severe perinatal stress, indicating the need to refocus the emphasis about diagnosis and remediation from "reproductive casualties" to the "environmental casualties" [Werner et al., 1968, p. 125].

OBSTETRIC MEDICATION

"In sorrow shalt thou bring forth children" were God's angry words to Eve after he learned that she had eaten of the forbidden fruit in the Garden of Eden. Or were they? Some biblical scholars believe that God meant to say, "In travail shalt thou bring forth children" (Tanzer & Block, 1972). Eve may have been punished by having to work hard, or labor, in childbirth—but she may not have been doomed to pain, as the more popular rendition of the biblical phrase seems to say.

In any case, most societies throughout history and around the world *have* associated pain with childbirth and have evolved a variety of techniques to hasten the delivery and make the mother more comfortable. In 1853, when Queen Victoria gave birth to her seventh child, Prince Leopold, under the influence of the anesthetic chloroform, she gave great impetus to the use of obstetric painkillers. By the beginning of the twentieth century, some type of anesthesia during childbirth was virtually taken for granted among Western middle-class women. These drugs affect the baby as well as the mother.

All drugs, including the analgesics, anesthetics, and amnesiacs taken during childbirth, pass through the placenta, enter the fetal blood supply and tissues, and reduce the amount of oxygen in the fetal bloodstream. Critics of Western obstetric practices attribute the relatively high rate of infant mortality in the United States, the richest country in the world, to our routine use of obstetric medication (Haire, 1972). One recent report showed that more than 85 percent of almost 20,000 newly delivered American mothers had received anesthetic at delivery (Benson et al., 1965, in Conway & Brackbill, 1970).

Just what *are* the effects on the newborn infant of medication that is given to the mother? All drugs given the mother during labor and delivery make their way to the fetus and affect the newborn baby's central nervous system for the first week of life, and possibly even longer. Obstetric medication clearly appears to affect the neonate's initial weight gain, his or her response to nursing, and the performance of early learning tasks (Brazelton, 1970). Although all narcotics used during labor will produce neonatal depression, the effect is less for infants born within one hour or after six hours following administration of the drug (Moya & Thorndike, 1962). Table 3-3 compares mortality rates for selected countries in 1968.

Newborn babies whose mothers received obstetric medication often have excellent Apgar scores at birth. They do well on appearance, pulse, grimace, respiration, and activity measures. But in a little while they often become unresponsive, showing little spontaneous motor activity, slow heart and breathing rates, and poor circulation (Brazelton, 1970). Since their sucking behavior is depressed for four days after delivery, they will not be able to nurse as vigorously as they should. As a result, they will have trouble gaining weight (Kron, Stein, & Goddard, 1966). Babies of medicated

Table 3-3   Infant Mortality Rates, Selected Countries, 1968

Rank	Country	Rate*
1	Sweden (1967)	12.9
2	Netherlands (1967)	13.4
3	Finland	14.0*
4	Norway (1966)	14.6
5	Japan (1967)	15.0*
6	Denmark (1967)	15.8*
7	Switzerland (1967)	17.5
8	Australia (1967)	18.3
9	New Zealand	18.7
10	United Kingdom	18.8*
11	Eastern Germany	20.4*
12	France	20.4*
13	UNITED STATES (1968)	21.7*
14	Canada (1967)	22.0
15	Federal Rep. of Germany (1967)	22.8
16	Czechoslovakia (1967)	22.9*
17	Belgium (1967)	23.4*
18	Ireland (1967)	24.4
19	Singapore (1967)	24.8
20	Austria	25.5*
21	Israel (1967)	25.9
22	Bulgaria	28.2*
23	Jamaica (1967)	31.0*
24	Spain	32.0*
25	Italy (1967)	32.8*
26	Greece	34.4*
27	Hungary (1967)	37.0
28	Poland (1967)	38.1
29	Trinidad and Tobago (1966)	41.8
30	Ceylon (1965)	53.2
31	Portugal (1967)	59.2
32	Romania	59.5
33	Yugoslavia (1967)	61.4*
34	El Salvador (1967)	63.1
35	Mexico (1967)	63.1
36	Costa Rica (1966)	69.9
37	Albania (1965)	86.8
38	Guatemala (1966)	91.5*
39	Chile (1967)	99.9

*Rates indicate deaths under one year of age per 1,000 live births; provisional data are starred.
Source: U. S. Department of Health, Education, and Welfare, Health Services and Mental Health Administration, National Center for Health Statistics.

mothers are more vulnerable than babies of unmedicated mothers and are in greater danger of dying because of birth injury and respiratory distress (Haire, 1972).

In one longitudinal study (Conway & Brackbill, 1970), the behavior of twenty-three infants was measured at two days, five days, and one month of age to determine the effects on them of the analgesics and anesthetics taken by their mothers during labor and delivery. The babies were tested by the Graham Scale, which scores muscle tension, vision, and maturation; the Bayley Scales, which score psychomotor and mental development; the Apgar ratings; and the extinction of the orienting reflex. The findings were significant: the more medication the mother had received, the less competent was her baby's performance on these ratings (Conway & Brackbill, 1970).

Aside from these sobering facts, obstetric medication has another effect. There probably is no such thing in humans as "maternal instinct." Much of a woman's motherly feeling comes about because of the positive responses she receives from her baby. A baby who nurses eagerly and who acts alert sets up positive feelings in his or her mother. What, then, we must ask, are the long-range psychological implications for the mother-child relationship when a drugged mother is interacting with a drugged infant? For both physiological and psychological reasons, then, we as a society should carefully reexamine the routine usage of obstetric medication. There *is* an alternative.

Childbirth without Drugs

As early as 1914, Dr. Grantly Dick-Read, an English obstetrician, began to question the inevitability of pain in a natural function like childbirth and to propound the theory of "natural childbirth." Dr. Dick-Read educated his patients in the physiology of reproduction and delivery and trained them in breathing, relaxation, and physical fitness, to eliminate the fear that he felt caused most childbirth pain. By the middle of the century, Dr. Fernand Lamaze, a French obstetrician, began to use the psychoprophylactic method of obstetrics, often termed "prepared childbirth." This method was built on Russian techniques that used the principles of conditioned reflexes to substitute new learned responses of special types of breathing and muscular activity to the sensations of uterine contractions, instead of the old responses of fear and pain.

Both these methods, which have been rapidly gaining adherents among mothers and physicians, stress a minimum amount of obstetric medication. Their rapid spread in recent years can be attributed to two principal factors. First, there are psychological benefits for the parents: for the awake mother who can actively participate in her baby's birth and thus know and enjoy the experience of childbirth, and for the involved father who can assist his wife throughout her labor and delivery and thus also know the joy of participating in the birth of his child. In the long run, however, the most far-reaching effects of these new types of childbirth will probably be felt by the babies themselves.

There will probably always be a need for obstetric medication in deliveries that run into complications. But for the vast majority of normal, uncomplicated childbirths, there are good reasons to use as little medication as possible.

Important Issues Concerning the Neonate

BREAST FEEDING

Baby bottles for feeding infants artificially were in use in Egypt and a few other countries as early as the first century A.D., but such artificial feeding used to be resorted to only by a tiny minority of wealthy women. In the United States today, however, artificially fed babies are in the majority. Only one newborn baby in three even begins to nurse at the mother's breast, only one in five is still nursing at the age of two months, and after that time the percentage drops off sharply (Mason, 1973). This fall from popularity of a once almost universal method of infant feeding has occurred all over the world, to the distress of public health experts everywhere (Berg, 1973). The one ray of hope seen by concerned nutritionists is the rising incidence of breast feeding among well-off, well-educated women (Salber, 1966), which may presage a more universal return to this ancient means of nurture.

Breast milk has been termed the "ultimate health food" (Olds & Eiger, 1973) because it offers so many physiological benefits to babies. Breast-fed children are protected in varying degrees against infantile diarrhea, respiratory infections, allergy, eczema, hay fever, asthma, colds, bronchitis, pneumonia, German measles, scarlet fever, and polio (Baum, 1971; Jelliffe & Jelliffe, 1971; Hodes, 1964). Furthermore, recent research indicates that the breast-fed baby is more likely to have healthy teeth (Tank, 1965) and less likely to be obese (Fomon, 1971) or to suffer from premature atherosclerosis (Fomany, 1971). Psychological benefits are also said to accrue from the close mother-child relationship and the abundance of body contact afforded by breast feeding (Montagu, 1971; Newton, 1967).

Breast feeding benefits the mother, also. While nursing, a woman is less likely to become pregnant, assuring a period of rest between pregnancies for her and a period of uninterrupted care for the infant; her uterus shrinks more quickly to its prepregnancy size; and she undergoes a distinct phase of female sexuality that many women find enjoyable (Olds & Eiger, 1973). The pleasurable aspects of breast feeding may have an element of species survival. If a woman enjoys nursing her baby, she will do so for a longer time, thereby assuring the infant of the benefits of breast milk.

Why, then, did breast feeding fall so sharply from favor during the first half of the twentieth century? The answer to this question is complex, due to many changes in our society, including changes in the status and life expectations of women (Olds & Eiger, 1973), a societal distaste for nudity leading to extreme modesty (Newson & Newson, 1962), and the increasing use of childbirth medications, which interfere with the new baby's ability to suck (Brazelton, 1961; Kron, Stein, & Goddard, 1966).

Lactation is a hormonally controlled process set in motion during pregnancy, when glandular changes in the breasts prepare them to produce milk. The altered hormonal balance in the mother's body that follows the delivery of the placenta causes the release of *prolactin*, a milk-producing hormone. As Vicky exercises the sucking reflex, she stimulates the nerve endings in her mother's nipples, which then send signals to the mother's pituitary gland. This gland continues to release prolactin and also sends out another hormone, *oxytocin*. Oxytocin controls the mechanism that takes the milk from the site in the breast where it is made, through the ducts, to Vicky. This process of getting the milk to the baby is known as the "let

Although breast feeding is preferable from several points of view, the quality of the relationship between mother and child appears to be more important than the feeding method.

(Erika Stone, from Peter Arnold)

down reflex," an elegant example of natural design that coordinates reflexes of mother and baby and aids the development of the early mother-infant attachment (Olds & Eiger, 1973).

Many factors influence the breast feeding relationship. Since the baby's vigorous sucking is essential for the ample production of milk, the personality and behavior of the baby can have positive or negative effects on the course of successful breast feeding (Newton & Newton, 1967). The mother's physical health and emotional attitudes also matter. Although a poorly nourished woman can nurse her baby for the first few months, the better nourished she is the longer she will be able to breast-feed (Kon & Cowie, 1961). And mothers with favorable attitudes toward breast feeding give more milk and are more successful than mothers with negative attitudes (Newton, 1955). All drugs—medicines, tobacco, alcohol, marijuana, and so forth—do go through the milk to reach the baby. Although some of these seem to have little or no effect, others should not be taken by the nursing mother (Shore, 1970; Catz, 1972; Arena, 1970).

Breast feeding is preferable from several points of view, but it is not the only way to nourish a baby, either physically or psychologically. A very small minority of women are physically unable to nurse their babies, and many others find the idea unappealing. There is no reason why babies fed with formula and raised with love cannot grow up to be healthy, well-adjusted individuals. In fact, long-term studies that have compared breast-fed children with those who had been bottle-fed have found no significant differences between the two (Schmitt, 1970). The quality of the relationship between mother and child appears to be more important than the feeding method (Olds & Eiger, 1973):

> A baby raised in a loving home can grow up to be a healthy, psychologically secure individual no matter how he receives his nourishment. While successful nursing is a beautiful, happy experience for both mother and child, the woman who nurses grudgingly because she feels she *should* will probably do more harm to her baby by communicating her feelings of resentment and unhappiness, than she would if she were a relaxed, loving, bottle-feeding mother [p. 18].

THE FATHER'S ROLE

In some primitive societies, biological paternity is not even recognized. The inhabitants of the Trobriand Islands in the South Pacific and the Aranda think that intercourse is for fun, not for babies (Mead & Newton, 1967). But most societies do recognize the father's role in procreation, and all prescribe their own mores for "social" fatherhood. Usually the man provides materially for his sexual partner and for their children; only rarely does he take an active role in the care of the children.

Even during pregnancy, the father's role varies a great deal from society to society. Since some primitive people feel that both the mother and the father are responsible for fetal development, the father in these societies observes the same restrictions on food or activity as the mother (Mead & Newton, 1967). The Ifugao tribe in the Philippines does not allow a man to cut or kill anything during his wife's pregnancy (Metraux, 1940), and the Lepchar father or Sikkim in the Himalayas takes part, with his wife, in a ceremonial cleansing during the fifth month of her pregnancy (Gorer, 1938). In the United States, the traditional role of the prospective father has been one of supporting and protecting his wife, but one in which he was relatively uninvolved with the pregnancy. Today, however, the rapid proliferation of classes for expectant parents in hospitals across the country has involved many more prospective fathers with the physiological and psychological aspects of pregnancy.

Paternal roles during childbirth vary, also. At this time the Kurtatchi father of the Pacific Islands must stop work, must refrain from lifting any heavy object or touching any sharp instrument, and must remain in seclusion until after the child is born (Blackwood, 1935). The *couvade*, a practice by which the father takes to his bed during and immediately after birth as if *he* were bearing the baby, highlights his responsibility to his wife and child. Couvade is still practiced in certain parts of Asia, North and South America, and Oceana (Mead & Newton, 1967).

In the past, in this country, when babies were customarily born at home, the father would stay with his wife to comfort her during her labor. Then, when the birth was actually taking place, he would welcome the doctor, supervise the activities of the household, and mind the older children. He played an important, necessary role that went well beyond Hollywood's view that his primary function was to boil plenty of water. But when childbirth moved to the hospital, the father was displaced. He could no longer remain with his wife in labor; he was often made to feel like an unwelcome visitor; he was relegated to a special room set aside for anxious fathers; and after the baby was born, he could see his child only by peering through the glass window of the nursery.

In 1970, a court case brought by a young father who wanted to stay with his wife throughout her labor and delivery in a Chicago hospital dramatized the changing mores in our country relating to the father's role during childbirth (Olds & Witt, 1970). With the growing popularity of prepared childbirth, during which the woman is active and participating, and of prenatal classes that include fathers, more and more men find that they do, indeed, have a valuable role during childbirth. A supportive husband can coach his wife in her breathing, can massage her back during contractions, can provide emotional encouragement, and can enjoy the feeling that he is actively participating in his child's birth, as he did in its conception.

Paternal patterns of child care are also changing. Although untold billions of words have been written in professional journals and popular magazines about mother-child relationships, most child-care professionals have virtu-

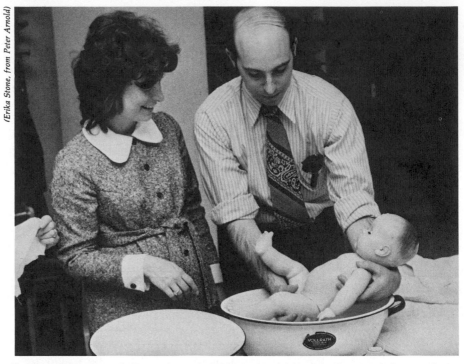

(Erika Stone, from Peter Arnold)

Rapid proliferation of classes for expectant parents has involved many fathers with the physiological and psychological aspects of parenthood.

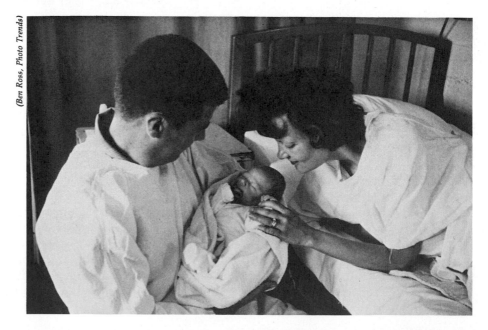

(Ben Ross, Photo Trends)

ally ignored the father's relationship to his child, especially in infancy. Those who have written on it have usually lamented the fact that it is practically nonexistent.

In the eighteenth century, an American physician, Dr. William Buchan, wrote (Byrne & Carey, 1803):

> The mother is not the only person concerned in the management of children; the father has an equal interest in their welfare, and ought to assist in every thing that respects either the improvement of the body or mind. It is a pity that men should be so inattentive to this matter . . . but men generally keep at such a distance from even the smallest acquaintance with the affairs of the nursery, that many would reckon it an affront were they supposed to know any thing of them. Not so, however, with the kennel or the stables: a gentleman of the first rank is not ashamed to give directions concerning the management of dogs or horses, yet would blush were he surprised in performing the same office for that being who derived its existence from himself, who is the heir to his fortunes, and the future hope of his country.

But now we see more and more examples of what one psychologist has called "the new father" (*Life*, 1972). This man "no longer considers child care to be strictly woman's work. He is much more aware of his child's emotional needs and he actively, intimately nurtures them." These changing attitudes among American fathers are probably due to broad changes in our society, in which increasing numbers of women pursue professions outside the home, men and women alike cast aside rigid stereotypes of "appropriate" sex roles, and men are waking up to the fact that they can give much more to their children and get much more in terms of emotional fulfillment. As a result, we are seeing many young men assume a larger role in child care, beginning in their offspring's infancy.

Perhaps our society will eventually reach the point attained many years ago by the Arapesh of New Guinea who consider the care of children to be the work of *both* men and women, so much so, that Margaret Mead says in *Sex and Temperament in Three Primitive Societies*, "If one comments upon a middle-aged man as good-looking, the people answer: 'Good-looking? Ye-e-e-s? But you should have seen him before he bore all those children.' [Mead, 1935, p. 55]."

SEX DIFFERENCES AMONG NEW BABIES
"Sugar and spice and everything nice"—or "snakes and snails and puppy dogs' tails." These descriptions have become so strong a part of our culture that we know the first is meant to describe the ideal girl, the second the ideal boy. Like all cultures, we have very firm ideas of a typical, or normal, girl and a typical, or normal, boy. In recent years, more and more research has sought the reasons behind the cultural dichotomy between male and female.

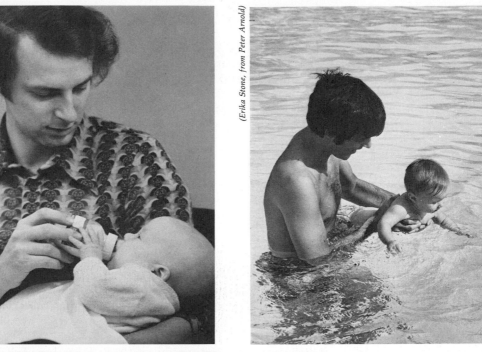

(Erika Stone, from Peter Arnold)

"The new father no longer considers child care to be strictly woman's work. He is much more aware of his child's emotional needs and he actively, intimately nurtures them."

(Mimi Forsyth, Monkmeyer)

Some critics of society state roundly that there are no differences between males and females other than the biological-reproductive ones and that since these do not matter until puberty, girls and boys should be treated exactly the same, "socialized" exactly the same, and be expected to perform alike in all spheres. Other observers of the sexual scene point to innate biological and hormonal differences between male and female, state that these differences play a large part in determining personality and attitude as well as physical form, and warn against the psychologically damaging effects of "unisex" treatment.

As with so many of the other issues in child development, this controversy has no single, clear-cut answer. Yes, some biological differences do show up even before infancy. But we also must recognize the very different ways we treat boys and girls based on our cultural expectations for them.

Biological Differences

In the discussion in Chapter 1 about the determination of sex at the moment of conception, some of the prenatal differences between the sexes were pointed out, showing the female sex to be anything *but* the weaker one. The male's greater vulnerability accelerates even more after birth, with more males than females dying during the first years of life (*Vital Statistics*, United States Department of Health, Education & Welfare, 1967, 1969) and more males subject to postnatal behavior disorders associated with brain damage during pregnancy (Pasamanick et al., 1956). Among premature infants, males are more likely to die, more likely to suffer neurological damage, and more likely to score poorly in both mental and motor development tests (Braine et al., 1966). Males are plainly at a disadvantage in physical, psychological, and neurological development from conception to about four years of age.

In one study of 15,000 patients in the first year of life (Singer, Westphal, & Niswander, 1968), the males had significantly lower Apgar ratings than the females. They also had a much larger number of abnormalities. Out of 187 abnormalities, 71.8 percent appeared primarily among males, 25.1 percent among females, and 3.1 percent equally between the two sexes. This finding is especially surprising in light of the heavier birthweight among males. Larger babies usually do better than smaller ones, but in this instance, the male babies' extra ounces did not help them.

What causes these sex differences? No one knows for sure, but their early appearance makes us hold the genetic code responsible. Maybe the X chromosome contains certain genes that protect females physiologically against the stresses of life. If this is so, females, who have two X's, one from each parent, benefit from their more varied active genetic material. Or maybe the Y chromosome contains genes that are actually harmful. Since the female has no Y's, she cannot be injured by them. Perhaps the differences lie in the different hormones secreted by male and female. The possibility has even been raised that some women become "allergic" to male fetuses. Substances produced by the male fetus may sensitize the mother, causing her to reject it or in some way to damage its central nervous system (Renkonnen & Makela, 1962, from Singer et al., 1968).

Other Physical Differences

Baby boys and girls differ in other ways, too. The electrical activity of the skin is different for a newborn male than for a newborn female (Maccoby, 1966). Baby girls are more sensitive to pain (Lipsitt & Levy, 1959), and they react more strongly when jets of air are directed to their abdomens and when a covering blanket is removed (Maccoby, 1966). These reactions may be survival mechanisms that help girls to cope with dangerous situations. Newborn boys and girls show different kinds of activity, too. While Johnny is more likely to show spontaneous startle reactions in which his whole body moves convulsively, Vicky shows more finer movements, like twitching, smiling, and sucking (Korner, 1969).

Johnny and Vicky are likely to show differences in state, too. Johnny is apt to be more irritable, crying and fussing more, and sleeping less than Vicky (Moss, 1967). When thirty first-born babies—fifteen boys and fifteen girls—were observed during the first three months of life, the researcher concluded that "much more was happening with the male infants than with the female infants [Moss, 1967]." The baby boys slept less and cried more, and, as a result, got more attention from their mothers. When the state of the infant was taken into account, the sex differences were no longer statistically significant. Thus sex apparently influences state, and state influences the way a baby is treated. The end result is different treatment for boy and girl babies, about which more will be said in Chapter 6.

It is very likely that the large differences in interests, abilities, and even personalities between adult men and women in our society must be due as much or more to differences in parental handling, starting in the cradle, as to any inborn differences between the sexes. For, ultimately, boy and girl children have more in common than they have differences. They have the same basic needs for food, shelter, and love. They approach the same developmental milestones intellectually, physically, and emotionally. And there are much greater differences between individual children of the same sex than there are between the "average" male child and the "average" female child.

Summary

1   The birth process occurs in three stages: during the first stage, uterine contractions cause the cervix to dilate; in the second stage, the baby descends from the uterus and emerges from the mother's body; the afterbirth is expelled in the third stage.

2   Neonate refers to a child from birth until about two weeks of age. This is the period of transition from intrauterine to extrauterine life. During this time, temperature regulation, the circulatory, respiratory, gastrointestinal, and nervous systems operate independently from the mother.

3   The systems for vision, audition, olfaction, gustation, and sensitivity to temperature and pain are all operational to some extent in the infant at birth, and then they improve. When assessing the abilities of the neonate, we must be aware of the *state* of the infant.

4   Just as during all other periods of development, individual differences are exhibited by the newborn.

5   Shortly after birth the neonate is assessed medically using the *Apgar Scale*. This scale measures five factors (heart rate, respiration, color, muscle tone, and reflex irritability) which indicate how well the newborn is adjusting to the extrauterine environment. Conditions such as prematurity, birth trauma, and obstetrical medication can influence early adjustment and continue to exert an influence later in life.

6   Breast feeding offers physiological benefits to the infant and facilitates formation of the mother-infant bond.

7   The father's relationship to the unborn and newborn child varies in different cultures. In America today, young fathers are assuming a larger role in child care than in the past.

8   There are biological differences, physical differences, and differences in the treatment of male and female infants.

Suggested Readings

Chess, S., Thomas, A., & Birch, H. G. *Your Child Is a Person: A Psychological Approach to Parenthood without Guilt.* New York: Viking, 1965. *A very readable book that translates the findings of the New York Longitudinal Study into practical words of wisdom and reassurance for parents. The major premise is that children differ temperamentally from birth and that parents will be most successful if they take these differences into account.*

Olds, S., & Eiger, M. S. *Complete Book of Breastfeeding.* New York: Bantam, 1973. *A comprehensive guide that pays particular attention to the benefits of breast feeding for mother and baby, and discusses the fall from favor of breast feeding in America and how it fits into family life. It includes beautiful photographs.*

Senn, M. J. E., & Hartford, C. *The Firstborn: Experiences of Eight American Families.* Cambridge: Harvard, 1968. *A description and interpretation of the experiences of eight representative American families with their first-born children. It examines what happens to two people when a new family member enters their home, and how early family experiences can, and do, affect the development and personality of the young child.*

Spock, B. *Baby and Child Care.* The "Bible" for millions of parents and still the most complete easy-to-read guide to all aspects of children's day-by-day development. From this guide you can get a picture of what children are like from infancy to adolescence. It includes the behavioral problems and physical disorders that are common to children.

CHAPTER FOUR
PHYSICAL DEVELOPMENT

IN WHICH VICKY EXHIBITS STARTLING
PHYSICAL GROWTH AND DEVELOPMENT

I'm like a child
trying to do everything
say everything
see everything
and be everything
all at once

(John Hartford, 1971*)

As an infant, Vicky is primarily a motor creature. By actually manipulating her toys, her bottle, and even her own fingers and toes, she learns about the world. Her first attempts at language are accompanied by physical gestures. As she says "bye-bye," she opens and closes her hand, and as she says "up," she raises her arms to be lifted. She talks not only with her hands but often with her whole body. Only later will the motor component drop out of her speech.

In the early months of life, Vicky does not completely differentiate herself from her surroundings. She has to learn what is her body and what is not. As she incessantly drops toys over the side of her crib, splashes water all over the bathroom during her bath, and hurls sand at her

*From "Life Prayer," by John Hartford, in Word Movies. Garden City, N.Y.: Doubleday & Co., 1971.

neighbors in the sandbox, she learns how her body and its activities can affect other objects in her environment. Her physical growth and developing coordination dominate her life.

We speak of Vicky as an average child, knowing full well that there's no such thing. Nor is there a "right" age when a child should be a certain height or weight or should be performing specific activities. The philosophy that "nature abhors identities" (Gesell, 1943) can be seen nowhere more clearly than in the unique course of growth and development followed by every individual. The range of normality is a broad one. But there are basic patterns that all of us follow as we go through life.

Normal development, for example, follows two principles of progression, both in physical growth and in motor development. The *cephalocaudal* principle (from the Latin "head-to-tail") dictates that development shall proceed from the head to the lower part of the body. Thus, an embryo's head, brain, and eyes develop before its trunk and legs, continue after birth to develop ahead of the lower parts, and are disproportionately large until the other parts catch up. The head of the two-month-old embryo is half the length of the entire body, and the head of the newborn infant is one-fourth his total body length and weight, while the head of the adult is only one-seventh the size of the rest of the body (see Figure 4-1). The brain of a one-year-old baby weighs 70 percent of its full adult weight, while the rest of the body still has far to go. Furthermore, infants learn to use the upper parts of their bodies before their lower parts. Vicky sees objects before she can reach them with her hands; she can control her head before she can control her trunk; and she learns to do many things with her hands long before her legs are very useful.

Figure 4-1 **Changes in Human Body Form Associated with Age** *(Robbins, 1929)*

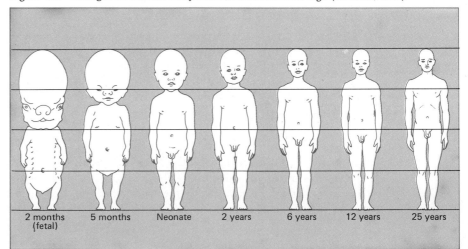

2 months (fetal)   5 months   Neonate   2 years   6 years   12 years   25 years

According to the *proximodistal* law (Latin, "near-to-far"), development proceeds from the central part of the body to the peripheral parts. Thus, the embryonic head and trunk develop before the limbs, and the arms and legs before the fingers and toes. Vicky first develops the ability to use her upper arm and upper leg (which are closest to the central axis), then her forearm and foreleg, then her hands and feet, and finally her fingers and toes.

Normal physical development follows an apparently preordained course, even though the time by which individual babies perform specific activities varies widely. In other words, almost all children progress in a definite order from certain activities to others. Only with specific environmental stimulation—such as is sometimes found in mother-child interactions in certain non-Western cultures—is the sequence altered noticeably. Thus, even though Vicky will be able to sit up at six months and Jason not until eleven months, both babies will hold up their chins before they hold up their chests, both will sit with support before they sit alone, and both will stand before they can walk. Just as children grow taller and heavier—and not shorter and lighter—they first perform simple movements before the more complicated ones.

Physical Growth, or What the Baby Becomes

"Curiouser and curiouser!" cried Alice. "Now I'm opening out like the largest telescope that ever was!"

While real live human babies do not shoot up quite so suddenly as Lewis Carroll's storybook heroine, their rapid growth in height and weight during the first three years of life helps to change their lives just as much as Alice's

(Gregor, Monkmeyer)

Just as children grow taller and heavier, they first perform simple movements before more complicated ones.

unexpected growth changed hers. Furthermore, not only do they grow in total body size, but the very proportions of their bodies change markedly during this time. Tables 4-1 through 4-4 show the patterns and the growth ranges for boys and girls up to three years of age. We see that babies gain about twice as much in height during their first year of life as during the second. In weight, the difference between the two years is even more dramatic, with most babies tripling their birthweight during the first year, and then gaining only about one-fourth of that during the second year. During the third year, increments in both weight and height are still smaller, and the three-year-old is quite slender, compared with the chubby one-year-old.

Table 4-1   Height Percentiles for Boys, Birth to Age 3

Age	Length (inches)						
	3%	10%	25%	50%	75%	90%	97%
Birth	$18^1/_4$	19	$19^1/_2$	20	$20^1/_2$	21	$21^1/_2$
1 month	$19^3/_4$	$20^1/_4$	$20^3/_4$	$21^1/_4$	22	$22^1/_4$	$23^3/_4$
6 months	$24^3/_4$	$25^1/_4$	$25^3/_4$	26	$26^3/_4$	$27^1/_4$	$27^3/_4$
12 months	28	$28^1/_2$	29	$29^1/_2$	$30^1/_4$	$30^3/_4$	$31^1/_2$
18 months	$30^1/_2$	31	$31^1/_2$	$32^1/_4$	33	$33^1/_2$	$34^1/_2$
24 months	$32^1/_2$	33	$33^3/_4$	$34^1/_2$	$35^1/_4$	36	$37^1/_4$
30 months	$34^1/_4$	$34^3/_4$	$35^1/_2$	$36^1/_4$	37	38	$39^1/_4$
36 months	$35^3/_4$	$36^1/_4$	37	38	$38^3/_4$	$39^1/_2$	$40^1/_2$

Source: From *Growth and Development of Children*, 5th edition, by Ernest H. Watson and George H. Lowrey. Copyright © 1967, Year Book Medical Publishers, Inc., Chicago. Used by permission of Year Book Medical Publishers.

Table 4-2   Weight Percentiles for Boys, Birth to Age 3

Age	Weight (pounds)						
	3%	10%	25%	50%	75%	90%	97%
Birth	$5^3/_4$	$6^1/_4$	7	$7^1/_2$	$8^1/_4$	9	10
1 month	$7^1/_2$	$8^1/_2$	9	10	$10^1/_2$	$11^1/_2$	13
6 months	14	$14^3/_4$	$15^1/_2$	$16^3/_4$	18	$19^1/_4$	$20^3/_4$
12 months	$18^1/_2$	$19^1/_2$	$20^3/_4$	$22^1/_4$	$23^3/_4$	$25^1/_2$	$27^1/_4$
18 months	21	$22^1/_2$	$23^3/_4$	$25^1/_4$	27	29	$31^1/_2$
24 months	$23^1/_4$	$24^3/_4$	$26^1/_4$	$27^3/_4$	$29^3/_4$	32	35
30 months	$25^1/_4$	$26^1/_2$	$28^1/_2$	30	$32^1/_4$	$34^1/_2$	37
36 months	27	$28^3/_4$	$30^1/_4$	$32^1/_4$	$34^1/_2$	$36^3/_4$	$39^1/_4$

Source: From *Growth and Development of Children*, 5th edition, by Ernest H. Watson and George H. Lowrey. Copyright © 1967, Year Book Medical Publishers, Inc., Chicago. Used by permission of Year Book Medical Publishers.

Table 4-3 Height Percentiles for Girls, Birth to Age 3

Age	Length (inches)						
	3%	10%	25%	50%	75%	90%	97%
Birth	$18^1/_2$	$18^3/_4$	$19^1/_4$	$19^3/_4$	20	$20^1/_2$	21
1 month	$19^3/_4$	$20^1/_4$	$20^1/_2$	21	$21^1/_2$	22	22
6 months	24	$24^1/_2$	25	$25^3/_4$	$26^1/_4$	$26^3/_4$	27
12 months	27	$27^3/_4$	$28^1/_2$	$29^1/_4$	30	$30^1/_4$	31
18 months	$29^1/_2$	$30^1/_4$	31	$31^3/_4$	$32^1/_2$	$33^1/_4$	34
24 months	$31^1/_2$	$32^1/_4$	$33^1/_4$	34	35	$35^3/_4$	$36^3/_4$
30 months	$33^1/_4$	34	$35^1/_4$	36	37	38	39
36 months	$34^3/_4$	$35^1/_2$	$36^3/_4$	$37^3/_4$	$38^1/_2$	$39^3/_4$	$40^3/_4$

Source: From *Growth and Development of Children,* 5th edition, by Ernest H. Watson and George H. Lowrey. Copyright © 1967, Year Book Medical Publishers, Inc., Chicago. Used by permission of Year Book Medical Publishers.

Table 4-4 Weight Percentiles for Girls, Birth to Age 3

Age	Weight (pounds)						
	3%	10%	25%	50%	75%	90%	97%
Birth	$5^3/_4$	$6^1/_4$	7	$7^1/_2$	8	$8^1/_2$	$9^1/_2$
1 month	7	8	$8^1/_2$	$9^3/_4$	$10^1/_4$	11	$11^3/_4$
6 months	$12^3/_4$	14	$14^3/_4$	$15^3/_4$	$17^1/_4$	$18^1/_2$	$19^3/_4$
12 months	$16^1/_2$	18	$19^1/_2$	21	$22^1/_2$	$24^1/_2$	$26^1/_2$
18 months	$19^1/_4$	21	$22^1/_2$	$24^1/_4$	26	28	$30^3/_4$
24 months	$21^1/_2$	$23^1/_2$	$25^1/_4$	27	$29^1/_4$	$31^3/_4$	$34^1/_2$
30 months	$23^1/_2$	$25^1/_2$	$27^1/_2$	$29^1/_2$	32	$35^1/_2$	$38^1/_4$
36 months	$25^1/_2$	$27^1/_2$	$29^1/_2$	$31^3/_4$	$34^1/_2$	$37^1/_2$	$41^3/_4$

Source: From *Growth and Development of Children,* 5th edition, by Ernest H. Watson and George H. Lowrey. Copyright © 1967, Year Book Medical Publishers, Inc., Chicago. Used by permission of Year Book Medical Publishers.

INFLUENCES ON HEIGHT AND WEIGHT

The most important determinant of our size and shape appears to be heredity. The genes we inherit have the biggest say in molding our basic body—whether we will be tall and thin, short and stocky, or just in between. Aside from the ordinary observation that tall parents tend to have taller children and short parents shorter children, studies of twins bear out the heritability of both height and weight (Mittler, 1971). Identical twins, raised either together or separately, are closely concordant for both height and weight, compared with fraternal twins.

Height and weight are also affected, though, by such environmental factors as nutrition, living conditions, and general health. The Ten-State

Nutrition Study carried out by the United States Department of Health, Education, and Welfare from 1968 to 1970 carefully examined and took personal histories of some 22,000 children, all under seventeen, who lived in various sections of the country. The survey found a number of relationships between family income, race, and children's growth.

Income

As might be expected, well-fed, well-cared-for children grow taller and heavier than their counterparts in poverty-stricken homes. This is probably due to better medical care. Furthermore, children from more comfortable circumstances mature sexually at an earlier age and attain their maximum height earlier. Their teeth erupt sooner, too. These differences are generally evident by the first year and remain consistent throughout life (American Academy of Pediatrics, 1973).

If you have seen suits of armor in a museum, you probably noticed their small size. Most of these fighting outfits would be far too small for the average man today, indicating that people have been growing taller over the years. This increase in height is particularly noticeable among children, who are growing taller and achieving maturity sooner than they did 100 years ago (Tanner, 1973). We don't know how long this trend has been going on, but it was commented upon as far back as 1876: "A factory child of the present day at the age of 9 years weighs as much as one of 10 years did in 1833—each age has gained one year in 40 years [Charles Roberts, 1876; in Tanner, 1968, p. 23fl."

Improved environmental and social conditions undoubtedly account for the increase and earlier attainment of height, since findings are consistent

Miscellaneous Facts about Infants' Size

First-born infants usually weigh a few ounces less than later-born infants in the same family. Why this is so is a mystery, especially since first-born children are no smaller in adulthood than their younger brothers and sisters.

The child of a small woman and a large man is usually smaller at birth than would be expected from his or her ultimate growth. Some factor may be operating to keep the infant from growing too large to pass comfortably through the mother's small birth canal.

Infants who will be large at birth are already large by the end of 24 weeks of gestational age.

(*Whipple, 1966*)

Taller children stand and walk earlier than shorter ones.

(*Garn, 1966*)

that children from more favorable environments grow taller sooner than their less-privileged contemporaries. Better nutrition, better medical care, the decrease in child labor, and the elimination of early marriage are some social factors that have had both direct and indirect effects on children's growth patterns over the years.

Race

Although the findings relating children's development to family income may have fulfilled the investigators' expectations, the discovered relationships between growth and racial backgrounds were less predictable. Even when the statistics had been corrected to eliminate different income levels, it was clear that the bones of the black children hardened earlier, their permanent teeth appeared sooner, they matured earlier, and they tended to be larger. The American Academy of Pediatrics (1973) in its review of the study concluded that "genetic factors outweighed economic factors in explaining differences in skeletal and dental development. These findings suggest the need for different standards for black and white children when assessing nutritional status during growth."

Sex

Another major influence on height and weight is, of course, sex. Boys are slightly longer and heavier than girls at birth and remain larger through adulthood—except for a brief period during puberty when the girls' growth spurts make them overtake the boys.

Physical Health

A child with some serious long-term illness will not grow as well as a healthy child. Congenital heart disease, nephritis, inborn metabolic disorders, and certain other illnesses can have grave effects on growth. A child who is ill for a long time may never achieve his genetically programmed normal stature because he may never be able to make up for the growth time he lost while he was sick. Better medical care, and especially the use of immunization procedures and antibiotic drugs, have played a part in making modern children larger than their forebears by decreasing the amount of serious illness likely to strike today's youngsters.

Emotional Factors

Infants who suffer emotional deprivation fail to gain weight normally, even when their nutrition and medical care are adequate (Whipple, 1966). This phenomenon is discussed more fully in Chapter 7. Although many child-care workers have noted the apparent effect of emotional deprivation on physical development, more research in this area is needed, specifically to separate the two factors that often go hand in hand: lack of adequate food and lack of adequate love.

OBESITY

A major nutritional problem among modern American children is the "overnutrition" that leads to obesity. Apparently there are some fat people whose undue size stems from the genetic inheritance that has endowed them with more subcutaneous fat or with a more sluggish metabolism. But current thought leans heavily to the view that "we are what we eat"—that most fat people have gained their surplus poundage because they eat too much food for the amount of energy they expend.

The Ten-State Nutritional Survey, for example, found that from infancy through adolescence obesity increased directly with income (American Academy of Pediatrics, 1973). And a new theory rapidly gaining currency among pediatricians and nutritionists is that many people become obese in later life because they are overfed in infancy. Recent animal research indicates that feeding infant rats too many calories causes them to develop an abundance of fat cells (Hirsch, 1972). The same process may be operating in human beings so that overfed infants develop extra fat cells that persist through life and cause stubborn obesity (Hirsch, 1972; Mayer, 1973; Jelliffe, 1974).

If these beliefs are borne out by more research, they are bound to change our traditional attitude that the fat, dimpled baby is the healthiest one, and they will most certainly bring about changes in infant feeding practices. Some pediatric nutritionists are even now advising parents to prevent obesity in children by breast feeding them as infants, waiting four to six months after birth before offering them solid food, and keeping a watchful eye on infant calorie intake (Mayer, 1973; Hammer, 1973; Jelliffe, 1974).

Motor Development, or What the Baby Does

It has been said that "actions are the bricks of all intellectual edifices [Crowell, 1967]." By this we mean that a child cannot learn how to think unless he learns how to *do*—first, through actual physical movement and then through mental activity. In an infant the only activity we can observe is the physical, and so this is the focus of child study at this age. We cannot tell what the infant Vicky is thinking—but we can *see* what she *does*. If we want to measure her intelligence or satisfy ourselves that she is developing normally, our only gauge is her level of motor skills. Developmentalists have found that there is a definite order for the acquisition of motor skills, proceeding from the simple to the complex.

With age, Vicky's motor development shows more control and a specificity of function. Her control of her body parts is *differentiating.* Thus she proceeds from good control of her hands, eventually, to good control of her fingers. After she has gained control over a variety of differentiated movements, these abilities are *integrated* into complex behavior patterns. Thus Vicky's control over her leg, feet, and arm movements are integrated to enable her to walk. Heinz Werner (1948) calls this *hierarchic integration,* or the integration of individual abilities into larger behaviors.

In the womb Vicky moved about a great deal, turning somersaults, kicking, and sucking her thumb. As a newborn baby, she could turn her head, kick her legs, flail about with her arms, and display a diverse array of reflex behaviors described in Chapter 3. These prenatal and early postnatal movements represent a very generalized type of activity. All of these early motor activities are under subcortical control, which begins to give way by about the fourth month of postnatal life to voluntary, directed movements that are controlled by the cortex. The cerebellum regulates balance and posture. It matures more rapidly between six and eighteen months than before. With this maturity we see improvement in the motor behavior.

Much early motor development appears to come about principally because of maturation, but there is also an element of interaction with the environment. Before Vicky can perform a specific behavior, she has to be physiologically capable of carrying it out, *and* her environment must permit its expression.

When Vicky's central nervous system, muscles, and bones have matured sufficiently and she is placed in appropriate positions with freedom to move, she will lift her head. She does not have to be taught to do this; it "just comes naturally." However, the more she practices this new skill, the more proficient she will become. Like almost all babies, Vicky is obsessed by each new level of skill. As soon as she first succeeds in lifting her head from a prone position, she continues to practice this interesting new pastime until she can do it perfectly. She transfers this obsession to each new motor activity in turn. And each newly mastered activity prepares her to tackle the next in the preordained sequence of motor skills (see Table 4-5). A baby cannot perform one activity without having mastered the movements in the previous stage. Regardless of individual differences in the age of acquiring the various behaviors, this sequence is true for all babies—whether full-term, premature, or postmature.

Table 4-5   The Normal Course of Motor Development

The following table is adapted from N. R. Haimowitz (1973), Shirley (1933), Lenneberg (1967), and Smart and Smart (1973). Although these ages are the averages for acquiring various abilities, there is a considerable range among babies for reaching each new skill level. These age norms, therefore, should not be taken as absolutes. The *order* of skill acquisition, however, is highly constant among all babies in our culture.

Birth   Motor behavior is highly variable and transient.
                   Wakefulness is not sharply differentiated from sleep.

Infant does not stay in one position for any length of time.

Exhibits reflex behaviors.

Turns head from side to side while lying on back, lifts head for short time when prone, but head sags when not supported.

1 Month

Head still not self-supporting.

Stares at surroundings.

Some eye-following.

Lifts chin when prone.

2 Months

Lifts chest.

Holds head erect when held.

3 Months

Steps when held erect.

Holds head erect and steady.

Reaches for ball but misses.

Turns from side to back.

4 Months

Head steady and self-supporting; lifts when prone, holds steady when held.

Hands open and close.

Reaches for objects close by but can't quite get them.

Contemplates objects held in hand.

Recognizes bottle.

Eyes follow more distant objects.

Plays with hands and clothing.

Holds up chest.

Shakes and stares at rattle placed in hand.

Sits with support.

5 Months

Sits on lap.

Grasps objects.

Rolls over (not accidentally) from back to side.

6 Months

When sitting, bends forward and uses hands for support.

Can bear weight when put in standing position, but cannot yet stand by holding on.

Reaches with one hand.

No thumb apposition yet in grasp. Can transfer objects from hand to hand.

Releases cube held in hand when given another.

7 Months

Sits alone, without support, for a while.

Holds head up.

Attempts to crawl.

Rolls over from back to stomach.

8 Months

Stands with help.

	Crawls (abdomen on floor, arms pull along body and legs).
	Shows thumb apposition.
10 Months	Creeps on hands and knees (trunk free; arms and legs alternate).
	Sits up easily.
	Pulls up to standing position.
	Can put one object on top of another.
12 Months	Walks with support.
	Seats self on floor.
13 Months	Climbs stair steps.
	Sits down.
14 Months	Stands alone.
15 Months	Walks alone.
18 Months	Runs in clumsy fashion, falls a lot.
	Can build tower of two or three objects.
	Pulls and pushes toys.
	Grasp, prehension, and reach are fully developed.
2 Years	Walks well.
	Runs fairly well, with a wide stance.
	Kicks large ball.
	Walks upstairs and downstairs alone.
	Builds tower of three objects.
	Jumps 12 inches.
	Turns pages of a book, one at a time.
2½ Years	Jumps into air with both feet.
	Stands on one foot about two seconds.
	Takes a few steps on tiptoe.
	Jumps from chair.
	Good hand-finger coordination.
	Can move fingers independently.
	Builds tower of five blocks.
3 Years	Stands on one foot.
	Rides tricycle.
	Draws circle.
	Pours from pitcher.
	Buttons and unbuttons.
	Tiptoes.
	Improved object manipulation.
	Can build six-cube tower.
	Runs smoothly.
	Walks up and down steps with alternate footing.

MILESTONES IN INFANT MOTOR DEVELOPMENT[1]

Head Control

At birth most babies can turn their heads from side to side while lying on their backs and can lift their heads somewhat to turn them while on their stomachs. The developmental sequence involves lifting the head while prone, to holding it erect when sitting, to lifting it when lying on the back. For approximate ages of developing this and other motor abilities, see Figure 4-2.

Sitting

Babies learn to sit two different ways: getting up from lying on the stomach or back, and sitting down from standing erect. They sit with support at an average of four months, in a high chair at six months, and alone at seven months (Shirley, 1933).

[1]The ages given here and in Table 4-5 are average ages. About half of all normal babies master these skills before the specified ages and about half master them afterward. As we said earlier, normality includes a wide age range.

Figure 4-2   The Development of Motor Abilities

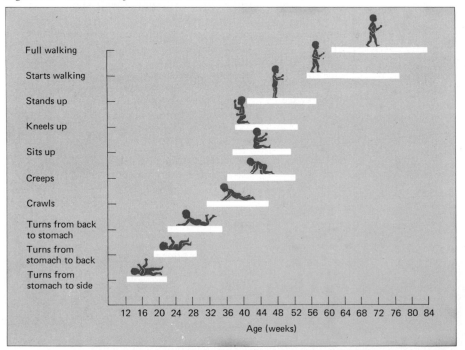

(Andrew Sachs, Editorial Photocolor Archives)

(Erika Stone, from Peter Arnold)

(Shelly Rusten)

Almost all babies become obsessed with each new level of skill—from holding their heads erect, to bear-walking, to walking alone—and they practice each interesting new pastime until they can do it perfectly; then they move on to the next.

Rolling Over
Babies roll over, first from back to side (five months), then from back to stomach (seven months).

Getting Around before Walking
Ames outlined fourteen steps in the development of *creeping* (see Chart 4-1), which involves crawling on hands and knees with trunk above the floor surface. Other prewalking means of locomotion, which may precede or substitute for creeping, are *hitching* or *scooting*, by which a baby moves along in a sitting position, pushing herself forward with her arms and legs; *crawling* (eight months), by which she wriggles on her belly, pulling along her body with her arms and dragging her feet behind; and *bear-walking*,

which is like creeping, except that the legs are straight and the feet, rather than the knees, touch the floor.

Standing Erect

If someone gives them a helping hand, babies can stand at an average age of eight months, stand holding onto furniture about a month later, pull themselves to a standing position at one year, and by grabbing a crib railing or a piece of furniture, stand alone at fourteen months (Shirley, 1933; see Chart 4-2).

Walking

Less than a month after a baby can stand without support, he ventures his first step, most likely tumbles to the floor with a look of surprise on his face, goes back to creeping for a while—and then tries another step, until within a few days he is walking regularly, if shakily. Babies can walk with help at an average age of eleven months and walk alone at fifteen months (Shirley, 1933; see Chart 4-3). We will see in the next section how genetic and environmental factors relate to the age of walking. Ugandan infants, for example, walk at about ten months, considerably before Europeans (Geber, 1956).

Chart 4-1   Fourteen Steps in the Development of Creeping (*Ames, 1937*)

1	One knee and thigh forward beside the body
2	Knee and thigh forward, inner side of foot contacting the floor
3	Pivoting
4	Inferior low-creep position
5	Low-creep position
6	Crawling
7	High-creep position
8	Retrogression
9	Rocking
10	Creep-crawling
11	Creeping on hands and knees
12	Creeping, near step with one foot
13	Creeping, step with one foot
14	Quadruped progression (creeping on hands and feet)

Note: This is a good example of cephalocaudal development. The baby uses his arms for prone progression until step 11, when the legs come into the picture for the first time as effective instruments in forward motion.

Chart 4-2   Steps in the Development of Erect Posture and Locomotion (*Shirley, 1931*)

1 Tensing the muscles when lifted
2 Sitting with support
3 Lifting the head when lying on the back
4 Sitting alone momentarily
5 Standing with support under the armpits
6 Sitting alone
7 Standing with support by holding
8 Sitting down from the standing position
9 Pulling self to the standing position
10 Standing alone

Chart 4-3   Development of Postural Control and Locomotion (*Adapted from Shirley, 1931*)

Stage	*Median Age, Weeks*
First-order Skills: Passive Postural Control of Upper Trunk	
On stomach, chin up	3.0
On stomach, chest up	9.0
Held erect, stepping	13.0
On back, tense for lifting	15.0
Held erect, knees straight	15.0
Sit on lap, support at lower ribs and complete head control	18.5
Second-order Skills: Postural Control of Entire Trunk	
Sit alone momentarily	25.0
On stomach, knee push or swim	25.0
On back, rolling	29.0
Held erect, stand firmly with help	29.5
Sit alone, one minute	31.0
Third-order Skills: Active Attempts at Locomotion	
On stomach, some progress	37.0
On stomach, scoot backward	39.5
Fourth-order Skills: Locomotion and Improved Postural Control of Body	
Stand holding to furniture	42.0
Creep	44.5
Walk when led	45.0
Pull to stand by furniture	47.0

(Continued)

Chart 4-3 (Continued)
Fifth-order Skills: Complete Postural Control during
   Locomotion
      Stand alone   62.0
      Walk alone   64.0

Manipulation Ability

Halverson (1931) analyzed films of manipulation ability (reaching and grasping cubes) in infants up to sixty weeks of age. The neonate shows the grasp reflex. When her palm is stimulated, she grasps the cube. At four months the infant does not grasp—either reflexively or voluntarily. Five-month-olds don't grasp firmly, but they do touch objects. At seven months prehension (grasping) does not include the thumb; at nine months it does. The fifteen-month-old child shows mature prehension using fingers and thumb together. Early grasping involves the entire arm. It is only at the end of this period that differentiation occurs and allows the child to coordinate thumb and forefinger. (See Figure 4–3.)

INFLUENCES ON MOTOR DEVELOPMENT

Maturation appears to be the most important determinant of what a baby can do and when he can do it. In general, motor development does not

Figure 4-3   The Development of Manual Skills *(After Halverson, 1931)*

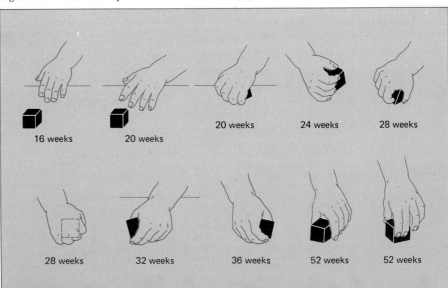

appear to be affected at all by a child's sex, geographical residence, or the level of parental education (Bayley, 1965). At certain age levels (six, seven, twelve, fourteen, and fifteen months), first-born children score slightly better than later-born children on the California Infant Scale of Motor Development (Bayley, 1965), which may be due to the fact that parents spend more time with their first children and probably stimulate them to greater activity. In any case, these small differences are probably temporary (Bayley, 1965).

Race

A number of different studies (Bayley, 1965; Geber, 1958; Geber & Dean, 1957) have shown that black babies appear to be more advanced in motor development than white babies, at least until the first year or first fifteen months of life. It is possible that some genetic factor accounts for the motor precocity of black babies. It is also possible that black parents may handle their infants in a way that stimulates motor development. Perhaps they are less likely to dress their babies in constricting clothing or to put them in playpens, or perhaps they encourage motor activity in some other way.

In Table 4–6 we can see some of the differences in motor development between black and white babies. These data illustrate differences in performance in some of the sixty items on the Bayley Infant Scale of Motor Development. In one study (Bayley, 1965), 1,409 babies, aged one to fifteen

Table 4–6   Scores of the Bayley Infant Scale of Motor Development for Babies by Race *(Bayley, 1965)*

Age (months)	White Babies			Negro Babies			Puerto Rican Babies		
	No.	Mean	Standard Deviation	No.	Mean	Standard Deviation	No.	Mean	Standard Deviation
1	41	6.34	2.03	41	6.39	2.98	5	7.00	1.00
2	45	9.31	2.20	37	9.89	2.22	6	11.17	2.40
3	42	12.12	2.57	41	13.39	2.82	5	13.20	1.79
4	47	14.57	3.20	31	16.29	2.92	8	14.88	1.36
5	41	18.83	3.32	40	21.25	3.46	4	20.75	1.50
6	44	25.73	4.40	42	25.76	4.78	5	27.80	3.77
7	47	28.47	4.88	41	30.46	4.64	9	30.33	5.50
8	61	34.41	5.27	51	35.67	5.02	5	39.00	3.00
9	54	37.13	4.06	44	38.95	4.17	4	37.25	8.18
10	53	40.11	3.62	40	41.32	3.93	5	42.80	1.30
11	43	42.84	3.06	26	44.00	2.99	8	44.13	1.36
12	49	44.22	3.16	43	45.88	4.42	5	46.20	1.64
13	44	46.45	6.49	36	47.08	3.27	7	46.14	2.41
14	48	48.33	3.01	38	48.68	4.03	3	49.00	1.73
15	46	49.35	3.08	36	48.39	3.42	4	50.00	.82

months, were tested. Of these, 55 percent were white, 42 percent black, and 2.3 percent of other races. The ratio of boys to girls was about equal at each age tested.

Not one of the sixty test items favored the white babies by as much as half a month, but the black babies did better by at least 0.7 month on eleven of the items. The particular skills on which the black babies did better are well distributed throughout the first year. They show no particular pattern of age superiority or superiority in any one kind of coordination. Two of the items indicate midline arm and hand coordination. The nine others all require muscle tone and strength. Of these, the ones classified as "antigravity" are the ability to hold the head steady, to balance the head when carried, to sit alone steadily, and to stand alone. "Locomotor" skills measured the ability to turn from side to back, to raise the self to a sitting position, and to make stepping movements, walk with help, and walk alone.

Environment

Although a child has to be physiologically ready to perform various activites, her motor development does not operate in a vacuum. The environment plays its part, too, in determining the acquisition of motor abilities.

How Environment Can Retard Development

By comparing the motor development and the ways of handling children in three Iranian institutions, Dennis (1960) dramatically showed the vital role played by environment in the chronology and style of a child's motor development.

In the two institutions whose children were extremely retarded motorically, the children were hardly ever handled by the overworked attendants. The younger babies spent practically all their time lying on their backs in their cribs. They drank from propped bottles. They themselves were never propped up in a sitting position, were never placed on their stomachs, had no toys, and were not taken out of bed until they were able to sit unsupported. This was often not till past the age of two (as compared with an average sitting age of nine months for normal, noninstitutionalized American children). Once the sitting child did reach the floor, he had no child-size furniture and no play equipment of any kind.

By contrast, the children in the third children's home, who showed normal levels of motor development, were fed in the arms of attendants who had received special training in child care. The babies were placed on their stomachs and propped up in sitting positions during part of their time in bed; they spent time in playpens from the age of four months; and they had many toys.

When the children in the first two groups did learn to get about, they scooted rather than crept. That is, they moved around in a sitting position, pushing their bodies forward with their arms and feet, rather than creeping on hands and knees. Since they had never been placed on their stomachs, they had had no opportunity to practice either raising their heads in this position or pulling their arms and legs beneath their bodies—the movements needed for creeping. Also, since they had never been propped in a sitting position, they had had no practice raising their heads and shoulders to learn how to sit at the usual age. It is amazing that they learned to sit at all. It is even more amazing that this retardation in motor development appeared to be only temporary. School-age children at the second institution, who presumably had been as retarded as toddlers as the children under study, played and worked normally, showing no indications of early motor retardation.

Such extremely severe levels of environmental deprivation as experienced by these first two groups of children are, fortunately, rare. They are cited here to show that environment does play a part in motor development—and that the more an environment departs from the typical, the more of an effect it will have.

Can Motor Development Be Accelerated?

Several experiments have tried to discover the effects of training babies to perform various developmental activities. In the 1920s, Arnold Gesell, the pediatrician who, working at the Yale Clinic of Child Development, first established normative ages for virtually every activity of early childhood, used the co-twin method to study the effects of training. T, one member of a pair of identical twins, was trained in such functions as stair-climbing, block-building, and manual coordination, while Twin C received no such training.

When the twins were forty-six weeks old (about ten months), T was trained in climbing stairs for ten minutes every day for six weeks. Within two weeks, she was climbing the special experimental five-step staircase, with a little help. At the end of the training period, when she was a year old, she was a "relatively expert climber" (Gesell, 1929). At a year, Twin C would not even try to climb the stairs, even with help. But when C saw the staircase again a week later, she climbed to the top without any help and without any previous training.

At this point, C received a two-week stair-climbing course. Motion pictures taken of T at fifty-two weeks of age (after six weeks of training) and of C at fifty-five weeks (after two weeks of training) showed that C was now just as good a climber as T, even though T had been trained three times longer and seven weeks earlier. Since T's advantage was more than overcome by the three weeks of C's added age, "the powerful influence of maturation of infant behavior pattern is made clear [Gesell, 1929]."

Some activities may respond more to training than do others. A recent study (Zelazo, Zelazo, & Kolb, 1972) indicates that training infants in walking, starting at one week of age when they still give reflexive walking responses, may indeed lead to early walking. In this study, twenty-four infant boys were assigned to one of four groups, from the beginning of their second week of life through the end of their eighth week. The babies in the *active-exercise* group had four 3-minute exercise sessions every day, during which they were held under the arms while the soles of their feet were allowed to touch a flat surface. The legs and arms of the babies in the *passive-exercise* group were gently pumped while the babies lay in their cribs, their infant seats, or on a parental lap. The babies in the *no-exercise* group received no training and were tested weekly. And a fourth group of babies was tested only once at the end of the program, just to be sure that the babies in the third group had not learned from being tested every week.

When the babies' parents later reported the age of walking, the researchers found that the babies in the active-exercise group walked at an average age of 10.12 months, while the average child in the control groups did not begin to walk till some time later—as late as 12.35 months for those in the fourth group. (The fact that all the babies walked earlier than the Gesell-Thompson 1934 norm of a little over fourteen months was probably due to heightened parental interest.) This study suggests that there is a critical period during which the walking response can be transformed intact from a reflexive action to a voluntary one. It is possible that the walking reflex has a definite function in helping the human infant to become more mobile; perhaps it should be stimulated rather than be allowed to fade with disuse.

Cross-cultural Perspectives on Motor Development

What is "normal" and typical for children in one culture may not be so for those in another, not only in the chronology of motor development, but even in its usually invariant sequence. For example, Margaret Mead (1935) has reported that the Arapesh of New Guinea hold their babies a great deal, "often in a standing position so that they can push with their feet against the arms or legs of the person who holds them. As a result infants can stand, steadied by their two hands, before they can sit alone [p. 57]." Other studies have demonstrated differences in motor development between black and white American children (Bayley, 1965), between African, European, and Indian children (Geber & Dean, 1957), and between African and American babies (Tronick, Koslowski, & Brazelton, 1971).

Newborn African infants seem to be precocious in motor development. A study that assessed Ugandan, European, and Indian children all born in Africa (Geber & Dean, 1957) found that the African infants had far superior muscle tone, could turn their heads from side to side, pursue moving objects with their eyes, and raise their heads before the other children. The African babies actually seemed to have been born at a more advanced stage of development, since many of their activities at less than a week corresponded to those performed by European children aged four to eight weeks.

Geber (1962, pp. 54–55) outlines specific precocity:

From the first day, placed in the sitting position, the newborn child can keep his head up, so that it does not tip backwards, and supported in a sitting position, his back remains straight. His gaze is lively, and he can focus on the examiner's face and follow an object moving horizontally a little way from his eyes.

At 1 month and a half he can hold his head upright, and smile.

At 3 months he can stay seated for 10 minutes, and smiles at his image in the mirror.

At 4 months he can sit without support, lean forward and regain his balance.

At 8 months he can stand upright on his own.

At 10 months he can walk.

At 11 months he can pick up a small object (a pellet), with precision, between thumb and index-finger.

At 14 months he can run.

According to the standards of the Gesell Test, these last two performances are those of a child of 24 months. . . .

This notable precocity lasts up to 18-20 months. Then it tends to disappear. . . .

Some genetic differences may be responsible for this precocity, especially since American black babies are also advanced in both gross and fine motor development during the first year of life (Bayley, 1965). Some of the difference, though, is probably due to the ways the babies are handled. Zambian mothers, for example, rouse their babies by picking them up under the arms and tossing them up and down. From as soon as twenty-four hours after delivery, a mother carries her baby in a dashiki, which provides no support for the infant's head. The baby quickly learns to keep his head steady. One study (Tronick, Koslowski, & Brazelton, 1971) tested Zambian and American infants on days one, five, and ten using the Brazelton Neonatal Behavioral Assessment Scale. On the first day, the Zambian infants reacted less than the Americans, showing the effects of a poor prenatal environment. But by the fifth day they had caught up, and by the tenth they had become much more attentive than Americans, presumably because of more vigorous, socially stimulating child-care practices.

Evidence that this motoric precocity of African children is environmental as well as hereditary comes from observation of differential activities before and after weaning and of those African children being raised European-style (Geber, 1958). Before children are weaned, their mothers sleep with them, breast-feed on demand, continually stimulate them by activities and conversation, and never leave them. After weaning, the very basis of a child's life is shaken. His mother not only stops giving him the breast but may also stop giving of herself, seeming to make a deliberate effort to separate herself from the child. When weaning causes a sudden change in a child's way of life, the child usually becomes less lively afterwards. Those children who are not weaned as abruptly generally remain vigorous. European-reared African children, who spent a lot of time in their cribs and

(Beryl Goldberg, Photo Trends)

Environment plays a part in development of motor abilities, too. How a baby is handled can make a difference.

were fed on schedule rather than on demand, were not precocious in motor development after the first month.

The program described earlier, which trained infants in walking by stimulating the walking reflex, seems to have incorporated into its research design some types of parental treatment that are common in African cultures. One psychologist who has studied infants among the Bushmen says, "in many infant care contexts the newborn reflex repertoire in general has functions (other than to be elicited by examiners) and . . . these functions may have survival value [Konner, 1973]."

But survival value in the African bush may be very different from optimum development in an urban or suburban setting. Before we counsel parents to deliberately try to accelerate their infants' physical development, we have to question the purpose behind such acceleration. It is possible that "forced" motor development might damage children in ways we are as yet unaware of.

TOILET TRAINING

At the age of twenty-seven months, Vicky is bladder-trained. Two previous attempts (one at nineteen months and one at twenty-three months, three months after the birth of her brother) were unsuccessful. At twenty-seven months, Vicky's mother decided that since *she* was ready for Vicky to be trained, Vicky should be ready, too. Thus her mother put "training pants" on Vicky (underpants made of very thick absorbent cotton). After one week of constantly wetting and changing her training pants, Vicky responded appropriately to the "potty chair" at a friend's house. From that day forward, despite an occasional accident, she has been emptying her bladder in the socially accepted place. Bowel training occurred three months later. One reason for the later arrival of bowel training, which in many children precedes bladder training, is Vicky's tendency to constipation, which often makes her reluctant to move her bowels on cue.

The control of elimination appears to rely heavily on maturational readiness. Initially, elimination of waste from the body is involuntary. When the infant's bladder or bowels are full, the appropriate sphincter muscles open automatically.

Before children can control their elimination, they have to learn a lot. They have to know what is expected of them—that there is a proper time

(Virginia Hamilton)

Children have to learn a lot. A certain level of maturation must exist for training to be effective.

and place to eliminate; they have to become familiar with the feelings that indicate the need to eliminate; and they have to learn to tighten the sphincter muscles to inhibit elimination and to loosen them to permit it.

One co-twin study (McGraw, 1940) tried to measure the effects of very early toilet training. One twin was placed on the toilet every hour of every day from the time he was two months old. Eighteen months later he started to show some control, and by about twenty-three months of age, he had achieved almost perfect success. His twin, who was never put on the toilet until he was about twenty-three months old, quickly caught up to his trained brother. It seems that a certain level of maturation must exist for training to be effective.

Generally, the later toilet training is begun, the faster a child learns. One study (Sears, Maccoby, & Levin, 1957) found that most parents begin bowel training at about eleven months, achieving success some seven months later. When training is begun before a child is five months old, it usually takes ten months to complete; but when it is begun later than twenty months, success comes after only about five months of training. This study also rated children in terms of the emotional upset connected with toilet training (Sears et al., 1957). Those babies whose training began between five and fourteen months of age, or after twenty months, seemed to take the whole business with the greatest degree of equanimity. And the parents

Table 4-7   Daytime Dryness Based on 859 Children by Three Criteria* (*From Oppel, Harper, & Rider, 1968*)

| Age (year) | A | | B | | C |
	Percent	Standard deviation	Percent	Standard deviation	Percent
1	8	1.2	7	1.1	6
2	55	2.2	51	2.3	55
3	84	1.5	78	1.8	84
4	89	1.4	85	1.6	88
5	95	0.9	91	1.2	92
6	99	0.5	94	1.0	96
7	99	0.5	95	1.0	96
8	99	0.4	96	0.8	97
9	99	0.4	96	0.8	97
10	99	0.4	96	0.8	97
11	100	0.3	98	0.6	98
12	100	0.3	99	0.4	99

*A: Percent dry by age of first attaining dryness (adjusted for race, sex, and prematurity).
 B: Percent dry by age of finally attaining dryness without further relapse.
 C: Percent dry at specific age (prevalence).

Table 4-8   Nighttime Dryness Based on 859 Children by Three Criteria* (*From Oppel, Harper, & Rider, 1968*)

Age (year)	A		B		C
	Percent	Standard deviation	Percent	Standard deviation	Percent
1	7	1.2	6	1.1	7
2	41	2.2	35	2.2	41
3	66	2.2	51	2.3	64
4	72	2.0	56	2.3	68
5	81	1.8	64	2.2	72
6	87	1.5	70	2.1	77
7	90	1.3	74	2.0	77
8	92	1.2	78	1.8	81
9	94	1.1	81	1.7	83
10	95	1.0	84	1.6	84
11	96	0.9	90	1.3	90
12	97	0.8	92	1.2	92

*A: Percent dry by age of first attaining dryness (adjusted for race, sex, and prematurity).
 B: Percent dry by age of finally attaining dryness without further relapse.
 C: Percent dry at specific age (prevalence).

who scolded and punished their children a great deal during the process did not complete the training any sooner than the more easygoing parents, but often produced emotional upset in their children.

According to a study of 859 children in Baltimore, Maryland, deemed to be "roughly representative" of all the children in the city (Oppel, Harper, & Rider, 1968), only 8 percent of one-year-olds had achieved initial dryness during the day. By the age of two, 55 percent were dry; by three, the figure rose to 84 percent; and by five, 95 percent didn't wet their pants. Nighttime dryness came a little later. Only 7 percent of one-year-olds ever stayed dry through the night, compared with 41 percent of two-year-olds, 66 percent of three-year-olds, 90 percent of seven-year-olds, and 97 percent of twelve-year-olds. (See Tables 4-7 and 4-8.) One out of four of these children relapsed at some point—lost bladder control once they had achieved it, accounting for most of those who were still wetting the bed after the age of six.

This study also produced some other interesting findings. Girls became dry—both during the day and at night—earlier than boys during the first two years of life, probably due to earlier maturation. Children who were low-birthweight infants had more trouble attaining bladder control than did those who were full-term babies, possibly due to neurological deficits. And white children were less likely to relapse—to lose bladder control once they had achieved it—than were black children. Since relapsing is probably due more to something in the social environment than to some organic cause, it is possible that different child-rearing practices in black families or different daily stresses undergone by black children account for this difference.

Summary

1 Physical growth and motor development follow two principles of progression: the *cephalocaudal principle* and the *proximodistal principle*. The cephalocaudal principle indicates that development progresses from "head to tail," and the proximodistal principle dictates that it proceeds from "near to far." In other words, development proceeds from the head down and from the central part of the body to the peripheral parts.

2 Normal physical and motor development proceeds in a preordained sequence, though there is a wide range of individual differences in ages at which the milestones of development are reached.

3 Environmental factors such as income, nutrition, race, sex, and physical health influence height and weight. Heredity also has a major effect.

4 Early motor development occurs when the child is maturationally ready to engage in certain activities, although environment may influence the expression of specific behaviors. Some studies indicate that black babies are more advanced motorically than white babies. This may in part result from

genetic factors, but it may also result from the way parents handle black infants. Infants who are raised in isolated, impoverished conditions, such as orphanages, may show motoric retardation. It seems that powerful environmental influences are needed to accelerate or retard motor development markedly. Short-term experiments aimed at acceleration of specific kinds of development such as stair-climbing and toilet training generally have had little effect.

Suggested Readings

Caplan, F. *First 12 Months of Life.* New York: Grosset and Dunlap, 1973. *A detailed description of physical, emotional, and behavioral development during the first year, well-illustrated with photographs and charts.*

Stone, L. J., Smith, H. T., & Murphy, L. B. (Eds.) *The Competent Infant.* New York: Basic Books, 1973. *A comprehensive handbook of research in the earliest phase of child development—infancy. It is divided into six sections and provides over 200 selections in infancy research, stressing new methods, findings, and theories.*

Tanner, J. M. *Education and Physical Growth.* New York: International Universities Press, 1971. *A brief and easily read text that summarizes the basic principles of physical and mental development. Tanner discusses growth from birth to maturity, developmental versus chronological age, growth gradients, critical periods, stage concepts, brain development, and the influence of heredity.*

CHAPTER FIVE
MENTAL DEVELOPMENT

IN WHICH VICKY EXHIBITS EQUALLY
STARTLING INTELLECTUAL DEVELOPMENT

I wish I could travel by the road that crosses baby's mind, and out beyond all bounds;
Where messengers run errands for no cause between the kingdoms of kings of no
* history;*
Where Reason makes kites of her laws and flies them, and Truth sets Fact free from its
* fetters.*

(Rabindranath Tagore, 1913)

Piaget's Theory of Intellectual Development

Little Lucienne, eleven months old, is playing a game. She hides her feet under a blanket, then picks up the blanket, peeks at her rosy little toes, and promptly hides them again. The casual observer might look at her in her crib, smile with delight at the way she is amusing herself, and think no more about the baby's pastimes. But Lucienne's game of hide-and-seek has been immortalized by her father, Jean Piaget, who saw in his baby daughter's play evidence that she "begins to study the effect of displacements [Piaget, 1952]."

Much of what we now know about the way children learn is due to the creative inquiry of this Swiss psychologist who has been called the "Giant in the Nursery." For more than fifty years Piaget has been applying his broad knowledge of biology, philosophy, and logic, as well as psychology, to his meticulous observation of children. From his observations and experiments with children, Piaget has constructed complex theories about the ways we human beings find out about the world we live in. These theories have spurred a great deal of research, most of which has tended to support Piaget's original conclusions about children's *cognitive*, or knowledge-acquiring, development.

According to Piaget, human cognitive development progresses through four major stages, each of which is very different from the others. He is an interactionist, who says that each stage occurs as the result of interaction between maturation and environment. Each stage shows a different way that the individual adapts to his environment. According to Piaget, intelligent behavior is the ability to adapt, and so even preverbal behavior is intelligent, since it is adaptive. In each of these stages, the organization and structure of the child's thinking differ in a qualitative way. Although development is gradual and continuous, the often imperceptible step between one stage and the next involves a great leap forward in the child's ability to handle new concepts.

The sequence of these four stages and of the substages they comprise never varies; and no stage is ever skipped, since each one rounds out the preceding stage and lays the groundwork for the next. The stages are somewhat related to chronological age. As with all development, however, each individual reaches each stage according to his or her own unique timetable. For this reason, and also because there is considerable overlapping between the stages and retention of some characteristics from preceding stages in those that follow, all age norms must be considered approximate.

In the *sensorimotor stage* (also spelled *sensorymotor*), which begins at birth and lasts till about the age of two, the infant changes from a creature who responds primarily through reflexes to one who can organize his or her sensorimotor activities in relation to the environment. A baby's activities are organized, not random. He engages in organized activities in which he directly manipulates objects. Through this active encounter, he progresses from the stage of reflexes to using trial-and-error learning and solving simple problems. He becomes more goal-oriented and differentiates himself from his surroundings—all before the age of two.

In the *preoperational stage* (roughly between two and seven years of age), the child's thought is egocentric and, by adult standards, illogical. In this stage, the child is beginning to be able to use symbols to represent objects, places, and people in the environment. This is manifest in language, dramatic play, and deferred imitation. Thus, Vicky uses words to stand for a person, place, or event. She represents her view of the world by acting it out in play. And she imitates what she has seen some time previously. She is thus developing a symbol system that is distinct from concrete reality, but one that represents it.

The child in the *concrete operations stage* (from about seven to eleven years of age) is gaining the ability to think logically, to understand concepts that he or she uses systematically to understand and deal with the immediate environment.

Finally, sometime between twelve and fifteen years of age, the child enters the *formal operations stage*, when he or she is capable of thinking in abstract terms as well as in concrete ones. By this time, the adolescent can deal with hypothetical situations as well as with real ones. We will discuss these four cognitive stages in detail in the appropriate places in this book as we follow the developing child.

To understand Piaget's theories, a few definitions are crucial. The *schema* (plural *schemata*) is the basic cognitive unit in Piaget's theory. It is a complex concept that involves both mental organization, or the child's conceptualization of a specific situation, and observable behavior. The schema is known by the behavior it involves, and so we have a schema of sight, for seeing; a schema of sucking, for eating; a schema of shaking, for playing with a toy; and so forth. The schema of sucking, for example, implies that Vicky recognizes her hunger, knows how to get food, and therefore sucks. This schema changes from a simple reflex action to a voluntary, controlled activity as she develops.

Two general principles, organization and adaptation, influence cognitive development through all stages. They are known as *functional invariants* because they operate at all stages of development, even though the structures they regulate undergo qualitative change from stage to stage. *Organization* involves the integration of all processes into one overall system. Initially the infant Vicky's schema of looking and her schema of grasping are quite different, resulting in faulty hand-eye coordination. Eventually she coordinates these schemata so that she can hold and look at an object at the same time. This is an example of organization.

Adaptation is the general term given to two complementary processes, *assimilation* and *accommodation*. Through this dual process of adaptation, Vicky creates new structures so that she can deal effectively with her surroundings. Adaptation is the essence of intelligent behavior.

Assimilation is the "taking in," or the incorporation, of a new object, experience, or concept into an existing set of schemata. Vicky, at any age, has a stock of mechanisms that she knows how to use. When she can use these actions to respond to a new stimulus, she is said to be assimilating. Once she knows how to suck at the breast, for example, she is presented for the first time with a bottle of milk. She assimilates the rubber nipple on the bottle into the schema of sucking and is able to respond to the new stimulus.

Accommodation is the process by which the child changes his or her actions to manage new objects and new situations. The mouth movements used in sucking milk from a rubber nipple are somewhat different from those used in nursing at the breast. When Vicky realizes that different motions of her tongue and jaws result in more efficient intake of milk, she will accommodate to the rubber nipple and develop a new schema of sucking.

These two processes, assimilation and accommodation, are constantly working together to produce changes in Vicky's conceptualization of the world and in her reactions to it. The state of balance between assimilation and accommodation is called *equilibrium*. This is a necessary state which protects Vicky from being overwhelmed by new experiences and new information and from overreaching herself in an attempt to accommodate to an environment that is changing too rapidly (Pulaski, 1971).

The acquisition of knowledge, then, is an active process that depends on interaction between the child and the environment. Vicky learns about the world through her active encounters with it. She is neither a passive recipient of stimulation from the environment, nor the possessor of a preformed set of intellectual capacities. In infancy, motor activity gives rise to thoughts (which Piaget calls mental operations). As Vicky develops, her motor activity increasingly gives way to cognitive activity, but her learning continues to be an active process (Piaget, 1952; Harter, 1968; Tuddenham, 1966).

The acquisition of knowledge is an active process that depends on interaction between the child and the environment.

(Phil Friedman)

SENSORIMOTOR STAGE (BIRTH TO ABOUT TWO YEARS)

This initial stage in intellectual development is a time of intelligent behavior before the development of language. During this period, Vicky formulates schemata that organize the information gained through the senses and that develop responses to environmental stimuli. Her behavior in infancy is *adaptive* in that she is constantly modifying schemata in response to the environment and is obviously, therefore, intelligent. These sensorimotor schemata "are the historical roots out of which later conceptual schemas develop [Baldwin, 1968, p. 190]."

Baldwin (1968) has described the major acquisitions of the sensorimotor period as:

1 The ability to coordinate and integrate information from the five senses (sight, hearing, touch, taste, and smell) to understand that the information received from different senses relates to the same object rather than to different, unrelated ones. Thus, Vicky does not at first associate the tinkling music she hears with the music box on the table; to her, they are two completely unrelated aspects of her environment. She has to learn that she can both see and hear—and also touch—the same object.

2 The capacity to recognize that the world is a permanent place, whose existence does not depend on the child's perceiving it. This is the schema of the permanent object.

3 The ability to exhibit goal-directed behavior. Vicky wants something. To get it, she is able to perform several different actions, even to construct new actions never before attempted. Since her actions in this period are very concrete, however, her ability to plan ahead is limited.

The *schema of the permanent object* (Piaget, 1953) is the most important acquisition of the sensorimotor period and the basis of later cognitive acquisitions. The permanent object is an object that continues to exist even though the child cannot see, feel, hear, taste, or smell it. If an object that Vicky has seen and responded to in some way is taken away, and if she begins to search for it even after she can no longer perceive it through any of her senses, she has a schema of the permanent object. If, on the other hand, she does not seem to remember the existence of the object once she cannot perceive it, there is no schema of a permanent object.

This schema is basic to the understanding of such vital concepts as space, time, and causality; for without an understanding that the objects in the environment are separate from Vicky herself, she cannot truly appreciate the nature of things as they are. "In other words, the person who believes that his wishes influence the movements of things, does not understand either self or things; the person who believes that the two are separate has a greater understanding of both [Ginsburg & Opper, 1969, p. 68]."

We will trace the development of the schema of the permanent object as we discuss the six substages of the sensorimotor phase.

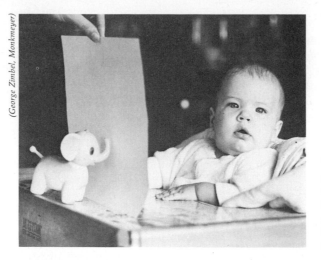

(George Zimbel, Monkmeyer)

The schema of the permanent object is the most important acquisition of the sensorimotor period; without it, such vital concepts as space, time, and causality are impossible.

SUBSTAGES OF THE SENSORIMOTOR STAGE

Stage One: The Use of Reflexes (Birth to One Month)

Even though reflexes are inborn reactions to stimulation, they are adaptive in the sense that they enable the infant to survive and learning to take place. Adaptive behavior is intelligent behavior. Reflex behavior is adaptive and therefore is intelligent, since it enables the infant to survive and allows later learning to take place. A good example is the sucking reflex, which is adaptive in that it enables Vicky to take in nourishment. Intelligent reflex behavior forms the basis for later intelligent activity. Vicky changes from a passive recipient of stimulation that elicits the reflex to an active seeker of stimulation.

It is easier to see Vicky as an active stimulation seeker as she gets a bit older. She babbles. If her babbling brings attention from her parents, cuddling, and smiles, she will babble more and more.

Stage Two: Primary Circular Reactions/The First Acquired Adaptations (One to Four Months)

As Vicky lies in her crib, blissfully sucking her thumb, she exemplifies a *primary circular response*. This is an active effort to reproduce something that was first achieved by chance, through some random activity. The actual content of Vicky's behavior—the ability to suck—is inborn. One day, quite by accident, she put her thumb in her mouth. Exercising her inborn sucking reflex, she sucked the object in her mouth—and liked it! Thus she made some acquired adaptations: deliberate efforts to put her thumb in her mouth, to keep it there, and to keep sucking it—not for food but just for the bliss of the sucking itself. She will suck all sorts of things, both for nutrition and for fun. She actively seeks to nourish the sucking schema.

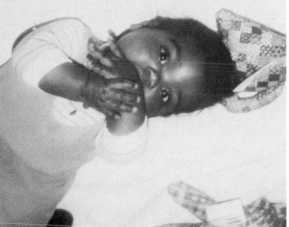

The primary circular response: an active effort to reproduce something that was first achieved by chance.

During Stage Two, Vicky starts to coordinate sensory information. She looks at her brother, listens to him, and touches him when he is within reach. She is now coordinating vision and grasping. When she hears him speak, however, she does not try to look at him unless she has just seen his face in motion (Beard, 1969).

At the age of three months seven days, Piaget's son, Laurent, had just grasped a piece of tinfoil with his left hand. He let it go. He turned his head to look at his empty hand. Then his father put the tinfoil in the baby's right hand. Laurent started to carry the tinfoil to his mouth, but before it had reached his lips, he suddenly saw it and looked at it for a while. Piaget relates this incident (1952, p. 113) to illustrate the typically Stage Two rudimentary development of coordination between vision and grasping.

Object permanence.   During Vicky's normal activity in Stages One and Two, she is constantly encountering, losing contact with, and reencountering objects—a pacifier, her father's finger, her mother's blouse. But when an object disappears, she does not look for it. As far as Vicky is concerned that object has ceased to exist when she cannot see it, feel it, hear it, smell it, or taste it. There is no object permanence yet.

Stage Three: Secondary Circular Reactions
(Four to Eight Months)

This stage marks the beginning of intentional action. While Vicky was in Stage Two, she repeated her primary circular reactions for the joy of the actions themselves. Now she is becoming interested in the results of her actions. New patterns of behavior continue to occur accidentally during random movement; she learns them; and then she repeats them *to see what results they will bring about.* She no longer focuses only on her own body, but is now concerned with external objects and events.

Piaget (1952, p. 161) describes this transition from actions for pleasure to actions for their effect on the environment:

At 0;2(25) [2 months, 25 days] I connect his [Laurent's] right hand to the celluloid balls but leave the string a little slack in order to necessitate ample movements of the right hand and thus limit the effect of chance. The left hand is free. At first the arm movements are inadequate and the rattle does not move. Then the movements become more extensive, more regular and the rattle moves periodically while the child's glance is directed at this sight. There seems to be a conscious coordination, but both arms move equally and it is not yet possible to be sure that this is not a mere pleasure reaction. The next day, same reactions. At 0;2(27) on the other hand, conscious coordination seems definite for the following four reasons: 1) Laurent was surprised and frightened by the first shake of the rattle which was unexpected. On the other hand since the second or third shake, he swings his right arm (connected to the rattle) with regularity, whereas the left remained almost motionless. Now the right could move freely without pulling at the balls. It therefore seems the swinging was intentional. 2) Laurent's eye blinks beforehand, as soon as his hand moves and before the rattle moves as though the child knew he was going to shake it. 3) When Laurent temporarily gives up the game and joins his hands for a moment, the right hand alone resumes the movement while the left hand stays motionless. 4) The regular shakes that Laurent gives the rattle reveal a certain skill; the movement is regular and the child must stretch his arm backward sufficiently to make the rattle sound.

Object permanence. When Piaget's son was seven months old, the father conducted an experiment to see whether Laurent had yet acquired the schema of the permanent object (Piaget, 1963):

At the time of his feeding I show him the bottle, he extends his hand to take it, but, at that moment, I hide it behind my arm. If he sees one end sticking out he kicks and screams and gives every indication of wanting to have it. If, however, the bottle is completely hidden and nothing sticks out, he stops crying and acts for all we know as if the bottle no longer existed, as if it had been dissolved and absorbed into my arm.

Stage Four: Coordination of Secondary Schemata and Their Application to New Situations (Eight to Twelve Months)

The infant can now solve simple problems by using responses that have been previously mastered. His or her actions are increasingly goal-directed. We can see how Piaget's daughter, Jacqueline, overcame the obstacle of her father's hand to get at her toy duck (Piaget, 1952, p. 219):

At 0;8(8) Jacqueline tries to grasp her celluloid duck but I also grasp it at the same time she does. Then she firmly holds the toy in her right hand and pushes my hand away with her left. I repeat the experiment by grasping only the end of the duck's tail; she again pushes my hand away.

Object permanence.   The Stage Four infant is truly beginning to develop the schema of the permanent object. During Piaget's experiments with all three of his children, he found that they would not search for a hidden object until the end of the first year, or Stage Four. At nine to ten months of age, the babies would look for an object behind a screen if they had seen it being hidden. But if it were moved from one hiding place to another while the baby watched, he or she would, curiously, look for it in the *first* hiding place. Not until Stage Five does the object exist independently of Vicky's own actions or perceptions. If it disappears, she looks for it, and she looks for it where she has seen it last (Piaget, 1963).

Stage Five: Tertiary Circular Reactions/The Discovery of New Means through Active Experimentation (Twelve to Eighteen Months)

This is the last cognitive stage that does not include mental representations of external events, or what we think of as *thought*, and the first that does include trying out new activities. Vicky is still making accidental discoveries of actions that produce some pleasing results, but she no longer repeats these accidentally discovered actions exactly. She varies them somewhat as she repeats them. She experiments to find out in what respect an object, event, or situation is new. In scientific language, she is "experimenting in order to see."

For the first time Vicky intentionally accommodates to find new solutions for new problems. As she tries out new behavior patterns to reach some goal, she is learning by trial and error. And as she varies her actions and causes new results, she is led to new complete acts of intelligence (Piaget, 1952). We see a child in Stage Five through the eyes of Piaget, as he describes his daughter (1952, p. 272):

> At 1;2(8) Jacqueline holds in her hands an object which is new to her: a round, flat box which she turns all over, shakes, rubs against the bassinet, etc. She lets it go and tries to pick it up. But she only succeeds in touching it with her index finger, without grasping it. She nevertheless makes an attempt and presses on the edge. The box then tilts up and falls again. Jacqueline, very much interested in this fortuitous result, immediately applies herself to studying it. . . . This discovery, instead of giving rise to a simple circular reaction, is at once extended to "experiments in order to see."
>
> In effect, Jacqueline immediately rests the box on the ground and pushes it as far as possible (it is noteworthy that care is taken to push the box far away in order to reproduce the same conditions as in the first attempt, as though this were a necessary condition for obtaining the result). Afterward Jacqueline puts her finger on the box and presses it. But as she places her finger on the center of the box she simply displaces it and makes it slide instead of tilting it up. She amuses herself with this game and keeps it up . . . for several minutes. Then, changing the point of contact, she finally again places her finger on the edge of the box, which tilts it up. She repeats this many times, varying the conditions, but keeping track of her discovery: now she only presses on the edge!

Object permanence.   Although Vicky in Stage Five has a schema of the permanent object and can follow a sequence of object displacements, she still has no conceptualization of the possibility of movement that she does not actually see. If her father were to do as Piaget did and put a toy in his hand, put his hand behind a pillow, leave the toy there, and bring out his closed hand for her to examine, Vicky would look for her toy in his hand. It would not occur to her that the toy might be behind the pillow, because she did not see him putting it there (Baldwin, 1968).

Stage Six: The Invention of New Means through Mental Combinations (Eighteen to Twenty-four Months)

By Stage Six, Vicky has considerable understanding of "the nature of objects, the relationships between different paths in space, and some understanding of causality [Baldwin, 1968, p. 217]." She develops the ability to picture events in her mind and to follow them through to some degree. In other words, she can think. This stage represents a great breakthrough, since she no longer has to go through the laborious process of trial and error in solving new problems. In effect, she can now "try out" solutions in her mind and discard the ones that she is sure won't work. She can also imitate actions even after whatever or whoever she is copying is no longer in front of her.

At the age of one year four months, Piaget's daughter Lucienne shows us the imitative and mental abilities of the Stage Six child (Piaget, 1952, pp. 337–338):

> Here begins the experiment which we want to emphasize. I put the chain back into the box, an empty matchbox, and reduce the opening to 3 mm. It is understood that Lucienne is not aware of the functioning of the opening and closing of the matchbox and has not seen me prepare the experiment. She only possesses the two preceding schemata: turning the box over in order to empty it of its contents, and sliding her finger into the slit to make the chain come out. It is of course this last procedure that she tries first. She puts her finger inside and gropes to reach the chain, but fails completely. A pause follows during which Lucienne manifests a very curious reaction bearing witness not only to the fact that she tries to think out the situation and to represent to herself through mental combination the operation to be performed, but also to the role played by imitation in the genesis of representations. Lucienne mimics the widening of the slit.
>
>   She looks at the slit with great attention; then, several times in succession, she opens and shuts her mouth, at first slightly, then wider and wider! . . . The attempt at representation which she thus furnishes is expressed plastically, that is to say, due to inability to think out the situation in words of clear visual images she uses a simple motor indication as "signifier" or symbol. Lucienne, by opening her mouth thus expresses, or even reflects her desire to enlarge the opening of the box. This schema of imitation, with which she is familiar, constitutes for her the means of thinking out the situation.

Object permanence.   The concept is now fully developed. Vicky can now understand visible and invisible displacements. She can see a series of displacements and look for an object in the last (not the first) hiding place. She will search for objects she has not actually witnessed being hidden.

RESEARCH BASED ON PIAGET'S THEORIES

Since Piaget's early work was based on his observations of his own three children, other researchers have sought to determine whether his theories apply to children in general. So far, the Piagetian constructs are holding up well under standardized testing programs. One study, for example, observed infants in their homes from four weeks of age to about two years and confirmed Piaget's invariant order for the progressive stages of the sensorimotor period (Uzgiris, 1972). Another studied the schema of the permanent object in six-month-old babies, following them until they were about a year old (Gratch & Landers, 1972). Again, Piaget's conclusions were affirmed.

Piaget's theories have also spurred other research projects as developmentalists seek to discover new information about the influences on the developing child. A study that looked at the effects of social class on cognitive development in infancy (Golden & Birns, 1968) found no differences related to socioeconomic status among twelve-month-, eighteen-month-, and twenty-four-month-old children from socially disorganized slum families, from stable low-income families, and from stable middle-income families, on either of two measures. The first measure was the Cattell IQ test, a measure of infant intelligence, and the other was an Object Permanence Scale, a standardized set of procedures that test an infant's readiness to search for an object hidden under one or more screens.

The translation of Piaget's complex theories into concrete, standardized testing situations provides researchers, then, with an additional tool for measuring the intellectual development of very young, preverbal children. Several scales of sensorimotor development (Corman & Escalona, 1969; Uzgiris & Hunt, 1967) are in fairly wide use today.

Learning in Infancy

As a newborn, Vicky started to make sucking movements with her mouth whenever the nipple was in it—but no sooner. Within weeks, she started to make the sucking movements as soon as she saw her mother. She had learned that the presence of her mother presaged good things for Vicky.

As an infant, Vicky was not afraid of any animals. At the age of eleven months, she was happily sitting on a neighbor's lawn, when a large, friendly St. Bernard loped over to her and, with one swipe of his tongue, licked her face, chin to forehead. She howled in fright and rage, and for the next year, cried whenever she saw a dog. She had learned to fear dogs.

What *is* learning? In psychological terms, it is the establishment of new relationships or the strengthening of weak relationships between two events, actions, or things. In both the above examples, new associations have apparently been established, since Vicky is responding differently at one point than she had in the past. This results in a relatively permanent change in behavior brought about through experience.

Learning can be much more complex than in these rather simplified examples, since a stimulus can cause a new response and the new response itself can cause still another response, establishing a learning chain. This happens in playing a piano piece. Other behaviors are not learned. Some, like the blink of an eye in response to a bright light, are occasioned by reflex activity. Other pursuits, like the one-month-old baby's lifting of his head as he lies on his stomach, appear to result from the driving force of maturation.

Among the lower animals, a great deal of very complex activity seems to be based on *instinct*, an inborn ability to perform certain functions. Such instinctual behaviors would be the food collecting of ants, the nest building of birds, and the nursing of cubs. Human beings, however, have hardly any abilities that we could call instincts. We come into this world with a handful of reflexes, a maturational timetable, and a capacity for infinite learning. This learning generally falls into one of several categories. Habituation has been discussed in Chapter 3, observational learning will be discussed in Chapter 9, and some other types of learning are explained below.

TYPES OF LEARNING DURING INFANCY

Classical, or Conditioned, Learning

In this kind of learning, a reflex action comes to be associated with a stimulus that does not ordinarily elicit it. The most famous case of this involves the dogs of Professor Ivan Pavlov. In the late 1890s, this Russian physiologist conducted experiments in conditioning (Pavlov, 1927). When he fed his dogs, he rang a bell. When the dogs saw and smelled the food, they salivated. After repeated feedings just after the bell had been rung, the dogs eventually salivated upon hearing the bell alone—even when no food was presented. The dogs' salivary reflexes had been conditioned to respond to the bell as they did to food. This type of learning is presented schematically in Figure 5-1.

Operant, or Instrumental, Conditioning

In this kind of learning, a nonreflexive response that an individual is capable of making comes to be produced as the result of the response's being rewarded, or *reinforced*, after it is first made. (The first time the response occurs may well be accidental.)

The classic example of this is B. F. Skinner's (1938) work with rats and

UCS (unconditioned stimulus) ⟶ UR (unconditioned response)
  Food   Salivation

CS (conditioned stimulus) ⟶ NR (no response)
  Bell

UCS + CS ⟶ CR (conditioned response)
  Food + Bell   Salivation

CS ⟶ CR
  Bell   Salivation

Figure 5-1   Classical, or Conditioned, Learning

pigeons. This American behaviorist devised a series of experiments. When the animals pecked on a particular bar, they received a pellet of food. They quickly learned to press the bar to get food. Further experiments rewarded the animals with food every time they pecked on a green bar and punished them with a mild electric shock when they pecked on a red bar. They soon learned to tell the colors apart. This type of learning is presented schematically in Figure 5-2.

This new relationship is between the response (pecking at the bar) and its result (getting food or getting a shock). The frequency of a response is increased when it is rewarded and decreased when it is punished.

In operant conditioning, the nature of the reinforcement stimulus is extremely important. If the reinforcer is not effective, learning will not take place. In these experiments with pigeons, food was an effective positive reinforcer, and electric shock an effective negative reinforcer.

In recent years, operant learning—often referred to as *behavior modification* or *behavior therapy*—has been used to teach children a variety of behaviors, from toilet training, to speaking, to behaving well in school. It has been most often used for children with special needs, such as retarded or emotionally disturbed youngsters. But these techniques have also been used successfully in the day-to-day management of normal children.

Classical and operant learning differ in certain ways. Whereas classical conditioning requires a reactive organism, operant conditioning demands

Figure 5-2   Operant, or Instrumental, Learning

AR (accidental response)⟶R (reinforcement)⟶DR (deliberate response)
  Animal pecks at bar.   Animal gets food.   Animal pecks at bar.

an active one. If the organism *never* makes the desired response, that response cannot be reinforced. Classical conditioning is an involuntary process, whereas operant conditioning involves actions under the organism's control. In both types of learning, *intermittent* reinforcement (reward or punishment after *some* trials) causes more durable learning than *continuous* reinforcement (after every trial).

Imitative Learning

When Vicky's mother smiles at her little daughter, she is often rewarded with a smile from the baby. When Vicky's father talks "baby talk" to her, she is wont to babble back to him. Observing what other people do and copying it is another form of learning that originates in infancy.

Piaget has described such learning occurring in his own three children. When someone would do something the babies already knew how to do (like making sucking movements), the babies would ape the acts. Then, later, the babies would engage in deferred imitation when they saw a new action, code and store it, and act it out after some lapse of time. In an effort to confirm Piaget's findings with a larger group of children, Uzgiris (1971) observed twelve babies between eight and twenty-four months of age. The experimenter came to the babies' homes on a regular basis, presented a

(Amman Photo Features)

Learning is the establishment of new relationships (or the strengthening of weak relationships) between two events, actions, or things.

variety of different acts to them, and watched what they did. To assess the babies' vocal imitation, the experimenter *cooed* to the babies, making "infant-like sounds consisting primarily of vowels" ("aah"); *babbled*, repeating sounds that combined a consonant and a vowel ("da-da"); made *novel sounds*, which do not occur in English ("zik"); spoke *familiar words*, which the infant already was using; and, finally, spoke *new words*, which the infant had not yet used. To see how the babies would imitate gestures, the experimenter performed *familiar actions* which the infant had already performed (patting a surface); *complex actions* which required the infant to combine actions in a new way (taking a block, putting it in a cup, and shaking the cup); *unfamiliar visible actions* which consisted of new actions that the baby could easily see (making and unmaking a fist); and *unfamiliar invisible actions* which involved facial gestures (blinking the eyes).

Uzgiris found the following four steps in the development of imitative behavior, a sequence that closely followed Piaget's order:

1   At three to four months of age, the infant responds to acts that are already familiar, which she already engages in spontaneously herself, like cooing.

2   At five to seven months, the infant regards the experimenter's acts as

(Erika Stone, from Peter Arnold)

a spectacle. When the experimenter pauses, the infant tries, by means of some gesture or vocalization, to set up the spectacle again. The infant may reproduce a part of the experimenter's act, without trying to copy the whole thing. For example, when the experimenter hits two blocks together, the baby may copy the sound and part of the hitting action by hitting the table with something.

3   The infant tries to copy the experimenter's actions but seems to realize his limitations in approximating them accurately. When the experimenter spins a toy, the baby may first get it to move by pushing it with his hand, then wiggling it in place, and finally, turning it with both hands.

4   Between nineteen and twenty-three months of age, the infant is able to repeat with some accuracy both familiar and unfamiliar sounds and gestures. Uzgiris attributes the late arrival of this ability to the fact that the experimenter was a stranger to these babies. Babies seem to imitate their parents at an earlier age.

CLASSICAL CONDITIONING IN INFANTS

There has been some controversy over whether newborn infants can be classically conditioned. Some early experiments seemed, however, to demonstrate this possibility. In one (Marquis, 1931), infants from one to ten days of age were divided into two groups. Five seconds before the babies in the experimental group were fed, a buzzer sounded. The control group also heard the buzzer but were not fed right after it sounded. By the fifth day, eight of the ten experimental infants made sucking movements and opened their mouths as soon as they heard the buzzer. They also tended to stop crying and moving their bodies when the buzzer sounded. The control babies showed no such feeding reactions. Like Pavlov's dogs, the experimental babies had apparently associated the buzzer with the act of feeding and responded to it with a conditioned sucking reflex.

Then there is the true story of little Albert (Watson & Raynor, 1920). When Albert was nine months old, he loved furry animals—rabbits and rats and such. He loved them so much that he reached out eagerly to them when he saw them. Then the experimenter, John B. Watson, the founder of behaviorism, stepped into the picture.

When Albert was eleven months old, Dr. Watson brought him into the laboratory. Just as the baby was beginning to grasp a white rat, Watson sounded a loud noise. The noise startled Albert and made him afraid. He jumped, fell forward, and cried. A week later, Albert was again presented with the rat. Again, the loud noise. Again, Albert's frightened tears. Eventually, as soon as Albert saw the rat, he started to whimper with fear. Not only did he fear the rat, but he also became afraid of such furry animals as a rabbit and a dog and of such furry objects as a seal coat, cotton wool, and a Santa Claus mask.

This experiment demonstrated that classical conditioning "works" in a young child, that an emotional reaction like fear can be conditioned, and that such conditioned fear can be *generalized*; that is, stimuli similar to those on which the original learning occurred can elicit the same reaction.

In the light of current ethical thinking, how does this experiment strike us? Albert, after all, was not an anonymous laboratory animal, but a real child. The son of a wet nurse in a children's home, Albert had been reared from birth in an institutional environment. The experimenters chose to work with him because they considered him "stolid and unemotional" and felt that their experiments could do him *"relatively little harm* [Watson & Raynor, 1920, p. 2; emphasis added]." The fact that they did recognize the possibility of long-lasting effects from this one experiment is apparent from a statement in their report (Watson & Raynor, 1920):

> These experiments would seem to show conclusively that directly conditioned emotional responses as well as those conditioned by transfer persist, although with a certain loss in the intensity of the reaction, for a longer period than one month. *Our view is that they persist and modify personality throughout life* [p. 12; emphasis added].

Today an experiment like this would have virtually no chance of being carried out. Modern ethical standards require researchers to protect a child who is a subject in an experiment from *any* foreseeable harm.

OPERANT LEARNING IN INFANTS

In a good operant conditioning study, several phases are required. First, the base rate of the response under study has to be determined. The experimenter has to find out how often the subject exhibits that behavior under ordinary conditions. Second is the actual conditioning, the attempt to increase this base rate. And last, the new conditioned response should be *extinguished*; by failing to reward the response, it should disappear. When all three of these steps are followed, we can see whether a response is amenable to operant conditioning and how strong it is.

During a study of smiling in infants (Brackbill, 1958), eight $3\frac{1}{2}$- to $4\frac{1}{2}$-month-old babies were picked up every time they smiled, then returned to their cribs. After an increase in smiling had occurred for all the babies, four were intermittently reinforced, four continuously. During the extinction phase, smiling was never rewarded by picking up. The study found that picking up the babies made them smile more and that all the babies smiled less during extinction, when they were not picked up. Those who had been intermittently reinforced, however, continued to smile more than those who had been reinforced continuously. Apparently, intermittent social reinforcement influences infant smiling.

Another study of three-month-old infants (Rheingold, Gewirtz, & Ross,

1959) determined that infants babbled more if, after babbling, the experimenters smiled broadly at them, made "tsk" sounds, and touched them lightly on the abdomen. Based on these two studies, it appears that the responses of adults exert considerable influence on infant social responsiveness.

In this latter study, it was assumed that the infants babbled more to elicit the adult responses. Is it possible, though, that the adult's smile, approving sounds, and light touch are stimuli that in and of themselves cause the infants to babble? That is, which is cause and which is effect? Does the adult's attention cause the baby's babbling? Or does the baby babble more because she is rewarded when she does so? To try to answer these questions, another experiment was devised, with excellent controls that took into account all the relevant factors in the relationship (Weisberg, 1963). A group of three-month-old infants was divided into six groups:

Group 1 received *contingent* social reinforcement as in the former study. The experimenter smiled, made an approving sound, and rubbed a baby's chin every time the baby babbled. The adult actions were contingent on the babies' babbling.

Group 2 received the same type and the same amount of adult attention during the conditioning phase, but it was *noncontingent*. The adults paid attention to the infants at times not directly related to their babbling.

Group 3 received contingent *nonsocial* reinforcement. Every time these babies babbled, they heard door chimes. Group 4 heard the door chimes at times unrelated to their babbling.

Groups 5 and 6 were controls. These babies had no contact with the experimenters.

The door chimes (the nonsocial reinforcer) produced no change in the babies' babbling, whether they had been sounded on a contingent or a noncontingent basis. Apparently, infants couldn't care less about hearing chimes, making them an ineffective means of reinforcement. The adult smiles, sounds, and touch (the social reinforcer) increased infant babbling only when they were contingent. When they were noncontingent, they produced no such changes. When the social reinforcer was withdrawn during extinction, the rate of infant babbling tended to fall off.

If the babies were babbling because adult smiles, approving sounds, and touch elicit babbling, then the babies who received the noncontingent social reinforcement would have increased their babbling as much as the babies in the contingent group. That they did not indicated that the babies were learning to babble because their babbling was rewarded by adult responses.

Another study (Todd & Palmer, 1972) sought to determine the degree to which human presence is necessary in conditioning infant babbling. When the 2½- to 3½-month-old babies in one group babbled, they heard a tape of a human voice saying, "Hello, baby," "pretty baby," "nice baby." No adult was in the room. The other group heard the same tape, while an adult experimenter stood expressionless at the head of the crib. Since both groups increased their babbling and there was no significant difference between them, it may be the human voice—rather than the human presence—that is the primary reinforcer of infant babbling.

Operant conditioning has also been used to teach ten-week-old infants to move their heads to make a crib mobile move (Watson, 1972). A group of 40 eight-week-old infants were divided into three groups. Every mother hung a mobile about 18 inches over the baby's head every day for ten minutes a day, fourteen days in a row. In the experimental group, the mobile was rigged up in such a way that it would move in response to the baby's head movements. One control group had a mobile that moved in a noncontingent way; it did not respond to the baby's own movements. The other control group had a nonmoving mobile, or, more accurately, a stabile. The mothers recorded the number of head movements their babies made during each ten-minute session.

The babies in the experimental group increased the number of head movements they made over the two weeks of the experiment, whereas the control groups' movements didn't change at all. Not only had the experimental babies learned how to work the mobiles; they were enjoying the experience immensely. They were smiling broadly and cooing heartily to the mobiles, so much so that some of their mothers eventually used the mobiles as "baby sitters" when they wanted to amuse the babies. A large part of the infants' pleasure was undoubtedly due to their ability to control the movements of the mobiles.

This study shows that Piagetian secondary circular reactions, which are concerned with the effects one's own actions have on the enviornment, can occur, with stimulation, at least one month earlier than Piaget's norms would indicate.

COMPLEX LEARNING IN INFANTS: COMBINED CLASSICAL AND OPERANT CONDITIONING

There is some indication that these two types of learning interact to produce increasingly complex activities on the part of infants, as brought out by the work of Papousek (1959, 1960a, 1960b, 1961). Infants who ranged in age from one to twenty weeks were exposed to complex learning situations with combined aspects of classical and operant conditioning techniques.

In the *operant* phase of the experiment, the babies were taught to turn their heads left at the sound of a bell; when they did this they received milk. This is considered an operant procedure since the babies learned to make a response to get a reward. No unconditioned stimulus was used to elicit head turning. Those infants who did not learn to turn their heads to get the milk were *classically conditioned* to do this. When the bell was sounded (CS), the left corner of the baby's mouth was stimulated (UCS); this would cause him to turn his head (CR), whereupon he would get his milk. When the babies were from four to six weeks of age, they learned to turn their heads for milk when hearing the bell (CR).

Another aspect of the study was begun once the babies learned—through either operant or classical conditioning—to turn their heads for the milk. The infants were then trained to differentiate the *bell* from a second stimulus, a *buzzer*. They were fed on the left when the bell rang and on the right when the buzzer sounded. At about three months of age, the babies had learned to turn to the appropriate side to be fed. Infants four months old even learned to reverse the response to bell and buzzer, demonstrating the remarkable complexity of infants' capacity to learn.

Learning the Language

At three months of age, Vicky laughs out loud. At four months, she coos when someone talks to her or when she wakes up in the morning. At eleven months, she says "dada," and at twelve months, "mama." At thirteen months, she introduces her own word into the language: "ha-dja," which her parents interpret as meaning, "I want that." At seventeen months, she says "ma" for more, "me" for give it to me, "ha" for hot, "ca" for bread, cracker, or pretzel. At twenty-two months, she knows the rhyming words for "Hey Diddle-Diddle," and loves to shout them out when someone gives her her cues. And, at twenty-six months, Vicky says her first four-word sentence.

Vicky picks up her pajamas in her chubby little hands and holds them out to her father, commanding, "Daddy—on my jamans." Her father says, "You want me to put your pajamas on for you?" Vicky chortles, nods, and holds out her dimpled arms to welcome the pajama sleeves. Vicky's first "long" sentence may not be grammatical in a conventional way. But it is, according to her proud parents and to linguists, of a relatively high order of communication. Before she spoke this sentence, she went through several well-defined stages of speech development. Within the year, she will be at the culminating stage of grammatical speech.

All children in all countries go through the same basic, well-defined stages in the acquisition of language. According to one linguist (Lenneberg, 1967; see Chart 5-1), the onset of speech is:

> a gradual unfolding of capacities; it is a series of generally well-circumscribed events which take place between the second and third year of life. Certain important speech milestones are reached in a fixed sequence and at a relatively constant chronological age [p. 127].

Before we discuss the various theories that attempt to explain how and why children learn a language, let us trace these stages.

Chart 5-1   Language Development *(Lenneberg, 1967)*

3 Months	Markedly less crying than at 8 weeks; when talked to and nodded at, smiles, followed by squealing-gurgling sounds usually called *cooing,* which is vowel-like in character and pitch-modulated; sustains cooing for 15-20 seconds.
4 Months	Responds to human sounds more definitely; turns head; eyes seem to search for speaker; occasionally some chuckling sounds.
5 Months	The vowel-like cooing sounds begin to be interspersed with more consonantal sounds; labial fricatives, spirants and nasals are common; acoustically, all vocalizations are very different from the sounds of the mature language of the environment.
6 Months	Cooing changes into babbling resembling one-syllable utterances; neither vowels nor consonants have very fixed recurrences; most common utterances sound somewhat like ma, mu, da, di.
8 Months	Reduplication (or more continuous repetitions) becomes frequent; intonation patterns become distinct; utterances can signal emphasis and emotions.
10 Months	Vocalizations are mixed with sound-play such as gurgling or bubble-blowing; appears to wish to imitate sounds, but the imitations are never quite successful; beginning to differentiate between words heard by making differential adjustments.
12 Months	Identical sound sequences are replicated with higher relative frequency of occurrence and words (mamma or dadda) are emerging; definite signs of understanding some words and simple commands (show me your eyes).
18 Months	Has a definite repertoire of words—more than three, but less than 50; still much babbling but now of several syllables with intricate intonation patterns; no attempt at communicating information and no frustration for not being understood; words may include items such as "thank you" or "come here," but there is little ability to join any of the lexical items into spontaneous two-item phrases; understanding is progressing rapidly.
24 Months	Vocabulary of more than 50 items (some children seem to be able to name everything in the environment); begins spontaneously to join vocabulary items into two-word phrases; all phrases appear to be own creations; definite increase in communicative behavior and interest in language.

(Continued)

Chart 5-1 (Continued)

30 Months   Fastest increase in vocabulary with many new additions every day; no babbling at all; utterances have communicative intent; frustrated if not understood by adults; utterances consist of at least 2 words, many have 3 or even 5 words; sentences and phrases have characteristic child grammar; that is, they are rarely verbatim repetitions of an adult utterance; intelligibility is not very good yet, though there is great variation among children; seems to understand everything that is said to him.

NORMATIVE DEVELOPMENT

Understanding Language

Children learn to understand language before they learn how to speak it themselves, and this understanding follows a developmental pattern. Eleanor and George Kaplan (1971) have distinguished five stages in the development of the understanding of language:

Stage 1.   At birth, infants respond to auditory stimulation. At only a few minutes, they can determine where sounds are coming from. Neonates are also able to tell the difference between various sounds, based on their frequency, intensity, duration, and tempo.

Stage 2.   At about two weeks of age, infants begin to recognize the difference between voices and other sounds. The human voice is more effective than other sounds (like whistles and rattles) in bringing out smiles and cooing and in calming crying babies.

Stage 3.   At the end of the second month, babies begin to pick up emotional cues in the utterances they hear. They tend to withdraw from angry voices and to smile and coo at friendly ones. They can also tell the difference between familiar and unfamiliar voices and between male and female.

Stage 4.   At about five or six months, babies learn to discriminate among several kinds of linguistic information. They are conscious of intonation and rhythm and will respond intelligently to phrases in a strange language that have the same overall intonation pattern that the infants are used to hearing.

Stage 5.   Toward the end of the first year, babies become able to distinguish among the various *phonemes,* or individual sounds, of their language. They can tell the difference between pairs of words that differ only in their initial sound (like *cat* and *bat*).

Prelinguistic Speech

Before Vicky will say her first real word, she will go through the following six, and perhaps seven, stages of speech (Eisenson, Auer, & Irwin, 1963; Lenneberg, 1967):

1 *Undifferentiated crying.* With "no language but a cry," babies come into this world. Early crying is a reflexive reaction to the environment produced by the expiration of breath. We generally consider crying to be a reaction to discomfort, although at this stage it is often impossible to determine just what that discomfort might be. Crying is thus a reflexive form of communication, since it is the infant's only means of signaling her needs. And as anyone who spends much time with babies can affirm, they spend a lot of time signaling these needs, with some babies crying more than others.

2 *Differentiated crying.* After the first month of life (and of crying), the

Through a series of stages, children learn to understand language before they learn how to speak it themselves.

(David S. Strickler, Monkmeyer)

close listener can often discriminate a difference between a baby's cries, depending on their causes. Vicky's parents can sometimes tell by the different patterns, intensities, and pitches of her cries whether she is hungry, sleepy, angry, or in pain. In this sense, crying is becoming a more precise means of communication, although this is not conscious on the part of the baby.

3 *Cooing.* At about six weeks, chance movements of Vicky's vocal mechanisms produce a variety of simple sounds called cooing. These squeals, gurgles, and bleats are usually emitted when she is happy and contented. The first sounds are vowels, and the first consonant is h. Although cooing has been elicited by visual material by the fifteenth day of life (Stechler, Bradford, & Levy, 1965), it generally comes later.

4 *Babbling.* These "vocal gymnastics" begin at about three or four months, as Vicky playfully repeats a variety of sounds. Again, she is most likely to babble when she is contented and when she is alone. As she lies in her crib or sits in her infant seat, she loquaciously, and often loudly, spouts forth a variety of simple consonant and vowel sounds: "ma-ma-ma-ma-ma," "da-da-da-da-da," "bi-bi-bi-bi-bi," and so forth. While most children babble, a few seem to skip this stage. Deaf children babble normally for the first few months of life, but then appear to lose interest when they cannot hear themselves (Clifton, 1970). We can interpret babbling in Piagetian terms. First, a baby babbles for the joy of it (primary circular reaction), and then, later, for its effect on the environment (secondary circular reaction).

5 *Lallation, or imperfect imitation.* Sometime during the second half of the first year, Vicky seems to become more aware of the sounds around her. She will become quiet listening to some sound. When it stops, she babbles in excitement, accidentally repeating the sounds and syllables she has heard. Then she imitates her own sounds.

6 *Echolalia, or imitation of the sounds of others.* At about the age of nine or ten months, Vicky seems to consciously imitate the sounds made by others, even though she still does not understand them. Since babies raised in middle-class families seem to vocalize more in this stage than babies from working-class homes (Rheingold, Gewirtz, & Ross, 1959), it is probable that parental vocalizing encourages infant vocalizing.

During the last three stages of prelinguistic speech, Vicky acquires her basic repertoire of sounds. Once she knows how to reproduce these sounds and how to invest them with meaning, she is ready to learn the language of her culture.

7 *Expressive jargon.* During the second year, many children use *expressive jargon.* This term, coined by Gesell, refers to a string of utterances that *sound* like sentences, with pauses, inflections, and rhythms,

but that are made up of "words" that, for the most part, are nothing more than meaningless gibberish. Speech is not yet communicative.

Linguistic Speech

During stages 4 to 6 of prelinguistic speech, Vicky has been acquiring a basic repertoire of sounds that her vocal mechanisms are capable of producing. She has even made a number of sounds—such as the German vowels and the French guttural—that do not have a place in the language of her culture, English (Miller, 1951). She has also been picking up some understanding of the speech she hears, and she understands the meaning of words long before she can say them. When she does begin to utter meaningful speech, she again goes through distinct stages (Eisenson et al., 1963).

1   *One-word sentence ("holophrase").*   At about a year, Vicky points to a cracker, a toy, a pacifier, and says, "da." Her parents correctly interpret the command as "Give me that" or "I want that." She points to the door and says, "out." Depending on the situation, she may mean, "I want to go out" or "Mommy went out." Her single word thus expresses a complete thought, even though her listeners may not always be able to divine what that complete thought may be. When they expand on Vicky's one-word sentences, she hears new words that will eventually be added to her vocabulary.

2   *Multiword sentence.*   Some time about the age of two, Vicky strings together two or more words to make a sentence. When she wants to feed herself with no interference, she says imperiously, "Mommy 'way." When she has finished eating, she says proudly, "All gone." When she sees her father putting on his coat, she says, "Me go." In the middle of a crying fit, she looks at her mother, says "Bicky cwy," and resumes her bawling.

The earliest of these multiword sentences are combinations of nouns and verbs. Other parts of speech, such as articles, prepositions, and adjectives, are lacking. Although these sentences are far from grammatical, they do communicate. This is *telegraphic speech*; it contains only words that carry meaning.

3   *Grammatically correct verbal utterances.*   At about the age of three, Vicky has an impressive command of the language. She now has a vocabulary of some 900 words; she speaks in longer sentences that include all the parts of speech; and she has a good grasp of grammatical principles. (Her grammar is not the same one used by adults because she makes little allowance for exceptions to the linguistic rules she has assimilated. So, she says, "We goed to the store.") Her vocabulary and the complexity of her

sentences are increasing rapidly and constantly. In Chapter 8 we will discuss some factors that influence the development of language.

THEORIES OF LANGUAGE ACQUISITION

For thousands of years, philosophers have been postulating theories about why and how children learn languages, and there is still no agreement among the many students of linguistics. The major theories, which range along a continuum on the relative influences of environment and heredity, fall into four categories—behaviorism, cultural relativism, interactionism, and preformationism, discussed below (Houston, 1971).

Behaviorism

The behaviorists are environmentalists. They believe that language is learned through operant conditioning procedures. Since parents and teachers selectively reinforce infant vocalizations, they shape language behavior. Parents usually respond with delight to their babies' babbling, talking back to the babies and thus reinforcing the babbling. Gradually adult reinforcement goes more and more to those sounds that approximate adult language. In this way, according to the behaviorists, babies proceed from meaningless babbling to meaningful speech. Thorndike (1943) calls this the "babble-luck theory," because the infant randomly emits sounds and gets reinforced for those that "sound like" meaningful language.

Various studies do show the effect of reinforcement on early speech. Babies in institutions (where babbling is less likely to be noticed and reinforced by adults) vocalize less often and make fewer kinds of sounds than babies reared at home (Brodbeck & Irwin, 1946). And, as we pointed out earlier, babies raised by middle-class parents vocalize more than babies from working-class homes, possibly because middle-class parents tend to talk more to their children from infancy onward.

According to the behaviorists, a child learns the structure of language because she makes a stimulus-response connection that results in a *response class*. For example, when Vicky hears the phrases, "John is eager to please" and "John is easy to please," she presumes that both these sentences possess the same structure, and she assigns the words "easy" and "eager" to a single category since they both occur in the same context (Houston, 1971). Because of their association with "John is," "easy" and "eager" are comprised by a response class.

Mowrer (1960) claims that a child learns language by imitating a model (that is, the parent) and by having his own utterances reinforced (by the parent). The infant learns to associate the human voice with need gratification, since the adults whom he hears are the ones who meet his needs. Because of this association, his own voice—particularly when it makes sounds that imitate his parents—is reinforcing. Another behaviorist, Braine (1963), states that a child's language learning is due to contextual generalization. After learning the approximate position for a word in a sentence, the child learns to understand and eventually to use the word in the same position in other sentences.

Cultural Relativism and Cultural Determinism

Both of these anthropological approaches (dominated by Sapir and Whorf) are somewhat less environmentalist than behaviorist. But they still emphasize the role of culture and minimize the importance of individual differences and heredity in the acquisition of language. Their adherents believe that children have innate predispositions for learning language but that it is learned because it is a social necessity. From field observations of cultures where children are not specifically taught to use language (as they are in our society), they conclude that children learn language naturally.

These theories emphasize the differences among languages, rather than their similarity. Sapir (1921) feels that each individual linguistic system is unique and that it is difficult to express the dominant cultural themes of one linguistic group in another language. The Whorfian Hypothesis (Whorf, 1956) says that the specific language we learn influences our mental processes, so that people who speak different languages perceive the world differently and think differently.

Interactionism

This body of thought is exemplified by Piaget's theories that the development of language comes about through the interaction of heredity, maturation, and encounters with the environment. Children learn language not because of parental reinforcement, but because they are born with the capacity and the need to acquire language. Language is an essential part of human development.

At about the age of two, a child begins to connect sounds with actual events, persons, and situations in the environment. She develops a representational, or symbol, system by which certain words represent certain people or objects. Such a system is essential for further cognitive development. Language and thought are parallel, interconnected processes. According to this theory, "language develops along with the child's capacities for logical thought, judgment, and reasoning, and reflects these capacities at each stage [Houston, 1971, p. 267]."

Preformationism and Predeterminism

According to these theories, which are the most popular among contemporary linguists, human beings have an innate, biological predisposition for language. Language occurs naturally, without training, just as walking does. These bodies of belief rest on a number of findings that relate to universal trends in the acquisition of language.

All normal children learn their native language, no matter how complex it is, and they all master the basics sometime between four and six years of age. In all cultures, children display remarkable similarities in learning language. They follow the same stages for both prelinguistic and linguistic speech. They use the same kinds of one- and two-word sentences, in the same kind of "telegraphic" speech, innocent of articles, prepositions, and word endings. Since there are universal aspects of acquisition and of linguistic structure common to *all* languages, there must be inborn mental structures that enable children to build grammars, or systems of rules.

These structures have been termed the *Language Acquisition Device* (LAD). Common to all languages, its operation is as follows (McNeill, 1966, pp. 34–35):

> LAD receives a *corpus* of speech, which is a set of utterances, some grammatical, some not. . . . Upon receipt of this corpus, LAD creates a *grammatical system.* . . . LAD creates a grammar by passing the evidence contained in the corpus through some kind of internal structure. The sequence can be represented by a simple flow diagram:

> Corpus of speech   LAD   Grammatical system

> Like LAD, children are exposed to a corpus of speech, and like LAD, they develop grammatical competence on the basis of this corpus. Moreover, in the case of both LAD and children some kind of internal structure converts a corpus of speech into a grammatical system. Since the same corpus is input and the same grammatical structure is output, LAD's internal structure therefore corresponds to the fundamental human capacity for language.

The preformationist-predeterminist points of view challenge behaviorism in several ways. First, they claim that the knowledge of language is infinite, in the sense that we can always create new and longer sentences; it would be impossible to have learned all the language we are capable of expressing by simple operant conditioning. Also, small children do not imitate adult speech. When they try to, they typically repeat only some of the words and omit parts of speech. Apparently, "much of what children say reflects what is presumably their internal grammar at that stage, not the speech of others [Houston, 1971, p. 272]." These facts, plus the universality of language, point to the heritability of the neurological mechanism for language, if not language itself.

Measuring Infant Intelligence

An adoption agency is trying to decide into which of several prospective homes a baby would best fit. A psychologist at a child development center wants to know how to answer the worried parents who ask, "Our baby isn't doing the things our other children did at his age—is he normal?" A school district wants to find out how many children will need special teaching geared for slow learners.

In just such a practical situation was the concept of the IQ (intelligence quotient) born. At the beginning of the twentieth century, the school administrators of Paris wanted to relieve the overcrowding in the schools by removing from the rosters those youngsters who did not have the capacity to benefit from an academic education. They called in psychologist Alfred Binet and asked him to devise a test to identify those children. Binet's test, which is still being used in somewhat amended forms, was the precursor for a wide variety of current tests that attempt to measure intelligence.

DIFFICULTIES IN MEASURING INTELLIGENCE OF PREVERBAL CHILDREN

Intelligence can be variously defined as an ability to understand concepts and the relationships between them, as an ability to learn and use knowledge, or as a capacity to perform well in certain situations. An intelligence test measures only what the framers of that test have defined as intelligence. At best, intelligence is an elusive quality to define, much less

An examiner cannot ask questions to test a baby's ability to think or reason; the way to test intelligence is to observe behavior.

(Erika Stone, from Peter Arnold)

measure. And the intelligence level of infants is the most elusive of all, primarily for three reasons.

First, infants do not have a command of language. An examiner cannot ask questions to test a baby's ability to think or reason, and the baby cannot show by spoken or written answers how well he understands and can respond to a question. The only way to test a baby's intelligence is to observe his behavior in various situations. But this raises a second problem: infants have a limited range of behaviors. They just don't do all that much. The most that can be determined about a very young infant is his level of sensory functioning and of rudimentary postural control, and then, a little later, of his motor coordination. The third obstacle to accurate measurement of infants' intelligence is the inability to control their motivation. If, for example, a six-month-old baby does not pick up a block offered to him, we do not know whether he doesn't know how to pick it up—or just doesn't feel like picking it up at that particular time. Infants' lack of motivation may even cause them to fall asleep during a test.

One writer has even said, "Attempting to measure infantile intelligence may be like trying to measure a boy's beard at the age of three [Goodenough, 1949, p. 310]," suggesting that there may be no justification for even speaking of intelligence in infancy. This statement is based on the almost complete lack of predictability between babies' scores on various intelligence tests and their intelligence tests in adulthood, or even later in childhood. Many researchers have tried in vain to find a relationship between babies' scores in the most commonly used tests of infant intelligence and their test scores later in childhood. At present, there is almost no basis for predicting the intellectual functioning of normal children from the scores they make as infants. This may be because the early intelligence tests, which measure a lot of motor activity, are so different from the heavily verbal later tests. The tests may actually be measuring two different things.

The *only* predictive value in infant testing appears to be in very general terms (see Table 5-1). Infant scores can sometimes tell us whether a baby is mentally retarded, normal, or unusually superior, and we can more often predict the future performance for the deficient child than for the average or superior one. When psychologists and pediatricians add their assessments of a baby's level of development to the test score, we can obtain a more accurate prediction of that child's future school achievement level (Knobloch & Pasamanick, 1963; Werner, Honzik, & Smith, 1968).

At the age of twenty months, 639 children were tested on the Cattell Infant Intelligence Scale, examined by pediatricians, and evaluated by psychologists. At the age of ten, these same children were tested for intelligence and rated for school achievement. Those who had an IQ of 72 or less on the Cattell at twenty months had problems in school at the age of ten. All three children who had, at twenty months, been rated defective by the psychologist and three-fourths of the ninety-six rated below average

Table 5-1   Poor Predictability of Infant IQs (*Adapted from Anderson, 1939*)

Ages	Number of Children	Correlation Coefficients
3 months–5 years	91	.008
6 months–5 years	91	−.065
9 months–5 years	91	−.001
12 months–5 years	91	.055
18 months–5 years	91	.231
24 months–5 years	91	.450

had school problems at age ten, as did three-quarters of those who had been labeled "low normal" or "retarded" by pediatricians (Werner, Honzik, & Smith, 1968). When both the pediatrician and the psychologist had agreed on the status of the infant, they were better able to predict the child's future status.

A child's home environment exerts a very important influence, so much so that Werner, Honzik, and Smith (1968, p. 1074) say that "the combination of retarded development and a deprived environment in infancy is more predictive of serious achievement problems at school age than either infant or family variables alone." And Anastasi (1968) maintains that when there is no marked physical defect, we can predict such environmental factors as childhood IQ better from knowing the education levels of a baby's parents than from knowing the infant's test scores.

THE INFANT INTELLIGENCE TESTS

What They Measure

At 2.3 months, Vicky can follow a moving pencil with her eyes; at 6.5 months she can reach for a block with one hand; at 13.1 months she can dangle a ring on a string; and at 17.2 months she can put two round blocks in two round holes in a formboard (Bayley, 1935). These skills are test items on the Bayley Scales of Mental and Motor Development, also called the California Infant Scales. These scales, the Gesell Developmental Schedules, and the Cattell Infant Intelligence Scale are the three most often used tests of infant mental development.

All these tests work on basically the same principle. Through careful observation of a large number of babies, researchers determine what most of them can do at particular ages. The researchers then develop a standardized scale, assigning a developmental age for each specific activity. (See Chart 5-2 for more examples of infant test items.)

The child's DQ[2] (*developmental quotient*) is computed by dividing the child's score on the test, given as a *mental* age, by the child's *chronological*

[2]The Gesell score is computed as a DQ; the Cattell and Bayley tests yield an IQ.

age, and multiplying this figure by 100. A quotient of 100 means that the child has passed all the items that the testers have listed as appropriate for his or her age level, and no items for the next higher age level. A score below 100 means that the child has not passed the items passed by at least 50 percent of children the same age, and a score over 100 means that the child has passed some items that half the children of the same age cannot pass. In other words, 100 is average; a score considerably below 100 indicates developmental retardation; and one considerably above 100 indicates acceleration.

The Tests

The three most popular tests are quite similar.

The Gesell Developmental Schedules (Gesell & Amatruda, 1947), which are not tests so much as standardized observations, measure four major areas of development and cover an age range from four weeks to six years. They emphasize *motor behavior*: holding the head erect, sitting, standing, creeping, walking, jumping, and hopping. They also measure certain forms of *adaptive behavior*: eye-hand coordination in reaching for and handling things; solving problems, like putting round and square forms in round and square holes; and exploration of new objects and new surroundings. As the child develops, *language behavior* is assessed: how well the child seems to understand other people and how he reacts by facial expression, gesture, body movements, babbling, and, eventually, speech. Finally, the child's *personal-social* behavior is evaluated: How does she respond to other people and to the culture? Is she toilet-trained? Does he feed himself? When does he smile and at whom?

The Cattell Infant Intelligence Scale, a downward extension of the Stanford-Binet test, covers the span from two to thirty months. It uses some Stanford-Binet items, some Gesell items, some items from other tests, and some new ones. It is composed largely of items testing perception (paying attention to a voice or a bell, or following movement with the eyes) and motor abilities (lifting the head or using the fingers). Recognizing that it is impossible to hurry a baby, the devisers of this scale wisely avoided setting any time limits for any of the tasks.

The Bayley Scales, which cover babies from birth to fifteen months, also use items from several other tests, as well as some new ones. (See Chart 5-2 for a comparison of these three tests.)

INFLUENCES ON INTELLIGENCE

Heredity versus Socioeconomic Status

As the evidence presented in Chapter 2 showed, intelligence seems to have a large genetic component. This seems particularly true of infant development, which appears to be less readily influenced by social class and parental education levels than are later measures of intelligence.

Chart 5-2   Comparison of Gesell, Cattell, and Bayley Tests

Gesell and Amatruda (1941; yields DQ)	Cattell (1940; yields IQ)	Bayley (1933; yields IQ)
(Key age, 28 weeks) Lifts head. Sits erect momentarily. Radial palmar grasp of cube. Whole hand rakes pellet. Holds two cubes more than momentarily. Retains bell. Vocalizes m-m-m and polysyllabic vowel sounds. Takes solid food well. Brings feet to mouth. Pats mirror image.	(Key age, 6 months) Secures cube on sight. When child is sitting in upright position before table a one-inch cube is placed within easy reach. Lifts cup. Place straight-sided aluminum cup upside down within easy reach of child as he is sitting at table. Fingers reflection in mirror. While child is in sitting position, a framed mirror is held before him in such a manner that he can see his reflection but not that of his mother or other persons. Reaches unilaterally. Child sits with shoulders square to front and both hands an equal distance from examiner. A two-to-three-inch door key or peg is presented in perpendicular position. Reaches persistently. One-inch cube is placed on table just out of child's reach. Credit if child reaches several times.	5.8 mo. Exploitive paper play. Present a piece of paper to child so he may grasp edge of it. 5.8 mo. Accepts second cube. When child is holding one cube, place a second in easy reach. 5.9 mo. Vocalizes pleasure. 5.9 mo. Vocalizes displeasure. 6.0 mo. Reaches persistently. Place cube just far enough away from child so he cannot reach it. Credit if he reaches persistently. 6.1 mo. Turns head after spoon. Hold spoon so that it protrudes over edge of table by child's side and when he is interested, suddenly drop it to floor. 6.1 mo. Mirror image approach. Hold mirror before child, bringing it close enough so that he may reach it easily. 6.2 mo. Picks up cube deftly. *(Continued)*

Gesell and Amatruda (1941; yields DQ)	Cattell (1940; yields IQ)	Bayley (1933; yields IQ)
	Approaches second cube. Child is presented with one cube and as soon as he has taken it a second is held before him in such a position as to favor his grasping, but is not actually placed in his hand.	6.3 mo. Says several syllables.
(Key age, 52 weeks) Walks with one hand held. Tries to build tower of cubes, fairly. Dangles ring by string. Tries to insert pellet in bottle. Two words besides "mama" and "dada." Gives toy on request. Cooperates in dressing. Releases ball towards adult. (56 weeks).	(Key age, 12 months) Beats two spoons together. Two spoons are taken, one in each hand, and beaten gently together while child watches, then they are presented to child, one in each hand. Places cube in cup. Aluminum cup and one-inch cube are placed before child and he is asked to put "block" in cup. If no response, placing cube in cup is demonstrated and request repeated. Marks with pencil. Piece of paper and pencil are placed before child with request, "——write." If no response writing is demonstrated and request repeated. Credit if child makes any marks on paper.	11.5 mo. Inhibits on command. When child puts an object in mouth or on some other pretext, say "no, no." Credit if he inhibits. 11.6 mo. Repeats performance laughed at 11.6 mo. Strikes doll. Place small rubber whistle doll on table. Hit it smartly to produce whistle, encourage child to do the same. Credit if he imitates the hitting motion. 11.7 mo. Imitates words. Say several words, as mama, dada, baby, etc., and credit attempts to imitate.

(Continued)

Gesell and Amatruda (1941; yields DQ)	Cattell (1940; yields IQ)	Bayley (1933; yields IQ)
	Rattles spoon in cup. Aluminum cup is placed before child and spoon is moved back and forth in it, hitting edges; then spoon is placed beside cup with handle toward child.	12.1 mo. Spoon imitation. Rattle spoon in cup with stirring motion. Credit if child succeeds in making a noise in cup by a similar motion with spoon.
	Speaking vocabulary —two words. "Ma-ma" and "da-da" are not credited.	12.2 mo. Holds cup to drink. Hand cup to child saying, "Take a drink." Credit if he takes it in his hands, and holds it adaptively to drink.
	Hits doll. Rubber doll with whistle is put face up on table before child, and hit gently with open hand several times. Credit if child makes a definite attempt to hit doll.	12.6 mo. Adjusts round block. Three-hole (Gesell) form board is laid on table with round hole at child's right. Give round block to him with no directions. Credit if child puts block in round hole.

The Louisville Twin Study, mentioned in Chapter 2, tested 261 pairs of identical and fraternal twins at three, six, nine, twelve, eighteen, and twenty-four months of age, with the Bayley Scales of Mental and Motor Development. The twins were from homes that represent "nearly the full spectrum of conditions under which urban families live, ranging from the welfare case to the wealthy professional family [Wilson & Harpring, 1972, p. 286]." There was *no* correlation between the socioeconomic status of the babies' families and their mental or motor development. There *was* a high degree of concordance between identical twins in both mental and motor development at every age tested—much higher than between fraternal twins. The differences between unrelated children appear, then, to be due largely to the genetic blueprint. Only in extreme cases of serious prematurity, an impoverished environment, or brain injury will this genetic factor be outweighed (Wilson & Harpring, 1972).

As children grow older, their facility with language becomes more important in their overall functioning. Then their home environments assume a more important role, as we shall see in our discussion of children's school achievements. But in infancy, the genes seem to be the important determinants of development.

More than 1,000 babies from one to fifteen months of age, from socioeconomic backgrounds representative of the United States population, were tested on the Bayley Scales to uncover relationships between infant development and several other factors (Bayley, 1965). No relationships were found on either the mental or the motor scale for sex, birth order, education of either parent, or geographic residence. Nor were differences between black and white babies found on the mental scale, although the black babies consistently scored higher on the motor scale.

Although socioeconomic status does not appear to be related to infant mental or motor development, it is a good predictor of the *direction* of DQ change from infancy to preschool age. The test scores of children in middle-class and superior working-class homes increase after infancy; children from average working-class homes stay pretty much the same; and children from culturally deprived working-class homes show a decline (Knobloch & Pasamanick, 1963). As the child grows, then, the home environment assumes more and more importance.

This can be seen in the rising level of racial differences in DQs as children grow older. At forty weeks, there is no difference between overall DQs of black and white infants, despite the black babies' precocity on several motor abilities. Even when there are considerable disparities in the amount of education of the children's mothers, the children's DQs do not reflect this. By three years of age, though, the picture is very different. White children score better, even when the mothers of both white and black babies have had similar amounts of education (Knobloch & Pasamanick, 1963). Intelligence testing of black and white children will be discussed in detail in Chapter 11.

Nutrition
Severe malnutrition in infancy may retard general mental development. Evidence that early malnutrition may have devastating and irreversible effects on mental development can be seen in the findings that infants who died of the protein deficiency disease marasmus had fewer brain cells than did normal babies of the same age (Winick & Rosso, 1969), and the brains of children who were malnourished in early childhood were found to weigh less than those of normal children (Stoch & Smythe, 1963).

Brockman & Ricciuti (1971) compared twenty severely malnourished children from Lima, Peru, ranging in age from about 1 to about $3^1/_2$ years of

(UNICEF/Ling)

Heredity and environment, again: Whenever we discuss the influences on the development of children, we have to consider the overall milieu in which they spend their days.

age, with a control group in their ability to perform ten sorting tasks. The undernourished children then received twelve weeks of nutritional treatment, after which they took the sorting test again. Not only did the undernourished children perform much more poorly than the control children—at least six to eight months behind them—but they showed no significant increase in test scores even after nutritional therapy, leading to the gloomy conclusion that early malnutrition may indeed do irreversible damage to intellectual functioning. It is possible, though, that a longer nutritional treatment might provide more beneficial results.

Interaction between Biological and Social Factors

The nutrition studies cited above would appear to contradict the conclusions of the study cited in Chapter 2 (Stein et al., 1972), showing no differences in intellectual performance among Dutch men who had been conceived, carried, or born during periods of famine, compared with nonfamine babies. Perhaps a physiological influence like malnutrition assumes greater importance when it occurs in conjunction with unfavorable social conditions, as well. The Peruvian children cited above, for example (Brockman & Ricciuti, 1971), may have been especially vulnerable to any biological insult because of general social deprivation. A similar relationship has been seen in the effects of birth complications. The study of Hawaiian children cited in Chapter 3 (Werner et al., 1968) indicated that severe perinatal stress tended to have little effect on the later intelligence of middle-class children, but the same stress in a child born to poor families often had catastrophic effects. Whenever we discuss the influences on the development of children, we have to consider the overall milieu in which they spend their days.

Child-rearing Techniques

Let's take a look at two preschoolers—the same age, the same nursery school—but oh, so different! Why is it that when something gets in Vicky's way, she will figure out a way around it, while Jason will either burst into tears, pitch a tantrum, or just give up? How does Vicky know where to look for her mother's keys, while Jason stares vacantly when asked to get them? How can Vicky anticipate the consequences of her actions, while Jason seems unable to think ahead?

The Harvard Pre-School Project set out to determine what makes preschool children competent in ways such as this. After extensive testing and observation of some 400 preschoolers from a variety of backgrounds, the researchers identified a group of "A" children, who showed all-around excellence, a group of "B," or average, children, and a group of "C" children, who had great trouble coping with daily life (White, 1971).

What made the A children excellent? They knew how to get and hold the attention of adults in socially acceptable ways, to use them as resources, and to show them both affection and hostility. With other children, they were able both to lead and to follow, to compete, and again to express both affection and hostility. They were proud of their accomplishments, and they showed a desire to grow up and to act in more grown-up ways. They used language well; they demonstrated a range of intellectual abilities (such as dealing with abstractions and taking the perspective of another); they could plan and carry out relatively complicated activities; and they were able to "dual-focus"—that is, to keep their attention on the task at hand while keeping in touch with what was happening around them. The B children were less able in these skills, and the C children were markedly deficient (White, 1971). Follow-up studies two years later showed a notable stability in the classifications (Pines, 1969).

Since the researchers found that A children were already different from C children by the age of three, they tried to locate differences in the early environments of these two extremes. Thus they identified A's and C's who had younger siblings, and dispatched a corps of observers into their homes to see how these infants and toddlers were being brought up. They found an enormous difference in kinds of mothering being given these two groups of children—and concluded that the way children's mothers treat them during the years between one and three can determine "much of the basic quality of the entire life of an individual [White, 1971, p. 100]." The Harvard researchers focused on the mothers, since they felt that so few fathers spent much time with children of this age that they were not influential.

How the A and C Mothers Differed

During much of the first year of life, most of the mothers seemed to treat their babies similarly. But starting at about eight months of age, differences became more apparent, both in the parents and in the children. At this time, children are starting to understand language, and so the ways—and the amount—that their parents talk to them gain in importance. They begin to crawl, a development some mothers react to with pleasure, others with annoyance. They become attached to the person they spend most of their time with, making that person's personality more important. And they also develop a growing sense of who they are.

Burton White, director of the Harvard Pre-School Project, feels that

> the behavior of parents really begins to diverge during the child's second year, when the growing baby—now walking around and talking—forces himself on the attention of adults. The toddler's insatiable curiosity at that age, his zest for learning, and his obvious grasp of language, all lead the effective mother to produce a rich flow of talk and try in various ways to satisfy his drives. To other types of mothers, however, this growth means only two things: danger to the child, and much more work for them [Pines, 1969, p. 159].

Mothers from all socioeconomic groups were in both groups, with some welfare mothers raising A children and some middle-class women raising C's. But by and large, the A mothers were more likely to be of the middle class. The middle-class children in this study spent much less time than the poor children just sitting around and doing nothing, and much more time in games of make-believe, in making things, or in practicing new skills (Pines, 1969). Basically, what were the differences between the A and C mothers?

The A mothers.   These women had many traits in common, whereas the C mothers were a more diverse group. The A mothers generally had positive attitudes toward life, enjoyed being with young children, and generously gave of themselves to their children. They were energetic, patient, tolerant of the mess that babies make, and relatively casual about letting their children take minor risks. They did not devote their entire lives to their babies, though. A number had part-time jobs, and those who did stay home generally spent less than 10 percent of their time interacting with their infants (White, 1971).

The time they did spend was fruitful. They tended to go about their daily routines but to make themselves available for a few seconds—or less often, a few minutes—at a time when their children needed them. They would take time out to answer a question, to label some object in the child's world, to help a toddler learn how to climb stairs. They served as "designers" and "consultants" to their children. They designed a physical environment full of interesting things for their children to see and touch, although these things were just as likely to be common household objects as expensive toys. And they were pretty much, although not totally, "on call" when their babies needed them.

The C mothers. These women were a diverse group. Some were overwhelmed by life, ran chaotic homes, and were too absorbed by daily struggles to spend time with their children. Others spent too much time with their babies—hovering over them, being overprotective, pushing them to learn, making the children very dependent on them. Some were physically in the home but rarely made real contact with their children, apparently because they really didn't enjoy the company of babies and toddlers. These mothers tended to provide for their children materially but to confine the children much of the time in cribs or playpens. Many mothers who are conscientious and do love their children might be able to help their children by following the guidelines drawn up by the staff of the Pre-School Project.

Improving Children's Language, IQ, and General Competence by Working with Parents

Very often the difference between an able child and an inept one is a class difference. Yet the evidence seems to show that lower-class parents love their children just as much as middle-class parents and are just as eager for them to succeed. Is it possible, then, to intervene in poor families in such a way as to raise the sophistication level of the parents and, ultimately, the ability of the children?

Before we begin to impose middle-class values on families in a different subculture, we have to weigh very carefully the effects of such intervention. What will it do, for example, to the parents' own self-esteem? Will they think less of themselves if they have to be taught how to relate to their children? Will it interfere with the parent-child relationship if a mother feels that her competence is being judged by her child's competence? A great deal of sensitivity is required in any program that attempts to alter basic styles of living and interrelating. But the justification for such steps lies in the reality that success in our society tends to come to the person with verbal, academic, and general coping skills. Since most parents want their children to succeed, many are receptive to any help offered to them or their children. It seems that we need a society in which people are respected for their cultural subgroup membership *and* are also encouraged to achieve verbal, academic, and coping skills without totally rejecting their own cultural values.

We will probably see a growing emphasis on teaching parents in

(James R. Smith)

(Charles Gatewood)

Before we impose middle-class values on families in a different subculture, we have to weigh the effects: A great deal of sensitivity is required in any program that attempts to alter basic styles of living and interrelating.

disadvantaged families how to deal with their children more effectively. For example, the conclusions drawn from the Harvard Pre-School Project are now being tested in an experiment in a Boston suburb (Reinhold, 1973). The Brookline Early Education Project, with a staff of some thirty doctors, psychologists, teachers, and other professionals, is working closely with 225 parents of infants, counseling some and not others. If those families who receive the most counseling end up producing the most competent children, the directors of BEEP hope to induce the government to fund more programs that focus on very young children.

Other programs have concentrated on developing children's abilities to use our language. These efforts do not make a frontal attack on parental language patterns, which would probably be ineffectual, if not absolutely impossible. Instead, they try to change certain aspects of parent-child interaction.

Karnes, Teska, Hodgins, and Badger (1970), for example, recruited twenty poor mothers of one- and two-year-old children to attend a two-hour meeting once a week for fifteen months to learn how to teach their children. Fifteen mothers completed the entire program. The emphasis during the meetings was on the need for the mothers to respect their children, to maintain a positive approach that focuses on success and minimizes errors, to teach a task by breaking it down into separate components, and to keep learning "fun."

At the end of the program, these mothers' children and a matched control group of children whose mothers received no training, were tested on the Stanford-Binet Intelligence Test and the Illinois Test of Psycholinguistic Abilities (ITPA). The experimental children scored much higher in language and intellectual functioning on both tests than the controls.

Another study attempted to stimulate the verbal interactions between mothers and their two- and three-year-old children (Levenstein, 1970). Fifty-four children, aged twenty to forty-three months, and their mothers were divided into three groups. Over the course of seven months, the mothers and children in the experimental group received an average of thirty-two home visits by a social worker, called a Toy Demonstrator. She would bring a variety of educational toys and books and show the mother how to use them to play with her child. The Toy Demonstrator was instructed to treat the mother "as a colleague in a joint endeavor in behalf of the child [Levenstein, 1970, p. 429]." The children in one control group were visited regularly by a social worker who brought noneducational toys but didn't do much with then and had little contact with their mothers. And the children in the other control group were not visited at all.

All the children were tested at the beginning and at the end of the program, and the children in the experimental group improved in intellectual functioning, although those in the two control groups did not.

In all three of these programs, and in other similar ones, parents have shown enthusiasm for the opportunity to learn how to help their children; and in the latter two, the children have made definite gains. Although we do not know how well the experimental children's advantages will hold up over time, it does seem fruitful to continue to investigate ways in which professionals can work with parents to help children develop their cognitive and linguistic abilities.

Emotional Climate in the Home

Do the emotional attitudes of parents have a significant effect on children's development? According to the Berkeley Growth Study, they do. In this longitudinal study (Bayley & Schaefer, 1964), sixty-one children were followed from infancy to the age of eighteen and tested periodically. The children's mothers were assessed for the degree of emotional warmth or coldness they showed their children early in life. Surprisingly, the mothers' attitudes seemed to affect their sons and daughters differently.

According to these findings, warm, affectionate mothers of boys who grant their sons a certain degree of autonomy are likely to have happy, calm babies who make below-average mental scores in infancy but end up with high IQs in later life. The baby daughter of this same type of mother is likely to make above-average mental scores in her first three years. After this time, though, there seems to be no relationship between the daughter's IQ score and the mother's attitude—except for a negative one between IQ and maternal intrusiveness.

In other words, we could predict a high IQ for a six-month-old boy who is happy, inactive, and placid, has a loving, accepting mother, and a father in a professional occupation, even though he tests rather low now. But if we want to predict a six-month-old girl's IQ, we can only try to correlate it with her parents' education, her father's occupation, and her mother's intelligence. Good mothering in infancy is apparently more important for boys than it is for girls—at least as far as it affects intellectual achievement.

This may be still another bit of evidence pointing to the ability of girls to withstand an unfavorable environment. Boys may be more susceptible to environmental influences psychologically as well as physically. Maybe this has something to do with the preponderance of boys who develop learning and behavior problems and who get into trouble with the law (Elkind, 1967).

In another study of parent-child relationships (Kagan & Freeman, 1967), girls whose mothers were critical tended to have higher IQs. The authors of both these studies warn against drawing rigid conclusions. Correlation is not necessarily causation, and there may be other factors at work. But findings like these indicate the webbed complexity of what we call intelligence and its susceptibility to many different influences, some of which we may not even be aware.

Summary

1 According to Piaget's interactionist theory of cognitive development, the child progresses through a series of four sequential stages of cognitive

development between birth and adolescence: *sensorimotor* (birth to two); *preoperational* (two to seven); *concrete operational* (seven to eleven); and *formal operational* (twelve years and beyond). Each stage is attained through an interaction of maturational and environmental factors and is qualitatively different from the other stages. Much of Piaget's work is based on meticulous, detailed observations of his own three children and has generally received empirical support by other experimenters using more highly standardized, regimented procedures.

2   During the time a child is in the *sensorimotor stage* of development—although still a preverbal creature—intelligent (adaptive) behaviors are exhibited. The infant also develops from a primarily reflexive individual to one who shows rudimentary foresight into his or her behavior. An aspect of this stage is the development of the concept of *object permanence.* At the beginning of this stage an object ceases to exist for the infant once it is out of range. By the end of this stage the object permanence concept is fully developed and the child understands the implications of visible and invisible displacements. The child then possesses a mature object concept.

3   *Learning* is establishing a new relationship or strengthening a weak relationship between two events, actions, or things. The type and extent of infant learning has been the subject of much recent controversy. However, there is evidence that the very young infant is capable of several types of learning: *habituation, classical conditioning, operant conditioning*, and *imitation.*

4   Some time during the second year the infant begins to speak the language. Even before this milestone, certain verbal utterances have been understood. There is little agreement on how to theoretically account for language acquisition. Theories of language acquisition have ranged from those stressing environmental (e.g., *behaviorism*) and cultural (*cultural determinism* and *cultural relativism*) factors to those stressing innate, maturational (*preformationism* and *predeterminism*) explanations. *Interactionism* (Piagetian theory) acknowledges the mutual influence of heredity, maturation, and environmental stimulation on language.

5   It is difficult to assess infant intelligence because (*a*) infants do not have language and cannot be tested verbally; (*b*) infants have a limited range of behavioral capacities which can be assessed; and (*c*) motivation in the testing situation cannot be controlled to insure that infants will perform "their best." Scores on infant intelligence tests are poor predictors of later intelligence. Intellectual ability is greatly influenced by emotional climate in the home.

Suggested Readings

Church, J. (ed.). *Three Babies: Biographies of Cognitive Development.* New York: Vintage, 1966. *An absorbing and very personal life history of three babies from birth to two years as recorded by their mothers. It includes notes by Church on laboratory data on children and theoretical views of child growth and development.*

Ginsburg, H., & Opper, S. *Piaget's Theory of Intellectual Development.* Englewood Cliffs, N.J.: Prentice-Hall, 1969. *A clear, readable discussion of Jean Piaget's research on intellectual development. It includes outlines of his basic ideas, Piaget's early research and theory, Piaget's use of logic as a model for the adolescent's thinking, and a discussion of the implications of Piaget's work.*

Piaget, J. *The Origins of Intelligence in Children.* New York: International Universities Press, 1952. *Piaget's presentation of the six sequential stages of the sensorimotor period. Abundantly illustrated with observations of his own children.*

CHAPTER SIX
PERSONALITY DEVELOPMENT
IN WHICH VICKY SHOWS US HER PERSONALITY

The heart of childhood is all mirth:
We frolic to and fro
As free and blithe, as if on earth
Were no such thing as woe.

(John Keble, The Christian year, 1827)

Most adults tend to romanticize the past, leading to such unrealistic reminiscences as those so quaintly expressed above. Have we already forgotten the fears and worries of our childhood years, the uncertainties, the pain, the rage, the frustration? Of course, the joy and the laughter and the innocent moments of delight are all part of childhood, too. But only part. It is the total range of emotions in these early years—and the people and experiences that evoke them—that have far-reaching effects in determining our personalities.

As we pointed out in the Introduction, it is virtually impossible to separate social and emotional development from the formation of personality, even though each describes a slightly different facet of the feeling, acting, human being. Vicky's personality begins to show up in infancy, almost from the day of birth. In the first month of life, she is already manifesting her own unique temperament; she is already gaining a subliminal sense of the world as a friendly, caring place; and she is both responding to and evoking responses from the people around her.

What Emotions Do Babies Have?

It is easy to tell when the newborn Vicky is unhappy. She emits a piercing cry in an ever-rising crescendo; she flails her arms and legs about; and she stiffens her tiny body until it is rigid. It is harder to tell when she is happy. We know that during the first month she quiets at the sound of a human voice or when she is picked up, and she smiles when her hands are moved together pat-a-cake style (Bayley, 1933; Griffiths, 1954; Wolff, 1963). With every passing day, she responds more and more to people—smiling, cooing, reaching out to, and eventually going right to them. But are these early moments of quiet positive expressions of happiness, or do they tell us only that Vicky is not unhappy? It is hard to tell whether she is really happy

(Annan Photo Features)

What emotions do babies have? How early? And can we "correctly" separate rage, fear, distress, anger, pain, and frustration?

or more-or-less neutral until about the third month of life, when her more frequent smiles and delighted coos signal her times of joy.

The time at which infant emotions appear has long been a controversial topic. In 1919 John B. Watson, the behaviorist, claimed that infants are born with three major emotions—*love, rage,* and *fear.* Behaviorism soon became very fashionable, and so did its corollary that these three basic emotions are unconditioned responses to unconditioned stimuli, which, through conditioning, became elaborated and attached to new stimuli.

According to the behaviorists, cuddling was the unconditioned stimulus for *love,* which the baby showed by quiet behavior; withdrawal of support and loud sounds caused *fear,* which the baby demonstrated by crying, blinking his eyes, and pulling back his body; and restraining a baby's movements caused *rage,* which he showed by crying and flailing his arms and legs. Only through conditioning, behaviorists said, would other stimuli come to elicit love, rage, or fear.

Before the decade was out, however, other investigators who tried to confirm Watson's theories found that observers who had not actually seen the stimuli that elicited infants' reactions had trouble identifying the babies' emotional states. An observer who had seen an infant being dropped would identify his subsequent crying as fear. But an observer who simply saw a film of the same crying infant—without having seen her being dropped—was unable to "correctly" identify the emotion as fear. People were most likely to identify a baby's cries as those of anger—whether the precipitating cause had been hunger, being dropped, being restrained, or being stuck with a needle. Sherman (1927) thus concluded that infant emotional states are generalized and not nearly so specific as the behaviorists had believed.

By 1932, K. M. B. Bridges was making the point that newborn infants show only one emotion, an undifferentiated excitement (called "distress" by later workers) and that the baby's emotions *differentiate* as he grows older; that is, his emotions proceed from the general to the specific. More recent research has shown that the specific emotions identified by Bridges do not appear in the precise timing and form she indicated, and both she and Watson have been criticized for projecting certain adult emotional responses on infants (like "disgust" for a six-month-old baby). Bridges' principle of the differentiation of emotions is still considered valid, but babies may, from an early age, have a wide range of emotions that they cannot express specifically or that our techniques are not refined enough to identify.

A more recent study of crying in infants indicates that this differentiation may begin much sooner than had been thought. By recording infant cries on magnetic tape and then showing them visually as sound spectrograms (see Figure 6-1), Peter Wolff (1969) has found different patterns between infants' basic rhythmic cries and their cries of anger, pain, and frustration.

Why Infants Cry *(Adapted from Wolff, 1969)*

First Week

Hunger. Hungry babies cry more than full ones, and it is the feeding that quiets them, not just picking them up.

Temperature. Babies cry more and sleep less in an environment of 78° F than in one of 88–90° F.

Being naked. Undressing a baby causes crying, even in a warm environment, and dressing him stops the crying.

Pain. The pain of a needle or unanesthetized surgery causes crying; apparently, so does intestinal discomfort.

Disruption of sleep. During a state of drowsiness, infants who wake themselves up by spontaneous jerking often cry.

Not wet or dirty diapers. Infants who were undiapered and then rediapered with the soiled diapers stopped crying after the "sham" change just as often as those who were given clean diapers.

Second Week

All the above, plus:

Interruption of feeding. When the bottle is taken away from a baby after she has taken an ounce or less of formula, she will cry vigorously; this response lasts till the end of the first month or the middle of the second. Breastfed babies do not begin to protest the interruption of a feeding till the end of the first month, possibly because they sucked longer before the first interruption and became drowsy sooner.

Third Week

A variety of stimuli when presented in a fussy state. A silent, nodding head, a human voice, or pat-a-cake motions, which elicit indifference or smiling when the baby is content, may cause crying when the baby is active or fussy.

Fourth Week

Solid food. When first presented with cereal, some babies cry, but few react this way to fruit.

Being tickled while fussy. Tickling the armpit or groin, which may make a baby laugh in some states, will make him cry when fussy.

1–2 Months

Departure of adult. The baby cries, not because of the absence of a person in the room, but because of the experience of being left alone; he cries just as much upon the departure of a stranger as of his mother.

Removal of familiar toy animal. Again, it is the removal of the toy, not its absence, that makes the baby cry; when it is returned to its usual place, she stops crying.

2–3 Months

Stronger reaction to departure of adult or removal of toy, often accompanied now by *thumb-sucking,* which becomes a specific response to psychological distress.

Besides showing up differently on the spectrograms, the cries also sound somewhat different, sometimes enabling parents to identify their babies' needs by the rhythm and tone of the cry.

Four examples of infant cries that Wolff has recorded are

Basic rhythmical cry: This is often called the hunger cry, but it need not be associated with hunger. Sooner or later, the infant always reverts to this pattern of crying.

Mad, or angry, cry: In this variation of the basic pattern, the baby forces excess air through the vocal cords.

Pain cry: This is distinguished by a sudden onset of loud crying without preliminary moaning and an initial long cry, followed by an extended period of holding the breath.

Cry of frustration: This starts from silence as does the cry of pain, but there is no long breath-holding. The first two or three cries are long and drawn out.

SMILE—AND THE WORLD SMILES WITH YOU

Vicky's winning smile is one of her most powerful tools for making people—especially her parents—fall in love with her. All higher animals send nonverbal messages to others of their species that serve a specific function in perpetuating the species. A baby's smile is a basic means of communication that sets in motion a beautiful cycle. It is a rare adult who can resist a baby's smile—especially when that baby is one's own. As Vicky smiles at her parents, they smile back at her, and enjoy being with her. This, in turn, makes her smile more, tending to cement the bonds between her and the important people in her life. A recent research project proved the power of a baby's smile when it found a probability of from 0.46 to 0.88 that an infant's smile would elicit a smile from an adult (Gewirtz & Gewirtz, 1968).

Infants vary considerably in the amount of smiling they do (Tauterman-nova, 1973), and the differences among them are significant for their effects on others and the others' subsequent behavior toward them. The happy, cheerful baby who rewards her parents' caretaking efforts with smiles and gurgles is almost certain to form a more positive relationship with them than will her sister, who smiles less readily.

The smile appears early in life. One-week-old babies smile spontaneously and fleetingly when their stomachs are full or when they hear soft sounds. These smiles become more frequent and more socially oriented (that is, become directed more toward people) at about the age of one month. The four- or five-week-old baby is likely to smile at a variety of different stimuli—having his hands clapped together as in a game of pat-a-cake (Wolff, 1963), seeing a rotating cardboard oval (Salzen, 1963), or hearing a familiar voice (Kreutzer & Charlesworth, 1973). But not until a baby is about

(Shelly Rusten)

The power of a baby's smile: The probability is great that an infant who rewards parents' efforts with smiles will form a more positive relationship.

3¹/₂ months old will she smile more to a familiar face than to an unfamiliar one (Kreutzer & Charlesworth, 1973).

Theoretical Perspectives on Personality Development in Infancy

For centuries, philosophers have been expounding theories about the origins of personality, and many, in their time, have had enormous influence over the ways that parents brought up their children. In this category is the psychoanalyst Sigmund Freud. As Freud, at the end of the nineteenth century and the beginning of the twentieth, attempted to help Viennese adults overcome their neuroses, he formulated a broad philosophy to explain how these neuroses had developed. In so doing, he attempted to explain how all children develop emotionally. Erik Erikson, a student and disciple of Freud, disagreed with some aspects of his theory and expanded upon others.

Table 6-1   Comparison of Freud's Psychosexual and
Erikson's Psychosocial Stages of Development

Chronological Stages	Freud's Stages	Erikson's Stages
Infancy	oral	basic trust vs. mistrust
1½–3 years	anal	autonomy vs. shame, doubt
3–5½ years	phallic	initiative vs. guilt
5½–12 years	latency	industry vs. inferiority
Adolescence	genital	identity vs. role confusion
Young adulthood		intimacy vs. isolation
Adulthood		generativity vs. stagnation
Maturity		ego-integrity vs. despair

Freud and, to a lesser extent, Erikson have had a tremendous impact on Western society. Their ideas have been assimilated as unquestioned truths by so many child-care professionals that there is probably no one under the age of forty whose upbringing does not owe something to them. Because of the nature of their theses, neither Freud's nor Erikson's ideas have generated much research to support their findings. And many developmentalists now question many aspects of their theories. But because of their great influence on child rearing in our society, it is important to be familiar with their ideas. (A summary is presented in Table 6-1.)

THE PSYCHOSEXUAL THEORIES OF SIGMUND FREUD

Freud's original and creative thinking made definite contributions to our beliefs about children—and adults. It was he who made us aware of infantile sexuality, of the nature of our subconscious thoughts and emotions, of the importance of children's relationships in their earliest years, of the significance of dreams, and of many more aspects of emotional and intellectual functioning. He has incontestably expanded our understanding of ourselves and our fellow human beings. And yet we need not take everything he says as gospel. His is only one body of thought about the ways that children develop.

According to Freud, there are three parts to the personality structure: the *id,* the *ego,* and the *superego.* The id is the unconscious source of motives and desires, which operates on the "pleasure principle." That is, it strives for immediate gratification. The ego, which may be thought of as reason or common sense, mediates between the id, the outside world, and, eventually, the superego. The ego develops when the infant's gratification is delayed. It operates on the "reality principle" and seeks an acceptable way to obtain gratification. The superego, or conscience, is the incorporation of the morals of society, largely through identification with the parent of the same sex.

The id is present at birth. The infant is egocentric in that he does not differentiate himself from the outside world. All is there for gratification, and the baby's feelings (such as hunger or wetness) are the feelings of all. Only when gratification is delayed (as when he has to wait for food) does he develop his ego and begin to differentiate himself from the surroundings. Thus the ego develops relatively soon after birth. The superego does not develop until the age of four or five, at the end of the Oedipus complex (see Chapter 9).

In Freudian thought the human organism goes through several different stages of psychosexual development. The stages are defined and named for those parts of the body that come to the fore during each phase as primary sources of libidinal gratification. Thus we have in infancy, the *oral* stage and then the *anal.* The experiences during these critical early stages determine an individual's adjustment patterns and the personality traits he will have as an adult. An individual may be *fixated* at a particular stage if his needs at this level of development have not been met—or, conversely, if he has been overindulged. Freud is vague, however, about the way fixation occurs.

The Oral Stage (Birth to Twelve to Eighteen Months[1])

During this stage, when the baby is "all mouth," she attains most of her gratification from sucking, most obviously during her frequent feedings.

[1]All ages are approximate.

(Wayne F. Miller, Magnum)

In Freudian thought, fixation in the oral or anal stage can determine an individual's adjustment patterns and personality traits.

Her erogenous zones are her lips and mouth; the erotic objects that gratify her libidinal instincts are nipples, bottles, fingers, and anything else that can go into the mouth. She views these sources of gratification positively and *cathects* them, that is, forms attachments to them.

During this stage of "primary narcissism," the infant is concerned only with her own gratifications. She is all id, as she operates on the pleasure principle and strives for immediate gratification of her needs.

The oral stage has two substages: the *oral-dependent,* when the infant can do nothing more assertive than cry to be fed, and the *oral-aggressive,* when the teething infant can bite the nipple as well as suck it.

A Freudian may speak of an adult as having an "oral personality," meaning that this person was fixated during the oral period. Such a person may derive a disproportionate amount of satisfaction by literal use of his mouth—kissing a lot, smoking, biting his nails, overeating, or drinking too much. Since food plays a large part in the oral stage of infancy, a person fixated in this stage may equate food with love, and either overeat or compulsively overfeed his children. Oral fixation may also take other forms, explains Baldwin (1968, p. 357): an "imperious demand for the love object when desire is high together with ignoring it the rest of the time" (just as the baby demands a feeding when he is hungry but is not interested in food at other times), or "a passive, unrealistic optimism that someone will appear to solve one's problems" (just as the infant waits for someone to feed him).

(Reg Innell, Annan Photo Features)

The Anal Stage (Twelve to Eighteen Months to Three Years)

The child's greatest pleasure now comes from moving his bowels, and the way toilet training is handled determines the effective resolution of this stage. The "anal personality" may be shaped by two different aspects of this period: the concern with cleanliness that is inevitably a part of toilet training, or the view of one's feces as gifts to one's parents.

In the first instance, a person may become obsessively clean and neat or defiantly messy. Or, extending to other areas of life, she may become pedantic, obsessively precise, and rigidly oriented to schedules and routines. Fixation to the gift-giving aspects of anality may make one hoard his possessions as he once withheld his feces or may cause him to identify love with the bestowal of material objects.

THE PSYCHOSOCIAL THEORIES OF ERIK H. ERIKSON

Whereas Freud stresses the biological determinants of behavior, Erikson looks to the cultural/societal influences on it. Erikson's major concern is with the growth of the ego, and especially with the ways that the society into which we are born shapes our ego development. In each of Erikson's "Eight Ages of Man" (1950) crises occur that influence ego development. The ways these crises are resolved determine the course of ego development. Two of these crisis stages occur during the first three years of life.

Crisis I: Basic Trust versus Basic Mistrust (Birth to Twelve to Eighteen Months)

> The general state of trust . . .implies not only that one has learned to rely on the sameness and continuity of the outer providers, but also that one may trust oneself and the capacity of one's own organs to cope with urges; and that one is able to consider oneself trustworthy enough so that the providers will not need to be on guard lest they be nipped [Erikson, 1950, p. 248].

During early infancy, the foundation for later development is laid. The creation of trust through sensitive care of the infant's needs—both physical and emotional—is the basis of later identity. The trusting baby sleeps deeply, eats well, and enjoys bowel relaxation, thus showing his secure feeling that the world is a good place to live in. (This theory does not take into account temperamental differences that appear in infancy which prevent some children from showing their trust in these ways; see "Individual Differences in Temperament" later in this chapter.)

The Mother-Infant Relationship

According to Erikson (1950), this bond is an important determinant of the infant's sense of trust, especially in the feeding situation, with the *quality* of the mother-child relationship more important than its *quantity:*

The infant's first social achievement . . . is his willingness to let the mother out of sight without undue anxiety or rage, because she has become an inner certainty as well as an outer predictability [p. 247].

As the infant "finds that more and more adventures of the senses arouse a feeling of familiarity, of having coincided with a feeling of inner goodness," she correlates these comfortable, remembered sensations and images, and those that are only anticipated, with her world's "population of familiar and predictable things and people [p. 247]."

Erikson's period of trust versus mistrust coincides with Freud's oral stage, both in chronology and in the importance of early feeding experiences. Feeding alleviates the infant's generalized sense of discomfort, provides its own sensual satisfaction, establishes the infant's primary contact with the outside world, and has a certain regularity and consistency.

The mother, or caring person, brings the social world to the infant. The environment expresses itself through the mother's breast, or the bottle substitute. Love and the pleasure of dependency, which is so important in this phase, are conveyed to him by the mother's embrace, her comforting warmth, her smile, and the way she talks to him [Maier, 1969, p. 35].

Crisis II: Autonomy versus Shame and Doubt (Eighteen Months to Three Years)

The child's sense of trust in his mother and in the world leads him to a realization of his own sense of self. Realizing he has a will, he asserts himself. At the same time, however, he realizes the limitations of his abilities, and his continued dependency makes him *doubt* his ability to be autonomous. If he does not receive enough control from adults, he will develop his own "precocious conscience," and with it, a sense of *shame,* or "rage turned against the self."

Outer control at this stage, therefore, must be firmly reassuring. The infant must come to feel that the basic faith in existence, which is the lasting treasure saved from the ravages of the oral stage, will not be jeopardized by this about-face of his, this sudden violent wish to have a choice, to appropriate demandingly, and to eliminate stubbornly. Firmness must protect him against the potential anarchy of his as yet untrained sense of discretion. As his environment encourages **him** to "stand on his own feet," it must protect him against meaningless and arbitrary experiences of shame and early doubt [p. 252].

If a child fails to develop a sense of autonomy, either because of overly controlling or too permissive parents, he may become compulsive about controlling himself; for his fear of a loss of self-control may inhibit his self-expression, cause him to doubt himself, to be ashamed of himself, and, consequently, to suffer a loss in self-esteem.

(Annan Photo Features)

In Erikson's view, concepts of trust and autonomy are two key stages in ego development.

The push toward autonomy is partly maturational, as the child tries to use his developing muscles to do everything himself—to walk, to feed and dress himself, to eliminate when he feels like it and not when his parents want him to—in short, to expand his own boundaries whenever possible. Language markedly enhances a child's ability to make his wishes understood and, thus, to be autonomous. During the first phase, a mutual trust grew up between mother and child in which the child accepted doing what her mother wanted. Now, for the sake of her growth, this "agreement to agree" must be violated in her relentless quest to do everything herself, without her mother's guidance, direction, and help.

Parents play an important role in a child's search for and attainment of autonomy. They provide a safe harbor, with secure limits, from which she can set out and discover the world—and keep coming back to them for support.

The "terrible two's" are a normal manifestation of autonomy. Two-year-old Vicky tries out her independence by saying "no!" to everything, and the shift from the docile and agreeable baby she was to the terrible-tempered two-year-old she is now is normal. She has to test the new notion that she is an individual in her own right, that she can make her own decisions, and that she has new, hitherto undreamed-of powers.

(Jo Marks, Monkmeyer)

The Infant in the Family

Most theories and research projects on the emotional development of children have been based on the premise that a baby ideally grows up in a nuclear family, with both mother and father in the home, but no other adult relatives; that the mother assumes the primary, almost total, care of the infant, while the father's main role is to encourage and support the mother; and that the most important factor in a child's emotional well-being is the mother-baby bond. When a child turns out to be well adjusted, his mother is praised; when he has problems, she is blamed.

Although some psychological literature does use terms like "caretaker" or "caring person" instead of "mother," the almost universal implication is that a child's healthy emotional development is fostered almost entirely by good mothering. This emphasis on the importance of the mother has been influenced by our societal patterns, and, in turn, has reinforced these same patterns of family life. The father has been almost ignored by child developmentalists, who only now are recognizing the importance of doing more research on his impact on his children's development. As one psychologist (Wortis, 1971) has said:

> It is scientifically unacceptable to advocate the natural superiority of women as child-rearers and socializers of children when there have been so few studies of the effects of male-infant or father-infant interaction on the subsequent development of the child [p. 739].

We also need to know a great deal more about the influence of substitute parents on children's development.

In 1969, some 25 percent of all mothers of children under three years of age were in the labor force (Women's Bureau, 1970). Obviously, then, one-fourth of the nation's children under three do not receive the ministrations of an ever-present mother. These children are cared for in their mothers' absence by their fathers, other relatives, baby-sitters, day-care workers, and so forth. We need to know the crucial elements that encourage healthy development—physical, intellectual, and emotional—for these youngsters.

Children are reared in many ways—in the extended family; communally, as in Israel, Russia, and isolated spots in the United States; in two-parent families in which the father plays as large a role as the mother, or an even larger one; and in a combination of home and community, by which children spend much of their day in a group nursery and the rest of the time with their parents. It is quite likely that new theories of child development will evolve to keep in tune with the changing styles of family life.

For the bulk of this book, however, we will discuss the child in the context in which most children in our society grow up today—as one member of an individual nuclear family. And we will cite the research and the thinking based on this pattern of child rearing that have advanced our understanding of the emotional development of children. But always, we have to remember to keep an open mind, to reevaluate constantly, to add new knowledge to old, and to be ready to modify formerly cherished beliefs.

The kind of nurturance an infant receives within the family depends on a host of life circumstances: whether the pregnancy was planned and welcomed; the parents' personalities, life experiences, health, and ages; their financial circumstances; the number of adults living in the home; and the infant's own sex, inborn temperament, health, and birth order.

SEX DIFFERENCES IN INFANCY

As soon as a new baby is born, the parents' first question is, "Is the baby normal and healthy?" In the same breath, they ask, "What is it?" Once they know whether it is a boy or a girl, they know a basic fact of the infant's identity that will have a major effect on the child's development. First, this fact of sex may determine the degree of pleasure with which the baby is welcomed into the family. Then, in virtually every society, boys and girls are apt to develop considerably differently in social roles and in personality.

The moment a baby's sex is determined, it becomes an important factor in the way the baby will be treated. In the hospital, the infant wears a bracelet that says "Baby Girl Bernstein" or "Baby Boy Ciecuk." Baby Bernstein is swaddled in a pink blanket, Baby Ciecuk in blue. Baby Bernstein's first waterproof panties have ruffles, Baby Ciecuk's a baseball emblem. Baby Bernstein's first toy is a doll, Baby Ciecuk's a pair of squeaky rubber baseball gloves. As one psychiatrist has said, "From birth the child is allocated to one sex or the other and society begins to implant in him motives, interests, skills and attitudes appropriate to such membership [Kuffler, 1969]."

These differences in parental handling, which cover a wide range of activities, are often subconscious. Mothers, for example, are more likely, after their babies are three months old, to babble back to their infant daughters than to their sons (Moss, 1967), thus reinforcing verbalization and perhaps paving the way for verbal superiority in girls. Fathers talk to their baby boys in "a sort of hail-baby-well-met style," saying things like, "Come here, you little nut," or "Hey, fruitcake," while talking to and treating their baby girls much more gently (Shenker, 1971). And mothers are more indulgent and warmer toward their baby daughters than toward their sons (Sears, Maccoby, & Levin, 1957). It is probable that parents reward what they consider sex-appropriate behavior (little girls' nurturant play with dolls, sociability, and obedience, and little boys' attempts to be independent and self-reliant) with smiles and approval and encouragement, while punishing, or discouraging, sex-inappropriate behavior.

Early Behavior Differences between the Sexes

It has been only in recent years that studies of sex differences in children have gone into the nursery. One recent experiment sought to observe sex differences in mother-child relationships and in children's behavior (Goldberg & Lewis, 1969). Sixty-four infants, half boys and half girls, were seen on three occasions: at twelve weeks, six months, and thirteen months. As early as twelve weeks after birth, the mothers looked at and talked to their baby girls more than to their infant sons. In the first six months, they had more physical contact with their baby sons, but then the situation reversed so that the girls received more physical, as well as nonphysical, contact.

At thirteen months, the babies were observed individually in a playroom. For fifteen minutes, the baby was in a free-play situation with the mother present; then a fence was erected between mother and child. Significant differences showed up between the boys and the girls. The girls touched their mothers more, looked at them more, talked more to them, spent more time close to them, and were more reluctant to leave their side. After the barrier was erected, the girls spent more time crying and calling for help, whereas the boys spent more time trying to get around the barrier.

For the most part, boys and girls both liked the same toys: the lawnmower, the blocks, and the quoits. The girls were slightly more likely, though, to choose toys involving fine muscle coordination (the blocks, the pegboard, the toy dog and cat), while the boys chose toys involving gross motor coordination (the mallet, the lawnmower, and such nontoys as the doorknob and the electric outlet in the room). And the boys were more active, tending to run when they played.

Why were these girls more dependent on their mothers? One theory (Lewis, 1972) turns to the ways mothers treat their infants for an explanation. Since mothers in our society tend to believe that girls should be sociable and able to develop close relationships, they encourage their daughters to be close to them. But, believing that boys should be more independent, they encourage their sons to go off on their own. The children pick up on parental cues and respond accordingly. Another theory attributes the girls' greater dependency on their mothers in a strange situation to their more advanced maturation. "Since the major cause of fear in the first year of life is exposure to unfamiliar events, then the more acute your awareness of the world, the more vulnerable you will be to fear," says psychologist Jerome Kagan (Lang, 1973). In a sense, then, the price of girls' developmental precocity may well be more frequent anxiety. The girls are frightened in this situation because they realize its strangeness, but the boys don't recognize the elements of strangeness and don't become anxious.

(Annan Photo Features)

The moment a baby's sex is determined, it becomes an important factor in how the baby is treated; verbalization and dependency are two aspects of personality that can be affected.

There may well be some innate biological differences between males and females that help to determine their personality differences. Work with primate animals, for example, has found that the frequency and intensity of aggressive behavior is closely related to levels of the male hormone *testosterone* (Rose, 1972). Recent work with mice has shown that trace amounts of testosterone have an imprinting effect on the infant nervous system, without which aggressive behavior is not elicited in adult life (Bronson & Desjardins, 1969); and the hormone *prolactin,* which is released in a woman's body after childbirth, has been shown to induce motherly behavior, even when artificially administered to virgin or male animals (Levy, 1966).

Even if biological differences do exist, though, they provide no more than a hint of the direction that a child may follow. Society appears to do 90 percent of the job in determining which "sex-related" characteristics each individual child will assume. Ultimately, boy and girl children have more in common than they have differences. They have the same basic needs for food, shelter, and love. They approach the same developmental milestones intellectually, physically, and emotionally. And there are much greater differences between individual children of the same sex than there are between the "average" male child and the "average" female child.

INDIVIDUAL DIFFERENCES IN TEMPERAMENT

The way Vicky is cared for is due, not only to her parents' personalities, but to her own personality as well. Like all infants, she develops, soon after birth, her own unique style of approaching people and situations, or what we call her *temperament.* In Chapter 2 we discussed nine different facets of personality in which babies differ almost from the day they are born. Such innate traits help to set the climate in the home.

Vicky, for example, wakes up happy. At a year of age, she wakes up occasionally in the middle of the night, but instead of crying for her parents, she amuses herself till she falls asleep again by playing with a musical crib toy. By contrast, Jason wakes up with a howl. His mouth opens to cry before his eyes open to see. Such differences in disposition, which tend to be consistent over a variety of situations and over the years, are bound to influence the way a child's parents feel about and act toward him or her.

Aside from overall mood, babies show other temperamental differences that make them easy or difficult to care for, and to love. Since Vicky has a very regular biological time clock and gets hungry and sleepy at predictable times, it is relatively easy for her parents to put her on a schedule and to toilet train her. It is much easier for them to plan their own schedules than it is for Jason's parents, who never know when he will wake to eat, when he will move his bowels, or when he will get sleepy. Whereas Vicky eagerly welcomes new situations, Jason needs more time to warm up to a new person, a new place, or even a new food; this is another factor in the

(Enid Elliot)

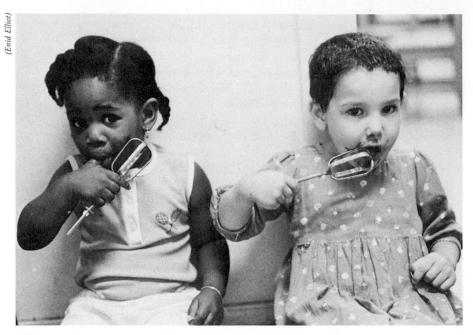

Differences in temperament also account for individuality and bring important practical considerations for parents.

child-rearing equation. Overall, then, Vicky is an easy baby, Jason a difficult one.

Knowledge of inborn personality differences bears important practical considerations for parents. First, an awareness that each child brings with him into this world his own stock of predispositions should relieve parents—most especially the parents of a difficult baby—from feeling guilty. A baby may be a poor sleeper, a poor eater, and a constant cryer, not because of emotional deprivation, but because that's the way he is. Realizing this, parents can shed their guilt and respond more positively to their child.

Recognition of a child's unique way of approaching life should also help parents adapt their child-rearing practices to an understanding of their own child's characteristics and needs. Although most children are fairly adaptable to a variety of child-rearing practices, there always seems to be a minority for whom a particular approach will not work. This is because of the very special needs of individual children. Because of these needs, "there can be no universally valid set of rules that will work equally well for all children everywhere [Thomas et al., 1963, p. 150]." Thus the parents of a highly rhythmic child like Vicky can use a "demand" feeding schedule, letting the baby set the pace, whereas the parents of a highly irregular child like Jason will do better to institute a flexible schedule that is based on the needs of both baby and parents. Jason's parents have to learn to gradually introduce new people, foods, and places. The parents of Emily, who is highly sensitive to sensory stimulation, have to learn the necessity of changing her diapers as soon as they are soiled, of keeping room temperatures even, and of avoiding bright lights and loud noises, and so on (Chess, 1965).

Most of all, a recognition of a child's basic temperament relieves parents of a feeling of omnipotence—that they, and they alone, are responsible for turning her out in a certain mold.

BIRTH ORDER

If you were your parents' first child, you may be more likely than your younger brothers and sisters to want company in times of stress, to be enrolled in an elite college, to make it into the pages of *Who's Who*, and to become an astronaut. Since 1874, investigators have sought to determine the influence of position in the family on personality and achievement. Although their findings are often inconsistent and contradictory, some interesting relationships have turned up.

When participants in a study of gregariousness were given the choice of waiting alone or with someone for an electric shock, more first-born and only children wanted company than did later-borns (Schachter, 1959). In 1874, Sir Francis Galton found more first-born and only children in the ranks of eminent scientists than the laws of chance would dictate, and since then similar findings have been made for listees in *Who's Who in America*, enrollees at academically selective colleges, and National Merit Scholarship finalists (Irwin, 1969). All seven of the original Mercury astronauts were first-born or only children; twelve of fifteen candidates for the Gemini project were eldest or only male children; and sixteen of the twenty-eight Sealab aquanauts were eldest or only children (Helmreich, 1968). When 400,000 nineteen-year-old Dutch men were tested for intelligence on the Raven Progressive Matrices, a definite birth-order relationship showed up (Belmont & Marolla, 1973).

> Within each family size (i) firstborns always scored better on the Raven than did later borns; and (ii) with few inconsistencies, there was a gradient of declining scores with rising birth order, so that firstborns scored better than secondborns, who in turn scored better than thirdborns, and so forth. At each family size, earlier borns performed better on the Raven than those in the adjacent birth order position [p. 182].

We can explain the greater competitive drive, greater achievement, and greater sociability of first and only children (Helmreich, 1968) in several ways. First, these children have only adult models on whom to base their behavior. Although this may inspire them to try harder to overcome the awesome gap between adult and juvenile competence, it may also make them less sure of themselves as achievement of this goal eludes them. Then, parents treat their first child differently. They are more consumed with his upbringing: they devote more time to him, proudly admire his every little achievement, take more photos of him, expect more of him, punish him more, and give him more responsibilities. At the same time, they are more unsure of themselves than they will be with later children, and their own anxiety is bound to affect the child they learn on.

In the minds of most researchers, though, birth order as a factor in personality is still subordinate to such other elements as intelligence, inborn temperament, socioeconomic status, and overall parental values.

THE MOTHER'S ROLE IN PERSONALITY DEVELOPMENT

Judging from the literature, most child developmentalists appear to agree with Napoleon, who once said, "My opinion is that the future good or bad conduct of a child entirely depends upon the mother." In our society, as in most societies around the world, the mother has traditionally been the person who gives primary care to a child. And the nature of the relationship between a child and her primary caretaker has a great and long-lasting influence on her emotional and social development. But it has not been proved that the primary caretaker has to be the child's biological mother. Nor has it been proved that a baby cannot thrive just as well with two or three primary caretakers. More research is needed on adult-child relationships with caring adults other than the mother—father, grandparents, baby-sitters, day-care workers, and so forth. For now, however, the information that we have usually refers to the relationship between a child and his mother, and there is no doubt that this is a vital, basic bond.

Imprinting

In 1873 the English naturalist D. A. Spalding found that newly hatched chicks would follow the first moving objects they saw, whether this object was a member of their own species or not, and would become increasingly attached to the object they first followed. In 1937 the Austrian ethologist Konrad Lorenz described this behavior as *imprinting*, an innate, instinctual, rapid form of learning that takes place during a critical period in the animal's life to enable it to form its first social relationship.

Usually this first attachment is to the mother, but if the natural sequence of events is altered for any reason, other, often bizarre, attachments will take place. Lorenz found that if he waddled, honked, and flapped his arms, and presented himself thus to a newborn duckling, that duckling would "love him like a mother [Lorenz, 1937]." In childhood it would follow him about, and at sexual maturity it would court human beings instead of animals of its own species (Lorenz, 1952; 1957). Chicks and ducks have responded similarly to footballs, cubes, and dangling tin cans.

Among higher animals, like sheep, goats, and cows, imprinting occurs through certain standardized rituals between mother and child that occur during a critical period right after birth. If these rituals are prevented or interrupted, neither the mother nor the baby will recognize each other, and no mother-child attachment will ever take place. The results for the baby are devastating—either physical withering and eventual death or abnormal, neurotic development (Blauvelt, 1955; Scott, 1958; Moore, 1960).

Although it is valuable to seek relevance for human development in such a phenomenon, it is always dangerous to extrapolate animal findings too completely to human beings. As much more complex creatures, we rely far less on instinct than do the lower animals, and except in extreme situations, we can often overcome early adverse experiences. Thus, while there is evidence that there is a specific time period during which the mother-infant bond is formed—the second half of the first year of life—its absence during this time may be overcome by later, compensatory parental or substitute-parental care. Children who have been institutionalized during this time of life and have then been adopted before the age of two have recovered both physically and mentally (Dennis, 1973). Furthermore, most adopted children form close, loving ties with their adoptive parents and grow up to be well adjusted.

The significance of our studies of imprinting in animals may well be to determine just what behaviors do take place on the parts of both mother and child that help to form this bond and, thus, to better understand it.

Harry and Margaret Harlow's studies on mother-infant relationships among rhesus monkeys have pointed to a number of factors that seem to be important in forming this essential bond among these animals, who are so close to human beings in so many ways. In one study, a critical period for establishing the mother-child bond appears to have been set, since infant monkeys who were removed from their mothers for a crucial three weeks showed intense emotional distress after separation. They rocked and stared and remained isolated, and at sexual maturity were unable to mate normally (Harlow & Harlow, 1962).

In another famous study, Harlow separated rhesus monkeys from their mothers six to twelve hours after birth and raised them in the University of Wisconsin Primate Laboratory. The infants were placed in cages with one of two surrogate mothers. One "mother" was a plain wire mesh cylindrical form, and the other was covered with terry cloth. Some of the monkeys were fed from bottles connected to the wire monkey; others were "nursed" by the warm, cuddly cloth "mothers." The cloth figures turned out to be much better "mothers" than the wire ones.

When the monkeys were allowed to spend time with either surrogate mother, they all spent more time clinging to the cloth ones—even if they were being fed totally by the wire mother. When the babies were placed in an unfamiliar room, those "raised" by the cloth mothers showed more of a natural interest in exploring than did those "raised" by the wire mothers, when the appropriate "mothers" were present (Harlow & Zimmerman, 1959). The monkeys remembered the cloth mothers better, too; after a year's separation, the cloth-raised monkeys eagerly ran to embrace the terry cloth forms, whereas the wire-raised monkeys showed no interest in the wire forms after such a separation (Harlow & Zimmerman, 1959).

From these studies, Harlow concluded that the essential feature of the mother-infant relationship is not the mere provision of nutrients, but, instead, the comfort provided by close bodily contact. Only the cloth mothers were able to satisfy the baby monkeys' innate need to cling, for example. Unfortunately, though, even the cloth-raised monkeys did not grow up normally. Although they seemed normal on the surface, a major problem showed up when, at maturity, Harlow wanted to mate them to produce more experimental animals. It was only then that he found that these monkeys, even the cloth-raised ones, were sexually inadequate—unable to mate normally (Harlow & Harlow, 1962). It is not surprising that

(Erika Stone, from Peter Arnold)

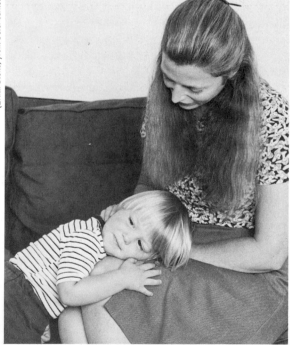

It isn't surprising that a cloth dummy cannot provide the kind of stimulation that a normal, live, species-specific mother does.

a cloth dummy should not provide the same kind of stimulation that a normal, live, species-specific mother does, and one of the most important thrusts in modern psychology is to find out just exactly what parents do to achieve normal emotional development in their children.

Attachment between Mother and Child

In psychological terms, this attachment is an active, affectionate, reciprocal relationship specifically between these two individuals as distinguished from all other persons. The interaction between the two continues to reinforce and strengthen their bond.

When Vicky's mother first set eyes on her new baby, she was dismayed and guilt-ridden to realize that she felt no great surge of love for this infant she had borne. But there was nothing abnormal about this young mother. Maternal love is not an instinct; it does not come about automatically with the birth of a baby, but, in fact, takes time to develop. In one study (Robson & Moss, 1970), only about half of a group of fifty-four new mothers said that they had had positive feelings when they first saw their babies; only 13 percent identified those feelings as love; and 34 percent had no feelings at all for their babies on first sight. They said things like "I felt nothing" or "it was neutral [p. 978]."

It took most of the mothers about three weeks to begin to feel love for their babies. This love was strengthened by the babies' own behavior. As the babies smiled at their mothers, looked into their eyes, or watched them as they moved, their mothers' love grew toward them. By the end of the third month, most of the mothers were strongly attached to their babies.

A mother's own general attitude toward children, her own life experiences (the kind of childhood she had herself, for example), her present circumstances, and her personality all play a part in awakening mother love. And so do actions initiated by the baby. Virtually any activity on the baby's part that leads to a response from an adult caretaker is an attachment behavior. Such behaviors are sucking, crying, smiling, clinging, choking, hiccoughing, moving the body, changing the rhythm of breathing, sneezing, burping, looking into the mother's eyes, and even soiling the diapers (Bowlby, 1958; 1959; Robson, 1967; Richards, 1971).

Vicky initiated some of these behaviors right from birth, and as early as the eighth week of life was initiating them more toward her mother than to anyone else. Her overtures were successful because her mother responded warmly by giving her frequent physical contact and freedom to explore and showing delight in dealing with her (Ainsworth, 1969). Her mother's sensitive responses to Vicky's signals gave the baby a sense of consequence for her own actions and a feeling of power and self-confidence in her ability to bring about results. Some infant behaviors that are important in the formation of mother-child attachment are shown in Chart 6-1.

Chart 6-1 Patterns of Attachment Behavior Shown by the Infant in Interaction with His or Her Mother *(Adapted from Ainsworth, 1964)*

"This catalogue of thirteen patterns of attachment behavior omits behavior associated with feeding . . . because I wanted to distinguish attachment to the mother as a person from mere attachment to the breast as a need-satisfying object [Ainsworth, 1964, p. 609]."

This chart is based on Dr. Ainsworth's observations of twenty-eight African babies, aged two to fifteen months. They may have been more accelerated in their development of attachment than American babies because they were accelerated in development in general, because all but one were breastfed, and because they were almost always with people, as opposed to remaining alone for long periods in their cribs. But while the timing of these behaviors may vary from culture to culture, the behaviors themselves are universal, and the sequence probably holds true for babies everywhere.

Behavior	Earliest Observation	Commonly Observed
Differential crying (cries when held by someone else, but stops when picked up by mother)	8 weeks	12 weeks
Differential smiling (smiles more readily to mother)	(9 weeks)	(32 weeks)
Differential vocalization (babbles and coos more to mother)	(20 weeks)	

Ainsworth (1964), who studied attachment in African babies aged two to fifteen months, noted four overlapping stages of attachment behavior during the first year:

1 First the infant responds indiscriminately to anyone.

2 Beginning at about eight to twelve weeks, the baby cries, smiles, and babbles more to the mother than to anyone else, but continues to respond to others.

3 At six or seven months, the infant shows a sharply defined attachment to the mother, with a corresponding waning of indiscriminate friendliness to others. He follows her more, cries more when she leaves, and uses her as a secure base from which to explore the world.

4 Overlapping this stage, the baby develops an attachment to one or more familiar figures other than the mother, such as the father or the siblings. Anywhere from six to eight months, fear of strangers usually appears.

Chart 6-1 (Continued)

Visual-motor orientation (keeps looking at mother, even when apart from her)	(18 weeks)	
Crying when mother leaves the room	15 weeks	25 weeks
Following (creeps or walks after mother when she leaves the room)	17 weeks	25 weeks
Scrambling (climbs over mother more often than over others, exploring her person, playing with her face, hair and clothes)	(10 weeks)	(30 weeks)
Burying the face in mother's lap (this was observed only in relation to mother)	(22 weeks)	(30 weeks)
Exploration from mother as a secure base (leaves her side but returns from time to time; in contrast to distress when mother herself gets up and goes away)	28 weeks	33 weeks
Clinging (when afraid of stranger, when ill, or when mother returns after an absence)	25 weeks	40 weeks
Lifting arms in greeting (after mother's absence)	(17 weeks)	(22 weeks)
Clapping hands in greeting	(28 weeks)	(40 weeks)
Approach through locomotion (creeping or walking to mother as soon as possible after she returns from an absence)	(26 weeks)	(30 weeks)

The fact that babies who have the chance to interact with other people besides the mother become attached to them, too, supports Bowlby's position and Harlow's findings that an infant does not become attached to his mother only because she feeds him. This would appear to be a strong argument for opening up the mothering experience to others besides the biological mother. Even though the mother is the only one who can nurse her baby, she is not the only one who can comfort him by holding him close, provide security from a threatening world, play with him, and so forth. Fathers, grandparents, friends, and baby-sitters can do this, too.

How the infant's personality affects attachment. In many ways, the parent-child relationship is similar to the marital tie. And yet parents can't choose their infants as they choose their spouses. Brian's parents, for example, are lively, exuberant people who are always on the move, always eager to try new experiences, and always doing things quickly. They are impatient with their son's personality, since he is quiet and shy, and such a "good," docile baby that they consider him somewhat namby-pamby.

On the other hand, Nancy's parents are quiet people who like to live according to a fairly well-established routine. Nancy drives them to distraction because she has a highly irregular body rhythm, is completely unpredictable, always in motion, and likely to react intensely to each new experience. If these two babies could have been switched around in one of those hospital mix-ups that, in these days of instant foot-printing and wrist-banding, never seem to happen anymore, both families might find the going easier. But since the likelihood is that both Brian and Nancy will stay with their own families, their respective parents will have to learn how to adapt to their children's personalities.

The New York Longitudinal Study, mentioned in Chapter 2 (Thomas, Chess, & Birch, 1968), found wide variations among children's personalities, right from birth. Parents are likely to react differently to their children, depending on the children's personalities and how well they mesh with their own. Ainsworth and Bell (1969) emphasize the importance of *both* members of an attachment bond:

> Whatever role may be played by the baby's constitutional characteristics in establishing the initial pattern of mother-infant interaction, it seems quite clear that the mother's contribution to the interaction and the baby's contribution are caught up in an interacting spiral [p. 160, quoted in Stone et al., 1973].

Schaffer and Emerson (1964) looked at the formation of the mother-infant bond with "cuddlers" (infants who enjoyed physical contact) and "noncuddlers" (those who usually tried to break free). They found that not all infants eagerly seek physical contact. This was determined in an interview study of thirty-four normal infants of working-class parents. Interviews with the mothers took place every four weeks during the first year, and once more at eighteen months. Nineteen infants were cuddlers, nine were noncuddlers, and nine were in the middle, accepting cuddling with reservation. The noncuddlers sought visual, rather than physical, contact with their mothers for reassurance. They protested *close* physical contact. They accepted other kinds of physical handling—being swung, kissed, and tickled—but they did not want their movements restrained.

The degree of the babies' attachment was assessed "by the reaction to the object's withdrawal in any of the separation situations which tend to occur in the everyday life of all infants [p. 5]," such as being left alone or with other people, or being put down. By twelve months, the noncuddlers had formed less intense attachments. But by eighteen months, no differences were found between cuddlers and noncuddlers. Reduced physical contact seems to be associated with the establishment of social attachments to only a minor extent. This ties in with Rheingold's belief (1961) that visual rather than physical contact may be at the root of human sociability.

Stranger Anxiety

What has happened to Vicky? She used to be such a friendly baby, smiling at anyone who took the trouble to pay any attention to her, going freely to strangers, continuing to coo happily when her parents left the room, as long as someone—anyone—was around. Now, at eight months, she seems like a different baby. She howls when a new person approaches her or when her father tries to leave her with a baby-sitter. Has she changed her disposition? No, she has just become astute enough to recognize the difference between the people she knows and the ones she doesn't. Thus stranger anxiety is one indication that attachment has occurred.

One study (Morgan & Ricciuti, 1968) observed the onset of stranger anxiety in eight boys and eight girls, aged $4^{1}/_{2}$, $6^{1}/_{2}$, $8^{1}/_{2}$, $10^{1}/_{2}$, and $12^{1}/_{2}$ months. In two different situations—seated on the mother's lap and with the mother 4 feet away—the baby was approached by a stranger and was presented with Halloween masks that showed a smiling face and a distorted face. The younger babies smiled at the strangers and the masks, but at about $12^{1}/_{2}$ months, the babies started to cry and frown. Some infants also reacted negatively at $6^{1}/_{2}$, $8^{1}/_{2}$, and $10^{1}/_{2}$ months. The intensity, though, was greatest by $12^{1}/_{2}$ months. There were no sex differences. The infants of $8^{1}/_{2}$ months and older reacted more negatively when separated from their mothers by 4 feet, but the younger infants showed no difference in lap-sitting and separation conditions. The older the babies, then, the more important was their physical closeness to their mothers in determining how they would react to strangers.

Children of all ages reacted positively to the masks, although the older ones liked them better. The older children reacted more positively to the masks than to the stranger, with a slight preference for the distorted mask. It's possible that the children liked the masks because they saw them as toys rather than as distorted faces.

The number of adults a baby is familiar with influences her degree of stranger anxiety. Babies raised around few adults show more stranger anxiety than those raised by a greater number (Schaffer & Emerson, 1964), and those raised by many adults, as in a kibbutz, don't show stranger anxiety at all (Spiro, 1958).

Not surprisingly, parents' behavior affects their babies' social behavior. The more suppressive and critical a mother is of her baby, the less responsive he will be to her. And the more he responds to his mother, the less he will respond to a stranger (Beckwith, 1972). Thus stranger anxiety seems to bear an inverse relationship to a baby's closeness to his parents.

Stranger anxiety also seems to be related to the way a mother stimulates the baby in the first three months of life. When fifty-four first-time mothers and their babies were observed for degree of maternal stimulation at one and three months of age, and then for degree of stranger anxiety at 8 to $9^{1}/_{2}$ months, an inverse relationship showed up. The more auditory and visual stimulation a baby received, the less stranger anxiety he was likely to show (Moss, Robson, & Pederson, 1969).

Infants whose mothers sat them in front of a television set, shook toys in front of their faces, or put them close to radios and music boxes were less

Social Development in the First Year (*Adapted from Caplan, 1973*)

1 Week

Smiles spontaneously and fleetingly to sensory stimulation like soft sounds. Shows excitement and distress.

1 Month

May smile back at face or voice. Eyes fix on mother's face in response to her smile. Makes eye-to-eye contact. Looks at faces and quiets down. Responds positively to comfort and satisfaction, negatively to pain.

2 Months

Shows distress, excitement, delight. Smiles at people besides the mother (father, siblings, etc.). Quiets when held.

3 Months

Smiles immediately and spontaneously. Crying decreases dramatically. Knows several people. May stop or start crying according to who holds him. Cries differentially when mother leaves, versus other people. Smiles, babbles, orients differently to mother's presence or voice. Chortles, squeals with frustration, whimpers with hunger, smacks lips.

4 Months

Vocalizes moods, enjoyment, indecision, protest. Laughs while socializing; wails if play is disrupted. Shows anticipation, excites, breathes heavily. Is much more sociable. Interested in mirror image.

5 Months

Shows fear and anger. Discriminates self and mother in mirror. Smiles to mirror image, human faces and voices. May distinguish familiar and unfamiliar adults. Smiles or babbles to make social contact. Stops crying when spoken to. Expresses protest—resists adult who tries to take toy. Frolics when played with. Plays with rattle, pats bottle or breast. Raises arms to be picked up.

6 Months

Smiles at mirror image, other children. Distinguishes children from adults. Plays peek-a-boo, come-and-get-me, go and fetch. Tries to imitate facial expression. Turns when hears own name.

7 Months

May fear strangers and cry at their presence. Shows humor; teases. Resists pressure to do something he doesn't want to. Distinguishes friendly and angry talking. Plays with toys.

8 Months

Tries to kiss mirror image. Fears strangers, separation from mother. Awakens or quiets to mother's voice. Shouts for attention. Pushes away what he doesn't want. Rejects confinement.

9 Months

Perceives mother and probably father as separate persons. Performs for home audience; repeats act if applauded. Cries if other children cry, is interested in other people's play. Initiates play. Plays pat-a-cake, so-big, bye-bye, and ball games. May play out new fears. Fights for disputed toy. Begins to evaluate people's moods and motives.

10 Months

Increases dependence on mother. Tries to alter mother's plans through persuasion or protest. Asserts self among siblings. Obeys commands. Seeks approval but is not always cooperative. Establishes meaning of "no." Shows guilt at wrongdoing. May tease and test parental limits. Plays parallel to, not with, another child.

12 Months

Expresses many emotions and recognizes them in others. Distinguishes self from others. Fears strange people and places. Reacts sharply to separation from mother. Develops sense of humor. Is affectionate to humans and objects. Negativism increases. Refuses eating; resists napping. May have tantrums. Plays games with understanding; may give up toys on request. Definitely prefers certain people to others.

Social development during the first year is a process of learning who's who. Parents, self, and strangers are discovered.

(Horst Schaefer, Photo Trends)

likely to fear strangers later on. The authors of this report (Moss, Robson, & Pederson, 1969) explain this relationship in these terms:

> Children who are accustomed to experiencing novel auditory and visual stimulation may have a better "set" for coping with and assimilating "strangeness." Strange stimuli are less novel and thus evoke less of a sense of subjective uncertainty for these children [p. 246].

Cross-cultural Styles of Mothering

Different styles of mothering can influence infant personality development, as seen, for example, by looking at Zinacanteco Indian mothers in southern Mexico during their babies' first nine months of life (Brazelton et al., 1969). These mothers maintain close physical contact with their infants throughout the early months, nurse them at the littlest whimper, and swaddle them, restraining their physical movement. The mothers rarely talk to their babies **or look** closely into their faces to get a response. At nine months of age, the infants are quite different from American babies. They hardly babble or mouth their hands; they never suck their fingers; and they maintain alert states for a much longer time. The researchers (Brazelton et al., 1969) explained these differences as follows:

> Zinacanteco mothering practices, while culturally uniform, seemed well fitted to [the controlled and alert] characteristics of their infants. By swaddling the infant,

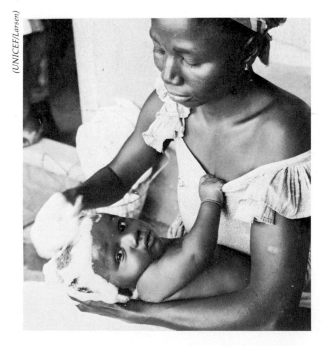

(UNICEF/Larsen)

Styles of mothering in different cultures—or subcultures—also influence development of social behavior.

through the close physical contact maintained with the child during all the early months, and by nursing at the earliest signs of restlessness or vocalization, these mothers seemed to establish and maintain a kind of physical kinesthetic communication with their babies which re-inforced the suppression of extraneous motor activity and enhanced the fluid and moderate characteristics of the infants' state behavior. [M]other and child interaction appeared to foster quiet alertness conducive to imitation and conformity. . . . Imitation seems to be the chief mode of learning. Fantasy play, games of imagination, and innovation are rarely seen in Zinacanteco children [pp. 287–288].

Mothering styles differ even between subcultures in the same society, as indicated by a study (Tulkin & Kagan, 1972) that compared American middle-class and working-class mothers and their ten-month-old babies. The middle-class mothers talked more to their babies, tried harder to entertain them, gave them more toys, and responded more to their fretfulness. No class differences showed up, however, in the amount of time the mothers spent close to their babies, in the amount of time they held

(Elliott Erwitt, Magnum)

them, in the number of times they said "no" to them, or in their positive responses to the babies' nonverbal behaviors. The greatest differences that appeared were *within* the two groups, which may indicate that mother-baby interaction is more a function of the individual personalities involved than of any class differences.

The middle-class mothers' tendency to talk more to their infants may reflect different concepts of babyhood. Since the working-class mothers felt their babies could not communicate, they thought it was foolish to talk to them. The middle-class mothers, though, felt strongly that they could influence infant development even in the early months. And so they talked.

Maternal Deprivation

What happens to infants who are deprived of their mothers early in life? For years, child-care professionals have maintained that such deprivation—in the absence of a single mother-substitute—could bring about long-term deficits in physical, emotional, and intellectual development. This would appear to be not only because of the absence of the mother, but also because of the sensory deprivation her absence would imply. What, after all, do mothers (and mother-substitutes) do? For one thing, they give babies a wide spectrum of sensory stimulation. They pick them up, they cuddle them, they rock them, they speak to them, they play with them, and, most of all, they love them. The effects of separation from the mother would seem to be borne out by the dismal record that foundling homes have had throughout history, with from 31.7 to 90 percent of the babies in their care dying by the end of the first year of life (Spitz, 1945).

The devastating effect of institutionalizing healthy children for long periods of time has been termed *hospitalism*, as distinct from hospitalization, which refers to the hospital care of a seriously ill child (Spitz, 1945). To investigate hospitalism, René Spitz (1945, 1946) compared 134 institutionalized children under one year of age with a control group of 34 home-reared children. At the end of the first year, the control children and those in *one* of the institutions ("Nursery") were "well-developed and normal." Those in the other institution ("Foundling Home"), whose status had at first been almost as high as the best of the others, had "spectacularly deteriorated."

How did these two institutions differ? The babies in Nursery were the offspring of delinquent girls, many of whom were either emotionally disturbed or mentally retarded. Those in Foundling Home came from a variety of backgrounds, many of which were far more favorable than those of the Nursery babies. The children in Nursery had more toys and enjoyed a brighter, more interesting, and more stimulating environment. But the most significant difference between the two homes revolved around the amount of personal attention given to the babies. In Nursery all the babies received full-time care from their own mothers or from individual full-time substitutes. In Foundling Home each nurse took care of eight children.

It is obvious that the amount of care one nurse can give to an individual child when she has eight children to manage is small indeed. These nurses are unusually motherly, baby-loving women; but of course the babies of Foundling Home nevertheless lack all human contact for most of the day [Spitz, 1945, p. 781].

Spitz concluded:

We believe that the children in Foundling Home suffer because their perceptual world is emptied of human partners, that their isolation cuts them off from any stimulation by any persons who could signify mother-representatives for the child at this age. The result is a complete restriction of psychic capacity by the end of the first year [p. 784].

For the Foundling Home children, hospitalism brought more than psychic disturbance. Their physical development was retarded on both height and weight, and they were much more susceptible to disease, often fatally so. Furthermore, their developmental quotients, which had started out at 124, sank to 75 by the end of the first year, and plummeted to 45 by the end of the second.

Spitz's studies were significant in pointing out the urgency of providing foster care that approached "good mothering" as closely as possible. As Stone et al. (1973) comment:

The ensuing spate of interest in maternal deprivation produced both research and social reform. Practically, Spitz's work hastened the trends toward use of foster homes rather than institutions and toward much earlier adoptions; it obviously made no sense to follow the common practice of the 1930's and 1940's of delaying adoption until a better IQ determination could be made (for purposes of matching infant and adoptive parents) if the delay itself resulted in severe damage to the very IQ that was to be studied [p. 754].

In another effort to assess the effects of a young infant's separation from his mother, John Bowlby (1960) observed the reactions of fifteen- to thirty-month-old infants who had to be hospitalized. These babies went through three fairly well-defined stages of what Bowlby termed *separation anxiety*: *protest*, *despair*, and *detachment*.

In the *protest* stage, the infant actively tried to get his mother back by any means at his disposal; he cried, shook his crib, threw himself about, and continually expected her to return. Then *despair* set in, with increasing hopelessness. The child diminished his active movements, although he was likely to cry monotonously or intermittently. He became withdrawn and inactive and, because he was so quiet, was often assumed to be in a state of positive acceptance of the situation. In the final stage, *detachment*, the child accepted care from a succession of nurses; he ate, played with toys, and even smiled and was sociable. But the clue to his distress appeared when his mother visited. Rather than cling to her, he remained apathetic and even turned away from her. Children between the ages of six months and four years of age are most likely to react in this way, but even within this age range not all show this degree of disturbance (Rutter, 1971).

The studies of Spitz and Bowlby indicate that total replacement of a child's primary caretakers and familiar environment, with an around-the clock institutional setting, can produce severe emotional disturbance, at least on a short-term basis. But Rutter (1971) concluded, after conducting his own studies of children who had experienced various types and lengths of separation from one or both parents and after reviewing the literature, that "children can be separated from their parents for quite long periods in early childhood with surprisingly little in the way of long-term ill effects [p. 238]."

Rutter found that children separated from *one* parent for at least four consecutive weeks (his criterion of a separation experience) were no more likely to develop any kind of psychiatric or behavior disorder than were children who had never been separated. It did not seem to matter how old the child was when the separation occurred, nor which was the absent parent—the father or the mother. Children separated from *both* parents were more likely to develop a psychological disturbance, but even in this case it was not only the *fact* of separation that was important, but the *reason* behind the separation. When the separation was due to family discord or deviance, children were four times as likely to show antisocial behavior than if the separation was due to a vacation or to physical illness of either child or parent. Furthermore, children separated from both parents were more likely to become disturbed if the parents' marriage were rated "very poor" than if it were rated "good" or "fair."

Many observers have claimed that full-time mothering, especially in the early years, is essential for the healthy development of children. Rutter, though, found that some separation experience may actually be beneficial, since "children used to brief separations of a happy kind are less distressed by *unhappy* separations such as hospital admission [p. 237]." He also looked into the situations of working mothers whose children are cared for during the day by one or more caretakers other than their mothers, and concluded (1971):

> There is no evidence that children suffer from having several mother-figures so long as stable relationships and good care are provided by each (Moore, 1963). This is an important proviso but one which applies equally to mothers who are not working. A situation in which mother-figures keep changing so that the child does not have the opportunity of forming a relationship with any of them may well be harmful, but such unstable arrangements usually occur in association with poor quality maternal care, so that up to now it has not been possible to examine the effects of each independently [p. 238].

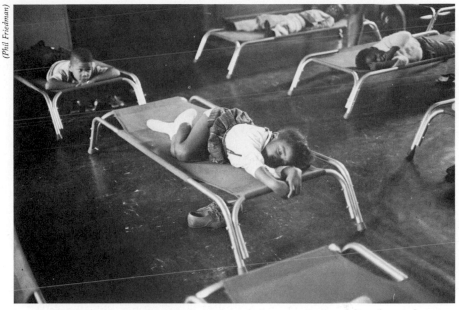

An around-the-clock institutional setting can produce severe emotional disturbance, but some separation experience may actually be beneficial.

Nothing has been found to indict day-care services for infants. There is no evidence that removing a child from her home for part, or even most, of her day and then returning her to her own home and family on evenings and weekends has any ill effects (Yarrow et al., 1962; Yudkin & Holme, 1969).

Separation anxiety is more severe in the second half of the first year of life than in the first (Yarrow, 1963). A group of adopted children who were separated from their primary caretakers before three months of age rarely showed any disturbance at the move, but when the separation occurred at six months, most infants showed disturbed behavior. Those separated between seven months and a year showed such severe emotional reactions as blunted social responses, clinging, crying, apathy, sleeping and eating problems, and a decline in IQ and abilities.

Enriching the environment of the maternally deprived child. In one effort to determine the effects of substitute mothering on institutionalized babies, Rheingold (1956) herself mothered a group of eight 6-month-old infants. For 7½ hours a day, 5 days a week, for 8 weeks, she played with them, fed them, diapered them, and did whatever a mother would do. A group of eight control infants got the usual institutional care, which meant adequate attention to their physical needs from a variety of caretakers.

After two months, the mothered babies were dramatically different from the control babies, much more likely to smile and babble not only to the experimenter but also to other adults. A year and a half later, the experimental babies still vocalized more than the control babies, but there were no other differences between the two groups of babies, all of whom were now in foster or adoptive homes. This might be because the period of enrichment was too brief to bring about any lasting changes. Or possibly the individual care all the babies eventually received in their new homes had made up for their initial institutional experience.

Another study of enrichment for institutionalized children did yield striking long-term results (Skeels & Dye, 1939; Skeels, 1969). Thirteen apparently retarded two-year-olds were moved from an orphanage to an institution for mentally retarded young adults. In the institution, the retarded adolescent girls and young women doted on the babies and spent a lot of time playing with, talking to, and training "their" children. As adults, all thirteen of these children were functioning in the community, married, with normal children of their own. Four had attended college. By contrast, a control group of twelve youngsters who had remained in the orphanage until later placement had a much lower average IQ, and four were still in institutions.

More recently, old people in a Foster Grandparent program (Saltz, 1973) rocked, fed, walked, and talked to a group of eighty-one institutionalized babies for four hours a day, five days a week. They read stories, played games, talked with, and taught skills to older children. After four years of foster grandparenting, these children had made considerable gains in IQ and in social competence as compared with a control group in a similar institution without foster grandparents. This study, like the two previous ones, indicates that individual attention from a warm, affectionate person can compensate to a considerable degree for the absence of a close mother-child relationship.

THE FATHER'S ROLE IN PERSONALITY DEVELOPMENT

John Bowlby (1951), who attributes great psychological importance to the mother-baby relationship, has expressed the traditional view of the infant's father: "In the young child's eyes, father plays second fiddle and his value increases only as the child's vulnerability to deprivation decreases [p. 363]." This prejudice against fathers is rampant in our society and in most others, but it appears to be losing some ground. Finally, more attention is being paid to the father-baby relationship.

One research team (Rebelsky & Hanks, 1972) made six 24-hour tapes of father-baby interaction for each of a group of ten lower-middle-class to upper-middle-class fathers of two-week-old to three-month-old babies. The tapes showed that these fathers spoke very little to their infants. The average father in the group spent 37.7 seconds per day doing things with or for his baby, and the most devoted spent less than $10\frac{1}{2}$ minutes a day with his baby. Initially, these men spent more time talking to their infant

(Erika Stone, from Peter Arnold)

Our new awareness of the father's importance to his children comes at a time of social change, when more men are assuming larger roles in the care of their children.

daughters, but by the time the babies were three months old, the sons were getting more attention. By the end of the study, the fathers were spending less time talking to their babies than they had at the beginning, and especially to their baby daughters. These findings are actually the reverse of mother-baby interactions, which are more frequent in the beginning for baby boys, and after three months, shifted to baby girls (Moss, 1967). The mother's differential treatment is explained by the baby boys' being more likely to be awake and irritable in the beginning, and the baby girls' being more likely to reward their mothers' attention. It is possible that the fathers switch sex preference at this age because, for many men, having a son is ego-boosting.

How does a father's presence or absence in the home affect his baby's development? According to one study of fifty-four poor and lower-middle-class black babies (Pedersen, Rubenstein, & Yarrow, 1973), the more attention a father pays to his baby son, the brighter, more alert, more inquisitive, and happier that baby is likely to be at five or six months of age. No similar results were found for baby girls. The father's influence on his son may come from the extra stimulation he provides, and the differential finding for boy and girl babies may be due to these fathers' greater interest in their sons than in their daughters. Again, boys may be more "vulnerable" to their environment than girls.

Another study of father-infant relationships (Pedersen & Robson, 1968) rated forty-five young middle-class fathers on the amount of care they gave their babies, their emotional investment in them, the amount and kind of playing they did, their irritability levels, degree of apprehension over the baby's well-being, authoritarian attitudes, and time spent in the home. The attachment the infants had for their fathers was judged by the babies' smiling, babbling, and general excitement upon seeing the father.

This particular sample of fathers showed a great deal of involvement with their infants. As a result, three-fourths of these babies, who were seen at 8 months of age and again at 9½ months, showed real attachment to their fathers. For the boys, attachment seemed to be related to the fathers' interest and involvement, but, surprisingly, there was no such correlation for the girls. Different attachment systems may operate between fathers and their baby girls, as opposed to their baby boys. Possibly this may be because the fathers act in subtly different ways, playing more vigorously with their sons and more gently with their daughters, for example.

To counter the traditional assumption that the mother-infant relationship is unique, and perhaps even biologically rooted, a recent study (Kotelchuck, 1973) sought to determine the nature of the infants' ties to their fathers, as well as to their mothers. A total of 144 boys and girls were observed at six, nine, twelve, fifteen, eighteen, and twenty-one months of age. Each child sat in an unfamiliar playroom, surrounded by toys, as his parents read quietly at one end of the room. A stranger came in, and with the mother and father, took turns leaving the room at regular intervals.

The six- and nine-month-old babies did not protest anyone's departure from the room, but from twelve months onward, the children protested the departures of both parents, but not the stranger. Their responses were quite similar to both their mothers and fathers, from twelve months on, with the babies following either parent to the door when he or she left, staying there and crying, and continuing to cry while clinging to the parent upon his or her return. They avoided the strangers, and used both parents as bases of security, typically choosing to stay close to both of them.

Although just over half the children were more likely to go to their mothers while both parents were in the room, one-quarter showed a preference for the father, and the others showed no preference for either parent. The extent of father involvement in caretaking did not seem related to the child's behavior in the experiment, suggesting that neither "quantity of interaction nor specific caretaking practices are the critical issues in the formation of a relationship [Kotelchuck, 1973, p. 8]."

This study shows that children form an active and close relationship with their fathers during infancy, and that fathers are much more important to their young children than has previously been acknowledged. Our new awareness of the father's importance to his children comes at a time of social change, when more men are assuming larger roles in the care of their children. It is likely that burgeoning interest in his role will bring about new theoretical perspectives on father-child relationships. Theorists will have to reckon with the presence of the male parent in the nursery, as well as with the mother.

Summary

1   There has been considerable disagreement over the nature of emotions and emotional development in infants. The behaviorist, James B. Watson, believed infants are born with three emotions (love, rage, and fear), and that emotional development is a conditioning procedure. K. M. B. Bridges, another early researcher, claimed that infants have only one emotion— excitement—which gradually *differentiates* into a wider range of emotional manifestations. Today, both of these theories are regarded as limited interpretations of infant emotions.

2   Recent research indicates that differentiation between crying and smiling responses begins quite early in life. Wolff isolated four different crying patterns—the basic rhythmical cry and cries of pain, anger, and frustration.

3   Two major developmental theories are the psychosexual theory of Sigmund Freud and the psychosocial theory of Erik Erikson. Freud stresses the influences of biological/maturational factors on development, and Erikson stresses cultural influences.

4   According to Freud, the infant, from birth to 1½ years, is in the *oral stage* and receives pleasure and gratification through oral stimulation. From 1½ to 3 years, the child is in the *anal stage* and receives pleasurable stimulation primarily from moving his or her bowels. During the early infancy period the baby is primarily *id*, operating on the "pleasure principle," striving for immediate gratification. When gratification is delayed, the *ego* develops and operates on the "reality principle," which strives to find acceptable ways to obtain gratification. Events during these and later psychosexual periods are thought to influence adult personality.

5   Erik Erikson maintains that the infant from birth to 1½ years experiences the first of a series of eight crises which influence psychosocial development through life. The first crisis focuses on the development of *basic trust or mistrust.* Like the Freudian oral stage, the development of trust or mistrust is greatly influenced by events surrounding the feeding situation and by the quality of the mother-child relationship. The infant of 1½ to 3 years is developing a sense of *autonomy* or a sense of *shame and doubt.* The child also develops a sense of mastery over him or herself (as seen in the ability to control bowel and bladder functions) and environment (as seen in

"negativism," primarily toward parental requests). Parental modes of dealing with their children highly influence the success of this stage.

6   Individual differences during infancy include sex and temperment differences, as well as differences influenced by birth order.

7   The relationship between infant and mother, and factors affecting this relationship, have received more theoretical and empirical attention. Harlow has pointed out the importance of *contact comfort* in the establishment of the mother-child bond, which is influenced by both baby and mother. Once the relationship has developed, *stranger anxiety* is normal and generally occurs in the second half of the first year.

8   Studies of maternal deprivation—generally conducted with institutionalized orphans—point to the need for consistent mothering in a stimulating environment for the emotional, intellectual, and physical health of the

child. Attempts at enriching orphans' environments have provided remarkable gains for these children.

9   The role of the father has received less empirical support than the role of the mother. Studies indicate that a father-child attachment also develops early in life.

Suggested Readings

Escalona, S. K. *The Roots of Individuality.* Chicago: Aldine, 1968. *A collection of separate but related approaches to the understanding of what takes place during the first half year of normal development in human beings.*

Guillaume, P. *Imitation in Children.* Chicago: University of Chicago, 1971. *Guillaume provides a theoretical discussion of imitative learning in very young children. He discusses the role of instincts, memory, perception, mental images, the acquisition of language, and the learning of affect.*

PART THREE
THE PRESCHOOL YEARS
Ages Three to Six

Even though Vicky, amid some tears and second thoughts, started nursery school at the age of three, we still call the years from three to six the preschool years. This is partly by tradition, since *formal* schooling does not begin until the first grade, and partly in recognition that until that time Vicky is still tied more to the home than to any outside social institution.

Vicky changes enormously during these three years. She looks different as she loses some of her babyish rotundity. She acts differently as she becomes much more proficient at a variety of tasks ranging from tying her shoelaces to riding a two-wheeled bicycle. She thinks differently as she leaps forward in her ability to handle a wide range of intellectual concepts, and to express her thoughts and feelings in the language of her culture.

These are critical years for personality development, as well. During the preschool years, Vicky's conception of herself grows stronger. She knows she's a girl—and she wants everyone else to know it, too. She identifies with her mother more than her father. She develops a sense of right and wrong, and tries to live by her conscience, hard though that may be at times. All aspects of her development—physical, intellectual, emotional, and social—continue to intertwine to make her the unique person she is. With her shiny new pencilcase full of newly sharpened pencils, Vicky walks into the first-grade classroom. A veteran of school after having attended both nursery school and kindergarten, she is not at all shy or anxious about entering the unfamiliar room. On the contrary, like most new scholars, she finds the idea of school exhilarating. For that first day of school is indeed a milestone, signaling to all that Vicky has entered a distinctly new stage of development.

CHAPTER SEVEN

PHYSICAL DEVELOPMENT

IN WHICH VICKY IS NO LONGER A BABY, PHYSICALLY

"I love you,"
said a great mother.
"I love you for what you are
knowing so well what you are.
And I love you more yet, child,
deeper yet than ever, child,
for what you are going to be,
knowing so well you are going far,
knowing your great works are ahead,
ahead and beyond,
yonder and far over yet."

(Carl Sandburg)

It is the morning of Vicky's third birthday. She leaps out of bed at her usual early hour and runs to the mirror. As she stands there, first on one foot and then on the other, she examines her mirror image closely, then runs to her parents' room. "Mommy, Daddy!" she squeals into sleepy ears, "I'm three!" But then a note of disappointment creeps into her voice as she acknowledges sadly, "But, I don't look no diff'runt."

Vicky's change from the day before may be infinitesimal—but in terms of what she was a year ago, she is very "diff'runt" indeed. She is bigger, and she is capable of bigger things. Her next two years will show still greater changes.

Physical Growth

Although Vicky's height increase is no longer so rapid as it was in infancy, she has grown almost 4 inches during the last year. The pencil mark on the wall that marks her height at three years is now $37^3/_4$ inches from the floor, and the old yardstick won't reach the tip of her head anymore. Over the next few years, she will grow a steady 2 to 3 inches per year, until she reaches the growth spurt of puberty. Knowing Vicky's height at five years of age enables us to predict with some accuracy her adult height. (The means of prediction and its reliability will be discussed in some detail in Chapter 10.)

As an "average" three-year-old girl, Vicky tips the scales at $31^3/_4$ pounds, and she will continue to gain weight slowly but steadily, commensurate with her height increases. She is only slightly smaller and lighter than the average boy of the same age, and this small difference will hold true until puberty, when she will shoot up ahead of her male classmates—and then see them begin to overtake her in height. (See Tables 7-1 to 7-4.)

Although Vicky still has a prominent potbelly, it will slim down over the next two years as her trunk elongates, along with her arms and legs. Her

Between the ages of three and six, girls are slightly smaller and lighter than boys; later they will shoot ahead.

(Photo Trends)

Table 7-1   Height Percentiles for Boys, Ages Three to Six

Age	Length, Inches						
	3%	10%	25%	50%	75%	90%	97%
3 years	$35^3/_4$	$36^1/_4$	37	38	$38^3/_4$	$39^1/_2$	$40^1/_2$
$3^1/_2$ years	37	$37^3/_4$	$38^1/_2$	$39^1/_4$	$40^1/_4$	41	42
4 years	$38^1/_2$	39	$39^3/_4$	$40^3/_4$	42	$42^3/_4$	$43^1/_2$
$4^1/_2$ years	$39^1/_2$	$40^1/_4$	41	42	$43^1/_4$	$44^1/_4$	45
5 years	$40^1/_4$	$41^1/_4$	$42^1/_4$	$43^1/_4$	$44^1/_2$	$45^1/_2$	$46^1/_2$
$5^1/_2$ years	$41^1/_2$	$42^1/_2$	$43^3/_4$	45	$46^1/_4$	$47^1/_4$	48
6 years	42	44	45	46	48	50	51

Source: From *Growth and Development of Children*, 5th edition, by Ernest H. Watson and George H. Lowrey. Copyright © 1967, Year Book Medical Publishers, Inc., Chicago. Used by permission of Year Book Medical Publishers.

head is still relatively large; but the rest of her is catching up, and her proportions are steadily becoming more similar to adult proportions. By the time she is ready to enter the first grade, she will have lost her top-heavy look.

Other changes are also taking place in Vicky's body. Her muscular and nervous systems are maturing, as is her skeletal growth. Cartilage is turning to bone at a faster rate, and her bones are becoming harder. All the primary, or *deciduous*, teeth are in now, and she can chew anything she wants to.

Nutrition has a strong influence on bone growth—the thickness, the shape, and the number of bones in the body. Malnourished children show retarded bone development and smaller head circumference than do

Table 7-2   Weight Percentiles for Boys, Ages Three to Six

Age	Weight, Pounds						
	3%	10%	25%	50%	75%	90%	97%
3 years	27	$28^3/_4$	$30^1/_4$	$32^1/_4$	$34^1/_4$	$36^3/_4$	$39^1/_4$
$3^1/_2$ years	$28^1/_2$	$30^1/_2$	$32^1/_4$	$34^1/_4$	$36^3/_4$	39	$41^1/_2$
4 years	30	32	34	$36^1/_2$	39	$41^1/_2$	$44^1/_4$
$4^1/_2$ years	$31^1/_2$	$33^3/_4$	$35^3/_4$	$38^1/_2$	$41^1/_2$	44	$47^1/_2$
5 years	34	36	$38^1/_2$	$41^1/_2$	$45^1/_4$	$48^1/_4$	$51^3/_4$
$5^1/_2$ years	$36^1/_4$	$38^3/_4$	42	$45^1/_2$	$49^1/_4$	53	$56^1/_2$
6 years	38	41	45	48	52	58	67

Source: From *Growth and Development of Children*, 5th edition, by Ernest H. Watson and George H. Lowrey. Copyright © 1967, Year Book Medical Publishers, Inc., Chicago. Used by permission of Year Book Medical Publishers.

Table 7-3   Height Percentiles for Girls, Ages Three to Six

Age	Length, Inches						
	3%	10%	25%	50%	75%	90%	97%
3 years	$34^3/_4$	$35^1/_2$	$36^3/_4$	$37^3/_4$	$38^1/_2$	$39^3/_4$	$40^3/_4$
$3^1/_2$ years	$36^1/_4$	37	38	$39^1/_4$	$40^1/_4$	$41^1/_2$	$42^1/_2$
4 years	$37^1/_2$	$38^1/_2$	$39^1/_2$	$40^1/_2$	$41^1/_2$	43	$44^1/_4$
$4^1/_2$ years	$38^1/_2$	$39^3/_4$	$40^3/_4$	42	43	$44^3/_4$	$45^3/_4$
5 years	40	41	42	43	$44^1/_4$	$45^1/_2$	$46^3/_4$
$5^1/_2$ years	$41^1/_4$	$42^1/_2$	$43^1/_2$	$44^1/_2$	$45^3/_4$	$46^3/_4$	48
6 years	42	43	45	46	48	49	51

Source: From *Growth and Development of Children*, 5th edition, by Ernest H. Watson and George H. Lowrey. Copyright © 1967, Year Book Medical Publishers, Inc., Chicago. Used by permission of Year Book Medical Publishers.

well-nourished children (Scrimshaw, 1967). Nutrition also affects tooth development. One of the greatest problems among American children is tooth decay. More than half of all two-year-olds in the United States have at least one cavity; and by the time the average child is ready to go to school, she has three or more decayed primary teeth (American Dental Association, 1966). Dental problems are, of course, much more common among economically deprived children (Schiffer & Hunt, 1968).

ABNORMAL GROWTH

The parents of an unusually small child often become alarmed, in fear that some abnormal condition is interfering with normal growth. In many such instances, the child's small size reflects nothing more than a familial

Table 7-4   Weight Percentiles for Girls, Ages Three to Six

Age	Weight, Pounds						
	3%	10%	25%	50%	75%	90%	97%
3 years	$25^1/_2$	$27^1/_2$	$29^1/_2$	$31^3/_4$	$34^1/_2$	$37^1/_2$	$41^3/_4$
$3^1/_2$ years	$27^1/_2$	$29^1/_2$	$31^1/_2$	34	37	$40^1/_2$	$45^1/_4$
4 years	$29^1/_4$	$31^1/_4$	$33^1/_2$	$36^1/_4$	$39^1/_2$	$43^1/_2$	$48^1/_4$
$4^1/_2$ years	$30^3/_4$	33	$35^1/_4$	$38^1/_2$	42	$46^3/_4$	51
5 years	33	$35^1/_2$	38	41	$44^1/_2$	$48^3/_4$	$52^1/_4$
$5^1/_2$ years	35	38	$40^3/_4$	44	$47^1/_4$	$51^1/_4$	$55^1/_2$
6 years	35	39	43	47	52	56	61

Source: From *Growth and Development of Children*, 5th edition, by Ernest H. Watson and George H. Lowrey. Copyright © 1967, Year Book Medical Publishers, Inc., Chicago. Used by permission of Year Book Medical Publishers.

tendency to shortness, but in other cases, lack of growth may be due to illness or to malfunction of the pituitary gland. This gland, located at the base of the brain, secretes the hormone that assures normal growth. When growth retardation is due to growth hormone deficiency, injections of the hormone can often dramatically increase the rate of growth. But it is not always the answer.

Emotional Deprivation Can Retard Growth

Doctors were puzzled when a five-year-old girl whose small size had been diagnosed as growth-hormone deficiency failed to respond to administration of the hormone. Suspecting that a poor home situation was interfering with the course of treatment and the child's growth, they stopped the hormone treatment and sent the little girl to live with an aunt. During the time she lived away from home *without* the hormone treatment, the child grew at about twice the rate as when she had been getting the treatment but living at home (Frasier & Rallison, 1972). This case is one striking example of many that seem to point to the conclusion that growth is affected by other than physical factors.

One group of thirteen very short children between the ages of three and eleven were originally thought to have a condition called *idiopathic hypopituitarism,* a type of growth-hormone deficiency, until investigation into the children's family constellations revealed abnormal home environments and emotional disturbances. Five of the eleven sets of parents (two pairs of children were siblings) were divorced or separated, two others had marital strife, and five were engaging in extramarital affairs. At home, the children were suffering hostility and abuse at the hands of ill-tempered parents, when the parents bothered to spend time with them at all. Although the youngsters were abnormally small, many had huge appetites. Several were retarded in IQ, speech, and social maturity.

A radical increase in height and weight occurred when these children were hospitalized and given no treatment other than good nutrition and good all-around care, indicating that distorted parent-child relationships may have caused their growth lags (Powell, Brasel, & Blizzard, 1967).

HOW PHYSICAL DEVELOPMENT INFLUENCES
PERSONALITY DEVELOPMENT

As Vicky grows, so does her opinion of herself. She recognizes that she is getting bigger, that she is not a baby anymore, and that she is coming to look more like the idols in her life—her parents. Furthermore, each new motor ability adds to her growing confidence and mastery of her environment.

Physical development is associated with personality in other ways, too, as in this mistrustful comment by Shakespeare's Julius Caesar:

> Let me have men about me that are fat,
> Sleek-headed men and such as sleep o' nights.
> Yond Cassius has a lean and hungry look,
> He thinks too much: such men are dangerous.

By putting these words into Caesar's mouth, Shakespeare acknowledged an age-old tendency to associate certain aspects of physique with certain types of personality. Through the years various researchers have pigeonholed people into body-type categories, with an eye to associating body type with psychiatric disorders, criminal behavior, or, simply, personality.

In the 1920s, Kretschmer described three basic body types: the *pyknic* (fat), the *athletic* (muscular), and the *asthenic* (thin). In 1942, Sheldon used somewhat different terms to describe the same three basic body types. He called the round, plump person an *endomorph;* the muscular person, a *mesomorph;* and the tall, thin person an *ectomorph.* Both these investigators claimed various correlations between body types and personality traits, which have since been questioned by other researchers. They found fat people to be jolly, athletically built ones to be aggressive, and "string-beans" to be shy and withdrawn.

During the preschool years, after children have lost their baby fat, their bodies noticeably assume the characteristic proportions they will probably retain throughout their lives. How *does* body type affect personality?

In one of a series of studies by Walker (1963), 147 upper-middle-class parents were asked to rate their two- to six-year-old children on various personality traits, while the children were categorized independently, by Sheldon's body types. The parents seemed to see their children differently according to body type, and their perceptions were influenced by the children's sex. Endomorphic sons were rated as aggressive, bossy, awkward, and jealous, whereas endomorphic daughters were loving, cooperative, easygoing, and extroverted. Both mesomorphic girls and boys were energetic: in the boys this excess energy was associated with bossy, bold, impudent, destructive, aggressive, and assertive behavior, whereas the girls were seen as more cooperative. Ectomorphic boys were seen as socially reserved, shy, not aggressive, eager to please, well-coordinated, and not easily discouraged, whereas ectomorphic girls were tense, unstable, uncooperative, moody, lacking in energy and appetite, fault-finding, quarrelsome, afraid of failure, and likely to feel unloved.

There are several possible explanations for these findings. The first would be that differences in body type reflect underlying differences in body composition and function, which may also affect such temperamental characteristics as energy level. These then affect one's behavior and the reactions of other people toward one. Another explanation may be that parents treat short, fat children differently from tall, thin children and "just right" children, thus producing certain personality traits. And the third

(Horst Schaefer, Photo Trends)

(Shelly Rusten)

In the preschool years, physical development is rapid and includes a wide range of activities.

possibility is that the children are not actually different from each other, but are only perceived so. Children may form stereotypes of what a "fat" or "skinny" or "muscular" child *should* behave like. This is a fairly sophisticated reaction, probably more likely to be seen among older children.

Motor Development

When we see what Vicky can do at the age of three, we realize how rapid her physical development has been in these last months and how wide her range of activities. One minute, she puts on her ballet tutu and walks on her tiptoes; the next, she's back in her overalls, whipping around corners or riding her tricycle. Next year, at four, she'll be skipping and hopping on one foot and reliably catching the ball her father tosses to her; and on her fifth birthday, she'll be skipping on alternate feet, jumping rope on the sidewalk, and starting to skate and swim.

Vicky is a little behind her same-age cousin, Jason, on large-muscle coordination. He's a little stronger and has a little more muscle, even at this tender age (Garai & Scheinfeld, 1968), and he's more proficient in throwing a ball, jumping from one place to another, and going up and down ladders (McCaskill & Wellman, 1938). But Vicky outshines him at hopping, skipping, and galloping (Gutteride, 1939). And when it comes to small-muscle coordination, Vicky shows her female proficiency, always being one step ahead of her masculine counterpart. It is possible that these different proficiency levels are due to skeletal differences between the sexes, but it is just as possible that they reflect different societal attitudes that encourage different types of activities for boys and girls.

At three, Vicky has made big strides in eye-hand and small-muscle coordination. She can sit down with a crayon and a big sheet of newsprint and draw a circle. She can pour her own milk into her cereal bowl, letting her parents sleep a little later. And she can button and unbutton well enough to dress and undress herself after a fashion and to tend to her own toilet needs. At four, she will be able to cut on a line with scissors, to draw a person, to make designs and crude letters, and to fold paper into a double triangle. And at five she'll be good at stringing beads and at controlling a pencil or a crayon. She'll be able to copy a square, as well as other designs, letters, and numbers. By the age of five, she will also show a preference for using one hand more than the other. About one child in ten is left-handed—and this child is more likely to be a boy.

Yes, Vicky is a "diff'runt" physical creature—and even more sweeping changes are taking place in her intellectual and personality development (Chapters 8 and 9).

Abused and Neglected Children

A six-month-old baby will not stop crying and spitting up his pablum. In a fit of rage, his mother snatches the infant from his feeding chair and hurls him from the window of their second-floor apartment. When she rushes down the stairs to pick him up, he is, miraculously, still alive. She takes him to the bathroom, where she proceeds to drown him in the tub.

In a middle-class suburban family with five children, one boy is chosen to be the object of excruciating cruelty. His brothers and sisters are permitted to take food from him so that he is systematically starved. He is burned with lighted cigarettes, beaten with a steel wire, and refused all treats and recreations. When his mother attempts to hang him, his sad plight finally comes to the attention of the authorities, who remove him from the home.

A policeman chasing a mugger up a fire escape abandons the chase when he hears the persistent, though weak, wailing of an infant. When he investigates, he finds an emaciated one-year-old girl lying in a filthy crib, alone in a stinking, squalid apartment.

The American Humane Society has estimated that 10,000 cases of child abuse were reported across the nation in 1969, and the number of neglected children who came to the attention of authorities in New York City alone in 1970 also came to 10,000 (Solomon, 1973). But most authorities estimate that these figures constitute only the most minute tip of a horrifying iceberg, and that as many as 2½ million children may be abused or neglected by their parents each year.

The children, known as "battered babies," are kicked, beaten, burned, thrown against walls and radiators, strangled, suffocated, and even buried alive. Bones are broken, teeth are knocked out, eyesight is destroyed, and internal organs are injured. Inevitably, many children who survive such brutal treatment suffer irreparable mental, physical, and emotional damage. Most of these tragic victims have not yet seen their fourth birthday (Solomon, 1973).

Neglected children suffer from hunger, dehydration, festering sores, and rashes that cover their entire bodies. Varying degrees of neglect may go on for a child's entire life and can also result in permanently retarded development (Young, 1964).

Although neglecting parents are usually equally indifferent to all their children, abusing parents sometimes pick one scapegoat among their children. This one child in the family who bears the brunt of parental anger may have the misfortune to resemble a hated relative, may be of the "wrong" sex, may have been the cause of a forced marriage, may have been born with a birth defect, or may have a personality that one or both parents simply cannot stand. Usually only one parent inflicts the actual injuries, but by allowing mistreatment to exist, the other parent demonstrates his or her own inadequacy as well (Steele & Pollack, 1968).

ABUSING PARENTS
Who are the parents who abuse their children? They come from all segments of the population: from all income levels, all ranges of intelligence, and all cultural, religious, and racial groups. They may be young school dropouts or successful professionals (Steele & Pollack, 1968). Incidents of reported abuse occur most often in large, poor families (Gil, 1970). This preponderance of reported abuse among the poor is due partly to the fact that children mistreated by more prosperous parents are more likely to be seen by private physicians, who are less likely to report such abuse than are representatives of public clinics. Another explanation is the strong positive relationship between child abuse and general life stresses, stresses felt more by poor people. The poor cannot take a vacation away

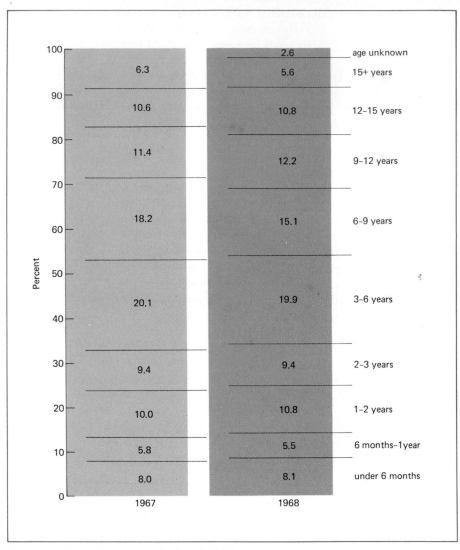

Figure 7-1   Age Distribution of Abused Children, 1967–1968

from their children, cannot hire nannies and baby-sitters, cannot fill their lives with other pleasures. "It is the poor . . . who are expected to be perfect mothers seven days a week [Kempe, 1973]."

Abusing parents are emotional cripples. Typically, they themselves were often beaten as children and were emotionally deprived in other ways as well so that they never developed that "basic trust" that Erikson (1950) holds essential. They are likely to be unhappy in a marriage into which they were forced at an early age because of an unplanned, unwanted pregnancy.

And they often have money troubles (Solomon, 1973). They are isolated from other people and usually have no one whom they can depend upon to help them in times of distress. They have painfully low opinions of themselves (Helfer, 1973).

Because of their great needs, which went unfulfilled by their own parents and continue to go unmet by their spouses and others, these parents often turn to their children. They expect their children to care for them as no one else ever has. They virtually reverse the parent-child relationship. Able to think only of their own needs, they are oblivious to those of their children and are unrealistic in their expectations. Helfer (1973) tells of a mother who ignored her twenty-month-old daughter's crying when the child fell and hurt herself. But about ten minutes later, when the mother herself began to cry about something else, the baby ran to comfort the mother. When children are unable to meet their parents' emotional needs, the parents turn on them.

In their own pathetic way, these parents often do love their children and are remorseful to see the damage they have inflicted.

Steele and Pollack (1968) give examples of high parental demands and lack of understanding of babies:

> Henry J., in speaking of his sixteen-month-old son, Johnny, said, "He knows what I mean and understands it when I say 'come here.' If he doesn't come immediately, I go and give him a gentle tug on the ear to remind him of what he's supposed to do." In the hospital it was found that Johnny's ear was lacerated and partially torn away from his head.

> Kathy made this statement: I have never felt really loved all my life. When the baby was born, I thought he would love me; but when he cried all the time, it meant he didn't love me, so I hit him [p. 309]."

A societal factor that may contribute to our high rate of child abuse is the general acceptance of the role of physical force in rearing children. In those cultures that have strong taboos against striking children, such as the American Indians, such abuse is extremely rare (Gil, 1970). Many abusing parents are carrying societal mores just one step further. Their pathology lies in the inappropriateness of their expectations and the severity of their punishments. It is different in degree, but not very different in kind from any parent striking any child in anger. One common justification given for spanking children is that "it makes the parent feel better." In this way, the needs of the (presumably normal) parent take precedence over the needs of the child.

HELPING ABUSED CHILDREN AND THEIR FAMILIES

What can be done for these unhappy families? Parents can be and frequently are criminally prosecuted. They are not always convicted, though, and when they go back home may be even harsher than ever. The authorities can step in and remove a child from an abusing home, which is, of course, often done. In such cases, the parents feel unjustly punished and may transfer their brutality to one of their other children. And since abusing parents are at times kind and loving, their children may genuinely grieve to be removed from the home. The ideal solution, then, is to help the entire family as a unit. This has proven to be exceedingly difficult.

Traditional psychotherapy is often ineffective with these parents, who tend to deny reality, blaming the child for his injuries instead of recognizing themselves as the injurers. Since abusing parents are "exquisitely sensitive to desertion and rejection in any form [Steele & Pollack, 1968, p. 314]," help for the children depends upon focusing attention almost entirely on the parent.

One psychiatric aim is to help abusing parents establish better relationships with their own parents, and most especially their mothers. When a mother feels that she is accepted and approved of by her own mother, she can identify with the "good" mother and be one herself (Steele & Pollack, 1968). Use of warm, compassionate "mother surrogates" is a help to some families. These are lay persons who visit abusing parents, help them with details of day-to-day living, show sympathy for their problems, and most of all, show interest in them as people (Kempe, 1973).

Two other approaches seem to be having some success in helping these families. Parental Stress Service, a twenty-four-hour telephone hotline, is a voluntary private agency in California which serves as a crisis intervention unit. The service takes calls from parents who have either abused their children in the past or fear they are about to lose control. About 40 percent of the hotline's calls are precipitated by acute crisis situations. The telephone volunteer can often solve the present crisis by talking to the distraught parent, by arranging for temporary baby-sitting, or by finding more long-lasting resources for the family (Johnston, 1973). Parents Anonymous, a New York City group based on the principles developed by Alcoholics Anonymous, depends on parents helping each other. Abusing parents meet in small groups, talk about their problems, and offer each other understanding and support. When this emotional sustenance comes from other adults, the parents do not have to seek it in vain from their small children (Nemy, 1972; Helfer, 1973).

Summary

1 Physical development increases rapidly during the preschool years with no significant changes in growth between boys and girls until puberty. The muscular, nervous, and skeletal systems are maturing and all primary teeth are present.

2 Factors such as nutrition and emotional deprivation can affect growth. Malnourished children show retardation in bone development and have smaller head circumferences than well-nourished children. Some children in conditions of extreme emotional deprivation are abnormally small but height and weight increases upon removal from a hostile environment. The "battered child syndrome," in which children are neglected or physically abused, has received medical documentation recently; family therapy is recommended.

3 Physical development influences personality. There is a relationship between body type and various personality traits.

4 Motor skills in the preschool years are vastly improved. Children show improvement in large-muscle, small-muscle, and eye-hand coordination.

Suggested Readings

D'Ambrosio, R. *No Language but a Cry.* Garden City, N.Y.: Doubleday, 1970. *This book is the story of Laura, a child born to psychotic, alcoholic, and cruel parents. She is born with crossed eyes, a hunched back, and suffers from facial burn scars and varicose veins. Yet, with the help of her doctor and an order of Catholic sisters, she overcomes these obstacles.*

Gil, D. G. *Violence against Children: Abuse in the U.S.* Cambridge, Mass.: Harvard University Press, 1970. *This book is a comprehensive and systematic study of child abuse in the United States.*

Kempe, C. H., & Helfer, R. E. *Helping the Battered Child and His Family.* Philadelphia and New York: Lippincott, 1972. *A series of essays that provide a child-abuse treatment program and outline the variety of professional people useful in such treatment. This book is divided into four separate but interrelated parts including discussions of the parents' need and desire for help and the world of the battered child.*

Thomas, A., Chess, S., & Birch, H. G. *Temperament and Behavior Disorders in Children.* New York: New York University Press, 1968. *A report of the ten-year-old New York Longitudinal Study. It emphasizes the different temperamental characteristics that show up right from birth and the ways these characteristics combine with certain methods of child rearing to create problems for children.*

CHAPTER EIGHT

MENTAL DEVELOPMENT

IN WHICH VICKY'S BUSY MIND DEVELOPS
AT PLAY AND IN SCHOOL

*[H]er voice and acts were full of love, and I was content, for I loved her as she loved
me. I never thought of her grey, pock-marked, wide face, and her loose, colorless hair,
and her dark tight clothes that strained across the full shapes of her old womanly arms
and bosom and belly. She was to me neither young nor old, beautiful nor ugly. She
belonged to me, and was therefore worthy. All persons seemed to commit their acts for
my benefit, and all events were interesting only as they pleased me or met my needs.*

(Paul Horgan, 1964*)

Vicky, at age four, is bothered by a big, black, buzzing fly. After waving her
arms around to no avail, she finally tries a new tack: "Fly," exhorts Vicky,
"go home to your mother." We see that our young friend is now more
likely to try to solve her problems with the use of language, since her
command of it has grown enormously. She still thinks in egocentric terms,

*From *Things as They Are*, by Paul Horgan. New York: Farrar, Straus & Co., 1964.

though, as shown by her belief that other creatures, like the fly, have lives and feelings just like hers—and that she can get them to do what she wants.

During the years from three to six, Vicky is becoming more competent in the areas of cognition, intelligence, language, and learning. She is developing the ability to use symbols in her thought and action, and she is able to handle more efficiently such concepts as age, time, space, moral judgments, and relationships between various objects. Yet she has still not completely separated the real from the unreal, and much of her language ability is egocentric. She is unable to consider fully another's viewpoint. She is a fascinating creature to observe and to get to know. Let's take a look.

Piaget's Preoperational Stage (Two to Seven Years)

During her preschool years, Vicky is smack in the middle of Piaget's second major stage of cognitive development, the *preoperational*. She enters it at about the age of two, as she is coming out of the sensorimotor stage, and she emerges from it at about the age of seven, as it overlaps the concrete operations stage.

The preoperational stage marks a major qualitative leap in Vicky's

Smack in the middle of cognitive development: egocentric, focused, active, reasonable.

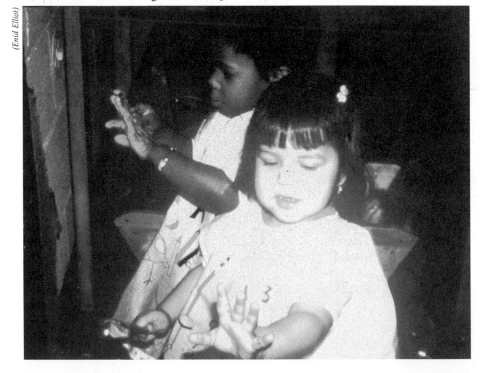

(Enid Elliot)

thinking because it ushers in the *symbolic function*. Her thought processes used to be chained to the actual, the present, the concrete. But now that she is able to use symbols to represent the objects, places, and people in her world, her mind can soar above the here and now. Her thinking can dart back to events of the past, can surge forward to anticipation of the future, and can dwell on what might be happening somewhere else in the present.

In the sensorimotor stage, Vicky understood individual actions but was not able to view them sequentially. Piaget has compared sensorimotor intelligence to a slow-motion film that shows one static frame after another but can give no simultaneous, all-encompassing viewing (Flavell, 1963). In the sensorimotor stage, Vicky moved her body to pursue concrete goals. Now she still acts, but not necessarily in a motoric way. Her mental processes are active, but they are also, for the first time, reflective. Once Vicky enters the preoperational stage, her ability to represent things with symbols enables her to share a symbol system with the fellow members of her culture.

THE SYMBOLIC FUNCTION

Back in the early sensorimotor state, Vicky could deal only with those parts of her world that came to her through her five senses. If she could not, at any given moment, see, feel, hear, smell, or taste something or someone, that object or person did not exist for her. By the end of the sensorimotor stage, she had developed very primitive representational abilities. When she heard her mother's voice, for example, she recognized it as a symbol (called a "sign") of her mother, and she displayed the same kind of excitement upon hearing that beloved voice as she did when her mother actually walked into her room. Similarly, the sight of her bottle had become a symbol (called a "signal") of food, which she responded to with the joy of the feeding situation itself.

But in Piagetian terms, Vicky was still not thinking in true representative fashion, because before the preoperational stage, she did not yet have the ability to evoke for herself—with no external clues—some symbol of a person or event. Not until Vicky can internally evoke some word or image in her mind is she capable of true symbolic thought. She will have attained the ability to think symbolically only when she can lie alone in her crib and *think* of her mother's voice without actually hearing it, or conjure up in her mind's eye the mouth-watering sight of her nighttime bottle. In Piagetian language, these mental representations are called *signifiers*, and the objects or events (the mother, feeding situation, etc.) that they represent are called *significates*.

Signifiers may be of two kinds. They may be *symbols*, which are very personal representations that involve a visual or auditory image, or even a kinesthetic one; they bear some resemblance to the object they represent. Another kind of signifier is a *sign*, such as a word or a mathematical symbol. A sign is an arbitrary representation in the sense that it doesn't look or sound like the object it stands for but is a socially agreed-upon representation for a certain object or concept. Young children think first in *symbols* and continue to think in them even after they become proficient with language and other socially accepted *signs*.

Mental Symbols

During the sensorimotor stage, babies imitate the objects around them. Thus, at one point Lucienne opens her mouth to imitate the opening of a matchbox, and at another time she sways back and forth at the same speed as her father's bicycle. By acting like these objects, she is able to grasp their essence. By the end of the sensorimotor period, though, the child is no longer imitating things overtly, but has, rather, internalized her imitation. Now Lucienne might imitate the bicycle by moving her muscles so slightly that her movements are imperceptible. These internal movements constitute for her the mental symbol of a bicycle.

Such internal imitation, or mental symbolism, makes possible *deferred imitation*. This concept explains the mechanism whereby a child may see something, form a mental symbol of it, and later—when he no longer sees the activity—imitate the behavior. Three-year-old David, for example, sees his father shaving in the morning. When David goes to nursery school that afternoon, he may head for the housekeeping corner and promptly begin to "shave." He obviously has a mental representation of his father's shaving behavior, or he would not be able to carry out such similar actions.

Symbolic Play

When children make one object stand for something else in a playful way, they are using concrete symbols rather than mental ones. At the age of fifteen months, Piaget's daughter Jacqueline found a cloth whose fringed edges reminded her of her pillow. She treated it as she would her pillow, and laughed unreservedly. Her laughter is our clue that she knows this piece of cloth is not her pillow and that she is engaging in symbolic play.

> Symbolic play . . . is an appropriate means of providing an adjustment to reality. [It allows the child to] assimilate the external world almost directly into his own desires and needs with scarcely any accommodation. He can therefore shape reality to his own requirements. Furthermore, in symbolic play, he can act out the conflictual situations of real life in such a way as to ensure a successful conclusion in which he comes out the winner, and not, as is usually the case in real life, the loser. In brief, symbolic play, serving a necessary cathartic purpose, is essential for the child's emotional stability and adjustment to reality [Ginsburg & Opper, 1969, p. 81].

Language

This third aspect of the symbolic function will be discussed in some detail later in this chapter. For the moment, let us say only that the preoperational

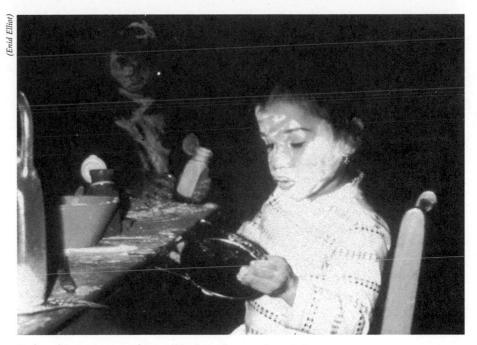

(Enid Elliot)

Deferred imitation—made possible through mental symbolism

child can use words to stand for absent things or events and therefore has invested them with a symbolic character. This linguistic neophyte uses words in very idiosyncratic ways—and quite differently from the way he will use them in adulthood, or even later in childhood.

CHARACTERISTICS OF PREOPERATIONAL THOUGHT
The preoperational child has made such a leap forward from the sensorimotor stage that it comes as somewhat of a shock to realize just how rudimentary her thinking still is. Its primitiveness comes across clearly in the following characteristics of thought at this stage, as identified by Flavell (1963, pp. 156–162).

Egocentrism
Vicky is unable to take the role of another person. The only viewpoint that exists is hers. When she is asked to look at a three-dimensional model and describe what it would look like to someone on the other side, she persistently describes it only from her own point of view. She cannot remotely imagine that someone else would have a point of view different from hers.

At the age of four, Vicky is seeing the ocean for the first time. Awed by the constant thundering of the waves, she turns to her father and asks, "But when does it stop?" "It doesn't," he replies. "Not even when we're *asleep*?" asks Vicky incredulously. Her thinking is so egocentric that she cannot consider anything—even the mighty ocean—as having a life of its own when she isn't around to see it! Also, when Vicky covers her eyes she thinks that since she can't see you, you can't see her.

This egocentrism is especially noticeable in the use of language. Listening to a conversation among children this age is like being in the theater of the absurd. Several children may be sitting with each other, apparently conversing, but when we listen to their words, we realize that none of them is paying the slightest attention to what any of the others is saying. They may politely wait for each other to finish, alternate sentences, and stay remotely within the same subject area. But what emerges from all this garrulity is a set of separate monologues; each child speaks what is on his mind, without knowing or caring whether the other children are interested or are listening to what he has to say.

The following conversation between two four-year-olds as they "do the dishes" in the housekeeping corner at nursery school is an eloquent example of dual monologues:

Jason: What will we have for supper tonight?
Vicky: Christmas is coming.
Jason: Cake and coffee would be good.
Vicky: I have to do my shopping soon.
Jason: I really like chocolate cake.
Vicky: I think I will buy some slippers and candy.

Centration

The preoperational child tends to *center*, or focus, on one aspect of a situation and neglect the importance of other aspects, thus leading to patently illogical reasoning. We say that the child in this stage cannot *decenter*. One of Piaget's most famous experiments, involving the concept of *conservation* (which is discussed in Chapter 11), illustrates this inability to decenter.

Eric is shown two identical glasses, each one short and wide, each one holding the same amount of water. When asked which glass has more water, Eric, five, readily answers, "They're both the same." While he watches, the experimenter pours water from one of the wide glasses into a tall, thin one. She then asks him, "Now which glass has more water in it?" Unhesitatingly, Eric points to the short, wide glass. The experimenter repeats the operation, pouring the water back and forth several more times. Eric persists in claiming that the short glass has more water. When asked why, he says, "This one is bigger this way," pointing with pudgy fingers to the width.

Other children say that the tall glass contains more water. What children of this age cannot do is to consider both height and weight simultaneously. They center on one or the other and cannot logically solve the problem. One reason why they have difficulty is their *perception* of the two glasses. Because one looks larger than the other, they are fooled by appearance into thinking that it *is* larger. Their faulty perception inhibits their ability to think logically.

Focus on States

Again we think of Piaget's reference to thought as a slow-motion film made up of one static frame after another. The preoperational child still focuses on successive states and is not able to understand the meaning of the transformation from one state to another. We can see this in the conservation experiments referred to above. It is also illustrated by an experiment that asks children to identify the successive movements of a bar that falls from an upright position to a horizontal one, as when a pencil drops after one has tried to balance it on end (Flavell, 1963). Preoperational children find it very difficult to reconstruct the various positions occupied by the quickly falling bar.

Action Rather than Abstraction

The preoperational child thinks and learns by running off "reality sequences in his head just as he might do in overt action [Flavell, 1963, p. 158]." One result of this is an overemphasis on realism, to the extent that even such intangibles as dreams, thoughts, and moral obligations are considered by the child to be "quasi-tangible entities." The child does not yet completely differentiate reality from fantasy.

Irreversibility

Going back to the classic conservation experiment with the glasses of water, we see that Eric fails to grasp the idea that the pouring operation is reversible. If he could conceptualize the possibility of restoring the original state by pouring the water back into the other glass, he would realize that the amount of water in both glasses is the same. He does not; therefore his thought is illogical.

Irreversibility of thought is also apparent when we ask five-year-old Vicky whether she has a sister. She'll tell us "yes," but when we ask her whether her sister has a sister, she'll say "no." By the age of seven, 60 percent of children can handle this correctly; by the age of nine, 75 percent can (Piaget, 1928).

Transductive Reasoning

The child's earliest concepts are *preconcepts*. Active and concrete, rather than schematic and abstract, they do not permit the child to recognize stable identity in changing circumstances or, on the other hand, to consider different individuals of the same type as anything but one and the same. What is the same object in different situations—and what are different objects of the same class? The preoperational child cannot answer this question.

Vicky saw her mother wearing a new pair of huge sunglasses that practically covered the top half of her face. "Who are you?" she asked. When her mother took off the glasses, Vicky said, "Now you're Mommy." On the other hand, every time the preoperational Jacqueline saw a slug, she called it *"the* slug," never dreaming for a moment that what she was seeing were different members of one class (Piaget, 1951a, from Flavell). She thought that the same slug kept turning up all over, even though the same one could not possibly have slithered to all the spots where she had seen them.

Logical reasoning is of two basic types: *deduction* and *induction.* Deductive reasoning, which goes from the general to the particular, is expressed in this syllogism: *All people are mammals. I am a person. Therefore, I am a mammal.* The following is an example of inductive reasoning, in which we go from the particular to the general: *Investigation has shown that the red blood cells of horses, porpoises, tree shrews, people, and other mammals lack nuclei. Therefore, we can probably assume that the red blood cells of all mammals lack nuclei.*

The preoperational child reasons along neither of these lines. Instead, he goes from one particular to another particular without taking into account the general. Thus transductive reasoning may ascribe a cause-and-effect relationship to two unrelated events (I had mean thoughts about my brother. My brother got sick. Therefore, I made my brother sick); may fail to grasp a relationship that exists (that Mother is still Mother, even when she wears new sunglasses); or may completely misinterpret the actual relationship (assuming that all slugs are the same slug instead of realizing that they are related by species).

Cognitive Concepts of the Preschool Child

During the years from three to six, Vicky is learning how to deal with many concepts. Time is no longer one amorphous blob; it can be divided, albeit with some difficulty, into past and future (even though for a while Vicky calls every day in the past "yesterday" and every day in the future "tomorrow"). Space becomes a reality in terms of understanding the difference between "near" and "far," "small" and "large," and so forth. She is also developing a rudimentary awareness of causation, a recognition that certain events cause others, even though she still attributes causative powers to events that are merely correlative. Some concepts that come to the fore most markedly during the preschool years are the ability to perceive items in serial relationships, the ability to classify objects into various meaningful categories, the ability to judge age, and the ability to begin to make moral judgments.

SERIATION

Children show that they have a grasp of serial relationships when they can arrange objects in a sequence along one or more relevant dimensions. For example, they may order a series of sticks along the dimension of height, from shortest to tallest. Piaget (1952) used sticks of different sizes in his experiments to trace the development of relational concepts. He would give the children a handful of sticks of differing heights and pose several problems.

At the most elementary level, he asked the child to pick the smallest and largest sticks. Most children were able to do this consistently at about four or five years of age.

Then he would build a staircase effect with ten sticks, thus:

He would show this to the child, demolish it, and ask the child to reconstruct it. Children of five or six years of age could do this, with some difficulty. Younger children accomplished the staircase effect—but only on the top, not on the bottom, so:

Younger children also built several smaller series of a few sticks.

A child who had passed the previous test was given another set of sticks of various heights to insert in the series, so that the final result would look something like:

Children could accomplish this at six or seven years of age. Younger children (five or six years) could do the initial seriation but could not deal with the inserts.

The children's mistakes illustrated the primitive characteristics of pre-operational thought; for example, getting the staircase effect on one dimension (the top) but not on the other (the bottom) indicated that the child was centering only on one dimension and not seeing all the relevant dimensions of the problem. Not until six or seven years of age did the children develop a true relational concept, embodying the principle of always choosing the smallest or largest stick from the pile to construct an ordered series. And although those children who were able to construct a staircase *appeared* to have the idea, their lack of a sophisticated relational concept was betrayed by their difficulties with the inserts.

CLASSIFICATION

When a child can *classify*, or sort objects into categories according to particular attributes, he demonstrates his perception of the characteristics involved, such as color, shape, size, and so forth, as well as his understanding of the overall notion of categorization. Verbal ability comes into play here since it is important to be able to label what he perceives. Counting the ability to classify as an important measure of intelligence, Piaget conducted a number of studies on this topic.

Children of various ages were given pieces of plastic of different colors and shapes and told to "put together those that are alike [Piaget & Inhelder, 1959]." From the ages of $2^{1}/_2$ to $4^{1}/_2$, the children made *figural* collections. That is, they did not sort out shapes according to their differences, but used the plastic circles, triangles, and squares to make their own shapes—usually a line or a circle.

From the ages of $4^{1}/_2$ to 6 or 7, children made quasi-classifications, jumping capriciously from one basis of classification to another. Typically, a child would sort some of her materials by color and others by shape, ending up with a pile of red triangles and circles, and another pile of red, blue, and yellow squares. By the end of this age grouping, the children would sort by one dimension at a time, but only one—like color, or size, or shape.

Children aged seven or eight and older classified exhaustively. They were now able to deal with several dimensions, or classes, simultaneously. They would end up with piles of large red circles, small red circles, large blue circles, small blue circles, large yellow triangles, small yellow squares, and so forth.

Inclusion Relations

At this stage, children still have trouble understanding the relationship between a whole and its parts. This difficulty is brought out by an example (Piaget & Inhelder, 1959, p. 108; cited in Flavell, 1963):

> The (5;6). "If I make a bouquet of all the primroses and you make one of all the flowers, which will be bigger?—*Yours.*—(the experimenter takes 4 primroses and 4 other flowers and repeats the question.)—*The same* [p. 308].

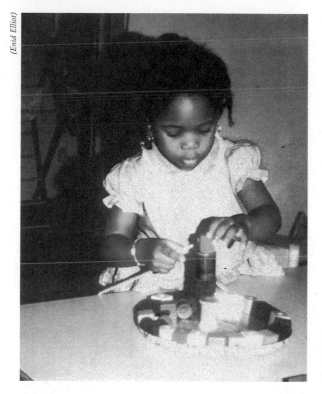

(Enid Elliot)

When a child can classify, the characteristics have been perceived, and categorization is understood.

This child does not understand that the part (some, namely the primroses) is less than the whole (all, namely flowers). We say he lacks the *class inclusion* principle. Between the ages of seven and eleven, children develop this principle and can understand that the class of "flowers" includes the subclass of "primroses."

ACCELERATING THE PIAGETIAN CONCEPTS

What about concepts like seriation, classification, and conservation, which seem to come naturally to children at certain developmental stages? Can children be taught these ideas before they discover them for themselves? The evidence seems to indicate that they can if the children are maturationally ready and if the training programs are specific to the types of ability involved. Children who respond to such training are generally those who are in a transitional cognitive period. They are on the verge of discovering a specific concept. A structured learning experience may serve to push such children into an earlier acquisition of an ability.

In one study of sixty 3- to 5-year-old urban middle-class children (Burke-Merkle & Hooper, 1973), children were trained in seriation, classification, or a combination of the two. The children who received training in seriation did better than those who were trained in classification, probably because children grasp the concept of seriation at an earlier age than they do that of classification. A small child who has neither concept will, then, respond more to seriation training. In this study, the older children did better than the younger ones, showing the importance of maturation.

The final important element in evaluating such training programs is the makeup of the posttest (the test given to the children after training). In general, the closer the posttest requirements are to the training experience, the better the child will do. In other words, after training, the child may pass a task very similar to those on which he was trained (this is called "near transfer"), but may or may not pass a test that is less similar (this is called "far transfer") because the specific learning during training failed to generalize to other tasks. Reese & Lipsitt (1970) point out five aspects of training that contribute to its success or failure: (1) the child's level of development at the start of training, (2) the particular method of training, (3) the specific tasks used, (4) the amount of training, and (5) the criteria for success (near or far transfer).

According to Pulaski (1971), Piaget himself has some reservations about such training programs:

> This is not true learning in his view; it is an artificial, verbally acquired, "deformed" response, a rote memorization of responses to a specific situation only. It is neither stable nor permanent; children will revert quickly to the usual errors, nor can they generalize to similar situations. The logical structure can be acquired only through internal equilibrium, Piaget insists. Until a child is around seven he is not capable of grasping the notion of conservation because he does not have the logical structures, the mental organization for dealing with them [pp. 33–34].

Children may, then, be better off spending their time making mud pies, playing with blocks, or going to the park than engaging in "accelerating" activities.

CHILDREN'S JUDGMENT OF AGE

A rather petite psychologist was sitting in a circle discussing age with a group of four-year-olds. When she asked Peter whether everyone in the circle was four and he nodded, she said, "*I'm* a lot older than four." He looked at her, saw a small-boned person who was able to sit comfortably on a child-sized chair, and retorted, "Well, if you're not four, you're awful little!"

Peter's perception and thinking were both typical of a four-year-old. He did not see the considerable differences between this young woman and the four-year-olds around her, and he unhesitatingly and unquestioningly equated age with size.

During the first two or three years of life, children realize that there is a correlation between age and size. But then they center on this correlation, and it takes them several years to learn that "the bigger you are, the older you are" is not an inflexible rule. Preschoolers are misled by their faulty perception and their tendency to center on such aspects as tallness and fatness, to the exclusion of such other physical clues to age as body proportions, skin texture, clothing styles, and so forth. Recent studies point out that children gradually develop the ability to take into account factors other than size when estimating age and that it is about the age of eight that they stop making errors in age judgment based on size (Looft, 1971; Looft, Rayman, & Rayman, 1972; Kratochwill & Goldman, 1973).

Children aged three through nine were shown paired photos of males and females at four age levels: infant, child, adolescent, and middle-aged adult (Kratochwill & Goldman, 1973). The photos were reproduced in two different sizes, then duplicated and paired into twenty-eight different combinations of same-sex pairs. When the children were asked, "Which one is older, or are they the same age?" fewer than half the three-year-olds were able to give the right answers for all the pairs, whereas almost all the seven-year-olds and *all* the nine-year-olds had perfect scores. The youngest child to get all the age relationships right was five years old.

The children's mistakes in stating which of the pair was older were virtually all due to their preoccupation with the size of the figures. The preschoolers said things like, "He's older because he's bigger," "She's taller," or "Same because look, these two are both big." One four-year-old who looked at the same figure shown in two sizes pointed out that both figures were the "same people," that they were wearing the same pants and shirts, and so forth—and then announced that the larger figure was older.

Although American children center on height as the definitive clue to age, a similar study with Malaysian children showed fatness to be the salient characteristic that determined the children's judgments of age (Looft, Rayman, & Rayman, 1972). These children also became more accurate in their judgments as they grew older.

Learning in Preschoolers

Vicky's parents are conscientious people who want to do right by their child. One day they come home from their local library, their arms loaded down with books with such titles as *Teach Your Baby* (Painter, 1971), *Blueprint for a Brighter Child* (Sparkman & Carmichael, 1973), and *How to Raise a Brighter Child: The Case for Early Learning* (Beck, 1967). These books and others like them have extrapolated the findings from experimental studies of children's learning and applied them to the home situation. Following the guidelines in the books, Vicky's parents set up a daily schedule of activities. A bit concerned that they had not begun to set up a preplanned schedule right from the day of Vicky's birth, as some of the books recommended, they decided to plunge in at the preschool level.

At regular times every day they sat down with Vicky, teaching her to classify cutouts by number and shape, teaching her to seriate by putting different-size plastic circles on a stick, teaching her left from right, and showing her how to draw circles, squares, and triangles. How far did these planned activities go toward turning Vicky into a child prodigy? This is hard to say. Although we can assess the effects of training done under carefully controlled experimental conditions, it is harder to evaluate individual programs within the home. We do know, of course, that even infants are capable of learning. And since the developmentally advancing preschooler can learn so much more, she seems to some educators and parents an irresistibly fertile subject for scheduled teaching. Exactly how much *can* she be taught?

NURSERY SCHOOL

There goes four-year-old Vicky, scooting around in a wheelchair, since she broke her leg in a sledding accident three weeks ago. Is she staying home to recuperate? Far from it. She is back at nursery school, wheelchair, cast, and all, making paper placemats, painting pictures, building with blocks. She has had to curb her more energetic activities for the time being. But Vicky is

The nursery school, where work is child's play.

(Ben Ross, Photo Trends.)

a typical student at a good nursery school in not wanting to miss school—and in feeling that a day without nursery school is an incomplete day.

Public nursery schools were first established in 1919, began to flourish within the decade, and by 1972, more than 4 million children between three and five years of age were enrolled in public and private nursery schools (Stocker, 1973). The number of children in these programs increased by more than 1 million between 1964 and 1972, and by 1980, more than $7^1/_2$ million children are expected to be enrolled. Federal funding for preschool programs was nonexistent in 1960. By 1972 it amounted to about 1 billion dollars and is expected to keep rising.

These nursery schools cover a wide range. They may be commercial or nonprofit enterprises or parent-run cooperatives. Teachers may be accredited and certified—or untrained. Some run two or three half-days a week, other five full days. They are located on campuses, in churches, in apartment buildings, and at shopping centers. Very few are run by public school systems. Some are models of what early childhood education should be while others are no more than glorified baby-sitting services. And sometimes even the baby-sitting is inadequate.

What Children Do in Nursery School

Despite their differences, most nursery schools have a great deal in common. The following schedule would probably be typical for the vast majority (Evans, 1971):

Arrival and health inspection
Outdoor and/or indoor play   20–30 minutes
Toilet and clean-up   10 minutes
Music   10–20 minutes
Snack time   10–15 minutes
Rest (may include listening to
   records, looking at books, etc.)   15 minutes
Indoor free play   20–30 minutes
Story time: toilet and clean-up   15–30 minutes
Outdoor play and departure

Even today, many people still feel that nursery school is nothing but a baby-sitting service where children can play. But the experience can offer much more than that. We have to remember that play is the work of children. Keeping this in mind, it is easy to understand how a well-run, well-equipped nursery school can, through children's play, foster their development.

A Typical Day

As Vicky arrives at nursery school, at 8:50 A.M., she takes off her jacket and hangs it up on the hook labeled with her name in large block letters. She greets her teacher with a kiss on the cheek and her best friend, Bobby, with an excited announcement about the kittens she saw "being borned" yesterday. Bobby and she scamper over to the dress-up corner, where they both don hard hats and play for a while at being construction workers. When this palls, she wanders over to the easel to paint a bright blue picture. After she has finished it to her satisfaction, she goes into the washroom, which is shared by both sexes, and chats there while washing the paint off her hands.

Up to her elbows in soap, Vicky is summoned by the teacher to come out to join the other children. She rinses off and finds a spot in the circle the children have formed around Tom, their new student teacher. Tom has brought his guitar to school today and is about to teach the group a lively action song. After several simple, catchy songs, it is time for apple juice and graham crackers.

Today it's Vicky's turn to pour the juice for her table. No one scolds her when she spills some on the floor. As the children sit at the tables, conversation goes on at a brisk pace about baby brothers who spit up their dinner, Sunday visits to the zoo, overflowing toilets, new shoes, and all sorts of other important experiences in a preschooler's life.

Through play with others, a child learns to cooperate toward common goals and develops a sense of other people's perspective and feelings.

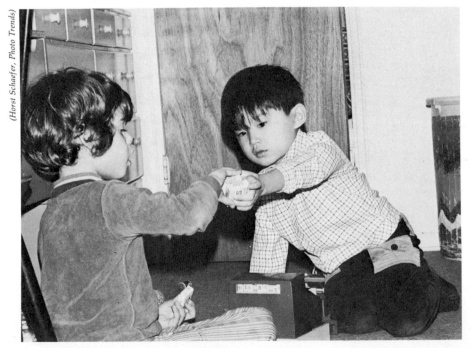

(Horst Schaefer, Photo Trends)

At rest time today, Vicky decides to sit quietly on the floor, putting together some simple wooden puzzles that show various "community helpers." After she has put the completed puzzles back on the shelf, she seeks out Bobby, and the two of them take turns being a baby and pushing each other around in a sturdy wooden carriage. Before they realize it, it's time to put away the carriage and the baby bottle they've been using as a prop, and to go over to hear the teacher read a story.

Thumb in mouth, Vicky listens to the adventures of a brave little rabbit. After the rabbit is safely home, the children put on their jackets, with varying degrees of skill and help from the teachers. They dash out to the playground, where, with whoops and hollers, yowls and squabbles, they climb on the jungle gym, go up and down on the seesaw, thread their way through the crowd on tricycles, crawl in the corners, or stand around trying to decide what to do. At 11:45, Vicky's father comes to pick her up. Another day at nursery school is over.

How Children Develop in Nursery School
Early childhood education may well make a deeper, longer-lasting impression than later educational experiences. For these first few years are the "root years" for psychosocial development, concept formation, language, and creativity (Mukerji, 1965). These are also years when physical development is proceeding rapidly, and when both large- and small-muscle coordination are fostered by nursery school activities.

Psychosocial Development
During the nursery school years Vicky learns about herself, developing a sense of who she is. Her sense of autonomy flourishes as she picks and chooses from the many activities available to her. Since these activities are tailored to her interests and her abilities, she experiences many successes. And with each one, her confidence grows and her self-image prospers. Through play with other children, she has many opportunities to cooperate toward common goals and to develop a rudimentary sense of understanding other people's perspective and feelings. And when cooperation turns into conflict, she learns how to deal with frustration, anger, and hurt feelings. Preschool experiences are particularly valuable in helping children from small families to learn how to get along with other people, both adults and children.

Cognitive Development
Formal teaching of academic skills may or may not take place in nursery school, depending on the orientation of the particular school. Those schools that are based on the theories of Piaget or the Italian educator Maria Montessori have a strong cognitive bent. Some schools place heavy

(Enid Elliot)

Even when no formal instruction takes place, cognitive development can be advanced.

emphasis on teaching the alphabet and numbers to children; others feel that this can wait for kindergarten.

Even when no formal instruction takes place, the teachers in a good nursery school usually try to advance the children's cognitive development to some degree. They provide a variety of experiences so that children learn by doing. They offer a rich, well-balanced program that stimulates the children's senses—through music, art, and tactile materials like clay, paint, water, sand, and wood. They are always alert to ways they can nurture the children's powers of observation, their sense of curiosity, their flights of creativity, and their proficiency in language skills. They provide opportunities in the daily play schedule for the children to learn such concepts as space, time, age, size, and many other relationships between people and things. They encourage the children to solve problems—social, practical, and intellectual. And, throughout everything, they encourage the children to talk about their responses to their daily experiences. As Schermann (1966) puts it, the ideal teacher is—among other things—"an astute observer and a skillful conversationalist [p. 273]."

Vicky's language develops rapidly in the preschool years. Her vocabulary grows every day—although not all her new words are equally delightful to her parents. She is forced to abandon her egocentric speech in order to make her teachers and playmates understand her. She becomes more familiar with books and stories and thus is getting ready for the more serious language learning that awaits her in first grade.

In the final analysis, though, nursery school's most important contribution to Vicky's future academic career is the feeling that she gets in these years that school is fun, that learning is satisfying, and that she is competent in the school situation.

PRESCHOOLS FOR CULTURALLY DEPRIVED CHILDREN

Michael, the only child of middle-class suburban black parents, is about to go to his first day of kindergarten. It seems that the first five years of his life have been skillfully engineered to prepare him for this day. His parents have engaged him in conversation from infancy, taught him nursery rhymes, and answered his every question. Today he is quite proficient in his use of words. He has his own favorite picture books, which he knows by heart, and he is used to seeing other people reading for pleasure and information. He has a wealth of toys that have been specially designed to help him learn such concepts as color, size, and shape, and to encourage him to use his imagination. He also has his own crayons and scissors, which he handles with dexterity. He has been to many of the places he will read about in his first school readers—the zoo, the circus, the park—and even a real working farm, where his parents took him on a vacation.

Wendell, the eldest of four children of a poor black family trying to get by in an overcrowded slum apartment, is also going to kindergarten. For him it is like setting foot on another planet, a strange world where the teacher will have trouble understanding what he says, even though they both ostensibly speak the same language. The utterances that serve Wendell adequately in his daily life will strike his teacher as slurred, ungrammatical, and almost incomprehensible.

Wendell will not realize when she calls him by name because at home he is always called by his nickname, "Junior." As a matter of fact, Wendell is spoken to very little at home, by any name. Caught up in the daily struggle for survival after her husband's desertion, Wendell's mother has little time or inclination for answering his questions, telling him stories, or teaching him nursery rhymes. Theirs is not a verbal household.

Wendell has never seen a book at home, much less had any of his own. He has had pitifully few toys, and these have been cheaply made and easily broken. He has never colored with a crayon nor cut with a scissors. The few times he has been out of his immediate neighborhood—either to accompany his mother to the welfare office or to visit his grandparents—have been major events. These trips were not undertaken for his pleasure, and the fears and anxieties they engendered in him were neither recognized nor dealt with. (These descriptions of Michael and Wendell were based on comparisons in Crow, Murray, & Smythe, 1966, pp. 205–208.)

Michael and Wendell will have very different experiences in kindergarten and throughout their school years. Although Michael's parents are of a minority racial group, they are solidly middle-class, and so is he. As such he is likely now to see school as a comfortable and enjoyable place to be, and eventually as a vehicle for success. On the other hand, Wendell's impoverished background will give him trouble when he tries to learn how to read. Frustration and failure will be his constant companions through school.

For more than fifty years, educators have recognized that children from the lower social classes enter school with a considerable handicap. Not until the last decade, though, have large-scale programs been developed to help the Wendells of our society *before* they reach the age of formal schooling. Such programs try to compensate for all the experiences that these children miss out on during the early years—the experiences with language, with the use of a variety of materials, with the handling of educational implements, with the opportunity to see and learn about a wide variety of events.

The best known of the compensatory preschool programs is Operation Head Start, the federally funded program launched in the mid-1960s under the aegis of the Office of Economic Opportunity. Head Start attempted to give poor children a boost early in life by tending to their physical health, their family's social welfare, and their educational needs. Through Head Start, millions of children received medical checkups and whatever follow-up care was needed; an enriched school curriculum where they did all the things children in standard nursery schools do, but with extra, individual attention; and special attention in learning how to speak and listen, in overcoming shyness with strangers, and in developing both large-motor and fine-motor coordination.

Head Start became a very political program, with its proponents claiming great gains in IQ and educational prowess for the children enrolled in it, and its opponents calling it a waste of public funds. Follow-up studies (Westinghouse Learning Corporation, 1969) have shown that the rises in IQ of Head Start children have not persisted through their later school years. But instead of being an indictment against the program itself, this finding probably means that the type of intensely individualized education that it offers on the preschool level should be started earlier and continued for at least some of the elementary grades.

DAY-CARE CENTERS

Vicky's mother left her job as a copywriter in an advertising agency three weeks before Vicky was born. Her father continued to work as a teacher. Now Vicky is three years old, and her mother wants to go back to work. She misses the work she had enjoyed and had done well; she does not enjoy being home with a small child; and, with the cost of everything constantly on the rise, she feels that added income could provide many extras for the entire family.

But Vicky's parents know that the first few years of life are important ones for children's development, and so they want to provide the very best day care possible. As soon as they begin to explore the facilities in their community, though, they find that there is no day-care program that they consider adequate. They are now faced with a difficult decision. Should Vicky's mother take the full-time job she has been offered and settle for less than ideal care for her child; should she look for part-time work that would mesh with her husband's schedule; should he change his schedule; or should one of them stay home until Vicky goes to school all day?

Vicky's parents are caught on the horns of the same dilemma that faces millions of parents across the nation. The situation in their community is typical. There is a woeful inadequacy of day-care services for all the children who need them now, let alone for all those who *would* need them if their mothers went out to work. There are more working mothers now than ever before, and the availability of day care has not kept up with the need.

There are in the United States now about 6 million children under six whose mothers work outside the home (Stocker, 1973). But only 625,000

There is a woeful inadequacy of day-care services for all the children who need them now, let alone all those who would need them if their mothers went out to work.

(Shelly Rusten)

(Marcia Keeger, Photo Trends)

Day care: comprehensive, developmental, or custodial

can be cared for in licensed private and nonprofit day-care centers (Keyserling, 1972). Where are the rest? Some are cared for at home by the father or another relative. About 2 million are cared for in another person's home, and less than half of these "day-care homes" are licensed (Keyserling, 1972). Many of them are inadequate, with "too many horrifying examples of children neglected and endangered in both licensed and unlicensed centers [White House Conference, 1970, p. 274]."

What constitutes good day care? The Office of Child Development of the United States Department of Health, Education and Welfare has defined three types of child care (Stocker, 1973):

1   *Comprehensive child development programs*, which embrace all or nearly all the needs of a growing child and his family—educational, nutritional and health—plus involvement of parents through instruction in the fundamentals of child development and family counseling.

2   *Developmental day care*, which is designed to enable mothers of young children to work and to provide their children with an opportunity for social and educational development. It involves trained people working with children, availability of books and toys, meals meeting nutritional requirements, and some medical care.

3   *Custodial child care*, which involves little more than ensuring the supervision and physical safety of children while their mothers are at work.

People in charge usually have little or no training in child development; there are few books or educational toys; and entertainment is generally provided by a TV set [p. 8].

The first type of care is very expensive. It is unnecessary for middle-class children, but desirable for disadvantaged youngsters. The third type is inexpensive—and common, but inadequate. The second type is the most realistic goal for most day-care programs. A good day-care center of this type has many of the same activities as a good nursery school. It runs for a longer time, though—possibly from 7:30 A.M. till 5:30 P.M., instead of the two- or three-hour morning or afternoon program of the typical nursery school. Since children spend so much time in the day-care center, it must provide more of what the good home provides. The younger the child, the smaller the group should be, and the fewer adults should become involved in his or her care. Poor day care can be a negative experience in a child's life, but a good, creative, well-run program can expand a child's horizons while it expands those of her parents.

KINDERGARTEN

Kindergarten is a transitional year between the relative freedom of nursery school and the relative structure of formal schooling. In 1972, more than

Kindergarten: An extension of nursery school that helps prepare children for formal education

(Shelly Rusten)

2¹/₂ million five-year-olds were attending kindergarten (Stocker, 1973), almost all in programs run by their local public school systems.

In many ways, kindergarten is an extension of nursery school. Some of the functions of kindergarten, for example, as expressed by Widmer (1967), would apply equally to nursery school. Widmer defines the purposes of kindergarten as helping to promote and maintain children's health and physical development; providing the opportunity to broaden social contacts; offering a rich environment for living, thinking, and learning; cultivating the foundations for the three R's; providing opportunities for the expansion of language as a means of communication and expression; broadening children's understanding of the social and scientific worlds; providing satisfying esthetic experiences; and providing opportunities for children to develop a sense of responsibility.

Kindergarten *is* different from nursery school, though. The kindergarten teacher usually has to be certified by the state, as compared with the nursery school teacher who often needs no more than a warm heart, a strong back, and a feeling for children. The kindergarten is usually located in the same neighborhood public school where its students will go through the primary, and maybe all the elementary, years. And there is usually a fair amount of emphasis in kindergarten on preparing children for the first grade, by teaching them their letters and their numbers, in addition to all the other activities that are similar to those offered in nursery school. As Evans (1971) sees it:

> The flexibility of a kindergarten curriculum . . . enables a good teacher to infuse daily activities with ample doses of basic language, mathematical, science, and social studies concepts if she so desires. In fact, both the nursery school and kindergarten settings provide an extensive opportunity for a teacher to "do her own thing," at least by comparison to most upper grades, where parameters are typically firmer [p. 7].

Several studies have indicated that children who attend kindergarten generally do better later on with reading skills, like improved word recognition, word comprehension, and reading rate (Evans, 1971). Although this is not true of all children, nor of all kindergartens, the value of the kindergarten experience appears to be well accepted both by the educational community and by the general public.

Language in the Preschooler

"I'm never going back to Pittsburgh any, any more!" announced Vicky, age three, shortly after a family move. Her speech is now at quite a sophisticated level. Her grammar is now about as complex as that of most adult everyday speech, although she does, of course, still make a fair number of mistakes. Almost everything she says is intelligible, even to strangers. And her vocabulary has grown from the 300 words she understood at the age of two to a comprehension of about 900 words (Smith, 1926; see Table 8-1).

NORMATIVE LANGUAGE DEVELOPMENT IN THE PRESCHOOL YEARS

Between three and four years of age, Vicky uses three- to four-word sentences that are termed "telegraphic" because they include only the most essential words. She asks many questions and can give and follow simple commands. She names familiar things, such as animals, body parts, and the important people in her life. She uses plurals and the past tense, and uses "I," "you," and "me" correctly. Her vocabulary is somewhere around 900 to 1,200 words.

Between four and five, Vicky's sentences average four to five words. She can now deal with such prepositions as "over," "under," "in," "on," and "behind." She uses verbs more than nouns, and she now understands and speaks a total of some 1,500 to 2,000 words.

Between five and six, she begins to use sentences of six to eight words. She can define simple words, and she knows some opposites. She is using more conjunctions, prepositions, and articles in her everyday speech. Her speech is fairly grammatical, although she still neglects the exceptions to

Table 8-1 Vocabulary Understood and Spoken by Preschool Children (*Smith, 1926*)

Age*	Number of Words
0–8	0
0–10	1
1	3
1–3	19
1–6	22
1–9	118
2–0	272
2–6	446
3	896
3–6	1,222
4	1,540
4–6	1,870
5	2,072
5–6	2,289
6	2,562

*Where there are two numbers, the first indicates years, the second indicates months.

rules. Her language is becoming less egocentric and more socialized, and she now has a vocabulary of 2,000 to 2,500 words.

Between the ages of six and seven, Vicky's speech becomes quite sophisticated. She now speaks in compound, complex, and grammatically correct sentences, uses all parts of speech, and has a vocabulary of 3,000 to 4,000 words.

DEVELOPMENTAL PATTERNS OF SPEECH

Not only does the form of children's speech change as they mature, but its very functions become radically different. The meaning of the infantile speech is very different from that of an older child's utterances. After having observed speech changes in many children, including his own, Piaget (1955) characterized preschool speech as being of two types: *egocentric* or *socialized*.

Egocentric Speech

Egocentric speech consists of repeating words and syllables for pleasure, of *monologue* (talking to oneself), and of *collective monologue* (two or more children talking *at* each other, with no communication intended). Because this kind of speech fails to consider the other person's point of view, it is not communicative. But it does have other functions. Just as the sensorimotor infant babbled for the sheer pleasure of it, the preoperational child repeats words and phrases just to exercise verbal schemata. Also, the child talks to himself, partly because he does not yet fully differentiate the word he says from what that word represents. His speech becomes part of his activity. Another purpose served by the monologue is wish fulfillment. If a child cannot attain her goal, she may speak as if she can. Thus, afraid of the thunder, Vicky might scold it and say, "Be quiet, thunder. You bother me."

The younger the preschooler, the greater the proportion of egocentric speech. When Vicky enters school and must communicate with her teachers and the other children, her use of egocentric speech will diminish sharply.

Primary Social Attachment Speech

After studying developmental speech patterns of preschoolers, Schacter (1973) described this category, comparable to Piaget's egocentric speech. Before the age of three, most speech is involved with getting what one wants ("more paste"), making me-too statements (Jane: "I'm making whip cream." John: "I'm making whip cream, too"), learning about the world ("What's that?"), and reporting ("I'm going to get the paste"). In this stage children do not differentiate much between themselves and others. Speech at this level is full of desire requests to adults and, in fact, is directed mostly to adults, thus fostering caretaker-child attachment.

A Conversation between Two 4-year-olds

Boy 1	If you make faces you will turn into mudpies, so don't make them.
Boy 2	I'll make you shut up. I'll make you shut up.
Boy 1	Can't
Boy 2	Can
Boy 1	The books are going to fall down and smash your motorcycle.

Socialized Speech

This more advanced preschool speech *is* for communication. Piaget (1955) divides it into four categories: *adapted information* (an exchange of information between speaker and listener); *criticism*; *commands, requests, and threats*; and *questions and answers*. See Table 8-2.

Schacter (1973) divides this category into *secondary sociable speech*, which appears at about age three, and *tertiary socialized speech*, which develops at age four or five. Secondary sociable speech includes ego-

Table 8-2   Analysis of Preschool Speech *(Piaget, 1955)*

Type of Speech	Proportion of Total Speech, Percent
Repetition Repeating words and syllables for pleasure	1–5
Monologue Talking to oneself	5–15
Collective Monologue Talking at another person with no communication intended. The presence of another person seems to stimulate speech.	23–30
Adapted Information Exchange of information between speaker and listener	15
Criticism	5
Commands, Requests, Threats	10–15
Questions	15
Answers	15

enhancing boasts ("Look at my big house!") and speech patterns addressed principally to other children: joining statements ("Let's jump") and collaborative statements ("The garage goes there"). By this time, there is an increasing degree of self-differentiation. Tertiary socialized speech includes a lot of explanations, justifications, explanations, rationalizations, and expressions of disagreement. Children now increasingly show an ability to take the listener's point of view.

THE RELATIONSHIP BETWEEN LANGUAGE AND THOUGHT

This association is a controversial one, with Piaget and Vygotsky, the Russian linguist, at opposite poles. To Piaget, thought comes first, and then linguistic expression of it. Language does not structure thought, but is the vehicle for communicating it to another. To Vygotsky, on the other hand, speech regulates cognitive behavior and guides one's actions. Vygotsky (1962) has considered three types of speech: *external*; *egocentric*, or private; and *inner*.

External speech is seen (or, rather, heard) when Vicky talks out loud and acts at the same time, but her speech is not guiding her actions. One morning, for example, Vicky's father walked into his daughter's room to see her crayoning huge circles on the wallpaper, even as she said to herself, "Mommy said I must not write on the walls; I must not write on the walls; I must not write on the walls." Luria (1961) looked at the effects of external speech on the actions of three-year-olds. They were told to say, "Don't squeeze" every time they saw a green light. Later they were given a bulb that could be squeezed. When they saw the green light they squeezed the bulb, even while saying, "Don't squeeze." Thus, their words did not guide their actions.

Egocentric, or *private*, *speech* is considered noncommunicative by Piaget, who feels that children talk out loud because they have not yet fully differentiated thought from action. Vygotsky, though, feels that idiosyncratic private speech helps to guide children's behavior and helps them to solve problems. Kohlberg, Yaeger, and Hjertholm (1968) have hypothesized five levels, or types, of private speech based on Vygotsky's theories:

Level I. Presocial Self-stimulating Language
   1. *Word play and repetition.*—Repeating words or phrases for their own sake (. . . "A whats, a whats. Doodoodoo, round up in the sky.")

Level II. Outward-directed Private Speech
   2. *Remarks addressed to nonhuman objects.*—For example, "Get back there," addressed to a piece of sticky paper clinging to the child's finger.
   3. *Describing own activity.*— . . . Remarks about the self's activity which communicate no information to the listener not apparent from watching him, that is, describing aspects of the self's activity which are visible to the other person

whose attention does not need to be directed to it. The description is in a form which has no task-solving relevance or planning function. It is present tense rather than past tense. (Similar to Piaget's 1926 category of "collective monologue.") [Example: "I'm playing with this."]

Level III. Inward-directed or Self-guiding Private Speech
   4. *Questions answered by the self.*—For example . . . "Do you know why we wanted to do that? Because I need it to go a different way."
   5. *Self-guiding comments.*— . . . "The wheels go here. We need to start it all over again." . . . these comments are task or goal oriented. Speech precedes and controls activity rather than follows it. Such speech often involves cognitive analysis or inferring, for example, reasons for action, analysis of the situation, or reference to nonvisible attributes of the activity.

Level IV. External Manifestations of Inner Speech
   6. *Inaudible muttering.*—Statements uttered in such a low voice that they are indecipherable to an auditor close by.

Level V. Silent Inner Speech or Thought [pp. 707–708].

Inner speech, to Vygotsky, is egocentric speech that "goes underground." He feels that overt speech eventually becomes internalized as verbal thought, or, as he puts it, "thinking in pure meanings [1962, p. 149]."

HOW CHILDREN LEARN LANGUAGE

The preschool Vicky is now saying an untold number of novel sentences, saying things that have never been said exactly the same way before. She obviously knows a limited set of rules from which she can generate an infinite number of sentences. These rules are the grammar of her language; the way she learns how to use this grammar is termed *language acquisition*.

Does a child learn to speak through imitation, which is then reinforced? Probably not. The kinds of early grammatical mistakes that children make do not reflect usage they are likely to hear. Vicky talks about "mouses" instead of "mice"; she tells us that her mother "goed" to work, instead of saying she "went" to work. She overgeneralizes those rules that she has become aware of, and even hearing the correct version does not ensure proper imitation, as can be seen from the following exchange (Gleason, 1967, cited in Cazden, 1971):

She said, "My teacher holded the baby rabbits and we patted them."
I asked, "Did you say the teacher held the baby rabbits?"
She answered, "Yes."
I then asked, "What did you say she did?"
She answered again, "She holded the baby rabbits and we patted them."
"Did you say she held them tightly?" I asked.
"No," she answered, "She holded them loosely."

Conversations like this make us question the possibility that an imitation-reinforcement model can explain language acquisition. Further evidence against it is the fact that parents rarely bother to correct their small children's incorrect grammar. Adults intuitively realize that this is unnecessary. As long as children hear well-formed sentences spoken by those around them and take part in conversations about things they care about, they will learn their native tongue. Eventually they will absorb the appropriate grammatical rules and exceptions and end up speaking as grammatically as those around them.

There is abundant evidence that twins take longer to learn language than do singly born children. This has been brought out by Luria and Vygotsky and confirmed by studies in this country and in England (Mittler, 1970). This language retardation among twins may be due to their general developmental immaturity. Or it may be due to other causes, as suggested by Vygotsky (Mittler, 1970):

> The closer the social relationship, the less the need to make meaning fully explicit; communication goes forward against a backcloth of shared identification and affective sympathy which removes the need for elaborated verbal expression [p. 755].

LANGUAGE AND SOCIAL CLASS

One of the most pressing problems in our society can be summed up by the following statement (Hess & Shipman, 1965):

> Children from deprived backgrounds score well below middle-class children on standard individual and group measures of intelligence (a gap that increases with age); they come to school without the skills necessary for coping with first grade curricula; their language development, both written and spoken, is relatively poor; auditory and visual discrimination skills are not well developed; in scholastic achievement they are retarded an average of 2 years by grade 6 and almost 3 years by grade 8; they are more likely to drop out of school before completing a secondary education; and even when they have adequate ability are less likely to go to college [p. 870].

Socioeconomic influences on intellectual development and academic achievement can be seen most clearly in the area of language. Children who come from lower-class homes acquire language more slowly, retain immature pronunciations longer, know fewer words, and speak shorter sentences than do middle-class children (Cazden, 1968). In our highly verbal society, developmental retardation in language is a crippling handicap. Through *sociolinguistics,* the study of the interaction between language and its social setting, researchers are trying to discover the precise mechanisms that cause these different patterns of speech, which appear to be different in a qualitative way, as well as a quantitative one. In other words, lower-class children are not simply less mature in their language development than middle-class children; their language is also different in kind.

Sociolinguistic studies have focused on social-class differences in language behavior, in mother-child interaction and teaching styles, and on the efficacy of teaching parents more efficient ways of dealing with their children. The major voice in this new science has been that of Basil Bernstein, an English sociologist whose findings seem as relevant in the United States as they do in Great Britain. Bernstein (1961) identified two patterns of speech that he called codes: the *restricted code* used by the lower social classes, which uses short, simple sentences and offers little detail or precision of concepts and information, and the *elaborated code* of the middle class, in which messages are more complex, more individualized, and more specific to a particular topic, situation, or person. Early experience with these ways of communicating affects much more than one's language facility and intellectual development. Since language is a form of social behavior, the way it is used in the home influences the way children relate to their parents and to the larger world.

Parent-Child Interaction

Bernstein (1964) also distinguishes two different types of family control, paralleling the two linguistic codes and pointing up the social significance of language. Families who use elaborated codes are more likely to be person-oriented. In their dealings with their children they are more likely to consider the unique characteristics of an individual child, rather than the demands of a particular role for that child (such as "smart boy" or "good girl"). Users of restricted codes are more status-oriented. Their behavior with their children is more likely to be governed by their own expectations that the child will automatically obey the more powerful parent and will fulfill a particular role. In status-oriented families, "there is little opportunity for the unique characteristics of the child to influence the decision-making process or the interaction between parent and child [Hess & Shipman, 1965, p. 871]." See Chart 8-1.

Hess and Shipman (1965) interviewed 163 black mothers from four socioeconomic groups: professional, skilled blue-collar, semiskilled or unskilled, and families on public assistance. They taught the mothers three simple tasks, asking them to teach these tasks to their four-year-old children. When the experimenters observed the mothers and children together, they noted very little difference among the four groups in mother-child emotional attachment, but great difference in verbal and cognitive styles.

The middle-class mothers were much more efficient teachers. They were more likely to offer explanations, along with specific information; they clearly defined the tasks their children were expected to perform; and they offered various kinds of support and help. They criticized their children as much as the lower-class mothers, but they praised them a great deal more. By contrast, the lower-class mothers had little success in teaching their children. They had trouble getting the ideas across because they were vague

Chart 8-1   Two Parent-Child Interactions *(After Hess & Shipman, 1965)*

Child is playing noisily in the kitchen with pots and pans; phone rings:

Person-oriented, elaborated-code family
Mother: Would you keep quiet a minute? I want to talk on the phone.

Mother's statement helps the child to relate his behavior to the situation and probably helps him look for action sequences in his own and others' behavior.

Status-oriented, restricted code family
Mother: Be quiet.

Mother's message cuts off thought and offers little opportunity to relate what she said to the context for saying it.

in their instructions, in their expectations, and in the overall problems involved. Furthermore, instead of encouraging their children to solve the problem at hand, the lower-class mothers stressed compliance and passivity, implying that the children were supposed to follow orders unquestioningly, to do what they said just because they said it, and not for any other reason.

The authors conclude (Hess & Shipman, 1965):

The effect of restricted speech and of status orientation is to foreclose the need for reflective weighing of alternatives and consequences; the use of an elaborated code, with its orientation to persons and to consequences (including future), tends to produce cognitive styles more easily adapted to problem-solving and reflection. . . .
The picture that is beginning to emerge is that the meaning of deprivation is a deprivation of meaning—a cognitive environment in which behavior is controlled by status rules rather than by attention to the individual characteristics of a specific situation and one in which behavior is not mediated by verbal cues or by teaching that relates events to one another and the present to the future. This environment produces a child who relates to authority rather than to rationale, who, although often compliant, is not reflective in his behavior, and for whom the consequences of an act are largely considered in terms of immediate punishment or reward rather than future effects and long-range goals [p. 885].

In a similar study (Bee et al., 1969), researchers looked at the interaction between 114 middle-class and lower-class mothers and their four- and five-year-old children. The experimenter made a house out of blocks, asked the child to build one like it, and told the mother she could help her child as

(Erika Stone, from Peter Arnold)

Family control parallels linguistic codes; elaborated codes are likely to be person-oriented, while restricted codes tend to be status-oriented.

much or as little as she wanted. Considerable differences in style showed up between the two groups of mothers. The middle-class mothers paid more attention to their children in the waiting room, giving them more approval and fewer orders. They spent more time helping their children, gave fewer specific suggestions, and were more likely to tell them what they were doing right than to point out errors. The language of the middle-class mothers was much like Bernstein's elaborated code, with more words, longer sentences, more complex syntax, greater use of adjectives and verbs, and less use of personal pronouns. With their children, they were person-oriented more than status-oriented. They let the children work at their own pace, offered general suggestions, encouraged exploration, and emphasized success rather than failure. The lower-class mothers were more controlling, restrictive, and disapproving, and they paid less attention to their children.

Improving Children's Language by Working with Mothers

The evidence seems to show that lower-class mothers love their children just as much as middle-class mothers and are just as eager for them to succeed. Is it possible, then, to intervene in poor families in such a way as to raise the sophistication level of the parents and, ultimately, the language ability of the children? Before we begin to impose middle-class values on families in a different subculture, we have to weigh very carefully the effects of such intervention. What will it do, for example, to the mothers' own self-esteem? Will they think less of themselves if they have to be taught to relate to their children? Will it interfere with the mother-child relationship if a mother feels her competence is being judged by her child's competence? A great deal of sensitivity is required in any program that attempts to alter basic styles of living and interrelating. But the justification for such intervention lies in the reality that success in our society tends to come to the person with verbal and academic skills. We have to develop ways of helping people with these skills while encouraging them to be proud of their own unique heritage. It is probable that we will see a growing emphasis on teaching parents in disadvantaged families how to deal with their children more effectively. Such programs do not make a frontal attack on parental language patterns, which probably would be ineffectual, if not absolutely impossible. Instead, they try to change certain aspects of parent-child interaction.

Karnes, Teska, Hodgins, and Badger (1970), for example, recruited twenty poor mothers of one- and two-year-old children, to attend a two-hour meeting once a week for fifteen months (fifteen mothers completed the entire program) to learn how to teach their children. The emphasis during the meetings was on the need for the mothers to respect their children, to maintain a positive approach that minimizes errors, to teach a task by breaking it down into separate components, and to keep learning "fun."

At the end of the program, these mothers' children and a matched control group of children whose mothers received no such training were tested on the Stanford-Binet Intelligence Test and the Illinois Test of Psycholinguistic Abilities (ITPA). The experimental children scored much higher in language and intellectual functioning on both tests than the controls. Although we do not know how well the experimental children's advantage would hold up over time, it does seem fruitful to continue to investigate ways in which we can work with parents to help children develop their cognitive and linguistic abilities.

Working Directly with Preschool Children
The verbal deficiencies of culturally deprived children involve much more than a smaller vocabulary and a tendency to use words less than middle-class children. Blank and Solomon (1968) have postulated that many of these children cannot think abstractly, that they have no "symbolic system by which to organize the plentiful stimulation surrounding them [p. 380]." To develop such abstract concepts as time, space, direction, and com-

parison, children need feedback from an articulate older person who can help them clarify their ideas. Such feedback is often missing in lower-class homes. Believing that most attempts to enrich cognitive development in disadvantaged children do not focus specifically on the development of abstract thinking, Blank and Solomon developed a specialized language tutoring program, which, when put to a controlled test, appears to increase IQ.

Twenty-two urban slum children, ranging in age from three years three months to four years seven months were divided into four groups matched for age, sex, and IQ. The first group received individual tutoring for fifteen to twenty minutes a day, five days a week; the second received the same tutoring three days a week; the third group had daily one-to-one sessions with the same teacher who did the tutoring (to control for the factor of individual attention) but without any tutoring; and the fourth group took part in the regular nursery school program.

The tutoring sessions used a variety of techniques, each one geared to overcome a particular deficiency, such as *selective attention, relevant inner verbalization, ability to categorize, sustained sequential thinking*, and so forth. The youngsters were constantly encouraged to look for the meanings in language, to reason, and to respond in words. After drawing a circle, for example, a child would be asked to draw something "other than a circle" to show that she understood the characteristics of a particular category. After a child located a doll on a table, he might be asked, "Where would the doll be if it fell from the table?" to increase his capacity to imagine future events. To understand cause-and-effect reasoning, a child might be asked, "What is the weather outside today?" and then "Why can't we go out to play?"

After four months, the children in the first two groups showed IQ increases of 14.5 and 7.0, respectively, whereas those in the untutored groups remained substantially the same. Furthermore, several of the tutored children—but none of the untutored—showed changes in behavior and attitudes, including "an apparent joy in learning and the feeling of mastery [p. 388]." The difference between the tutored and untutored groups was striking, strongly suggesting "that exposure to materials, a school-like situation, and an interested adult is not sufficient for learning [p. 388]." The authors recommend maintaining such a program for about two or three years, to consolidate the gains and enable the children to maintain them on their own.

Measuring Preschool Intelligence

Vicky, now four, is sitting in a little room with a man she has never seen before. The man places a toy automobile, a dog, and a shoe in a row on the table in front of Vicky and asks her to name each object. Then he says, "Shut your eyes tight now so that you can't see them." He puts a screen between the child and the objects, and then he covers the dog. Removing the screen, he says to Vicky, "Look! Which one did I hide?" Vicky exclaims, "The doggie!" and gets credit for answering the question correctly.

This task is part of the revised Stanford-Binet Intelligence Test (Terman & Merrill, 1937). This is the famous—or, in some circles, infamous—IQ test. It is only one of a great variety of tests designed to measure the intelligence of children. Intelligence testing has become a major interest of psychologists, educators, and other social scientists.

Intelligence test scores are often used to determine children's acceptance to selective schools, their need for special remedial education, their suitability for foster placement with a particular family, and, sometimes, whether a behavior disorder is related to inappropriate school placement. IQ scores predict future school performance fairly accurately and, to a limited extent, future occupational success.

During the preschool years the intelligence test really comes into its own as a way of measuring childhood intelligence and of predicting adult potential. We have already noted that there is virtually no correlation at all between the scores children under the age of three make on intelligence tests and the scores they will make later on in childhood. This is partly due to the nonverbal nature of infant intelligence tests. But with the advent of language, the tests can now include verbal items. Facility with language is the key that differentiates the baby from the child. From this time on, there is a relatively steady correlation between the preschool child's intelligence scores and those that the same person will make later in life (Honzik, Macfarland, & Allen, 1948). But before we can discuss the ramifications of intelligence testing, it behooves us to give some thought to the nature of intelligence itself.

WHAT IS INTELLIGENCE?

Abstract words and concepts are formidable stumbling blocks to communication. You and I may appear to be having a discussion of "intelligence," when in reality your definition of the word and mine are poles apart, and our conversation breaks down into a "dual monologue."

There is no scarcity of definitions of intelligence. There are, in fact, nearly as many different definitions of this elusive quality as there are people talking about it. At one pole, intelligence is seen as a genetically endowed, inborn, general capacity to develop a number of intellectual abilities. Another view sees it as the ability to do a variety of specific things and to engage in rational, productive behavior.

Wechsler (1944) defines intelligence as the ability "to act purposefully, to think rationally, and to deal effectively with the environment [p. 3]." This would coincide with Piaget's emphasis on adaptive behavior as the basic component of intelligence. Terman (1921), an early student of intelligence, described it as the ability to think abstractly. This definition would preclude its existence in young children, since the capacity for abstract thought does not develop until adolescence. Most contemporary psychologists would be more likely to agree with Piaget (1952), who finds evidence of intelligence in the newborn infant's first adaptive behaviors. And pragmatists define intelligence as "whatever intelligence tests measure."

Obviously, then, there is no one correct definition of intelligence. When we discuss this characteristic, we must remember its complexity and the wide range of meanings subsumed in the word "intelligence." To gain a better understanding of what it can mean, let us look at some of the more important theories about the nature of intelligence.

Intelligence as a General Factor

Some of the early theorists, such as Binet, Simon, Goddard, and Terman, believed that intelligence was an all-encompassing factor that influenced one's abilities in all spheres of activity. The more intelligent you were, the better you were at everything. This general factor was believed to be genetically determined and to be stable throughout life. It was modifiable to some degree, but only within limits.

The Two-factor Theory of Intelligence

Charles Spearman (1927) proposed that intelligence is composed of two factors. The g factor, which represents general intelligence, influences all-around performance. Typical IQ tests (for example, the Stanford-Binet) tend to measure the g factor. This "general fund of mental energy" explains the positive correlations individuals often show in the performance of different kinds of tasks, that is, the common phenomenon of an individual's scoring high on one task and also on others. The s factor, which influences specific abilities, accounts for the differences between an individual's scores on different tasks, that is, the situation in which a person's verbal scores are much higher than his math scores.

Primary Mental Abilities

These abilities, defined by Thurstone (1941), correspond to Spearman's s factors. Thurstone used *factor analysis* on the scores of a large group of children who had taken a variety of intelligence tests. Factor analysis is a statistical technique used to determine a factor common to a variety of items. A factor is composed of a group of measures that have high intercorrelations. Vocabulary tests and reading tests, for example, both measure a common factor of verbal comprehension. The same person taking both tests would probably have scores that correlate highly with each other. Through factor analysis, Thurstone was able to identify seven separate factors that combine to make up intelligence: memory, reasoning, number, perceptual speed, space, verbal comprehension, and word fluency. He devised tests to measure these factors.

The Structure of Intellect

Taking factor analysis several steps further, Guilford (1959) proposed the three-dimensional model of intelligence seen in Figure 8-1. This important theory views intelligence not as a unitary construct but as a complex one, with many facets. According to Guilford, intelligence is made up of 120 different intellectual abilities. These components of intelligence are the result of the interaction of the three major dimensions listed in Chart 8-2. *operations,* or the ways we think; *contents*, or what we think about; and *products*, or the results of the application of a certain operation to a certain content (in other words, our thinking a certain way about a certain issue).

Guilford's theoretical model provides a jumping-off point for devising many different tests of intelligence, each one geared to assess a different facet. To test that component that results from the *cognition* of *figural units*, for example, a person may be asked to recognize pictures of familiar objects even though parts of the silhouettes of these objects have been blocked out. To test the ability to make *transformations* of meaning in *semantic relations*, the testee may be asked to state several ways in which two objects, such as an apple and an orange, are alike. To test the ability of *divergent production*

Figure 8-1   A Three-dimensional Model of Intellect *(Guilford, 1959)*

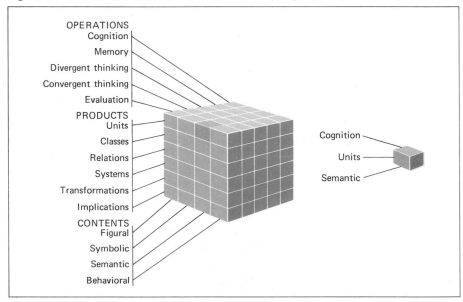

Chart 8-2   Three Dimensions of Intelligence (*After Guilford, 1959*)

Operations are the *ways* we think:
1 Cognition (discovery or recognition)
2 Memory (retention)
3 Divergent thinking (seeking new answers by exploring different avenues of thought)
4 Convergent thinking (leading to one right, or best, answer)
5 Evaluation (deciding about adequacy of knowledge)

The *contents* of our intellectual functioning—*what* we think about—may be:
1 Figural (concrete information perceived through the senses)
2 Symbolic (words and numbers)
3 Semantic (verbal meanings or ideas)
4 Behavioral (social intelligence)

Products are the *results* of our thinking a certain way about certain issues. In other words, a *product* is the result of the application of a specific *operation* to a kind of *content*.
1 Units (a single word, number, or idea)
2 Classes (a set of related units)
3 Relations (relationships between units or classes)
4 Systems (ideas organized in a logical way)
5 Transformations (changes, including modifications in arrangements, organization, or meaning)
6 Implications (seeing certain consequences from the information given)

of *symbolic units*, the examinee may be asked to list as many words as possible beginning with the letter *s*.

> Winston Churchill must have possessed this ability to a high degree. Clement Attlee is reported to have said about him recently that, no matter what problem came up, Churchill always seemed to have about ten ideas. The trouble was, Attlee continued, he did not know which was the good one. The last comment implies some weakness in one or more of the evaluative abilities [Guilford, 1959, p. 355].

To test *divergent production* of *semantic transformations*, more usually known as "creativity" or "original thinking," examinees are presented with a story, for which they are asked to list as many appropriate titles as possible. People who come up with titles that are appropriate but not original are given credit for ideational fluency. But to get credit for originality, they have to come up with many clever, novel, or unusual answers.

We see, then, that the possibilities are almost limitless for devising tests to evaluate these 120 components of intelligence. Instead of saying that someone is "very intelligent," we can say, "John has a good memory for symbolic classes" (he knows the multiplication table) or "Mary can use figural relations to arrive at the right solution" (she's a whiz at fixing cars). These tests, then, have many implications for assessing various kinds of aptitudes and abilities.

Interplay between Neurological Factors and Cultural Learning in the Development of Intelligence

Hebb (1949, 1959) explains intelligence as a neurological function. Early sensory stimulation from the environment—a particular sight or sound, for example—builds up *cell assemblies* in the brain. These cell assemblies are neural activities that correspond to a particular sensory event (such as the tactile stimulation a baby receives when her hand touches a rattle). The cell assembly corresponds to the simplest form of an image or an idea; its activity continues even after the original sensory event is over. A series of cell assemblies make up a *phase sequence,* or "one current in the stream of thought [Hebb, 1959, p. 629]."

Intelligence depends on early stimulation since the cell assemblies are built up slowly in infancy. Therefore, infants from an environment lacking in stimulation do not build up enough cell assemblies to enable learning to take place. Building on his work with animals, Hunt (1951, 1961) confirms this view that intelligence is more than an inherited, genetically determined capacity. The child's earliest experiences determine her intellectual capabilities. Within broad hereditary limits, a child's early encounters with her environment determine how much of her potential will be actualized. Intelligence, then, is a dynamic process, which requires constantly challenging environmental experiences to use inborn abilities.

Ferguson (1954, 1956) describes intelligence as "a collection of distinguishable learned abilities [Reese & Lipsitt, 1970, p. 514]." An individual acquires the ability to reason or to work with numbers, for example, through experience with the environment. But every environment is different, and the abilities developed by any individual will depend, in large part, on those valued and rewarded by the prevailing culture. Thus, children growing up in our society, which stresses verbal and reasoning skills, would be more likely to develop these abilities than would children growing up in an isolated community in Newfoundland, where perceptual and motor abilities are essential for survival (Burnett, 1955). In this view, then, there is "not one 'intelligence' but many, corresponding to the diversity of cultural demands [Reese & Lipsitt, 1970, p. 515]."

The distinction between "fluid" and "crystallized" intelligence is proposed by Cattell (1965) and Horn (1967, 1968, 1970). Fluid intelligence, which reflects neurophysiological structure, increases with neural maturation up to early adolescence and then begins a slow, steady decline. Physiologically based, fluid intelligence is relatively free from the influences of education and culture. It is involved in such activities as rote memory, classification, and reversed digit span (Horn, 1970).

Crystallized intelligence is dependent upon cultural influences unique to a particular society, such as the level of formal schooling. Based on the recall of stored information, it is bolstered by techniques that are usually acquired within a cultural context. Crystallized abilities are measured by questions on vocabulary, general information, and social situations (Horn, 1970).

A Working Definition of Intelligence

Taking these various theoretical definitions of intelligence into account, we can boil them down to a concept that we can work with. When we refer to intelligence in this book, we will consider it a constantly active interaction between inherited ability and environmental experience, which results in an individual's being able to acquire, remember, and use knowledge; to understand both concrete and abstract concepts; to understand the relationships between objects, events, and ideas, and to apply this understanding; and to use all of the above in his or her functioning in daily life.

INTELLIGENCE TESTING

Although defining intelligence is a theoretical exercise, testing it is a pragmatic task, and one that has absorbed the energies of American psychologists for most of the twentieth century. Thinkers who have developed their own theories of intelligence generally agree that this elusive property is composed of several different abilities. And designers of intelligence tests generally aim to measure all the important aspects of intelligence. In actual practice, though, most of the tests are heavily verbal. This may be because our culture is a very wordy one, or because, as the authors of one test say (Terman & Merrill, 1937):

> Language, essentially, is the shorthand of the higher thought processes, and the level at which this shorthand functions is one of the most important determinants of the level of the processes themselves [p. 5].

The widespread administration of intelligence tests has become a highly controversial political issue in our country. The tests are used by some to demonstrate supposed superiority of certain ethnic or racial groups over others. They are castigated by others as racist instruments designed to keep minority groups from attaining full equality. Just how and why are intelligence tests used, and how much information can or cannot be obtained from them?

The Intelligence Quotient (IQ)

The IQ is the "sitting duck" of the field of psychological testing. By itself it is nothing more than a mathematically computed score of a certain type of test, but a great mystique has grown up around it, setting it up as a prime target for attack.

The concept of the intelligence quotient was first developed in France by Alfred Binet, as explained in Chapter 5, and then brought to this country. It is expressed by a number that is the ratio of a person's mental age to his chronological age multiplied by 100, or

$$IQ = MA/CA \times 100$$

The IQ is determined by the administration of a test, whose tasks are set up in order of increasing difficulty. Each task is given a numerical value, and the final score is the child's mental age (see Table 8-3). The child whose mental age is the same as his chronological age has an IQ of 100, which is average. The child whose mental age exceeds her chronological age has an IQ over 100. One whose mental age is less than the chronological age has an IQ under 100. An individual is not likely to get exactly the same IQ score on different intelligence tests, due to the different character of each test.

Test Construction

The constructors of a test must decide what the test is supposed to evaluate and what it is supposed to predict. Then they choose items that seem to fit into the framework of the test and try out these sample items on a group of subjects of the type for whom the test is to be devised. In other words, if the test is supposed to predict the ability of slum children to benefit from a particular educational program, it should be standardized on a sample of poor children, rather than on middle-class ones. The test constructors refine some items, eliminate some, and add others. They determine the ages by which most children master the various tasks, retain those that seem to discriminate between children of different ages and abilities, and discard those that don't. Then they administer the refined test to the *standardization* sample, a different group of children who are also similar in type to those for whom the test is ultimately intended. After seeing how well these children do, norms of achievement are drawn up and usually published in the test manual. An individual child's score is assessed in relation to the scores of the standardization sample. Both reliability and validity must be calculated during test construction.

Reliability of Intelligence Test

A test is *reliable* when a person who takes it on several different occasions obtains consistent scores. The reliability of the IQ as a *group* measure is quite good. That is, if one group of children are retested, there will be about the same number of 100s, the same number of 85s, and the same number of 115s as were obtained at the original time of testing.

Table 8-3   The Meaning of Various IQ Scores Obtained on the Revised Stanford-Binet

The Child Whose IQ Is:	Equals or Exceeds (percent)	The Child Whose IQ Is:	Equals or Exceeds (percent)
136	99	98	45
135	98	97	43
134	98	96	40
133	98	95	38
132	97	94	36
131	97	93	34
130	97	92	31
129	96	91	29
128	96	90	27
127	95	89	25
126	94	88	23
125	94	87	21
124	93	86	20
123	92	85	18
122	91	84	16
121	90	83	15
120	89	82	14
119	88	81	12
118	86	80	11
117	85	79	10
116	84	78	9
115	82	77	8
114	80	76	8
113	79	75	6
112	77	74	6
111	75	73	5
110	73	72	4
109	71	71	4
108	69	70	3
107	66	69	3
106	64	68	3
105	62	67	2
104	60	66	2
103	57	65	2
102	55	65	2
101	52	64	1
100	50	63	1
99	48	62	1
160			1 out of 10,000
156			3 out of 10,000
152			8 out of 10,000
148			2 out of 1,000
144			4 out of 1,000
140			7 out of 1,000

Source: Reproduced with the permission of the publishers from *Supplementary Guide for the Revised Stanford-Binet Scale* (L) by Rudolph Pinter, Anna Dragositz, and Rose Kushner. Stanford: Stanford University Press, 1944, p. 135.

The IQ of an individual, though, can fluctuate somewhat between different times of taking the test. Some factors that can cause inconsistent test results include fatigue, distractions like noise, a poor choice of test items, and poor test administration and scoring (Reese & Lipsitt, 1970, p. 522). If these factors are present at one test administration but not at another, an individual's score may fluctuate widely.

We determine the reliability of a test by calculating the *correlation* between scores at the two times of testing. The higher the correlation, the closer the scores, and thus, the higher the reliability of the test. Correlation in this sense is a mathematical procedure designed to determine the *degree* and *direction* of the relationship between variables. A positive correlation means that the variable factors vary in the same direction. A negative one means that they vary inversely: As one goes up, the other goes down. Correlations range from −1.0 to +1.0, with −1.0 being a perfect inverse relationship and +1.0 being a perfect positive relationship. The symbol for correlation is *r*.

Generally, the older the child and the shorter the time lapse between test and retest, the more stable the IQ score will be (see Table 8-4). There is very poor reliability on IQs obtained by testing a child under the age of five, and virtually none on those obtained under the age of three (Honzik et al., 1948; Anderson, 1939).

The important thing to remember about the IQ is that it is not a score that we are born with, which we carry about unchanged for the rest of our lives. A better emotional and cultural climate can bear fruit in better IQ

Table 8-4　Reliability of IQ Tests* (*From Honzik et al., 1948*)

The shorter the time span between tests, the more reliable the test.

Age at First Testing	Age at Second Testing	Correlation (*r*)
6 years	7 years	.82
6 years	9 years	.80
6 years	14 years	.67
6 years	18 years	.61

The older the child, the more reliable the test.

Age at First Testing	Age at Second Testing	Correlation (*r*)
4 years	6 years	.62
8 years	10 years	.88
12 years	14	.92

* Test used was the Stanford-Binet.

scores, and a poorer one can bring them down. Thus it is dangerous and unwarranted to pigeonhole children from an early age because of one, or even more, IQ scores.

Validity of Intelligence Tests

A test is valid if it measures what it is supposed to measure, as judged by how well the test scores correlate with other measures.

What are intelligence tests supposed to measure? Wechsler (1966), the developer of several tests, feels they should measure the ability to learn, to comprehend, and to adapt. He also quotes Lorge's definition on what intelligence tests try to measure: "the ability to learn and to solve the tasks required by a particular environment [p. 305]." If we assume, then, that in order to succeed in our culture, one must be able to handle words well and to do well in school, then the intelligence tests are useful, if limited.

The intelligence tests in use today correlate very well with success in school. The Stanford-Binet is especially good at predicting success in such heavily verbal courses as English, history, and reading comprehension, and is less good at predicting success in arithmetic. IQ tests are moderately successful in predicting some types of vocational success—those that depend on "book-learning," but is virtually useless in predicting success in any career that depends on personality, creativity, drive, or some special talent, like music or art. Since they do not measure social maturity, they cannot tell us much about the way an individual will conduct herself in daily life. Since they don't measure original, or divergent, thinking, they can't tell us how well someone will be able to come up with new ways of doing things. Furthermore, the predictive values of the IQ tests are only valid when we apply them to people who are like the children on whom the tests were standardized, namely, white middle-class children.

The IQ is not an *aptitude* test that measures what an individual might learn from an optimal learning environment. It is, rather, a measure of what an individual has already learned. As such, the child who comes from a more favored learning environment will do better in the beginning and continue to do better than a child whose cultural milieu does not provide the same opportunities for learning. Furthermore, the basic skills and attitudes picked up in the early years facilitate later learning. Therefore, the more one has learned in the early years, the more one is able to learn. Compensatory education programs such as Head Start operate on this principle, attempting to reach children early in an effort to improve later learning (Anastasi, 1968). In Chapter 11 we will discuss some of the problems in testing minority-group children in our society.

The Preschool Tests

Tests for preschoolers are administered to one child at a time. Anastasi (1960) describes the preschool test taker:

[T]he subject can walk, sit at a table, use his hands in manipulating test objects, and communicate by language. At these ages, the child is also much more responsive to the examiner as a person, whereas for the infant the examiner serves chiefly as a means of providing stimulus objects [p. 457].

The Stanford-Binet

Standardized for use with children from 2½ to 18 years of age, this test is in actual practice usually used with children between the ages of 3 and 8. In 1916, Lewis Terman revised the Binet-Simon into the Stanford-Binet, and further revisions occurred in 1937 and 1960. Each time, a new standardization procedure was carried out. This is an individual test that requires about thirty to forty minutes to administer to a preschool child. The tester begins by confronting the child with questions below the child's expected mental age to determine the highest level at which the child can answer *all* the questions. This level then becomes the *basal age*, and the lowest level at which the child fails to answer *any* questions is the *ceiling age*. When the ceiling age is reached, the administration of the test comes to an end. At various levels, the test asks the child to give the meanings of various words, to string beads, to build with blocks, to identify the missing parts of a picture, to trace mazes, and to show an understanding of numbers. The way the child responds to the test items is considered a measure of practical judgment in possible real-life situations, memory, and spatial orientation.

The Wechsler Preschool and Primary Scale of Intelligence (WPPSI)

In 1939 David Wechsler designed a test to measure adult intelligence. About ten years later he produced a version suitable for school children (the WISC), and in 1967 developed the WPPSI for use with children aged 4 to 6½. It takes about an hour to administer and is sometimes given in two separate sessions, since children this age are distractible and tire easily. Like the WISC described in Chapter 11, the WPPSI is divided into eleven subtests, grouped into two separate scales: Verbal and Performance. Thus, with this test we can obtain a Verbal IQ, a Performance IQ, and a Full Scale IQ. The subtests for the WPPSI are similar to those in the WISC (see Chapter 11).

Influences on Intellectual Achievement

We'll assume that you, the reader, are a typical college student. As such, you have taken many intelligence tests over the course of your academic career, possibly beginning in nursery school and undoubtedly running through your high school years. The aptitude tests that you took to gain admission to college are one type of intelligence test. As we indicated in the previous section, your scores on these tests were influenced by a host of factors that had nothing whatsoever to do with any inborn intellectual faculty.

(Charles Gatewood)

Intellectual functioning is closely related to emotional functioning; development is greatly influenced by parental attitudes and child-rearing practices.

Your personality, your cognitive style, the socioeconomic climate in your home, your ethnic background, and your ease in the testing situation all affected how well you did in the tests and how well you have done in school. Recent evidence points to other factors that are important influences in the preschool years on test scores and school functioning. Such factors are nutritional status, social and emotional adjustment, and probably most important, the interaction between parents and child.

SOCIAL AND EMOTIONAL DEVELOPMENT

Intellectual functioning is closely related to emotional functioning. It is also related to temperament, in the sense, say, that an active child, who is assertive, curious, and likely to use initiative, does well on intelligence tests and in school. Now we have evidence that a child's social and emotional functioning during the preschool years appears to influence how well he will do in the first and second grades of school.

A group of 323 three-year-old children attending public day-care centers in New York City were rated on their socioemotional functioning, and then followed up in first and second grades. At this time their scores on the

Metropolitan Readiness Test, the Metropolitan Achievement Test, and their teachers' first- and second-grade academic ratings were assessed and compared with their preschool socioemotional ratings. The study found a strong relationship between preschool social and emotional functioning and later intellectual achievement. Report Kohn and Rosman (1972):

> These findings suggest that the child who is curious, alert, and assertive will learn from his environment and that the child who is passive, apathetic, and withdrawn will, at the very least, learn less about his environment because of his diminished contact; he may even actively avoid contact [p. 450].

The same study came up with negative findings related to anger and defiance. There seems to be no relationship between angry, defiant behavior during the preschool years and later intellectual functioning, except for one. Girls who had been angry, defiant preschoolers did poorly on their second-grade achievement tests. These girls may have managed to alienate their teachers in such a way as to interfere with their learning, and this situation may be truer of girls, because teachers may be more likely to put up with angry, defiant behavior in boys.

PARENT-CHILD INTERACTION

Parental influence is much more all-encompassing than a particular study, or even a few studies, would lead us to believe. In the typical experimental study, the researcher chooses one or two variables to examine and pretty much ignores everything else that is going on in the child's life. In reality, of course, everything in a child's life is related to everything else. And although in this chapter we are concerned with the intellectual development of children, we have to realize that parental attitudes and child-rearing practices influence much more than a child's score on the Stanford-Binet. They affect health, emotional functioning, personality development, value systems, and codes of morality, as well as those measures of intellectual development that can be judged by test or classroom performance.

The Effect of Parental Warmth on Academic Achievement

Radin (1971, 1972) defines parental warmth, or nurturance, as the degree of physical or verbal reinforcement a parent gives a child; the degree to which he or she consults with or asks a child to share in some decision; and his or her sensitivity to the child, in anticipating the child's requests or feelings.

Radin (1971) observed fifty-two lower-class mothers, both black and white, and their four-year-old children. In relating her ratings of the mothers' warmth with the children's scores on standard IQ tests, she found a significant correlation. The children of warm mothers were more highly motivated to take the Stanford-Binet test and to do well in school; their IQs on the Stanford-Binet and the Peabody Picture Vocabulary Test were

(Erika Stone, from Peter Arnold)

Parental warmth can motivate a child toward academic achievement.

higher; and they made greater IQ gains during their preschool years. The only group of children for whom this correlation did not hold true were four-year-old white boys. The researcher felt that these boys might be responding more to the influence of their fathers, rather than their mothers.

Accordingly, Radin (1972) then studied the relationship between paternal warmth and the intellectual functioning of four-year-old boys. She found that the more nurturant the fathers were, the higher their sons' IQs were likely to be, and the more restrictive the fathers were (threatening, ordering without explanation, and scolding or spanking), the lower the boys' IQs on the Stanford-Binet.

Sharp class differences showed up. The middle-class father-son pairs showed a positive, significant relationship between IQ and nurturance that was not present in the lower classes. In both groups, however, one component of nurturance—a father's tendency to ask information of his child—showed a positive relationship to the boy's IQ. This may be because fathers are more likely to seek information from brighter children, but it may also indicate that boys whose fathers ask them questions are encouraged to acquire knowledge, to get used to answering questions, and even to ask questions of themselves.

Following these boys up a year later, Radin (1973) found that paternal warmth and interest still exerted a strong influence. The sons of the more nurturant fathers were still scoring higher on IQ tests. The lower-class boys, though, were still not responding similarly to their fathers' warm interest, and, in fact, a negative correlation now appeared between the lower-class boys' IQs and their fathers' expectations. The higher the father's expectations of his son, the lower the boy's IQ.

Maternal Acceleration and Children's Achievement

Maternal acceleration refers to a mother's concern with her child's growth, achievement, and development during the first three years of life—the degree to which she tries to push her child and show off his skills, for example. When forty-four middle-class mothers were rated for acceleration, a surprising sex-related correlation showed up with regard to the children's IQs at age three and six (Moss & Kagan, 1958). Maternal acceleration was related to boys' high IQs at age three, but not girls', and bore no relation to the six-year-old IQs of either sex. Thus it appears that mothers' "pushiness" has no real lasting effect on their children's achievements.

Play in the Life of the Preschool Child

Vicky wakes up to see her clothes for the day laid out for her. She tries putting her overalls on backwards, her shoes on opposite feet, her socks on her hands, and her shirt inside out. When she finally comes down to breakfast, she pretends that the little pieces of cereal in her bowl are "fishies" swimming around in the milk, and, spoonful by spoonful, she goes fishing. After breakfast, she hops on a little stool by the kitchen sink, plunges her arms in soapsuds up to the elbows, and "washes" the dishes.

Throughout the long, busy morning, she plays. She puts on an old hat of her father's, picks up the discarded briefcase he has given her, and is the "daddy" going to work. Next, she becomes the doctor. "There, there, dolly, this'll hurt a little but then you won't get sick," she says in a soothing voice as she administers a "shot" to her doll. She runs outside to splash in the puddles, comes in for an imaginary telephone conversation, turns a wooden block into a truck and makes the appropriate sound effects, and so on, and on, and on. Vicky's day is one round of play after another. She makes a game of everything—and all (or nearly all) becomes play.

An adult might be tempted to smile indulgently at Vicky at play, envy her, and dismiss her activities as a pleasant, if trivial, way to pass the time. Such a judgment, though, would be grievously in error. For play is characteristic of all young mammals and is the work of the young.

Children progress from playing alone to cooperative play
with interaction.

(Singer, Amman Photo Features)

(Charlotte Kahler, Photo Trends)

Through play, children grow. They learn how to use their muscles; they develop the ability to coordinate what they see with what they do; and they develop a sense of mastery over their bodies. Through play, children learn. They find out what the world is like and what they are like. They acquire new skills and learn the appropriate situations for using them. They "try out" different aspects of life. Through play, children mature. They cope with complex and conflicting emotions by reenacting real life in play. They make "their lives more encompassable and endurable [Biber, 1971]."

The preoperational child "may be said to play his way through his life [Maier, 1969, p. 120]." Play is so much a part of his life that he does not completely differentiate reality from fantasy. A child may play that one wooden block is a rabbit and another is the carrot that rabbit is eating. To the child, these blocks actually *become* the rabbit and the carrot, and he treats them as such.

The preschool child engages in many types of play. He tickles his senses by playing with water, sand, and mud. She masters a new skill, like riding a

Chart 8-3   Types of Play among Preschool Children (*From Parten, 1932*)

Unoccupied behavior—The child apparently is not playing, but occupies himself with watching anything that happens to be of momentary interest. When there is nothing exciting taking place, he plays with his own body, gets on and off chairs, just stands around, follows the teacher, or sits in one spot glancing around the room [p. 249].

Onlooker—The child spends most of his time watching the other children play. He often talks to the children whom he is observing, asks questions, or gives suggestions, but does not overtly enter into the play himself. This type differs from the unoccupied in that the onlooker is definitely observing particular groups of children rather than anything that happens to be exciting. The child stands or sits within speaking distance of the group so that he can see and hear everything that takes place [p. 249].

Solitary independent play—The child plays alone and independently with toys that are different from those used by the children within speaking distance and makes no effort to get close to other children. He pursues his own activity without reference to what others are doing [p. 250].

Parallel activity—The child plays independently, but the activity he chooses naturally brings him among other children. He plays with toys that are like those which the children around him are using, but he plays with the toy as he sees fit, and does not try to influence or modify the activity of the children near him. He plays *beside* rather than *with* the other children. There is no attempt to control the coming or going of children in the group [p. 250].

tricycle. He engages in dramatic play, pretending to be someone or something other than himself. And she delights in formal games with their predetermined routines and rules, like ring-around-a-rosy or simple card games.

Children progress from playing alone, to playing alongside other children but not with them, and finally to cooperative play, in which two or more children actually interact.

HOW CHILDREN PLAY

In the 1920s, Mildred B. Parten observed a group of two- to five-year-old children during their free play periods in nursery school. After some preliminary observation, she distinguished six different types of play that these children engaged in (see Chart 8-3). Parten (1932) then observed these children systematically to determine the proportion of time spent in each type of play, and she charted the activities of the thirty-four for whom she had the most complete records.

In 1969, Barnes (1971) set up a study along the same lines and found that

---

Chart 8-3 (Continued)

Associative play—The child plays with other children. The conversation concerns the common activity; there is a borrowing and loaning of play material; following one another with trains or wagons; mild attempts to control which children may or may not play in the group. All the members engage in similar if not identical activity; there is no division of labor, and no organization of the activity of several individuals around any material goal or product. The children do not subordinate their individual interests to that of the group; instead each child acts as he wishes. By his conversation with the other children one can tell that his interest is primarily in his associations, not in his activity. Occasionally, two or three children are engaged in no activity of any duration, but are merely doing whatever happens to draw the attention of any of them [p. 251].

Cooperative or organized supplementary play—The child plays in a group that is organized for the purpose of making some material product, or of striving to attain some competitive goal, or of dramatizing situations of adult and group life, or of playing formal games. There is a marked sense of belonging or of not belonging to the group. The control of the group situation is in the hands of one or two of the members who direct the activity of the others. The goal as well as the method of attaining it necessitates a division of labor, taking of different roles by the various group members and the organization of activity so that the efforts of one child are supplemented by those of another [p. 251].

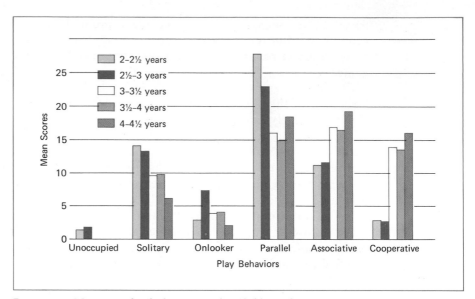

Figure 8-2   Mean Preschool Play Norms for Children Three to Five *(Barnes, 1971)*

the three- and four-year-olds whom he observed played quite differently from those in Parten's group (see Figure 8-2). *If* Barnes' children were typical of children in 1969 and *if* Parten's were typical of those in 1927—a difficult conclusion to draw, since both researchers used comparatively small numbers (thirty-four for Parten, forty-two for Barnes)—then we can draw some inferences about changes in children's play over the years.

From these two studies, it appears that children of today play much less socially than did those of forty years ago. Barnes offers several possible explanations: modern children spend a lot of time watching TV, and therefore less time playing with other children; elaborate modern toys encourage solitary play more than did the simpler ones of the past; and children now grow up in smaller families, with fewer opportunities for playing with brothers and sisters.

Whatever the reason, if children entering school today have fewer social skills than did children of the past, parents and teachers will have to respond in different ways to their needs. It's an area worth exploring.

IMAGINARY PLAYMATES

As Vicky's aunt starts to sit down next to her at the dinner table, Vicky cries out, "You can't sit there!" Pointing to the empty chair, she says, "Schwartzie's sitting there." Puzzled, her aunt turns to Vicky's father, who explains, with a discreet wink, "Schwartzie—he used to be called 'Mr. Schwartz'—is Vicky's friend. He *always* sits next to her." When Vicky spills her milk, she turns to the invisible Mr. Schwartz and says, "Schwartzie, I don't know what to do with you. Why do you spill your milk so much?" During a lull in the conversation, Vicky pipes up with, "Do you know what Schwartzie did today? He climbed all the way up to the top of the jungle gym and he jumped off. And he didn't even hurt himself." (Vicky is still working up her courage to climb to the top of the jungle gym.)

"Schwartzie" is a normal manifestation of childhood. Some 15 to 30 percent of children have imaginary companions between the ages of three and ten (Schaeffer, 1969). These invisible friends usually come into a child's life sometime between the ages of 2½ to 6, and they usually drop out at about the time the child goes to school (Ames & Learned, 1946). The imagined person or animal seems real to the child, who talks to it, plays with it, and refers to it in conversation.

At this age, there's nothing pathological about playing with someone who isn't there. Children who do usually also play well with other children, and when they do so, they don't bring their imaginary companions along. Only and first-born children seem to have them more than do children with older siblings, indicating that these children have found an ingenious way to overcome loneliness (Manosevitz, Prentice, & Wilson, 1973). Bright, creative children are more likely to have imaginary companions than are children of limited intelligence (Jersild, 1968; Schaeffer, 1969).

THEORIES OF PLAY

Play is a multifaceted activity that transcends all levels of a child's life. It engages the emotions, the intellect, the culture, the behavior. As such, it can be explained variously, according to psychoanalytic, cognitive, and learning theories.

Cognitive Dynamics

Piaget (1951) sees play as a way to learn about new and complex objects and events, a way to consolidate and enlarge concepts and skills, and a way to integrate thinking with actions. The way a child plays at any given time depends upon her stage of cognitive development. Thus the sensorimotor child plays in a concrete fashion, moving her body, manipulating tangible objects. Then, as she develops the symbolic function, she can pretend that something exists when it does not; she can play in her mind, so to speak, rather than with her whole body.

In Piagetian terms, "Play is characterized by the assimilation of elements in the real world without the balancing constraint of accepting the limitations of accommodating to them [Ellis, 1973, p. 67]." In other words, the child at play is not developing new cognitive structures (accommodation), but is trying to fit his experiences into preexisting structures (assimilation).

Psychoanalytic Theory

According to Freud and Erikson, play helps a child to develop ego-strength. Through play a child can work out conflicts between the id and the superego. Motivated by the pleasure principle, play is a source of gratification. It is also a cathartic response that lessens psychic tension and gives the child mastery over overwhelming experiences. (When Vicky gave her doll a shot, she was helping to work through her own feelings of fear and helplessness when she herself had received an injection.)

Freud (1955) explains the meaning of play in these terms:

> It is clear that in their play children repeat everything that has made a great impression on them in real life, and that in doing so they abreact the strength of the impression and, as one might put it, make themselves master of the situation. But on the other hand it is obvious that all their play is influenced by a wish that dominates them the whole time—the wish to be grown up and do what grown up people do. It can also be observed that the unpleasurable nature of an experience does not always unsuit it for play. If the doctor looks down a child's throat or carries out some small operation on him, we may be quite sure that these frightening experiences will be the subject of the next game; but we must not in that connection overlook the fact that there is a yield of pleasure from another source. As the child passes over from the passivity of the experience to the activity of the game, he hands on the disagreeable experience to one of his playmates and in this way revenges himself in a substitute [p. 16].

Learning Theory

According to Thorndike (Kimble, 1961), play is learned behavior. It follows the "law of effect," which says that reinforcing a response increases the probability of its occurring again, and punishing a response decreases the probability of its occurring again. It is different from work in that it is not critical for survival, but it is influenced by learning just as work is. Since play depends on its reinforcement by adults in the community, it has a large measure of cultural control. Each culture or subculture values and rewards different types of behavior, and therefore the play of children in different cultures reflects these differences.

Roberts and Sutton-Smith (1962) studied differences in child-rearing patterns and in the games played by children in three separate societies. They found strong relationships between these two factors. Children raised in societies that emphasize responsibility and doing what one is told to do will tend to play games of chance. These games respond to the players passive roles in life and hold out the promise of lifting them out of their lives of humdrum responsibility. Children in societies that value achievement or performance like to play games of physical skill. They can compete in these games in a relaxed fashion since the outcome is less critical than it is in their pressured performances of daily life. And children raised to be obedient tend to play games of strategy. They can thus displace their aggressive tendencies by controlling others in the game.

Testing the Theories

Gilmore (1966) tested the relative influences of the cognitive aspects of play (children want to play with novel toys) and the psychoanalytic aspects (children want to use toys to alleviate their anxieties). He offered different types of toys to two groups of children, aged four to eleven. Those in one group were hospitalized for tonsillectomy, and the others were a matched group of schoolchildren. Some of the toys, like a toy stethoscope, syringe, thermometer, and scissors, were relevant to the hospital experience, whereas others were not; some were novel, others familiar.

All the children in this study preferred novel toys to familiar ones; the hospitalized children were more likely to prefer the hospital-relevant toys than were the control children, but they were also more likely to prefer the novel toys. Therefore, in this case, the children's toy choices could be explained by both the cognitive and the psychoanalytic theories, with the cognitive influences apparently the more important. In other words, the anxiety of the hospitalized children affected their toy choices to some degree, but it was not so strong an influence as the relative novelty of the toys.

This study illustrates the intertwining of cognitive and emotional factors, an intertwining, as we said, that runs through the entire fabric of a child's life.

Summary

1   According to Piaget's *preoperational* stage of cognitive development, the *symbolic function* develops and enables the child to represent and reflect upon people, places, and events in his or her world. Thought is more flexible than during the sensorimotor stage but is still not mature in the adult sense, since the child cannot yet deal with abstractions. The presence of the symbolic-function is manifest through *language, deferred imitation,* and *symbolic play*. However, the preoperational child is still burdened with cognitive limitations such as *egocentrism* and *irreversibility*. The child uses *transductive* reasoning rather than deductive or inductive. During the preoperational stage the child makes forward strides in dealing with concepts such as age, relationality, and classes. Some evidence indicates that carefully designed "training studies" can accelerate cognitive development.

2   Many children from three to six years of age attend preschools and kindergartens. These preparations for formal schooling are of many types and focus on the child's cognitive, emotional, and physical growth.

3   A preschooler's speech is of two main types: *egocentric* and *socialized*. The meaning of egocentric speech has been debated by theoreticians such as Piaget and Vygotsky. Egocentric speech, which fails to take into account the listener's needs, may be used to guide behavior rather than to communicate. Socialized speech is for communication. Generally, the younger the child, the greater the proportion of egocentric speech.

4   During the preschool period, the environment influences, to some extent, a child's facility with language. *Sociolinguistics* is the study of interactive relationship between language and its social setting. Through the study of sociolinguistics we learn that the language of lower-class children is different from that of middle-class children. This difference is largely a result of parent-child interaction, or how parents (particularly the mother) verbally communicate with their children. Improvements in children's language have been brought about by instructing mothers how to teach their children effectively.

5   No one definition of intelligence is accepted by all developmentalists, and no one theory of intelligence is accepted universally. Intelligence appears to be a multifaceted construct: Many different abilities contribute to what we call intelligence. There is a wide variety of preschool intelligence tests, all of which must be assessed in terms of *validity* and *reliability*. The tests tend to be verbal rather than motoric. Intelligence is influenced by one's inherited potential, home life, relationship with parents, and personality.

6   There are many kinds of *play* and many theoretical interpretations of their purpose. Through play, children grow and exercise their physical capabilities, learn about their world, and cope with conflicting emotions by reenacting real-life situations. Types of play range from playing alone, to playing alongside other children but not with them, to playing in cooperation with others. Some children have imaginary companions during childhood. This phenomenon is normal and often reduces loneliness. First-born children have imaginary companions frequently, and highly creative adolescents in literary fields report a number of imaginary companions in childhood.

Suggested Readings

Anastasi, A. *Psychological Testing* (3d ed.). New York: Macmillan, 1968. *Intended as a college text, this is a comprehensive view of current psychological tests and testing problems. It provides material dealing with individual intelligence tests, measurement of intellectual impairment, projective techniques, and other personality tests, as well as a description of the principles of test construction, and problems with psychological testing.*

Ellis, M. J. *Why People Play.* Englewood Cliffs, N.J.: Prentice-Hall, 1973. *A scientific approach to what play is and why people play, including classical, recent, and modern theories of play.*

Flavell, J. H. *The Development of Role-taking and Communication Skills in Children.* New York: Wiley, 1968. *Flavell's experimental background provides a basis for discussion of children's ability to discriminate role attributes in other persons. This text is particularly valuable to behavioral scientists and students of the research process.*

Hunt, J. M. *Intelligence and Experience.* New York: Ronald, 1961. *An examination of* *the concept of intelligence including discussions of the effects of early experience on later problem-solving capacity of humans.*

Hutton, R. E., & Sutton-Smith, B. *Child's Play.* New York: Wiley, 1971. *A complete and well-planned study of the many variables involved in play behavior and the relationship of play to child development. It includes a historical review, normative studies, ecological approaches, and some of the major modern approaches.*

Kellogg, R. *Analyzing Children's Art.* Washington, D.C.: National Press Books, 1969. *A discussion of critical analyses of over half-a-million drawings, paintings, and clay models by children.*

Keyserling, M. D. *Windows on Day Care.* New York: National Council of Jewish Women, 1972. *What the members of the National Council of Jewish Women found in local communities in terms of day-care services and needs in the United States.*

Piaget, J., & Inhelder, B. *The Psychology of the Child.* New York: Basic Books, 1969. *Piaget's own synthesis of his theory of cognitive development. With the assistance of his long-time collaborator Barbel Inhelder, he traces the stages of cognitive development over the entire period of childhood, from infancy to adolescence.*

CHAPTER NINE

PERSONALITY DEVELOPMENT

IN WHICH VICKY DEALS WITH
SEX TYPING, AGGRESSION, AND SUCH

I hear my father and my mother and they are my giants, my king and my queen beside whom there are no others so wise or worthy or honorable or brave or beautiful in this world.
I need never fear: nor ever shall I lack for loving-kindness.

(James Agee, 1957*)

At the age of five, Vicky has definite opinions about people, as about everything else in her life. She says, "I like Daddy. He's a nice daddy. He's not a mad daddy. He's a teasing daddy, and I love him."

Her classmate, David, is another matter altogether. When David commits the social blunder of inviting Vicky to his birthday party, she refuses to go. She explains to her mother, "I don't want to go to David's party because he's too sloppy. Sometimes at school his pants slide down and he doesn't feel it and he doesn't pull them up and I don't like to look at it. And besides, his nose drizzles down and he doesn't blow it and I don't like the way that looks."

While Vicky as an infant displayed, as does every infant, her own unique temperament, it is during the preschool years that she emerges more fully as an individual person in her own right. During these years, her characteristic ways of relating to people are becoming more pronounced, and she is developing many aspects of the personality that will stay with her throughout her life: the conscience that will enable her to make moral judgments of right and wrong, her feelings about herself as an individual and as a member of her sex, and the degree to which she identifies with her parents.

Throughout our study of children, we are interested in the similarities among them as they work their way through different developmental stages, and also in their idiosyncratic ways of approaching life. In this chapter, we will discuss some aspects of psychosexual development, some of the influences that strengthen children's sense of gender, and the ways in which parents influence their children's personalities.

Average Ages for Acquisition of Certain Abilities

Three Years
  Can point out and perhaps name body parts
  Can match primary colors
  Can name familiar animals

Four Years
  Can count to 5
  Can repeat back four digits
  Defines things in terms of function (apple is to eat instead of apple is fruit)
  Recognizes names of colors (which is blue? which is red?)
  Can name shapes (cross, triangle, circle, . . .)

Five Years
  Knows right and left of self, not others
  Can deal with simple opposites
  Counts to 10
  Recognizes coins
  Names colors (the telephone is yellow)
  Has time concepts of day (morning, afternoon, night) and week (yesterday, today, tomorrow)

Six Years
  Repeats five digits back
  Can give uses of some simple objects
  Names at least five colors
  Counts to 100
  Has concepts of space, time, number, and shape

Theoretical Perspectives on Preschool Personality Development

THE PHALLIC (EARLY GENITAL) STAGE OF SIGMUND FREUD

According to Freud, the primary zone of psychosexual pleasure changes at about the age of three or four, when the child passes from the anal stage into the *phallic*, or *early genital*, stage. Interest and pleasure are now concentrated in the genital area, although the child is hardly at the stage of mature adult sexuality. Preschool children exhibit an inordinate amount of interest in anatomical differences between girls and boys and between adults and children, in finding out where babies come from, and in learning about the adult sex act. Their conversation is full of "dirty" jokes, although more of these still seem to be centered around the bathroom rather than the bedroom.

The Oedipus Complex

In the ancient Greek play by Sophocles, Oedipus was the king's son who had been placed in infancy with a foster family. When he grew to manhood, he killed a man, not realizing that the man was the king in disguise—and his own father. He married the widowed queen, never dreaming that she was his mother. Upon learning the truth, he put out his own eyes and sent himself into exile. Freud gave the name of this tragic hero to his concept that every little boy falls in love with his mother and has murderous thoughts toward his father.

According to this theory of the Oedipus complex, during the years from about three till about six, a little boy lavishes love and affection, with decidedly sexual overtones, on his mother, thus competing with his father for the mother's love and affection. Subconsciously, the little boy wants to take his father's place with his mother; yet at the same time he is realistic enough to recognize that his father is much more powerful than he. The little boy is caught up in a whirlpool of conflicting feelings toward his father—genuine affection, tempered by hostility, rivalry, and fear. In the child's strivings to possess his mother for himself, he subconsciously wishes that his father were dead. At the same time that he is experiencing these powerful feelings, he has begun to notice that while he has a penis, certain other children, namely little girls, do not. In his childish mind, his guilt feelings about his yearning for his mother and his resentment of his father combine with his lack of comprehension of anatomical differences, and he fears that what "has happened" to those little girls will happen to him, too. He will be castrated! And the agent of such mutilation will be his angry father. Thus the *castration complex* comes about.

The fearful child represses his sexual strivings toward his mother. He also represses his anxiety over the whole messy situation, stops trying to rival his father, and begins to identify with him, accepting his values. Anna

Freud, the daughter of Sigmund Freud and a psychoanalyst who has concentrated upon the study and treatment of children, calls this "identification with the aggressor [1947]."

The Electra Complex

Freud named the female counterpart of the Oedipal dilemma after Euripides' heroine, who spurred her brother on to kill their mother and stepfather, whom she hated, and thus avenge the murder of their father, whom she had adored. While Freud was vague about its specific mechanisms, he claimed that the Electra complex is similar to the Oedipus—that the little girl desires her father, fears her mother, represses these feelings, and eventually identifies with the same-sex parent. Neither he nor his followers have been able to reconcile this explanation with such unanswered questions as: How does a little girl's sexual attachment to her father develop? (The boy's to his mother develops through his early attachment to her, but the girl presumably has this same primary attachment to her mother rather than her father.) Or, how can a little girl fear castration at the hands of her mother—when both she and her mother are already "castrated"? (The usual explanation is that she believes she has already been castrated—but that even worse may happen to her.)

Penis Envy

At the age of three, Vicky saw a naked little boy for the first time, after a trip to the beach, when her friend John came home with her. As they were about to step into the bathtub to wash off the sand, she pointed to John's penis and asked in wonderment, "What's that?" Her mother answered, "That's something little boys have and little girls don't." "How did he get it?" asked Vicky. "He was born with it," answered Mother.

Some years later, remembering the incident, Vicky's mother asked her, "Were you upset when you realized that John had a penis and you didn't?" Now a sophisticated eleven-year-old, Vicky, who remembers the incident well, answers, "To tell you the truth, I thought it was kind of funny-looking."

Freudian thinkers would dismiss Vicky's statement as nothing more than a cover-up of her true feelings. Freud was quite specific about penis envy in little girls, saying,

> The first step in the phallic phase . . . is a momentous discovery which little girls are destined to make. They notice the penis of a brother or playmate, strikingly visible and of large proportions, at once recognize it as the superior counterpart of their own small and inconspicuous organ, and from that time forward fall a victim to envy for the penis [1905, quoted in Schaeffer, p. 16].

According to Freud, a little girl just can't win. If she succumbs to penis

(Shelly Rusten)

Preschool children exhibit an inordinate amount of interest in anatomical differences between girls and boys and between adults and children, in finding out where babies come from, and in learning about the adult sex act.

envy, she hopes against all odds to get one for herself and to become a man; if she does not, she is "denying" her envy, which could cause adult neurosis. In either case, the little girl inevitably develops a sense of her own inferiority because of that "strikingly visible" organ which she does not have, is likely to become a jealous person, and to turn against her mother, who, she reasons, is the person responsible for her lack of a penis. Eventually, if the girl develops normally (for a female, that is), she

> gives up her wish for a penis and puts in place of it a wish for a child: and *with this purpose in view* she takes her father as a love-object. Her mother becomes the object of her jealousy. The girl has turned into a little woman [quoted in Schaeffer, p. 19].

We see then that in the Freudian paradigm, the very desire for motherhood is the result of penis envy. He takes this belief a step further by claiming that a woman's procreative urge is most fully satisfied by the birth of a son, "who brings the longed-for penis with him."

Womb Envy

Karen Horney, a psychoanalyst who challenged Freud's views of the all-encompassing nature of penis envy, wrote, "I, as a woman, ask in amazement, and what about motherhood?" She later said, "when one begins, as I did, to analyze men . . . one receives a most surprising impression of the intensity of this envy of pregnancy, childbirth and motherhood, as well as of the breasts and the act of suckling [Cherry & Cherry, 1973]."

Development of the Superego

Freud explains the preschooler's superego development as an upshot of the Oedipus situation. By identifying with the parent of the same sex, the child actually takes the parent's personality into her own. In psychoanalytic terms, this is called *introjection.*

> When the boy introjects his father, or the girl her mother, either child constantly then carries around a conscience, representing the parent's wishes, values, and standards. When the child transgresses, this inner voice reprimands him and makes him feel guilty; it is part of the child's own wishes and values [Baldwin, 1968, p. 367].

Thus the superego is comparable to what we think of as the conscience. Because the preschooler's desires for the parent of the opposite sex are so very strong, the new superego has to be very strong to combat these desires. At this stage, therefore, a child's conscience is very rigid. The daughter of parents who value cleanliness and neatness, for example, may become so compulsive about being neat and clean that she will want to change her clothing five or six times in the course of a day. Or a little boy may be tormented by guilt because he fought with a friend, even though his parents do not disapprove of harmless tussling among children of the same size. Only with maturity does the superego, or conscience, become more realistic and flexible, allowing an individual to function according to higher principles while also considering self-interest.

If we are to hew to the Freudian theory, we would be convinced that girls, because of their very anatomy, are functionally incapable of developing a conscience. Explains Freud:

> In girls the motive for the destruction of the Oedipus complex is lacking. Castration has already had its effect, which was to force the child into the situation of the Oedipus complex. Thus the Oedipus complex escapes the fate which it meets within boys, . . . I cannot escape the notion (though I hesitate to give it expression) that for women what is ethically normal is different from what it is in men. Their superego is never so inexorable; so impersonal, so independent of its emotional origins as we require it to be in men. Character traits which critics of every epoch have brought up against women—that they show less sense of justice than men, that they are less ready to submit to the great necessities of life, that they are more often influenced in their judgments by feelings of affection and hostility—all these would be amply accounted for by the modification in the

formation of their superego which we have already inferred. We must not allow ourselves to be deflected from such conclusions by the denials of feminists, who are anxious to force us to regard the two sexes as completely equal in position and worth; but we shall, of course, willingly agree that the majority of men are also far behind the masculine ideal [quoted in Bronfenbrenner, 1960, p. 18].

This statement does not explain how a female could develop feelings of guilt, for surely guilt is a function of the superego. And yet guilt is more commonly manifested by females than by males (Bronfenbrenner, 1960).

Freud's Phallocentrism

We plainly see Freud's "phallocentric" orientation—his belief that the male is the norm and the ideal by which both males and females are to be judged. His very terminology betrays sexual prejudice, when he refers to this stage of genital gratification as the *phallic* stage, using a word that refers almost always to the male genital organ.

We must recognize the mighty contributions of Freud's original and creative thinking. It was he who made us aware of infantile sexuality, of the importance of our subconscious thoughts and emotions, and of the significance of dreams. As he addressed himself to the origins of conscience, the process of internalization, and to many more aspects of emotional and intellectual functioning, he has incontestably expanded our understanding of ourselves and our fellow human beings. And yet we must look for explanations of sex-related differences in personality beyond the theories of this man who was rooted in nineteenth-century Victorian culture and unalterably convinced of the superiority of men and the weakness of women.

ERIKSON'S THEORY: CRISIS III: INITIATIVE VERSUS GUILT (THREE TO SIX YEARS)

Preschool children are still trying to gain and maintain a sense of autonomy. The guidance of their parents and their new ability to express their needs and thoughts in words help them to be more "on their own." According to Erikson, children at this stage are energetic, and ready and eager to learn to try new things and to work cooperatively with other children.

At this time they turn from a total *attachment* to their parents, to an *identification* with them. This identification comes about, partly as a result of Oedipal rivalry and guilt, but more so from "a spirit of equality experienced in doing things together [Erikson, 1950, p. 258]."

The basic personality conflict of preschoolers is between *initiative*, which enables them to undertake, plan, and carry out their activities, and *guilt* over the things they want to do. The guilt is caused partly by the Oedipal conflict and partly by the rigidity of the developing superego. This conflict

(Shelly Rusten)

Taking the initiative: Preschoolers are energetic and ready to try new things on their own.

can be characterzed as a split between that part of the personality that remains a *child*, full of exuberance and a desire to try new things and test out new powers, and the part that is becoming an *adult*, constantly examining the child's motives and actions, to determine their propriety. Children have to learn how to regulate these two aspects of their personality, so that they will develop a sense of moral responsibility but still be able to enjoy life.

If the superego becomes too strict and leaves too large a residue of guilt, the child may overcontrol and overconstrict himself until his own personality has been totally obliterated, she may over-obey her parents to a far greater extent than they either expect or want, or he may develop a lasting resentment of the parents who do not live up to his exacting new conscience.

Adults who did not develop a sense of initiative during these years are likely to suffer from deep repression of their wishes. They may develop psychosomatic illness, paralysis, inhibition, or impotence; they may try to overcompensate by showing off; or they may become self-righteous and intolerant of others, concerned more with the negative aspects of prohibiting their own impulses and those of others, than with the positive task of guiding initiative.

Detachment from Parents

With the development of autonomy and initiative during the preschool years, we see children detaching themselves from the object of their first attachments, their parents. One study of detachment (Rheingold & Eckerman, 1970) found that children's readiness to leave their mothers increases regularly with age. For each added month of age, forty-eight children ranging in age from one to five years went about 1/3 meter farther away from their mothers. After the second year, the children varied considerably in the distance they were willing to travel away from their mothers.

Where do children go when they leave their parents? They go to explore new territory, to learn about new games, and to form relationships with new people. The most significant type of new relationship in the preschool years is that between peers. At this time, children begin to form real friendships with other children and to be influenced by them. These influences continue to grow until, by the middle years of childhood, peers are as important as parents, if not more so. (Peer influences will be discussed in detail in Chapter 12.)

Identification

Both Freud and Erikson consider the child's identification with the parent of the same sex as an important—perhaps *the* most important—event of the

(Enid Elliot)

The child's identification with the parent of the same sex is an important event of the preschool years.

preschool years. The Harvard psychologist Jerome Kagan defines identification, not in psychoanalytic terms, but in learning-theory terms, also
seeing it as an important development of the preschool period:

> Identification is, in part, the belief of a person that some attributes of a model (for
> example, parents, siblings, relatives, peers, and fictional figures) are also pos-
> sessed by the person. A boy who realizes that he and his father share the same
> name, notes that they have similar facial features, and is told by relatives that they
> both have lively tempers, develops a belief that he is similar to his father. *When
> this belief in similarity is accompanied by vicarious emotional experiences in the
> child that are appropriate to the model, we say that the child has an identification
> with the model* [Kagan, 1971, p. 57; italics in the original].

According to Kagan (1971), four interrelated processes establish and
strengthen identification:

1 "The P[erson] believes that he or she shares particular physical
or psychological attributes with the M[odel]." When Vicky hears people
say, "You look just like your mommy" or "You tell jokes just like
your mommy," she will start to think of herself as being like her
mother.

2 "The P[erson] experiences vicarious affective reactions that are appropriate to events that the M[odel] is experiencing." When Vicky sees her
mother cry upon the death of her own brother, Vicky feels sad and cries,
too—not because of the death of an uncle whom she barely knew, but
because she is vicariously experiencing her mother's grief.

3 "The P[erson] wants to acquire the attributes of the M[odel] that the
P[erson] perceives to be desirable and wishes to have access to the positive
goal states that he or she believes the M[odel] to possess." Vicky recognizes
that her mother has a great deal of independence and authority, and the
ability to do whatever she wants whenever she wants to do it (or so it seems
to Vicky.) So Vicky feels that the more she is like her mother, the more she
will be able to do the things her mother can do.

4 "The P[erson] adopts and practices the attitudes and behaviors
displayed by the M[odel], because the P[erson] feels that by increasing his
or her similarity to the M[odel], he or she might command the M[odel]'s
desirable attributes." So Vicky acts more like her mother, adopts her
mother's opinions on a wide range of topics, in the hopes that some day she
will be more like her mother. Her mother has already had the somewhat
startling experience common to most parents, of hearing her daughter in
play, adopting her mother's mannerisms, voice inflections, and very
words—and not only the ones that she wants her to copy.

(Leonard Freed, Magnum)

Through sex typing children acquire the behavior and attitudes regarded by their culture as characteristically masculine or feminine.

Sex Typing

Vicky, age five, is playing house with Michael, who lives in the next apartment. "I'm the mommy," she says, as she busily cooks and cleans and takes care of her "babies," while Michael puts on a hat and "goes out to work." A minute later, Michael comes home, sits at the table, and says, "I'm hungry. Where's dinner?"

Vicky and Michael at play exemplify the results of sex typing, the process by which children acquire the behavior and attitudes regarded by their culture as characteristically masculine or feminine. Vicky has absorbed at least one value of her society, the belief that "woman's place is in the home." Michael has accepted the notion that adult masculinity involves leaving the house to go to work—and returning to eat the food that a woman has prepared.

Sex typing, though, goes much deeper than this little anecdote might indicate. It involves the very motives, emotions, and values that help us to direct our lives from infancy to the grave. One writer has even said, "Whether the child is born a boy or girl is perhaps the single most important determinant of personality characteristics [Lidz, 1968, p. 207]." Even in these days, when there is a great deal of blurring of the traditional sex-related expectations, most of us grow up with strongly defined notions of the behavior, opinions, and emotions that are appropriate for a male and those that are suitable for a female. Children develop these notions very early, as we pointed out in Chapter 7, and their sex-role patterns remain remarkably stable throughout life (Hetherington, 1970).

HOW SEX TYPING COMES ABOUT

The extent to which the differences between males and females are biological or cultural is the source of great controversy. On the one hand, there are certain differences between the sexes that seem to show up inexplicably soon after birth. On the other hand, if male and female behavior were unalterably established by nature, we could not have patterns such as those described by Margaret Mead (1935).

Mead reported on three New Guinea tribes. Among the Arapesh, both the men and the women are "placid and contented, unaggressive and non-initiatory, non-competitive and responsive, warm, docile, and trusting [p. 56]." Both sexes are nurturant toward children. Among the cannibalistic Mundugumor, "both men and women are expected to be violent, competitive, aggressively sexed, jealous and ready to see and avenge insult, delighting in display, in action, in fighting [p. 213]." The occasional mild man and nurturant woman are considered social misfits. In the Tchambuli tribe, there are different expectations for males and females; these expectations are noteworthy, though, because they are directly opposite to those in most societies around the world. The Tchambuli woman is dominant, impersonal, and hard-working, while the man is less responsible, more concerned about personal appearance, and more dependent emotionally.

True, these three societies are different from the norm in most communities around the world, but the fact that they exist at all is proof that sex roles are not preordained by nature but are subject to considerable cultural influence.

Other evidence against natural preordination of sex-determined personalities can be seen in the variations among individuals in every society in terms of their ability to meet their own culture's standards for sex-appropriate characteristics. It can also be deduced from research on persons whose sex is ambiguous at birth, due to genital anomalies. If such a child is dubbed a girl at birth, and later chromosomal or hormonal evidence indicates that "she" is more properly a "he," it will be possible to reassign the child's sex without severe psychological stress *only* if the change is made before the child is two years old (Money, 1963). Otherwise, the child's sexual orientation will be too strongly entrenched to make an effective change, even though such sexual orientation may be contradictory to the child's biological sex.

There *is* evidence, however, that hormones also influence sex-typed behavior. Probably, characteristically male or female behavior is determined by some combination of hormonal and environmental influences. This conclusion is borne out by research with laboratory animals. Female guinea pigs, for example, whose mothers had received testosterone while pregnant exhibited masculine behavior when they reached maturity (Dantchakoff, 1938), the administration of testosterone to young female rats made them act in typically masculine patterns (Gray et al., 1969), and female rhesus monkeys who had been masculinized *in utero* acted more like normal male monkeys than like female in initiating play, engaging in more rough-and-tumble play, and in other activities (Phoenix, 1966).

Animals are not people, of course, and the behavior of human beings is determined socially to an infinitely greater extent than is that of any animal. Furthermore, we cannot confirm animal studies with those on human beings, since it would be unthinkable to try to deliberately alter the sex-typing of children. We can, though, observe—and draw inferences from—those occasional individuals in whom, for some reason, sex assignment is not clear-cut. Of particular interest are two studies involving a total of twenty individuals. We have to be wary of drawing conclusions based on such small numbers. But we also have to remember that the kinds of sexual abnormalities that appear in these subjects are, fortunately, so rare that we are not likely to find large numbers of such persons.

In the first study (Ehrhardt & Money, 1967), ten girls, age three to fourteen, had been born to women who had received synthetic progestins during their pregnancies to avert threatened miscarriages. Nine of these girls were born with abnormal external sexual organs, which had to be surgically corrected to make them look like normal girls or to enable them eventually to participate in sexual intercourse. Internally, they were females capable of normal reproduction. All these children were raised as girls from birth and generally looked forward to assuming the role of wife and mother. But, as children, they were closer to the male stereotype than to the female. Nine of the ten were called "tomboys" because they liked to compete with boys in active sports and liked playing with trucks, guns, and other "boys' toys" better than with dolls and other "girls' toys." Tomboyishness *is* fairly common among middle-class girls (as these were), and there is nothing pathological about it. But Ehrhardt and Money, while acknowledging that tomboyishness "does not preclude eventual romance, marriage, child bearing and full-time home and family care [p. 96]," still raise the possibility that there might be something in fetal masculinization that affects that part of the central nervous system that controls energy-expending behavior. From an early age, boys are more active than girls. How much of this is hormonal and how much cultural? So far, we don't know.

The ten people, aged thirteen to thirty, in the other study (Money, Ehrhardt, & Masica, 1968) looked like females, but were chromosomally male. They had testes instead of ovaries, and they were unable to bear children, since they could not ovulate. Their condition appeared to have been inherited, and the particular mechanism may have involved an inability to utilize androgen during prenatal development. Since these individuals looked like normal girls, they had been brought up as females. All were "typically female" in their behavior and outlook. They all considered marriage and raising a family to be very important, and all had had repeated dreams and fantasies about bringing up children. Eight of the ten had played primarily with dolls and other "girls' toys," and the seven who reported having played "house" in childhood had always taken the part of the mother. There was no ambiguity in their psychological sex role. The experiences and attitudes of these individuals, who were playing out their culturally determined female roles, shows the strong influence of environment on sex typing.

In most cultures men are more aggressive and have more authority than women, and they usually do the dangerous, physically strenuous jobs, while the women generally perform routine jobs closer to home. These patterns undoubtedly grew up because of the anatomical differences between adult men and women. Since the average man is taller, heavier, and more muscular than the average woman, it is only natural that he would be assigned the more arduous tasks. And since it is the woman who bears and nurses the babies, it makes more sense for her to perform those tasks that can be done while staying close to the children. Today, however, when most work in an industrial society can be performed as well by a 90-pound woman as by a 200-pound man, and when women are bearing fewer children and nursing them more briefly (if at all), the old bases for assigning work along sex lines do not seem so relevant. Many in our society are now questioning the ways by which children become sex typed and assume their gender roles.

What Is Sex Typing?

This is the process by which a person develops the behavior, personality characteristics, emotional responses, attitudes, and beliefs that his or her culture has deemed appropriate for his or her sex (Mussen, 1969). Through sex typing, Vicky learns that she should pay attention to her physical appearance and try to be pretty; that she should develop nurturant attitudes toward dolls, and eventually, toward babies; that it's "not nice" to beat up little boys in the sandbox. Jason learns that "boys don't cry"; they don't play with girls' toys like housekeeping sets and dolls; they help little girls with hard jobs, and so forth. While many of these sex-stereotyped attitudes are irrelevant and may actually be damaging to the emotional health of specific individuals (the emphasis on passivity for girls, for example, and the strictures against boys' expressing certain emotions), the entire complex of such attitudes gives a person an extra dimension to his or her own self-identity.

Sex typing comes about, partly because of the differential ways in which boys and girls are treated and partly because of children's own recognition of their own sex.

THEORETICAL EXPLANATIONS OF SEX TYPING

Biological Differences

Boys and girls are biologically different even before birth, as we pointed out in Chapter 3. They have different reproductive organs, different hormonal levels, and different skeletal development. Furthermore, we have seen that they also show many differences in behavior very soon after birth. "Although the female infant is more mature and in some ways more responsive to stimulation, the male infant interacts more violently and actively with his environment [Hetherington, 1970, p. 195]."

Pursuing these apparently inborn differences, one line of research attempts to relate the higher activity level in male neonates with the greater degree of aggression in boys and men. Another research thrust seeks to determine the effects of hormones at critical periods in prenatal development. It is possible that different levels of hormones may predispose males to more aggressive behavior and females to more nurturant behavior, and it will be interesting to follow the recently increased research activity along these lines. Even if such predispositions do exist, though, their eventual flowering or withering on the part of one or both sexes depends in large part on the ways children perceive the sex-oriented values of their culture.

Psychoanalytic Theory

According to Freud and other analysts, sex typing is the indirect result of anatomical differences, an integral part of the identification process, and an upshot of the Oedipus complex. While a little boy loves his father, he also resents him as his rival for the love of the mother. The guilt engendered by this rivalrous resentment makes the child fear his strong and powerful father. The little boy in this ambivalent situation eventually *represses* his striving for the sexual love of his mother and identifies with his erstwhile rival, his father. He has not totally given up on his dream of winning his mother, and so he takes on many of his father's attributes, in the hope that if he becomes more like his father, the woman who loves his father will love him, too. The child assimilates as his own his father's expressed attitudes and behavior, many of which are related to sex-role expectations. The little boy also identifies with the idealized values of the father's superego, becoming, in effect, more like the ideal father than his father is himself.

The little girl's identification with her mother proceeds along somewhat different lines. Since, according to the psychoanalytic view, she is already castrated, this fear does not have the same sudden impact upon her that the fear of castration does upon a little boy. She does fear further injury, but not so dramatically. Her concern, rather, is more that she will lose the love of the parent of the same sex. Motivated by this fear, she develops *anaclitic identification*, or identification through fear of loss of a loved object (Bronfenbrenner, 1960). In an effort to hold onto the love of her mother,

(Inge King)

The vestiges of a preliterate society: It is more efficient to train people for adult roles from early childhood than to wait until adolescence.

she attempts to be more and more like the mother. In this process, she assumes those aspects of feminine behavior and attitudes that she associates with her mother.

Learning Theory

According to this viewpoint, sex typing comes about as a result of parental rewards and punishment. Parents are important to the child because of the care they give the child and because of the child's dependency on them. The parents have strong convictions about the desirability and undesirability, from a sex-role point of view, of various behaviors. By their responses to these behaviors, they either encourage or discourage their children from pursuing them.

It is more efficient to train people for adult roles from early childhood than it would be to wait until adolescence for such training. This is why most societies socialize boys and girls differently from an early age, in anticipation of adult responsibilities, even though there is no need for them to act in sex-differentiated ways during childhood. When Barry, Bacon, and Child (1957) looked at sex differences in 110 cultures, they found that most of these societies, most of which were nonliterate, raise their daughters and sons differently and that the differences vary somewhat from culture to culture. While there are some reversals of the usual roles and some instances of no discernible sex differences, most societies socialize their children along fairly similar lines, in response to anatomical differences.

Cultures that place a high premium on superior strength and strenuous physical tasks, such as the hunting or tending of large animals, the raising of grain rather than root crops, a nomadic way of life, and warfare as a way of life, usually raise their sons and daughters in sharply divergent ways. Boys are encouraged to be more self-reliant, so that they will be able to leave home as the economy deems necessary, and to be physically active and strong, so that they will be able to perform those strenuous activities required of adult males. Girls are trained to be nurturant, obedient, and responsible on a daily basis, since as adult women they will be expected to be the ones who stay home, care for the children, cook, carry water, maintain family gardens, and keep up the day-to-day home-related responsibilities.

These investigators also found that those societies that favor large family groups, with a great deal of cooperative interaction, are more likely to be highly differentiated in regard to sex roles than are societies where families live in relatively isolated nuclear units. "To the extent that the nuclear family must stand alone, the man must be prepared to take the woman's role when she is absent or incapacitated, and vice versa. Thus the sex differentiation cannot afford to be too great [Barry et al., 1957, p. 331]."

Thus, in our technological economy, in which most tasks can be performed equally well by a brawny man or a slightly built woman, and in which the most usual mode of life is the isolated nuclear family, it would appear that a minimal degree of role differentiation would be required. Yet in many ways our society retains the vestiges of a preliterate society that depends on male strength and female nurturance.

Cognitive-Developmental Theory

In this view, sex typing comes about not from anatomy, not from deep-seated emotions, and not from cultural patterning, but rather as a natural corollary of children's cognitive development. Boys act like boys and girls like girls, because children organize their "social world along sex-role dimensions [Kohlberg, 1966, p. 82]."

First, babies hear and learn the words "boy" and "girl," are labeled as one or the other, and by the age of two or three, know the appropriate labels for themselves. They then organize their lives around these labels. While children are learning what they are, they are also learning what to do. They generally learn what activities, opinions, and emotions are considered masculine or feminine, and they incorporate the appropriate ones into their daily lives.

Vicky knows that she is female. Her self-concept requires her to value those things that are consistent with or like herself. So when she understands what things are considered feminine, she will choose those that are consistent with her self-label. When she has acquired sex-appropriate values, she will tend to identify with other females, especially her mother. She begins to imitate her mother more, and becomes more attached to her (Maccoby & Masters, 1971).

As cognitive development progresses, children think in terms of cross-cultural stereotypes, which "are not derived from parental behavior or direct tuition, but rather, stem from universal perceived sex differences in bodily structure and capacities [Mussen, 1969, p. 411]." Thus, when they themselves notice the differences in male and female bodily structure and capacities, they consider dominance and aggression as appropriate male characteristics and nurturance as an appropriate female trait. They try to live up to these stereotypes, as well as trying to copy directly the attitudes and activities of individual adults of the same sex.

SEX TYPING IN THE UNITED STATES

While our society is less rigid in its sex-role definitions than are many others, it is still far from being a culture with no sex-role distinctions. On the contrary, even though many changes have taken place, indications are that sex typing is very much with us. Hetherington (1970) says:

> Some writers have attempted to differentiate between the male and female role by stressing the greater demands for competence in the male role. It might be more accurate to say that the areas of competence differ for males and females. Masculine competence is manifested in coping independently and effectively in competitive achievement situations associated with the male's functions as a provider and protector. In contrast, feminine competence is demonstrated in being attractive, loving, and supportive in social relationships, particularly in her role as a wife and mother [p. 194].

Comparing these two "areas of competence" in this way implies an equality between the two, but our society consistently undervalues abilities that fall within the purview of "feminine competence." For example, while women in other cultures are proud of their skills in caring for children, our girls learn from an early age to devalue these tasks—and yet to associate them with femininity. The little girl, then, is in a double bind. She identifies with her mother's skills in caring for children and in keeping the home—and at the same time she picks up all the nuances in the culture that let her know that this work, "woman's work," is not nearly so important as "man's work."

These attitudes become crystallized quite early. In one study, 120 children ranging in age from just under three to just under six were shown a series of photos of boys and girls. They were asked, "Which of these children will grow up to be a doctor? A dentist? A teacher?" and so on. With a series of adult photos, the children were asked, "All of these people are scientists (or artists, or teachers, etc.). Who is the best?" The children were also tested for intelligence.

All the children tended to give highly stereotyped answers, with the brightest children giving the most traditional responses. They were most likely to see boys growing up to be doctors and dentists, girls being teachers, and adult males being the smartest scientists (Greenberg & Peck, 1974). They had very early picked up the cues from their society. Even in the preschool years, girls expect that their adult roles will be more limited than those of boys, and are more likely to see themselves in adult life as a mother, a nurse, or a teacher, whereas boys look forward to a wide range of possible occupations (Kirchner & Vondracek, 1973).

The superior position and privileged status of the male permeates nearly every aspect, minor and major, of our social life. The gadgets and prizes in boxes of

Most parents look with mild amusement at the antics of a "tomboy," whereas they react strongly and negatively to "sissyish" behavior in boys.

(Enid Elliot)

breakfast cereal, for example, commonly have a strong masculine rather than feminine appeal. And the most basic social institutions perpetuate this pattern of masculine aggrandizement. Thus, the Judeo-Christian faiths involve worshipping God, a "Father," rather than a "Mother," and Christ, a "Son," rather than a "Daughter" [Brown, 1958, p. 235].

Because masculinity is considered more important in our culture, there is much more pressure for boys to adopt male-oriented behaviors than there is for girls to adopt female ones, at least in early childhood. Most parents look with mild amusement at the antics of a tomboy, whereas they react strongly and negatively to "sissyish" behavior in boys—crying, passivity, and an interest in so-called feminine activities, like playing with dolls, interest in the arts, and helping around the house. And as the "tomboy" approaches adolescence, she too is expected to shed her childish interests in active sports, and "boyish" games, and to assume the accouterments of femininity.

It is not surprising, then, that one study of seventy-four preschool boys and girls (Flammer, 1971) found that boys with a highly masculine sex-role orientation had greater self-esteem than boys with moderate or low sex-role orientation, and girls with low sex-role adoption had greater self-esteem than those with moderate or high sex-role adoption. The girls in general had a greater sense of self-esteem, indicating that the preschool years may be more comfortable for girls. This may be because the traits that are encouraged in girls—passivity and dependence—allow preschool children to feel secure and comfortable with themselves, whereas the pressure on boys to become "manly" and independent is threatening for such young children.

Socioeconomic Differences

The pressure on children to conform to sex-role expectations is more marked in the lower socioeconomic groups. Lower-class boys show a strong preference for "boys'" toys at the age of four or five, lower-class girls and middle-class boys show preference for "sex-appropriate" toys at about the age of seven, and middle-class girls do not show a preference for "girls'" toys until they are about nine (Rabban, 1950). The girls' tendency to show sex-role preferences later than the boys in both social groups probably reflects an early recognition on the part of both sexes of the tendency in our culture to value masculine activities more highly, as well as the greater tolerance of their parents for "tomboyish" interests.

The earlier sex-role identification in the lower classes may be due to the more stereotyped "masculine" and "feminine" models offered by lower-class adults, which more rigidly conceptualize sex-appropriate behaviors. Lower-class fathers, for example, are more likely to work in traditionally masculine occupations involving heavy labor, and lower-class women in such traditionally feminine service-oriented occupations as cleaning and cooking. Lower-class fathers rarely help around the house or take care of the children, as compared to middle-class fathers, who are more likely to change diapers, shop for groceries, or dry dishes. And middle-class mothers are usually more assertive within the home and more likely to participate in a variety of activities or in a profession not generally regarded as feminine.

PARENTAL INFLUENCES ON SEX TYPING

While anatomical differences between the sexes may predispose the direction that personality differences will take, the actual molding of these differences appears to be more a result of cultural conditioning than of biological predetermination. First, a child's parents transmit the values and attitudes that they consider appropriate for one sex or the other, and then this job is taken over by other forces in the society, such as the school, the church, and the mass media. Thus, the first important relationship in the development of sex typing is that between parent and child. In the preschool years, this appears to be the most important factor in the development of sex-appropriate, or sex-stereotyped, attitudes and behaviors. How, then, do parents transmit these sex-role values?

Parental Attitudes

We all know of the little girl who "can twist her father around her little finger" or the little boy who "can get away with murder" with his mother, but not with his father. These popular interpretations of the Freudian concepts of the Oedipal and Electra periods in children's psychosexual development have given rise to scientific curiosity. Do fathers and mothers treat their sons and daughters differently? Are the differences based on the sex of the child and the sex of the parent? How influential are these differences in determining sex-role development?

A number of studies have investigated the ways children see their parents. Young children of both sexes usually see their fathers as the parent more likely to punish them. Both boys and girls report being kissed more by the parent of the opposite sex, and they tend to see the same-sex parent as "less benevolent and more frustrating [Rothbart & Maccoby, 1966]."

Kagan and Lemkin (1960) interviewed 67 three- to eight-year-olds to determine how they perceived their parents. They asked the children a series of direct questions, and then a series of indirect questions (Kagan & Lemkin, p. 441). The results from this study confirm those in others along the same lines, with children seeing their mothers as more nurturant, and their fathers as more punitive, more competent, and more powerful. The girls in this study saw their fathers as both more affectionate and more punitive, implying more power in both positive and negative ways. It is quite possible that these children were influenced in their answers as much by the way the mass media, the books they read, and other children portray stereotyped masculine and feminine roles, as by what their parents are actually like.

Other studies have looked at the parents themselves. Fathers report different expectations for and participation in different activities with their sons and daughters, while mothers tend to treat both sons and daughters similarly. Mothers do, however, report that they permit more aggressiveness from boys when it is directed toward parents and toward children *outside* the family. (They are no more likely than their husbands to let their sons beat up their brothers and sisters.) Fathers appear to be more concerned about sex typing than are mothers (Rothbart & Maccoby, 1966).

In an effort to study parents' reactions to specific behaviors of children, Rothbart and Maccoby (1966) studied a group of upper-middle-class parents of nursery school children—ninety-eight mothers and thirty-two fathers. They achieved some surprising results in testing a hypothesis that grew out of social learning theory (Rothbart & Maccoby, 1966):

> The greater incidence of dependent behaviors for girls than boys, and the reverse situation with respect to physically aggressive behavior, seems directly explicable in social learning terms. Dependent behaviors are less rewarded for males, physically aggressive behaviors are less rewarded for females in our culture, and, consequently, there are mean differences between the sexes in the frequency of such behaviors after the first few years of life [p. 238].

All the parents heard the recorded voice of the same child in a variety of hypothetical situations, but some were told that the child was a boy, and others that it was a girl. The parents were also questioned on their feelings about the degree to which boys and girls should and actually do differ on selected characteristics. The parents were tested in four separate groups: fathers who heard a "girl's" voice, fathers who heard a "boy's" voice, mothers with a "girl's" voice, and mothers with a "boy's" voice.

The parents were asked to imagine that they were at home reading, while a four-year-old daughter (or son) was playing with a puzzle in the next room. A year-old baby was with the preschooler. The parents were asked to write down what they would say or do in response to each of the child's statements, which included phrases such as "Daddy (or Mommy), come look at my puzzle"; "Come help me"; "Tell the Baby he can't play with my puzzle—it's mine!"; "Leave my puzzle alone or I'll hit you in the head! (to the baby)"; "I'm going across the street to play."

The mothers turned out to be more permissive toward their sons and fathers toward their daughters on comfort-seeking, dependency, allowing the child to stop the game, and siding with the older child against the baby. Fathers allowed more aggression toward themselves from girls, and mothers from boys. Only one effect was significant, regardless of the child's sex:

fathers allowed the children to be more autonomous than did mothers. Parents who felt that sex roles should be highly differentiated showed larger differences in the way they treated boys and girls than did low-differentiation parents, but *not* by promoting dependency in girls and assertiveness in boys. Rather, they showed more permissiveness to the opposite-sex child on both traits.

So the study did not bear out its hypothesis, and the authors concluded (Rothbart & Maccoby, 1966):

> Rather than consistent reinforcement of sex-typed behavior by both parents, inconsistency between parents seems to be the rule, and while a parent may treat his child in a manner consistent with the cultural stereotype in one area of behavior, in another he may not [p. 242].

It is possible that other societal factors have more influence in developing sex roles than parents do, and it is also possible that parents shift their encouragement toward sex typing as the children grow older. In any case, this study brings out the great difficulty in trying to ascribe single causes for the very complex behaviors of human beings in society.

Parental Warmth

The degree of warmth that parents show their children exerts a strong influence on whether those children will emulate the parents of the same sex. Boys who are rated highly masculine, for example, see their fathers as more rewarding and nurturant than do low-masculine boys, and the warmth of both fathers and mothers appears to be positively related to high levels of femininity in girls (Hetherington, 1970). The influence of the father appears to be especially important in sex typing, since fathers usually respond differently to their sons and daughters, while mothers treat their children of both sexes more similarly (Hetherington, 1970).

The Father's Role

Psychoanalytic theory emphasizes the *negative* forces underlying a little boy's identification with his father—the resentment and fear that make him defensively "identify with the aggressor." In direct contrast, learning theory emphasizes the *positive* forces that facilitate father-son identification.

> If the father is an important source of nurturance, reward, and satisfaction, his responses and characteristics acquire secondary reward value and the boy imitates his father's behavior in order to "reproduce bits of the beloved and longed for parent [Mussen & Distler, 1959, p. 350]."

Mussen and Distler's study (1959) of 38 five-year-old boys indicates that highly masculine little boys perceive their fathers as more rewarding and

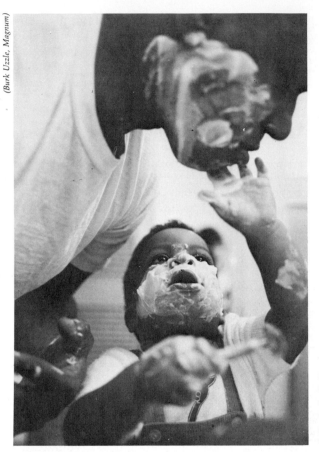

The first important relationship in the development of sex typing is between parent and child. Fathers report different expectations for sons and daughters, while mothers tend to treat both similarly.

nurturant, and also as more punitive and threatening, than do boys who are rated low on an index of masculinity. A boy, then, seems to model himself after his father when he views him as the more powerful parent who doles out both reward and punishment.

The Effect of Father's Absence

If the father's influence is so important to his children's sex-role development, what happens when the father is not in the home? Biller (1969) looked at thirty-four kindergarten boys: half of their fathers had not been living at home for at least one year and had been absent an average of three years; the fathers of the other seventeen were living at home. Both groups of boys were assessed on sex-role orientation, sex-role preference, and sex-role adoption, and the boys' mothers were rated on the degree to which they encouraged their sons' masculine behavior.

Sex typing has three major dimensions: *sex-role orientation*, or how masculine or feminine an individual views himself or herself; *sex-role preference*, or the individual's desire to adhere to the socially defined cultural standards for his or her own sex; and *sex-role adoption*, or how masculine or feminine the individual's actual overt behavior seems to other people.

The most commonly used test for measuring sex-role preference or sex-role orientation is the IT Scale for Children (Brown, 1956). The ITSC is a projective test consisting of thirty-six picture cards. One card shows "IT," a stick figure of undetermined sex, and the other cards in the series depict objects, figures, and activities that have masculine or feminine connotations. The child is shown the IT figure, and then asked to choose from among various pairs of toys (a truck versus a doll), clothing (overalls versus a dress), and activities (sports versus doll play) and asked which of the pair IT would like. It is assumed that children will project themselves into the IT role, and that their choices for IT reflect the children's own choices, which they may be inhibited from expressing more directly.

Sex-role adoption is usually measured by having a teacher or someone else rate various aspects of the child's behavior on a scale of masculinity/femininity, which includes such characteristics as assertiveness, aggressiveness, competitiveness, and independence (all considered masculine), and passivity, dependency, and timidity (all considered feminine).

Biller found that the father's absence seems to affect his son's sex-role orientation and his sex-role preference, but does not appreciably affect the boy's overt behavior—his assertiveness, aggressiveness, competitiveness, independence, and activity directed toward physical prowess and mastery of the environment. When the father is absent, the mother's role in encouraging masculine behavior becomes more important. For the fatherless boys in this study, the more their mothers encouraged masculine behavior, the more the boys were likely to prefer masculine games and the higher their scale on overt masculinity was likely to be.

Biller and Bahm (1971) found that the loss of the father at age five or earlier affected a little boy's masculine identification, but that no effect was seen if the loss occurred after this time. The mother's role emerged as an important one in this study, too. The boys who felt that their mothers encouraged aggression had more masculine self-concepts than those who did not sense this encouragement.

After a boy enters school, there are many more ways to compensate for the absence of his father. He can pick up cues for masculinity from other boys, other men, and the mass media.

Very little research has been done on the effects of father absence on girls or the effects of mother absence on either boys or girls. While a great deal of research has been done on fatherless boys, the results are far from clear-cut, as we will see in the discussion in Chapter 12 of the one-parent family.

OTHER INFLUENCES ON SEX TYPING

As Kraft (1966) wrote in his essay on child rearing on the Israeli kibbutz:

> With the exception of those rare and for the most part monstrous examples of children reared in complete isolation (for example, the child kept locked up in the attic by an insane grandmother), the world thrusts between the caretaker and the child an endless bombardment of influences which serve to mitigate the effects of even the most painstaking and elaborate of child-rearing regimens [p. 197].

Nowhere is this intrusion of the outside world more obvious than in the realm of sex typing. While an individual family may live a relatively egalitarian life, the children in it will often base their own ideas of what is appropriate not on what they see at home, but on what the outside world says they should see. Thus we learn that

> a child whose mother is a teacher was asked what job her mother had. "She does the dishes," she said. "Is that all?" we asked. "Well, she cleans, too [Smith, 1974]."

So Vicky's view of sex-appropriate behavior depends not only on the attitudes and behavior of her parents, but also on what she observes at school, in the library, on television, in the homes of her friends, and in the activities of her siblings. Let us look at some of these influences.

Older Siblings

It seems reasonable that a little girl who has older brothers will be more likely to play football and baseball than will the youngest of three sisters. When sibling relationships are examined scientifically, this is what usually happens. Koch (1956) found that children whose older siblings are of the same sex are more likely to behave in ways culturally associated with that sex than those children with opposite-sex older siblings, and Brim (1958) found that teachers of children from two-child families are more likely to rate boys masculine and girls feminine when their older siblings are of the same sex.

Television

When we talk about today's children, we have to consider the impact of television. Ninety-six percent of all American homes have at least one television set, and most children start to watch TV for at least two hours a day by the age of two or three (Surgeon General's Report, 1972). During the preschool years, children spend more time in front of the TV set than they do in any other single activity except sleep (Sternglanz & Serbin, 1973).

What do these impressionable preschoolers see on the little screen? A

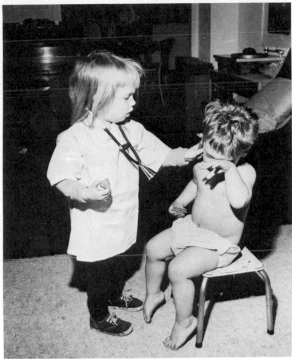

(Ray Shaw, Photo Trends)

But on television, four out of five female lead characters are witches.

more restricted world than the real one. One study that tried to analyze the ten most popular commercially produced children's shows for depictions of male and female roles had to eliminate four of the top ten, because no female characters showed up consistently (Sternglanz & Serbin, 1973). On the ten favorite children's shows that do show females regularly, viewers still see males twice as often as they see females. And these ever-present males are aggressive and constructive. They do more than the females and are more likely to reap rewards for their efforts. But females, who usually defer to males on TV, tend to be ignored for inconsequential behavior or punished for very active behavior. The only way around this for some TV women is to be a witch, which four out of five female lead characters are. The authors of this study conclude that on TV

both male and female roles are limited because certain behaviors are considered appropriate primarily for one sex. A child who identified with the female characters would be shown that it is inappropriate for her to make plans and carry them out or for her to be aggressive. . . . Boys, on the other hand, are shown that it is sex role inappropriate for males to defer to another's plan or suggestion or to express admiration of others. On a still more specific level, female children are taught that almost the only way to be a successful human being if you are female is through the use of magic. By using magic one may manipulate others without their being aware of it, and may manipulate them effectively. One may imagine the shock to the little girls at the age of 10 or so when they realize that witchcraft is not really a viable career [p. 13]!

When these same young viewers stick around for the commercials, what do they see? More of the same. In a study of 1,241 TV commercials, women were almost always shown inside the home, while men were portrayed as engaging in a wide range of activities from politics to fishing (Hennessee & Nicholson, 1972). Only 0.3 percent of the advertising messages monitored in this study showed women as autonomous, independent people.

In most ads women's lives are dreary. It's the men, children and even the family dog who have the fun while women do the work. In 54.4 per cent of the food commercials and 81.2 per cent of the cleaning commercials men are the beneficiaries [p. 13].

Sesame Street, the highly acclaimed public television program designed to help teach letters and numbers to culturally deprived preschoolers, has also come under fire from feminists for its heavy emphasis on male characterization (Bergman, 1972). But both commercial and noncommercial producers, as well as the sponsors and the advertising agencies responsible for the commercials, have responded somewhat to pressures from women's groups. It is possible that between the time we write and you read this book the television picture may well have become more egalitarian.

Children's Books
Vicky loves her picture books. Seated on a parent's lap, she relishes hearing the same story over and over again. She learns the stories by heart, spends hours poring over familiar and beloved illustrations, and will remember some of these tales and pictures well into her adult years. Since she is first exposed to these books at a time when her sexual identity is becoming established, they are an important element in sex typing. What do they teach young children?

According to a study of prize-winning picture books, Vicky gets the same message about sex roles from her carefully selected library that she would get by flipping on her television set (Weitzman et al., 1972). In a five-year selection of books that won the Caldecott Medal, the most coveted prize for picture books, females are almost invisible. For every illustration of a female person or animal, eleven males are pictured. In one-third of these books, there are no females at all. And again, when the girls and women do appear, they play traditional female roles. They are the helpless victims rather than the brave rescuers; they are passive rather than active; they are constricted by their pretty clothes; the men pursue a variety of interesting occupations, while the women serve only as subservient wives and mothers. The boys in these books never cry; they must be "fearless, brave, and clever at all times [p. 1138]."

These same patterns appear in three other influential groups of children's books assessed by the same authors: the Newbery Award winners (for third- to sixth-graders), the best-selling Little Golden Books, and the etiquette books, which prescribe proper behavior for boys and girls.

If the books that young children read—or have read to them—exerted total influence over their lives, women would hardly ever take off their aprons and would never take on any job other than that of teacher or nurse, men would never experience grief or fear and would never care for their children, and the adult roles of both sexes would be much more constricted than they actually are in real life. The sex-role stereotyped thinking that does limit most men and women in our society, though, may be due at least partly to those images in the picture books of our childhood.

School

One day at nursery school, Vicky hung a toy stethoscope around her neck and proceeded to examine all the dolls in the doll corner. Completely in charge of the situation, she alternated with another little girl between playing mother and doctor. But then Stephen, a slight youngster about a head shorter than the "doctor," stepped into her "office." Vicky unhesitatingly handed her stethoscope to Stephen, saying, "*You* be the doctor and I'll be the nurse." She had already received and acted on the message that a girl has to defer to a boy.

Vicky's school is probably the most outstanding and progressive nursery school in her community. The director believes strongly in treating children as individuals and in avoiding constricted sex-role stereotypes. Yet the school perpetuates traditional thinking in many subtle ways. A poster of a hospital scene, for example, portrays patients, doctors, and nurses: the doctors are all men, the nurses all women. The wooden figures in the block corner show people in different occupations. The police officer, the firefighter, the storekeeper, and the construction worker are all men; only the housewife-mother and the teacher are women. When Vicky's teacher handed out painting caps to the children, she said, "Here, Billy, put this hat on." To Vicky she said, "This hat will keep your pretty curls clean."

For many years, nursery school teachers have been influenced by psychoanalytic theories that teach that children's healthy sexual identification depends on distinct differentiation between the male and female roles. As a result, many conscientious teachers have tried to help children by emphasizing the differences between the sexes. More recent thinking, however, has shifted to the view that strongly differentiated sex roles *impede* the intellectual and the psychological development of both boys and girls (Maccoby, 1966; Slater, 1964).

A View of a Nonsexist Classroom: Checklist for Observation in a Preschool*

Classroom has both male and female teachers.

Both teachers share jobs equally (i.e., male does not teach while female serves juice and cookies).

Teachers greet boys and girls equally (i.e., teacher does not shake hands with boys while telling girls "how pretty they look").

Block area accessories include doll furniture as well as trucks, animals, etc.

Community Helper figures are interracial.

Community Helper figures are not sex-role stereotyped.

Dress-up area includes hard hats, police badges, and firefighters' hats as well as crinolines and lace scarves.

Boys and girls are encouraged to use housekeeping and/or dress-up area.

Books and records are strongly nonsexist in title selection.

Girls and boys are encouraged to use climbing equipment.

Musical instruments are not sex-typed in usage (i.e., girls play the bells while boys get the drums).

All children use carpentry equipment equally.

Teacher-made equipment, such as lotto games and puzzles, are not role stereotyped.

Pictures on walls are interracial and depict women and men in nonstereotypic roles.

Art materials are used equally.

Toilets are coeducational.

All children are allowed to express affection physically.

All children are allowed (if not encouraged) to get messy.

Teachers approach all noise, fights, emotional outbursts of anger or crying the same, regardless of sex involved.

Teachers value and encourage independent and assertive behavior.

*It's Never Too Early, by Merle Froschl. Copyright © 1973 by the Feminist Press.

Many modern teachers and school administrators are making strong efforts to overcome old ideas. They are recruiting male teachers to let children know that men, too, can enjoy being with, teaching, and caring for children. They are renaming the "doll corner" the "family corner," and are stocking it with tools as well as with dolls and dishes, so that boys and girls can play together there comfortably. They are not emphasizing what *boys* can do or what *girls* can do—but what *children* can do. Some of the efforts being made can be seen in the above checklist.

Children's Fears

Vicky's parents treasure a large wooden African mask that a peripatetic friend once gave them. But every time four-year-old Vicky has to pass the room where the mask hangs, she shields her eyes and hurries past. Asked why she is afraid of it, she just shrugs.

People of every age are afraid of some things. While some fears, like Vicky's of the mask, seem irrational, many are essential aspects of the instinct for self-preservation. If we did not have a healthy fear of fast cars, deep water, and fire, for example, few of us would be here today. Even babies just starting to crawl will not cross what appears to them to be a deep cliff (Walk & Gibson, 1961). It appears, then, that some of our fears may be inborn mechanisms for our own protection. This seems most apparent in the fears of infants under a year old, who are frightened by directed physical stimuli—loud noises or people or things associated with them, the sensation of falling, sudden movements, flashes of light, people or objects associated with pain, and strange people, things, or situations (Jersild, 1946).

With time, some of these fears diminish and new ones take their place. It

(Enid Elliot)

One of the things they "know" is that there are a lot of things in this world to be afraid of, and their imaginations tend to go wild.

is usually not until the second year, for example, that children are afraid of the dark or of being left alone.

The years from two to six appear to harbor the greatest number of new fears. By this time, children have a broader view of the world around them. They're likely to have had some frightening experiences, like being lost in a department store, being bitten by a dog, or falling off a high ledge. Furthermore, they've heard of scary things that have happened to others, either in real life, in stories, or on television. They *know* so much more at this age. And one of the things they "know" is that there are a lot of things in this world to be afraid of. Their imaginations tend to go wild. They worry about being attacked by a lion (even though lions are not likely to prowl the asphalt below their apartment windows), about being in the dark, being left alone, going up to high places. They shiver over witches, ghosts, and other imaginary creatures. They are also afraid of criminals and snakes (Jersild, 1935).

CAUSES OF CHILDREN'S FEARS

Since so many childhood fears are of objects or events that are far removed from their daily lives, it is often hard to find their roots. Some fears are, indeed, linked to an actual event. A child who has been bitten by a dog may generalize her fear to all dogs. One boy who had been hit by a car had nightmares about traffic accidents, and became afraid—not only of crossing the street, but also of being alone in a dark room (Jersild & Holmes, 1935, in Jersild, 1946).

Parents sometimes instill fear in their children. Youngsters are more likely to be afraid of thunder and lightning, dogs, and insects when their mothers are frightened by them, too (Hagman, 1932). Dentists who have worked with children often groan when they hear a parent tell a child, "There's nothing to be afraid of," because such assurances often *put* fear into a child's mind. Parents who are overprotective give their children the feeling that the world is a dangerous place, full of fearsome things.

Freudian thinkers believe that the upsurge of fears during the preschool years result from children's anxiety about being injured (due to the castration complex) and to their guilt feelings over their emotions toward their parents (due to the Oedipus complex), which make them feel as if they deserve some sort of intense punishment.

As we said, fear is partly a function of age; as children grow older, bigger, and more competent, some of the things that used to seem so menacing lose their fangs (see Figure 9-1). Girls express more fears than boys (Jersild, 1933; Croake, 1973). This may be due to parental acceptance of girls' fears and discouragement of those of boys, or it may be possible that more dependent children are more fearful and girls are encouraged to be more dependent. Poor children are afraid of more things than children from more comfortable circumstances (Jersild & Holmes, 1933; Croake, 1969), perhaps

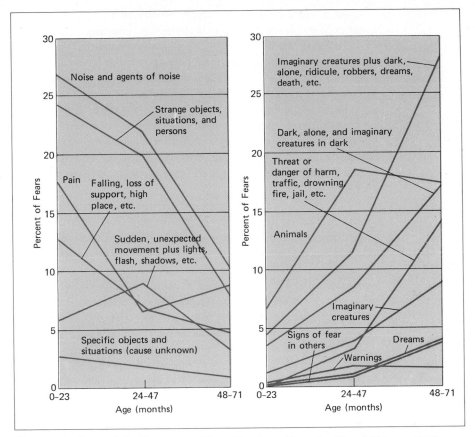

Figure 9-1   Age and the Frequency of Fear Situations *(From Jersild and Holmes, 1933)*

because poor children are less secure about life in general, and their anxiety is reflected in a greater number of specific fears.

Fear is also related to the society a child lives in. For example, while school-age American children used to fear supernatural beings and events above all else, they are now more worried about war and Communists (Croake, 1973). This change is probably at least partly due to the influence of television, which brings war and politics into our living rooms. TV and movies themselves are often frightening to children, and some children have nightmares after every "cops and robbers" show they see. The shows themselves probably do not make a child fearful, but they do provide frightening images in which to cloak his anxieties.

HELPING CHILDREN OVERCOME THEIR FEARS
As children grow older, losing their sense of powerlessness, many of their fears evaporate. When they do not, such fears can interfere with a child's

living a normal life. Parents sometimes try to rid a child of fears through ridicule ("Don't be such a baby!"), coercion ("Come on, pat the nice doggie. He won't hurt you."), logical persuasion ("How can you be afraid of a bear, when the closest one is twenty miles away, locked up in a zoo?"), or ignoring them. None of these approaches work (Jersild, 1935), and some may even aggravate a child's fearfulness.

The best ways to help children overcome their fears—which they are usually quite eager to shed—involve activity on the part of the children themselves. Children are most successful when they become more competent in finding practical methods of their own to deal with what they fear, and when they are helped to gradually experience the situations that frighten them.

Explanations can help children shed their fears, when these reassurances are combined with active conditioning to the frightening situations. For example, one investigator helped children who were afraid of the dark, by repeatedly setting up situations whereby the children were encouraged to go into a dark room to retrieve a ball that had rolled in. The investigator reassured the children of the room's safety and went with them into the room. After three to seven exposures, thirteen of the fourteen children in the experiment entered the dark room alone (Holmes, 1936).

Modeling, or showing fearlessness in others, is also useful in helping fearful children. A group of nursery school children who were afraid of dogs took part in eight brief sessions in which they observed an unafraid child their own age playing happily with a dog. Afterwards, two-thirds of the fearful children were willing to climb into the playpen with the dog (Bandura, Grusec, & Menlove, 1967).

Setting up a situation in which children have actual contact with the object they fear is quite effective. In one study (Murphy & Bootzin, 1973), 67 first-, second-, and third-grade boys and girls who were afraid of snakes and could not touch one for 10 seconds were divided into two groups. Those in the experimental group were gradually induced to have closer and more frequent contact with nonpoisonous snakes. These children were again divided into two groups to compare active and passive desensitization techniques. The youngsters in the active group performed the steps listed in Chart 9-1 after seeing them modeled by the experimenter at each step. Those in the passive-treatment group remained still; the experimenter would approach each child and manipulate the snake's body so that it touched the subject's hand.

Both active and passive desensitization proved to be equally effective as fast ways to overcome fear of snakes. Ten days after the treatment ended, thirty-nine of the forty-five children in the experimental group (86.7%) were able to sit with a snake in their lap, their hands touching it, for 15 seconds. Only five of the twenty-two control subjects (22.7%) were able to do this. A definite plus in this treatment was the brevity of the treatment

Chart 9-1   Steps in the Desensitization of Fear of Snakes
(From Murphy & Bootzin, 1973)

Pretest Steps
(Used initially to test children for fear of snakes, then used during treatment, and as posttest criteria)

1   Enter room and stand 15 ft. from snake
2   Stand 10 ft. from snake
3   Stand 5 ft. from snake
4   Stand in front of the snake
5   Touch the snake
6   Touch the snake for 10 seconds
7   Hold the snake with both hands for 5 seconds
8   Hold the snake with both hands for 10 seconds

Additional Posttest Steps

9   With glove on, hold snake with one hand 5 seconds
10   With glove on, hold snake with one hand 10 seconds
11   With bare hand, hold snake with one hand 5 seconds
12   With bare hand, hold snake with one hand 10 seconds
13   Hold snake (both hands) 5 inches from face 5 seconds
14   Hold snake (both hands) 5 inches from face 10 seconds
15   Sit with snake in lap 5 seconds
16   Sit with snake in lap 10 seconds
17   Sit with snake in lap, hands touching snake, 10 seconds
18   Sit with snake in lap, hands touching snake, 15 seconds

time—an average of 15 minutes per child, in 1.9 sessions and a maximum of 32 minutes (four sessions of 8 minutes each).

Children's Feelings about Death

Children two or three years old rarely get upset by the sight of a dead animal or the news of a dead person, because children this age generally have no idea what death means. They confuse it with sleep—or they just ask in puzzlement, "Why doesn't it move?"

Children vary considerably in the age when they begin to comprehend the concept of death, and in their reactions to it. A very few seem to begin to understand death—and to become anxious about it at about the age of three, but it is more typical for these feelings to emerge at about the age of five or six (Anthony, 1965). And even then, children are usually puzzled by death, don't understand its permanence, and often consider it an unnatural event caused by violence.

The notion of reincarnation is believed by many children. Anthony (1965) tells of two 5-year-olds who believed that dead people are reborn as babies: One, whose father had died two years previously, asked, "Mama, is papa borned yet?" and another, who saw a coffin, said, "Of course the person who went away in the coffin will become a baby." He explained this statement by saying that when his baby brother was born, "someone must have died [p. 321]." This belief in rebirth and the impermanence of death is fed by fairy tales like *Little Red Riding Hood,* in which the dead grandmother comes back to life by emerging from the wolf's body, and by animated cartoons, which regularly show characters falling from airplanes and cliffs, being blown up in explosions, being mashed flat by steamrollers —and always coming back to life in the next frame.

When anxiety about death does appear, it may have several roots. A child may worry that a parent or some other loved adult will die, forsaking him and leaving him with no one to take care of him. Or a child who loses a parent, sibling, or playmate through death may suffer from guilt that leads to depression or an overwhelming fear of punishment. Her thinking may still be egocentric enough to make her believe implicitly that her angry feelings had caused the death. Ultimately, children come to realize that they themselves will die someday, and this realization may be the most frightening of all. Said one four-year-old, "Every day I'm afraid of dying . . . I wish I might never grow old, for then I'd never die, would I? [Anthony, 1965, p. 324]"

Sometime about the age of seven, eight, or nine, many children become consumed with questions about death. They ask their parents when they will die. One little girl, who used to play with her grandmother's jewelry, kept asking, "Nana, will you give me this when you die?"—much to Nana's discomfort. By the twelfth year, virtually all children realize that death comes to everyone and that its coming need not be seen as a punishment or an act of violence, but as part of the normal life cycle.

Most human beings remain anxious about death as long as they live, and starting in childhood they deal with their anxiety through songs, jokes, and games.

How Child-rearing Techniques Affect Personality Development

Why does Nicole hit and bite the nearest person when she is unable to complete a jigsaw puzzle? What makes David sit there with that puzzle for hours, until he has solved it? Why does Michele walk away from it, after she first realizes she can't do it right away? What accounts for the fact that Tommy hardly gives his father a backward wave when he is dropped off for the first day of nursery school, while Denise clings to her mother and insists that she stay in the room for the next two weeks? The big question in child psychology is: What makes children turn out the way they do?

We are light-years away from having all the answers to this question, although we do have some partial clues. We know, for example, that children are born with varying degrees of biological hardiness, intellectual capability, and temperamental leanings. Yet in each of these three major areas, the kind of environment the child lives in during the first few years of life exerts a strong influence on the eventual outcome in development.

The most important facet of children's emotional environment involves the ways their parents raise them. We have seen the effects of parenting on intellectual development (see Chapters 5 and 8). Parental child-rearing techniques are probably even more influential in molding children's personalities.

When parents get their child to do what they want by reasoning, playing on the child's sense of guilt, or withdrawing parental approval and affection, the child is much more likely to develop a strong conscience and to suffer from guilt feelings, and much less likely to become aggressive than is the child who is disciplined by physical punishment, threats, or the withdrawal of privileges. Since parents are more likely to use the former methods with girls and the latter with boys, this may explain why girls are more likely to exhibit feelings of guilt and why boys become more aggressive (Sears, Maccoby, & Levin, 1957). This is one specific type of parental behavior that brings about specific kinds of behavior in children. Much research has investigated the antecedents of other types of behavior that children exhibit.

AGGRESSION

What makes some children so ready to hit, bite, scream, be "mean" to others, and destroy property? One newspaper article offers "A Sure Formula for Raising a Violent Child":

> This is how you raise a violent child:
> Ignore, humiliate, and tease him. Yell a lot. Show your disapproval for everything he does. Encourage him to fight with his brothers and sisters. Fight a lot, especially physically, with your spouse. Hit him a lot.
> And if all that doesn't do the trick, plop him down in front of a television set and give him carte blanche to watch every violent show that's available [Kramer, 1973].

This reporter based her "advice" on sound theoretical ground. For each of the above directives reflects the findings of numerous studies that have explored the origins of aggression. Usually when we discuss aggression, we think of it as behavior that is intended to injure someone or damage something. But if we leave out the factor of intent, we can define it as behavior that *could* injure or damage *if* it were to be aimed at a vulnerable person or thing (Bandura & Walters, 1963). By using the latter definition, a number of investigators, most notably Albert Bandura and his colleagues, have conducted laboratory experiments on the factors that seem to encourage aggressive, violent behavior on the part of young children.

Frustration

"Ignore, humiliate, and tease him. Yell a lot. Show your disapproval for everything he does."

Frustration involves imposing limitations upon what a person wants to do, or limiting an individual's self-concept. Punishment, insults, and fears can bring about a state of frustration. Frustration does not always lead to aggression, but a frustrated child is more likely to act aggressively than a contented one (Bandura, Ross, & Ross, 1961).

Modeling

"Fight a lot, especially physically, with your spouse. Hit him a lot."

Hitting a child provides a double incentive to make him violent: Aside from suffering frustration (the pain and the humiliation of being hit), the child sees an example of an adult with whom he identifies acting aggressive-

(Burk Uzzle, Magnum)

Hitting a child provides a double incentive to make him violent: In addition to the frustration of being hit, he sees an adult with whom he identifies acting aggressively.

ly. When parents spank a child, they provide a "living example of the use of aggression at the very moment they are trying to teach the child not to be aggressive [Sears, Maccoby, & Levin, 1957, p. 266]."

Just how influential the action of an aggressive model can be has been brought out by a number of studies. In one, seventy-two children three to six years old were divided into three groups—two experimental and one control (Bandura, Ross, & Ross, 1961). Each group had an equal number of boys and girls. One by one, each of the children in the first experimental group went into a playroom equipped with interesting toys. An adult model (male for half the children, female for the other half) quietly played in a corner with some toys. The model for the second experimental group began to assemble tinker toys, but after about a minute, the model spent the rest of the ten-minute session acting aggressively toward a five-foot inflated Bobo doll.

> The model laid Bobo on its side, sat on it and punched it repeatedly in the nose. The model then raised the Bobo doll, picked up the mallet and struck the doll on the head. Following the mallet aggression, the model tossed the doll up in the air aggressively and kicked it about the room. This sequence of physically aggressive acts was repeated approximately three times, interspersed with verbally aggressive responses such as, "Sock him in the nose . . . ," "Hit him down . . . ," "Throw him in the air . . . ," "Kick him . . . ," "Pow . . . ," and two non-aggressive comments, "He keeps coming back for more" and "He sure is a tough fella [Bandura, Ross, & Ross, 1961, p. 76]."

The children in the control group saw no model. After the experimental sessions, each child in all three groups was subjected to a mild degree of frustration by being offered a group of tantalizing toys, and then told that he or she could not play with them. After this experience, each child was taken individually into still another room, containing nonaggressive toys like a tea set, crayons and paper, a ball, dolls, and trucks, and aggressive toys like a three-foot Bobo doll, a mallet and peg board, and dart guns. The children spent twenty minutes in this last room, during which their behavior was observed.

The subjects in the second experimental group, who had seen the aggressive model, were much more aggressive than those in either of the other two groups. They said and did many of the very same things they had seen the aggressive model do. Both boys and girls who had seen an aggressive male model were more strongly influenced than those who had seen the aggressive female model, apparently because the children were responding in terms of behavior considered appropriate only for one sex. The children said things like: "Who is that lady? That's not the way for a lady to behave," or "You should have seen what that girl did in there. She was just acting like a man. I never saw a girl act like that before. She was punching and fighting but not swearing." Both boys and girls approved of male aggression, in such comments as "Al's a good socker," or "He's a good fighter like Daddy" (Bandura, Ross, & Ross, 1961, p. 581). Boys were more aggressive than girls.

The subjects who had been with the quiet models were less aggressive than the controls, indicating still further how adult models can influence children's behavior in more than one direction.

Does Television Cause Aggressive Behavior?

The day after a televised movie featured a switchblade knife fight, a California boy was knifed in a reenactment of that fight (*San Francisco Chronicle*, 1961). Two days after a television show portrayed teen-age boys dousing tramps with gasoline and setting them on fire, the nation was shocked to learn that a group of Boston youths had poured gasoline on a young woman and burned her to death (Morgan, 1973). Is this, then, the effect of "plopping" children in front of violent television shows?

In 1972, a special committee organized under the auspices of the National Institute of Mental Health presented five volumes of research and a 279-page summary report to the Surgeon General of the United States. The report, titled *Television and Growing Up: The Impact of Televised Violence*, concluded that there is some relationship between exposure to television violence and aggressive tendencies, but that this relationship applied only to deviant children and that the relationship between viewing violence and putting it into action was often activated by a third, unknown variable.

Many observers have criticized the report, partly because the committee that produced it included several persons with known ties to the television industry and because industry representatives were permitted to veto the appointment of some highly vocal critics (Holden, 1972). Some of these critics state that the relationship between viewing and doing violence is far stronger than indicated in the report, and that this relationship exists with children who are not necessarily predisposed to violence. Studies such as the following give support to these views.

Of 136 boys and girls aged five to nine, an experimental group watched a $3\frac{1}{2}$-minute segment from a popular TV series. In these $3\frac{1}{2}$ minutes were a chase, two fist-fights, two shootings, and a knifing. A control group watched $3\frac{1}{2}$ minutes of athletic competition. After the televiewing, the children were asked to take part in a "game," which involved pushing either a *help* button that could help an unseen child win a game, or a *hurt* button that would make a handle touched by that unseen child so hot that it would hurt. There was, of course, no such mysterious child; the only child in the experiment was the one pushing the buttons. The disturbing result of this study was that children who had watched the violent programming (which is typical of much TV fare) were more willing to hurt the unseen child and more willing to inflict more severe pain than were those who had watched the neutral sports program (Liebert, 1972).

In another study by Bandura, Ross, and Ross (1963), ninety-six preschool boys and girls were divided into three experimental groups and one control group of twenty-four subjects each (twelve boys, twelve girls). Experimental group 1 observed real-life aggressive models, group 2 saw films of these same models acting aggressively, group 3 saw a film featuring an aggressive cartoon character, and the control group saw no models. Each child was then brought into a playroom, frustrated slightly, and then taken into another room that contained both aggressive and nonaggressive toys.

The children who had seen the real-life aggressive models, the filmed aggressive models, or the cartoon aggressive model all showed much more aggression that did children who had seen none of these. Of this normal group of children, 88 percent of the youngsters who saw real-life or filmed human models and 79 percent who saw an aggressive cartoon model, imitated in some way the aggression they had just witnessed. The children who had seen the filmed people seemed to have been influenced the most, a finding that has grave implications for children's viewing of violent TV shows and movies.

Both these studies and other similar ones involved normal children, not deviant ones, and both showed a marked rise in aggression. The jury is still out, though, as to whether such influences carry over from the laboratory to real life. The tragic incidents related at the beginning of this section may indicate that they do.

Rewarding Aggressive Behavior

Since children learn to do things that bring reinforcement, we have to ask what kinds of rewards exist for aggressive behavior. Sometimes the reward is attention, even if the attention is negative. Nursery school teachers have been able to decrease the amount of aggression exhibited by three- and four-year-old boys by ignoring their aggressive behavior and rewarding their cooperative activities (Brown & Elliott, 1965). Fathers or mothers who permit aggressive behavior by not interfering with it communicate their implicit approval of such behavior to their children. Other parents actively reward and encourage children's aggression toward other children, while discouraging it toward themselves (Bandura, 1960). As a result, the children learn not to hit their parents, but they become quite aggressive toward other children.

PASSIVE AND DEPENDENT BEHAVIOR

On the first day of nursery school, Jamie, three, cried as if his heart would break the moment he thought his mother was going to walk away and leave him. After several weeks, he transferred his attachment, first to his teacher and then to another little boy, whom he tagged after most of the time. Quiet and shy, he hung back in every new situation, often going to one adult or another to help him out.

Jamie is an extremely passive and dependent child. Passivity in this sense is more than a state of inactivity; it is, rather, the state of being done to, rather than doing, or failing to initiate behavior. And dependency can be defined as the opposite of self-sufficiency. It can involve a wide variety of behaviors, all of which demonstrate the individual's need for reassurance, love, approval, and help from others (Hetherington, 1970).

Dependency on others as a lifelong character trait does not develop until the school years, and often not till past the age of ten. So the child—generally the boy—who is passive and dependent as a preschooler may come into his own during the school years to emerge as an independent adult. What differences can we see between the early environments of children who will eventually be dependent or independent? Since our society considers dependence more appropriate for girls than for boys, how does it encourage this differentiation, to the extent that one writer (Hetherington, 1970) can say:

> If a man wished to have a car door held open for him, this would probably be classified as dependent behavior. This would not be true if the behavior had been emitted by a woman or a two-year-old child [p. 210].

Attempting to answer these questions, investigators have looked at children and young adults and have drawn several conclusions.

Stability of Dependent Behavior

Two little girls are in nursery school. At three, Amy is independent and capable. She has a strong, intense personality and tends to be quite stubborn. At five, she is a successful leader who can organize a group on a hike, directing them and arranging things. She consistently shows a strong drive for achievement—and for doing everything herself, with a minimum of help. Barbie couldn't be more different. At three, she is timid and tense. She tends to follow meekly behind one particular friend. When the friend is absent, Barbie trails along with the teacher. At four, she still stays close to the teacher and goes along with whatever an adult asks of her. When she wants a turn on the slide, she asks the teacher to get it for her, instead of handling the situation for herself.

What kinds of women do these girls grow up to be? At twenty-one, Amy is a senior at college—still strong-minded and independent. She still has an intense drive for achievement, she is trying to be independent of her mother—and of other people as well, and she has an aversion to appearing "helpless and weak." At twenty-three, Barbie is working and living with her parents. She depends on her friends for advice, she likes being close to her family, she accepts her dependency on people she considers authority figures, and she tends to see herself as inadequate when faced with problems.

"Amy" and "Barbie" (not their real names) are among twenty-seven men and twenty-seven women observed by Kagan and Moss (1960). These adults were assessed on various measures of dependency—how much they needed security on the job; how much they depended on their husbands, wives, parents, and friends; how much they withdrew from possible failure-producing situations; and how conflicted they were over dependent behavior. (To rate the last variable, there were shown a series of pictures to determine how readily they recognized dependent situations. When they did not recognize them, they were considered to have conflicts in this area.) Since these adults had participated in a longitudinal study from the age of three, information was also available on their degree of dependency in the preschool and early school years. As children, they had been evaluated on such factors as their passivity when faced with obstacles and their tendency to seek help and affection from adults.

Kagan and Moss (1960) found little or no relationship between the children's dependency in the *preschool* years and their dependency in adulthood.

> Passive and dependent behavior for ages 6 to 10 showed a better relation to adult dependent behavior than the ratings for 3 to 6 years of age. This finding indicates that important age changes occur between ages 3 and 10 and that behavior displayed during the first few years of school is a better index of adult functioning than the earlier preschool behavior patterns [Snadowsky, 1973, p. 201].

This was particularly true for girls. If they were independent from ages six to ten, they were likely to be independent as adults, and vice versa. More of the boys shifted from high dependency during childhood to independent behavior as adults, and more of the men were conflicted over dependent behavior than the women.

It seems that girls are more likely to maintain passive behaviors because they are rewarded for them. Boys, on the other hand, are more likely to switch from dependent to independent behavior since they are rewarded for being independent.

How Parents Encourage Dependency

Other investigators have attempted to identify the specific ways by which parents encourage dependency in children. Hartup (1970) claims that dependent, passive, clinging persons are those who are frustrated in infancy, rejected and punished severely during the preschool years, scolded when they cling to their parents or want to sit in their laps (but are allowed to do so anyway) and, in general, are treated inconsistently. And Hetherington (1970) attributes dependency in children to overprotective, excessively controlling, and dominating parental practices.

INDEPENDENCE AND ACHIEVEMENT

Right from infancy, children differ in their inborn drives to persist in overcoming obstacles to achieve some goal (Thomas et al., 1963). By the preschool years, these differences become much more evident, but so much so that we wonder whether inborn personality is the only factor that accounts for the difference. Why does Vicky keep trying to scale the jungle gym, day after day, until she makes it to the top—while Denise gives up after one unsuccessful effort? While innate temperamental differences do exist between the two girls, we also see considerable differences in the ways the girls' parents treat them. When Vicky tries something new, her parents encourage her, and when she succeeds they are quick to praise her and to show their approval. They are quite chary of responding to her pleas for help or for emotional support in most of her little problems, and as a result she tends to do more things on her own. Denise's parents show less approval for her achievements, but come to her aid more when she is frustrated. And so she does not try as hard, and when she runs into trouble, is more likely to go to her mother's knee rather than to keep trying.

The two girls reflect two different kinds of achievement behaviors and parental practices, as uncovered by a study of thirty preschoolers and their mothers (Crandall, Preston, & Rabson, 1960). The investigators rated the children in free-play situations at home and in nursery school for their efforts to accomplish tasks requiring skill and effort, and for the degree to which they sought approval and praise for their accomplishments, adult help with their problems, and emotional support, sympathy, or reassurance. The researchers also assessed the amount of affection the children's mothers expressed to their children, and the degree to which the mothers rewarded each of the four patterns of child behavior described

---

Children Learn What They Live*

If a child lives with criticism, He learns to condemn.
If a child lives with hostility, He learns to fight.
If a child lives with ridicule, He learns to be shy.
If a child lives with shame, He learns to feel guilty.
If a child lives with tolerance, He learns to be patient.
If a child lives with encouragement, He learns confidence.
If a child lives with praise, He learns to appreciate.
If a child lives with fairness, He learns justice.
If a child lives with security, He learns to have faith.
If a child lives with approval, He learns to like himself.
If a child lives with acceptance and friendship,
He learns to find love in the world.

*Dorothy Law Nolte.

above (achievement-effort, approval-seeking, help-seeking, and emotional support-seeking).

The mothers who frequently rewarded their children's efforts to achieve were usually intolerant of the children's efforts to get help or emotional support. They did not reward dependent behaviors. They did reward approval-seeking, perhaps because they linked this to achievement development rather than to dependency. The children did achieve, and depended less on adults for help and for emotional support. The children behaved fairly consistently at home and in school, and no differences showed up between boys and girls on any of the four behaviors studied. Nor was there any connection between the amount of affection a mother displayed toward her child and that child's achievement behavior.

GLOBAL STYLES OF CHILD-REARING

So far we have been talking about fairly specific aspects of child-rearing—how parents discipline their children, or how they encourage or discourage aggression, dependence, independence, and achievement. While it is possible to pick apart discrete aspects of parental behavior, the overall style of the way parents relate to a child affects *all* the child's behavior.

In the fairly short history of the United States, we have had fashions in child-rearing, just as we have had fashions in clothing. For much of our country's early history, the "father knows best" school of bringing up children held sway. According to this view, the parents know everything and the child knows nothing. It is, therefore, incumbent upon the parents to make their will known to the child and to enforce it strictly.

About a third of the way into the twentieth century, as the psychoanalytic theories had gained wide acceptance, the pervasive theme shifted to permissiveness, or a belief that the child knows everything and the parent knows nothing. Since parents and professionals alike were convinced of the harm done when children were not satisfied in the oral, anal, and genital stages of psychosexual development, the feeling seemed to be that children should set their own pace for feeding, weaning, toilet-training, and other childhood activities.

Now, what we might call the democratic way of bringing up children appears to have the most adherents, that is, that parents probably know best in many things, but children know something, too. Therefore, the parents should guide their progeny through childhood, but with respect for the child.

Most children seem to have thrived equally well throughout the shifting tides of parenting fashions, although with each method, a few children have been unable to adapt to their parents' handling. Say one group of authors (Thomas et al., 1963):

The small proportion of children who fail to adapt and thrive with one type of child care practice may be totally different from those who fail to thrive with another type of practice. During the centuries when infants were fed whenever they were hungry, most children apparently adapted to this approach. When feeding by the clock according to a predetermined schedule became the advocated pattern, most children adapted to this. When once again it was decided to feed children when they were hungry—now called "self-demand feeding"—in response to the awareness that a small group of children did not adapt to clock feeding, again most, but not all, children adapted to this method. . . .

The enormous variety of child care practices which have succeeded in maintaining the race does not, however, attest to the equality of excellence. With the understanding that no general rule of child care practice will be appropriate for every child, it nevertheless can be argued that some general rules will be optimal for a higher percentage of children than other modes of practice. Defining such optimal practices still remains a goal, even though it will always be necessary to deviate from such general rules with some children [p. 151].

Current Styles of Parenting

In an effort to determine the ways by which present-day American parents are bringing up their children, and then to measure the effectiveness of their practices, Baumrind has defined three prototypes of parental practices: the *authoritarian*, the *permissive*, and the *authoritative*, and has examined preschool children with reference to their parents' styles of handling them (Baumrind, 1966; Baumrind & Black, 1967).

The authoritarian parent. These parents try to control their children's behavior and attitudes and make them conform to a set and usually absolute standard of conduct. They value unquestioning obedience; they punish their children forcefully for acting contrary to parental standards. Authoritarian parents believe in "keeping the child in his place, in restricting his autonomy, and in assigning household responsibilities in order to inculcate respect for work [Baumrind, 1966, p. 890]." They are more detached, more controlling, and less warm than other parents. As rated in Baumrind and Black's study of 103 nursery school children (1967), their children are more discontent, withdrawn, and distrustful.

The permissive parent. These parents make few demands on their children, allow them to regulate their own activities as much as possible, and avoid imposing their own standards. They consider themselves resources for their children to draw upon, but not standard-bearers or ideal models. They explain to their children the reasons underlying the few family rules that do exist, consult with them about policy decisions, and hardly ever punish them. They are noncontrolling, nondemanding, and relatively warm, and their children as preschoolers are immature—the least self-reliant, the least self-controlled, and the least exploratory.

The authoritative parent. These parents try to direct their children's activities rationally, with attention to the issures rather than the children's fear of punishment or of loss of love. They exert firm control when they consider it necessary, but they explain the reasoning behind their stands, and they encourage verbal give-and-take, so that the children feel free to voice their objections to parental policies. They value "both autonomous self-will and disciplined conformity." While they have confidence in their ability as adults to guide their children, they respect their children's interest, opinions, and unique personalities. They are loving, consistent, demanding, and respectful of their children's independent decisions, but firm in maintaining their own standards and willing to impose limited punishment at times. They combine control with encouragement. Their children apparently feel secure in knowing that they are loved, and also in knowing what is demanded of them. As preschoolers, these children are the most self-reliant, self-controlled, self-assertive, exploratory, and content youngsters in the group.

Why Children of Authoritative Parents Seem to Be the Most Successful

Children whose parents expect them to perform as well as they can, to fulfill their commitments, and to participate actively in family duties as well as in family fun, are learning how to formulate goals. They are also experiencing the satisfaction that comes from meeting responsibilities and achieving success. The essential factor here, then, appears to be the parents' reasonable expectations and realistic standards.

> Authoritarian control and permissive noncontrol may both shield the child from the opportunity to engage in vigorous interaction with people. Demands which cannot be met or no demands, suppression of conflict or sidestepping of conflict, refusal to help or too much help, unrealistically high or low standards, all may curb or understimulate the child so that he fails to achieve the knowledge and experience which could realistically reduce his dependence upon the outside world. . . . Spirited give and take within the home, if accompanied by respect and warmth, may teach the child how to express aggression in self-serving and prosocial causes and to accept the partially unpleasant consequences of such actions [Baumrind, 1966, p. 904].

Children from permissive environments receive so little guidance that they often become uncertain and anxious about whether they are doing the right thing. Children from authoritarian homes are so strictly controlled, either by punishment or the manipulation of guilt, that they are often prevented from making a conscious choice about the merit of a particular behavior because they are overly concerned about the parental consequences of that behavior. They are not free to judge the behavior on its own merits. But in authoritative homes, children know when they are meeting expectations, learn how to judge those expectations, and are able to decide when it is worth risking parental displeasure or other "unpleasant consequences" in the pursuit of some goal.

Harmonious Parents

Baumrind (1971) also identified a small group of eight sets of parents whom she termed "harmonious parents." These parents could not be rated on control, because while they almost never *exercised* control, they seemed to *have* it in the sense that their children generally sensed what the parents wanted and tried to do it. These parents, generally from the highest educational levels, encouraged independence and individuality in their children, enriched the children's environments, and were nonconformists themselves.

> [Harmonious parents] focused upon achieving a quality of harmony in the home, and upon developing principles for resolving differences and for right living. Often they lost interest in actually resolving a difference once agreement upon principles of resolution had been reached. These parents brought the child up to their level in an interaction but did not reverse roles by acting childishly, as did some Permissive and Nonconforming parents. Harmonious parents were equalitarian in that they recognized differences based upon knowledge and personality, and tried to create an environment in which all family members could operate from the same vantage point, one in which the recognized differences in power did not put the child at a disadvantage. They lived parallel to the mainstream rather than in opposition to it. In their hierarchy of values honesty, harmony, justice, and rationality in human relations took precedence over power, achievement, control, and order, although they also saw the practical importance of the latter values [p. 101].

One harmonious mother described her 4-year-old daughter:

> She's strong-tempered, which comes up because she's always been taught that her opinions are valid. So if you disagree with her, she'll stand there and argue all day if she feels differently. But all of the things that make her hard to deal with are again the same things that make her very appealing. She's a very individualistic person. She tries very hard to please people and to communicate with people and to amuse them, but she's not a follower, really. And she doesn't need other people—she's not dependent, really. Psychologically she's not dependent on other people—I don't think she feels so, although she knows she couldn't do a number of things herself [Baumrind, 1971a, p. 101, Lavatelli & Stendler, 1972].

The mother then discusses her philosophy about obedience:

> *Mother*: I only think that obedience is practical. I've taught my kids to do whatever you want to do, but you're responsible for your actions and therefore also suffer the consequences of whatever you want to say. For instance, in the sense of society, if you break a law and are cognizant of the fact, and you know that if you're going to go out and play the game, if you break the rules, you're going to have to take the consequences.
>
> *Interviewer*: What decisions does Nina make for herself?

Mother: She makes all her own decisions and then we argue about them. She really does. She decides all her own things. She decides her clothes, what she'll eat; but they're sort of in the context of what's happening. She goes to the store and she decides what she'll wear by what she'll see. Or if she gets dressed in the morning, she'll decide what she'll wear by what she can see around her [p. 101].

While the harmonious parents identified by Baumrind constitute a tiny group, it is possible that this is the direction that American child-rearing practices are taking. If so, it would be worthwhile trying to locate more such families, with an eye to discerning how their children turn out in the long run.

Summary

1   According to Sigmund Freud, the preschool child is in the *phallic stage* of psychosexual development and receives pleasure from genital stimulation. This sexuality is not like the mature adult's, however. Freud postulated the male *Oedipus complex* and its female counterpart, the *Electra complex*, to account for a child's feelings toward the opposite-sex parents. Because of the conflict a child feels, he or she eventually represses sexual urges, identifies with the same-sex parent, and enters latency. The *superego* (or conscience) develops when the complex is resolved.

2   Erik Erikson maintains that the chief developmental crisis of the preschool period focuses on the development of a sense of *initiative* or *guilt*. The successful resolution of this conflict enables the child to undertake, plan, and carry out activities. Success or failure is strongly influenced by parental dealings with their children.

3   During the preschool period the child identifies with appropriate models and develops sex-appropriate behaviors. There are many theoretical interpretations of identification and sex typing. In psychoanalytic terms, the child identifies with the same-sex parent at the resolution of the Oedipus/ Electra complex. According to social learning theory, the child adopts the behaviors and attitudes of a model in order to possess the desirable attributes of that model.

4   Theoretical explanations of sex typing (the acquisition of sex-appropriate behaviors, values, motives, and emotions) range from those which focus on biological-hormonal differences between the sexes, psychosexual factors, learning (primarily through parental rewards and punishments for "appropriate" or "inappropriate" behaviors), or cognitive development. Sex typing is influenced by one's particular cultural membership (different cultures regard different behaviors as sex-appropriate), the attitudes of one's parents, one's socioeconomic status, and factors such as television programming, schools, textbooks, and children's books.

5   Child-rearing techniques influence children's personalities. Traits such as aggression, passivity, dependence, and independence are molded by the particular way parents deal with their children. Baumrind has isolated four types of parenting styles: *authoritarian, permissive, authoritative,* and *harmonious.* Each produces certain personality traits in children.

Suggested Readings

Fricke, I. *Beginning the Human Story: A New Baby in the Family.* Glenview, Ill.: Scott, Foresman, 1967. *Twelve large color charts are designed to instruct children four to eight years of age on sex education within the framework of family living. Each card has information on the back to aid in use of the card and discussion.*

Maccoby, E. E. *The Development of Sex Differences.* Stanford: Stanford University

Press, 1966. *A compendium of articles by different authors relating to differences between the sexes in behavior other than specifically sexual behavior, with a focus on how and why these differences develop. An extensive annotated bibliography summarizing a great deal of research in this area.*

Peterson, C. C. *A Child Grows Up.* New York: Alfred Publishing, 1974. *Offers the theory of developmental psychologists and the written observations of a real-life father. A textbook and a diary that offer entries of Candida's father as well as explanations with the latest in research about a child growing up.*

Sears, R. R., Maccoby, E. E., & Levin, H. *Patterns of Child-rearing.* New York: Harper & Row, 1957. *A report on the child-rearing practices of 379 working-class and middle-class suburban women, during the first five to six years of their children's lives. The mothers were interviewed at length on how they handled feeding, toilet training, aggression, and dependency. The authors draw some conclusions about the techniques that appeared most successful.*

PART FOUR
THE MIDDLE YEARS
Ages Six to Twelve

Vicky is still growing, growing, growing. She's getting taller, heavier, and stronger. She's learning new skills and concepts. But these are years of consolidation more than years of novelty. She learned how to throw a ball during the preschool years; now she can aim it better and throw it farther. She began to run as a toddler; now she can run farther, faster, and for a longer time. Some of her personality traits began to show up in infancy; now they are etched in more deeply as she encounters more situations calling for independence or dependence, aggression or cooperation, activity or passivity. She learned the rudiments of numbers, got the general idea of what reading was all about, and began to understand concepts of size, space, and time. Now she can apply them meaningfully in many concrete situations.

She is still learning new skills, though. She can read a book, write her name, figure out how soon two trains will crash if one is going 60 miles an hour and the other 80 miles an hour. She can hit a ball with a bat, she can knit, and to her parents' disgust—she can now belch at will, cross her eyes, and sew the tips of her fingers together. In short, she has better control over her body.

Vicky's parents are still extremely important in her life—but not as all-important as they used to be. In the absence of serious family problems, life is relatively tranquil at home. She doesn't fight her parents, but she doesn't worship them the way she did as a preschooler. She tends to take them for granted. Even though the way they feel and act toward her influences her self-esteem, her academic progress, and her creatvity, her parents often seem to move to the background of her life these days.

Who's in the foreground? First of all, other children. This is the age when the peer group comes into its own. Vicky wants to do things with her friends, wants to cultivate the skills they consider important, wants to be popular. She also responds to other outside influences—the mass media, especially television; other adults, such as her teacher, her Scout leader, her gym coach; and also to her older brothers and sisters.

Her thinking is developing along with her realization that she is not the center of the universe. With this realization, she can understand diverse points of view, see physical facts with some objectivity, and deal logically with many concepts. Her moral judgments, which were "black or white" during the preschool years, now become more flexible as she learns to think through the issues involved.

School has become the focus of Vicky's life. She spends more time in class and on the way to and from school than she spends with her parents. Her intellectual progress is keyed to the academic curriculum. Her social life revolves around her classmates. When she's happy in school, she's happy in general; and when she's unhappy there, she's miserable.

During these middle years, Vicky solidifies many aspects of her personality. We begin to see the kind of adult she will turn out to be as more and more of her characteristics and competencies emerge. But let's not project her into adulthood yet. Vicky is living a full, rich, and interesting childhood.

(Virginia Hamilton)

CHAPTER TEN

PHYSICAL DEVELOPMENT

IN WHICH VICKY GROWS TALLER
AND THROWS FARTHER

When I was the sissy of the block who nobody wanted on their team
Sonny Hugg persisted in believing that my small size was an asset
Not the liability and curse I felt it was
And he saw a use for my swift feet with which I ran away from fights.

*   *   *

But I will always have this to thank him for:
That when I look back on childhood
(That four psychiatrists haven't been able to help me bear the thought of)
There is not much to be glad for
Besides his foolish and delicious faith
That, with all my oddities, there was a place in the world for me
If only he could find the special role.

(Edward Field, 1963*)

*From Stand Up, Friend with Me, by Edward Field. New York: Grove Press, 1963.

Physical Growth during the School Years

If we were to walk by a typical elementary school just after the ringing of the three-o'clock bell, we would see a virtual explosion of children of all shapes and sizes. Tall ones, short ones, fat ones, skinny ones would be dashing helter-skelter through the school doors into the freedom of the open air.

These six- to twelve-year-olds look very different from their preschool brothers and sisters. (See Tables 10-1 through 10-8). They're much taller, for one thing. And they're a lot thinner; most are fairly wiry, although, on the average, the girls do retain somewhat more fatty tissue than the boys, a

Table 10-1   Percentile Distribution of Height in Inches for White Males (*Age Defined at Subject's Last Birthday*)

Age	N (Total = 2973)	3rd	10th	25th	50th	75th	90th	97th
6	250	42	44	45	46	48	50	51
7	268	45	46	47	49	50	52	54
8	261	47	49	50	51	54	56	58
9	259	48	50	51	53	55	57	61
10	221	50	52	53	55	57	59	62
11	228	51	53	55	57	59	61	66
12	222	54	56	57	59	62	64	66

Source: Reprinted by permission from J. L. Rauh, D. A. Schumsky, and M. T. Witt, "Heights, Weights, and Obesity in Urban School Children," *Child Development*, **38**, 515-530. Copyright The Society for Research in Child Development, Inc.

Table 10-2   Percentile Distribution of Height in Inches for Nonwhite Males (*Age Defined at Subject's Last Birthday*)

Age	N (Total = 1208)	3rd	10th	25th	50th	75th	90th	97th
6	110	43	44	46	47	49	51	51
7	115	45	47	48	49	51	52	56
8	128	47	49	50	52	54	55	59
9	121	48	51	52	53	55	56	69
10	89	50	51	54	55	57	60	63
11	101	51	54	55	58	59	61	64
12	101	55	57	58	60	62	64	68

Source: Reprinted by permission from J. L. Rauh, D. A. Schumsky, and M. T. Witt, "Heights, Weights, and Obesity in Urban School Children," *Child Development*, **38**, 515-530. Copyright The Society for Research in Child Development, Inc.

physical characteristic that will persist through adulthood. If this school is among the minority of racially integrated grammar schools in the United States, we will be able to see that the black children tend to be slightly larger than the white (American Academy of Pediatrics, 1973).

Strolling along, hand in hand, are a sixth-grade boy and girl, the twelve-year-old Juliet half a head taller than her Romeo. While there is very little difference in weight and height between the younger boys and girls, the boys are generally slightly heavier and taller. But at about the end of this stage, the girls reach their pubescent growth spurt before the boys, and tend to be larger. (This is apparent to every dancing-master—if, in these

Table 10-3 Percentile Distribution of Height in Inches for White Females (*Age Defined at Subject's Last Birthday*)

		Percentile						
Age	N (Total = 3010)	3rd	10th	25th	50th	75th	90th	97th
6	264	42	43	45	46	48	49	51
7	251	43	45	47	49	50	52	54
8	260	45	47	49	50	53	54	57
9	247	47	49	51	53	54	56	59
10	268	49	51	53	55	57	59	62
11	252	52	54	56	58	60	62	66
12	259	54	56	58	60	62	64	66

Source: Reprinted by permission from J. L. Rauh, D. A. Schumsky, and M. T. Witt, "Heights, Weights, and Obesity in Urban School Children," *Child Development,* **38,** 515-530. Copyright The Society for Research in Child Development, Inc.

Table 10-4 Percentile Distribution of Height in Inches for Nonwhite Females (*Age Defined at Subject's Last Birthday*)

		Percentile						
Age	N (Total = 1289)	3rd	10th	25th	50th	75th	90th	97th
6	132	42	44	45	47	48	50	54
7	132	44	46	48	49	51	53	57
8	137	46	48	50	51	53	56	59
9	108	46	50	51	53	55	58	60
10	88	50	53	55	57	59	61	64
11	104	52	55	58	59	61	63	64
12	103	56	58	59	61	63	65	68

Source: Reprinted by permission from J. L. Rauh, D. A. Schumsky, and M. T. Witt, "Heights, Weights, and Obesity in Urban School Children," *Child Development,* **38,** 515-530. Copyright The Society for Research in Child Development, Inc.

days of bluejeans and workboots instead of white gloves and patent leather shoes, such persons still exist.)

During these middle years of childhood, children grow regularly but quite slowly, compared to the rate at which they grew during infancy and the preschool years, and to the way they will shoot up during the adolescent growth spurt. They also exhibit very little change in overall body proportion.

Normal children of the same age show a wide range in height, reflecting the wide variations among individuals in all aspects of development. This

Table 10-5   Percentile Distribution of Weight in Pounds for White Males (*Age Defined at Subject's Last Birthday*)

Age	N (Total = 2973)	Percentile						
		3rd	10th	25th	50th	75th	90th	97th
6	250	38	41	45	48	52	58	67
7	268	42	46	50	53	58	63	77
8	261	44	50	55	61	67	75	83
9	259	51	54	60	66	74	87	98
10	221	54	62	66	73	82	96	110
11	228	59	64	70	81	96	111	131
12	222	68	74	80	91	104	125	141

Source: Reprinted by permission from J. L. Rauh, D. A. Schumsky, and M. T. Witt, "Heights, Weights, and Obesity in Urban School Children," *Child Development*, **38**, 515-530. Copyright The Society for Research in Child Development, Inc.

Table 10-6   Percentile Distribution of Weight in Pounds for Nonwhite Males (*Age Defined at Subject's Last Birthday*)

Age	N (Total = 1208)	Percentile						
		3rd	10th	25th	50th	75th	90th	97th
6	110	36	41	44	49	53	59	62
7	115	43	47	50	55	60	65	69
8	128	45	51	56	61	68	75	82
9	121	51	56	59	66	72	81	89
10	89	52	58	66	72	81	94	110
11	101	65	69	74	80	88	97	106
12	101	71	74	83	93	104	117	142

Source: Reprinted by permission from J. L. Rauh, D. A. Schumsky, and M. T. Witt, "Heights, Weights, and Obesity in Urban School Children," *Child Development*, **38**, 515-530. Copyright The Society for Research in Child Development, Inc.

range is so wide, in fact, "that if a child who was of exactly average height at his seventh birthday grew not at all for two years, he would still be just within the normal limits of height attained at age nine [Tanner, 1973, p. 35]."

If the school we have stopped to observe is in a relatively affluent community, the children are somewhat larger and more mature than are children from lower socioeconomic groups. This earlier maturation and consequent larger size is due in large measure to the better nutrition among the upper classes. The fat children—the overnourished—mature earliest of

Table 10-7 Percentile Distribution of Weight in Pounds for White Females (*Age Defined at Subject's Last Birthday*)

Age	N (Total = 3010)	Percentile						
		3rd	10th	25th	50th	75th	90th	97th
6	264	35	39	43	47	52	56	61
7	251	37	43	46	52	58	65	72
8	260	42	47	52	57	65	76	89
9	247	47	51	57	63	75	87	99
10	268	51	56	62	70	84	98	116
11	252	57	63	73	87	99	113	124
12	259	64	72	82	95	110	120	133

Source: Reprinted by permission from J. L. Rauh, D. A. Schumsky, and M. T. Witt, "Heights, Weights, and Obesity in Urban School Children," *Child Development*, **38**, 515-530. Copyright The Society for Research in Child Development, Inc.

Table 10-8 Percentile Distribution of Weight in Pounds for Nonwhite Females (*Age Defined at Subject's Last Birthday*)

Age	N (Total = 1289)	Percentile						
		3rd	10th	25th	50th	75th	90th	97th
6	132	34	38	42	46	50	54	67
7	132	39	44	48	51	58	63	86
8	137	42	47	52	58	67	76	84
9	108	46	53	58	65	76	89	104
10	88	51	58	67	78	89	116	131
11	104	62	67	80	90	105	118	134
12	103	67	77	86	99	113	127	144

Source: Reprinted by permission from J. L. Rauh, D. A. Schumsky, and M. T. Witt, "Heights, Weights, and Obesity in Urban School Children," *Child Development*, **38**, 515-530. Copyright The Society for Research in Child Development, Inc.

(Shelly Rusten)

Normal children of the same age show a wide range in height; they're growing regularly but slowly, compared with earlier rates.

all, and heavy girls attain *menarche*, or age of first menstruation, earlier than do their slender classmates. So we see that malnutrition hinders growth, while overnutrition accelerates it.

If our school is an international one that draws students from many different countries, we are likely to see an even wider range of sizes among children the same age. One study of eight-year-old children in different parts of the world yields a range of about 9 inches between mean heights of the shortest children (mostly from Southeast Asia, Oceania, and South America) and the tallest (mostly from northern and central Europe, eastern Australia, and the United States) (Meredith, 1969). While genetic differences probably account for some of this diversity, environmental influences also play a part. The tallest children come from parts of the world "where nutritious food is abundant and where the infectious diseases are well controlled or largely eliminated [Meredith, 1969]."

Children of this age have much keener vision and sight than they did earlier, due to maturation of the relevant organ systems. By six years, for example, their binocular coordination is well developed, enabling them to focus their eyes better. Brain development is virtually complete now. The child before six tends to be farsighted since his eye has not fully matured— and it is different in shape from an adult's.

When we take a close look at the school-age Vicky, we see that the proportions of her face have changed. In accordance with the cephalocaudal principle of development, the upper part of her head originally grew at a faster rate than the lower, mostly because of the growth of her brain. Now the lower half of her face catches up, her forehead is not so high any more, and her facial features become more prominent and more distinctly individual.

Between the ages of six and ten, children are in a constant cycle of losing their primary teeth and growing in their permanent ones. This is most noticeable in the winning toothless smiles of first- and second-graders, whose front teeth have fallen out, to be replaced by much larger ones. Shirley Temple, the child movie star of the 1930s, wore false teeth to cover the gap in her grin during this stage, but today the gap-toothed look is considered childishly charming enough so that we see children in the television commercials lisping their messages through their incomplete dentition. Among children this age, the loss of teeth is a big event, signaling a developmental milestone. (It's an even bigger event for those fortunate youngsters who can look forward to the visit of a "tooth fairy" who leaves a quarter under the pillow, in exchange for every grown-out tooth.)

HEIGHT PREDICTION

England's Royal School of Ballet maintains strictly narrow height limits for its dancers—they must be neither too short nor too tall. But since it takes years of study to become a ballet dancer, students enter the school when they are only from nine to eleven years of age, before their ultimate height is known. Those students who end up too short or too tall to be accepted into the corps de ballet will have wasted years of their lives, and suffered bitter disappointment, besides. If adult stature can be predicted for children about to enter ballet school, those whose adult heights would be unacceptable can be weeded out at an early age, so that they can set their vocational sights elsewhere (Tanner, 1973).

This is one practical reason for developing some method of predicting adult height. There are others that are appropriate for children who are developing normally. More poignant, though, are the cases of those children who appear to be growing unusually slowly or unusually quickly. In former days, the parents of such children could do nothing more than stand by the sidelines, wonder about their children's eventual stature, and hope to shrink or stretch them to optimal size.

In recent years, researchers have developed several ways of predicting adult stature and of treating abnormal growth. Under optimal circumstances, height can often be predicted within a range of about 2 inches in either direction. In other words, a boy whose height is predicted, according to the best methods, to be 5 feet 10 inches will probably end up no shorter than 5 feet 8 inches, and no taller than 6 feet (Tanner, 1973).

Channelwise Progression

This theory of height prediction makes the assumption that a child in the sixtieth percentile at age eight will still be in the sixtieth percentile at age eighteen, leading to the conclusion that if we can measure a child's stature at any point in development, then we can predict what it will be at a later age (Garn, 1966).

Percentage Relationship

Another method of predicting size depends on measurements of children's growth, as gleaned from a longitudinal study. It determines the percentage of final growth at each age level. For example, six-year-old girls are about 70 percent of their final size; at age eleven they are about 90 percent, and so on. If we know, then, the average percentage relationships between size at a given age and final body size, we can calculate a series of multipliers for stature prediction. To use this method we have to know the measured size of the child, the age of the child (either chronological or skeletal age, as explained in the next section), and the multiplier appropriate for the age and sex of this child.

Since girls mature earlier, they are at any given age closer to adult height than are boys of the same age. Therefore, the multiplier for a girl is smaller than that for a boy at any given age. Furthermore, the multiplier is different for each age, since a child at age six has achieved a different proportion of adult height than has a child at age ten.

This system is effective only for people of average size, and it is further limited by the fact that it doesn't take into account differing rates of growth at different ages.

Skeletal, or Bone, Age

When the human skeleton first begins to form in the second month of prenatal life, it starts out as cartilage, a tough elastic tissue, which gradually changes to hard bone. This process of bone formation is called *ossification*, and it continues until an individual achieves full growth, at about the age of eighteen. Bone shows up in an x-ray photograph; cartilage does not. The rate of ossification is an important measure of growth. We can make much more accurate predictions of final height if we have access to skeletal age, rather than chronological age.

In practice, a child's bone age is derived by looking at an x-ray, usually of the hand and wrist, to determine how much of the cartilage has turned into bone and how closely fused the ends of one bone are to the one next to it. The closer the bones in the hand are fused together the more advanced the skeletal age. By comparing a particular child's x-ray to x-ray photos standardized for age, we can determine that child's bone age. And knowing the bone age, we can predict ultimate height more accurately.

Thus, we can look at two girls, both nine years old, both 53 inches tall.

Even though height predictions based on bone age and comparisons to norms are somewhat closer than a guess, children do not grow along percentile lines.

Using the multiplier determined by researchers at the Fels Institute to calculate adult stature, we would predict an adult height for each girl of about 5 feet 5 inches. But when we look at the girls' hand-and-wrist x-rays, we see that Anne, an early maturer, has a skeletal age of eleven years, and Barbara, a late maturer, one of only eight years. Anne, then, has a shorter future span of growth than does Barbara. Knowing the girls' bone ages, we change our predictions for their ultimate growth, and look ahead to a height of 4 feet 11^1/$_2$ inches, for Anne, and one of 5 feet 8^1/$_2$ inches, for Barbara.

Ironically for the children themselves, who are usually self-conscious when their growth is either ahead or behind most of their contemporaries, people destined to be tall usually reach their full growth sooner than the average, and short people take a longer than average time to reach full growth. So, in those late middle years and early adolescent years when physical appearance is so important to children's self-concepts, the tall get taller and the short stay shorter.

Size Standards

Any method of height prediction is necessarily based on an accurate set of tables to measure average sizes attained by large groups of children. One of the problems in assessing children's height is our general lack of up-to-date size standards for American black children, or for children of Chinese or Japanese ancestry. Recently some researchers (Wingerd, Solomon, & Schoen, 1973) have addressed themselves to this problem, but for the most part, in assessing the growth of these children, doctors, nutritionists, and public health personnel have to guess at average heights in these groups.

Limitations of Size Prediction

Even though our prophecies of height based on bone age and comparisons to norms are somewhat closer than a guess, they are still not so accurate as we would like them to be, for a number of reasons. Most children do not grow neatly along percentile lines. Size at one age is not necessarily an indication of size at a later age—especially for children of very short or very tall parents, or of one short and one tall parent. Children may grow quickly at one stage, slowly at another. The timing and magnitude of the adolescent spurt and the amount of postspurt growth affect ultimate stature, but so far these factors are unpredictable.

> In projecting human stature, then, the following generalization should be borne in mind. The later the projection is made, the more it makes use of skeletal rather than chronological age, and the more nearly the child conforms to the characteristics of the group, the better the prediction. Conversely, the earlier the size prediction is made, the more it depends on chronological age alone (or early skeletal age estimates), and the more the child deviates from the averages for the group, the poorer the size prediction will necessarily be [Garn, 1966, p. 538].

TREATMENT OF ABNORMAL GROWTH

Tamara Dobson is an extraordinarily beautiful and successful actress and model, who has capitalized on her statuesque height of 6 feet 2 inches. And many historians have felt that Napoleon became a noted military leader to compensate for his short stature. But these two individuals are notable, partly because they are exceptions to the general rule. In our society, it is a distinct social disadvantage for a man to be too short or a woman too tall. Since so much of children's—and also adults'—self-concept is related to how well they fit into a normal spectrum of physical characteristics, the parents of excessively short or tall children are often eager to do what they can to alter their children's growth patterns. Today, physicians administer various types of treatment, depending on the reasons behind the aberrant growth pattern.

If a doctor finds out that a child will grow to average height and is just maturing early or late for his age, she can reassure the parents and the child, and urge patience until final growth is eventually reached. If, however, height predictions point to unusual tallness or shortness, the doctor may choose to treat the abnormal growth.

If hormonal tests show that a child's malfunctioning pituitary gland is

Tamara Dobson: At 6 feet 2 inches, an exception to the general rule that makes it a disadvantage for a man to be too short or a woman too tall.

retarding normal growth, it is sometimes possible to accelerate development by injecting human growth hormone, a precious commodity presently in very short supply. To do any good, the hormone must be injected on a regular basis before puberty, when growth slows down markedly.

Health Problems of Children

Vicky, ten, is home in bed with a cold, her second of the year. She sneezes, snoozes, watches a lot of TV, pulls out her old coloring book—and, in general, enjoys being sick. Vicky is lucky. She has had no other illnesses this year other than the two colds. Her good health reflects great strides in medical progress over the past several decades.

Children born in the 1920s and 1930s—of all social classes—were prone to many diseases whose rates have dropped sharply over the years. They were likely to contract whooping cough, mumps, chickenpox, and measles;

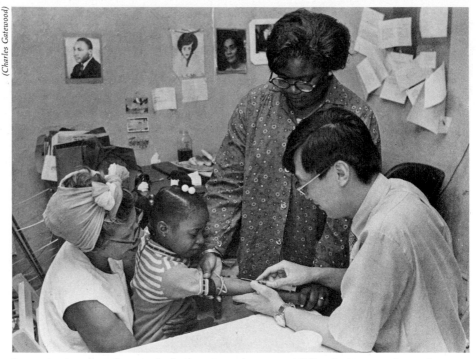

(Charles Gatewood)

Immunization has decreased death rates of many childhood diseases, but others—tuberculosis, veneral disease, hepatitis—remain a threat.

scarlet fever, diphtheria, and polio were also common dangers (Bayer & Snyder, 1950). These diseases were often serious and sometimes fatal. Vicky, though, has been inoculated against all these diseases, and she has never had any of these classic childhood ailments.

ILLNESSES

There are many children in the United States today who are not as fortunate as Vicky. True, the incidence and death rate from many childhood diseases—most notably diphtheria, polio, measles, and whooping cough—*have* decreased, due to immunization, improved diet, and improved sanitation (Profiles of Children, 1970). But too many children are still suffering from too many preventable illnesses.

Tuberculosis, syphilis, gonorrhea, and hepatitis are a major health problem among children under fourteen. Tuberculosis is a particular threat to children of minority races.

ACCIDENTS

The leading cause of death among children is not illness, though, but accidents. Some 15,000 American children under the age of fifteen die each year and another 19 million are injured severely enough to seek medical care or to restrict their usual activity (Profiles of Children, 1970, p. 28). Most of these accidents occur in or around the home. Children are killed by automobiles; they drown in pools, lakes, rivers, and oceans; they are fatally burned in fires and explosions; they drink a variety of poisonous substances; they fall from heights; they get caught in various mechanical contrivances. The tragic list goes on and on.

Children are naturally venturesome, and naively ignorant of the dangers that surround them. Their innocence puts a large burden on parents and other adult caretakers who must tread a delicate line between supervising children adequately and smothering them with oversolicitousness. The greatest burden, though, should be on society at large. Federal laws have already been passed to require children's-size pajamas to be flame-retardant, to require "child-proof" caps on medicine bottles, and to require minimum spaces between the bars on babies' cribs, so that they cannot get their heads caught and strangle. Many more regulations are needed to ensure that the normal curiosity and playfulness of children will not lead to their untimely death. Manufacturers of bicycles, playground equipment, and swimming pools, for example, should be required to adhere to governmentally established safety standards.

POVERTY

Poverty is the most serious health problem among American children today. Some 20 percent of our total population does not have enough money to maintain an adequate standard of living. And when people don't have money, they live in substandard, crowded, unsanitary housing; they don't eat enough of the right kinds of foods; they don't go to doctors and dentists often enough; and parents are too busy keeping body and soul together to provide adequate supervision for their children. Poverty is unhealthy.

The problems of poor children begin long before birth, as we have pointed out earlier. Poor mothers don't eat well themselves and don't get adequate prenatal care. They are more likely to have premature and low-birthweight babies, and babies who are born dead or who die soon after birth. More poor children are born with venereal disease, drug addiction, and hepatitis. We have already discussed the implication of perinatal factors for later development in Chapter 3.

As poor children grow a little older, they are more likely to contract diseases like tuberculosis. They have a higher rate of untreated dental cavities. Lead poisoning and rat bites are diseases of poor children living in urban slums. Poor children are less likely than middle-class children to be fully protected by immunization. American Indian children are still suffering from typhoid, dysentery, tuberculosis, hepatitis, diphtheria, and trachoma (White House Conference, 1970).

(Hugh Rogers, Monkmeyer)

Poverty is unhealthy: We need to work on the social conditions that breed disease.

In view of the overwhelming health problems among the poor—which have far-reaching effects on their intellectual and emotional development—it is imperative to make massive efforts to serve them. Some progress has been made in providing health services to the poor; much more is needed. Free or low-cost health clinics have been set up in many low-income areas, and such clinics have reduced the rate of infant mortality in city slums. But there is a great need for many more preventive health services to poor children and their families. Such programs should include immunization schedules, along with parent education on the need for such immunization and help in getting the children to the clinics. The clinics should emphasize dental care, an often neglected service. More extensive prenatal care is needed. Concurrently, society has to work on the social conditions of poverty that breed disease. We have to help more low-income people get better housing, free from the rats that bite their babies and the lead paint that poisons their toddlers. We have to help people break out of the cycle of poverty, illiteracy, unemployment, and despair, if we are going to make the promise of medical progress become a reality for all our citizens.

Motor Development

Back in that school yard at 3:00 PM, we see the grade-school children running pell-mell on their way out of the building. Were we to follow them home, we'd see them as they leap up onto narrow ledges and walk along, balancing themselves, and as they jump off, trying to break distance records but occasionally breaking a bone instead. After dashing into the house to drop their books, go to the bathroom, and get a snack, they'll be out on the street again. They'll be jumping rope, playing sandlot baseball, roller-skating, bicycling, sledding, throwing snowballs, or jumping into the old swimming hole, depending on the season, the community, and the child. A few may be learning how to ride a horse, skate on ice, dance the ballet, or contort their bodies on gymnastics apparatus. It's astonishing how far these children have come in terms of getting their bodies to do what they want them to do. They keep getting stronger, faster, and better coordinated, and they derive great pleasure from testing their bodies and achieving new skills.

Since running, jumping, and throwing are common elements of many childhood games, Espenschade (1960) based her study of age changes and sex differences on these three activities. By examining a large number of reports in the literature of child development, giving measures of children's abilities in running, in doing a standard broad jump, in jump-and-reach, and in throwing, she found wide individual differences and some sex differences. (See Figures 10-1 through 10-4.) At all ages, she found, ability is closely related to size and build. The effect of maturation can be seen in the improvement, with age, of balance and coordination, which have little relationship to physique or strength. She also found that children's abilities

Figure 10-1 **Age and Sex Differences: Running** *(Espenschade, 1960)*

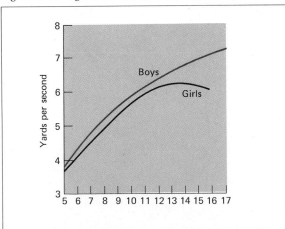

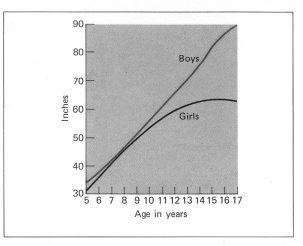

Figure 10-2   **Age and Sex Differences: Standing Broad Jump** *(Espenschade, 1960)*

in one activity correlate with their skills in another, and so the good runners tend to be good at throwing and jumping, too.

Distinct differences showed up between boys' and girls' abilities in the activities measured by these reports. Boys were found to improve in performance from ages five to seventeen, while girls improved through their early school years, hit a peak of performance at about age thirteen, and then declined or stayed the same from then on (see Table 10-9). Since girls, as well as boys, continue to grow taller and stronger after the age of thirteen, it is hard to explain their poorer showings thereafter on the basis of the attainment of physical maturity. Some authors have tried to explain

Figure 10-3   **Age and Sex Differences: Jump and Reach** *(Espenschade, 1960)*

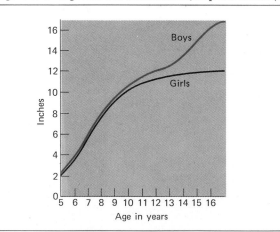

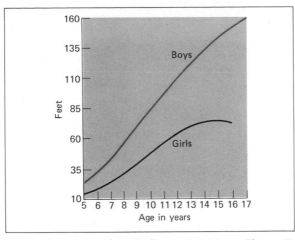

Figure 10-4   Age and Sex Differences: Distance Throw *(Espenschade, 1960)*

this "topping out" of female physical abilities on the basis of their development of secondary sex characteristics with the advent of adolescence. A social explanation of this phenomenon seems more likely.

After this age, there is less motivation for girls to excel in physical activities. Traditionally, this has been the age when girls have been encouraged to put aside their "tomboyish" ways and give themselves over to their "true" feminine natures. The contemporary awakening interest in physical education for adolescent girls may bring about a different state of affairs.

While the boys do somewhat better than the girls on all skills, according to Espenschade, their superiority is very slight until puberty, when they show sharp increases in their skills, and the girls either decline or level off.

To determine the relationship between gross motor skills and children's developmental status, Govatos (1959) examined 101 children six to eleven years old. The youngsters were measured for height, weight, bone structure, strength, IQ, and the number of permanent teeth they had. Then their running, jumping, throwing, and kicking abilities were assessed.

Some definite developmental relationships showed up. Both sexes, for example, increased their performances as they matured, getting better at different skills at different age levels. The children's dental and grip ages (the number of permanent teeth and the strength of hand grip in kilograms, converted into age values) correlated significantly with their abilities in jump-and-reach, soccer, kicking for distance, and over- and underhand distance ball throw. These measures correlated better with these skills than did height and weight. There was no correlation between reading ability or IQ and motor skills.

Table 10-9   Age Changes in Motor Performance (*Espenschade, 1960*)

Age	Run (Yards Per Second)	Standing Broad Jump (Inches)	Jump and Reach (Inches)	Distance Throw (Feet)
Boys				
5	3.8	33.7	2.5	23.6
6	4.2	37.4	4.0	32.8
7	4.6	41.6	6.1	42.3
8	5.1	46.7	8.3	57.4
9		50.4	8.5	66.6
10	5.9	54.7	11.0	83.0
11	6.1	61.0	11.5	95.0
12	6.3	64.9	12.2	104.0
13	6.5	69.3	12.5	114.0
14	6.7	73.2	13.3	123.0
15	6.8	79.5	14.8	135.0
16	7.1	88.0	16.3	144.0
17	7.2	88.4	16.9	153.0
Girls				
5	3.6	31.6	2.2	14.5
6	4.1	36.2	3.5	17.8
7	4.4	40.0	5.7	25.4
8	4.6	45.9	7.7	30.0
9		51.3	8.7	38.7
10	5.8		10.5	47.0
11	6.0	52.0	11.0	54.0
12	6.1		11.2	61.0
13	6.3	62.1	11.0	70.0
14	6.2	62.7	11.8	74.5
15	6.1	63.2	12.2	75.7
16	6.0	63.0	12.0	74.0
17	5.9			

Boys and girls of similar size tended to do equally well in running and jumping, but the boys generally outdid the girls in throwing and kicking. It is not clear how much of this difference is related to basic anatomical differences, which are slight at this age, or to differential practice in various activities. In other words, do girls play tag and jump rope because they're good at running and jumping, or does playing tag and jumping rope improve their running and jumping abilities? And similarly with boys, do they play football and soccer because they're good throwers and kickers, or do they become good at throwing and kicking from playing football and soccer?

In any case, it appears that maturation plays an important part in the development of motor skills, but culture influences their maintenance.

Relationships between Physical Development and Personality

BODY TYPE

Tom is short and pudgy, Dick is tall and thin, and Harry has a muscular, athletic build. How do these boys' body types affect their personalities? In Chapter 7 we referred to a study showing that parents tend to see their preschool children differently, according to the children's body types. Schoolchildren, too, see other children according to body-type stereotypes.

In one study (Staffieri, 1967), 90 six- to ten-year-old boys who attended the University School at the University of Indiana were categorized as being endomorphs (like Tom), ectomorphs (like Dick), or mesomorphs (like Harry). They were asked which body type they would like to be, which they actually were, and they were also asked to apply any of a selected list of adjectives to silhouettes of fat, thin, and muscular boys. These ninety boys were then evaluated for their popularity, as follows: The boys and girls in all classes from Grades 1 through 5 in their school were asked to write down in order the names of their five best friends in their class, and also the names of the three children they "did not like so well," also in order.

The mesomorph body type clearly emerged from all these measures as the representative of the ideal male physique. The mesomorphs were the most popular children in their classes, the boys looking at the silhouettes wanted to look like mesomorphs themselves, and all the adjectives used to describe the mesomorph silhouette were favorable (see Figure 10-5).

Since people tend to live up—or down—to other people's expectations of them, it is probable that, from an early age, children are cast into certain stereotyped personality molds by other people, and the children quickly learn to accommodate themselves to these molds.

HANDEDNESS

When we use the word "sinister," we conjure up an image where somewhere evil and danger lurk. In the original Latin and in present-day Italian, "sinister" also means "on the left." Possibly because of ancient beliefs that anything on the left betokened auguries of evil or inauspiciousness, many cultures have actively discouraged left-handedness. But is there anything intrinsically bad about it?

In a society that imposes no deprecatory judgment on left-handedness, there is not. Left-handers are no less intelligent, no clumsier, nor any more apt to have difficulties with reading than are right-handed children (Young & Knapp, 1966). But in a culture that considers left-handedness a moral and personal defect, the picture is quite different. In a study comparing

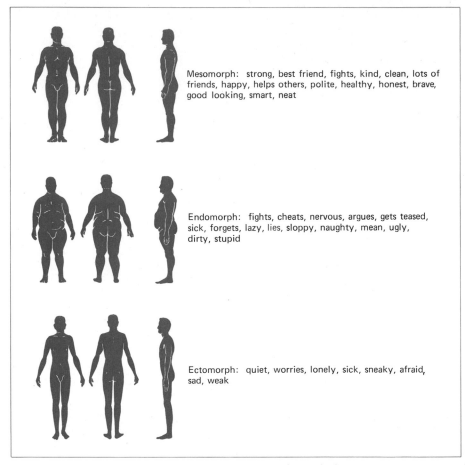

Mesomorph: strong, best friend, fights, kind, clean, lots of friends, happy, helps others, polite, healthy, honest, brave, good looking, smart, neat

Endomorph: fights, cheats, nervous, argues, gets teased, sick, forgets, lazy, lies, sloppy, naughty, mean, ugly, dirty, stupid

Ectomorph: quiet, worries, lonely, sick, sneaky, afraid, sad, weak

Figure 10-5   Body Types and Adjectives Most Commonly Applied

left-handed Boston children of Italian ancestry with left-handed children in Italy, where they are forced to convert to use of the right hand, Young and Knapp (1966) found that the Italian "lefties" are more demanding, impatient, subjective, dependent, and hypochondriacal. This would appear to be due to the social opprobrium attached to left-handedness in Italy, and to the strains of being forced "to abandon their natural disposition or face the disadvantage of social penalties [Young & Knapp, 1966, p. 40]."

Lefties also have their problems in Japan. One child brought to a psychiatrist for treatment of a severe tic turned out to be a left-hander, whose mother had been binding the hand with tape in an effort to make the girl use her right hand. The tic disappeared when the mother stopped binding her. A Japanese psychiatrist, concerned about the high rate of neuroses among left-handed children, has been trying to dispel these old ideas by educating adults, publishing a monthly bulletin that talks about such famous lefties as Michaelangelo and Harry Truman, and helping left-handed children to solve some of the practical problems involved in being left-handed in a right-handed society (*Time*, 1974).

Implications for Child-care Practices

Eleven-year-old Maria Pepe of Hoboken, New Jersey, liked to play baseball, and she was good enough to be put on the local Little League team—until the team was ordered by the national organization to kick her off. After the National Organization for Women took Maria's case to the New Jersey Division on Civil Rights, the division ruled that Little League had to permit girls to play on all its local teams in New Jersey. The ruling followed six days of expert testimony, which included that from a pediatric orthopedic surgeon, who said that any disparity in strength between the bones of eight- to twelve-year-old girls and boys was negligible and that, if anything, girls' bones tended to be more break-resistant than boys'. The division obviously concluded that there was no medical reason why boys and girls of this age could not play baseball together (Cook, 1973).

The fact that boys and girls are so nearly equal in most physical measures has implications for raising and teaching them.

(Horst Schaefer, Photo Trends)

Maria's case is one example of the implications for raising and teaching children, based on the issues discussed in this chapter. The fact that boys and girls are so nearly equal in most physical measures, for example, and particularly running and jumping, means that there is no reason to separate boys and girls for physical education, at least on the grade-school level. The fact that girls' physical skills deteriorate or fail to improve after puberty points to the need for greater encouragement of adolescent girls' physical activities. The importance of maturation in the development of various motor skills indicates the problem of putting boys of the same chronological age, but of widely differing maturational levels, on opposing teams.

The greater psychological difficulties of left-handed children who have been forced to convert bear a message to those societies that still impose such restrictions.

Children's universal admiration for a single body type—the mesomorph—means that they are learning one lesson from their society and makes us ask whether they shouldn't be learning others. Shouldn't children, for example, learn to accept and admire a wide diversity of shapes that human beings come in? Shouldn't the heroes and heroines of their books represent the range of human body types, instead of almost always hewing to the mesomorphic ideal?

And, of course, the great health problems of poor children are the shame of our nation. They require a massive expenditure of funds and effort on every governmental level. It is to solve problems such as these that we turn to the study of child development.

Summary

1   Physical development is less rapid in middle childhood than in the preschool years. Though boys are slightly taller and heavier than girls at the beginning of this period, girls attain the adolescent growth spurt at an earlier age and thus tend to be larger by the end of it. Wide individual and cross-cultural differences exist in height and weight.

2   It is possible to predict adult weight from height at middle childhood. Of the techniques available, the most efficient is determination of *skeletal*, or *bone, age.* But all techniques are somewhat limited, and accuracy is greater the later the assessment is made. Hormone therapy can help the child who is not growing normally.

3   In the middle years children's facial and bodily proportions change, and their vision becomes keener. Brain development is virtually complete.

4   As a result of medical advances such as innoculations and antibiotics, many diseases which previously plagued the middle child have been controlled. But a large proportion of the problems in these years are

accidents and diseases such as tuberculosis, syphilis, gonorrhea, and hepatitis.

5 Because of improved motor development and coordination, boys and girls can engage in a wider variety of physical activities than preschoolers. By adolescence, boys tend to outstrip girls in physical achievements. Social factors (it is "unfeminine" for girls to excell athletically) must be considered along with physical explanations.

6 Body type and personality traits are interrelated, but we cannot be certain that the relationships are predetermined; children learn early to behave in expected ways.

CHAPTER ELEVEN

MENTAL DEVELOPMENT

IN WHICH VICKY'S INTELLECT ADVANCES HER MORAL JUDGMENT, REASONING, AND CREATIVITY

Above all things we must take care that the child, who is not yet old enough to love his studies, does not come to hate them and dread the bitterness which he has once tasted, even when the years of infancy are left behind. His studies must be made an amusement.

(*Marcus Fabius Quintilianus, c.* A.D. *35–c. 95*)

With her shiny new pencilcase full of newly sharpened pencils, Vicky walks into the first-grade classroom. A veteran of school after having attended both nursery school and kindergarten, she is not at all shy or anxious about entering the unfamiliar room. On the contrary, like most new scholars, she finds the idea of school exhilarating. For that first day of school is indeed a milestone, signaling to all that Vicky has entered a distinctly new stage of development.

It is hardly coincidental that the usual starting age for school, at least in the Western world, coincides with a number of qualitative jumps in Vicky's thinking abilities. It also coincides with a new Piagetian stage of cognitive development.

Piaget's Stage of Concrete Operations (About Six to Eleven Years)

Somewhere between the ages of five and seven, Vicky becomes what Piaget calls an *operational* child. She now becomes able to use symbols in a rather sophisticated way to carry out *operations*, or mental activities, as opposed to the physical activities that were the basis for her earlier thinking. Her use of mental representations of things and events allows her to become quite proficient at classifying, seriating, dealing with numbers, and understanding the principles of conservation. She can *decenter*, that is, take all aspects of a situation into account when drawing conclusions, instead of getting stuck on one aspect as she did during the preoperational stage. And she understands the reversible characteristic of most physical operations.

At about this time, Vicky's galloping egocentrism is diminishing, and she is beginning to conceive of herself as a being distinct and separate from the rest of the universe, including other people. In the words of the old Indian proverb, she is learning how "to walk in another's moccasins," and thus to understand other people's points of view. The ability to put herself in the place of another improves her ability to communicate. It also affects her ability to make moral judgments, which are becoming more flexible with maturation and with peer interactions.

Primitive concepts such as realism, animism, and artificialism (which will all be discussed in this chapter) are dropping out of Vicky's thought. Her thought is becoming stable and logical, but she is still not able to deal with abstract ideas.

PIAGET'S CLINICAL METHOD

When Piaget first began to pose questions to children in connection with his work in standardizing the Simon-Binet intelligence test, he became more interested in the wrong answers he heard from the children than in the right ones, since he felt that in these wrong answers lay many of the clues to the way they reasoned. Accordingly, when he decided to study the content of children's thought, he developed a new method of examination, called the *clinical method.*

This method is a flexible way of assessing childhood thinking by tailor-making the test situation to the child being questioned so that no two children are questioned in exactly the same fashion. Its open-ended, individualized method is quite different from the standardized testing technique that aims to make the testing situation as similar as possible for all subjects. With the clinical method, the experimenter can probe further into responses that seem especially interesting, can use language that the particular child understands, and can even change to the language that a child is spontaneously using.

There are definite drawbacks to this method of inquiry. While it does enable an investigator to probe more deeply into children's thought than the standard method possibly could, its very flexibility means that we have

(Sepp Seitz, Magnum)

The operational child: less egocentric, more autonomous; able to understand others' points of view, to communicate and to make moral judgments.

to have a great deal of confidence in the interviewer's ability to ask the right questions and to draw the right conclusions. The only check on this method is to provide it to a great number of investigators who have varying points of view and then to see whether their results corroborate each other. One thing, though, is certain. If Piaget had not used this method to explore children's thinking on a wide range of subjects, our knowledge about the way thought processes develop would be far poorer. By his overwhelming curiosity and interest in children, Piaget has opened our eyes to their distinctive thought processes, as will be seen in some of the examples of the clinical method that follow in this chapter.

THE CHILD'S IDEAS OF REALITY: REALISM, ANIMISM, ARTIFICIALISM

When we look closely at children's jumbled notions of what is real and what is unreal, of what is the product of their own minds and what exists in tangible form, of what has life and what is inanimate, and of their explanations for the existence of many natural phenomena, we cannot help being struck by the similarity between the reasoning of children and the elaborate belief systems of many primitive people (Pulaski, 1971).

Realism

When children confuse psychological events with objective reality, and see names, pictures, thoughts, and feelings as actual entities, they are in the throes of what Piaget calls *realism.* He has brought this out most clearly in his investigations of children's ideas about their own dreams, and has characterized their thought into three stages.

First stage (beginning at age five or six).   Children consider the names of things as real and immutable as the things themselves. For children in this stage, "a rose by any other name" would not only not smell as sweet—it could not even exist. Their immature thinking in this regard is illustrated by Vicky's experience in first grade, upon meeting a classmate, also named Vicky. Since the other Vicky was a shy, quiet child, our Vicky felt that, sharing the same name, she had to make an effort to be shy and quiet, too. Not understanding exactly what a name signified, Vicky invested it with a strange power that created an almost magical bond with this other Vicky.

Children in this stage believe that their dreams come from outside and take place within the room. They dream with their eyes and are able to "see" what they dream. Because of their confusion between moral laws and physical laws, they believe that bad dreams come as a punishment for misbehavior (see the section "Moral Development" later in this chapter).

The following conversation, which grew out of the clinical method, exemplifies this first stage:

Interviewer: Where do dreams come from?
Zeng (six years old): They come from the night.
Int: How?
Zeng: I don't know.
Int: What do you mean by "they come from the night?"
Zeng: The night makes them.
Int: Does the dream come by itself?
Zeng: No.
Int: What makes it?
Zeng: The night.
Int: Where is the dream?
Zeng: It's made in the room.
Int: Where does the dream come from?
Zeng: From the sky.
Int: Is the dream made in the sky?
Zeng: No.
Int: Where is it made?
Zeng: In the room.   [Piaget, 1929, p. 94]

Second stage (beginning at age seven or eight). Children now think that dreams originate in the head, in thought, in the voice, and so forth, but that the dreams are in the room, in front of them. They recognize that dreams are unreal and not true, but they still see them as images outside the person, which are seen with the eyes.

Interviewer: You know what it is to dream?
Mith (7½ years old): Yes.
Int: What do we dream with?
Mith: With the eyes.
Int: Where does it come from?
Mith: The heart?
Int: Where is the dream while you are dreaming?
Mith: In the dream, in the mind.
Int: Is it really and truly there?
Mith: No.
Int: Where is it?
Mith: Outside.
Int: Where?
Mith: In the room.   [Piaget, 1929, p. 113]

Third stage (beginning at about nine or ten). Children now recognize that names have been given to objects by people and that dreams are the products of thought, which take place inside the head.

Visc (eleven years old): You dream with the head and the dream is in the head.
Interviewer: It isn't in front?
Visc: It's as if you could see.
Int: Is there anything in front of you?
Visc: Nothing.
Int: What is there in your head?
Visc: Thoughts.
Int: Do the eyes see anything in the head?
Visc: No.   [Piaget, 1929, p. 119]

Animism

Young children's egocentric tendency to endow inanimate objects with life, consciousness, and will—like themselves—is known as *animism.* Children are less and less likely to attribute life to inanimate objects as they mature, and they eventually reach a point where they consider animals and plants the only live things in the universe.

First stage (until about age six or seven). Children regard everything that has a use of any sort as alive.

Interviewer: Is the sun alive?
Vel (8½ years old): Yes.
Int: Why?

Vel: It gives light.
Int: Is a candle alive?
Vel: No.
Int: Why not?
Vel: Yes—because it gives light. It is alive when it is giving light, but it isn't alive when it is not giving light.
Int: Is a bicycle alive?
Vel: No, when it doesn't go it isn't alive. When it goes it is alive.
Int: Is a mountain alive?
Vel: No.
Int: Why not?
Vel: Because it doesn't do anything.
Int: Is a tree alive?
Vel: No; when it has fruit it's alive. When it hasn't any, it isn't alive.
Int: Is a watch alive?
Vel: Yes.
Int: Why?
Vel: Because it goes.
Int: Is a bench alive?
Vel: No, it's only for sitting on.
Int: Is an oven alive?
Vel: Yes, it cooks the dinner and the tea and the supper.
Int: Is a gun alive?
Vel: Yes, it shoots.
Int: Is the play-bell alive?
Vel: Yes, it rings.

Vel even goes so far as to say that poison is alive "because it can kill us."
[Piaget, 1929, p. 196]

Second stage (till about eight or nine).   Anything that moves or can be moved is alive.

Interviewer: Are you alive?
Vag (8½ years old): Yes.
Int: Why?
Vag: I can walk and I go and play.
Int: Is a fish alive?
Vag: Yes, because it swims.
Int: Is a bicycle alive?
Vag: Yes.
Int: Why?
Vag: It can go.
Int: Is a cloud alive?
Vag: Yes.
Int: Why?
Vag: Because it can go.
Int: Is the moon alive?

Vag: Yes.
Int: Why?
Vag: It guides us at night.   [Piaget, 1929, p. 200]

Third stage (till eleven or twelve).   Things that move spontaneously are alive, but those that require an outside agent to move them are not.

Interviewer: You know what it means to be alive?
Sart (12½ years old):   Yes.
Int: Is a fly alive?
Sart: Yes.
Int: Why?
Sart: Because if it wasn't alive it couldn't fly.
Int: Is a bicycle alive?
Sart: No.
Int: Why not?
Sart: Because it's we who make it go.
Int: Is a horse alive?
Sart: Yes.
Int: Why?
Sart: He helps man.
Int: Are clouds alive?
Sart: Yes.
Int: Why?
Sart: No, they're not.
Int: Why not?
Sart: Clouds aren't alive. If they were alive they could come and go as they wanted. It's the wind that drives them.
Int: Is the wind alive?
Sart: Yes.
Int: Why?
Sart: It's alive, because it's the wind that drives the clouds.
Int: Are streams alive?
Sart: Yes, because the water is flowing all the time.
Int: Is a motor?
Sart: No, it's the engine that makes it go.
Int: Is the engine alive?
Sart: No, it's a man who makes the engine go.
Int: Is the sun alive?
Sart: Yes, it makes the sunshine and gives light during the day.
Int: Is the lake alive?
Sart: No, because the lake is all alone and it can't even move by itself.
                                                              [Piaget, 1929, p. 202]

Fourth stage (from about eleven or twelve).   Only plants and animals, or only animals are alive.

Artificialism

The egocentric child, considering herself the center of the universe, develops a feeling of omnipotence. She feels that she, or other human beings like herself, have created everything in the world. People have made the sun, the moon, and the stars, and put them in the sky. Only by stages, with adult instruction, does she achieve the realization that human activity is not involved in the creation of natural phenomena. We see vestiges of artificialism in the Old Testament, which describes God creating the world; in the ancient Greek myths, which attribute to the gods the creation of such natural phenomena as the Milky Way, the seasons of the year, and the presence of mountains, flowers, and trees; and, in fact, in the creation stories of religions around the world.

First stage (till seven or eight years).   In this stage of complete artificialism, the child explains the presence of the sun and moon as the creation of human or divine agents.

> *Interviewer:*   How did the sun begin?
> *Fran (nine years old):*   It was a big ball.
> *Int:*   How did it begin?
> *Fran:*   By getting bigger and bigger and then afterwards they told it to go up in the air. It is like a balloon.
> *Int:*   Where did this ball come from?
> *Fran:*   I think it is a great stone. I believe it is made of a great ball of it.
> *Int:*   Are you sure of that?
> *Fran:*   Yes, sure.
> *Int:*   How did it get made?
> *Fran:*   They made it into a big ball.
> *Int:*   Who did?
> *Fran:*   Some men.   [Piaget, 1926, pp. 265-266]

Second stage (begins at about eight years).   In this transitional stage, the child gives the origin of the solar system as half natural, half artificial.

> *Interviewer:*   What is the sun made of?
> *Brul:*   Of clouds.
> *Int:*   How did it begin?
> *Brul:*   It began by being a ball.
> *Int:*   Where did this ball come from?
> *Brul:*   From the clouds.
> *Int:*   What are the clouds made of?
> *Brul:*   Of smoke.
> *Int:*   Where does this smoke come from?
> *Brul:*   From the houses.   [Piaget, 1926, p. 275]

Third stage (begins at about nine to eleven years).   By this time, the child, with the help of adult instruction, realizes that no human activity was involved in the creation of the solar system.

Interviewer: What is the sun made of?
Not (ten years old):   Of flames.
Int: Where do these flames come from?
Not: From the sun.
Int: How did they begin, did something make them?
Not: They made themselves.
Int: How?
Not: Because it was warm.
Int: How did they begin?
Not: The sun was made of flames of fire.
Int: How?
Not: Because it was warm.
Int: Where?
Not: In the sky.
Int: Why was it warm?
Not: It was the air.

The sun then is the product of incandescent air, and according to Not, the moon is also made of air.

[Piaget, 1926, p. 276]

CONSERVATION

Probably the most well known of Piaget's work is his study of the ability to understand *conservation,* which we mentioned in Chapter 8. The ability to conserve involves the child's ability to recognize that two equal quantities of matter remain equal (in substance, weight, length, number, volume, or space) even if the matter is rearranged, as long as nothing is added or taken away. Let us look at three different types of conservation—that of substance, of weight, and of volume. In the conservation of substance, a child is shown two equal balls of clay, and he agrees they are equal. Then, he observes one ball being rolled into the shape of a worm, or perhaps divided into several smaller balls. He is said to conserve substance if he then recognizes that the original ball and the "worm" have equal amounts of matter. In weight conservation, the child is asked whether the ball and the worm weigh the same. And in conservation of volume, the child is asked to judge whether both the ball and the worm displace an equal amount of liquid when placed in glasses of water.

While each of these types of conservation is based on the same underlying principle, children develop the different types at different times. First, at age six or seven, they are able to conserve substance; then, at nine or ten, weight; and last, at eleven or twelve, volume. *Horizontal decalage* is the term Piaget uses to describe this phenomenon of the child's inability to transfer what he has learned about one type of conservation to a different type, for which the underlying principle is identical.

This decalage, or lack of immediate transfer, illustrates how concrete is the thought of the child during the ages of about 7 to 11 years. His reasoning is tied to

(James R. Smith)

The middle, operational child shows a qualitative cognitive advancement: Thinking is reversible, and transformation is seen as a perceptual alteration.

particular situations and objects; his mental operations in one area may not be applied to another, no matter how useful this might be [Ginsburg & Opper, 1969, p. 165].

Before they master any type of conservation problem, children go through three stages. In the *first*, they fail to conserve. They center on one aspect of the situation, they are fooled by looks, they cannot recognize the reversible nature of the operation. The *second* is a transitional stage, when children vacillate in their responses, sometimes passing and sometimes failing. While children in this stage tend to concentrate on more than one aspect of the situation, they do not realize the interrelationships between such dimensions as height and width or length and thickness, and they fail more often than they pass.

In the *third* and final stage in conservation, children conserve and give logical justifications for their answers. These justifications may take the form of *reversibility* (as: "If the clay worm were shaped into a ball, it would be the same as the other ball"); *identity* ("It's the same clay; you haven't added any or taken any away"); or *compensation* ("The ball is shorter than the worm, but the worm is longer than the ball, so they both have the same amount of clay"). So we see that the middle, operational child shows a qualitative cognitive advancement over the preoperational preschooler. His thinking is reversible, he decenters, and he is aware that whatever transformation has taken place is only a perceptual alteration.

Training in Conservation

Reversibility, or the awareness that a given operation can be reversed to bring back the original situation, is one of the principles underlying conservation. One group of six- and seven-year-old children, all of whom had failed number conservation tasks, were trained in reversibility (Wallach & Sprott, 1964). The experimenter showed each child some dolls in doll beds, then took the dolls from their beds and placed them sometimes close together, sometimes far apart. From time to time the experimenter added or removed a bed. After each manipulation of the beds, the experimenter asked the child, "Can you put a doll in every bed now?"

In this way all the children but one learned that the number of dolls and beds remained the same, regardless of whether the dolls were placed close together or far apart, as long as no beds were added or removed. They were then able to transfer their number abilities to checkers and cards, as well as dolls and beds. None of the children in a comparable untrained group developed number conservation. In the normal course of events, these children should have developed number conservation within a short time; they were thus ready for training and susceptible to its impact.

Transitivity

Closely related to conservation is *transitivity*, the ability to recognize a relationship between two objects, by knowing the relationship between each of them and a third. Let us suppose that Vicky is shown three sticks: a yellow one, a green one, and a blue one. She is shown that the yellow stick is longer than the green one, and the green one is longer than the blue. There is never a direct comparison of the yellow and blue sticks, but Vicky is asked about their relationship, based on her knowledge of the relationship each of these holds to the green stick. Among four- to ten-year-old children, most either pass both conservation and transitivity tests, or else they fail both measures (Smedslung, 1963).

Influences on Conservation Ability

Piaget stresses the maturational components of conservation, that is, that children will learn this concept when their cognitive structures are mature enough and that it is only minimally subject to training. But factors other than maturation also affect conservation. We must assume this, since children who learn conservation skills earliest are those with high grades, high IQs, high verbal ability, and nondominating mothers (Goldschmid & Bentler, 1968; Almy, Chittenden, & Miller, 1966).

Cultural Influences on Conservation Ability

The Wolofs are members of the dominant ethnic group in Senegal, on the westernmost tip of what used to be French West Africa. Wolof children who live in Dakar, the capital city, live in a cosmopolitan environment and go to French-style schools. Wolof children who live in Taiba N'Diaye in the bush country live in primitive isolation; some attend French-style schools, and some don't go to school at all.

When a Harvard University researcher (Greenfield, 1966) conducted conservation tests on Wolof children who lived and went to school in Dakar, on those who lived and went to school in the bush, and on those who lived in the bush but had never gone to school, she found that there was a wider difference between schooled and unschooled rural children than between schooled urban and schooled rural children. By eleven or twelve, virtually all the schoolchildren could conserve liquid quantity, compared to only half of the unschooled.

Obviously, something that the children are learning in school is helping them to understand the principles of conservation. This experiment, like others on uneducated adults, indicates that maturation alone cannot account for conservation development. Greenfield suggests, in fact, "that, without school, intellectual development, defined as *any* qualitative change, ceases shortly after age nine [1966, p. 234]."

A number of studies have shown that children from various countries— Switzerland, the United States, Great Britain, and others—achieve conservation at different ages. Greenfield's work indicates that the education the children receive probably affects conservation more than other aspects of the culture. In her analyses of the Wolof children's thinking, as revealed in the explanations they gave for their answers, she concluded that the Senegalese children's cognitive thinking was quite different from that of American children, that they tended to give different reasons for their answers than do Western children, and that some of these differences were dramatically reflected in their native language, which had no words for some of the concepts taken for granted in previous conservation studies. And yet, the educated Senegalese children still achieved conservation, illustrating how "different modes of thought can lead to the same results [p. 255]," although some modes of thinking may be more suited to one type of life style than others.

Moral Development in the School-age Child

Is a seven-year-old child morally mature? This question is being hotly debated these days among the hierarchy and laiety of the Catholic Church. The Church's long-standing tradition of requiring children to confess all their sins before they may receive first communion is at the heart of the controversy. Catholic youngsters usually receive their first communion, which marks their first formal acceptance of their religion, at about the age of seven. But since the Second Vatican Council of 1962 to 1965, more than half of all American dioceses have been acting on the belief that seven-year-olds do not understand the difference between right and wrong, and have been allowing children to postpone their first confession until they are

Some say moral development coincides with cognitive development, mostly as a result of interaction with peers and adults.

about ten or eleven (Fiske, 1973). These diocesan decisions are right in line with current thinking about the awakening of moral sensitivity in children, spurred by the work of Jean Piaget and Lawrence Kohlberg.

But why are we even discussing morality in a chapter on intellectual development of children? Isn't moral thinking an outgrowth of personality, of emotional attitudes, of cultural influences? A growing number of psychologists and educators are adopting the views of Piaget and Kohlberg that the development of moral values is a rational process that coincides with a child's cognitive development. In this view, children cannot make moral judgments until they achieve a certain level of cognitive maturity, which involves shedding much of their egocentric thinking. They attain this cognitive maturity partly through the normal maturational process, but mostly as a result of interaction both with their peers and with adults. How does this take place?

We can explain Vicky's moral development according to the social learning theory proposed by Piaget, as explained by Ginsburg and Opper (1969). When Vicky goes to school, she begins to move beyond the world of her parents; she spends less time with them and more with other people.

She gradually learns to make her own decision. As she does so, she sees herself as the equal of older people—like parents and teachers—whom she once accepted as absolute authorities. Furthermore, as Vicky grows older, she has ever-increasing contact with a wide range of points of view, many of which contradict what she has been taught at home. In an effort to reconcile what she has learned at home and what other people—whom she also respects—believe, Vicky comes to the conclusion that there is not one unchangeable, absolute standard of morality, but that individuals can formulate their own codes of right and wrong. She decides which rules she is going to follow, and is on the way to formulating her own moral code.

According to the cognitive-developmental approach to moral thinking, true morality is consonant with true cognitive maturity. On the road to cognitive and moral maturity, a person goes through definite, distinct, qualitatively different stages. In any one stage, an individual behaves with relative consistency in regard to different aspects of morality, although at any one time, a developing child may be half in and half out of a particular stage. Due to environmental influences and varying timetables of cognitive development, different persons go through different stages at different times. But the sequence is always the same. A person cannot go from an advanced state to a more primitive one; movement is always in one direction. No stage can be skipped; each builds upon the one that has gone before and contributes to the one that will come next. Let us see more specifically how Piaget and then Kohlberg define these stages of moral development.

PIAGET'S STUDIES OF THE MORAL JUDGMENT OF THE CHILD
By approaching the problem of investigating moral thought in new ways, Piaget was able to study how children think about rules, about the motivation behind various actions, about lying, cheating, adult authority, punishment, and responsibility. By speaking with a large number of children of different ages and then analyzing their answers, Piaget (1932) drew conclusions about the qualitative changes in children's moral thinking that come with maturation. He postulated a series of developmental stages to coincide with these qualitative changes (see Chart 11-1). While these

Chart 11-1   Piaget's Stages of Moral Judgment

Piaget's theory of moral development in children can be summarized by broadly dividing children's moral thinking into two major sequential stages. *(Adapted partly from Kohlberg, 1964, and Hoffman, 1970.)*

Moral Concepts	**Stage I** Morality of Constraint or Heteronomous Morality	**Stage II** Morality of Cooperation or Autonomous Morality
Point of View	Child views an act as either totally right or totally wrong, and thinks everyone sees it the same way. Cannot put himself in place of others.	Child can put herself in the place of others. Not absolutistic in judgments, she sees possibility of more than one point of view.
Intentionality	Child tends to judge an act in terms of actual physical consequences, not the motivation behind it.	Child judges acts by their intentions, not their consequences.
Rules	Obeys rules because they are sacred and unalterable.	Recognizes that rules were made by people and can be changed by people. Considers himself just as capable of changing them as anyone else.
Respect for Authority	Unilateral respect leads to feeling of obligation to conform to adult standards and obey adult rules.	Mutual respect for authority and peers allows child to value own opinion and ability more highly and to judge other people more realistically.
Punishment	Favors severe, expiatory punishment. Feels that punishment itself defines the wrongness of an act; an act is bad if it will elicit punishment.	Favors milder, reciprocal punishment that leads to restitution of the victim and helps the culprit recognize why her act was wrong, thus leading to her reform.
"Immanent Justice"	Confuses moral law with physical law and believes that any physical accident or misfortune that occurs after a misdeed is a punishment willed by God or some other supernatural force.	Does not confuse natural misfortune with punishment.

stages hold true statistically for a large group of children, they overlap considerably for any individual child, who may be at a more primitive stage in one aspect of moral thinking than in another.

Children's Attitudes toward Rules

The young psychologist, pointing to some marbles and a piece of chalk lying on a table, would say to his companion, a Swiss boy who might be anywhere from four to thirteen years of age:

> Here are some marbles. . . . You must show me how to play. When I was little I used to play a lot, but now I've quite forgotten how to. I'd like to play again. Let's play together. You'll teach me the rules and I'll play with you [Piaget, 1932].

The seemingly ignorant psychologist had already learned the rules of the game as it was played in Switzerland. (Piaget devoted more than eight pages of his book *The Moral Judgment of the Child,* 1932, to a careful explanation of the rules of marbles.) Piaget and his coworkers listened to the children's explanations, observed pairs of boys at play, and posed specific questions to them ("Can you invent a new rule?" "Would it be all right to play that way with your pals?" "Is this a fair rule like the other rules?" "Have children always played marbles as they do today?" "Did your daddy play this way?" and so forth).

But why pay so much attention to so trivial an activity as a game of marbles? Because of Piaget's conviction that "all morality consists in a system of rules, and the essence of all morality is to be sought for in the respect which the individual acquires for these rules." It is especially difficult to study the reasoning behind people's adherence to the larger rules of our world—those that regulate the ways people relate to each other and to society at large. But by finding out how children think and how they act in reference to child-propagated rules, as for example, those that govern a childhood game, we are able to analyze children's thinking about rules. What children do does not always correspond to what they believe, and so the evolution of the way children practice rules goes through different stages, at somewhat different times, than does the progression of children's thinking about rules (see Chart 11-2). Eventually, practice and thinking arrive at approximately the same point of cognitive development.

Children's Understanding of Intentionality

Once upon a time there were two little boys. Augustus noticed one day that his father's inkpot was empty, and decided to help his father by filling it. But while he was opening the bottle he spilled the ink and made a large stain on the tablecloth. Julian played with his father's inkpot and made a small stain on the tablecloth (Piaget, 1932). Which boy is naughtier, and why?

Chart 11-2   Children's Practice of Rules and Their Thinking about Rules *(Adapted from Piaget, 1932.)*

Children's Practice of Rules	Children's Thinking about Rules
Stage I: Motor Activity	
Children handle marbles in an individual way to see what they can do with them.	*Stage I:* Absolutism (from four to seven)
	Rules are considered as interesting examples, not obligatory realities. Children consider rules sacred and untouchable, although in practice they are willing to accept changes, possibly because they don't recognize them as changes.
Stage II: Egocentrism (beginning anywhere from two to five years)	
Children have a general idea of what rules are and they like to think they're playing by the rules. Actually, though, they play by their own idiosyncratic systems and change the rules about when it suits their purpose.	*Stage II:* Morality of Constraint (from seven to ten)
Stage III: Incipient Cooperation (begins about seven or eight)	Children are constrained by their respect for adults and older children. Whatever these authorities say must be so. They refuse to accept any change in rules.
Each player tries to win and wants to play by a set of rules. But children's ideas are still vague and three children playing together will give three different explanations of the rules.	*Stage III:* Morality of Cooperation (from ten on)
	Children see rules as laws due to mutual consent. Most children have by now cast aside their belief in the infallibility of parents and other authority figures. They see themselves as equals of others and believe that since people made the rules, people can change them. And they see themselves as just as able to change them as is anyone else. They no longer accept adult authority without question.
Stage IV: Codification (begins about eleven or twelve)	
Children know every detail of procedure. All children in a group know and play by the same rules.	

Most adults and older children would consider Julian the guiltier party, since the small stain he made was caused by his doing something he should not have been doing, while Augustus's larger stain was an accidental by-product of a completely laudable intention. But the child under seven is more likely to consider Augustus the greater offender, since he made the greater stain (Piaget, 1932).

Children's responses to stories such as this underscore Piaget's contention that moral development reflects a child's cognitive maturity—or lack of it. The egocentrism of the child under seven causes him to make immature moral judgments, since he is more concerned with the magnitude of an offense rather than the intention behind the act. The child under seven thinks rules are sacred and unchangeable since they have been created by an Authority, professes to follow them but actually does not understand them, and often follows her own rules for games and conduct in general. Furthermore, the young child is "amoral" since he does not distinguish between justice, and duty or obedience. He obeys his parents and follows the rules they lay down, but his egocentrism prevents him from understanding the purpose of rules. But even a very young child does begin to develop a sense of fairness and social justice.

In an effort to measure the ability of preschool children to make moral judgments about guilt and innocence, apology and restitution, and accidental versus intentional misdeeds, Irwin and Moore (1971) conducted a study working within the Piagetian framework. They told a series of stories to 65 three- to five-year-old children (see Chart 11-3), divided into a younger and an older group, and asked the children to provide endings for the stories.

The children's tendency to be more just than unjust showed that children develop some conventional notions of social justice before the age of six. The older children showed a more highly developed sense of fairness. The authors attribute this to their diminished egocentrism and the accompanying ability to tune in to the viewpoints and perspectives of others, and also to their greater experience in forming reciprocal peer relations based on mutual rather than unilateral respect.

The children in both groups, though, had trouble differentiating between actions on the basis of the intentions behind them. This corroborates a finding of Piaget (1932), who reports the following conversation about Augustus and Julian, with a seven-year-old girl:

Experimenter: Which is the most naughty?
Child: The one who made the big blot.
Exp.: Why?
Child: Because it was big.
Exp.: Why did he make a big blot?
Child: To be helpful.

Chart 11-3 Examples of Stories Told to Preschoolers to Determine Their Understanding of Social Justice *(Irwin & Moore, 1971)*

Guilt and Innocence

Betsy and Sharon are each playing with dolls. Gale comes over and takes Betsy's doll away from her. Now Betsy does not have a doll, while Gale and Sharon each do. Which of the two girls' dolls should the teacher take away and give to Betsy?

Apology and Restitution

Bill, Joe, and Mike are having a snack. Billy and Joe each steal one of Mike's crackers. Billy then gives back Mike's cracker, but Joe just says that he is sorry and eats the cracker anyway. Which boy should Mike be more angry at?

Intent and Accident

Karen and Susie are helping their mother bake cookies. Karen accidentally breaks three glasses while getting a bowl for her mother while Susie accidentally breaks one glass while reaching for some gum that her mother told her not to touch. Which girl should the mother be more angry at?

Exp.:   And why did the other one make a little blot?
Child: Because he was always touching things. He made a little blot.
Exp.:   Then which of them is the naughtiest?
Child: The one who made a big blot [p. 126].

This little girl's thinking is still sufficiently concrete so that even though she recognizes the two boys' different intentions, she is more concerned with what actually *happened.* Since Augustus's was the bigger inkspot, his was the greater guilt.

Exquisitely sensitive to the feelings of youngsters, Piaget points out how important clumsiness is to them. Repeatedly scolded or punished for accidents caused by their carelessness or ineptness, the children come to attach meanings to the accidents themselves, rather than to the intentions behind them. In a rather unusual aside in *The Moral Judgment of the Child,* Piaget urges parents to show sympathy to their children, to place themselves on the children's level, and to make the children feel like equals by emphasizing the parents' own needs, difficulties, mistakes, and the consequences of all of these.

In this way the child will find himself in the presence, not of a system of commands requiring ritualistic and external obedience, but of a system of social relations such that everyone does his best to obey the same obligations, and does so out of mutual respect. The passage from obedience to cooperation thus marks a progress analogous to that of which we saw the effects in the evolution of the game of marbles: only in the final stage does the morality of intention triumph over the morality of objective responsibility [Piaget, 1932].

Children's Attitudes toward Punishment

While Billy is playing in his room, his mother asks him to go out to get some bread for dinner. Billy says he'll go "in a minute." By the time dinner is ready, he still has not gone. Billy's father thinks of three possible punishments for the boy. He could forbid Billy to go to the fair the next day, he could give him hardly any dinner, or he could refuse to help Billy the next time *he* needs help, because Billy did not help when he was asked to. Which is the fairest punishment?

By posing problems like this to about 100 six- to twelve-year-old children, Piaget (1932) studied the development of children's ideas about justice and punishment. He found younger children to be more in favor of *expiatory* punishment, or punishment unrelated to the misdeed. And the younger the child, the more severe is the favored punishment (at least for *other*, hypothetical children!). The younger children were more likely to want to punish Billy by keeping him home from the fair, "because the child wants to

Piaget's conviction that "all morality consists in a system of rules, . . ." makes even a game important.

(Fujihira, Monkmeyer)

go and he's not allowed to." Older children tend to favor *punishment by reciprocity*, or, as in the Gilbert and Sullivan song, making "the punishment fit the crime." So an eleven-year-old said that the fairest punishment would be "not to give him any help because it's doing about the same thing to him as he had done" and that the next fairest would be "not to let him have any bread because he didn't fetch any [Piaget, 1932]."

As children mature, they judge the value of a punishment not by its severity but as much as possible by the direct material consequences of the misdeed, feeling that reciprocal punishments will make miscreants appreciate the results of their own actions.

KOHLBERG'S STUDIES OF THE CHILD AS A MORAL PHILOSOPHER

Inspired by Piaget, Lawrence Kohlberg embarked on his own major study of moral development in children. For twelve years, he studied a group of seventy-five boys, who were from ten to sixteen years old when his study began. He has also explored moral development in other cultures—Great Britain, Canada, Taiwan, Mexico, and Turkey. Kohlberg's research confirmed Piaget's findings that the level of a child's moral reasoning depends on the child's age and maturity. Kohlberg refined this theory further by defining different types of moral reasoning, which he classified into three levels. He feels that children arrive at their own moral judgments in a surprisingly independent fashion, rather than merely "internalizing" the standards of their parents, their teachers, or their peers (Kohlberg, 1968).

Kohlberg also used stories to test the levels of children's moral reasoning on twenty-five basic moral concepts, such as the value of human life, the motives for moral action, concepts of rights, the basis of respect for social authority, and so forth. He was less interested in the ways in which children would solve the hypothetical dilemmas posed than in the reasoning behind their answers, which indicated their stage of moral development.

Kohlberg's Six Stages of Moral Reasoning

Level I. Premoral (ages four to ten years).   Emphasis in this level is on external control. The standards are those of others, and they are observed either to avoid punishment or to reap rewards.

   Type 1. Punishment and obedience orientation.   "What will happen to me?" Children obey the rules of others to avoid punishment.

   Type 2. Naive instrumental hedonism.   "You scratch my back, I'll scratch yours." They conform to rules out of self-interest and consideration for what others can do for them in return.

Level II. Morality of Conventional Role Conformity (ages ten to thirteen). Children now want to please other people. They still observe the standards of others, but they have internalized these standards to some extent. Now they want to be considered "good" by those persons whose opinions count.

They are now able to take the roles of authority figures well enough to decide whether some action is "good" by their standards.

Type 3. Maintaining good relations, approval of others. "Am I a good girl [boy]?" Children want to please and help others, can judge the intentions of others, and develop their own ideas of what a good person is.

Type 4. Authority maintaining morality. "We need law and order." People are concerned with doing their duty, showing respect for higher authority, and maintaining the social order.

Level III. Morality of Self-Accepted Moral Principles (age thirteen, or not until young adulthood, or never). This level marks the attainment of true morality. For the first time, the individual acknowledges the possibility of conflict between two socially accepted standards, and tries to decide between them. The control of conduct is now internal, both in the standards observed and in the reasoning about right and wrong. Types 5 and 6 may be alternate methods of the highest level of reasoning.

Type 5. Morality of contract, of individual rights, and of democratically accepted law. People think in rational terms, valuing the will of the majority and the welfare of society. They generally see these values best supported by adherence to the law. While they recognize that there are times when there is a conflict between human need and the law, they believe that it is better for society in the long run if they obey the law.

Type 6. Morality of individual principles of conscience. People do what they as individuals think right, regardless of legal restrictions or the opinions of others. They act in accordance with internalized standards, knowing that they would condemn themselves if they did not.

RECENT RESEARCH ON THE COGNITIVE DEVELOPMENTAL THEORIES

While Kohlberg's theories have been formulated so recently that there have been few independent research projects on them, there have been many attempts to follow up the theories that Piaget put forth in the 1930s. Kohlberg himself followed up the Piagetian ideas, studied children in various cultures, and concluded that children develop basically the same ways in regard to moral reasoning, no matter what their society or their religion. Furthermore, age, social class, and IQ have all been found to correlate positively to moral judgment (Hoffman, 1970).

One team of investigators following up Piaget's findings told two of his stories and two new ones to 160 American working-class and middle-class children, aged six to twelve (Boehm & Nass, 1962). The stories were about physical aggression, lying, material values, and dependence on authority figures. The children were asked to judge a boy who, in play, unintentionally hit a playmate and made his nose bleed; two children who were asked for directions, one of whom tried to be helpful but gave the wrong directions and the other who deliberately misled a stranger; two children who broke cups, one who quite innocently broke fifteen by accident and another who accidentally broke one while committing an act of disobedience; and a boy who gets conflicting advice on decorating a room from his unartistic teacher and from a talented classmate, and has to decide whose counsel to follow. Those answers that took motivation into account for the first three stories, and the boy's talent over the teacher's authority in the fourth, were judged the most mature.

Working-class and middle-class children, and boys and girls responded similarly to the stories, with the age of nine a "crucial turning point toward greater maturity [Boehm & Nass, 1962, p. 164]." Most of the nine-year-olds in this study gave mature answers to the issues posed by the stories, compared to only half the Swiss nine-year-olds studied by Piaget. This difference may be due to cultural differences between the United States and Switzerland or possibly to the fact that children of the 1960s mature earlier than did children of thirty or forty years before.

Not all research findings bear out Piaget's theory. Even intelligent adults sometimes confuse intentionality with consequence, as was found by a study that showed college students more likely to judge someone responsible for causing an accident with severe consequences than one with minor results, even though the hypothetical person was said to have taken identical safety precautions in both cases (Walster, 1966; cited in Hoffman, 1970).

Further evidence against the universality of Piaget's stages comes from studies of American Indians that have shown, among some tribes, an *increase* with age in the belief of "immanent justice" and an *increase* in "the conception of rules as rigid, fixed, and unchangeable entities [Hoffman, 1970]."

Other studies have shown that children's responses can be modified, in either a forward or a regressive direction, by being exposed to a model who espouses exactly the opposite point of view (Utech, 1972). The fact that children can be influenced to make more immature judgments than they had previously made simply by observing an "immature" model casts question upon the "invariant sequence" notion of Piagetian moral reasoning. It is possible, though, to view this experiment as an indication that children may recognize that what is appropriate to say or do in an experimental situation is not necessarily what they really believe or act upon in real life.

Another finding that contradicts Piagetian thought emerged from a study that set up four different groups to train children to give more mature responses to moral dilemmas (Lickona, 1973). The four training techniques included focusing on the various issues involved, exposing the subject to another child who gave the more mature response, exposure to two adults with conflicting points of view (each of whom used reasoning to support the stand taken), and just telling the child the "right" answer. While all the training conditions brought about more mature moral reasoning in a posttest, the big surprise was that the greatest increase came about in those children who had just been *told* the right answer. This finding would flatly contradict both Piaget's and Kohlberg's convictions that children actively work out their own moral systems, and that moral reasoning is consonant with a child's stage of cognitive maturity.

Obviously, a great deal of research still remains to be done in this area. Enough of what has been done, though, indicates that the cognitive-developmental theory can help us understand children's thinking about right and wrong.

LEARNING THEORY APPROACHES TO MORALITY

Another way of explaining the development of conscience, or inner controls over behavior, is to say that children learn the moral values of their culture, principally by identifying with or modeling themselves after their own parents. They also learn to make moral decisions by being rewarded by their parents for making the "right" decisions and punished for the "wrong" ones. When they fail to comply with parental standards, they feel guilty, even when their parents are not in a position to know what they have done, much less to reward or punish them. When this happens,

While there is a relationship between what parents say and do and how their children act, research does not confirm the generalization of moral standards from the home to other situations.

(Sam Falk, Monkmeyer)

learning theorists say that the child has internalized parental standards and achieved a certain level of morality.

Research does not, however, confirm the generalization of moral standards from the home to other situations. When Hartshorne and May (1928–1930) performed a landmark series of experiments to assess children's moral behavior, they found that there was no one global moral standard by which children would always act in an "upright" way. Rather, they found that children apply situational morality. They act in different ways in different situations, even when the same principle is involved. Thus, they are more likely to resist the temptation to cheat if knowing the answers is not that important to them and if there is a good chance of getting caught.

Hartshorne and May found they could not divide children into groups of "cheaters" and "noncheaters," but that there was a "normal distribution" of cheating in experimental situations. "Almost all of the children cheated, but they varied in how much risk and effort they would take to cheat [Kohlberg, 1963, p. 284]." Such studies seem to indicate that it is not morality as such that is learned, but the practicality of being moral in certain situations. Children learn when it is more prudent to be honest than dishonest.

This is not to say that children do not learn moral values from their parents. There certainly seems to be a relationship between what parents say and do, and how their children act. Sears, Maccoby, and Levin (1957), for example, noted that children who are praised frequently for good behavior and isolated or deprived of love for bad are more likely to develop strong consciences than those who are disciplined by being spanked. (They considered that a child had a strong conscience if she felt bad after a misdeed, did not deny it, and needed to be forgiven for it. Girls generally had stronger consciences than boys.) Typically, psychological, as opposed to physical, techniques are most efficient in homes with a loving atmosphere. Obviously, if there is no love to withdraw, this cannot be an effective means of discipline.

Another recent study (Stouwie, 1971) bears out the frequently heard advice that parents should worship at the altar of consistency. When two adults gave conflicting directions about the permissibility of playing with some toys in an experimental room, second- and third-grade children experienced conflict and uncertainty about what to do, sometimes playing with the toys, sometimes not.

Parental influence extends beyond being pleased or angered by children's actions. The old admonition, "Do as I say, not as I do" recognizes that children do imitate the behavior of persons whom they take as models. This was brought out experimentally by a study of fourth-grade boys (Stein, 1967). One by one, the boys were put in an experimental situation in which they were asked to perform a boring task while an interesting movie was being shown just outside their range of vision. To see the movie, they would have to disobey their instructions. The boys in the first experimental group saw an adult male leave his own boring job to sneak a few peeks at the movie; those in the next two groups saw models who resisted the temptation to look at the movie, either by performing their own boring tasks or by doing nothing; and those in the fourth group were controls, who saw no model.

Those children who saw the model yield to temptation were more likely to do so themselves than were boys in any of the other three groups. The boys' attitudes and feelings about disobeying rules, as indicated by their answers to a Moral Behavior questionnaire, had less to do with whether they resisted temptation than whether or not they saw the model. In real life, of course, parents are strong models for their children's moral behaviors and influence them in this regard—but not in every situation.

> The traditional view that moral behavior is determined by internalization does not receive very strong support. Situational influences appear to be more important [Stein, 1967, p. 168].

Obviously, learning does enter into children's moral development, but the precise mechanisms by which it takes place are complex and not completely understood.

VALUES CLARIFICATION

Within the past few years many teachers, parents, and other adult leaders across the country have been implementing a new approach called "values clarification." This program has been designed to help children make moral judgments by giving them a set of skills that help them to analyze the values they say they hold and the values they actually live by (Raths, Harmin, & Simon, 1966). These skills are

> (1) seeking alternatives when faced with a choice, (2) looking ahead to probable consequences before choosing, (3) making choices on one's own, without depending on others, (4) being aware of one's own preferences and valuations, (5) being willing to affirm one's choices and preferences publicly, (6) acting in ways that are consistent with choices and preferences, and (7) acting in those ways repeatedly, with a pattern to one's life [Harmin & Simon, 1973, p. 13].

Values clarification makes use of a variety of game-like exercises, called "strategies," which pose provocative questions to the children and ask them to make judgments. The object is not to teach a prescribed set of values, but rather to teach the children how to form their own values.

The following strategies, from Simon, Howe, and Kirschenbaum (1972), are all designed for use with elementary school children:

Rank Order:

What would you do if you saw your best friend steal some candy from a store?
_____report him
_____pretend you didn't see
_____ask him to share it with you [p. 83]

Values Continuum (Children are asked to place themselves somewhere on a continuum between two extremes):

How far would you go to be popular with your group?
DO ANYTHING, IN-   DO NOTHING
CLUDING RISKING   .   .   .   .   AT ALL
SAFETY
[p. 120]

Public Interview: Children are asked to take center stage in the classroom and publicly affirm and explain their stands on various issues; they are given the opportunity to "pass" on any of the questions, which may include questions like "What would you do if you couldn't watch TV?", "How do people get rich? Why are some people poor?", and "Do you have any friends of different religions or races?"

Research testing the efficacy of this approach is still scant and inconclusive, but it does seem to hold promise as a practical extension of the theories of Piaget and Kohlberg, by encouraging children to reflect upon values and get practice in making moral judgments.

The Development of Communicative Abilities in Schoolchildren

LANGUAGE

Let us imagine that you are looking out the window at a snow-covered driveway and you ask how you are going to get the family car out of the garage. If you don't receive a not-too-gentle suggestion that an able-bodied young adult should be able to figure that one out without any help, you might get either one of the following answers:

"John promised Mary to shovel the driveway," or
"John told Mary to shovel the driveway."

Depending on which answer you received, you know whether that bundled-up figure just coming into view, shovel in hand, is John or Mary. But many children under five or six years of age do not understand the syntactic differences between these two sentences, and think that they both mean that Mary is to do the shoveling (Chomsky, 1969). Their confusion is understandable, since almost all English verbs that might replace *told* in the second sentence (such as *ordered, persuaded, wanted, advised, allowed, expected,* etc.) would put the shovel in Mary's hand.

Most six-year-olds have not yet learned how to deal with the exception to the grammatical rule exemplified by the word *promise* in the first sentence above, even though they know what a promise is and are able to use and understand the word correctly in other sentences. By the age of eight, most children can interpret the first sentence correctly. They know the concept attached to the word *promise,* and they know how the word can be used.

The above example shows us that even though six-year-old Vicky speaks on a rather sophisticated level, using complex grammar and a vocabulary of some 2,500 words (Lenneberg, 1967), she still has a way to go before she masters the syntactic niceties of her native language. Since she was about four, Vicky has been speaking in longer sentences and using more complicated grammar. During her early school years, she rarely uses passive sentences, verbs that include the form *have,* and conditional sentences ("If you were to do this, I could do that").

Children develop increasingly complex understanding of syntax up to and possibly after the age of nine (Chomsky, 1969). By testing the understanding of various syntactic structures by 40 five- to ten-year-old children, Carol Chomsky found considerable variation in the ages of children who knew them and those who did not (see Table 11-1).

EGOCENTRISM

> Once upon a time there was a lady who had twelve boys and twelve girls, and then a fairy a boy and a girl. And then Niobe wanted to have some more sons. Then she was angry. She fastened her to a stone. He turned into a rock and then his tears made a stream which is still running today [from Piaget, 1926, p. 102].

Anyone listening to eight-year-old Gio tell this story would be hopelessly confused as to the persons that all those *he's* and *she's* refer to. The story was actually Gio's rendering of the following tale, which Piaget told to a

Table 11-1   Acquisition of Complex Syntactic Structures (*Chomsky, 1969*)

Structure	Difficult Concept	Age of Acquisition
John is easy to see.	Who's doing the seeing?	5.6 to 9 yrs.*
John promised Bill to go.	Who's going?	5.6 to 9 yrs.*
John asked Bill what to do.	Who's doing it?	Some 10-year-olds still haven't learned this.
He knew that John was going to win the race.	Does the "he" refer to John?	5.6 yrs.

*All children nine and over know this.

number of six- to eight-year-old children to see how well they could tell it to another child who did not know the story:

> Once upon a time, there was a lady who was called Niobe, who had 12 sons and 12 daughters. She met a fairy who had only one son and no daughter. Then the lady laughed at the fairy because the fairy only had one boy. Then the fairy was very angry and fastened the lady to a rock. The lady cried for ten years. In the end she turned into a rock, and her tears made a stream which still runs to-day [Piaget, 1926, p. 82].

While further questioning revealed that most of the children understood the story themselves, their ability to relate it meaningfully was limited by their overweening egocentrism. Unable to take the viewpoint of the listener, young children omit much information that is crucial to understanding the story. The older the children, the better their ability to communicate. This ability, according to Piaget, reflects children's diminishing egocentrism, which is brought about by social pressure from peers and adults to develop communication skills.

Flavell (1966) pursued the emerging ability of the young child to assume the viewpoint of another, for the purposes of communication. He showed children, from the second to the eleventh grades, a sequence of seven pictures that told a story of a boy walking along, seeing a dog that is running after him, climbing an apple tree to get away from the dog, and

(Arman Photo Features)

Older children's ability to communicate better reflects their diminishing egocentrism, which is brought about by social pressure.

eating an apple while waiting for the dog to go away. All the children could easily narrate this story. After a child had done so, the experimenter removed three pictures, making the four remaining tell a very different story of a boy walking along, seeing an apple tree, climbing it, and eating an apple, with an innocent-looking dog in the background. The child is then asked to tell the story another person would tell about the *four*-picture story. The second- and third-graders had a lot of trouble telling this story, because their own perspective was so different from that of the supposedly naive observer who saw only the four pictures. They could not erase from their mind what those other three pictures had meant to them. But 70 to 90 percent of the fourth-graders and older children were able to explain the second story, without showing the influence of the first.

In another test of communication skills, experimenters taught a simple competitive game to children by playing the game with them and using gestures when necessary. No words were spoken. Then the children were asked to tell another adult, who had not seen the game being played, how to play it. The children were not allowed to touch the game materials, and the adults did not give the children any feedback about the adequacy of their instructions. Half the children at each age level (ranging from second to eleventh grades) had to teach a blindfolded experimenter; half had a sighted "pupil."

Some of the youngest children "blithely spoke of picking up 'this' and putting it 'over there,' and the like, when trying to explain the game to the unsighted adult [Flavell, 1966, p. 173]." But the older the children were, the more useful information they gave to the adults, and the better they were able to take into account the special circumstances of the blindfolded adults.

Children's points of view have a great effect, then, on their ability to communicate with other people. As they grow in their realization that other perspectives exist, they develop the ability to predict other people's responses, even though they may be foreign to the children's own perspective. The inability to take the role of another often explains much of a child's thoughtless, seemingly cruel behavior.

Measuring Intelligence in Schoolchildren

During the school years, children may be tested for a variety of reasons. In most public schools all children receive group intelligence tests every few years, partly to determine individual ability and partly to assess the school's standards. Youngsters are often tested on an individual basis either for admission to a selective school, or because they may be having problems in school. Intelligence testing will sometimes yield results that indicate that Johnny has specific learning disabilities, that Jenny should be in a less demanding classroom, that Joey may be getting into trouble in school because he isn't being challenged enough, or that Janie should be receiving some form of special help.

TESTS FOR SCHOOLCHILDREN

The Stanford-Binet
While this individual test, described in Chapter 8, is sometimes still used during the school years, many psychologists feel that it has definite drawbacks. Since it emphasizes verbal skills so heavily, it penalizes the child with a specific language problem—and masks the problems of a child who is highly verbal but has perceptual or motor deficits.

The Wechsler Intelligence Scale for Children (WISC)
This individual test was designed to be used with children aged five to fifteen, and is used mostly for youngsters between seven and thirteen. The WPSSI, described in Chapter 8, is a downward extension of the WISC. The WISC measures verbal and performance abilities separately, yielding separate scores for each, plus a total score. When a child's verbal score is significantly lower than his performance score, this points to probable problems with language development. When, on the other hand, a child's verbal IQ is high, but her performance IQ is low, we would investigate the possibility of retarded perceptual and/or motor development.

The WISC verbal subtests are Information, Comprehension, Arithmetic, Similarities, Vocabulary, and Digit Span. The performance subtests are Picture Completion, Picture Arrangement, Block Design, Object Assembly, Coding, and Mazes (see Table 11-2).

The Otis-Lennon Mental Ability Test, Primary Level
This group test is meant for children in kindergarten and first grade. Children of this age should be tested in small groups of ten or fifteen, so that the adult can be sure that the children understand and follow the instructions. Each child receives a booklet with the test items, which consist of pictures and diagrams. No reading is required. The teacher gives the instructions orally. The test takes about half an hour to administer and is given in two parts, with an intermission. It asks children to classify items, to show an understanding of verbal and number concepts, to display general information, and to follow directions.

The Lorge-Thorndike Multi-Level Battery
This group test is designed for children from fourth grade through high school and is divided into several levels, suitable for different age groups. It asks children the meaning of words, to complete sentences, to classify words, to do arithmetic problems that require reasoning, and to show an

Table 11-2 The Wechsler Intelligence Scale for Children

Verbal Scale	Performance Scale
1. General information A series of questions covering a wide range of information which children presumably have had an opportunity to acquire (e.g., "Who discovered America?"). Specialized knowledge is avoided.	*1. Picture completion* Picture cards from which some part (e.g., the whiskers of a cat) is missing.
2. General comprehension Items in which the child must explain what should be done in given circumstances, why certain practices are followed, and so on. An example: "Why is it better to build a house of brick than of wood?"	*2. Picture arrangement* Sets of picture cards are shown to the child; he must rearrange them so as to tell a story.
3. Arithmetic Simple, orally presented arithmetic problems, to be solved without paper or pencil.	*3. Block design* The child is given a set of blocks, with red sides, white sides, and sides that are both red and white. His job is to reproduce a pattern shown by the examiner.
4. Similarities Questions such as "In what way are a piano and a violin alike?"	*4. Object assembly* Cardboard puzzles which the child is to assemble.
5. Vocabulary Increasingly difficult words are presented orally and visually; the child is asked to tell what each means.	*5. Coding* A code substitution test in which symbols are to be paired with digits.
6. Digit span Orally presented lists of digits, which are to be repeated (in order or backward).	*6. Mazes* Eight printed mazes are presented; the child must trace in pencil the correct route out.

understanding of verbal analogies. On the fourth-grade level, the test takes about an hour.

Cross-cultural Testing

As far back as 1910, researchers recognized the difficulty of devising tests to measure the intelligence of diverse cultural groups (Anastasi, 1968). Since then, they have tried in many different ways to devise tests that can measure innate intelligence without introducing cultural bias. The task has proved virtually impossible.

It *has* been possible to design tests that do not require any language for their administration. Testers use gestures, pantomime, and demonstrations to let the test-takers know what they are supposed to do. And the tasks required have been such nonlanguage abilities as maze tracing, finding absurdities in pictures, putting the right shapes in the right holes, and completing pictures. But it has not been possible to eliminate any cultural content at all. Thus, if a person is finding absurdities in a picture or completing the picture, the picture has to be of something with which the test-taker is familiar. And the very conventionalities of art in the culture will affect the way the test-taker views the picture. For example, when a group of Oriental immigrant children in Israel were shown a picture of a face that had no mouth and were asked to provide the missing detail, the children said that the *body* was missing, not the mouth. They were not used to considering a drawing of a head as a complete picture and "regarded the absence of the body as more important than the omission of a mere detail like the mouth [Anastasi, 1968, p. 252]."

Recognizing that it is impossible to design a test that is *culture-free*, test-makers have attempted to produce tests that are *culture-fair*, which deal with experiences that are supposed to be common to various cultures. But even if the test content is so structured, it is almost impossible to screen for different, culturally determined values and attitudes. Anastasi (1968) lists some of the conditions that differ from one culture to another as "the intrinsic interest of the test content, rapport with the examiner, drive to do well on a test, desire to excel others, and past habits of solving problems individually or cooperatively [p. 251]." There are other cultural attitudes, too. A child from a society that stresses slow, deliberate, painstaking work is bound to be handicapped in any test that stresses finishing a task within a set time period. A child from a culture that stresses sociability and cooperation in performing tasks is likely to be handicapped doing a task all alone, with no company.

The difficulty of devising culture-fair tests can be seen in the great discrepancies upon the so-called performance, or nonverbal, tests between black and white children. We would expect there to be smaller differences in nonlanguage tests than in language tests, but many studies with various cultural groups in different countries "have found larger group differences in performance and other nonverbal tests than in verbal tests [Anastasi, 1968, p. 252]." It seems, then, that these nonlanguage tests are loaded more heavily with cultural baggage than their authors had hoped. And because this baggage is largely invisible, it is hard to allow for it.

Furthermore, if we *could* devise a test that had no relevance to any culture, what would we be measuring? Doesn't intelligence have something to do with how well a person perceives and adapts to the culture? Isn't culture so pervasive that it is bound to affect every aspect of a person's intelligent functioning?

Two examples of cross-cultural tests are the *Cattell Culture Fair Intelligence Test* and the *Raven Progressive Matrices Test.* The Cattell is a paper-and-pencil test available in three levels, for children from four to eight and mentally retarded adults; for children eight to thirteen and average adults, and for high school and college students and superior adults. Test-takers are asked to select the correct item to complete a series; or the proper item to complete a *matrix,* or design; or one item in a group that does not belong. They then are asked to insert a dot in a design so as to meet the same conditions as in the sample design.

The Raven, developed in Great Britain to measure Spearman's *g* factor of general intelligence, requires the ability to deal with abstractions. It asks the subject to choose the proper insert for sixty designs from which one part has been removed. The easier items require only accurate discrimination, but the harder ones involve analogies, permutation and alternation of pattern, and other logical relationships.

Both these tests require some kind of instruction: The Cattell administrators give them in a foreign language or in pantomime, and the Raven administrators issue very simple oral instructions, which can be given in a common language or can be translated into that of the subject.

Neither one has proved to be as culture-fair as its authors had hoped. The Cattell test gets similar results from test-takers from cultures that are fairly similar to our own, but not in very different ones. And the Raven test reflects the degree of education of subjects and is susceptible to the effects of practice in taking the test.

Is IQ Testing Unfair to Minority-Group Children?

The assumption behind an intelligence test is that if two people have grown up in identical environments and if one does much better on the test than does the other, then that one is smarter. In some nonreal world, this might actually be the case. But in the world we live in, no two children—even identical twins—ever grow up in *exactly* the same environment. If this is true for two children in the same family, how much truer it is for children from very different subcultures! The experience of an American Indian child in a family of eight growing up in dire poverty on a reservation is vastly different from that of a middle-class white child being raised as an only child in a suburban split-level. The different scores these two children will probably receive on an identical intelligence test will reflect not only an innate difference in intellectual capacity that *may* exist, but to a much greater extent will reflect the enormous differences in their environments that definitely do exist. Even the middle-class white child and the middle-class black child who live on the same block, attend the same schools, and

(Charles Gatewood)

The different scores two children receive on an identical intelligence test reflect not only an innate difference that may exist, but the enormous differences in environment that always do exist.

watch the same TV programs still reflect cultural differences between their diverse backgrounds.

The issue of IQ testing and children from minority groups has become most political as it refers to black children, even though it also affects the future of hispanic and Indian children, children of certain Caucasian subgroups, and others. Since the testing of blacks has received the most research and critical attention, and since many of the points made about differences between black and white youngsters also apply to those of other ethnic and racial groups, we will focus on the black child. We cannot talk about racial differences without talking about socioeconomic differences, because in our society there is such a disparity between the economic situation of the average black and the average white family. Even in the case of middle-class families who have overcome the barriers of class, we do not know how much they are affected by being part of a generally discriminated against and financially depressed group.

Intelligence of Black and White Children

In our society, black children tend to test lower than white children on intelligence tests (Carson & Raybin, 1960). The mean IQ for black samples is usually about 85, or about 15 points below the mean for whites, and rural southern blacks test lower than urban northern whites (Baughman, 1971). There is some overlap in the IQ distributions of the two groups. Some blacks will score higher than almost all whites, and many blacks will score higher than most whites (Pettigrew, 1964). The range of scores within *any* ethnic or racial group goes from very low to very high, indicating that the differences among individuals of the same group are much greater than the differences in average scores between the groups.

During the first two years of life, the only significant difference in motor or intellectual development between black and white babies is the motor precocity of the blacks (Bayley, 1965; Geber, 1957). But starting at about two or three years of age, black children begin to lag behind white children in their intelligence scores, and this gap widens as the children grew older (Golden & Birns, 1968).

How can this widening gap be explained? One explanation is that infant tests of development do not measure intelligence, and that this is why no difference shows up. A likelier explanation is that the older a child becomes, the more verbal ability is called for in the tests, the more influential his cultural environment becomes in his attitudes and set toward learning, and the more intelligence tests tap his already learned store of knowledge. It is also possible that the lower self-esteem among black children—even at this age—also may affect test differences.

The same pattern that exists between black and whites in our society also holds true between middle-class American children and deprived rural and mountain youngsters, and between middle-class English children and children from canal-boat and gypsy families (Pettigrew, 1964). As we said, it is impossible to completely separate socioeconomic status from race, even when surface attributes appear similar.

What factors, then, other than racial differences could account for the growing differences in intelligence? Let us look at the typical black child in America. He is likely to have been born to a poor woman who ate a poor diet before, during, and after her pregnancy—and we know that fetal and infant malnutrition may have devastating effects on intellectual development (Brockman & Ricciuti, 1971). He is likely to be premature—and prematurity and low birthweight are often associated with retarded development (Braine et al., 1966). His parents are likely to be undereducated, underemployed, and beset with the problems of surviving from day to day. They rarely have the time or the inclination to provide a richly stimulating intellectual environment. He is likely to attend an overcrowded, undermaintained city or country school, staffed by inexperienced teachers from a completely different social milieu. Certain personality traits that he may have adopted to get along in the predominantly white culture—such as passivity and slowness—work to his disadvantage when he takes an intelligence test (Davidson, Gibby, McNeil, Segal, & Silverman, 1950). His teacher may believe that black children are not as able intellectually as white children, may thus expect less of her black pupils and, as a consequence, receive less from them. And, finally, the IQ tests themselves are mostly middle-class creations, which refer to objects and situations unfamiliar to many poor children.

> One test item, for example, asks what the child would do if he were sent to buy bread and the grocer had no more. The only acceptable answer is that he would go to another store. But Kagan (1972) notes that many black children living in an eastern city reply that they would go home—a reasonable answer if only one neighborhood store exists, but scored as incorrect nonetheless [Liebert, Poulos, & Strauss, 1974, p. 282].

THE ROAD AHEAD

When children and adults do not fulfill their potential, this represents a tremendous waste, not only for the individuals involved, but also for society, whose greatest resource is the people in it. For this reason, it is worth making large outlays of money to solve those problems that we know are at the root of many of the problems of many poor, minority-group children in our society.

We must set up free prenatal clinics, where poor pregnant girls and women can get excellent care, complete with dietary supplementation. We must provide first-class maternity care for everyone, the poor as well as the rich, to reduce the risk of bearing premature and brain-injured babies. We must explore ways of working with community leaders among minority groups to enrich the environments of babies, both verbally and in other ways. We must develop programs of compensatory education beginning in early childhood and continuing through secondary school.

This approach need not deny that there will still be some differences in intelligence, possibly hereditary, among individuals. Pettigrew (1964) likens intelligence to longevity. The tendency to live a long life seems to run in certain families; therefore it probably has something to do with the genes we inherit. But life span is also affected by the environment, a fact borne out by the doubling of the average American's life expectancy over the past century. We have not shrugged and said that certain groups of people are bound to live longer than others; on the contrary, we have concentrated on finding out and implementing those factors that will lengthen the life span of everyone. Rather than concentrate our energies on seeking racial superiority or inferiority, we must continually seek for ways by which everyone can fulfill his or her true intellectual potential.

Not until children from all racial and ethnic groups can grow up free from the debilitating effects of poverty, racial prejudice, and intellectual deprivation can we make any attempt to compare group levels of intelligence. Until then, talking about inborn differences between groups is in the same intellectual category as debating how many angels can dance on the head of a pin.

Correlates of Cognitive Functioning

Why does David score high on IQ tests and get high grades in school, while Mark does poorly in both? As we brought out in Chapter 2, there do seem to be some genetic influences on cognitive ability. But there are also many other ingredients in the intellectual pie. Recent research points to such disparate influences on children's cognitive functioning as inborn temperamental characteristics, conceptual style, parental attitudes, and child-rearing practices. All of these—and probably many other factors, besides—affect our intellectual functioning all through life.

TEMPERAMENT

Nancy is so active and moves around so much in class that she often misses the teacher's instructions. Brad, slow to warm up to any new situation, usually lags behind the rest of the class in any new task, but, with time, help, and understanding, eventually catches up. Carl is so distractible that the slightest noise or movement in the corridor takes his attention away from the math problems before him. Temperamental characteristics like these, many of which seem to be inborn, play a major role in the ways children function in school. They affect the ways children approach learning tasks, the ways they relate to the teacher and the other children, and the ways they get along in school generally (Chess, 1968; Stewart & Olds, 1973). When parents and teachers can recognize children's unique temperaments and can adapt their own tempo to that of the child, such traits need not be a bar to learning.

COGNITIVE STYLE: IMPULSIVITY VERSUS REFLECTIVITY

Sara is impulsive. When faced with a problem, she blurts out the first answer that comes to mind, rarely taking any time to think of possible alternate solutions. Rose is reflective. Before she answers any question, she devotes a fair amount of time to considering a variety of possible answers and choosing the best one.

Not surprisingly, Sara makes more mistakes than Rose does. Generally, the longer a child's response time, the fewer errors she will make. Impulsive children, for example, are more likely to have problems with reading—to mispronounce, to substitute wrong words, to add words not in the test, to omit words, or even to skip entire lines (Kagan, 1965).

What makes a child impulsive or reflective? We don't know for sure, although we do know that a proclivity for one trait or the other seems to be fairly stable over time. During the preschool and early school years, children who will later be judged impulsive behave quite differently from those who will turn out to be reflective. Impulsive children seek quick success, and reflective children try to avoid failure. Impulsive children relish taking risks and enjoy active social participation in new situations, while reflective youngsters tend to avoid physically dangerous activities like climbing high or walking a narrow plank, and they avoid peer-group interaction and don't like strange social situations. While they seem more worried about making mistakes, they choose harder tasks to work on and they stick with them for a longer time (Kagan, 1965).

While the tendency to be impulsive or reflective may be partly an inborn personality trait, it may also be a function of upbringing, since children from the lower social classes tend to be more impulsive than those of the middle-class (Kagan, 1966). Their lower IQ scores may reflect their impulsiveness in answering the questions on intelligence tests more than the children's innate capacities. In any case, whether impulsivity is inborn or acquired, it *is* subject to training. For those children whose school failure is linked with a tendency to be impulsive, special training techniques are often effective (Kagan & Kagan, 1970; Stewart & Olds, 1973).

CONCEPTUAL STYLE: ANALYTIC VERSUS FUNCTIONAL/RELATIONAL THINKING

Before you go on to read this section, look at Figure 11-1. In each group, select two pictures that are alike in some way.

Types of Relationship

There are four possible kinds of relationships between these pictures (Kagan & Kagan, 1970), and the one that came to your mind says something about your cognitive style.

1   *Superordinate* or *categorical:* characterizing class membership of the objects as wholes (such as *shirts* in picture 2, *men* in picture 5, or *leaves* in picture 8).

2   *Functional-relational*: classifying objects because of the thematic relation between or among members of the class (the match lights the pipe; the man wears the watch).

3   *Functional-locational*: relating to a common location shared by the members of a class (the men and the woman all live in a town).

4   *Analytic*: categorizing objects that have a similar component (both the zebra and the shirt have stripes; the leaf and the page are both torn; the house and the pipe give off smoke; the watch and the ruler measure things).

Developmental Trends

Some interesting findings have emerged from studies of children's conceptual styles. Young children are more likely to see functional relationships

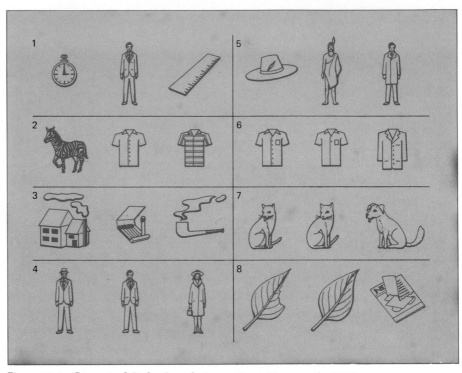

Figure 11-1 Conceptual Style: Sample Items *(From Kagan et al., 1964)*

while other children use analytic and superordinate categories (Kagan, Rosman, Day, Albert & Phillips, 1964). Reflective, attentive children are more likely to be analytic than are impulsive children (Kagan et al., 1964). And analytic children tend to be more active, striving, and independent, while relational children are more dependent (Kagan et al., 1963). Analytic children do better on a task requiring them to put pictures together in a logical sequence (Kagan et al., 1964). The relevance of the material to be categorized affects the style that a child will use: when children work with pictures, the tendency to be analytic increases with age; when working with words, it decreases (Mussen, Conger, & Kagan, 1969). Conceptual style should be considered in devising teaching techniques for children. Also, efforts should be made to match teacher and student on the basis of tempo to enhance learning.

PARENTAL INFLUENCES

By walking into Vicky's home, we can make a number of successful predictions about how well she will do in school and in intellectual work in general. We can predict a bright intellectual future for her when we observe the warm, positive, and democratic atmosphere in her home, and when we recognize that her parents make every effort to accelerate their children's intellectual development.

It is not the size of the home that matters nor the opulence of its furnishings. Rather, it is the atmosphere within the home. Is this a home that values intellectual achievement? Is there mutual respect between parents and children? Is there warmth between them? All these factors have been found to increase the rate of growth of children's intelligence, and most especially their verbal ability (Bing, 1963).

One recent study found that differing child-rearing practices can even affect differing intellectual attributes. Bing (1963) has found that ten-year-old children whose verbal abilities are much higher than their abilities in either numbers or spatial relations tend to have mothers who reinforce dependent behavior in the child. The mothers of these children—as opposed to the mothers of children whose spatial and numerical abilities are much higher than their verbal abilities—talk to their youngsters much more in infancy and early childhood, buy more story books for them, let them

(Leonard Freed, Magnum)

We can predict a bright intellectual future for a child when we observe a warm, positive, and democratic atmosphere in the home, and when parents make every effort to accelerate their children's intellectual development.

(John Briggs)

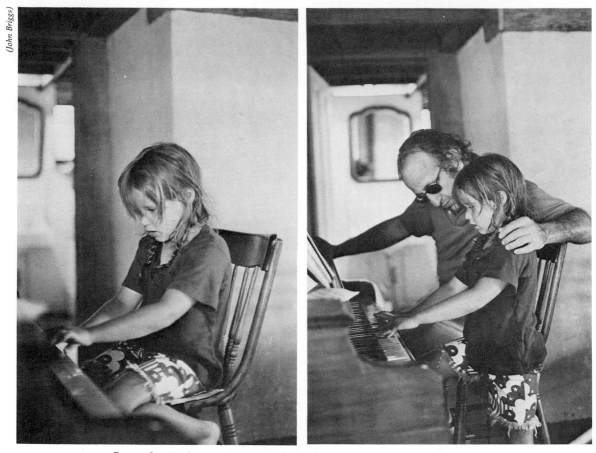

Parental attitudes can foster proficiencies.

participate more in conversations, remember more of their early accomplishments, punish them less for poor speech but criticize them more for poor academic achievement, are more restrictive and less permissive, and train them to be cautious by arousing anxiety. They are much more emotionally involved with their children. Their babies get more attention and stimulation, but when the children grow older, they are more highly pressured, restricted, and controlled.

The mothers of the children whose spatial and numerical abilities outweighed their verbal abilities allowed their children more freedom to experiment on their own. This may be the crucial factor in developing these nonverbal skills, since spatial ability requires interaction with the physical environment, and number facility requires the ability to concentrate and carry through a task by oneself. A greater degree of independence would, then, foster both these skills. This study may provide us with some clues to explain girls' general verbal superiority and boys' superiority in spatial and numerical tasks. Different parental attitudes may foster different proficiencies.

The Gifted Child: Intelligence and Creativity

A few years ago the twelve-member admissions committee of a prestigious New England prep school voted unanimously not to admit a certain thirteen-year-old boy. The rejection was not surprising. The boy's academic record contained failing or barely passing marks in almost every subject but English, and his teachers' negative comments ranged from "lazy" to "rebellious." After its decision, the committee learned that it had just passed judgment on the school record of the young Winston Churchill (Fleming & Fleming, 1970). This story points up a major dilemma for psychologists, educators, and parents: how to recognize children of exceptional talent and how to nurture their talent as fully as possible.

IDENTIFYING AND STUDYING GIFTED INDIVIDUALS: THE RETROSPECTIVE APPROACH

Attempts to study giftedness have taken two basic forms, the retrospective and the longitudinal. The retrospective method of studying gifted individuals locates adults who have achieved eminence, and then attempts, through biographical material, to identify those factors that appear to have contributed to their greatness.

The Studies of Sir Francis Galton

Hereditary Genius, written by Galton in 1869, has become something of a classic. As the title implies, Galton was convinced of hereditary, race, and class bases for achievement. To bolster his conviction, he identified eminent men in nine fields of endeavor (judges, statesmen, commanders, authors, scientists, poets, musicians, painters, and theologians) and then sought to show that achievement runs in families.

Galton selected his men of distinction in various ways, partly from biographical dictionaries, and then classified them somewhat subjectively, according to three levels of distinction:

(a) Illustrious men among whom "many are as one in a million, and not a few as one of many millions. . . . They are men whom the whole intelligent part of the nation mourns when they die; who have, or deserve to have, a public funeral; and who rank in future ages as historical characters"; (b) eminent men—those who have "achieved a position that is attained by only 250 persons in each million of men, or by one person in each 4000"; (c) the third and lower grade is that of English judges—their average ability "cannot be rated as equal to that of the lower of the two grades" described above [Stein & Heinze, 1960, p. 20].

From his studies, Galton estimated the chances for relatives of the most eminent men to achieve eminence themselves:

> The chance of a father is 1 in 6; of a brother, 1 in 7; of each son, 1 in 4; of each grandfather, 1 in 25; of each uncle, 1 in 40; of each nephew, 1 in 40; and of each grandson, 1 in 29. For all more remote relatives, the chances are about 1 in 200, except first cousins whose chances are about 1 in 100 [Stein & Heinze, 1960, p. 23].

Women are conspicuously absent from Galton's study, except as relatives and breeders of eminent males. Because of the smaller number of transmissions along the female line, Galton wondered about "an inherent incapacity in the female line for transmitting the peculiar forms of ability we are now discussing" or the possibility that the "aunts, sisters, and daughters of eminent men do not marry, on the average, so frequently as other women [Stein & Heinze, 1960, p. 24]."

The Studies of Catharine Cox (1926)

During the 1920s, Cox and two assistants at Stanford University selected 300 eminent individuals, as determined by the space devoted to them in biographical dictionaries, after eliminating those born before 1450 and those whose intellectual achievement had not contributed to their eminence.

Through careful study of all biographical material about these personages, three psychologists independently arrived at approximate minimum IQ scores that could account for a subject's known childhood performances. For example, Francis Galton learned to read at 2½, wrote a letter before he was 4, and had mastered almost the entire multiplication table by the age of 5. According to the weights given all these tasks in present-day intelligence tests, the child would have had to have had an IQ of 200, at the very least. The average minimum IQ score for the group as a whole was 155. Cox concluded that most eminent persons would have been identified as gifted children by standard intelligence tests, and also that those gifted children who did go on to great achievement were also characterized "by persistence of motive and effort, confidence in their abilities and great strength or force of character [Cox, 1926; cited in Terman, 1947]."

For more than half of Cox's group, later achievement was strongly foreshadowed by childhood interests—which were often disregarded by parents and teachers who tried to fit these youngsters into other molds. A genuine problem of vocational guidance for gifted children arises from their extreme versatility. Most of Cox's subjects, for example, were extraordinarily able in five to ten fields (White, 1931; cited in Terman, 1947).

The Studies of Victor and Mildred Goertzel

The Goertzels studied the childhoods of 400 eminent Americans who lived into the twentieth century, were described in a standard reference work, and had received a certain amount of biographical attention. In their book, *Cradles of Eminence* (1962), the Goertzels report having found a love for learning in almost all the childhood homes of the 400, as well as a high degree of opinionativeness among their parents. Most came from middle-class homes, were early readers, disliked school and teachers, and had trouble making friends. Many were faced with such major problems as poverty, broken homes, unhappy relationships with their parents, or physical handicaps, but practically none had nuclear family members who had to be hospitalized for mental illness.

> Many of the children of the past who were to become eminent, like the intellectually gifted children of today, tended to possess superior ability in reasoning and in recognizing relationships. They showed intellectual curiosity, had a wide range of interests, did effective work independently. . . . Most of them would probably have tested high on today's intelligence tests [Goertzel & Goertzel, 1962, p. x].

THE LONGITUDINAL APPROACH

The Studies of Lewis M. Terman

Many children may have the potential for greatness, but very few achieve great success in life. What determines which ones will shine—and which will be overshadowed? Recent research has attempted to solve this problem by identifying gifted children early in life and then following them to see which ones achieve success. The most eminent investigator of this type has been Lewis M. Terman of Stanford University.

Terman's original interest was in the study of *genius*, which he identified as "the ability to acquire and to manipulate concepts, the shorthand symbols without which abstract thinking cannot proceed [1947]." He recognized, though, that many people can master concepts and that not all of them turn out to be those rare individuals who display such brilliance and creativity that the world considers them geniuses. He eventually decided to focus on a longitudinal study of more than 1,300 intellectually superior individuals.

In 1922, Terman approached a number of teachers in California and asked each one to give him the names of the three brightest children and that of the youngest child in her classroom, as well as that of the brightest child she had taught the year before.[1] By this and other methods Terman

---

[1] Goertzel and Goertzel (1962) comment, "The teacher's ability to choose the child in her class who subsequently scored highest on the Stanford-Binet intelligence test was less than chance [p. 279]," but they also make the point that teachers are more likely to select children who score high on intelligence tests, but relatively low in creativity (see next section).

located more than 1,300 children capable of earning an IQ of 140 or higher, a score reached by only 1 child in 200.

These children were then tested for intelligence, school achievement, character, personality, and interests. They were examined medically, their physical measurements taken, and their parents and teachers interviewed for case-history material and ratings of the children's personalities. The data that emerged demolished the popular stereotype of the bright child as a puny, pasty-faced bookworm. On the contrary, Terman's gifted children were superior all-around. They tended to be taller, healthier, and better coordinated than the average child. They were also better adjusted and more popular with other children (Wallach & Kogan, 1965).

When these youngsters were followed up as adults, they still presented a picture of superiority, most notably in intellectual ability, scholastic accomplishment, and vocational achievements (Terman & Oden, 1959). They also were healthier than the population in general, and numbered proportionately fewer alcoholics. They were just as likely as anyone else, though, to have problems in marriage, to suffer a mental breakdown, or to take their own lives.

How had these children's early promise been fulfilled? In middle age, most were still scoring close to the 99th percentile in mental ability, even those who had not achieved great career success. They were ten times more likely than an unselected group to have graduated from college, and, once there, three times more likely than other students to have been elected to the honorary societies Phi Beta Kappa or Sigma Xi. Because of different societal attitudes toward careers for men and those for women, the sexes were evaluated separately. Both sexes made a good showing: They were highly represented in listings such as *American Men of Science* (which also includes women), the *Directory of American Scholars,* and *Who's Who in America.* Both men and women had many publications to their credit, and 86 percent of the men were in the two highest occupational categories: the professions, and the semiprofessions and higher echelons of business. By 1955, several dozen of the men had achieved national reputations, and eight or ten international ones.

Terman's group was bright, but not notably creative. None became outstanding in the arts, music, or great literature. Terman himself said that he would be surprised to find more than sixty subjects achieving national reputations, more than twelve becoming really eminent, or even one of them considered among the thousand most eminent persons of history (1947). He compared the superiority of the children in his group, estimated at 1 in 200, to the 1 in 4,000 ratio of Galton's eminent men, the 1 in about 2,000 of listees in American *Who's Who*, and the 1 in 20,000 of scientists listed by Cattell.

Terman recognized the great difficulties in predicting greatness on the basis of childhood ability when he said that genius and eminence are far from perfectly correlated. Why they are so poorly correlated, what circumstances affect the fruition of human talent, are questions of such transcendent importance that they should be investigated by every method that promises the slightest reduction of our present ignorance. So little do we know about our available supply of potential genius; the environmental factors that favour or hinder its expression; the emotional compulsions that give it dynamic quality; or the personality distortions that make it dangerous! And viewing the present crisis in world affairs who can doubt that these things may decide the fate of a civilization [1947, p. 42]!

While most of these adults were more successful than the average person in our society, there was a range of achievement in the group itself. When the 150 most successful and the 150 least successful men were compared in relation to their life histories and personalities, a number of differences emerged. They differed most widely in "persistence in the accomplishment of ends," "integration toward goals," "self-confidence," and "freedom from inferiority feelings [Terman & Oden, 1947]." The two groups differed most in "all-round emotional and social adjustment, and in drive to achieve [Terman & Oden, 1959, p. 149]."

Creativity in Children

Terman's group of children were tested for intelligence, where they performed brilliantly, but they were not tested for creativity. Perhaps if this had been one of the important criteria for selection, more of the Terman group might have been slated for the halls of greatness, rather than those of valuable competence. What is creativity? It is the ability to see things in a new and unusual light, to see problems, for example, that no one else may even realize exist, and then to come up with new, unusual, and effective solutions to these problems. Creativity involves *divergent*, rather than *convergent* thinking, in Guilford's (1959) terms. Instead of trying to come up with one right answer with which everyone will agree, the creative person tries to pursue a problem along as many paths as possible, to come up with new alternatives.

Creative people often spend a great deal of time turning over problems in their minds, just letting their ideas bubble forth. While great discoveries almost always follow intensive work in a particular area, the new thought itself seems to spring full-blown from an observation of the moment. For example, when Archimedes saw his bath water rise as he stepped into the tub, he suddenly realized that he could solve the problem of measuring the volume of the king's crown by displacement of water. When Marie Curie realized that the radioactivity she was studying could not be accounted for by a description of any of the known elements, the daring thought that she might have discovered a new one popped into her head. Further research identified it as radium. When Margaret Mead was trying to fit together the anthropological puzzle of culturally determined sex roles, she suddenly hit

(Bill Anderson, Monkmeyer)

The creative person tries to pursue a problem along as many paths as possible, to come up with new alternatives.

upon the notion of inborn temperamental types. None of these discoveries could have come about if their creators had not prepared themselves by years of arduous work. But neither could they have been born if their creators had not been willing to consider and been able to see startlingly new possibilities.

Studying Creativity in the Laboratory

Thanks to some creative psychologists who have devised a variety of imaginative tests (see Figure 11-2), we can make a stab at assessing children's creativity. In Guilford's (1967) Unusual Uses Test, a child is asked to suggest all the different ways that various objects may be used. In another test, children are shown various simple abstract drawings and are asked to tell all the things that each drawing might represent. And in still another, children are asked to tell the similarities between two objects. In all these tests, the number and the uniqueness of the child's answers are rated to arrive at a measure of creativity. Children who produce many original ideas are considered creative.

THE RELATIONSHIP BETWEEN INTELLIGENCE AND CREATIVITY

We all know bright people who do well in school and well on the job, but exhibit "little evidence of the quality that advances rather than enhances the status quo [Goertzel & Goertzel, 1962, p. 280]." These people are high in intelligence but low in creativity. We also know people who do not score well on intelligence tests and generally muddle their ways through school, but constantly come up with original, inventive ideas. These people are high in creativity, low in intelligence (as measured conventionally).

In an effort to measure creativity as an ability separate from intelligence and to draw some conclusions about children, Wallach and Kogan (1967) used the tests described above in their study of 151 fifth-grade middle-class children. The experimenters took special pains to test the children in a relaxed, untestlike situation, acting on their conviction that

> creative awareness tends to occur when the individual—in a playful manner—entertains a range of possibilities without worry concerning his own personal success or failure and how his self-image will fare in the eyes of others [p. 88].

These children were also tested for intelligence, and the results of both tests were analyzed to produce four different groups of children: the

Figure 11-2 Some Tests of Creativity *(From Wallach & Kogan, 1967)*

	Common answer	Creative answer
How many things could these drawings be?		
(four circles over a rectangle)	Table with things on top	Foot and toes
(triangle with three circles)	Three people sitting around a table	Three mice eating a piece of cheese
(flower-like figure)	Flower	Lollipop bursting into pieces
(two arches)	Two igloos	Two haystacks on a flying carpet
What do these things have in common?		
Milk and meat	Both come from animals.	Both are government-inspected.
[Other examples]		
How many ways could you use these objects?		
Newspaper	Make paper hats.	Rip it up if angry.
[Other examples]		

intelligent and creative, intelligent but not creative, creative but not intelligent, and neither intelligent nor creative.

1   *Intelligent and creative children.* These youngsters, who score high on both types of measures, are superior from virtually every viewpoint. They are friendly and popular with other children, they concentrate well on academic work, and they exude self-confidence. They are somewhat disruptive in the classroom, which may be a reflection on the conventional conformity required in most classrooms. They see possible connections between events that do not have much in common and show considerable insight and sensitivity to emotional clues in the environment. They report experiencing some anxiety—not so much as to cripple them, but enough, perhaps, to energize them.

2   *Intelligent children who score low in creativity.* These youngsters avoid risks. They hesitate to express their opinions, are "model" students, and make very conventional responses, unless they are specifically asked to think of unusual answers—when they perform quite well. Other children want to be friendly with them, but they tend to stay aloof. Their fear of error and of criticism seems to pervade most of their behavior. Since they do conform to expectations and do well in school, they exhibit very little anxiety. But the price of this anxiety-free state is rather constricted behavior.

3   *Creative children who score low in intelligence.* These children have the most trouble in school. They are least able to concentrate on their work, the most disruptive in the classroom, and the most socially isolated. Other children keep away from them, and they keep to themselves. Not surprisingly, they are abysmally low in self-confidence and self-esteem. Yet they do give evidence of creative thinking in the unpressured testing situation, seeing relationships between dissimilar events. Their cognitive abilities may be stifled by the pressures of being evaluated that are present in intelligence and achievement testing situations and in the classroom.

4   *Children who score low in both creativity and intelligence.* These children make up for their low intellectual status with social success. They are outgoing and relatively confident and self-assured.

Helping Children Make the Most of Their Potential

Since success and happiness in life often depend on the extent to which we can fulfill our potentialities, and since the children in the two middle groups seem to be capable of better performance and better mental adjustment, it is worth trying to think of ways in which we can help such youngsters reduce the disparity between their intellectual and their creative abilities.

Wallach and Kogan (1967) suggest that these two groups of children are handicapped, not by lack of ability, but by personality problems that may be due to pressures at home or in school. The intelligent, uncreative children seem worried about what other people think of them, and so they try to avoid making mistakes. They are particularly at sea when there is no clear standard of evaluation for them to judge themselves by. On the other hand, the creative, unintelligent children are afraid of evaluation and perform best when they know they won't be judged. If both these groups of children could learn to relax in those situations that are presently hard for them, the likelihood is that they would all perform better.

The Child in School

Vicky is now in second grade. She goes with the rest of her class to the auditorium, where they are to hear a guest speaker, the author of a book about the brain. After her talk, the speaker asks the 200 or so assembled children whether they have any questions. Shyly, Vicky raises her hand and asks, "Do headaches come from the brain?"

Ten years later, Vicky remembers that day with pain. "That lady laughed at me. The way she smiled and the tone of voice she used made me feel that I had asked the dumbest question in the world. I was really embarrassed. And I think that's one of the things that happened to me when I was little that made me the way I am today. I *hate* to ask questions in class!"

How a child does academically and how he or she gets along with teachers and classmates affect self-confidence, self-esteem, and the basic approach to life.

(Jack Marshall, Annan Photo Features)

School takes up so many hours and assumes such a central place in the lives of children that it affects every aspect of their development. It is, of course, the hub of their intellectual development, where they pick up all sorts of useful (and useless) information, where they learn the intellectual concepts and skills that their society deems valuable, and where they are inculcated with the values of their society. Those rare schools that have extensive, well-planned physical education programs help children pick up skills in street games and help them to achieve a state of physical fitness. And, of course, schooling has incalculable effects on children's personalities.

Sometimes a single incident, such as the one that stayed with Vicky, can leave an indelible mark on a child's psyche. More commonly, though, it is the overall atmosphere of the school that affects social and emotional development. How a child does academically and how he gets along with teacher and classmates will affect his self-confidence, his self-esteem, and much of his basic approach to life.

THE IDEAL SCHOOL

For thousands of years, writers have been trying to define the purpose of education and the ideal vehicle for its transmission. Bringing these definitions into the classroom, Nyquist and Hawes (1972) have come up with a particularly effective delineation of the ideal classroom:

> This is a classroom where freedom, responsibility, self-discipline, and consideration for others are learned by having to be practiced all the time. This is a classroom that accommodates the full range of individual differences, where individuality can be richly prized and given full expression—to such an extent that children of different ages often work together in it. This is a classroom where all children learn respect and trust by being treated with respect and trust. This is a classroom that provides abundant opportunities to develop intellectually in the way in which research has shown children naturally acquire powers of thought and logic—through their own action. This is a classroom where, with a skilled teacher, each child learns the meaning of good work, and in time becomes able to produce it in at least some things he or she attempts [p. 2].

Such classrooms herald the rise of a reform movement in American education. Reform is nothing new to American schools. Throughout our history, one writer after another has proposed methods whereby children would learn more in school and would enjoy the learning process more. The most recent wave of reform washed over the schools in the 1970s, after a spate of critical books indicted them for being inhumane and uncaring in general, and particularly inept in educating disadvantaged children. The public schools of America were charged with being oppressive, grim, and joyless places where more information was being imparted than ever before—but where children's spirits were being mutilated every day (Silberman, 1970). Too often, the schools were hewing to outdated, irrelevant curricula, avoiding meaningful social and personal issues, and ignoring the needs of individual children.

The Open Classroom

In response to such criticisms, many American school systems have begun to institute a form of education referred to as the "open," or "informal," classroom. Originated in the "infant schools" of Great Britain, these classrooms differ from the traditional classroom in many ways. The open approach builds on the findings of Piaget and other researchers about the ways children learn. Since children seem to learn best by doing, and not by listening, reading, or memorizing, open education emphasizes the children's involvement in their own education.

The curriculum in the open classroom is much more flexible than in the traditional school, responding more to the needs and interests of individual children than to a state-mandated syllabus. Whereas the traditional curriculum is heavily subject-oriented, the open curriculum is more child-oriented. The course of study is tailored to fit the child, rather than the child to fit the curriculum.

In the open classroom, it is rare for all the children to be engaged in the same activity at the same time. They do not sit at rows of desks, dutifully listening (or pretending to listen) as their teacher lectures in front of the room. Instead, they tend to be scattered around the room—at tables, on couches, or on the floor—working individually or in small groups. A typical view of an open classroom might show us two youngsters stretched out on a rug reading books they have chosen from the classroom library. The teacher is at the math table, showing a small group of children how to use a set of scales to learn about relative weights. Two children in the writing corner are playing a word game. And one child is taking notes on the nursing behavior of the class guinea pig. Other children are working individually or in small groups at desks or tables. A sense of purpose pervades the room, attesting to the children's interest in their various learning activities.

Open education, though, is not a panacea for all school problems. Not all children can function in this relatively unstructured environment—and neither can all teachers. Probably many of the principles of the open classroom will be incorporated into basically traditional classrooms, to the benefit of both teachers and pupils. But in the long run, the structure of education—whether traditional or open—is probably less important than the attitude behind it.

If children are respected as valuable human beings with their own individual educational needs instead of receptacles of a lot of useless information; if the curriculum is designed according to what the children want and need to know instead of what the schools have been teaching for

(Shelly Rusten)

In the long run, the structure of education—whether traditional or open—is probably less important than the attitude behind it.

the past twenty years; if the teachers provide helpful guidance rather than rigid command; if the emphasis is on the children's successes and not their failures; and if warmth, understanding, and acceptance fill the room instead of sarcasm and ridicule—then it matters little whether the children sit at desks, at tables, or on the floor. Their education will be a happy, satisfying experience that advances their development instead of stunting it.

INFLUENCE OF THE TEACHER
During Vicky's first couple of years in school, it is obvious how much she identifies her teacher with her mother. She not infrequently calls her teacher "Mommy," and her mother, "Miss Wolf." She usually catches herself and corrects the misnomer—but it is plain that the two women merge in her thinking. The fact that Vicky's mother and her teacher are both of the same race and the same social class makes the identification that much stronger.

A teacher's influence is particularly strong during the early years of school, when a child is in his or her company for five or six hours of every day. The teacher becomes a parent-substitute, an imparter of values, a contributor toward the child's self-concept.

What Children Want in a Teacher

Children recognize the importance of their teachers. When the superintendent of one upper-middle-class suburban school district asked the 2,000 children in kindergarten through the eighth grade, "What makes a good school?", teachers headed the list as the prime requisite (McPhee, 1966). And "understanding" emerged as the prime requisite of a good teacher. This attribute appeared again and again as the teacher's most valued virtue.

In one kindergartener's ideal school, "your teacher likes you even when you are bad," a second-grader said, "teachers shouldn't scream and yell over nothing," and a sixth-grader felt that "a web of understanding should envelop the teacher with his or her pupils."

But children want more than just a friend in their teachers; they want them to teach. One first-grader showed his grasp of education this way: "When you don't know something you ask the teachers and if you're wrong it's all right because that's why you're in school." And another said, "School is good when you have teachers that can get through to you, when they tell you something and you can understand them."

These children confirm the results of Jersild's 1940 survey of 526 elementary school children, who reported on the teachers they liked best. Judging from their comments, the ideal teacher is, first of all, a good teacher who explains things in a way that his or her pupils learn. Next in importance are the teacher's human qualities as a person: she is kind, sympathetic, considerate, and interested in her pupils as persons. She or he is also fair, consistent in her discipline, interested and enthusiastic—and attractive.

About two-thirds of these children also described the teachers they liked least. They focused on these teachers' use of ridicule, scolding, lack of sympathy, rigid or inconsistent discipline, ill temper, and a tendency to assign too much homework.

Self-fulfilling Prophecy

No child in the above surveys was reported to have desired a teacher "who thinks I'm smart." But there is reason to believe that when teachers feel that a certain child will do well in school, that child will in fact do well. The "self-fulfilling prophecy"—a phenomenon by which people (and even animals) act as they are expected to—has been documented in many different situations (Rosenthal & Jacobson, 1968).

In the "Oak School" experiment, some teachers in this California elementary school were told at the beginning of the term that some of their pupils had shown unusual potential for intellectual growth. Actually, the children identified as potential "bloomers" had been chosen at random. There was absolutely no basis for thinking that their IQs would rise any more than would those of any other children. But on subsequent tests several months or more later, many of the selected children—especially the first- and second-graders—showed unusual gains in IQ scores. (There were only small, nonsignificant differences in grades three to six.) Furthermore, the teachers seemed to like the "bloomers" better.

> The children from whom intellectual growth was expected were described as having a better chance of being successful in later life and as being happier, more curious and more interesting than the other children. There was also a tendency for the designated children to be seen as more appealing, better adjusted and more affectionate, and as less in need of social approval [Rosenthal & Jacobson, 1968, p. 22].

It is hard to know just how these teachers influenced their pupils to put on a spurt of intellectual growth. They do not appear to have spent more time with them than with the other children, nor to have treated them differently in any obvious ways. The authors feel that subtler influences were at work.

> The teacher's tone of voice, facial expression, touch and posture may be the means by which—probably quite unwittingly—she communicates her expectations to the pupils. Such communication might help the child by changing his conception of himself, his anticipation of his own behavior, his motivation or his cognitive skills [Rosenthal & Jacobson, 1968, p. 23].

While the data from this one experiment are not clear-cut, and the experiment itself has certain procedural flaws, the principle itself is probably valid.

> Regardless of where one stands concerning Rosenthal and Jacobson's original data, work by a large number of investigators using a variety of methods over the past several years has established unequivocally that teachers' expectations can and do function as self-fulfilling prophecies, although not always or automatically [Brophy & Good, 1974, p. 32].

The principle of the self-fulfilling prophecy has particularly important implications for minority-group and poor children. Since many middle-class teachers are convinced (often at a subconscious level) that their lower-class pupils have definite intellectual limitations, they may in subtle or not-so-subtle ways convey their limited expectations to their pupils and end up getting the little that they expect.

One teacher has written of the advice he received from another teacher on his first day in a big-city ghetto school:

> Jim, you ever work with these kids before?
> No, I admitted.

I thought so. Well, now, the first thing is, you don't ever push 'em, and you don't expect too much. If you do, they'll blow sky-high and you'll have one hell of a time getting them down again. May never do it. Now, it's not their fault, we all know that. But you have to take them as they are, not as you and me would like them to be. That means, you find out what they can do, and you give it to them to do [Herndon, 1968, p. 14].

Like Teacher, Like Pupil

In everyday life, it is a common enough axiom that "like attracts like." People seem to get along best with other people who are like themselves. They tend to marry persons of similar background and thinking; they tend to socialize with "kindred souls"; they tend to employ them. Teachers are not immune from this tribalism, even though they do not always choose to teach children whose backgrounds are similar to their own.

What happens, then, when teacher and child hold very different attitudes and opinions? According to one study, the closer a student comes to having the value system that his teacher would like him to hold, the higher his grades are likely to be (Battle, 1957).

This advantage conferred on like-thinking students may be the result of more favorable interaction between teacher and student, which encourages the student to learn better, or it may be the product of bias—either conscious or unconscious—in the grading process. In any case, it is obvious that teachers have to make conscious efforts to accept all their pupils, even those whose value systems differ most from their own.

Effects of Children's Socioeconomic Status

It is often difficult for teachers, who have either been born into or adopted the standards of the middle class, to understand or to get through to children of lower socioeconomic status. Goals that the teacher may take for granted—like neatness, punctuality, and competitiveness—may not be held by the child's associates. When a child's family and friends hold values that are markedly different from those of the teacher, the child will tend to be loyal to the familiar values and unimpressed with those of the teacher. This may be upsetting to the teacher, with a resultant problem in the teacher-pupil relationship.

Looking back on his youth as a poor child in Chicago, the comedian and civil rights worker Dick Gregory has written of the gulf between him and his unsympathetic, uncomprehending teacher:

The teacher thought I was stupid. Couldn't spell, couldn't read, couldn't do arithmetic. Just stupid. Teachers were never interested in finding out that you couldn't concentrate because you were so hungry, because you hadn't had any breakfast. All you could think about was noontime, would it ever come? Maybe you could sneak into the cloakroom and steal a bite of some kid's lunch out of a coat pocket. A bit of something. . . .

(John Briggs)

Students like teachers who are kind, fair, consistent, interested, and enthusiastic; they dislike ridicule, scolding, lack of sympathy, inconsistency, and too much homework.

The teacher thought I was a troublemaker. All she saw from the front of the room was a little black boy who squirmed in his idiot's seat and made noises and poked the kids around him. I guess she couldn't see a kid who made noises because he wanted someone to know he was there [Gregory, 1964, p. 44].

Socioeconomic status does seem to affect the treatment that children get from their teachers. One study of nineteen white middle-class teachers and their white third-grade pupils of varying social status found that a child's social class does not affect the *amount* of attention she gets from her teacher, but it does affect the *quality* of that attention (Hoehn, 1954). While lower-class children got just as much attention as their upper-class classmates, the kind of attention they received tended to be less positive in nature.

A factor other than class may also have been operating. These teachers were also found to favor their high-achieving pupils, and for a variety of reasons children from higher social classes usually do better in school. So it is possible that some of the teachers' partiality may have had as much to do with the high achievement of certain children as with their social class. In either case, the danger of favoring some children over others is obvious.

Do Teachers Like Girls Better?

In the United States, elementary school is a girls' world, especially in the early grades. The girls read and write better, they are less likely to repeat grades or to get into trouble, and their teachers like them better (Maccoby, 1966; Brophy & Good, 1973; Baughman, 1971). It is unlikely that this is due to biological differences between the sexes, since the boys come out ahead in some other societies (Brophy & Good, 1974).

An often-repeated explanation for these differences among the sexes has dwelt on the overriding femaleness of the typical public school. Women teachers, it has been said, understand and like girls better, and are less able to put up with the dirt and noise and aggression that swirl around little boys. The solution, then, seemed simple: recruit more male teachers.

A number of recent studies, however, indicate that the sex differential in elementary school is more complex than that, since those studies that have compared children taught by men with those taught by women have not found that the male-taught boys do any better (Clapp, 1967; Asher & Gottman, 1972; Lahaderne & Cohen, 1972; all cited in Brophy & Good, 1973). Other studies have shown that male teachers tend to show the same kinds of attitudes toward boys and girls that female teachers do, generally scolding the boys more but also praising them more (Brophy & Good, 1973; Etaugh & Harlow, 1973).

The problem seems to lie in a conflict between the kind of behavior that our society says is appropriate for boys and the kind of behavior that is deemed appropriate for children in the classroom. The ideal American boy is active, independent, and aggressive, while the ideal pupil is passive, docile, and quiet. (There is no such role conflict for girls, who usually get the message that they are supposed to be passive, dependent, and "nice" out of school as well as in it.) When these two sets of expectations collide, it is usually the schoolboy model that falls by the wayside, since it is more important for most boys in our society to show their friends and families that they are "real boys" than to show their teachers that they are "good students." As education allows children to be more active, assertive, and inquiring about their education, both sexes should benefit.

THE CULTURALLY DISADVANTAGED CHILD IN SCHOOL

During our discussion of preschool education in Chapter 8, we met Wendell and Michael—two boys of the same age and the same racial background, but of very different social class. Probably the biggest problem facing American education today is the need to help the Wendells of our society to make the most of their potential, to get the best education they possibly can, and to see school as a place where they can succeed and where they can escape the depressing cycle of poverty, unemployment, and alienation.

The Wendells of this country have been called "culturally limited," "culturally deprived," "underprivileged," or "disadvantaged." The terminology doesn't matter. What does matter is an understanding of the reasons why children like Wendell have trouble in school.

These youngsters may be black or white, native- or foreign-born, urban or rural. They usually belong to one of the minority subcultures in our society—black, Puerto Rican, American Indian, Mexican-American, Appalachian white. They tend to come from large families, where poverty is the most important fact of the family's existence. They may speak little or no English, or such an impoverished English that they have great trouble communicating. Their parents—often separated from each other—are so overwhelmed by the crushing problems in their lives that the struggle of day-to-day existence makes many of the middle-class amenities impossible. Instead of being able to rely on their parents' interest in them and in their school work, they are often on their own for much of the time. Instead of a close bond between school and home, there is often distance, suspicion, and lack of understanding. The parents may be too shy and embarrassed to come to school, and the school personnel may have no empathy with the parents and their way of life.

Wendell starts school without a feeling of comfort about words and how they can be used, without a strong sense of motivation to do well, without a rich fund of experiences with other people and other places. He comes from a home where discouragement and alienation are the dominant themes. He has received poor medical and dental care, and his diet falls far short of the nutritional ideal. But there he is, on the first day of school, wanting—and having the inalienable right—to learn whatever our schools can teach.

The schools did not create Wendell's problems. They did not create poverty and discrimination. They did not force Wendell and his family to live in crowded, substandard housing. They did not rob his parents of a job in life. But they are the largest institution in Wendell's life—and the first he comes into direct contact with. On them rests the obligation to try to compensate for all the things that he doesn't have. They have to discover the strengths that he does have, so that they can build his education on these strengths.

The schools have, in large measure, accepted this challenge and responsibility, and school systems across the country have tried a variety of approaches to help diminish the educational gap between middle-class and poor children. While no school district has yet solved this problem, some of the measures currently being tried appear to hold promise for the future.

Disadvantaged children need compensatory education, beginning in early childhood and continuing throughout their school careers. They need small classes, where they can receive individualized attention. They need special tutoring programs that emphasize the basic skills of reading, writing, and arithmetic. Because of their families' overwhelming social problems, they need extra health services, extra psychological services, extra counseling and social work services. They need cultural enrichment—not only the trips to zoos, museums, airports, and all the other places they've never been—but even more important, a sense of wealth in their own culture. They need to have pride in their own cultural heritage and their own identity. To foster this, the schools must recognize and teach the contributions that persons of many racial and ethnic groups have made to our world. And finally, in teaching deprived children—as in teaching any child—teachers and administrators must have an understanding of all the nonacademic factors that facilitate learning: the image a child has of himself the motivation to succeed, the feeling of belonging, the awareness that people care very much about his future.

SOME OTHER SCHOOL-RELATED PROBLEMS

Educating Handicapped Children

On May 2, 1972, Donald Lang, twenty-seven, was sentenced to a prison term of not less than fourteen years and not more than twenty-five, for the murder of a prostitute (Tidyman, 1974). Was he guilty? No one but Donald Lang—and the true murderer if, in fact, it was not he—will ever know. Because Donald Lang cannot communicate with anyone. Deaf and mute since infancy, Donald Lang does not know sign language, is unable to read lips, cannot read or write or talk.

Education for handicapped children has, in general, come a long way since the family of the deaf and blind Helen Keller had to travel to far-distant cities, and eventually hire a private tutor for their daughter. But Donald Lang is living proof that many handicapped children are still not receiving the education that could help them to become fully functioning members of society. When Donald was $2^{1}/_{2}$ and living with his mother in a Chicago slum, she took him to a nearby school for the deaf. But since the boy was not toilet-trained and since school personnel thought he might be retarded as well as deaf, they kept him only a few weeks. His mother tried again to enroll Donald in school when he turned six, but the local public school sent him home the same day. That was the end of Donald Lang's education. (See Figure 11-3)

It has been estimated that about half of the nation's 7 million handi-capped children are not being adequately educated (Flaste, 1974). These children—about 10 percent of the school-age population—are deaf, blind, mentally retarded, physically deformed, emotionally disturbed, speech-impaired, or afflicted with other problems that affect their entire lives, and most especially their education (see Figure 11-3).

There are many gaps in the educational structure, and too many of these handicapped children are slipping through the holes. Some do not attend school at all, because their local districts are unable or unwilling to meet their needs. Some are placed in regular classes where they cannot keep up, or are channeled into the wrong kind of special classes. Of those handi-capped children who do go to school, some attend special classes in their neighborhood public schools, some attend public or private day schools, and those whose problems are especially severe are cared for and schooled at special residential centers.

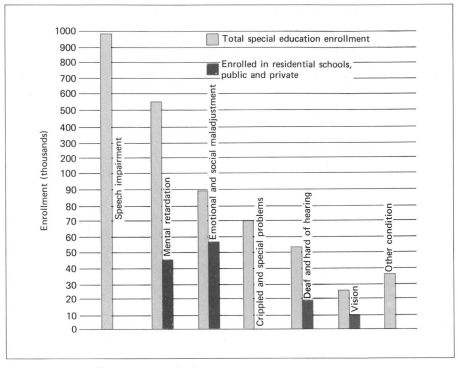

Figure 11-3   Enrollment in Special Education Programs for Handicapped Children, 1966 *(U.S. Bureau of the Census)*

One of the controversies in special education today centers around *mainstreaming* versus "segregated" special classes. Under the principle of mainstreaming, handicapped children are in regular classes with nonhandicapped youngsters, either for all or part of the day. Proponents of this approach emphasize the need for handicapped people to learn to get along in a society where most people do not share their impediments and the need for normal people to get to know and understand handicapped individuals. Obviously, mainstreaming requires sophisticated, specially trained teachers and innovative teaching techniques that meet the needs of all the students, handicapped or not. Critics of mainstreaming maintain that handicapped children can be taught better and more humanely in small classes with specially trained teachers, who can gear their lessons to the children's special needs.

The best solution for educating handicapped children is probably to combine the two approaches. Children who need special help can participate in some activities with their normal classmates, and can receive some instruction in special classes. A retarded child, for example, might be able to take physical education or shop in a regular class, while receiving academic instruction in a small group with other slow learners. Or a child with cerebral palsy might be in regular classes for academic work, but receive special physical training while her classmates go out for gym or recess. Of course, some children are too severely handicapped to take part in such programs. For them, separate education is the only possibility.

The goal of education for the handicapped is the same as the goal of education in general—to enable all children to fulfill their potential as much as possible, to lead rich lives in their homes and community, and to contribute to society to the best of their ability.

Learning Disabilities

Recently, educators have become aware of a large group of children— perhaps 10 percent of the general population—who suffer from a variety of learning difficulties known as "specific learning disabilities [Brutten, Richardson, & Mangel, 1973]." These children are of normal or above-normal intelligence, but for some not clearly understood reason, they have great difficulties in learning how to read, to write, or to work with numbers. The children see and hear perfectly well, but they seem to have trouble processing what they see or hear. Said one frustrated child to his teacher, "I know it in my head, but I can't get it into my hand."

Many of these youngsters have speech problems. They began to speak quite late, and their speech is still not so clear and well articulated as it should be. Others have difficulties with coordination. They are clumsy in their large-motor movements (running, climbing, playing ball) and inept in their fine-motor skills (tying shoelaces, coloring within the lines, writing with a pencil).

Since there is often a family history of reading disability, there is a possibility that the problems of some of these children are inherited. Other children are thought to have suffered bain injury before, during, or soon after birth. Some injuries may not have been severe enough to show up in any obvious way, but they may have been severe enough to affect the learning process. The rather vague term *mimimal brain dysfunction* has been coined to describe those children who do not seem completely normal, but whose difficulties cannot be precisely pinpointed. For unknown reasons, many more boys than girls are affected.

If learning-disabled children are diagnosed early enough and are given special attention, they can very often overcome their difficulties well enough to lead satisfying, productive adult lives. Some even go on to college and professional careers. On the other hand, those whose problems are not recognized and dealt with often grow up feeling stupid and inadequate failures. Some observers have linked learning disabilities with juvenile delinquency (Brutten et al., 1973).

After a child's difficulties have been diagnosed through a battery of specially designed psychological tests, a special educational program should be designed for him to build on his strengths and overcome his weaknesses. The child may leave his regular classroom for two or three hours a day of special instruction with a specially trained teacher. Or he may be placed in a special class. Or he may attend a public or private school, especially geared for children with special educational needs. The parents should receive counseling to help them learn how to help the child at home.

Hyperactivity

The story is an all too familiar one to many parents and teachers. Johnny can't sit still, can't finish a simple task, can't keep a friend, and is always in trouble. His teacher says, "I can't do a thing with him." The family doctor says, "Don't worry, he'll grow out of it." And the next-door neighbor says, "He's a spoiled brat." Finally Johnny's parents are told that he is a "hyperactive child."

What is hyperactivity? It is not a disease, nor is it an emotional disorder. Rather, it is a syndrome of personality traits that appear normally in all children, but more intensely in about 4 percent of the school population (Stewart, Pitts, Craig, & Dieruf, 1966) and possibly 9 percent of boys (Werner, Bierman, French, Simonian, Connor, Smith, & Campbell, 1968).

Hyperactive children probably represent one end of a normal spectrum of personality types (Stewart & Olds, 1973). They are much more active than the average child, especially in situations—like the classroom—where a great deal of activity is considered inappropriate. They are also more impulsive, excitable, impatient, and distractible. All these characteristics create problems for them in their daily life, especially in school.

The hyperactive youngster is likely to be of normal or above-average intelligence. Yet he has trouble with his schoolwork because he can't concentrate and can't show what he does know. It is difficult for him to sit in his seat long enough to hear a complete lesson or to complete a written assignment. When faced with an unfamiliar word or a perplexing arithmetic problem, he is more likely to blurt out the first thing that comes to mind instead of trying to work out the correct answer.

Parents and teachers can often help hyperactive children to do better at home and in school through the use of a variety of special techniques. First, they have to understand and accept the child's basic temperament. Then they can teach him how to break up his work into small, manageable segments; they can incorporate physical activity into the daily classroom schedule; and they can offer him alternate ways of demonstrating what he has learned (such as individual conferences or tape-recorded reports, which take the place of written reports).

Sometimes one of a family of stimulant drugs is prescribed for a hyperactive child. These drugs apparently help the children to focus their attention to the tasks at hand and thus to concentrate better. The drugs do not help all hyperactive children do better in school, though. And even

when they do appear to bring about an improvement in school performance, it is important to consider the long-range effects of giving drugs to
solve a nonmedical problem. If, as many observers believe, these are
basically normal children, what will be the ultimate effects of masking their
true personalities? Because we don't yet know the answer to this and other
equally important questions about the administration of stimulant drugs to
children, it is best to help these children by teaching their parents and
teachers the most effective ways of working with them (Stewart & Olds,
1973).

School Phobia

Linda wakes up on a Monday morning complaining of nausea and a
stomach-ache. She has been out of school for a week because of a bad cold,
but her parents were planning to send her back this morning. In view of her
new complaints, she is permitted to stay home, but as the day wears on, her
stomach troubles disappear. Next morning they reappear. Linda is not
trying to "put something over" on her parents. She is suffering from a
syndrome that has come to be known as *school phobia*, or an unrealistic fear
of going to school.

School phobia occurs most commonly in young children, from kinder-
garteners to fourth-graders (Millar, 1961). It is "one of the few forms of
psychological disorder for which boys do not outnumber girls [Ross, 1974,
p. 218]." Fear of school is found to about the same extent in both sexes
(Waldfogel et al., 1957).

Most children are occasionally reluctant about going to school, especially
after an unpleasant experience or an absence of any duration.

> If the parent deals with this reluctance in a matter-of-fact way and insists that
> school attendance is expected and required, nothing will come of the incident. On
> the other hand, if the parent begins to make lengthy inquiries into why the child
> does not want to go to school, eliciting more or less plausible and more or less
> factual rationalizations, and then agrees to let the child stay home, the basis of
> future school avoiding behavior may well be laid [Ross, 1974, p. 217].

Sometimes school phobia has little to do with anything that is happening
at school, but a great deal to do with a child's feelings about his parents. It is
the separation from the parent, usually the mother, that makes the child
anxious, and not the school itself.

> When these children are not attending school their concern over separation from
> mother is so great that they often need to keep her within sight, if not touch. One
> mother reported her child followed her about the house constantly, even sitting
> with his back to the bathroom door when she used that facility.
>
> The most constant anxiety fantasy reported by these children is of accident or
> injury occurring to their mothers while they are absent. It may be that the anxiety

observed in the classroom is related to pervasive obsessional thoughts of injury or accident having occurred to the parent while the child is at school [Millar, 1961, p. 561].

There is often a hostile interdependence between parents and child. The mother is subservient to the child and overprotective of him, largely due to the doubts she has about her adequacy as a mother. Unsure of what to do, she lets the child make many of the decisions for the family. The father may overidentify with the child or may compete as a sibling for the mother's affection (Waldfogel et al., 1957). The child attains power over the family, but the very control he exerts in manipulating his parents is likely to make him even more anxious, since by becoming "omnipotent" himself, he does not have the security of parental control.

In dealing with school phobia, it is vital to get the child back to school as soon as possible, even when this means getting her there by force, ignoring tears and tantrums and accusations, and returning her promptly if she comes home during the school day.

In fairly straightforward cases of school phobia, in which other aspects of the child's emotional life seem relatively stable, a matter-of-fact insistence on school attendance and a refusal to show sympathy for psychosomatic ailments will often clear the problem up quite quickly (Kennedy, 1965). In deep-seated cases where school phobia is only one of the emotional problems afflicting the family, psychotherapy for both parents and child may be indicated.

Summary

1   The child from six to eleven is in the stage that Piaget refers to as *concrete operations*. The concrete operational child uses symbols (mental representations) to carry out operations. He or she is becoming increasingly more proficient at classifying, seriating, dealing with numbers, and conserving. Egocentrism is diminishing, as are certain primitive concepts of realism, animism, and artificialism. Much of Piaget's information about children has come from utilizing the *clinical method*, a method in which the test situation is tailored to the child.

2   Both Piaget and Kohlberg regard moral development as a process that coincides with cognitive development. Moral development is influenced by a child's maturational level as well as by interactions with adults and other children.

3   Piaget regards moral development as a two-stage process. The first stage, *morality of constraint* (heteronomous morality), is characterized by rigidity. The second stage, *morality of cooperation* (autonomous morality), is characterized by flexibility. Piaget formed these conclusions through study of children's understanding of rules, intentionality, and punishment.

Kohlberg extended Piaget's view of morality to include six types of moral reasoning, and organized on three levels: premoral; morality of conventional role conformity; and morality of self-accepted moral principles.

4   Learning-theory approaches to studying moral development claim that children learn their culture's moral values by identifying with or modeling themselves after parents, who reward or punish moral decisions. But research does not confirm generalizations of moral standards from the home to other institutions.

5   Most school-age children have not yet mastered exceptions to grammatical rules. Children's understanding of increasingly complex syntax develops up to and perhaps even after nine years of age. A child's ability to communicate information to others improves with age and as egocentrism diminishes.

6   The intelligence of schoolchildren is assessed by individual tests (Stanford-Binet and Wechsler Intelligence Scale for Children) and by group tests (Otis-Lennon Mental Ability Test and Lorge-Thorndike Multi-Level Battery.)

7   A virtually impossible task confronting intelligence test constructors is to devise tests that measure innate intelligence without introducing cultural bias. But several *culture-fair* tests (Cattell Culture Fair Intelligence Test and Raven Progressive Matrices Test) are purported to deal with experiences thought to be common in various cultures. Even these tests are less fair than their authors intended, since it is almost impossible to screen for different, culturally determined attitudes and values. Intelligence tests currently used tend to be geared toward white, middle-class children; consequently, their use with children from minority-group backgrounds is inappropriate.

8   Cognitive functioning is correlated with individual temperment, cognitive style, conceptual style, and parental child-rearing practices.

9   Studies of intellectually gifted children have been of two types: *retrospective* (analysis of biographical materials of individuals who have already achieved eminence) and *longitudinal* (long-term follow-up studies of individuals identified as gifted during childhood). Gifted children tend to be superior in many respects—achievement, health, coordination, height, popularity—and as adults are superior in intellectual ability, scholastic accomplishment, and vocational achievement.

10   Creativity involves *divergent*, rather than *convergent*, *thinking.* The creative person sees things in new and unusual lights, and devises novel solutions to novel problems. It is not always easy to measure creativity—"creative" tests are required. When children are assessed both by measures of creativity and by measures of intelligence, four performance patterns may result: Children may (a) score high on both; (b) score low on both; (c) score high on creativity and low on intelligence; or (d) score low on

creativity and high on intelligence. Intellectual ability and creative ability are thus seen as separate constructs.

11   From six to twelve a child's development is influenced by the school and experiences that occur there. Academic and interpersonal successes (and failures) affect self-esteem, self-confidence, and basic outlooks on life. A child's school experience is influenced by various factors: type of classroom (open or traditional), teachers and attitudes, socioeconomic status, sex, and cultural membership. School-related issues include education of handicapped children, learning disabilities, hyperactivity, and school phobia.

Suggested Readings

Association for Childhood, Education International. *Migrant Children: Their Education.* New York, 1971. *A collection of fifteen brief, readable articles by people from around the United States who work in migrant education.*

Blackie, J. *Inside the Primary School.* New York: Schocken, 1971. *The author proposes alternatives to prescribed instruction and behavior modification of primary and elementary school children. Blackie relates his proposals to educational theory and child development.*

Cohen, D. H. *The Learning Child.* New York: Vintage, 1973. *This essay discusses both the excitement and danger facing children who are learning in school and in our world. It includes discussions of educational innovation, kindergarten and the parent, the meaning of reading and writing skills.*

Goertzel, V., & Goertzel, M. G. *Cradles of Eminence.* Boston: Little, Brown, 1962. *An absorbing study of the childhoods of some 400 prominent persons that seeks to relate early life factors to eventual success in life. It brings together biography, autobiography, and professional literature about gifted children and adults.*

Raths, L. E., Harmin, M., & Simon, S. B., *Values and Teaching.* Columbus, Ohio: Merrill, 1966. *An explanation of the theory behind values clarification, with examples of the strategies and a summary of some of the research in values.*

Simon, S. B., & Kirschenbaum, H. (Eds.), *Readings in Values Clarification.* Minneapolis, Minn.: Winston, 1973. *A collection of 38 articles on the identification and development of values, goals, and ideals, by writers such as Carl Rogers, Lawrence Kohlberg, and Urie Bronfenbrenner.*

Stewart, M. A., & Olds, S. W. *Raising a Hyperactive Child.* New York: Harper & Row, 1973. *A book for the lay reader that defines the characteristics of hyperactivity, explores possible causes, and offers practical suggestions to parents and teachers for the day-to-day management of hyperactive children.*

Task Force on Children Out of School. *The Way We Go to School: The Exclusion of Children in Boston.* Boston: Beacon, 1971. *The report of a Task Force on Children Out of School on the estimated 4,000 to 10,000 children of school age now excluded from classes in public school in Boston.*

Vernon, P. E. (Ed.) *Creativity.* Baltimore, Md.: Penguin, 1970. *A collection of works, both theoretical and applied, on creativity. This text studies genius, highly talented* *children, the nature of inspiration, personality characteristics of the creative individual, and special training in the development of creativity.*

Wees, W. R. *Nobody Can Teach Anyone Anything.* Garden City, N. Y.: Doubleday, 1971. *A book based on the author's premise that "whatever knowledge children gain they create themselves; whatever characters they create themselves."*

CHAPTER TWELVE

PERSONALITY DEVELOPMENT

IN WHICH VICKY'S PERSONALITY DEVELOPS
AMONG OTHER CHILDREN

I love you, Big World.
I wish I could call you
And tell you a secret:
That I love you, World.
      (Paul Wollner, 7)*

It doesn't hurt no place when I'm sad
I just know I'm sad.
            (Benny Graves, 6)*

Today is nine-year-old Vicky's big day. Narrator for the fourth-grade play. More lines to say than *anyone*. Right up there in front of the footlights she stands, knowing she looks her best. Her hair, freshly washed and neatly brushed. Her brand-new pantsuit fits to perfection. As the lights dim, her clear young voice reaches into every corner of the auditorium.

From the time Vicky was a baby, her parents have called her "The Calliope," because somehow she was always heard before she was seen. In the hospital nursery, her cry was the loudest; in nursery school, her shouts the most piercing; and at home someone was always saying, "Not so loud—I'm right next to you." But today "The Calliope" comes into her own. She who could project her voice so that others could hear her—really hear her—got the lead in the class play. Sometimes it's wonderful to be alive!

*From *Miracles: Poems by Children of the English Speaking World*, by Richard Lewis. New York: Simon & Schuster, 1966.

Theoretical Perspectives on Personality Development

FREUD'S THEORY OF PSYCHOSEXUAL DEVELOPMENT

According to Freudian theory, it is no accident that a child's sixth birthday marks the age for school entrance. By this time, most children have developed a functioning superego that allows them to internalize the morals and ethics of society, although somewhat rigidly at first. The superego makes them feel guilty over their misdeeds rather than afraid of parental punishment. They have resolved their Oedipal conflicts, they have comfortably wriggled into their sex roles, and they can now turn their energies to the acquisition of facts, skills, and cultural attitudes.

Freud termed the elementary school years the *latency period*, considering it an island of relative sexual quiescence between the turbulent preschool years with their Oedipal and castration conflicts, and the storminess of the adolescent search for sex partners. Freud's concept of sexual latency does not, however, imply the absence of sexuality. During the years from six to twelve, children continue to masturbate and to explore each other sexually. And they continue to think about and talk about sexual matters, as one eighteen-year-old brings out in her reminiscences of childhood (Maynard, 1973):

All fifth graders are obsessed with sex—the boys, with their mostly bathroom and bosom humor, of course, and—a bit more secretly, but more profoundly, the girls. . . . Boys, coming home from school at three, would weave and spin on their bikes, making little orbits around us as we walked, standing up on the seats when they passed us, to call out some new and thrilling combination of four-letter words, or taking their hands off the bars and giving us the finger. And we would clutch our neatly lettered notebooks to what we still shyly referred to as our "fronts" and speculate about the sex lives of our teachers [pp. 28–29].

Perhaps when Freud first formulated his theory, children in this age range expressed less sexual interest in each other than they do today. That sexuality is expressed at this age has been borne out by Broderick and Fowler's study (1961; cited by Muuss, 1970, p. 59) of fifth-graders, 90 percent of whom already had "steadies," 65 percent of whom had been kissed, and 40 percent of whom had gone on dates. Freud did acknowledge preadolescent sexuality, but he still considered it "latent" because at this age, he said, it no longer involves a conflict over the opposite-sex parent and does not yet involve what Baldwin (1968) has called the "reliving of the phallic stage" that takes place in adolescence.

Even those who adhere most closely to the notion of *sexual* latency acknowledge that these years are not marked by *behavioral* latency. The school years are characterized by a great deal of rebellious behavior, especially among boys. This seems to be manifest particularly in the school,

(Werner H. Muller, from Peter Arnold)

Freud termed the elementary school years the latency period, considering it an island of relative sexual quiescence; but even those who adhere to the notion of sexual latency acknowledge that these years are not marked by behavioral latency.

where boys are *supposed* to be polite and studious. But all along they have been conditioned to be independent and a bit aggressive.

Defense Mechanisms in Middle Childhood

The developing ego, or self-concept, of the school-age child is threatened on all sides. To uphold its strength, children develop a variety of defense mechanisms, many of which persist, in one form or another, throughout adult life. These are some of the most important defense mechanisms. There are others.

Regression.   During trying times, children often *regress*, showing behaviors of an earlier age, in an attempt to recapture past security. Thus, a child who has just moved or entered school, whose mother has just had another baby, or whose parents have separated, may go back to sucking her thumb, wetting her pants, or clinging to her mother. Generally, as soon as the emotional crisis is past, the "babyish" behavior, no longer needed, will disappear.

Repression.   The unconscious rejection of anxiety-producing situations may cause the child in this stage to *repress* those Oedipal feelings that he may formerly have freely expressed. These emotions are now so raw and uncomfortable that he cannot even let them rise to consciousness. Another kind of repression is referred to by Baldwin (1968), who describes young children who repress their desires for forbidden candy by turning around so that they cannot even see "the temptation they fear they cannot resist [p. 329]."

Sublimation.   By this process, children channel their sexual energy, which now makes them uncomfortable and anxious, into such acceptable activities as schoolwork, sports, and hobbies.

Projection.   When unacceptable thoughts and motives come to mind, one way of dealing with them is to attribute them to another. Thus, a child talks about how dishonest his brother is, how mean his sister, how bad the little boy next door, how jealous the baby is of him, and so forth.

Reaction formation.   When children say the opposite of what they really feel, they are exhibiting a *reaction formation.* This happens when Buddy says he does not want to play with Tony because he does not like him, when the truth is that Buddy likes Tony a great deal but is afraid that Tony does not want to play with him. The tendency for school-age children to play exclusively with other children of the same sex is considered a reaction formation.

ERIKSON'S THEORY OF PSYCHOSOCIAL DEVELOPMENT: INDUSTRY VERSUS INFERIORITY

An Arapesh boy learns to make bows and arrows and to lay traps for rats, and an Arapesh girl learns to weed and plant and harvest, to prepare food, and to care for babies. A young Eskimo learns to hunt and fish. And an American child learns to count, to read, and to form letters. During the school years, children learn the skills of their cultures so that they will eventually be able to work and provide for their families. Says Erikson (1950):

> Thus the inner stage seems all set for "entrance into life," except that life must first be school life, whether school is field or jungle or classroom [p. 258].

This is the age when productivity becomes important. No longer are children content to play; they must become workers and win recognition by their own efforts. Whether children are learning how to use bow and arrow, how to master the complexities of arithmetic, how to care for younger siblings, or how to read and write, their beginning efforts to handle the tools used by the adults in their society help them to grow and to form a positive self-concept. These are crucial years for the development of self-esteem, for if children feel that they cannot handle the tools of their culture, be they adzes or encyclopedias, they may feel hopelessly inadequate compared to their peers, and go "back to the more isolated, less

(James R. Smith)

Erikson sees this as the age when productivity becomes important. No longer are children content to play; they must become workers and win recognition by their own efforts.

tool-conscious familial rivalry of the oedipal time [p. 260]." They will feel inferior to their peers and will retreat to family situations.

> It is at this point that wider society becomes significant in its ways of admitting the child to an understanding of meaningful roles in its technology and economy. Many a child's development is disrupted when family life has failed to prepare him for school life, or when school life fails to sustain the promises of earlier stages [Erikson, 1950, p. 260].

On the other hand, children in this stage may give work too important a place in their lives, so that they identify themselves only through their work and neglect their relationships with other people. Perhaps the industrial tycoon who sits at his desk from dawn till well after dark, who lives, breathes, and dreams his business, and who rarely sees his family, is, in Erikson's words, "the conformist and thoughtless slave of his technology [1950, p. 261]." Perhaps this common archetype of business success was pushed in this direction during his school years.

Maier (1969) rephrases certain Eriksonian concepts:

> The "latent" child continues to invest as much of himself and his libidinal energy as he did before, and works incessantly on his bodily, muscular, and perceptive skills, as well as on his growing knowledge of the world, which becomes

increasingly important to him. Above all, he concentrates on his capacity to relate to and to communicate with the individuals who are most significant to him—his peers. A sense of accomplishment for having done well, being the strongest, best, wittiest, or fastest are the successes toward which he strives. The child wards off failure at almost any price. As long as ego tasks are mastered within the spheres of his own age group, the id and superego remain unchallenged and within safe boundaries. . . . He senses that if he proves his skills within the areas of his best competence, his successful future will be assured [pp. 54–55].

So Erikson, too, sees middle childhood as a time of relative physical and sexual latency—and rapid cognitive growth.

The Society of Childhood

Some observers of the contemporary scene bemoan the changing nature of childhood. Those long, lazy summer afternoons by the old swimmin' hole have now become these tightly scheduled days of day camp and Little League. Those years of innocence and gullibility have now become this age of precocious sophistication. Adults are different today, and so are children. They live differently, they act differently, and they think differently from children of years gone by.

Just as the great migration to the suburbs has changed the living patterns of millions of adults, so it has drastically altered the ways present-day children spend their time. Just as our country's nationwide mobility has meant the weakening of the bonds of the extended family, so it has meant the need for children to keep making new circles of friends and to grow up in communities where few adults outside a tight little circle know their names. Just as our relaxed views of morality have altered "polite" adult conversations, so have they changed the flavor of children's talk (and taken away some of the great mysteries associated with their once awesome ignorance). More leisure has given parents more time to spend with their children (or, as some put it, to interfere in the lives of their children). Our expanding knowledge of psychology has increased our interest in the way our minds work, and has altered the ways parents deal with their children, or, at least, the ways they think about the ways they deal with their children.

The technology of our time has changed the boundaries of children's worlds. A boy wails, "I'm ten years old and I've never been out of the United States!" An eleven-year-old gets her own private pink telephone as a birthday present. Travel, telephones, and television. Oh, television! Oh, the joy of it! Oh, the horror of it! Because of it, today's children are better informed and more constantly entertained. The events of a turbulent world—wars, riots, assassinations—are brought into our homes. Millions of children are wooed by multi-million-dollar advertising compaigns to eat

(Charles Harbutt, Magnum)

Children have their own lore, which they hand down to one another. They imitate, adapt, and make creative mistakes.

sugared cereals, play with expensive toys, and chew candy-coated vitamins. Because of television, children are not so sheltered from the adult world as they once were.

It would be incredible if today's children were not different in many ways from those of a generation ago. And yet there are still some eternal verities. Anyone who is in actual contact with real children will not be overly pessimistic about them. Yes, they may have absorbed some values of contemporary society that some of us lament. Yes, their tastes and their pastimes are often different today from what they were a generation ago. But they are far from passive little puppets, whose strings are pulled by parents, teachers, Madison Avenue, and Hollywood. The soul of a child who can sing verses like the following can't be moribund:

Jingle Bells, Santa Smells,　　　　When you're dancing with your honey
A thousand miles away . . .　　　　And your nose is kinda runny,
Blows his nose in Cheerios,　　　　You may think it's funny,
And throws 'em all away.　　　　　But it's snot.

Children's continuing insistence on singing their own songs, on telling their own jokes, on playing their own games, and on keeping among themselves what they don't want those alien intruders—adults—to know, underscores the truth of Douglas Newton's observation that "the world-wide fraternity of children is the greatest of savage tribes, and the only one which shows no sign of dying out [Opie & Opie, 1959]."

CHILDREN'S LORE
In 1954, a little girl in York City, England, skipped rope to this verse:

I had a little beer shop
A man walked in.
I asked him what he wanted.
A bottle of gin.
Where's your money?
In my pocket.
Where's your pocket?
I forgot it.
Please walk out.

More than 200 years earlier, in 1725, our tipsy hero had already become ensconced in a play-rhyme, incorporated in a ballad of the times:

Now he acts the *Grenadier,*
Calling for *a Pot of Beer;*
Where's his Money? He's forgot:
Get him gone, a Drunken Sot.

Peter and Iona Opie reproduced both these and ten other transitional verses on the same theme that were popular over the two-century span between them, in their intriguing book *The Lore and Language of School Children* (1959). After a ten-year study of some 5,000 British children, the Opies concluded that children have their own lore, which they hand down to one another. They rarely originate it. Rather, they imitate, they adapt, and they make creative mistakes. They pass along their pet superstitions— just ask Tom Sawyer how to get rid of warts. Or absorb what children were telling each other in this country earlier in this century (R. P. Smith, 1957):

What we knew as kids, what we learned from other kids, was not tentatively true, or extremely probable, or proven by science or polls or surveys. It was so. . . . If you eat sugar lumps, you get worms. If you cut a worm in half, he don't feel a thing, and you get two worms. Grasshoppers spit tobacco. Step on a crack, break your mother's back. Walk past a house with a quarantine sign, and don't hold your breath, and you get sick and die. Play with yourself too much, your brain gets soft. Cigarettes stunt your growth [pp. 18–20].

Children still parody the songs and poems of their elders, tell jokes that make fun of them, and play time-honored tricks on teachers, parents, grouchy neighbors, and each other. And as the verses above illustrate, they preserve a rich lode of traditional lore. With all their lively impudence, children are the great traditionalists. In line with Piaget's statements about the rigidity of children's conceptions of rules and morality, children pass on what they have heard as The Revealed Truth. They will not tolerate theories that contradict what they "know." Nor will they put up with alterations in familiar rhymes. While they eagerly seek out *new* jokes, stories, and rhymes, any slight variation in the old familiar ones is heresy. Young schoolchildren argue long and vociferously over a different word or phrase in a rhyme, with each saying, "No, you're not saying it right!" Eventually the majority rules, and the dissident is forced to yield to the most popular version.

The swift transmission of children's parodies is mouth-watering to advertising folk eager to get their messages around with dispatch or to record companies eager to make a hit. But the versions that fly the fastest are rarely the original commercial jingle or adult-composed song, but juvenile parodies of them. One example of this can be seen in the many take-offs on "The Ballad of Davy Crockett," which was wildly popular on American radio in 1955. In January 1956, schoolchildren in Sydney, Australia, were singing this take-off:

Reared on a paddle-pop in Joe's cafe,
The dirtiest dump in the U.S.A.
Poisoned his mother with D.D.T.,
And shot his father with a .303.
  Davy, Davy Crockett,
  The man who is no good.

In April, July, August, and September, various versions of the Davy Crockett song bubbled from children's lips, with one, practically identical to the above, being eagerly sung thousands of miles away in Swansea, England:

Born on a table top in Joe's Cafe,
Dirtiest place in the U.S.A.
Polished off his father when he was only three,
Polished off his mother with D.D.T.
  Davy, Davy Crockett,
  King of the Wild Frontier.
                    [Opie & Opie, 1959, p. 292]

These verses illustrate an important function in children's rhymes—a safety valve for the release of anger, frustration, and aggression against parents and such other family members as pesky little brothers and sisters (Butler, 1973), which can also be seen in the following jump-rope rhyme:

I had a little brother,
His name was Tiny Tim.
I put him in the bathtub
To teach him how to swim.
He swam down the river,
He swam down the lake,
He died last night
With an awful bellyache.

CHILDREN'S GAMES

Two little girls gracefully assume the familiar posture of jacks players. But these children, captured in terra cotta by an artist working in the year 800 B.C., are tossing and catching the original knucklebones, after which our modern jacks are modeled (Brewster, 1956). Marbles have been found in excavations of the Mound Builder Indians of Mississippi (Ferretti, 1973). A mural in an ancient Egyptian tomb shows two players in a furious game of *morra*, still played by Italians and persons of Italian background. This arithmetical game has two players both putting out any number of fingers from one to five, and both simultaneously guessing the total number extended (Tylor, 1879). Ball games, wrestling matches, imaginative play that imitates the work of adults, making figures with string, rolling hoops, throwing dice, moving checkers, playing tag, spinning tops, hiding and seeking are all venerable pastimes of children, popular today as they have been for hundreds, even thousands of years.

Children play games today for the same reasons that they always have. In play they discharge physical energy, prepare for life's duties, derive pleasure from achieving a difficult goal, and gain surcease from life's frustrations. They get the physical contact they crave, discharge their need to compete, act aggressively in socially acceptable ways, and develop their ways of getting along with a group. They give their imaginations free rein, learn the trappings of their cultures, develop the skills they'll need to get along.

> Play patterns are an integral part of all human culture wherever mankind is found and in whatever state of advancement the culture may be. A study of the play of primitive peoples will throw much needed light on the nature of the play tendencies of mankind as a whole. Moreover, a study of games and sports will reveal to us the nature and extent of civilisation of the race [Padmanabhachari, 1941; cited in Brewster, 1956].

One function of children's games is the teaching of sex-appropriate behavior. Several studies have examined differences in the play of boys and girls, and a 1960 investigation (Rosenberg & Sutton-Smith) chronicled some interesting shifts in popularity. When 187 fourth-, fifth-, and sixth-grade boys and girls indicated which of 181 games they liked to play, the

(Virginia Hamilton)

One function of children's games is the teaching of sex-appropriate behavior.

researchers found "an expansion of female role perception and a contraction of male role perception [p. 169]." Girls now like more games that used to be considered "boys'" pastimes, and they like to play more games than boys do. While only 18 of the 181 pastimes were chosen significantly more frequently by boys, 40 were chosen more often by girls. The other 123 showed no significant differences in appeal to one sex or the other.

Girls today have more variety in their play than boys. The girls continue to play "girls'" games, but they also play many games that have traditionally been considered the province of boys. But the boys are more restricted. While they spend as much time at play as boys used to do, they do fewer things. The authors of the study conclude, "The masculine role appears to have become confined, yielding fewer, widely acknowledged ways of seeing the self [p. 169]."

CHILDREN'S HUMOR
Amid whispers and giggles, Vicky's best friend, Dorie, seven, asks: "Do you want to hear a dirty joke?" To Vicky's eager nod, Dorie says, "A boy fell in the mud. Do you want to hear another one?" Again a nod. "A girl fell in the mud. Do you want to hear another? Yes? Okay, three came out." Raucous laughter follows snicker, and the joke is retold ad infinitum until every second-grader in the school knows it and repeats it to anyone who will listen.

As this sally into the world of juvenile humor points out, children's jokes are hardly subtle. Often, to an adult, they're not even funny. Children's stories do not have to have a surprise twist to make them laugh, and are often long, drawn-out "shaggy dog" stories, with no punch line. Much children's humor derives from their abiding interest in excreta and sexuality. By telling jokes about these taboo and often mysterious subjects, children can deal with things they'd like to understand better but are embarrassed to talk about more matter-of-factly.

In the opinion of one psychoanalyst (Wolfenstein, 1954), play on the ambiguity of words, one of the earliest forms of humor, draws upon the basic ambiguities of sex and emotion.

At about three, Vicky thinks it's the height of wit to say to a boy, "You're a girl." Behind this joke, says Wolfenstein, lies children's universal fears and wishes that their sex can be changed. As children become able to laugh at such comments directed toward themselves, they show their mastery of doubts about their own sex. At about four, Vicky may expand upon this game by calling a boy by a girl's name and vice versa. Sometimes, just mixing the names of two children of the same sex is funny. Thus, children learn to overcome doubts about their individual identities.

Older children base entire jokes on made-up names that have a sexual significance. At nine, Vicky loves the "Heinie" jokes, which rely for their humor on the double meaning implicit in stories like the following:

> A mother takes her little girl, named Heinie, out to buy her some underwear. She tells her child to wait in the alley while she goes into the store. When the salesman asks the mother what size underpants she needs, the mother answers, "Come out into the alley and I'll show you my Heinie."

Wolfenstein (1954) explains the humor in such jokes in this way:

> By setting up a situation in which the mother calls the child "my Heinie," the loving union of child and mother is achieved in a mocking way: the child becomes again a part of the mother's body. . . . While the mocking love name accomplishes a symbolic fusion of mother and child, the action of the joke consists in the mother's unwitting self-exposure. Her concern for her child keeps impelling her to reveal an intimate part of her body. . . . The mother is exposed as both sexually accessible and foolish. . . . Her image is degraded; from having been ideally desirable she becomes ridiculous [pp. 83–84].

And thus, the child telling the joke retaliates to some degree against the powerful figure of the mother.

Not all children's humor takes place in bathroom and bedroom, though. Children minimize their anxiety about many different situations with the gift of laughter. Whatever a child wants to gain mastery over, he tells a joke about, as we can see in the following stories:

(Charles Harbutt, Magnum)

Children's jokes are hardly subtle. By telling jokes about taboo and often mysterious subjects, they can deal with things they'd like to understand better but are embarrassed to talk about.

Hostility to siblings:
   "Boy, is my little sister spoiled!"
   "She is *not*."
   "Oh, no? You should see what the steamroller did to her!" (Third grade)

Fears about death:
   "How do you make a dead baby float?"
   "I don't know."
   "Take a dead baby, some soda, and a couple of scoops of ice cream . . ." (Sixth grade)

Doubts about own competence:
   "Why did the little moron throw the clock out of the window?"
   "He wanted to see time fly."

And then many jokes seem to be told for the sheer joy of showing mastery over the language—using mispronunciations and wrong words for effect, making puns, telling riddles, telling stories that depend for their humor on basic knowledge or on different meanings of a word, so that the child can show off what he knows. Goethe once said, "Men show their characters in nothing more clearly than in what they think laughable," and children often show their rate of development the same way.

LIFE IN THE PEER GROUP

The society of other children is much more basic to a child's life than as a telegraphic mechanism for transmitting skip-rope rhymes, rules for shooting marbles, or scatological stories. Children influence each other from the cradle. Even as a young infant, Vicky would begin to cry when she heard the wailing of other babies (Simner, 1971). By the time she reached nursery school, she was imitating the way the other children shared and fought—when they were not copying her style. Although she spent much of her time during those years in solitary play, she always enjoyed being in the presence of other children.

As a preschooler, Vicky's social behavior followed certain patterns that led up to her involvement with other children in her middle years. Hartup (1970) points out some of these early peer-oriented trends: From age two to five, children become more dependent on other children and somewhat less dependent on adults; they become more sympathetic and altruistic, on the one hand, and more competitive and aggressive, on the other. They quarrel less often, but the quarrels themselves last longer.

It is in middle childhood that the peer group really comes into its own. During these years, children spend more and more time away from their parents and more and more time with other children. Again, some observers here invoke "ontogeny recapitulating phylogeny." Just as our distant ancestors recognized at some point in development that the individual gains strength from being part of a group, so, too, do children

(Freda Leinwand, Monkmeyer)

In middle childhood the peer group really comes into its own; to compensate for their weak and powerless position in a society of giants, children hook up with each other.

compensate for their weak and powerless position in a society of giants by hooking up with other children.

Childhood subcultures exist in all societies around the world, and have always existed throughout recorded history. Their strength and importance vary, however, from one time and place to another. It is quite possible that at this time in the United States, the world of children may be stronger and more powerful than it has ever been before. Compared to other cultures with stronger family ties, our highly mobile society has had to find substitutes for the bonds of kinship. In some cases, the nuclear family becomes more cohesive; in most, the peer group achieves an overriding importance. This seems to be particularly true in heterogeneous urban settings, especially among working-class youths (Campbell, 1964).

Bronfenbrenner (1970) states that American children are no longer influenced by their parents as much as they once were, because they spend less time with them. He makes the point that our society is now age-segregated to an unprecedented extent.

Urbanization, child labor laws, the abolishment of the apprentice system, commuting, centralized schools, zoning ordinances, the working mother, the experts' advice to be permissive, the seductive power of television for keeping children occupied, the delegation and professionalization of child care—all of these manifestations of progress have operated to decrease opportunity for contact between children and parents, or, for that matter, adults in general [p. 99].

Increasingly, the peer group fills the void left by the absence of children's parents in their daily lives. In one study (Condry, Siman, & Bronfenbrenner, 1968), 766 sixth-graders said they spent an average of two or three hours a day over the weekend with their parents, while spending a little more than this with groups of friends and an additional two or three hours a day with a single friend. They were thus spending twice as much time with children their own age as with their parents.

Actually, in Victorian times, children were supposed to be seen and not heard by their parents—especially in affluent families, where their care was largely in the hands of nannies and governesses. So it is possible that children of today do not, after all, see that much less of their parent, than did children of seventy-five years ago. In any case, most American parents still feel keenly their responsibilities for helping their children develop values and behavior patterns. Furthermore, they are now concerned about their children's developing psyche, as well. By and large, though, the emphasis on parenting today is on the quality of the time parents spend with their children, rather than on its quantity.

Functions of the Peer Group

The time children spend in the company of their peers is often put to good use. It is within such groups that we see how we stack up with regard to others. It is often in the reflected opinions of others that we form our opinions of ourselves—or, in the words of the poet Robert Burns, we do "see oursels as others see us." The peer group thus provides a more realistic gauge for the development of skills and abilities than do our parents, who are so much bigger and wiser and more powerful, or our baby brothers and sisters. Only within a large group of our peers can we get a sense of how smart we are, how athletic, how skillful, how personable.

Peer groups help children to form their attitudes and values. While the family still does a great deal of this, the peer group provides a forum whereby we can sift through our parent-derived values and keep some while discarding others. Through the medium of other children from various backgrounds with differing value systems, we can test our opinions, our feelings, and our theories to see how well they hold up.

The peer group is a socializing agent that helps us learn how to get along in society. We learn how and when to adjust our needs and desires to those of others—when to yield and when to hold out for what we want and believe in. In modern times, societies such as Israel, Russia, and China have consciously and deliberately made use of the socializing nature of the peer group.

Generally, the peer group tends to be more homogeneous than not.

Racially and economically segregated housing patterns in most American communities ensure that a group of children who pal around together are all likely to come from similar backgrounds. Peer groups tend to be especially homogeneous with regard to sex, at least in the elementary school years. Groups are all-girl or all-boy, partly because of mutuality of interests within a sex, partly as an outgrowth of the group's function of teaching sex-appropriate behaviors, and partly due to the difference in maturity between girls and boys. In the Freudian view, this is also due to sexual latency. Children who play together are usually within a year or two of the same age, although an occasional neighborhood play group will form of a summer evening, including small children along with older ones. Too wide an age range brings problems with differences in size, interests, and ability levels.

Influence of the Group on the Individual

While the peer group serves a necessary role in wooing the individual away from the nest of the family and from parental dominance, it may impose its own dominance on the emerging individual. We need to function within the group but not be ruled by it. Who among us is immune to the pressures of the crowd? Probably no one. But there are differences in the extent of impressionability and willingness to go along with whatever the gang is doing. These differences have great implications for the behavior of children—and of adults—in society.

From time immemorial, parents have worried about the friends their children are seeing, with some justification, since peer-group pressures often induce youngsters to act in socially undesirable ways. It is usually in the company of their friends that children engage in petty shoplifting, smoke their first cigarette, chug-a-lug their first can of beer, sneak into the movies, and do a wide variety of antisocial acts. In the Condry, Siman, and Bronfenbrenner (1968) study of sixth-graders, children who were rated more "peer-oriented" reported engaging in more of this kind of behavior than did the "parent-oriented" children. Many children, though, do resist peer pressures. A number of investigators have tried to find out just how the group acts to influence the individual, and what differences exist between those who go along with the crowd and those who do not.

Citing that boldly nonconforming child in the nursery tale who dared to announce publicly, "The Emperor doesn't have any clothes on!", Berenda (1950) reports on an experiment that studied children's reactions to group pressures that contradicted what their own eyes told them. Ninety 7- to 13-year-old children were, one at a time, given a simple test whereby they were asked to compare the lengths of lines on twelve pairs of cards. They had already taken the same test in class. But this second time, the child being observed was tested in a room with the eight brightest children in his or her class, all of whom had been primed to give seven wrong answers out of the twelve.

The group influence was powerful. Almost all the children had given correct answers to the seven critical questions in the original control test, while only 43 percent of the seven- to ten-year-olds and only 54 percent of the ten- to thirteen-year-olds answered them right in the group-pressure situation. The children writhed uncomfortably in those instances when they felt pressured to give wrong answers. It is lonely to be the only dissenter in a group, but it is also a betrayal of oneself to deny the evidence of one's own senses.

> Lulled into security by the first two correct responses, each met the third (first wrong) answer with shock and bewilderment. Many a child would stand up in his seat, rub his eyes, look at all the others and then at the lines with a puzzled, embarrassed, and frightened expression on his face. Each child, without exception, felt ill at ease, fidgeted in his seat, or smiled uncomfortably at the others and at the experimenter. Many would whisper the right answer and turn to a neighbor for assurance. Some, after a few wrong group answers, would grow apathetic and look at the others in the group for the answer rather than at the lines. The situation was too puzzling; and being unable to explain it, they resigned themselves to it. There was always a note of relief when the majority gave the correct response [Berenda, 1950, pp. 231–232].

In talking about the experiment afterwards, the children expressed their anxieties. One eleven-year-old girl said:

> I had a funny feeling inside. You know you are right and they are wrong and you agree with them. And you still feel you are right and you say nothing about it. Once I gave the answer they didn't give. I thought they would think I was wrong. I just gave their answers. If I had the test alone, I wouldn't give the answers I gave [p. 232].

And a seven-year-old said:

> I felt funny. I know it will be silly, but when they said an answer and I didn't think it was right, I felt like my heart-beat went down [p. 232].

The brighter experimental children felt most anxious in this experiment. If a child had been thinking of herself as smart and if other children whom she knew to be smart all gave answers different from the ones she gave, where did this leave her? *All* those other smart kids couldn't be wrong. So she must be the wrong one. But she knew she *wasn't* wrong. There was just no rational answer.

When the material to be evaluated was ambiguous, the children's judgments were influenced most by the group. This alone carries grave implications for the individual trying to make sense out of an ambiguous world. Most moral issues are ambiguous. Is the decision to smoke marijuana a clear-cut issue? What about the morality of abortion? Dropping out of school? The person who goes along with the group despite his own convictions is going to betray himself by word or deed somewhere along the way.

While the egocentrism of the very young child (from about four to seven years) prevents her from conforming to the opinions of others, children become most susceptible to the influence of their peers in middle childhood, again becoming less conformist in adolescence (Costanzo & Shaw, 1966). Most studies have shown girls to be more conforming than boys (Mussen, Conger, & Kagan, 1969, p. 587), an understandable finding in view of our society's emphasis on girls' learning to be adaptable, to get along with people, and to avoid being assertive. Not surprisingly, the higher a child's status in the group, the less conformist he or she is likely to be.

To some degree, conformity to group standards is a healthy, self-serving mechanism of adaptation. It *is* important in human society to be able to get along with other people, even if this sometimes means sacrificing independent opinions. One study, for example, found that normal children responded more to the demands of a social situation than did hyperaggressive boys (Raush, Farbman, & Llewellyn, 1960; cited in Campbell, 1964, p. 312). Comments Campbell (1964):

> The reasonable implication is that "conformity" is not solely the province of the anxious, the dependent, the maladjusted; unwitting conformity in the face of ambiguity may be so, but conformity to the socially accepted demands of clearly defined situations seems a perfectly healthy response for a child (or for an adult, for that matter) [p. 312].

Various studies have shown that anxious boys, dependent boys, and boys who were not sure where they stood in the group were more susceptible to group influence (Campbell, 1964). One study of seven- to fifteen-year-old black and white boys and girls found no difference in conforming behavior between black and white boys, but did find that black girls were less likely to conform than white girls. This may have something to do with different sex-role expectancies and consequent different child-rearing practices between the two racial groups (Iscoe, Williams, & Harvey, 1964).

Popularity and Sociometry

We all want people to like us. From our earliest years to our hoariest, what our peers think of us matters terribly. Because acceptance by other people has such a major effect on our self-esteem and, ultimately, often on our success in life, researchers have devised *sociometric* techniques to answer some basic questions. Why are some children more sought out than others? Why are some ignored or rebuffed? What characteristics do popular children have? And what are unpopular children like?

Sociometric techniques take a number of forms, all of which can be translated into a *sociogram*, or a pictorial representation of popularity.

(James R. Smith)

While the peer group serves a necessary role in wooing the individual away from the nest of the family and from parental dominance, it may impose its own dominance on the emerging individual.

Researchers go into a classroom to observe which children seek out other children to play with, which ones are chosen most and learn least often, which ones are asked for help or advice, and so forth. They ask the children to name their three best friends in the group or the three children they like the least. Or the questions might be more specific: Which three children do you like to sit near? Do you like to walk home with after school? Do you like to serve with on a committee? Do you like to have on your gym team? And so forth. The data are then plotted as sociograms, which will be different for the same group, depending on which attribute is being measured: academic, organizational, creative, or athletic characteristics.

The popular child.   By establishing which children are chosen most often and which are chosen least often, researchers then try to correlate acceptance within the group with a wide variety of other factors. From various studies, a picture of the popular child takes form.

Popular children tend to be healthy and vigorous, well poised, capable of initiative, but also adaptable and conforming. They are dependable, affectionate, and considerate of others. And they are original thinkers (Bonney, 1947; cited in Grossman & Wrighter, 1948). They think moderately well of themselves, rather than showing extremely high or extremely low levels of self-esteem (Reese, 1961). They radiate self-confidence, without being overbearing or seeming "conceited." Popular children show mature dependence on other children: they ask for help when they need it and for approval when they think they deserve it, but they don't cling or make babyish plays for affection (Hartup, 1970). They are not goodie-goodies, but they make other people feel good to be with them (Feinberg, Smith, & Schmidt, 1958; Tuddenham, 1951).

While there is often a similarity in intelligence between children and their friends (Almack, 1922), popular children tend to be more intelligent than unpopular children. Once the minimum standard of normality is achieved, though, much greater intelligence does not make a child more popular (Grossman & Wrighter, 1948). The same relationship seems to hold true for social class. In one group that included children from professional, middle-class, and laboring or farm families, the minimum requirements seemed to be that of lower middle-class status. "More than lower middle class status did not help, but less than this level hindered [Grossman & Wrighter, 1948, p. 350]."

Good looks are valued in both boys and girls, and athletic ability is a plus for boys (Tuddenham, 1951). In sum, then, it seems that many of the same factors that influence adult popularity are already effective with children. The children whose company is valued by other children will probably grow up to be adults who are sought out by other adults.

The unpopular child. One of childhood's saddest figures is the child who is chosen last for every team, who hangs around the fringes of every group, walks home alone after school, is not invited to any of the birthday parties, and sobs in despair, "Nobody wants to play with me." Who is this child?

Children can be unpopular for many reasons. Sometimes because they are withdrawn or rebellious (Northway, 1944; Y. H. Smith, 1950). They are often the youngsters who walk around with a "chip on the shoulder," showing unprovoked aggression and hostility. Or they may act silly and babyish, "showing off" in immature ways. Or they may be anxious and uncertain, exuding such a pathetic lack of confidence that they repel other children, who don't find them any fun to be with. Extremely fat or unattractive children, children who behave in any way that seems strange to the others, and retarded or slow-learning youngsters are also outcast.

In any elementary school classroom, there is usually a small "inner circle" of extremely popular children, the "in" group. There are usually one or two isolates, with whom nobody wants to play. And then there is the large middle group who are neither extremely popular nor extremely unpopular. By any sensible standard then, most of the children should be fairly happy within the group. Far too often, though, the children in the outer circle, instead of banding with each other, spend all their time trying to make it into the inner circle. The cliquishness of schoolchildren being what it is, they are rebuffed time and again. They feel rejected, their self-esteem suffers, they do not value the friendship of the other children in the outer circle, and they remember these school years as ones of bitter unhappiness.

How Adults Influence Children's Peer-Group Dynamics

Grownups cramp kids' style. Or they help to guide them through life. Which of these points of view a given individual agrees with usually depends on whether that individual is a grownup or a kid. But either statement can be true. The personality, attitudes, and behavioral style of the adults who come into contact with groups of children exert a great influence on the individuals within those groups—and on the group dynamics themselves. Would the boys in Dickens' *Oliver Twist* or the girls in Muriel Sparks' *Prime of Miss Jean Brodie* have behaved differently under the tutelage of different adults? Undoubtedly. "Neither the idyllic events in *Peter Pan* nor the frightening denouement of William Golding's *Lord of the Flies* would have taken the same course with adult participation [Mussen, Conger, & Kagan, 1969, p. 583]."

One classic study (Lewin, Lippitt, & White, 1939) set up several clubs of ten-year-old boys under different styles of adult leadership, and found that the characters of the groups reflected the characters of the leaders. The groups in turn were run by authoritarian, democratic, and laissez-faire leaders (see Table 12-1 for a description of each style of leadership), so that each group experienced each type of leader.

The children in the democratically led groups were more spontaneous, friendly, and fact-minded, while those in the authoritarian and laissez-faire groups showed more hostility toward each other. Under authoritarian leadership there was either a high level of aggression or a high level of apathy, which quickly gave way to aggression when the leader left the room or during periods of transition to a freer atmosphere, indicating that the apathy reflected repressed aggression. There was also a difference in the boys' work style: When the autocratic leaders left the room, work slowed down, sometimes to a halt, whereas the boys in the democratic groups continued to work whether the leader was present or not.

The moral of these findings would seem to be, then, that groups of children do best when they have the leadership and guidance of a respected adult who respects them, and do least well with repressive adult leadership or with no adult leadership at all.

Adults can influence the popularity of individual children too. In one study of tenth-grade students, the teacher praised only those in the odd-numbered seats. A later testing of students' popularity indicated that those who had been praised were more popular with their classmates than those who had been sitting in the even-numbered seats (Flanders & Havumaki, 1960).

On the negative side, adults can make children unpopular. A common phenomenon is a situation whereby a particular child becomes a teacher's

Table 12-1   Authoritarian, Democratic, and Laissez-faire Leaders (*Lewin, Lippitt, & White, 1939*)

Authoritarian	Democratic	Laissez-faire
1 All determination of policy by the leader.	1 All policies a matter of group discussion and decision, encouraged and assisted by the leader.	1 Complete freedom for group or individual decision, without any leader participation.
2 Techniques and activity steps dictated by the authority, one at a time, so that future steps were always uncertain to a large degree.	2 Activity perspective gained during first discussion period. General steps to group goals sketched, and where technical advice was needed the leader suggested two or three alternative procedures from which choice could be made.	2 Various materials supplied by the leader, who made it clear that he would supply information when asked. He took no other part in work discussions.
3 The leader usually dictated the particular work task and work companions of each member.	3 The members were free to work with whomever they chose, and the division of tasks was left up to the group.	3 Complete nonparticipation by leader.
4 The dominator was "personal" in his praise and criticism of the work of each member, but remained aloof from active group participation except when demonstrating. He was friendly or impersonal rather than openly hostile.	4 The leader was "objective" or "fact-minded" in his praise and criticism, and tried to be a regular group member in spirit without doing too much of the work.	4 Very infrequent comments on member activities unless questioned, and no attempt to participate or interfere with the course of events.

"hostility sponge," who gets blamed for everything that goes wrong in class. The teacher's attitude infects the other children, and the child becomes unpopular with his classmates as well (Stewart & Olds, 1973). Philip came home to tell his mother how his first-grade teacher had rearranged all the seats in the room two by two, but left him sitting alone, saying, "No one would want to sit with you." Infected by the teacher's dislike of Philip, no one did. And a third-grader complained to her mother, "Louie spoiled our Halloween party because he was so bad the teacher made us stop." The teacher would have been more humane had she removed Louie instead of stirring up his classmates' resentment against him.

Societal Recognition of Peer-Group Influences

Relatively few societies consciously attempt to make use of peer influences in the socialization of children. But in some countries, conscious deliberate efforts have been made to use peer-group influences in molding new kinds of personalities to carry out the goals of new societies.

The Soviet Union

In Russia, children are spurred on to socially approved behavior by fostering a sense of the group (Bronfenbrenner, 1970). Nursery school teachers emphasize sharing, cooperation, and taking part in joint activities. In grade school, emphasis is placed on mutual responsibility between children, with a structure provided for older children to help younger ones. Teachers also motivate children to do better by encouraging competition between groups, rather than between individuals. Youngsters sit up straight, stay neat and clean, do their homework, and observe classroom rules, to make their row the best in the class. The children themselves exhort their classmates to do better, for the good of the entire unit.

The emphasis is generally positive, with those groups that make the best showing winning prizes. But "trials" by juries of their peers often reduce to tears of shame those youngsters who misbehave or fall behind in their schoolwork (Bronfenbrenner, 1970). Evidence that these methods are effective can be seen in studies that show that Soviet children appear much less willing to engage in antisocial behavior than American, English, and West German children (Bronfenbrenner, 1967).

A dramatic illustration of intercultural differences showed up in a study that tested Russian and American twelve-year-olds for their susceptibility to peer and adult influences (Bronfenbrenner, 1967). The children were confronted with thirty hypothetical situations involving their readiness to cheat, steal, play a practical joke on a teacher, neglect homework, and go against parental wishes in several specific ways. Some children were told that their classmates would see their answers, some that parents and teachers would see them, and some that no one but the researchers would see them. Both Russian and American children gave more socially approved responses when they thought adults would see their answers, although the Russian children were influenced more by adults and the Americans more by peers. Furthermore, the effects of peer-group pressures took different directions for the two groups of children. In Russia, peer-group pressure influenced children toward adult standards of behavior, while just the opposite held true in the United States. American children who thought their friends would see their answers were more likely to show a willingness to go against adult-approved standards.

Should we, then, adopt the Russian system of collective education? Not necessarily. Another study of Russian, American, English, and Swiss sixth-graders (Rodgers, Bronfenbrenner, & Devereux, 1968) found that

(Leonard Freed, Magnum)

Kibbutz children are raised together and forced to depend upon each other for virtually all companionship and comfort; adult kibbutzniks want the peer group to have such power, because on the kibbutz, as in the Soviet Union, the peer group reinforces standards and values society holds dear.

(Roy Pinney, Monkmeyer)

Russian children were more likely to be clean, orderly, and polite, but less likely to tell the truth and seek intellectual understanding. In our efforts to encourage individualism and a constant search for one's own values, do we perforce have to accept a certain amount of rebelliousness against adults? If so, how much? How can we find the golden mean between unquestioning docility on the one hand, and aggressive delinquency on the other?

The Israeli Kibbutz

About 90,000 Israelis, or some 2.8 percent of Israel's total population, live on the collective agricultural settlements known as kibbutzim (Government of Israel, 1973). Conceived in the spirit of a new nation, the kibbutz way of life involves communal living, collective ownership of all property, and the communal rearing of children (Spiro, 1954). The kibbutz's influence over Israeli society belies its small numerical standing, with former or present kibbutzniks accounting for disproportionately large numbers of elected governmental representatives and battle casualties (Bettelheim, 1969). It is the kibbutz that carries on the dream of the founders of Israel.

A cornerstone of the kibbutz life-style is the individual's relationship to the group, a bond that begins in earliest infancy. In most kibbutzim, as soon as mother and baby leave the hospital, the mother returns to the apartment she shares with her husband and the baby goes to live in the infants' house, to be cared for by a *metapelet*, or professional child-carer. From their first waking hours, babies see other babies, and Bettelheim (1969) says that a baby will often lose his appetite and become generally run down when a cribmate is taken out of the nursery.

The babies who live together in the infants' house will move on together to the toddler house, then to the kindergarten, and so forth to the other houses they will progressively occupy until they become adults. They are with each other constantly: They play together, they go to school together, they go on outings together. They become closer to each other than to their parents or their brothers and sisters. These age-mates look out for each other, comfort each other, and because they are so dependent on each other, exert group pressure on the behavior and attitudes of the individuals within the group. The individual rarely goes against the group.

At about the age of twelve or fourteen, children establish their own youth society, organizing along the same general lines as that of the kibbutz itself. They work, they vote, they make policy. And their influence over each other becomes even stronger. Bettelheim (1969) relates one incident:

> When I visited a class of high school seniors, they first asked me many questions about young people in America, about our educational system, about my reactions to the kibbutz, etc., and showed a lively interest and sharpness of mind. When I asked them what they would like to see changed in the kibbutz, they said, as usual, that everything in the kibbutz was just as it ought to be, though they felt

(like students anywhere) that school work was too hard, or too much. When I pressed for some specific change they would welcome, one said: "to have two movies a week instead of one."

In manner and tone his comment was matter-of-fact and straightforward. But the moment it was out, he felt the astonished, even agonized silence of the group, which until then had spoken up freely. Quite possibly they reacted this way because a kibbutz matter was being criticized to an outsider, and on so frivolous an issue as movies! But whatever the reason, he had gone against group opinion, and he sensed it immediately. Before anyone could say a word, he spoke hastily again, with what to me seemed an empty grin, saying "I meant this only as a joke" [p. 212].

If the kibbutz children were not raised together, if they were not forced to depend upon each other for virtually all companionship and comfort, if adults did not give the youth society the power to resolve most problems of the young people, the peer group could not wield the power it does. But the adult kibbutzniks want the peer group to have this power, because, by and large, on the kibbutz as in the Soviet Union, the peer group helps to reinforce the standards and values that the adults in the society hold dear.

The United States

Within the United States, a growing number of classroom teachers are learning how to improve children's behavior by enlisting the help of other children. In one case, for example, the teacher of Diane, an eight-year-old girl who regularly threw severe tantrums in class, instituted a new program. The teacher explained to the entire class that whenever Diane misbehaved, a teacher aide would hold her down in her chair, and everyone who did not turn around to look at her would receive a candy treat. On each half-day when there were no tantrums from Diane, the teacher would put a star on the board. When four stars in a row were awarded, there would be a little class party. Diane gradually threw fewer and milder tantrums until, by the last month of the school year (after the program had been in effect for just under three months), she was throwing no tantrums, was making friends, and was reacting positively both to the school and to her teacher (Carlson, Arnold, Becker, & Madsen, 1968). By giving the other children a stake in Diane's good behavior, the teacher was able to eliminate peer reinforcement of her tantrums and obtain a more peaceful classroom situation.

This is just one specific example of the ways that adults can capitalize on peer-group influences to bring about conformance to adult standards. Bronfenbrenner (1970) urges us to adopt a number of others. He suggests that teachers try to motivate children by using positive reinforcement, setting up teams, encouraging mutual help and "cooperative group competition." Schools, he says, should encourage older children to help younger children, both in and out of the classroom. And family, neighborhood, and the larger community should all involve themselves more fully in the lives of children.

> In the light of the increasing evidence for the influence of the peer group on the behavior and psychological development of children and adolescents, it is questionable whether any society, whatever its social system, can afford to leave largely to chance the direction of this influence, and realization of its high potential for fostering constructive development both for the child and his society [Bronfenbrenner, 1967, p. 206].

Self-concept

Probably the most important key to success and happiness in life is a favorable self-image. Lucky Vicky, who likes herself! Confident in her own abilities, she approaches life with an open attitude that will unlock many doors for her. She can take criticism without going to pieces, and when she feels strongly about something she wants to say or do, she is willing to risk making other people angry. She often challenges parents, teachers, and other people in authority. She feels she can cope with obstacles; she is not overburdened by self-doubt. She solves problems in original, innovative ways. Because she believes she *can* succeed in the goals she sets for herself, she generally *does* succeed. Her success renews her self-respect and makes it easy for her to respect and love others. They, in turn, admire and respect her and enjoy being with her.

On the other hand, Peter, who does not feel good about himself, is hampered wherever he turns. Convinced he cannot succeed, he does not try very hard. His lack of effort almost always assures continued failure, resulting in a downward spiral of lack of confidence and lack of success. He worries a lot about whether he is doing the right thing, he is destructive both of material things and of people's feelings, and he is constantly plagued by one psychosomatic pain after another. He tries hard to please others—often too hard, so that while he goes along with what other people want, he often strikes them as "wishy-washy." Because of his self-doubts, he's not much fun to be with, and so he has trouble making and keeping friends—which, of course, drives his opinion of himself to even lower depths.

Much of the above descriptions come from Coopersmith's studies (1967) of self-esteem in preadolescents. He focused intensively on the lives and backgrounds of eighty-five boys who were ten to twelve years old and whose self-esteem, as measured by various tests and rating scales, ranged from very low to very high. After interviewing the boys and their mothers separately to determine the relationships between self-esteem and other aspects of the boys' lives, Coopersmith concluded that people develop their self-concepts according to four bases. These are: significance (the way they feel they are loved and approved of by the important people in their lives); competence (in performing tasks they consider important); virtue (their attainment of ethical and moral standards); and power (the extent to which they influence their own lives and those of others). While people may draw favorable pictures of themselves if they rate high on some of these measures and low on others, the higher they rate on all four, the more highly they will rate themselves.

Much of Coopersmith's study was devoted to finding out what kinds of parental attitudes and practices were associated with children's high levels of self-esteem. He found that the parents of children with high self-esteem were likely to think well of themselves, that they loved and accepted their children totally or nearly so, but that acceptance was not synonymous with permissiveness. Far from it. The parents of the high self-esteem children made greater demands on their children for academic performance and for good behavior. Within the clearly defined and firmly enforced limits that they set, they showed a great deal of respect and latitude for individual expression and relied more on rewarding good behavior than punishing bad. Both parents led active, rewarding lives outside the family, while discharging their child-rearing responsibilities. What were these families like?

> Rather than being a paradigm of tranquility, harmony and open-mindedness, we find that the high self-esteem family is notable for the high level of activity of its individual members, strong-minded parents dealing with independent, assertive children, stricter enforcement of more stringent demands, and greater possibilities for open dissent and disagreement. This picture brings to mind firm convictions, frequent and possibly strong exchanges, and people who are capable and ready to assume leadership and who will not be treated casually or disrespectfully [Coopersmith, 1967, pp. 252–253].

A variety of factors affect a child's self-concept. Coopersmith found no relationship between self-esteem and height, physical attractiveness, or family size, and only a slim relationship to social status and academic performance. Sears (1970) contradicted some of these findings when he reported correlations between high self-concepts and high reading and arithmetic achievement, and small family size. Both found that first-born and only children, children with warm parents, and boys with dominant mothers had higher self-esteem. It is hard to say whether this last effect is because dominant fathers suppress their sons in some way, whether dominant mothers unconsciously play up to their sons, or whether some other interaction is at work. (In this context it is interesting to note that only 21 of the fathers of the 400 eminent persons in the Goertzels' 1962 study were considered dominating, as opposed to 109 mothers. The Goertzels suggest, "The mother's high expectations and performance are presumably not seen as competition by the son; but the son of the very capable father is often less sure of himself than is his father [p. 101].")

Evidence for the prestige of so-called masculine traits in our society can be seen in Sears' (1970) finding that higher scores of masculinity for both boys and girls were associated with higher levels of self-esteem. On the other hand, another study that compared fourth- and sixth-grade boys and girls found that girls at each grade level had higher self-concepts than boys (Bledsoe, 1964). The author theorizes that this may be due to girls' earlier maturation or to their more frequent contacts with adult women—their mothers and their teachers.

Both these findings may have a common source. Our society's emphasis on toughness, independence, strength, and achievement is communicated to both boys and girls, and it may be that the closer any child comes to meeting these demands, the higher will be that child's self-concept. But since the pressure is much greater for males, young boys who are not capable of all that toughness will feel their inadequacies all the more, with a resultant loss of self-esteem. Girls in our society have been able to comfort themselves with the reassurance that those are masculine traits, anyhow. Vicky can tell herself that whatever she achieves is fine, but if she doesn't meet all those standards, she's still doing okay, because she's "only" a girl. It will be interesting to see whether recently increased demands for achievement by girls and women will bring comparable pressures to young girls.

Age affects the way children see themselves. When ninety low-income black and white second-, fourth-, and sixth-graders were asked to answer the question "Who are you?" in as many ways as possible, they described themselves differently at each consecutive age (Sheikh & Beglis, 1973). The second-graders thought in basic units of identification, as "I am a boy," "I live on Main Street," and "I am part of the Brown family." The fourth-graders' responses reflected both their own individuality and their expanded worlds, as in "I get good marks in spelling," "I have a lot of friends," and "I like to play football." By the sixth grade, students were referring more to their futures, were more aware of the opposite sex, and the girls were talking about their physical appearance.

Some racial differences showed up, with the black children describing themselves more in terms of basic identification (sex, position in the family, address, year in school, etc.) and less often than the white children in terms of skills and accomplishments. The black sixth-grade girls tended to join their concern with looks with their feelings of racial identity and pride in statements like "I am black and proud" or "I am black and beautiful."

The impact of school entrance appears to raise children's estimates of themselves (Stendler & Young, 1951), perhaps because entering school is a well-recognized milestone of growing up. When 202 mothers of first-graders were interviewed, about eight months after the start of school, most of them reported that their children were more responsible now, more helpful, more self-confident, had more self-control, and got along better with their playmates.

Children generally become more accurate in evaluating themselves as they grow older, which can be seen in Piagetian terms as a manifestation of

(Magnum)

Probably the most important key to success and happiness in life is a favorable self-image.

decreasing egocentrism (Phillips, 1963). A group of fourth- and sixth-graders were asked to evaluate themselves and to compare their self-evaluations with the way they would like to be (McCallon, 1967). The closer the two scores were, the higher the children's self-concept. The girls and the older children seemed to feel they were closer to their ideal selves than the boys and younger children. This seems to indicate a relationship between maturity and self-esteem. Their ideal selves are the way they would like to be. The closer they feel to the way they'd like to be, the better they feel about themselves. Boys and younger children have greater discrepancy between ideal and real, probably due to greater immaturity.

Curiosity level has been found to correlate highly with self-esteem in fifth-grade boys (Maw & Maw, 1970). Very curious children tend to be more self-reliant, less prejudiced, more socially responsible, and to have a greater feeling of belonging. It is possible that children with poor self-esteem don't act very curious, because expecting to fail, they don't stick their necks out. Or uncurious children may not explore their surroundings as much and may fail to learn whatever might help them to gain a higher opinion of themselves.

By all expectations, children from economically deprived homes should have lower self-concepts than children from better-off homes. And undoubtedly this is true for some children. But at least two recent studies contradict this hypothesis, indicating that a child's intimate family situation probably exerts a greater influence on that child's self-image than does the broader social context. Soares and Soares (1969) looked at self-perceptions of 229 poor, mostly black and Puerto Rican children, and at those of 285 middle-class, mostly white children in elementary grades. On all five measures of the test, the disadvantaged children had higher self-perceptions than the advantaged children. Within the two socioeconomic groups, the poor boys had higher scores than the poor girls, while the middle-class girls thought more of themselves than the middle-class boys.

Trowbridge, Trowbridge, and Trowbridge (1972) examined 1,662 low-income and 2,127 middle-class children from the third to the eighth grades on Coopersmith's Self Esteem Inventory, and again found that the poor children had higher opinions of themselves than did the children from more prosperous homes. They were more likely than the middle-class children to identify with such statements as "I can usually take care of myself"; "I can make up my mind and stick to it"; "I'm pretty sure of myself"; "I can make up my mind without too much trouble"; and "If I have something to say, I usually say it." They see themselves as more popular and more likely to be leaders with other children.

Most surprising to anyone familiar with the generally lower academic ratings of disadvantaged youngsters is the fact that the ones in this study saw themselves as more successful in school than did their middle-class counterparts. They like to be called on in class, they're proud of their school work, and they don't have trouble talking in front of the class. But very few, compared to the middle-class children, feel they are doing the best work they are capable of. Children who think they are already doing the best work they can apparently consider their present status their upper limit, while those who feel they could achieve more if they tried harder can save face and hold onto a loftier image of their abilities. Furthermore, when these poor children do poorly in school, they blame the school or the teacher, while the middle-class children tend to blame themselves.

There must be some very special magic in the upbringing of the disadvantaged youngsters in these two studies. What is it that their parents or their communities have been able to impart to them to help them to maintain their dignity, their self-respect, and their enjoyment in life despite the handicaps of financial hardships and racial discrimination? When we can answer this question, millions of children may benefit.

How Prejudice Affects Children

Racism has been identified as "the number one public health problem in America today . . . a clear and present danger to the mental health of all

children and their parents [White House Conference, 1970, p. 295]."
Prejudice, of course, is also based on factors other than race. Children who
speak a different language, who worship in other ways, or who look or act
differently from the majority are frequently the butts of bigoted thinking.
Such thinking often makes youngsters hate themselves and hate their
backgrounds, with resultant emotional disturbance and antisocial behavior.

The roots of prejudice run deep in our society. While it does not appear in
infants, it begins to be demonstrated by children as young as two and
continues to flourish, with damaging results for both the one who harbors
prejudice and the one who is its target. Both are victims.

Morland (1966) found that preschool children from the South (Virginia)
and the North (Boston) are already aware of racial differences and already
imbued with the idea of white superiority. White children from both areas
preferred and identified with other children of their own race. The black
children also preferred white children, indicating a rejection of other
children like themselves, and, by projection, a rejection of themselves as
well. Mock and Tuddenham (1971) found that black fourth-, fifth-, and
sixth-graders were more conformist than were white children, especially
when they were in a group with a great many white children. Children of
both races consistently considered the judgments of white children to be
more valuable than those made by black children, again showing the
damage that prejudice does to children of minority groups. Since both black
and white children come to school with these attitudes, the public school
desegregation that is taking place today must be accompanied by an
understanding of these problems and an attempt to overcome these
damaging stereotypes.

"Children without Prejudice," the report of Forum 18 of the 1970 White
House Conference on Children, offers some fifty recommendations to
eliminate prejudice. These recommendations include the fostering of open
patterns of housing and education; greater educational emphasis on the
cultural contributions of American minority groups; expansion of scholarship programs for handicapped and socially or economically disadvantaged
children; recruiting and training minority-group teachers; requiring a
knowledge of cultural contributions of minority groups for teacher certifica-
tion; the allocation of 4 billion dollars a year "for renewed or new housing
for the 35 million Americans, mostly children, now living in substandard
surroundings [p. 302]"; the improvement of inner-city schools; the development of a drug education program for elementary school children; and
training programs in human relations for police officers, "particularly in the
areas of problems of children and youth [p. 303]."

The report states (White House Conference, 1970): The disparity between the
lofty ideals we preach and the sorry reality of practice can only continue to
undermine our institutions and our society. Discrimination perpetuates poverty,
crime, semiliteracy, poor education, and poor physical and mental health. Racial

policies and attitudes also prevent the achievement of a full measure of growth and development for all.

Eradicating racism will obviously be an immense task, expensive and difficult. But millions who would have been wasted human beings will become contributing members of society. As they will become new consumers for all national products, commercial relationships with other nations will be improved and welfare spending will be cut. To delay any longer will compound our national tragedy [p. 299].

And it concludes:

Children have a right to grow up in a society which stresses moral and ethical values, which teaches the concepts of love of fellow man, which respects the right of individual religious beliefs, which develops the child's personality to include the virtues of honesty, integrity, good character, fairness, compassion, and understanding in all human relations [p. 304].

We wholeheartedly agree.

Sex Typing in the Middle Years

In the 1950s, when a group of eight- to eleven-year-old boys were asked what men need to know and be able to do, they gave this picture:

They need to be strong; they have to be ready to make decisions; they must be able to protect women and children in emergencies; . . . they are the ones to do the hard labor, the rough work, the dirty work, and the unpleasant work; they must be able to fix things; they must get money to support their families; they need "a good business head." . . . They also need to know how to take good care of children, how to get along with their wives, and how to teach their children right from wrong [Hartley, 1959, p. 461].

And what do they think of women?

They are indecisive; they are afraid of many things; they make a fuss over things; they get tired a lot; they very often need someone to help them; they stay home most of the time; they are not as strong as men; they don't like adventure; they are squeamish about seeing blood; they don't know what to do in an emergency; they cannot do dangerous things; they are more easily damaged than men; and they die more easily than men. . . . They are not very intelligent; they can only scream in an emergency when a man would take charge. . . . Women do things like cooking and washing and sewing because that's all they can do [Hartley, 1959, p. 462].

One boy epitomized rigid sex-role concepts:

If women were to try to do men's jobs the whole thing would fall apart with the women doing it. . . . Women haven't enough strength in the head or in the body

(Mimi Forsyth, Monkmeyer)

In the 1950s, men needed to be "strong," and women did the dishes. In the 1970s, some do, some don't.

to do most jobs. . . . If we had a woman in Congress and taking over everything, probably the Russians would attack tomorrow if they knew about it—if we had a war, they would tell everybody to put down their arms. They'd probably make it life imprisonment for any boy or man who strikes a girl. I wouldn't even trust a woman as a doctor. You never know what they are going to do next [Hartley, 1959, p. 463].

In the 1970s, these attitudes seem amusingly obsolete. Surely in these days when woman's role has expanded into all spheres of modern life, children have very different ideas. Or do they? Some do, and some don't. A survey of 1,600 fourth-, sixth-, eighth-, and tenth-grade suburban students from various social classes revealed some decidedly stereotyped ways of thinking. But it also indicated that many of the students, most especially the older girls, express a willingness to "grant women greater participation in the social, economic and political spheres [Greenberg, 1972, p. 9]."

The students' responses to twenty questions relating to male and female roles gave some interesting clues to their thinking. While 70 percent of the boys thought a female doctor or dentist would be as good as a man, only 33 percent thought a trained female garage mechanic could fix a car as well as a man. And while 66 percent of the boys thought that "lady scientists" are as smart as male scientists, only 35 percent thought we should have female astronauts.

Contrary to popular belief that more privileged males are more liberal and privileged females more concerned about the equality of women, the social class of the students did not affect their answers. The differences that did show up had to do with sex and age. The girls were consistently more egalitarian than the boys, and the older students (after grade four for boys, after grade six for girls) more egalitarian than the younger ones, possibly because they understood and had thought more about the social issues involved, or possibly because they understood the questions themselves better.

THE SCHOOLS' INFLUENCE

We know, of course, that children come to school with many of their sex-typing attitudes already formed. Then the schools exert their own influences, confirming or adapting already held views. While little attention has been paid to the schools' role in this process, Minuchin (1965) did attempt to relate children's sex-role concepts to the kinds of schools they attended, as well as the kinds of families they came from. She measured the sex-role attitudes of 105 fourth-graders from two traditional and two modern schools in a large metropolitan area. The traditional schools emphasized facts, grades, competition, adult authority, and conventional sex roles, while the modern schools stressed "intellectual exploration and involvement, the shaping of curriculum to basic developmental trends, the individualized evaluation of mastery, and flexible, close relationships between teachers and children [p. 1035]" and flexible sex roles.

The children's families were also rated "traditional" or "modern," according to these definitions:

Traditional families . . . stress the social acceptability of the child's behavior and his adaptation to the expectations and standards of his society. In these families adults exercise authority as a fixed prerogative of the adult role. Modern families . . . stress the individual child's needs and rate of growth. They attempt to balance demands for socialization with provision for impulse gratification and individual expression, and they exercise authority in a relatively functional and flexible way [Minuchin, 1965, p. 1036].

Both school and home orientations seemed to influence the children's attitudes, with children from traditional families *and* traditional schools locked most tightly into conventional roles. Their play was most strongly sex-typed, the boys were more aggressive, and the girls more oriented to family life. The only boys who considered female lives dull and uninteresting were those who went to traditional schools, and the only girls who talked about female advantages in terms of attractiveness, clothes, and protection and deference to adult women were students of traditional schools. The more modern the background, the more open the child's attitude. The children who veered most from conventional attitudes were girls who attended modern schools, and whose families were both modern in outlook and of higher socioeconomic status.

Textbooks

While relatively little attention has been paid to the ways the schools themselves foster sex-typing, more interest has been shown in the books the schools use.

As far back as 1946, an analysis of commonly used third-grade school readers showed definite patterns of sex-role stereotyping (Child, Potter, & Levine, 1946). While than as now, girls made up about half the classroom population, girls and women accounted for only 27 percent of the characters in the readers. Male characters were more than $2^{1}/_{2}$ times as much in evidence. And when the females did appear, they were shown as helpless, passive, unintelligent, incapable, and in many ways morally inferior (twice as likely to be lazy or undesirably acquisitive).

Twenty-six years later, in 1972, the schoolbooks under Vicky's arm could still be described by that 1946 study. Females are still inadequately represented on their pages; even male animals outnumber female animals, 2 to 1. And women and girls in school readers are still passive, helpless, uncreative, incompetent in most respects, incapable of earning money or dealing with moral issues, overly concerned with looks, and destined to spend their lives in domestic servitude (Women on Words and Images, 1972).

At this writing, though, changes are finally taking place. Just as publishers a few years back made concerted efforts to rid their books of noxious racial stereotypes and to give various racial and ethnic groups their rightful place in children's readers, so today one publisher after another is revamping its schoolbooks to eliminate sex stereotyping.

The Child in the Family

"I'm home!" shouts Vicky as she bursts in the door, cheeks glowing from the cold and snow cascading from hat, mittens, and boots. She tries—she honestly does try—to take off all her dripping clothes before she reaches the new rug, but, bursting with news of the day to share with whoever's home, it isn't always possible to remember such trivia.

On this sunny day, with snow glistening on trees and telephone poles, Vicky has trudged her way to and from school, been pelted by a few snowballs in the morning and pelted back a few in the afternoon. Stepping into the house only long enough to stoke up her internal fires, changing to dry clothes, and going out again to play in the snow, it seems as if she is away from the bosom of her family more than she is within it. And yet during these busy middle years, Vicky's parents continue to exert an important influence on her personality and general development. Their attitudes and their styles of child rearing, set long before Vicky's first day of school, continue to affect all the children in the family.

While our discussions of development in infancy and the preschool years stressed the role of the mother, it is during middle childhood that the father's role appears to assume much more significance. Much research on family relationships with children in this age range focuses on the father's role, often as defined by his absence.

HOW CHILDREN VIEW THEIR PARENTS

Coopersmith (1967) was able to etch a detailed picture of the families of his high-esteem boys. In these homes, parental interest and affection runs through the fabric of everyday life. These parents know their children's friends, they are available in times of distress and discomfort, and they do things with their children. They are fairly strict, present many comprehensive demands which they enforce, largely through encouragement of desired behavior. When they do punish, they are more likely to isolate or take away privileges instead of spank or withdraw love from their children. They treat their children with respect and give them more rights and privileges as they mature and gain competence; they tolerate contrary and independent opinions from children; and they give youngsters a voice in planning and decision making. Their children consider them fair and reasonable, even in those instances when they might not appear so to an outsider.

Very often it is the way that children view their parents, as much as the parents' actual behavior and attitudes, that affects the children most strongly. Many studies have asked children, in a variety of ways, to indicate the way they regard their parents. Young children tend to fear their fathers more than their mothers and to see them as more punitive, more dominating, and less nurturant (Kagan, 1956; Kagan & Lemkin, 1960), but children over ten usually consider their same-sex parent as the most punitive one (Coopersmith, 1967). This may bespeak a greater rivalry with the parent of the same sex or may reflect more handling and disciplining by that parent.

In one study (Kagan et al., 1961), ninety-eight boys and girls six to eight years old were given tests designed to assess their perceptions of their parents and themselves, on a variety of symbolic dimensions. Problems were posed to the children relating to size, strength, nurturance, competence, punitiveness, dangerousness, dirtiness, darkness, coldness, meanness, and angularity; the children were asked to relate these concepts to their fathers, their mothers, or themselves. Both boys and girls conceptualized themselves as closer to the same-sex parent and characterized their fathers as "stronger, larger, darker, more dirty, more angular, and more dangerous [p. 635]" than their mothers.

Since adults and children in other cultures also characterize men and women similarly, and since children develop these attitudes by the time

(Mimi Forsyth, Monkmeyer)

Very often it is the way that children view their parents, as much as the parents' actual behavior and attitudes, that affect the children most strongly.

they are five or six years old, some factor outside the immediate family must be at work. After all, not all fathers are stronger, larger, dirtier, and more menacing than their wives; yet most children see them so. In western culture, the media help to confirm and communicate these views; it is possible that once a child has learned that his culture considers certain characteristics as masculine that he will then perceive his own father in these terms—whether or not his father actually fits the description.

Do children from different social classes view their parents differently? Apparently so, and especially as regards their fathers. The children's views reflect class differences in the ways their parents treat them (Rosen, 1964). Middle-class parents tend to be more tolerant of children's needs, more likely to take into account motives and intentions, more accepting and equalitarian, and more likely to correct their children by reasoning with them or appealing to their conscience, rather than hitting them. Lower-class parents tend to be more rigid and authoritarian and less accessible to their children. This is especially notable regarding fathers. The lower-class father's only role in child rearing, aside from financial support, is often as the agent of punishment, whereas the middle-class father is more of a companion, more involved in the daily life of his children.

When 367 lower-class and middle-class boys nine to eleven years old answered a structured questionnaire, definite class differences showed up in their answers (Rosen, 1964). The middle-class youths saw their parents as more able and more ambitious, and their fathers as more secure. The greatest difference, though, was in the ways the boys perceived their parents'—and especially their fathers'—acceptance and support of them. The middle-class boys were much more likely to feel their fathers were interested in their school performance and were meeting their requests for attention.

THE ONE-PARENT FAMILY

One out of every ten children in the United States today is growing up in a home with only one parent, and in some low-income black neighborhoods the percentage jumps to one child out of two (Biller, 1970). In about seven out of eight of these one-parent homes, the absent parent is the father; there are only about 600,000 father-only homes across the nation, compared to 4 or 5 million mother-only homes (LeMasters, 1970). How does growing up with only one parent affect children? It is hard to say. Practically no research has been done on the motherless family, and the voluminous research on the fatherless family is often contradictory.

The classic view (supported by some research and unsupported by other) is that long-term absence of the father affects children's psychological functioning adversely, with especially devastating effects on their sexual identification and functioning.

In an overview of the research on the effects of father absence on the personality of boys, Biller (1970) touches base with most of the points that have received investigative attention. According to the studies he cites, father-absent boys have more trouble achieving a strong masculine identity, especially if their fathers have been away during the boys' preschool years, because they have not been able to identify with their fathers. It is harder for them to control their impulses and accept delayed, rather than immediate, gratification, because they have not learned to trust other people, especially adult males. They're more likely to become delinquent. They score lower on tests of intelligence and academic achievement. They have more trouble making friends in childhood and developing long-term relationships with women later in life. They are more anxious and more likely to suffer a variety of emotional problems. And they are not so highly motivated to achieve, and, in fact, do not achieve as much career success as do men whose fathers had been present during their childhood.

But Biller and others (Herzog & Sudia, 1968) point out some of the problems of taking these conclusions at face value. Many of the studies on fatherlessness have severe methodological deficiencies. Often they do not specify the age of the child during the father's absence, the length of absence, the sex of the child, or the reasons for the absence (death, divorce, separation, illegitimacy, long business trips, etc.). Often the samples of children studied are so small as to preclude any generalization. After reviewing some 400 studies of children from fatherless homes, Herzog and

Sudia (1968) concluded "Existing data do not permit a decisive answer to questions about the effects on children of fatherlessness [p. 181]."

Children growing up in one-parent homes undoubtedly have more problems and more adjustments to make than children growing up in homes where there are two adults to share the responsibilities for child rearing, to provide a higher financial base raising a family, to more closely approximate cultural expectations of the "ideal family," and to offer a counterpoint of sex-role models and an interplay of personalities. But the two-parent home is not always ideal, and the one-parent home not necessarily pathological. In many societies, more than two adults play an active role in bringing up children; in those societies our two-parent nuclear family would be abnormal. While fatherless families are, on the average, poorer than two-parent families, this is more a reflection of our economic and social structure, rather than an indictment of the families themselves. In the United States today, men usually have greater earning power, women are usually expected to stay home and care for children, and the community takes virtually no responsibility for caring for the children of working mothers.

> It is obvious to any clinician that the two-parent system has its own pathology—the two parents may be in serious conflict as to how their parental roles should be performed; one parent may be competent but have his (or her) efforts undermined by the incompetent partner; the children may be caught in a "double bind" or crossfire between the two parents; both parents may be competent but simply unable to work together as an effective team in rearing their children; one parent may be more competent than the other but be inhibited in using this competence by the team pattern inherent in the two-parent system [LeMasters, 1970, p. 163].

Among a group of divorced women, one commonly cited advantage was the ability to raise one's children without having to cope with a spouse who disagrees with the day-to-day decisions about the children (LeMasters, 1970). Other research has concluded that the attitudes of a single parent are more important in determining the sexual attitudes of children than is the fact of single parenthood itself, that children of unwed mothers are no more likely to be emotionally disturbed than children with fathers (Klein, 1973), and that, in general, children grow up better adjusted when they have a good relationship with one parent than when they grow up in a two-parent home characterized by discord and discontent (Rutter, 1971).

Apparently this attitude is gaining ground, as shown by the growing tendency of adoption agencies, traditionally conservative institutions, to place children with unmarried adults. Perhaps the agencies are coming to realize that many eminently successful people have been raised by widows or widowers, by parents whose partners had deserted them and their children, and by mothers who never did marry the fathers of their children (Goertzel & Goertzel, 1962).

(Magnum)

The classic view is that long-term absence of the father affects children adversely, with devastating effects on their sexual identification.

To understand better how single-parent homes differ and how they affect children, it would be well to try to find answers to the following questions: How do tense, angry, unhappy intact homes compare with happy, well-ordered one-parent homes? How do the parents in successful one-parent homes differ from those whose children have more problems? What are the strengths of one-parent homes? How are they similar to, as well as different from, two-parent homes? Who are the role-models who substitute for absent parents and how effective are they? What are the differential effects of the timing and the reasons for parental absences? How do well-adjusted one-parent children differ from poorly adjusted ones and what might account for these differences?

CHILDREN OF DIVORCE

More than 6 million children in the United States today are experiencing the effects of their parents' decision to untie the marriage knot, a decision that occurs in one out of three marriages (McDermott, 1970; Sugar, 1970). Divorce is a traumatic event for everyone in the family. The final dissolution of a marriage stirs up powerful emotions of anger, hate, bitter disappointment, failure, and self-doubt in the husband and wife. And the children of the union react to the break-up of their parents' marriage even more severely than they would react to the death of a parent, as seen in the fact that children from homes broken by discord are more likely to get into trouble than those in homes broken by death (Rutter, 1971). They feel afraid of the future, guilty for their own (usually imaginary) role in causing the divorce, hurt at the rejection they feel from the parent who does not remain with them, and angry at both parents for making a shambles of their world. They may become depressed, hostile, disruptive, irritable, lonely, sad, accident-prone, or even suicidal; they may suffer from fatigue, insomnia, skin disorders, loss of appetite, or inability to concentrate; and they often lose interest in school work and in social life, partly because of shame and embarrassment (Sugar, 1970; McDermott, 1970).

The way a child reacts to parental divorce is affected by the youngster's sex, the age at the time of the break, the length of time the marriage is in serious difficulty, and the duration between the first separation and the formal divorce (Sugar, 1970). Probably the most important factor in determining how well the children will deal with this traumatic event in their lives is how well the parents deal with their children's sensitivities, fears, and anxieties. A husband and wife who engage in long drawn-out custody fights, who communicate their bitterness at each other through their children, who transfer their anger at their spouses to the children, and who suddenly impose adult responsibilities on them are exacerbating the problems that already exist.

The egocentrism of children often makes them feel as if they have caused the difficulties between their parents. One boy, for instance, knew intellectually that his parents were arguing because of his father's infidelity; yet he could not help feeling that if he had not broken a dish that day, the argument might not have taken place (McDermott, 1970). One of the most important tasks facing divorcing parents is the need to reassure their children that they are not responsible for their parents' breakup. Parents can also help their children by reestablishing a regular routine in the children's lives, by finding adults who can help fill the gap caused by the absence of one parent, and by not forcing the children to take sides between mother and father.

It is the emotional divorce, rather than the legal divorce that is hardest on children. And the emotional divorce—the divisiveness and discord between husband and wife—may go on for years in a legally intact marriage. While a divorce formalizes the problems in a marriage, it often creates a more harmonious home environment for the child and eases the relationship between parents and children. The initial break is always painful, but many children thrive in the atmosphere of hope for a better life that follows the end of a troubled marriage.

THE MOTHER WHO WORKS OUTSIDE THE HOME
One day, when Vicky was five, she and her mother were walking along, hand in hand, having one of those close moments that, thought Vicky's

mother, make parenthood so soul-satisfying. Out of the companionable silence, in utter love and admiration, Vicky turned to her mother and said, "When I grow up, I want to be nothing—just like you."

Was it this conversation that made Vicky's mother resolve to find employment outside the home once Vicky started school? Or was it a host of other factors that makes the time after the youngest child goes to school all day the most popular one for women to leave hearth and home for office or factory?

Which Mothers Work?

In our society, many factors mitigate against a woman's going out of the house to work while her children are babies or preschoolers. The children's needs during these years are great, and good day care is hard to find. When it is available, its cost often negates the second income. Also, many women find a sense of fulfillment in meeting the needs of very young children, but feel somewhat unnecessary once the children are away from the home six or more hours out of every weekday. So, while a third of all mothers with at least one child under six were in the labor force in 1970, this figure jumped to more than half of all mothers of six- to seventeen-year-old children (U.S. Dept of Labor, 1972). With a change in the social climate and increasing pressure for more and better day care, this difference may not continue to be so large. Already, the labor force participation rates of mothers of preschoolers have risen more rapidly than that of other mothers, jumping 60 percent during the 1960s, compared with a rise of 20 percent for other mothers (Waldman & Gover, 1971).

Because of more pressing financial needs and different vocational and sex-role expectations in the black community, black women are more likely to work than white women. In 1969, 73 percent of black mothers of children under eighteen and 58 percent of mothers of children under three were employed outside the home at some time throughout the year.

The fewer children a woman has, the older they are, the lower her husband's income, the higher her own education and the higher the market value of her employment skills—the more likely she is to seek a job (Howell, 1973a). Furthermore, millions of women are the sole support of themselves and their children. Most women work because they need the money, although many women in the higher-income brackets work less for the income than for the gratification they derive from using their abilities productively.

How Does a Mother's Outside Employment Affect Her Children?

Many studies have sought answers to this question, and a great deal has been written about the topic, often with no reference to any evidence other than the writer's own prejudices. Some of the problems that have dogged these inquiries have been bias on the part of investigators who sought to justify their own life-styles (often male researchers whose own wives did not work or female researchers who themselves were working mothers), the failure to take into account other factors that might affect both the mother's decision to seek employment and any problems of the children (such as financial or marital difficulties), a tendency to study families already identified as troubled, variable definitions of "maternal employment," and so forth. Also, research findings about children of abandoning, neglectful, depriving, or even dead mothers have been unjustifiably generalized to the children of working mothers (Howell, 1973b).

Today most investigators of maternal employment would probably agree with this statement (Howell, 1973b):

> Since parenting ability may be either enhanced or hindered by employment, it is not surprising that almost every childhood behavior characteristic, and its opposite, can be found among the children of employed mothers. Put another way, there are almost no constant differences found between the children of employed and nonemployed mothers; in general the more careful the methodology of a study, the smaller the differences found [p. 328].

Many observers feel that the timing of a woman's taking on a new job may affect her children adversely. All other things being equal, it is generally best if she can avoid going to work for the first time during the third quarter of her baby's first year, when mother-child attachments are being cemented, around the baby's second birthday, a crucial time for the development of language, and any time when a child has other major adjustments to make, such as the loss of a father through death or divorce, the move to a new home, the birth of a sibling, school entrance, and the like (Howell, 1973b).

On the other hand, maternal employment itself may have salutory effects. Children of employed mothers are more open in their sex-role views and have higher educational and career aspirations, and the daughters of employed mothers are more likely to select careers for themselves in traditionally male fields (Etaugh, 1973). And a study of 108 children of working mothers in an urban black ghetto found that the mothers who worked full-time were most consistent in disciplining in their children, who in turn were better adjusted, had higher IQs, and did better in school than the children of mothers who worked occasionally or parttime (Woods, 1972).

By most parameters, though, the families of women who earn a salary do not differ in any psychologically important way from those who engage in the work of homemaking. Neither group is more likely to undergo divorce. Their children do not differ with respect to peer relationships, school grades, IQ, emotional problems, or the dependency or independence of their behavior (Howell, 1973b).

In sum, the healthy development of children rests on the quality of the care they receive, and not the quantity of that care that is given by their own mothers. Whether the mother works outside the home or in it is less important than whether she enjoys what she is doing. Women who like their lives are more likely to communicate a sense of joy to their children, who, as a result, are likely to be better adjusted (Skard, 1965).

CROSS-CULTURAL PERSPECTIVES

In the novel *Anna Karenina* Leo Tolstoy writes, "All happy families are alike, but every unhappy one is unhappy in its own way." This sentence has a fine poetic ring to it but leaves much to be desired as social commentary. The role of the family differs from culture to culture, and even among subgroups within the same larger society. As practitioners of the new science of *family therapy* (in which an entire family, rather than a single member, is the patient) are beginning to learn, every family has its own dynamics. Then, when we recognize that the nuclear family is only one of a number of diverse family structures, we realize that it is virtually impossible even to define what a family is.

One classic definition of a family is

> a social group characterized by common residence, economic cooperation, and reproduction. It includes adults of both sexes, at least two of whom maintain a socially approved sexual relationship, and one or more children, own or adopted, of the sexually cohabiting adults [Murdock; cited in Spiro, 1954, in Skolnick & Skolnick, 1971].

If we were to accept this definition, we would have to exclude all the following as families: parents and children on the Israeli kibbutz, because they neither share a common residence nor divide the work among the family as such; childless couples; homosexual couples, no matter how long they have lived together; and a single parent with a child. Yet each of these excluded groupings would consider itself a family. Instead of being audacious enough to define what a family is, for all time and in all places, we'll look at various family structures and the way their members feel about them.

Most families are organized in some way around parents and their children. Some are *nuclear*, consisting of a man and a woman and their children; others are *extended*, including the above plus an assortment of grandparents, aunts, uncles, and cousins. *Patrilinear* families are organized around the father's lineage; *matrilinear* ones establish relationship through the maternal line. Families may be *monogamous*, with husband and wife staying together "till death do us part"; others are *polygamous*, characterized by multiple wives or husbands; and some could be described as *serial monogamy*, by which one man and one woman stay together until one or the other wants to dissolve the marriage, at which time both are free to form a new union.

The meaning that each family holds for the lives of its members differs, with either the emotional, the economic, or the child-rearing aspect coming to the fore. And, of course, within these structural divisions, the personalities of the individuals involved make every family unique. Let us take a look at some different family structures, especially as they relate to child-rearing and child welfare.

The Kibbutz

One of the strongest ideals of the founders of Israel was the equality between man and woman and their common goals in building a new state. Recognizing that women could never be free to shoulder their share of the work if they were confined by the duties of motherhood, the pioneers evolved a communal system for bringing up children. Husband and wife would live together in a room or an apartment with other adults, and all the children of the kibbutz would live together in a succession of children's houses. Under the direction of the kibbutz, specially trained persons would care for the children, inculcate them with values, educate them, and train them for work. Parents and children would visit with each other for two hours every day and on the Sabbath.

The parents' chief responsibility, then, is to provide their children with an emotional relationship. Some observers feel that since the parents do not have to teach, correct, and, inevitably, thwart their children, their love and affection will be untempered, and they become even closer to their children than do Western nuclear parents (Spiro, 1954; Talmon-Garber, 1954). On the other hand, Bettelheim (1969) sees some ambivalences in the relationship, whereby parents usually take their vacations without their children, keep from them any major family problems so as not to spoil their daily visits, and therefore avoid intense intimacy.

In any case, children seem to fare well in either setting. While some studies show kibbutz children to be more cooperative and more mature (Shapira & Madsen, 1974; Goldman, 1971), most of the research between kibbutz and nonkibbutz children reveals few or no differences between them in physical, intellectual, or personality development (Kraft, 1966; Kohen-Ray, 1968). And Kraft (1966) sums up the situation this way:

> By all means, we should be reassured. For, on the basis of the kibbutz experience, the conclusion seems to be that if a child is brought up in a humane and stable environment infused with love, tenderness, respect for work, and enlightened moral standards, then the basic product will be unspectacular but sound, irrespective of even major differences in child-rearing method [p. 197].

The Contemporary American Commune

They have mellifluous, exotic names like Morning Star, Raspberry, Rama Krishna, Oran. They enter this world in the presence of a throng of joyful adults and children. They are used to running around unfettered by clothing and are comfortable in the midst of adult nudity. They are the children growing up in the hundreds of *communes*, or "intentional communities," that have sprung up over the past several years across the United States, and especially on the west coast.

How are they faring? While it's too early to assess fully the effects of growing up in this branch of the counterculture, several observers from the fields of sociology, psychology, and medicine have drawn fairly sanguine conclusions about these youngsters.

Communes are made up of several adults and children who live cooperatively in pursuit of joint social goals. They vary widely as to family structure, economic organization and viability, drug use, religious orientation, and turnover. Most live as extended families, and adults may appeal to unrelated children to settle their quarrels with each other by saying things like "Janey is your sister, don't abuse her [Berger et al., 1971]." In some of the communes, men and women, either formally married or not, and their children are considered a family unit within the larger family; in some a woman will deliberately have sexual relations with several men so that no one of them can claim exclusive paternity; in many, all the adults consider themselves the parents of all the children.

This last attitude can sometimes produce ambiguity, as in one case when a man was sitting at the dinner table feeding a four-year-old girl on his lap. "The man was berating the mother for interfering with him and the child 'doing a dinner thing' together—suggesting that the 'mother' in this instance had no special rights over her child [Berger et al., 1971]." There are no specially designated caretakers, and the children usually spend most of their time with their own parents (Copans, 1972).

The major importance of communes may not be as a permanent lifestyle, but as an influence upon our dominant lifestyle, the nuclear family.

(H. Kubota, Magnum)

In most communes, the division of labor seems to fall along sex lines, with women milking the goats and doing the cooking and the men doing the heavy labor. In some, the communards are making concerted efforts to overturn sex-role stereotyping and to divide work along less traditional lines. In either case, the commune children have many role models, both male and female. Johnston and Deisher (1973) found that "where the status of women was significantly below that of the men, the status of children was consistently low [p. 323]."

The communards generally express a strong desire to raise their children free of many of the "hang-ups" they grew up with, and they make many conscious efforts along these lines. They tend to respect the feelings and opinions of children, sometimes giving them considerable responsibility at an early age and sometimes giving them the freedom not to conform to certain group routines, like daily meditation. Some communes run their own schools; some send their children to the closest public schools. Nutrition can be very good—with emphasis placed on "health" foods, organic farming, and lengthy breast feeding—or it can be deficient, reflecting marginal economic conditions, ideological adherence to an unsound diet, or parental irresponsibility.

Most observers are concerned about the effects of the constant comings and goings of commune members on the children. How do they cope with a turnover of some 20 to 80 percent? Johnston and Deisher (1973) conclude:

> Where the parental bond is not close and the stability of the individual parents is questionable, the existence of a high turnover rate correlates with children exhibiting directionlessness and apathy in their attitude and above average level of hostility in their behavior. Where the parental relationship is nurtural and secure, this dissolving of bonds appears to be experienced by the child as positive stimulation. Where the parental bond is not close, yet the relationships within the group are close and moderately stable, the child's source of security can be strong [pp. 322–323].

Or, put another way, in the words of one communard, "But we're not trying to teach our children attachment. . . . We're trying to teach them non-attachment [Copans, 1972, p. 20]."

At this time, it is impossible to draw conclusions about the degree to which these communes meet the needs of children, since almost all the communes under study had been in existence only from 6 months to 5 years at the time of observation. (In the kibbutzim, the third generation is now growing up.) It is possible that the major importance of such communes will not be as a permanent life-style, but as an influence upon the dominant life-style in this country, the nuclear family.

The Soviet Union
In its efforts to create a new socialist being, the Russians have emphasized social and collective child-rearing, combined with strong family involve-

ment. Family and school alike share in the upbringing of children. Anton Semyonovich Makarenko, one of the most important Russian educators and moralists, has had a strong influence on Soviet thinking. Of particular importance is his belief that parental authority over children is delegated by the state and that parental duties represent only one aspect of one's duties toward the state. When family values and needs conflict with those of society, it is society's values and needs that usually win out (Bronfenbrenner, 1962).

Makarenko's principal thesis about optimal personality development is that it can occur only through productive activity in a social collective. The first collective is the family, but this must be supplemented early in life by other collectives specially organized in schools, neighborhoods, and other community settings. The primary function of the collective is to develop socialist morality. This aim is accomplished through an explicit regimen of activity mediated by group criticism, self-criticism, and group-oriented punishments and rewards [p. 55].

While the Soviet Union has avowed its plans to make collective child rearing a possibility by setting up communal kitchens, dining halls, and laundries, and a network of children's homes and day nurseries, this intention, for the most part, is still unfulfilled (Geiger, 1968). Almost all Russian children are being raised at home and at school, much as in the American pattern, instead of according to the "ideal" collective system (Kraft, 1966). Most of the job of raising children still falls to the mother, and in Russia her burden is heavy indeed, since she is expected, even exhorted, to work outside the home and since it is the rare Soviet man who helps out with the children or the housework (Field & Flynn, 1968).

Vietnam

Just as families assume different structures in different societies, so do they perform different roles for their members. One study of Vietnamese and American children helps us to understand better what these children's families mean to them and how they prepare them for life in their respective societies.

Leichty (1963) gave sixty American children (nine to eleven years old) and forty-seven Vietnamese children (nine to fifteen years old) a sentence-completion test about their attitudes toward family and friends, their emotions, and their thoughts about the future. From their answers, two very different concepts of family emerge.

Vietnamese children see their family as the core of life—a life that revolves around work. The Vietnamese youngster feels that he owes his parents a debt of gratitude, a debt he can repay by assuming a responsible role in the family. In the relatively simple and set society of Vietnam, children are brought up to worship ancestors, to accept authority without question (especially the authority of the father), and to honor the unity of the family.

Vietnamese children see their family as the core of a life that revolves around work. By contrast, the American child's future is virtually open-ended.

By contrast, the American child's role in society is much less clearly delineated. The child's future is virtually open-ended. In preparation for this, they are much less dependent on their parents, less close with them, far freer to criticize and express negative feelings toward them, and much less likely to consider their parents' word as final. Along with these relatively independent attitudes go a weakening of family ties and a somewhat self-centered view of family life (Leichty, 1963):

[The American children's] relationships with their parents, in fact their outlook on life, revolves about themselves. Happiness is achieved by getting or having something material, something for the child himself. The father is the agent for doing something for the child, for giving him something. The mother goes somewhere or does something with the child, participates in the child's activities [p. 48].

Whereas work is the center of the Vietnamese child's life, recreation seems to be the dominant theme in the American child's existence. Leichty says, "These two groups of children seem to be growing up into quite different kinds of people [p. 49]." The values of their societies are reflected in the values of their families, which in turn are reflected in the goals and attitudes of the children themselves.

Essentially, then, what it comes down to is that children are reared according to the goals and values of the society they happen to live in. Children who are raised communally seem to have much easier and closer relationships with their peers but are less likely to have intense, intimate relationships with their families. It would be impossible to say that there is a single right way to raise children to be well-adjusted members of the community. It all depends on what the community is like, and on what kinds of citizens it wants to produce.

Summary

1   The middle child is in Freud's *latency stage*, a period of relative sexual quiescence compared to the stormier preschool and adolescent periods. However, children maintain interest in sexual functioning and masturbate, engage in bodily explorations of each other, and talk about sexual matters. *Defense mechanisms* are used by the school-age child to combat anxiety; these include *regression*, *repression*, *sublimation*, *projection*, and *reaction formation*.

2   Industry versus inferiority is the fourth of Erikson's eight developmental crises. Children learn those skills necessary for survival in their particular culture and face a sense of inferiority if they are much less successful in this pursuit than are their peers.

3   *Childhood societies* exist in all cultures and throughout all recorded history. Older children pass down traditional lores, rhymes, humor, and games to younger children.

4   The *peer group* assumes an important role during middle childhood, since a child spends more and more time away from the family and in the company of friends. The peer group is important in the development of identity, attitudes, and values, and as a socializing agent. The influence of the group is powerful, and a child's position in the group greatly influences self-concept. Adults also influence a child's standing in the group. In some cultures, such as Russia and Israel, the peer group has been used to carry out the goals of society. *Behavior modification* programs in American classrooms also might enlist the peer group to improve children's behaviors.

5   *Self-concept* refers to one's self-image. Coopersmith isolated four factors that influence self-concept development: *significance*, *competence*, *virtue*, and *power*. The higher an individual rates on all four variables, the higher the self-regard. Self-concept is influenced by parental characteristics, early birth order, small family size, school success, and personality traits.

6   Sex typing becomes more stable during the school years. Extra-family influences such as the school and textbooks are powerful in establishing sex typing.

Although a child spends a great deal of time with peers, the family still is an important influence. Children grow up in a variety of family situations —in homes with one or two parents, with mothers who work in or outside the home, in a nuclear family, in a kibbutz, or commune. In any of these home situations, an atmosphere of love, support, and respect for family members will provide an excellent prognosis for healthy development.

Suggested Readings

Avedon, E. M., & Sutton-Smith, B. *The Study of Games.* New York: Wiley, 1973. *A collection of game phenomena from the fields of anthropology, folklore, history, psychology, sociology, social psychology, medicine, psychiatry, military science, education, business and industry, and recreation. This book includes readings of representative fields of inquiry, many of which have not been generally available, and offers selected references from each field, indicating what material has been covered and what has yet to be touched.* The Study of Games *discusses history and origins, uses, and structure and function of games.*

Baughman, E. E. *Black Americans.* New York: Academic, 1971. *A readable and fair-minded report about black people in society today. It presents and discusses research findings about intelligence, school achievement, family styles, self-esteem, and psychopathology.*

Bettelheim, B. *The Children of the Dream.* New York: Avon, 1969. *A thorough study of communal child rearing in Israel. Babies are separated from their mothers at five days, weaned at six months, and raised in the kibbutz through adolescence. This book discusses both the strengths and weaknesses of this system and the possible future it has for ghetto children.*

Bronfenbrenner, V. *Two Worlds of Childhood: U.S. and U.S.S.R.* New York: Russell Sage Foundation, 1970. *A comparative study of child-rearing methods of the United States and the Soviet Union.*

Coopersmith, S. *Antecedents of Self-esteem.* San Francisco: Freeman, 1967. *A thorough and thought-provoking report of an in-depth study of eighty-five boys, ten to twelve years old, which correlated the boys' levels of self-esteem with parental attitudes and child-rearing practices, and with other aspects of the boys' functioning.*

Elkind, D. *A Sympathetic Understanding of the Child Six to Sixteen.* Boston: Allyn and Bacon, 1971. *A brief and informal discussion of some of the major aspects of child and adolescent development, dealing with such topics as children in school and the effects of sociocultural change upon children.*

Elkind, F., & Handel, G. *The Child and Society: The Process of Socialization.* New York: Random House, 1972. *A brief treatment, from a sociological viewpoint, of the ways children are socialized into modern society. It includes material on anthropology, human development, political science, psychiatry, psychology, and sociology.*

Eron, L. D., Walker, L. Q., & Lefkowitz, M. M. *Learning of Aggression in Children.* Boston: Little, Brown, 1971. *A detailed report of the guiding theory, methods, and results of a four-year field research program begun in 1955 to study the origin and maintenance of aggressive behavior in children.*

Skolnick, A., & Skolnick, J. H. *Intimacy, Family and Society.* Boston: Little, Brown, 1974. *A collection of readings that emphasize personal experience and interpersonal relations in the family.*

Steinzor, B. *When Parents Divorce: A New Approach to New Relationships.* New York: Pantheon, 1969. *A psychologist and family counselor provides an examination of marriage and divorce that includes practical sections on dealing with the legal and family problems of separation, child support, and remarrying.*

PART FIVE
ADOLESCENCE
Ages Twelve to Eighteen

The next two chapters offer us our last look at Vicky, who is now launched into adolescence. We see her as a girl-woman who has left childhood behind but has not yet reached adulthood. She looks different, as her figure changes with the hormonal events of puberty. She thinks differently, as she is better able to deal with abstractions and with what *might* be, instead of only what *is*. And she feels differently about almost everything.

Vicky will be an adolescent for a long time, compared with her counterparts in other places and at other times. Boys and girls today reach physical maturity sooner than they used to, and young people in a complex society that demands long years of schooling remain dependent on their parents for a longer time than do youths in simpler, more stable societies.

Adolescence is a relatively uncomplicated phenomenon in simple cultures where young people undergo a briefer transition period, assume adult responsibilities at an early age, and know from early childhood what the future will hold for them. But in our society, the passage from childhood to adulthood is amorphous and marked by no one *rite de passage.* No one will tell Vicky, ''You are now an adult.'' She has to force herself to become one and has to decide when indeed she has reached adult status. As she makes her way to womanhood, she often feels as if she is neither fish nor fowl, neither little girl nor mature woman. And in truth she is not. For the beginnings of adolescence and the beginnings of adulthood are both marked by a bewildering succession of physical, psychological, and cultural guideposts. One may pass one, two, three—but how does one know when one has passed them all?

The major task of adolescence is the establishment of adult identity. While Vicky emerged as a distinct and unique personality during the middle years, she was, nevertheless, still a child. Now she must establish herself as an adult. She becomes preoccupied with herself and with the ways that others perceive her. She blossoms into a sexual person, sometimes developing longings before her body is ready for them, sometimes remaining a child inside the body of a woman. She becomes absorbed with finding her own value systems and debates philosophical issues far into the night.

To find themselves in a society like ours that values individuality and change, adolescents often feel as if they must ''lose'' their parents. They chafe at the links between generations, seeing them not as a helpful guide but as a restraint. They must prove to themselves and to the world that they are their own persons and not just the latest version of their forebears. And yet not all do; some adolescents seem to cross the bridge to adulthood as easily as the Samoan girl or the Arapesh boy, as they accept the values of their parents and quietly pursue their own socially approved goals. These latter youths may even be in the majority, although it rarely seems so.

Adolescence can be an exciting time of life—if one is healthy enough to enjoy it, if one's sense of self-esteem is sturdy enough to withstand onslaughts ranging from acne to late development, if one has enough money to keep up with the latest fads, if one has had a good enough education to be able to look forward to a fulfilling career, and if one has grown up with the love that enables one to form relationships of love and friendship.

CHAPTER THIRTEEN
PHYSICAL AND MENTAL DEVELOPMENT

IN WHICH VICKY ENTERS THE PHYSICAL AND
INTELLECTUAL WORLD OF ADOLESCENCE

I saw the world today
I didn't know what to say.
                    (15-year-old girl)

The list shown on page 538 was found in Vicky's room on December 31, ten days after her twelfth birthday. It is reproduced verbatim.

The list itself is a microcosm of Vicky's life these days. While she has always been a social creature, her relationships with other people have now become more intense. Her best girl friend (item 1) is her constant confidante, and her boyfriend (item 5—whose name she won't even commit to paper, for fear of discovery) has changed her feelings about herself and intensified her interest in how she looks (items 3 and 7). She continues to work on increasing her competence in areas of special interest (item 6). Her intellectual powers are expanding to enable her to handle abstract concepts with new understanding (item 2). While she spends more time with her friends these days, her family still plays a central role in her life (items 8 and 10. Her superego is stronger, prodding her to perform socially expected tasks (items 4, 7, and 10). And yet she's still a kid. A free

Thursday, January 2 — First Day of School This Year

1. Bring Christmas present to Carol

2. Finish report on Aztecs' philosophy of death

3. Wear new red & white blouse & blue pants (maybe blue vest)

4. Thank Aunt Grace for $5.00

5. Find photo to give to D.N.

6. Gymnastics practice after school

7. Sew t-shirt (underarm)

8. Make cake for Mom's birthday

9. Take birthday card from ice cream store — get free cone

10. Shovel front path if it snows (surprise Daddy!!)

11. Watch "Horse Feathers" (Marx Brothers) — 8:00 P.M.

ice cream cone and a Marx Brothers movie still matter (items 9 and 11). The child/woman Vicky balances precariously on the threshold of adolescence.

What Is Adolescence?

Adolescence is the span of years between childhood and adulthood. Derived from the Latin word that means "to grow into maturity," it covers, in Western society, the time from the age of twelve or thirteen till the early twenties. Its beginning is heralded by *pubescence,* that stage of rapid physiological growth when reproductive functions and primary sex organs mature, and the secondary sex characteristics appear. Pubescence lasts about two years and ends in *puberty,* the point at which an individual is sexually mature and able to reproduce.

The end of adolescence is not so easily demarcated, being a combination of physical, intellectual, sociological, legal, and psychological factors. In some societies, adolescence ends at puberty, when an individual has completed sexual development and is capable of bearing or siring children, even though full stature will not be reached for another few years. Cognitive maturity is reached when a person is capable of abstract thought, or what Piaget has called "formal operations." Sociological adulthood may be said to have been attained when an individual is self-supporting, or has chosen a career, or has married, or founded a family. Legal adulthood comes when one can vote (age eighteen), marry without parental permission (usually eighteen for girls, twenty-one for boys), enlist in the army (seventeen), or be responsible for legal contracts (twenty-one). Insurance companies do not consider young men as adults until the age of twenty-five, at which time they no longer have to pay "young driver" premiums for automobile insurance. In the movies, one is either an adult at twelve, when one pays adult admission fee, or at seventeen, when one can view X-rated movies. And in the psychological sense, adulthood is considered to be reached when one has dealt with these tasks of adolescence: discovering one's own identity, becoming independent from one's parents, developing one's own system of values, and becoming able to form mature, interdependent relationships of friendship and love. By this criterion, it is obvious that some people never become adults, no matter what their chronological age.

Adolescence, then, is a combination of the physiological and the cultural, and is a relatively recent phenomenon as we know it. Contemporary adolescence is longer than it has ever been before: young people mature earlier physically, and they become more sophisticated at earlier ages, therefore entering adolescence sooner. Then, because of the many years of education needed in our increasingly complex society, many of them remain dependent on their parents—at least, financially—into their 30s.

In many contemporary primitive societies, children still move abruptly from childhood to adulthood upon the attainment of some preordained age, or with girls, upon the advent of the first menstrual period. Puberty rites, or *rites de passage* from childhood to adulthood, take different forms in different cultures. At one extreme they range from extremely severe tests of strength and endurance, which may include such bodily mutilation as circumcision (of both boys and girls), teeth filing, ear piercing, or elaborate tattooing or scarring (Muuss, 1970). On the other hand, such rituals are often relatively painless ceremonies that involve religious blessings, separation from the family, or performing acts of magic (Muuss, 1968). The Jewish Bar Mitzvah for thirteen-year-old boys and the coming-out party for eighteen-year-old debutantes each mark one aspect of adult status, but these rituals seem to be celebrated by fewer and fewer young people today. While high school or college graduation, passing one's driving test, or losing one's virginity are all *rites de passage* of a sort, in our modern western society, no *one* initiation rite signifies adulthood. The distinction between childhood and adulthood remains fuzzy.

Theoretical Perspectives on Adolescence

Many theories have been advanced to try to explain the full significance of the physiological changes of adolescence and their attendant effects on an individual's functioning in other spheres of life.

G. STANLEY HALL

The first psychologist to formulate a theory of adolescence, Hall, in 1904, wrote a two-volume work called *Adolescence.* Hall's *biogenetic* thesis is that genetically determined physiological factors bring about psychological reactions. He conceived of adolescence as part of his larger theory of recapitulation, that "ontogeny recapitulates phylogeny," and that adolescence represents a turbulent, transitional stage for the human race. It was Hall who first saw adolescence as a period of *Sturm und Drang,* or "storm

Some psychologists see adolescence as a time of "storm and stress" brought about by physiological changes; others find teenagers already quite independent and emancipated.

(Sybil Shackman, Monkmeyer)

and stress.'' Muuss (1968) sums up Hall's view of adolescence as a period of vacillating, contradictory emotions:

Energy, exaltation, and supernatural activity are followed by indifference, lethargy, and loathing. Exuberant gaiety, laughter, and euphoria make place for dysphoria, depressive gloom, and melancholy. Egotism, vanity, and conceit are just as characteristic of this period of life as are abasement, humiliation, and bashfulness. One can observe both the remnants of an uninhibited childish selfishness and an increasing idealistic altruism. Goodness and virtue are never so pure, but never again does temptation so forcefully preoccupy thought. The adolescent wants solitude and seclusion, while he finds himself entangled in crushes and friendships. Never again does the peer group have such a strong influence over him. At one time, he may exhibit sensitivity and tenderness; at another time, callousness and cruelty. Apathy and inertia vacillate with an enthusiastic curiosity, an urge to discover and explore. There is a yearning for idols and authority that does not exclude a revolutionary radicalism directed against any kind of authority [p. 35].

MARGARET MEAD

In sharp contrast to Hall's view, anthropologists who have studied adolescence in cultures other than the western have found that adolescence as we know it is not a universal phenomenon, and that it is often remarkably free from the storm and stress that have impressed Hall and most other observers of adolescents.

Margaret Mead made a great contribution to this literature when, in the 1920s and 1930s, she studied adolescence in Samoa (1961) and in New Guinea (1953). While not denying the influence of biology, Mead pointed to the importance of cultural factors in development. When a culture decrees a serene and gradual transition from childhood to adulthood, as does Samoa, there is no storm and stress, but only an easy acceptance of the adult role. Mead (1961) says:

The adolescent girl in Samoa differed from her sister who had not reached puberty in one chief respect, that in the older girl certain bodily changes were present which were absent in the younger girl. There were no other great differences to set off the group passing through adolescence from the group which would become adolescent in two years or the group which had become adolescent two years before [p. 196].

In a society that permits young children to see adult sexual activity, to watch a baby being born, to become close to death, to have important work to do, to exercise assertive and even dominant behavior, to engage in sex play, and to know precisely what their adult roles will involve, adolescence is relatively free from stress. In societies like our own, however, which consider children very different from adults, which have completely different expectations from them, and which shelter them from much of adult life and responsibilities, the shift from childhood to adulthood is much more discontinuous, and, as a result, much more stressful. Physical factors underlie one's being called an adolescent, but how one's culture handles these physical changes determines the nature of the transition.

ALBERT BANDURA

Even in contemporary society, adolescence may not be so stormy as popular opinion would have us believe. Albert Bandura, a social learning theorist, challenges the notion that *Sturm und Drang* need be synonymous with modern western adolescence. In a study of middle-class adolescent boys and their families, Bandura and Walters (1959) found that these teen-age boys were already quite independent and emancipated from their parents by the time of adolescence. In recognition of the boys' capabilities, the parents were quite permissive and trustful of their teen-age sons. They approved of their sons' friends and imposed few limits or restrictions. For the most part, this parental trust was well-founded and was met by the boys' opinions of their parents as supportive, guiding influences whose help and advice they could—and did—freely seek.

The following interview excerpts are typical:

M[other]:   I don't have to do anything like that any more. I think he's getting so mature now, he's sort of happy medium. I don't have to do much with him.
I[interviewer]:   What are some of the restrictions you have for him? How about going out at night?
F[ather]:   We trust the boy. We never question him.
I: Are there any things you forbid him from doing when he is with his friends?
F: At this age I would hate to keep telling him that he mustn't do this, or mustn't do that. I have very little trouble with him in that regard. Forbidding I don't think creeps into it because he ought to know at 17, right from wrong [Bandura, 1964, p. 224].

I: What sort of things does your mother forbid you to do around the house?
B[oy]:   Forbid me to do? Gee, I don't think there's ever anything. The house is mine as much as theirs . . . Oh, can't whistle, can't throw paper up in the air, and can't play the radio and phonograph too loud. Rules of the house; anybody, I mean, it's not just me. . .
I: Are you expected to stay away from certain places or people?
B: She knows I do. I'm not expected; I mean, she figures I'm old enough to take care of myself now. They never tell me to stay away from or where. Well, I mean, they don't expect me to sleep down on Skid Row or something like that. . . . [Bandura, 1964, p. 224].

Whence, then, came this mythology of adolescence? According to Bandura, it arose partly from an overemphasis on superficial signs of conformity, especially adolescent fad behavior; and from the sensationalism of the mass media, which has put forth a picture of the disturbed

Anthropologists stress that how one's culture handles physical changes determines the nature of the transition.

adolescent (as in Salinger's book *Catcher in the Rye*) or the delinquent (as the character played by James Dean in the movie *Rebel without a Cause*) as the typical teenager. Other forces that may act as self-fulfilling prophecies are the psychoanalytic and other "stage" theories, which emphasize the discontinuity of development and promote "the view that adolescence represents a form of stage behavior that suddenly appears at pubescence, and as suddenly disappears when adulthood is achieved [Bandura, 1964, p. 30]."

If a society labels its adolescents as "teen-agers," and expects them to be rebellious, unpredictable, sloppy, and wild in their behavior, and if this picture is repeatedly reinforced by the mass media, such cultural expectations may very well force adolescents into the role of rebel. In this way, a false expectation may serve to instigate and maintain certain role behaviors, in turn, then reinforce the originally false belief [Bandura, 1964, p. 230].

SIGMUND FREUD

In Freud's psychosexual theory of development, the *genital stage*, or the stage of mature adult sexuality, is the keynote of adolescence. This is a reawakening of the sexual urges of the phallic stage, which are now directed in socially approved channels—heterosexual relations with people outside the family. Because of the physiological changes of sexual maturation, the adolescent can no longer repress sexuality as he did during the latency stage; his biological needs make this impossible. Freud's view that masturbation becomes more urgent during these years was borne out by Kinsey's study, which found that the highest frequency of masturbation occurred between the years of about thirteen to fifteen (Kinsey, 1948). But a more recent study of teen-agers (Sorensen, 1973) found that more older adolescents (sixteen to nineteen years) and more nonvirgins masturbate, than do thirteen- to fifteen-year-olds and virgins. Facts like these force us to take a new look at Freud's—and many others'—belief that masturbation characterizes immature sexuality. While all the infantile forms of sexuality have pure pleasure as their aim, the changes of puberty now make reproduction, and the search for a suitable reproductive partner, an important component of sexuality.

Freud felt that during adolescence a boy is most likely to fall in love with an older woman, and a girl an older man. These first loves manage to surmount the incest barrier, since they represent mother and father figures. During adolescence, young people have to free themselves from the dependency upon their parents so that they can form mature relationships with persons of the opposite sex.

Freud postulated that adolescents typically go through a homosexual stage, which may manifest itself by hero worship of an adult of the same sex or by a close chum relationship. According to Freud, such a relationship cannot be satisfying, and the adolescent shifts from this into normal heterosexual relationships. A too-close dependence on a friend of the same sex can prevent this shift, leading to adult homosexuality. Some contemporary observers feel that this shift need not necessarily take place and that individuals who exhibit homosexual leanings are only showing a variant of normal sexuality. Homosexuality is discussed in further detail in Chapter 14.

Another Freudian view that has recently become controversial involves the female shift in libido from the *clitoris*, the erectile organ that corresponds to the male penis, to the *vagina*, the opening that leads to the uterus. According to Freud, the mature woman obtains sexual pleasure only from vaginal orgasm. Recent research has indicated, however, that a large number of normal adult women gain sexual pleasure from clitoral stimulation (Masters & Johnson, 1969). Most contemporary students of sexuality believe that women need not "shift over" from one kind of orgasm to another to be considered mature.

In Freudian terms, the adolescent uses ego defense mechanisms like intellectualization to avoid being overwhelmed by instinctual urges.

While Freud's theories on adolescent development are more meager than his elaborately presented theories on childhood development, he did give a nod to some of the other tasks of adolescence—the achievement of adult identity in such respects as career, cultural values, and individual ethics.

ANNA FREUD

Sigmund Freud's daughter spent more time than did her father in outlining adolescent development and the defense mechanisms employed by adolescents in their struggles to curb their new-found sexual urges. Compared to her father, who held that an adult's personality was formed in the first five years of life, Anna Freud considered the adolescent years important for the formation of character.

According to her, the glandular changes of puberty that produce the physiological changes also affect psychological functioning. The *libido,* the basic energy that fuels the sex drive, is reawakened. Corresponding to the id, the libido threatens the id-ego balance that has been maintained during the latency years. Since id strivings are strong, the ego, which tries to find acceptable ways to gratify the id, clashes with the superego. This conflict causes a temporary regression, a second Oedipal conflict, with a recurrence of castration fears in boys and penis envy in girls. These disturbing feelings produce anxiety, call forth the old standby defenses of repression, denial, and displacement, and may cause fears, anxiety, and neurotic symptoms.

To avoid being overwhelmed by instinctual urges, the adolescent employs several ego defense mechanisms. One defense, that of *intellectualization,* can be seen, felt Freud, in the predilection of many adolescents to engage in all-night abstract discussions on topics like religion, politics, philosophy, or the meaning of life. While much of the meat of these "bull sessions" relates to the adolescent's search for identity and values, and reflects his greater ability to deal with abstract thought, Anna Freud (1946) considers such intellectualism a defense because

> The abstract intellectual discussions and speculations in which young people delight are not genuine attempts at solving the tasks set by reality. Their mental activity is rather an indication of a tense alertness for the instinctual processes and the translation into abstract thought of that which they perceive. The philosophy of life which they construct—it may be their demand for revolution in the outside world—is really their response to the perception of the new instinctual demands of their own id, which threaten to revolutionize their whole lives [pp. 177–178].

Another defense is *asceticism.* Because the adolescent is afraid of losing control over his impulses, he seizes on an ascetic approach to life, whereby he overcontrols himself. The renunciation of many activities is not uncommon at this age. Recent trends toward the wearing of drab, shapeless clothing, toward vegetarianism, and toward the renunciation of many simple pleasures as espoused by some currently popular religious sects may be modern manifestations of adolescent asceticism. Later in life, as individuals gain confidence in their ability to control their dangerous impulses, they tend to relax and to be less strict with themselves.

ERIK ERIKSON

Adolescence is the fifth in Erikson's eight ages of man. The crisis of adolescence involves identity versus role confusion (1950). Rapid body growth and new genital maturity both bring home dramatically to young people the fact that they are different from the people they once were. These physical changes also signal the approach of full adulthood, with the question of their role in adult society. According to Erikson, the most important aspect of the search for identity is the decision one makes toward a career. (In this light, it is interesting to note that Erikson himself spent several years during his early manhood unsure of the career he would follow. For seven years after he left school at the age of eighteen, he wandered around Europe, tried out painting and wood carving, and eventually came into contact with a psychoanalytically oriented family in Vienna. This fortuitous meeting led to his decision to enter the profession of psychoanalysis.)

Erikson explains adolescents' tendencies toward hero worship as a form of overidentification, "to the point of apparent complete loss of identity [1950, p. 262]." He also sees the cliquishness of adolescence and its intolerance of those who are different as defenses against identity confusion. Similarly, falling in love during adolescence helps young people to define their own identities. By becoming intimate with another person and sharing thoughts and feelings, the adolescent offers up his own identity, sees it reflected in the loved one, and is able to clarify who he is.

Erikson sums up (1950):

The adolescent mind is essentially a mind of the *moratorium*, a psychosocial stage between childhood and adulthood, and between the morality learned by the child, and the ethics to be developed by the adult [pp. 262–263].

Physiological Changes of Adolescence

Tonight is Vicky's twelfth birthday, an event of some moment to her, as is her every birthday. This one is being celebrated by a slumber party, an event characterized by nine giggling, shouting, pizza-eating, joke-telling girls on the brink of adolescence. Toward bedtime, which does not come tonight till the early morning hours, the whispered conversation turns to serious things as the girls ask each other, "Have you had your period yet?" "Have you?" "Have you?" Two girls in the group own up to having passed this milestone of growing up, at which point they are besieged with questions by the others, to whom *menarche*, or first menstruation, is still a mystery.

"How did you feel?" "Weren't you scared to tell your mother?" "When did it happen?" "Do you know what Lisa did—she went around asking every girl in school whether she had got her period yet, and when she found out, she *told*!" "Barbara said the doctor told her she's going to get hers soon, because there was this tiny little brownish spot in her underpants." "My mother says I should be happy to get it because then I'll be able to have a baby, but it sounds like an awful lot of trouble to me. I don't know whether having a baby is worth going through this all my life!"

Menarche is the most dramatic and most widely accepted criterion of puberty for a young girl, and will be discussed more fully later. There are many other signs, though, that indicate to both boys and girls that they are entering a new phase of growth.

Puberty is the time of maturation of the reproductive organs. It begins with the gradual enlargement of the female ovaries (and other reproductive organs) and the growth of the male's prostate and seminal vesicles (Conger, 1973, pp. 94–95). This is accompanied by an adolescent growth spurt. The pituitary gland regulates growth, including sexual growth. The signal of the onset of sexual maturity is the menarche in girls, and—somewhat more debatably—the presence of sperm in the male's urine.

We do not know why maturation begins when it does, nor can we account for the precise mechanism that triggers it. We know only that at some biologically determined time—a time apparently chosen by the interaction of genes, individual health, and environment—the pituitary gland sends a message to a young person's *gonads*, or sex glands. Upon receipt of that message, a girl's ovaries sharply step up their production of estrogen, and a boy's testes increase the manufacture of androgen and testosterone.

While both males and females have been producing sex hormones all their lives, of both their own and the opposite sex, the amounts of the sex-appropriate hormones released into their bodies accelerate just before puberty. The presence of these *gonatropic* hormones in the young person's urine tell us that puberty has indeed occurred. These hormones are completely responsible for the production of mature egg and sperm cells, and partly responsible for the development of primary and secondary sex characteristics. The primary characteristics involve those physical organs directly involved in reproduction (see Chart 13-1).

THE ADOLESCENT GROWTH SPURT

One of the early manifestations of maturation is the *adolescent growth spurt,* a sharp increase in height that usually takes place in girls between the ages of 11 and 13, and in boys between 13 and $15^{1}/_{2}$. Before the adolescent growth spurt, boys are only about 2 percent taller; during the years from 11 to 13, the girls are taller, heavier, and stronger; but after the male growth spurt, boys are again larger, now by about 8 percent. The male spurt seems more intense, and its later appearance allows an extra period for growth, since prepubertal growth is faster than postpubertal growth.

For both sexes, the adolescent growth spurt is comprehensive, affecting practically all skeletal and muscular dimensions. Even the eye grows faster during this period, causing an upsurge of near-sightedness at about this age. The jaw usually becomes longer and thicker; both it and the nose project more; and the incisors of both jaws become more upright. These changes are greater in boys than in girls (Tanner, 1964), which helps to

Chart 13-1   Primary Sex Characteristics

Girls	Boys
ovaries	testes
fallopian tubes	penis
uterus	organs which transport
vagina	sperm from testes to penis

(Werner H. Muller, from Peter Arnold)

The adolescent growth spurt affects practically all skeletal and muscular dimensions.

explain how it could have been acceptable to an Elizabethan audience to see a teen-age male actor playing the part of Viola, the young woman in Shakespeare's *Twelfth Night*, who was passing as a young boy.

Aside from the difference in timing, boys and girls grow differently during adolescence, resulting in different body shapes. The male is not only larger overall, but his shoulders are wider, his legs are longer relative to his trunk, and his forearm is longer, relative to both his upper arm and his height (Tanner, 1964). It is during adolescence that the female pelvis widens, to facilitate childbearing, and that layers of fat are laid down just under the skin, giving the woman a more rounded appearance.

Before adolescence, boys are slightly stronger than girls on the average, but the difference is minuscule. After the adolescent growth spurt, though, the larger muscles of the male, his larger heart and lungs, and his greater capacity for carrying oxygen in the blood confers on him considerably greater strength and endurance (Tanner, 1964). While this is true on the average, there are many adult women who, because of their body build or their rate of physical activity, are stronger than many men.

The age for final attainment of full adult growth is just as variable as the age of the adolescent growth spurt, but while some boys continue to grow until about twenty-five years of age and some girls till about twenty-one, the usual age for attainment of adult height is probably about twenty-one in boys and seventeen in girls (Roche & Davila, 1972).

SECONDARY SEX CHARACTERISTICS

Hair Growth

One of the meanings of *pubescere,* the Latin word from which pubescence is derived, is "to grow hairy." The appearance of hair in new places on the body is a distinct phenomenon of adolescence. Straight, fine hair, slightly darker than other body hair, which begins to grow in the pubic area, is one of the first signs of pubescence for both boys and girls. After some months—or sometimes, years—this pubic hair becomes coarse and kinky. At about this time, hair, known as *axillary hair*, begins to grow under the armpits. And then, to the joy of adolescent boys, facial hair appears. The lesser amounts of facial hair that appear on some girls, often on the upper lip, is usually a cause of dismay and embarrassment, although it is perfectly normal, especially among dark-complexioned and dark-haired ethnic groups. Chest hair generally appears quite late in adolescence. Welcomed as a badge of manhood by boys, girls who may perceive some wispy strands of hair growing between their breasts or around their nipples may be concerned, although such a phenomenon is also perfectly normal.

Breast Development

Another early event in pubescence is the development of breasts. While a female's mammary glands begin to develop at about the sixth week of prenatal life and the principal milk ducts are already present at birth, outward manifestations do not appear before puberty. At this time, the nipples enlarge and protrude; the *areolas*, those pigmented areas surrounding the nipples, also enlarge; and the breasts themselves usually assume first a conical, and then a rounded shape, although mature breast shape may fall roughly into one of three categories: flat, round, or conical. The breasts usually achieve their full growth before menarche. Sometimes one breast grows more quickly than the other, but, while one generally remains slightly larger, this difference is not noticeable upon maturity. (This left-right asymmetry also appears with regard to size of feet, hands, testes, and virtually every other pair of body parts.)

About halfway through adolescence, some boys experience temporary breast enlargement. This lasts for some twelve to eighteen months before disappearing, to the great relief of the boys, who usually view this development with great embarrassment and concern.

Secondary sex characteristics are listed in Chart 13-2.

NOCTURNAL EMISSIONS

Very often the pubescent boy will awaken to find a wet spot or a hardened, dried spot in his bed. This will let him know that while he was asleep he had

Chart 13-2 Secondary Sex Characteristics

Girls	Boys
breasts	pubic hair
pubic hair	axillary hair
axillary hair	facial hair
increased width and depth of pelvis	body hair
	voice change

a *nocturnal emission*, or an ejaculation of semen. Often—but not always— such an emission occurs in connection with an erotic dream. Most youths who are not having sexual intercourse on a fairly regular basis experience these perfectly normal emissions. About 83 percent of the boys and men who responded to the Kinsey study (1948) reported that they had had nocturnal emissions, usually beginning in early adolescence.

SKIN CHANGES

The most obvious skin changes in adolescence are the outbreaks of pimples and blackheads that herald the appearance of *acne.* Caused by the increased activity of the sebaceous glands, which make the skin oilier, and by the enlargement of pores and coarsening of skin texture that occur at this time of life, acne is the bane of many a teen-ager's life. It is most troublesome in boys and is believed to be related to the increased amounts of the male hormone *androgen.*

The activity of the sebaceous glands also makes the hair oilier during adolescence, and the sweat glands also seem to be working overtime, causing body odor to become stronger.

MENSTRUATION

She is dangerous because she can dry up the well and scare animals, she is good and can increase the food supply, she is especially susceptible to enemy magic, she is possessed of a powerful supernatural blessing. Who is she? The menstruating girl, as seen by several different cultures (Muuss, 1968). *Menstruation*, the monthly sloughing off of the lining of the unfertilized womb, has different meanings in different societies and carries different significance for different women. In virtually all societies, it is accepted as a sign of sexual maturity, although it does not necessarily indicate reproductive maturity, since girls are usually not able to conceive for a year or more after the first menstruation.

The first menstruation appears to be accepted matter-of-factly by most American girls, with shame and embarrassment by some, and with joy and excitement by others (Conklin, 1933). The difference in attitude appears to be related to how well prepared a girl is for the onset of menstruation, and to what it means in her life. Generally, a girl has a more positive attitude if she knows what to expect ahead of time, if she does not experience much monthly discomfort, and if her family and friends do not treat the menses as a cursed burden of womanhood or as an illness.

Just knowing the facts about menstruation is not enough, though. The attitude in presenting these facts is crucial. A survey of 103 upper-middle-class women (Shainess, 1961) found that 21 percent had had no advance preparation at all for the menarche. Several of these naive girls had been afraid that their bleeding was due to some type of injury. Even more significant, 75 percent of those girls who *had* some advance knowledge still dreaded the onset of menstruation, or were fearful and worried about it. Perhaps their mothers had communicated their own negative feelings to them, since only 15 percent of all the mothers showed pleasure when their daughters told them that their menses had come.

As adults, only 13 percent of these women were "consistently free of symptoms of premenstrual tension. These were the same women whose mothers had adequately prepared them for menstruation and had received the news of its occurrence with pleasure [p. 24]."

The ambivalence felt by many girls can be seen in this excerpt from *The Diary of Anne Frank* (1952):

> I think what is happening to me is so wonderful, and not only what can be seen on my body, but all that is taking place inside. I never discuss myself or any of these things with anybody; that is why I have to talk to myself about them.
>   Each time I have a period—and that has only been three times—I have the feeling that in spite of all the pain, unpleasantness, and nastiness, I have a sweet secret, and that is why, although it is nothing but a nuisance to me in a way, I always long for the time that I shall feel that secret within me again [pp. 115–116].

Just as we do not know either the precise cause or the precise mechanism for maturation in general, so also are we ignorant as to why menarche begins when it does. Frisch (1972) has hypothesized that a critical weight triggers menarche, citing evidence that the mean weight at menarche of Caucasian girls has been about 106 pounds for more than a century. This explanation is interesting, but it leaves unexplained the variability in critical weights among menarcheal girls of different races.

We do know that menarche has been occurring earlier over the past century, as has the rate of maturation and growth in general (Tanner, 1968). This points to the influence of environmental factors. Despite the long-standing myth that girls from tropical countries mature earlier, there is now "almost unanimous agreement that climate in itself has little or no effect on menarche [Zacharias & Wurtman, 1969, p. 869]." Nigerian girls and Eskimo girls, for example, have remarkably similar average menarcheal ages.

A number of other environmental factors do seem to influence age of menarche. City girls mature earlier than country girls, girls from small

There is great variability in the time of maturation; young people today grow faster and bigger and reach sexual maturity sooner.

families earlier than girls from large families, mildly obese girls earlier than normal girls but normal girls earlier than extremely obese girls, girls born early in the year menstruate sooner than those born at the end of the year, and girls from high altitudes menstruate, on the average, three months later per 100 meters of increased altitude (Zacharias & Wurtman, 1969). All these relationships appear to be related to economic, and most especially nutritional, standards.

Genetics also appear to play a part in the age of first menstruation, even though the age of menarche is unrelated to adult stature (Damon et al., 1969) and to intelligence as measured on standard IQ tests (Reymert, 1940). Identical twins differ only 2.8 months in age of menarche, while fraternals differ by a year, sisters by 12.9 months, and unrelated women by 18.6 months (Hiernaux, 1968). Cuban Negro and Chinese girls attain menarche earlier than most Europeans, and eastern European girls begin to menstruate considerably earlier than western Europeans in similar economic circumstances (Tanner, 1968).

THE TIMING OF MATURATION

Any eighth- or ninth-grade class picture presents us with startling contrasts. We see flat-chested little girls next to full-bosomed, full-grown young women. We see scrawny little boys next to broad-shouldered, mustached young men. This individual variability is normal. There is about a six-year range for normal puberty in both boys and girls. Girls begin pubescence only about six months earlier than boys, but they achieve puberty about two years earlier (Tanner, 1973). The normal age range for puberty is ten to sixteen years for girls, with an average age of twelve, and twelve to eighteen for boys, with an average age of fourteen. Whether a youngster is an early or late maturer often has definite social and psychological consequences.

While there is great variability in maturation, the sequence of pubertal events is usually fairly uniform, although overlapping, among children around the world. These events are presented in Chart 13-3.

The Secular Trend in Growth and Maturation

In the seventeenth century, according to Hippolitus Quarinonius, writing in 1610, rural girls in Austria rarely began to menstruate "before their seventeenth, eighteenth or even twentieth year [Tanner, 1968]." In 1820, middle- and upper-class girls in Manchester, England, began to menstruate at about $14^{1}/_{2}$, and today girls in this socioeconomic group usually reach menarche sometime between twelve and thirteen years of age (Tanner, 1968). In technological societies around the world, the average age of menarche has been declining three or four months per decade for the last century, with girls in Britain, the United States, and Europe menstruating from $2^{1}/_{2}$ to $3^{1}/_{2}$ years earlier than they did a century ago (Tanner, 1968).

Boys, too, appear to be reaching sexual maturity earlier than they used to. The eighteenth-century records kept by Johann Sebastian Bach tell us that the boys in his choir could generally sing soprano until they were about eighteen years old; in 1959, the voices of London schoolboys were changing at the age of thirteen (Sullivan, 1971).

Chart 13-3   **Physiological Changes of Adolescence** *(After Muuss, 1968, p. 7; Tanner, 1964)*

Boys	Girls
Skeletal growth	Skeletal growth
Enlargement of testes and testicles	Straight pigmented pubic hair
Straight pigmented pubic hair	Breast development
Early voice changes	Enlargement of external genitalia
Ejaculation, often during sleep	Adolescent growth spurt
Kinky pigmented pubic hair	Kinky pigmented pubic hair
Adolescent growth spurt	Menstruation
Enlargement of penis	Axillary hair
Downy facial hair	Presence of gonatropic hormones in the urine
Axillary hair	Changes in complexion: skin texture coarsens, pores enlarge, acne appears
Late voice change	Stronger body odor
Coarse pigmented facial hair	Gradual deepening of voice
Chest hair	Changes in shape of body: pelvis enlarges, hips widen, more subcutaneous fat develops
Occasionally, enlargement of breasts	
Increase in erections	
Presence of gonatropic hormones in the urine	
Changes in complexion: skin texture coarsens, pores enlarge, acne appears	
Stronger body odor	

Furthermore, not only are people reaching sexual maturity sooner, but they are also growing faster, growing bigger, and attaining adult height earlier. This trend toward larger size and earlier maturation is known as the *secular trend*, since it has been observed from one century to another. In 1970, Muuss wrote:

> In the United States the normal healthy son will be as much as 1 inch taller and 10 pounds heavier than his father. The normal healthy girl will be $1/2$ to 1 inch taller, 2 pounds heavier, and will experience menarche about 10 months earlier than her mother. Boys are more strongly affected by the secular trend than girls, as boys in general react more strongly to various influences [p. 52].

Similar changes in size and age of maturity have occurred among Chinese, Japanese, New Zealander, Italian, and Polish children (Muuss, 1970).

The most obvious and the best explanation for this phenomenon appears to be the benign influence of a higher standard of living. As children are healthier, better nourished, and better cared for in general, they mature earlier and grow bigger. During periods of famine and economic crises, the secular trend is often reversed, attesting to the influence of socioeconomic factors (Tanner, 1968).

It is also explained as a function of hybrid vigor, or the "bicycle effect." When improved methods of transportation brought together young men and women from different geographical areas, the dominant genes for tallness were able to reach more people, with a concomitant increase in the height of the population at large.

Both these theories seem to explain growth better than maturational age. Since the two are related, it appears that a certain body size may trigger the onset of maturation, and that Frisch's (1972) theory of critical weight may help to account for earlier sexual maturation.

The secular trend is a relatively recent phenomenon, which seems to have begun about 100 years ago and may now be leveling off, at least in the middle and upper classes. We could not have an indefinite lowering of maturational age and increase in height, or we would have a race of giants who mature at birth. So it seems that when conditions have already been favorable, the age of maturation and the adult stature level off. This is borne out by such studies that show that boys entering Harvard from private schools in 1958 and 1959 were not taller than boys from these same schools in the 1930s, but that public school boys of the 1950s were taller than those of the 1930s, probably reflecting advances in living standards in less affluent families (Bakwin & McLaughlin, 1964).

FEELINGS ABOUT PHYSICAL APPEARANCE

By now, the scenario has become ritualized. Two or three times a week, Vicky, just turned thirteen, looks into the mirror for a while, turning this way and that, pulling in her stomach, sticking out her budding chest, striking various poses, inspecting her face for new blemishes, trying out new hairdos. After twenty or thirty minutes of this activity, she goes to her mother or her father and asks earnestly, "Am I pretty?"

The parent currently under interrogation looks at the girl/woman, thinks for a moment, and then carefully and ever-so-sincerely says, "Yes, you *are* pretty." Vicky immediately grimaces and says, "Well, of course *you'd* say that. I'm your *child*!"

Each time the ritual scene is reenacted as if it were scripted. As a girl in our society, Vicky feels freer to voice her concerns about her looks than a male adolescent, who may be just as worried. According to a "body image" survey by the magazine *Psychology Today*, boys are more likely to tease other boys about their physical appearance, often with long-lasting effects. Remembers one young man:

The horror of being 14 and standing in front of that mirror and seeing the skinny person crying in the disguise of a fat boy was the first time I saw the realities of life . . . I realized that no one, absolutely no one, would ever love me, a fat slob. The next month I lost 30 pounds [Berscheid, Walster, & Bohrnstedt, 1973, p. 122].

Most young teenagers of both sexes are more concerned about their physical appearance than about any other aspect of themselves (Jersild, 1952), and about one-third of all boys and one-half of all girls who took part in one longitudinal study at some point expressed their worries about at least one aspect of their growth (Stolz & Stolz, 1944).

What worries teenagers the most about their appearance? Everything. But some things more than others. Boys want to look like the tall, broad-shouldered, masculine ideal of our society, while girls want to be slim, though bosomy. Anything that makes a boy think he looks feminine (like a slight physique or a beardless, baby-face complexion) or a girl think she looks masculine (like a large-boned frame or facial hair) will make either one miserable. Both sexes want to look like everyone else they know and are uncomfortable when they mature either very early or very late, compared with their friends. On the other hand, both sexes have unrealistic

(Virginia Hamilton)

Almost everything worries teen-agers about their appearance, and this strongly influences one's self-concept.

ideals of appearance: "Adolescent girls long to look like fashion models; boys want to look like football pros [Dwyer & Mayer, 1968-69, p. 67]."

Both boys and girls fret about having to wear glasses or braces, having a bad complexion, and having features that are not perfect—a nose that's too big or too small, a face too round or too thin, ears too large or too protruding, and so on and so on.

Because good looks are stressed more for girls in our society, women are often pushed into defining themselves in terms of their appearance. As a result, teen-age girls agonize more about this than do boys. They are particularly concerned about being too tall and too fat—and teen-age girls who by any medical standard would be considered perfectly normal are forever going on diets. Girls also worry about being too flat-chested or too large-breasted or having hair that is too frizzy or too straight. Boys hate to be short, partly because our society demands that a boy be taller than the girl he dances with, and partly because the high-prestige teen-age sports—basketball and football—both favor tall youths, and the latter also favors brawny ones. So while fatness is deplored, bulk due to muscularity is adored.

Adolescent self-concepts depend largely on how attractive young people consider themselves. The *Psychology Today* survey found that "adolescent beauty . . . leaves its mark for years." People who consider themselves attractive during their teen-age years had higher self-esteem and were happier than less comely people well into their forties. Not until the midforties did the differences in happiness between those who had been attractive or homely adolescents disappear (Berscheid et al., 1973).

EFFECTS ON PERSONALITY OF EARLY OR LATE MATURING
Since one's appearance during adolescence exerts such a strong influence on one's self-concept, it is not surprising that the timing of maturation—which affects this appearance by determining when the body will assume more adult proportions and features—has important psychological effects during adolescence. Boys seem more affected by differences in timing than do girls.

Early- and Late-maturing Boys
The high school boy who has not yet experienced the adolescent growth spurt, whose voice is childishly high, and whose cheeks are smooth and hairless looks like a little boy next to his earlier-maturing classmates. He is so much smaller than many of them as to make athletic competition with them a mockery, if not an impossibility. The girls in his class are likely to consider him an amusing little "twerp" rather than a social equal. Because he looks immature, he is treated as a child. By contrast, the early maturer is generally considered and treated as more of a man, is more popular with his peers, and is more likely to be a school leader (Jones, 1957). It is not so

surprising, then, that this discrepancy between the way a boy may feel and how he looks should show up in psychological assessments.

The Thematic Apperception Test (TAT) was given to thirty-three boys seventeen years old; sixteen were early maturers, and seventeen were late maturers. The TAT is a projective test of personality, which offers the person being tested a series of pictures, about which he is asked to tell a story. After analyzing the boys' stories for underlying themes, Mussen and Jones (1957) concluded that boys who mature after most of their peers are more likely to feel inadequate, consider themselves rejected and dominated, be dependent, rebel more against their parents, and, in general, think less of themselves. The early maturers, on the other hand, showed self-confidence, independence, and the ability to play an adult role in interpersonal relationships. The two groups of boys did not differ in their needs for achievement or personal recognition.

In another study of early- and late-maturing boys, three observers who had known the youths over a period of years in conjunction with their participation in a longitudinal study, rated them according to their behavior, which was considered to reflect nine underlying drives. The early- and late-maturers differed on only two drives, one involving social relationships and one related to aggression. The late maturing boys tried harder to be accepted socially, but their attempts in this direction were often childish and affected. They also exhibited more aggressive behavior, probably because of their basic insecurity and feelings of inadequacy (Mussen & Jones, 1958).

Early- and Late-maturing Girls

Andrea, a fifth-grade classmate of Vicky's, ran out of the classroom in tears. The tallest student in the class and the only girl to have begun to menstruate and to wear a bra, Andrea was constantly teased by the boys and regularly pelted with curious questions from the girls. After a lecture on sexuality from the health teacher, Andrea found herself the recipient of head-turning stares, her self-consciousness became too much for her, and she fled in mortification.

Yet early maturation is not necessarily a distinct handicap for a girl. The findings on this are contradictory. When the TAT was administered to thirty-four early- and late-maturing girls, seventeen years old, the early maturers seemed to be better adjusted than the late maturers, although the differences were smaller than among the two groups of boys referred to above. Yet ratings of these girls by both peers and adult observers over the previous six years had seemed to favor the late maturers (Jones & Mussen, 1958).

Do Adult Personalities Reflect the Timing of Maturation?

How long do the differences persist between early- and late-maturing adolescents? Are they forgotten once adulthood is reached, or have they left their marks on adult personality? In an effort to answer this question, Jones (1957) contacted twenty 33-year-old men who had been among a group of early- or late-maturing boys. She found that most of the differences between the two groups had disappeared with the equalization conferred by adult status, but that a few vestiges remained.

There was no longer any differences between the two groups of men in size or physical attractiveness; nor were any found in educational attainment, marital status, and family size. While few personality differences showed up, the early maturers did seem to show earlier patterns of success in their chosen careers. They also seemed more concerned with "making a good impression" on other people. The late maturers showed more flexibility in their personalities, as measured by psychological tests; they were more assertive, insightful, self-indulgent, and touchy. Commenting on these differences in this group of men, Jones (1957) says:

> We might hazard the guess that some of the little boy behavior—the impulsiveness, playfulness and also the "touchiness" repeatedly noted in late-maturing adolescents is mirrored in the description of high scorers on the flexibility scale. We might speculate further that in the course of having to adapt to difficult status problems, the late-maturers have gained some insights and are indeed more flexible, while the early-maturing, capitalizing on their ability to make a good impression, may have clung to their earlier success pattern to the extent of becoming somewhat rigid or over-controlled [p. 120].

There is no question that during the adolescent years themselves, youngsters are exquisitely conscious of how they "stack up" with regard to their peers. One late-maturing boy in Jones's study became enthralled by the notion of participating in a study involving a growth-promoting hormone, describing himself as always having been small, underweight, and skinny. An early maturer was described as having been "embarrassed rather than pleased by his height," worrying about it and slouching to minimize it. And an eighteen-year-old girl recalls:

> There were girls who, from third grade on, hunched over with the weight and shame of early bras—I remember the shadow that showed through under white blouses, and the moment, each September in the locker room, when we pulled off our shirts and revealed just what had happened over the summer and just who would join the club. For some that moment came too early and for others, like me—scrambling frantically in the bathroom to get my gym suit on, snapping the fasteners that concealed an undershirt, while lines of girls formed outside the door and called "Hurry up in there, I've gotta go"—it came fatally late [Maynard, 1973, p. 42].

Yet the very small differences that showed up between the two groups of adult men, who had been early- or late-maturing boys, dramatically underscores the conclusion that the relationship between the time of maturation and personality is a complicated one, with no simple cause-and-effect ratio. Some young people are better able than others to accept being out of step for a few years. The quality of a single adolescence is determined largely by the young person's relationships with his or her parents and with peers, and with success in school and other areas of endeavor. Timing of maturation is just one more factor in the long list of influences that help to make us the people we are.

Intellectual Development in Adolescence

PIAGET'S STAGE OF FORMAL OPERATIONS
(AGE TWELVE AND BEYOND)

Over the years, Vicky has been presented several times with the pendulum problem, a typical Piagetian problem in formal reasoning. She is shown the pendulum, which consists of an object hanging from a string, and is then shown how she can change the length of the string, the weight of the object, the height from which the object is released, and the amount of force

(George W. Gardner)

The adolescent has arrived at the stage of formal operations and, for the first time, is capable of hypothetical reasoning.

she can use to push it. She is then asked to determine which of these factors, either alone or combined with others, determines how fast the object swings.

When Vicky first saw the pendulum, she was not yet seven years old. At that time she was unable to formulate a plan for attacking the problem, but instead tried one thing after another in a hit-or-miss manner. First she pushed a long pendulum with a light weight, then she swung a short pendulum with a heavy weight, and then she removed the weight entirely. Not only was her method completely slapdash, but she couldn't even understand or report what had actually happened. She was convinced that her pushes made the pendulum go faster, and even though this was not so, she reported it as observed fact.

The next time Vicky was faced with the pendulum, she was eleven. Her more advanced age showed in the way she tackled the problem this time. She did look at some possible solutions, and she even hit upon a partially correct answer. But she failed to try out every possible solution in a systematic way. She varied the length of the string, and she varied the weight of the object, and she thought that both length and weight affected the speed of the swing. She was still failing to keep one dimension constant while she varied the other.

Not until Vicky and the pendulum met again in adolescence did Vicky go at her old friend in a thorough, well-organized manner. She now realized that any one of the four factors, or some combination of them, might affect the speed of the swing. So she carefully designed an experiment to test all the possible hypotheses, holding constant one factor while she varied another. By carefully doing this, she was able to determine that one factor—the length of the string—is the only one that determines how fast the pendulum swings. (This description of age-related differences in the approach to the pendulum problem is adapted from Ginsburg & Opper, 1969.)

By solving the pendulum problem the way she did, Vicky illustrated her arrival in the stage of *formal operations,* a cognitive level usually attained at about the age of twelve. Once at this level, Vicky can think in terms of what might be true and not just what she sees in a concrete situation. Since she can imagine an infinite variety of possibilities, she is, for the first time, capable of hypothetical reasoning. Once she develops a hypothesis, she can then construct a scientific experiment to test that hypothesis and to deduce whether it is true. We say, then, that she is now capable of *hypothetico-deductive* reasoning. She considers all the possible relationships that might exist and goes through them one by one, to eliminate the false and arrive at the true. This systematic process of reasoning operates for all sorts of problems, of course, and not just mechanical or scientific ones. The person in the formal operations stage is better equipped to integrate what he has learned in the past with his problems of the present and his planning for the future. He applies these thought processes to the mechanics of day-to-day living, and also to the construction of elaborate political and philosophical theories.

Piaget (1957) describes adolescent thought as the ability to look at possibilities and test them out:

> The consequences of this new attitude are as follows. In the first place thought no longer proceeds from the actual to the theoretical, but starts from theory so as to establish or verify actual relationships between things. Instead of just coordinating facts about the actual world, hypothetico-deductive reasoning draws out the implications of possible statements and thus gives rise to a unique synthesis of the possible and necessary [p. 19].

As Vicky has grown, her neurological structures have developed; her social environment, which includes her schooling and the people she meets, has widened; and the opportunities she has had for experimentation have made their impression upon her. The interaction of these three factors brings about the maturation of her cognitive structures at about the age of sixteen, at which time her way of thinking is almost fully formed. After this time, while she will continue to learn, of course, her cognitive structures themselves will not undergo any more modification. In other words, there will be no further qualitative leaps to improved cognitive functioning. She's reached her peak—cognitively speaking, at least. Her mental structures, well enough developed now to enable her to handle a wide variety of intellectual problems, are said by Piaget to be in an advanced state of equilibrium.

If Vicky's culture or education had not encouraged her to engage in this kind of reasoning described above, she might never have attained this stage, even though she would have the necessary neurological development. So again we see Piaget's emphasis on the interaction between the individual and her environment. He stresses the impact of the environment here more than earlier.

FLEXIBILITY OF ADOLESCENT THOUGHT

We say that adolescent thought is flexible, because it is not tied down to a rigid way of looking at things. Explain Ginsburg & Opper (1969):

> The adolescent has available a large number of cognitive operations with which to attack problems. . . . He is versatile in his thought and can deal with a problem in many ways and from a variety of perspectives. . . . He is unlikely to be confused by unusual results because he has beforehand conceived of all the possibilities [p. 204].

Because of this new ability to consider all sorts of possibilities, adolescents are now capable of abstract thought. The intellectualism of adolescence, which Anna Freud sees as an ego-defense mechanism, is considered by cognitive theorists to be more of an exercise in the flexing of intellectual muscles. Elkind, for example, regards the major task of early adolescence as "the conquest of thought [1967, p. 43]," and Ginsburg and Opper (1969) summarize some of Piaget's thoughts about adolescent intellectual activity:

> Piaget finds repercussions of formal thought on several areas of adolescent life, although his remarks probably hold more particularly for European cultures than for American. In the intellectual sphere, the adolescent has a tendency to become involved in abstract and theoretical matters. He constructs elaborate political theories or invents complex philosophical doctrines. He may develop plans for the complete reorganization of society or indulge in metaphysical speculation. Having just discovered capabilities for abstract thought, he then proceeds to exercise them without restraint. Indeed, in the process of exploring his new abilities the adolescent sometimes loses touch with reality, and feels that he can accomplish everything by thought alone. In the emotional sphere the adolescent now becomes capable of directing his emotions at abstract ideals and not just toward people. Whereas earlier he could love his mother or hate a peer, now he can love freedom or hate exploitation. The adolescent has developed a new mode of life: the possible and the ideal captivate both mind and feeling [pp. 204–205].

THE EGOCENTRISM OF ADOLESCENCE

Despite the adolescent Vicky's abilities to conceptualize ideas and to take a scientific approach in looking at phenomena, her thought is not yet completely adult in nature, because of her lingering egocentrism. No longer a child, she now recognizes that other people have their own thoughts, too. However, since she is preoccupied with herself, she believes that these thoughts of others invariably focus on her. "It is this belief that others are preoccupied with his appearance and behavior that constitutes the egocentrism of the adolescent [Elkind, 1967, p. 1030]."

The Imaginary Audience

When Vicky hears her parents whispering, she "knows" they are talking about her. When she comes upon a couple of boys laughing raucously on a corner, she "knows" they are ridiculing her. When she catches the eye of a teacher, she wonders what that teacher is thinking about her at that moment. She feels under constant scrutiny from everyone she knows, and thinks that everyone is as admiring of her or as critical of her as she is of herself.

> In a sense, then, the adolescent is continually constructing, or reacting to, *an imaginary audience.* It is an audience because the adolescent believes that he will be the focus of attention; and it is imaginary because in actual social situations,

(Fujihira, Monkmeyer)

Despite adolescent abilities to conceptualize ideas and to take a scientific approach her thought is not yet completely adult in nature, because of lingering egocentrism.

this is not usually the case (unless he contrives to make it so) [Elkind, 1967, p. 1030].

The imaginary audience helps to explain the self-consciousness of early adolescence—why every pimple, every lock of hair, every article of clothing assumes such major importance. The hours that young adolescents spend in front of the mirror are devoted not only to self-criticism or self-admiration, but to projecting the way they will look to others.

When . . . young people . . . meet, each is more concerned with being the observed than with being the observer. Gatherings of young adolescents are unique in the sense that each young person is simultaneously an actor to himself and an audience to others [Elkind, 1967, p. 1030].

And yet this audience is not wholly imaginary. Young teen-agers *do* scrutinize each other with close attention to detail: they notice—and tell each other—when someone's hair needs to be shampooed, when a boy should start to shave (or grow a mustache), when a girl should wear a bra. It is almost as if, by noticing these minute details about others, they are legitimizing their concerns about themselves.

The Personal Fable

A counterpart to the imaginary audience, the *personal fable* is an adolescent's belief that, because so many people are interested in him, he must be special. Vicky *knows* that no one ever before in the history of the world has felt the way she does. No one ever loved so much, no one was ever so misunderstood, no one was ever so exquisitely sensitive to the injustices in the world. Her belief in her own uniqueness also leads to a belief that somehow she is not subject to the rules that govern the rest of the world. She is magically protected from the things that can happen to other people. It is the personal fable that makes a girl think that *she* can't get pregnant even if she engages in sexual intercourse without using contraceptives, or makes a boy think that *he* can't get killed even if he plays "chicken" racing in his car. Teen-age smokers feel protected from lung cancer; teen-age LSD users are convinced that they can never have a "bad trip." "These things only happen to other people—not to me" is the unconscious assumption that helps to explain much adolescent risk-taking.

Overcoming Adolescent Egocentrism

Elkind (1967) claims that the egocentrism of adolescence diminishes at about the age of fifteen or sixteen, when the young person "gradually comes to recognize the difference between his own preoccupations and the interests and concerns of others [p. 46]." At this point, the imaginary audience becomes the real audience, and the personal fable gives way to an understanding that other people are more like oneself than one ever dreamed possible.

Eventually the adolescent realizes that others are not preoccupied with him, but that they have their own concerns about themselves. With this realization and with the development of the ability to think about his own thought, the adolescent overcomes egocentric thinking. The more he talks about his own personal theories and listens to the personal theories of other young people, the sooner he will arrive at an adult level of thinking (Looft, 1971).

A factor of major importance in leading to more realistic thought is the pursuit of an occupation. When productive work becomes important to an individual, that person necessarily becomes less self-oriented and more attuned to the task at hand, to society in general, and to individuals within that society.

As the thought processes of adolescents mature, they are better able to think about their own identities, to form adult relationships with other people, and to determine how and where they fit into their society.

Summary

1   *Adolescence* is a period of transition from childhood to adulthood. It begins with *pubescence,* a period of rapid physical growth and maturation of reproductive functioning and primary and secondary sexual characteristics. Pubescence lasts about two years, ending with *puberty,* when sexual maturity and reproductive capacity are complete. The end of adolescence is not clearcut; in Western societies, no single sign indicates that adulthood has been attained. In some societies, adolescence ends at puberty and is signified by *puberty rites,* which take a variety of forms and typically occur in non-Western societies.

2   Various theoretical interpretations of adolescence exist. G. Stanley Hall views adolescence as a time of *storm and stress,* marked by vacillating, contradictory emotions. Margaret Mead is concerned with the way cultural factors influence adolescence; she claims that adolescence may be stressful or smooth, depending on how a particular society responds. Albert Bandura says adolescence, even in America, is not as stressful as Hall implies. Sigmund Freud places adolescents in the *genital stage,* the stage of mature adult sexuality. This stage is biologically determined and occurs when reawakened sexual urges no longer are repressed as during latency. Now sexual gratification is aimed at developing satisfying heterosexual relationships with people outside the family and in finding a suitable reproductive partner. Anna Freud expanded her father's discussion with sexual urges. These include *intellectualization and asceticism.* Erik Erikson's fifth crisis involves the adolescent's search for *identify,* or *role confusion.* Career choice is viewed as an important step in identity formation.

3   Dramatic physiological changes mark adolescence. Most notable and obvious is the appearance of *menarche* in females. Males experience *nocturnal emissions.* Both sexes undergo sharp growth in height, weight, and muscular and skeletal development—the *adolescent growth spurt.* A *secular trend* in growth and maturation occurs so that children reach sexual maturation and adult height earlier than before, a fact influenced by today's higher standard of living (improved nutrition and health care) that seems to be leveling off, at least in the middle and upper classes.

4   An adolescent's rapid body changes affect self-concept and personality. Particularly important is the effect of *early* or *late maturing,* an effect that is pronounced during adolescence but seems to disappear by adulthood.

5   The adolescent years correspond to Piaget's stage of *formal operations,* during which an adolescent develops the ability to think abstractly. This enables young people to deal flexibly with problems to test hypotheses, and to engage in hypothetical, deductive reasoning. Environment plays a more important role in the attainment of this stage than in earlier stages of cognitive development.

6   Although an adolescent is not egocentric in the sense that a child is, this concept does apply. *Adolescent egocentrism* is seen in the adolescents' notion that other people's thoughts are focused on them, just as they are preoccupied with themselves. Manifestations of adolescent egocentrism include the *imaginary audience* and *personal fable.* Adolescent egocentrism is gradually overcome as an adolescent realizes that other people have their *own* concerns. Selection of an occupation enables the individual to become less self-involved and thus contributes to the demise of adolescent egocentrism.

Suggested Readings

Cottle, T. J. *Time's Children: Impressions of Youth.* Boston: Little, Brown, 1971. *A well-written collection of essays about children's experiences, feelings, fears, and wants. It is an interesting observation on how children grow up and how the world around them affects their development.*

Fader, D. *The Naked Children.* New York: Macmillan, 1971. *A passionate story about the author's experience during one school year in a black ghetto junior high school in Washington, D.C., where he introduces his "English in Every Classroom" experiment.*

Goethals, G. W., & Klos, D. S. *Experiencing Youth: First Person Accounts.* Boston: Little, Brown, 1970. *A collection of cases dealing with the psychology of adolescence, divided into cases dealing with autonomy, identity, and sexual intimacy.*

Inhelder, B., & Piaget, J. *The Growth of Logical Thinking from Childhood to Adolescence.* New York: Basic Books, 1958. *An account of the research of Piaget on the development of intelligence through the various levels of human growth. Piaget and Inhelder show how a child's mind develops characteristics of adult thinking.*

Kohen-Ruz, R. *The Child from 9 to 13.* London: Aldine-Atherton, 1971. *A discussion of the interval between the end of childhood and the beginning of puberty and adolescence. It views adolescence as the beginning of a second phase of life.*

Minton, L. *Growing into Adolescence: A Sensible Guide for Parents of Children 11 to 14.* New York: Parents' Magazine Press, 1972. *A very readable book that uses many examples to explain the dynamics of early adolescence, as they revolve around such issues as burgeoning sexuality, need for independence, developing values, and the many day-to-day problems common in these years.*

CHAPTER FOURTEEN

PERSONALITY DEVELOPMENT

IN WHICH VICKY LOOKS EVERYWHERE FOR HERSELF

The great masses of the boys and girls of this country, with a newly acquired freedom, with unbounded opportunity for liberty and license, associated with a realization of the force that they are capable of exerting upon the community, have taken their newly acquired privileges, all of them laden with the stuff that just naturally leads to revolt, and have managed themselves with wisdom that should demand more respect and less criticism from adults, whose criticism is, after all, bred of fear of what is going to happen next.

(D. A. Thom, 1933*)

"The trouble is," said sixteen-year-old Vicky to her mother after an intense argument, "that I don't know who I am. You know who you are. You're Mary Smith Jones. You're a teacher. You're a wife. You're a mother. But who am I?

"You expect me to be just like you, to think just the way you do and to do whatever you would do if you were me. But you're *not* me. I don't know who *is* me. I wish I could be myself with you, but I always feel under all this pressure not to talk about the things I think or do that I know you wouldn't approve of.

*From *Guiding the Adolescent*. U.S. Department of Labor Children's Bureau Publication No. 225, 1933.

"Then when I do decide to open up a little bit of myself to you, it never seems to be a good time. I guess it's my fault. I don't pick the right times—whenever I want to talk, you always seem to be busy with something else and not have enough time to listen to me. But if we can't talk to each other, we'll never understand each other." And, unspoken and barely unthought, "and I'll never find out who I really am."

The Search for Identity

Vicky is not alone. Probably the most important task of adolescence is the quest to find out "who I really am." Teen-agers need to develop their own values, and to be sure that they are not just parroting the ideas of their parents. They have to find out what they can do and be proud of their own accomplishments. They want to develop close relationships with both boys and girls their own age, and to be liked and loved and respected for who they are and what they stand for. "The adolescent searches for his or her self-identity in many mirrors [Sorensen, 1973, p. 37]." Or, as Jones (1969) puts it:

Teen-agers need to develop their own values, and to be sure that they are not just parroting the ideas of their parents.

(Mahon, Monkmeyer)

The adolescent enters the threshold of personhood seeking an image he does not know in a world he rarely understands, with a body that he is just discovering. He has a mixed desire to be an individual who wants to assert himself while at the same time fearing to lose the little security and reassurance that only family can offer [p. 332].

Erik Erikson, the theorist who more than any other has delved into the adolescent search for identity, emphasizes the fact that this effort to make sense of the self and the world around is not "a kind of maturational malaise," but is instead a healthy, vital process that contributes to the ego strength of the mature adult (1960).

Implicit in this voyage of self-discovery is the young person's seesawing between childhood and maturity. At one moment Vicky climbs onto her father's lap, puts her arms around him, and talks baby talk. At the next she argues for the right to stay alone over a weekend and bitterly berates him for treating her like a child. Most teen-agers object when older people think of them as children, or even use the term "adolescents," even though they themselves are likely to concede, "In some ways, I still think and act somewhat like a child [Sorensen, 1973, p. 38]."

(Steve Aoki)

Adolescents want to come to their own conclusions—whatever the issue—and be taken seriously.

DEVELOPING VALUES

The year Vicky was fifteen, she participated in a street-corner demonstration against the killing of baby seals; went door-to-door to distribute leaflets on behalf of a political candidate; tutored underprivileged children two afternoons a week; applied (and was turned down for) nonpaying jobs on Indian reservations and in the Appalachian hills, and spent her summer on a work crew helping inner-city slum dwellers to rehabilitate their old apartments.

The adolescent years are a time of great idealism. At this time many adolescents become convinced of the need for social change, become outraged at the hypocrisy and the complacency of their society, and attempt to change the world. Their efforts are genuine, and when society can channel their energies constructively, their contributions can be meaningful.

During adolescence, the search for personal values is intense. "What is important to me?" asks Vicky. "What should I spend my time doing? How should I manage my life?"

In the Home

RELATIONSHIPS WITH PARENTS

Young people feel constant conflict between wanting to be independent of their parents and realizing how dependent they actually are. Boys see their fathers, with whom they identify, as their more powerful parent, and girls their mothers (Grinder & Spector, 1965). How hard it is to accept some of this power as one's own, without feeling swallowed up by that same-sex parent! In their pursuit of independence, adolescents often repulse their parents' attempts to guide them, dismiss their parents' opinions as hopelessly out-of-date and irrelevant, and deliberately say and do things that they know will shock and outrage their elders. As Erikson (1950) says:

> In their search for a new sense of continuity and sameness, adolescents have to refight many of the battles of earlier years, even though to do so they must artificially appoint perfectly well-meaning people to play their roles of adversaries [p. 261].

These "perfectly well-meaning people" are often, of course, their parents. It often seems as if the parents of teen-agers can't do anything right, as we see in this impassioned complaint from a seventeen-year-old girl:

> Lately they (her parents) have gotten into a thing with any guy who asks me out: "Oh, I think he really likes you." It's just garbage I don't feel I need. If he likes me, I can tell. I don't need my parents to say "I think he really likes you." or "Oh, good, he wants to take you out [Sorensen, 1973, p. 69]."

This tendency to cast their parents in the role of scapegoats who can be blamed for everything that goes wrong continues through the college years for many young people. At least one observer (Allport, 1964) feels that not until about the age of twenty-three are most people able to deal with their parents on a mature, adult-to-adult basis. And an earlier observer, Mark Twain, once said, "When I was 14 my father knew nothing, but when I was 21 I was amazed at how much the old man had learned in those seven years."

The teen-agers' ambivalent feelings are often matched by ambivalent feelings on the part of their parents, who are torn between wanting their children to be independent and wanting to keep them dependent on them. Ginott (1969) has said, "As parents, our need is to be needed; as teenagers their need is not to need us [p. 13]." Parents who find it hard to let go often give their teen-age children "double messages," saying one thing while communicating just the opposite meaning by their actions.

WHAT TEEN-AGERS WANT FROM THEIR PARENTS

In one workshop in which 30 teen-agers and 185 adults participated in a series of small groups, the adolescents were asked at one point during the week's activities, "What could adults do to make life better for you?" Among their answers:

> Adults could show us they care.
> Parents need to care.
> Parents need to understand that kids want to do things on their own.
> Love is more important than money.
> Authoritarian directions just squash us.
> Why not tell us what the rules are for or ask us to help make the rules?
> Parents should live what they tell us to do.
> Why are parents always running around earning money when they should be around with their kids? [Schindler-Rainman, 1969]

People trying to find their own values in a confusing society are very much concerned with the genuineness of the values of the people they look to as models. For this reason, they are quick to accuse their parents and teachers of hypocrisy whenever they detect any deviation from professed ideals and actual behavior. It is very hard for adolescents, embroiled in the job of finding the values that will define them, to understand that adults may have found their values but have a great deal of trouble living up to them. Parents are not always what they would like to be.

In adolescence the former images of our parents as perfect, all-knowing models come tumbling down, never again to be reassembled. From this time on, parents are only people like anyone else. But because we once invested them with much more power than any human being could possibly have had, this toppling of our ideal models comes as a grievous blow. If only our parents had been perfect, if only they had raised us perfectly—just think what paragons we could be! As Oscar Wilde once put it, "Children begin by loving their parents. After a time they judge them. Rarely, if ever, do they forgive them."

Adolescents need the freedom to make up their own minds. They want to know where their parents stand on issues, but they also want to come to their own conclusions. And while they are searching for answers, they want to be listened to, respected, and—above all—taken seriously.

Strife between parents and their teen-age children need not be a constant fact of life. The Bandura and Walters (1959) study cited in Chapter 13 showed a comfortable acceptance of each other by parents and teen-age sons. And another recent study found that, while parents are troubled by many facets of teen-age life, they are generally optimistic and positive about the young people themselves. Say parents who responded to a newspaper questionnaire, "We love their fresh insights, surprising evidences of maturity, their idealism and eagerness to learn"; "It's great becoming friends as well as parents"; and "They make me feel alive and involved. I was 'old' when they were young, but now I'm younger than my years [*McCall's*, 1973, p. 34]."

Another study that brings us the young people's own views tells us that most teen-agers feel they really know, like, and respect their parents (Sorensen, 1973). While this report focuses on adolescent sexuality, it also offers many insights into other aspects of adolescent thinking, such as self-concepts and relationships with parents.

The Sorensen study contacted 2,042 households randomly selected from a nationwide sample of 200 city or suburban neighborhoods and rural locations, in 103 areas throughout the continental United States, chosen "in accordance with accepted principles of area probability sampling [p. 20]." Eventually 411 boys and girls from these households filled out lengthy questionnaires, and an additional 200 young people aged thirteen to nineteen and representing different sectors of the teen-age population were interviewed at length. Parental permission was obtained for all study participants.

Three out of four of the young people who responded to the Sorensen study feel that they really know their mothers, and six out of ten that they really know their fathers. Seventy-eight percent feel strong affection for their parents, 88 percent have a lot of respect for them as people, and almost all feel that their parents, in turn, care for them.

Still there is a substantial minority of teen-agers who feel they have never really gotten to know their parents, and one teen out of four can't stand to be around them. Usually these youths blame their parents for having failed them in some specific way, showing a lack of understanding or an unwillingness to help with a problem in the youngsters' lives. Says one sixteen-year-old girl about her father:

I resent him because when I was in the seventh grade I didn't get along with my teachers in school. . . . And my father, from the time I was in seventh grade until I did, would say, "You're going to drop out." Every time something happened he'd say, "Why don't you just drop out now?"—which was not legal. . . .

My father showed no understanding. At that time he had no conception of a teacher being bad. To my parents, the teacher was always right. No matter what it was that I had done. . . . I got suspended for lighting incense in school and they thought it was to cover up the smell of dope and it wasn't. My parents took all my good clothes away from me and said you're only to wear these clothes. . . . I became very resentful about everything. I became very, very bitter [Sorensen, 1973, pp. 65-66].

COMMUNICATION BETWEEN PARENTS AND ADOLESCENTS

Most teens want to get along well with their parents, to be able to talk with them about things that really matter, and to feel free to ask their opinions—without being forced to abide by them. But often, in their struggle to be independent of their parents, they have trouble doing this. Some seem driven to find and discuss every point upon which they and their parents disagree, so that every conversation turns into an argument.

Most teens want to get along well with their parents, to be able to talk with them about things that really matter, and to feel free to ask their opinions—without being forced to abide by them.

(Michal Heron, Monkmeyer)

Others try to maintain family harmony by smoothing over any disagreements. They don't argue, but they don't really communicate, either.

Half of all the adolescents who took part in the Sorensen (1973) study think that their parents' ideas about most things are wrong, but with a magnanimous tolerance, they concede the old folks a right to their own opinions. Most would like to agree more about things in general, but given their parents' generally mistaken views, this poses some problems.

COMMUNICATION ABOUT SEX

Teen-agers find particularly frustrating their inability to talk freely with their parents about sexual behavior and sexual problems, and they seem to feel that this is largely because their parents don't know how to talk about sex. Very few young people say that their parents have discussed masturbation, birth control, or venereal disease with them. Less than one girl out of three and one boy out of four have heard about either birth control or VD from their parents, and even fewer have been told by them about masturbation (Sorensen, 1973). When parents and children do discuss sex, conversations are usually abstract rather than particular. In another study, college students reported that their *childhood* questions about sex were more likely to be answered satisfactorily than their inquiries during puberty and adolescence—when their sexual curiosity and anxiety are at their peak (Shipman, 1968).

Occasionally it appears that young people have indeed been taught about various sexual matters but they have resisted the information, denying even to themselves that they have heard such things from their parents' tongues. This phenomenon, as well as the tendency toward abstract discussions about sex, may be due to a universal taboo against incest, which affects both parents and children. In some nonliterate societies, the taboo may be expressed by avoiding the children at certain times or evicting them from the parental hut; in our society, it surfaces in the lack of communication about sex, especially between a child and parent of opposite gender (Shipman, 1968).

The ever-present adolescent ambivalence can be seen in young people's feelings about talking about sex with their parents. While they say they would like to be open and frank with their parents about their sexual behavior, they don't like to be questioned and they tend to consider their sexual activities nobody else's business. But when parents are obviously aware of their children's sexual activities and ignore them, the children often become puzzled and angry. Said one sixteen-year-old girl:

> I'm not going to pretend that I don't know what's happening. If my daughter comes in at five in the morning, her skirt backwards and wearing some guy's sweater, I'm not going to ask her, "Did you have a nice time at the movies?" . . . I don't plan to fail [Sorensen, 1973, p. 61]!

PARENTS VERSUS PEERS

Parents often express the fear that their teen-age children will become involved with sex, drugs, and delinquency just to go along with the crowd. An often-heard comment is, "A parent just can't win against a kid's friends!" The herd instinct *is* strong in adolescence, as is the desire to be accepted by the crowd. But the influence of the peer group is not all-powerful.

In one study (Brittain, 1963) 280 ninth- to eleventh-grade girls from both urban and rural high schools in Alabama and Georgia were posed a variety of hypothetical dilemmas involving a teen-age girl. For each instance, one solution was favored by the hypothetical girl's parents, a different one by her friends. By their answers, the girls showed that they valued the opinions of both their parents and their peers; whichever one carried more weight depended on the particular situation involved. When deciding how to dress, how to resolve school-centered situations, and other problems with immediate consequences, the peers' opinions carried more influence. But when deciding about which job to take, how to resolve a deeper moral conflict, or some other long-range issue, the girls tended to lean more toward parental opinions.

Teen-agers tend to hold the same political and religious attitudes as their parents (Bealer, Willits, & Maida, 1964). Students who are actively involved in campus protests, for example, tend to come from liberal, activist families. While their parents are often dismayed by the radicalism and illegality of their children's activities, the students themselves tend to feel they are just carrying their parents' ideas one step further (Keniston, 1967).

The conflicts between the generations are less often over broad values than over timing. Adolescents want to do things that their parents think they're not ready for. Once the parents and the child achieve some sort of balance between what is permitted and what isn't, the temporary nature of this type of conflict is over.

Teen Culture: Relations with Peers

As we enter the cafeteria of Vicky's high school, we see a broad spectrum of adolescents—eating, doing homework, talking, flirting, just "horsing around." And we notice that the large room is divided into several turfs, the boundaries of which all the students recognize by some unspoken agreement. At one table are the "heads," alienated middle-class or upper-middle-class teen-agers who seem to be marking time until they can legally leave school, and who spend much of their spare time using—and abusing—various drugs. At another are the "straights," students from all socioeconomic backgrounds who work and achieve recognition within the "system"—the student government leaders, the athletes, the honor students. At the far end are the black youths, who hang together, exchanging

(Charles Gatewood)

No matter which crowd a teen-ager is part of, she or he is more likely to identify with other adolescents than with people older or younger.

private jokes and forming their own "in" group. And over to the right are the "greasers," boys and girls mostly from working-class homes, who talk "tough and cool" and are likely to have had brushes with the law.

There is, then, no one peer group for all teens. The subgroup, or clique, that Vicky is drawn to depends partly on her socioeconomic status (since most adolescent cliques are class-bound), partly on the values she has picked up from home, partly on her own personality. Once Vicky has become part of a crowd, she influences its other members and they influence her. As much of a nonconformist as she considers herself, she will hew quite closely to the mores of her chosen group. If the other girls in the gang wear faded, patched jeans and work boots, Vicky will not come to school in a plaid skirt and saddle shoes. If her friends spend their evenings hanging around the drive-in restaurant, she will not—by choice—spend hers in the library. The set Vicky hangs out with will influence not only the way she dresses and wears her hair, but her social activities, her sexual behavior, her use or nonuse of drugs, her pursuit or nonpursuit of academic work, her vocational aspirations—the basic patterns of her life.

Not all adolescents run with the herd. Some are independent and individualistic even now, some are already pursuing life goals that keep them too busy, some prefer fewer but more intimate friendships, and some are excluded by every crowd in town.

No matter which crowd a teen-ager is part of—or even if he is a "loner," he is still more likely to identify with other adolescents, no matter what their background or interests, than with people older or younger than himself. American teen-agers are caught up in the grip of what Sorensen (1973) calls "generational chauvinism." They see themselves as part of a group, they think this group is better than any other, and they define the group strictly by age, taking seriously the catch phrase, "don't trust anyone over thirty."

Adolescents consider age the most important criterion for commonality. They tend to identify with other teen-agers, rather than with other people of their own race, religion, community, or sex (Sorensen, 1973). This may be because they feel that most other American teen-agers share their personal values, but that most older people do not. Since they are convinced that their values are superior, there is a basic wall between the generations, one erected by the young people themselves.

Comparing themselves to people in their forties and fifties, adolescents tend to consider themselves more idealistic, less materialistic, healthier in their sexuality, and better able to understand friendship and the important things in life (Sorensen, 1973). Perhaps young people have always thought thus, but in other countries or other times when society venerated the wisdom of old age, young people tacitly went along with the opinion that not until one reaches adult status does one have a true understanding of life. These days, when youth is venerated in our society, many young people tend to feel they have little if anything to learn from their elders. What their peers can teach them seems much more valuable, and for this reason they spend a great proportion of their time with people their own age.

WHAT THE CROWD DOES

"The trouble with this town," complains fifteen-year-old Vicky, "is that there's nothing to do." "What do you mean, there's nothing to do?" challenges her father. "There's a bowling alley, an ice-skating rink, two movies, school dances, lectures at the library. What do you want, a burlesque house?" "Well," says Vicky, "there's no place where you can just go to meet people and sit around and drink Cokes and talk."

Hanging Out

Most teen-agers like to do what Vicky likes—to go someplace where activity isn't organized but where other teens flock. Depending on the weather and the community, the favored place may be a beach, a corner drugstore, a drive-in restaurant, or a shopping center. Despite all the best intentions of civic leaders, a community-run "teen center" rarely becomes the "in" spot.

Dating

This hanging out seems to have replaced the somewhat formalized ritual of dating in most American communities. In very few adolescent circles does a boy call a girl early in the week to ask her to go out with him on Saturday night, to some event for which he will assume total financial responsibility. Today the pattern is more likely to be one in which a group of young people will congregate at the local hangout or at someone's house, or will go to a movie in a coed group, each paying his or her own way in . When pairing off does take place, it often leaps from large-group membership to "going steady," with nothing in between.

"We don't want to play those games," says Vicky. "Dating is so unnatural. You get all dressed up, you go someplace special, and you never really get to know the other person."

One result of this changed pattern of relationships among teen-agers may be the tendency for many adolescents to eliminate much of the necking and petting that once characterized dating relationships. Says Sorensen (1973), "Most adolescents are giving themselves little time for beginning sexual activities and move directly to sexual intercourse [p. 375]."

Dancing

As a popular adolescent pastime, dancing seems to go in and out of style. During the 1950s, weekly "sock hops" to that new "rock and roll" music were the rage. During the 1960s, an assortment of dances that incorporated erotic body motions while prohibiting body contact took over. And in the 1970s, sitting around listening to music appears to have largely supplanted moving in time to it.

Telephoning

An unbelievable amount of adolescent social life is expressed on the telephone, as anyone can testify who has ever tried to reach someone who shares a home (and a phone) with a teen-ager.

> The telephone is an ideal instrument for simultaneous physical distance and erotic proximity. One has a voice speaking intimately into one's ear and an ear at one's lips, and yet there are no possible complications if control over sexual feelings relaxes a little. In addition, the telephone provides the adolescent with a wonderful means of fulfilling the need for flight from his parents to his peers without ever leaving the home. Dial-a-peer and he is transferred out of one world and into the other, escaping too close family involvement by turning to others in the same predicament [GAP, 1968, p. 69].

Driving

Those teens who are old enough to drive and lucky enough to have cars tend to build their social lives around them. They may drive around aimlessly, picking up members of the opposite sex, as portrayed so well in the film *American Graffiti*. They may go beyond the confines of their own neighborhoods to attend parties and concerts in other communities. They may go to drive-in movies or to favored "lovers' lanes," where a boy and girl can have a measure of privacy for sexual exploration. In psychoanalytic thinking, the car may represent for the teen-ager, especially the male, the human body (hence the fascination in tinkering with its insides) or the penis (representing power, virility, and aggression) (GAP, 1968).

The car is an important symbol to the adolescent, symbolizing the attainment of adult status, independence from adult supervision, freedom of mobility, and access to sexual experience. While both boys and girls love to drive, boys are usually more "car-crazy." Their infatuation with the automobile leads to real problems. Almost two-thirds of deaths among eighteen- to nineteen-year-old boys are caused by cars and other motor vehicles. And some 48 percent of car thiefs are teen-age boys, many of whom have their first brush with the law for "borrowing" someone else's car for a joyride (FBI, Uniform Crime Report, 1970).

Sexuality

It is virtually impossible to separate sexuality from identity during adolescence, when sexuality is flowering and influencing a person's total being. Young people's images of themselves, their relationships with their peers, their relationships with their parents—all are inextricably bound up with their sexuality. At this age, sexual activity—from casual kissing to necking and petting to intercourse—fulfills a number of important needs, probably the least of which is physical pleasure. More important for most adolescents are its ability to enhance communication, to exemplify a search for new experience, to prove one's maturity, to be in tune with the peer groups, to find surcease from pressures, and to investigate the mysteries of love (Sorensen, 1973).

PARENTS AND SEX

Many parent-teen conflicts center around sexuality. Vicky's parents don't like her boyfriend, don't want her to see him when no adults are in the home, and don't want her to stay out so late with him. Protective of their daughter, they are somewhat uncomfortable with their own sexuality and extremely unsure of how to handle their little girl's transformation into a voluptuous young woman.

Furthermore, Vicky's parents expect different things from their daughter than they expected for themselves. Of the 3,000 parents who responded to a newspaper questionnaire, 45 percent of the mothers and 71 percent of the fathers had had sexual intercourse themselves before marriage. Yet almost

75 percent of them hoped that their daughters would not. Only 40 percent, however, *believed* their daughters would be virgin brides *(McCall's, 1973)*. The extent of parental confusion can also be seen in the parents' feelings about their sons. Only about half wanted them to be virgin grooms, and only one-sixth expected them to be. Yet these same parents—whose expectations differed so for their sons and daughters—condemned the double standard 5 to 1.

Many adults believe that today's teen-age sex scene is one huge orgy, with most girls on The Pill and ready to jump into bed with a boy as easily as her mother used to bestow a good-night kiss. The opposite viewpoint, as espoused by Bell (1966), is that the proportion of women who engage in sexual intercourse before marriage has not changed over the past three or four generations. What is the real truth? While some information on current sexual practices will be discussed in the next section, it is hard to

While communication about sex remains a problem, parents today seem more likely to stress maturity, mutuality of relationships, and the avoidance of exploitation and promiscuity rather than the need to "save oneself" for marriage.

(Charles Gatewood)

know how different today's young people are from their parents. Fewer studies were made in past generations, those that were are not always comparable to those of today (for example, the Kinsey reports were based largely on interviews with whites), and changing attitudes toward sex mean that today's young people may be more prone to tell the truth about their sexual behavior than were their parents and grandparents.

It does seem clear that attitudes *have* changed, not only among young people, but among their parents, as well. Many of today's parents are in a transitional stage. Remembering their own youth, they recognize and accept their children's premarital sexual activities, but enough vestiges of what their own parents taught them remain to block full acceptance of their children's behavior. Caught in the breezes of change, their ambivalence shows in their conflicting statements about the double standard. The single standard is gaining ground, though, as evidenced in the opinions of adults and high school and college students surveyed by Reiss (1964; cited by Bell, 1966). The students and the adults differed markedly in their willingness to condone sexual activities between engaged couples, but both age groups maintained fairly consistent standards for both males and females.

Parental values are unquestionably more liberal today than they have been in previous generations, especially as they concern female sexuality. Today's parents are less likely to punish or cast out a pregnant daughter than they are to help her. Today's parents may worry about where to put their daughter's boyfriend when she brings him home for a weekend visit; twenty years ago, they would not have admitted that they knew she was sleeping with him, much less have even entertained the notion of letting him sleep in her room.

While communication about sex still remains a problem for most parents and teen-agers, some parents have always communicated their values about sexual behavior to their children. Today, more seem likely to stress maturity, mutuality of relationships, and the avoidance of exploitation and promiscuity rather than the need to "save oneself" for marriage. Yet there are still many families in which parents and children avoid conflicts by avoiding the topic.

> For many parents and their children, the conflict about premarital sex will continue to be characterized by the parent's playing ostrich and burying his head in the sand, and the youth's efforts to keep the sand from blowing away [Bell, 1966, p. 44].

CURRENT SEXUAL PRACTICES

Despite the fears of some and the hopes of others, the teen-age virgin is not an extinct animal. More than half of all nineteen-year-old girls and almost half of all nineteen-year-old boys have not yet been initiated into sexual intercourse (Sorensen, 1973; Zelnik & Kantner, 1972). Zelnik and

Kantner's 1972 report, based on interviews conducted the previous year with 4,611 girls fifteen to nineteen years old found that 46 percent of all nineteen-year-olds were no longer virgins, and Sorensen (1973) came up with almost the same figure, 45 percent. The Zelnik and Kantner study involved girls only, but Sorensen, who also interviewed teen-age boys, found that 59 percent had sexual intercourse by the age of nineteen.

As we said in the previous section, it is hard to know exactly how these proportions compare with those of the past. Judging from the way today's adolescents talk and act in public, it certainly seems as if more of them—especially the girls—are more sexually active in private. And some comparative figures seem to bear this out. In 1953, for example, when Kinsey reported on his interviews with more than 5,000 white women, only 3 percent had parted with their virginity by the age of fifteen, and only 23 percent by twenty-one. A generation later, Zelnik and Kantner's figures for white females showed that 11 percent were no longer virgins at fifteen, 40 percent at nineteen. When the figures include black girls, who are more active sexually, the nonvirgin rates go up to 14 percent at fifteen and 46 percent at nineteen. Sorensen (1973) found that more than half (56 percent) of all nonvirgin girls, or 30 percent of *all* the girls surveyed, and almost three-quarters (71 percent) of the nonvirgin boys, or about 44 percent of *all* the boys, had had their first sexual intercourse by the age of fifteen.

So it is apparent that many young people today are having sexual intercourse at quite early ages. Young people who might in earlier days have contented themselves with necking and petting are now culminating their relationships with intercourse. This relative precocity may be a somewhat groping attempt to form "meaningful" relationships. Young people are acting in intimate ways, although they have not yet determined enough of a "sense of self," which Erikson (1950) postulates as a prerequisite for a genuinely intimate relationship.

Sorensen (1973) found that very few nonvirgins had waited till they were eighteen or nineteen to have sexual intercourse (see Table 14-1). This account contrasts with a 1969 study by Luckey and Nass, which found that of the 58 percent of college men and 43 percent of college women who were no longer virgins, the average age of first intercourse was 17.9 for the men and 18.7 for the women. These disparities in age may reflect different practices among college-bound and non-college-bound youth: The Luckey and Nass study surveyed only college students, while the Sorensen study surveyed young people from a range of socioeconomic circumstances. Young people from lower socioeconomic groups tend to become more sexually active at a younger age (Zelnik & Kantner, 1972).

This difference probably accounts for at least part—and perhaps all—of the difference in sexual activity between white and black teen-agers, since more blacks have been trapped in the lower classes. By way of comparison,

Table 14-1   Age of First Intercourse of Nonvirgin Adolescents *(Sorensen, 1973)*

	All nonvirgins	Nonvirgin boys	Nonvirgin girls
12 or under	13%	17%	7%
13	15	18	12
14	15	18	11
15	22	18	26
16	15	12	21
17	9	12	6
18 or 19	11	5	17
	100%	100%	100%

Zelnik and Kantner (1972) found that 32 percent of all fifteen-year-old black girls are no longer virgins, and by the age of nineteen, 81 percent have had sexual intercourse. The black girls, though, were less promiscuous than the whites, with 11 percent of the black nonvirgins reporting having had intercourse with four or more partners, compared to 16 percent of the white nonvirgins.

In general, teen-agers are not promiscuous. Sorensen found less sexual adventurism, which he defined as having several different sexual partners in a limited time period, than he found monogamy (without marriage). In other words, teen-agers tend to enter into sexual relationships that have meaning for them and that they plan to honor with fidelity. And Zelnik and Kantner found that 40 percent of the girls whom they interviewed had not had sexual intercourse at all during the past month, and 70 percent had engaged in it only one or two times. Sixty percent of the nonvirgins had had only one sexual partner, and half of these expected to marry him. In sum, it seems that teen-agers are more sexually active than they used to be, that this applies especially to younger teens and to girls, but that anyone looking for directions to the orgy will be hard put to find them.

CURRENT SEXUAL ATTITUDES

When we examine young people's attitudes toward sexuality, we see the "sexual revolution" in full flower. Vicky's mother, for example, may have had sexual intercourse with one or two young men before she met, bedded, and wedded her husband—but she kept her activities to herself, worried that her husband-to-be might not respect her, and experienced pangs of guilt from time to time over her sexual activities. In a popular novel of the 1950s, twenty-four-year-old Marjorie Morningstar agonized over the way she would tell the man who had just proposed to her that she had had an affair with another man:

(Virginia Hamilton)

Most sexually active young people do not engage in "recreational" sex, but instead perceive sex as part of a relationship, which may involve, love, affection, or friendship.

She woke a couple of hours later to an immediate and wretched problem: when and how should she tell him about Noel?

For she had not yet done so. No consideration in the world could have brought her to tell him, before she was sure he loved her and wanted to marry her . . . She knew she would have to tell him now, and the prospect made her sick, but she was ready to do it. . . . Quite possibly he might want to break off with her. Clearly he had assumed she was a virgin; it had never occurred to him to question the fact [Wouk, 1955, pp. 548-549].

What happened when Marjorie finally revealed the truth about her past to her fiance?

He never said anything about Noel thereafter; not for the rest of their lives. But she never again saw on his face the pure happiness that had shone there during the drive across the George Washington Bridge in the sunset. He loved her. He took her as she was, with her deformity, despite it. For that was what it amounted to in his eyes and in hers—a deformity: a deformity that could no longer be helped; a permanent crippling, like a crooked arm [Wouk, 1955, p. 553].

And today? Almost three-fourths of the teen-age boys questioned by the

Sorensen researchers say they do not lose respect for a girl who goes to bed with a boy before marriage. And 65 percent of the boys do not believe that girls should stay virgins till they find the boys they want to marry and do not insist on virginity for their future wives (Sorensen, 1973). Some of the pressures, then, against premarital sexual activity for girls have disappeared. While a few nonvirgins feel guilty, it is usually because they are uncomfortable about deceiving their family or friends, and not because of their sexual behavior itself.

Evidence that these attitudes have changed very recently comes from several quarters. As late as 1969, a team of developmentalists stated (Mussen, Conger, & Kagan):

> In no study available to us did a majority of students approve of premarital sexual relations for couples who are not in love or engaged, and in most studies, less than 50 percent approved even when there was a formal engagement [p. 640].

In the Sorensen study (1973), a whopping 76 percent of all boys and 66 percent of all girls approve of living together without marriage.

The winds of change have blown so that many young people now feel pressured *into* sexual relationships. College students sometimes worry about their normality if they are still virgins at the age of nineteen or twenty, often engage in sexual intercourse just to get rid of a burdensome virginity, and may feel that the pressures from family, friends, and society at large are forcing them into sexual activity before they are ready for it. A Yale University physician (Lee, 1973) comments:

> Adolescents are as ambivalent and anxious about sex as their elders ever were. Yes, there has been a youth rebellion against Victorian morality, but rather than liberating, it has transformed sex into an ideology. The new ideology is that sex is good and good sex means orgasm and anybody can. The result has been to turn the pleasures of sex into a duty. Along with all this goes the "knowledge" that if you don't have intercourse, you'll go crazy—and that virginity is a hang-up [p. 92].

Sex may be ethical these days, but there is still a sexual ethic. Young people have strong ideas of right and wrong, although these ideas may differ vigorously from those of their parents' generation. More than 8 out of 10 adolescents have strong feelings about what is right and wrong for them, as far as sex is concerned. But they are very tolerant of others, believing sex to be a private affair, and are reluctant to condemn others for participating in activities that they would not take part in themselves. The prevailing ethic is that "anything two people want to do sexually is moral, as long as they both want to do it and it does not hurt either one of them [Sorensen, 1973, p. 106]." Only a fourth of all adolescents surveyed believe it's immoral for unmarried persons to have sex, almost half believe that sex without love is still moral, but almost 9 out of 10 believe that it's immoral for a boy to force a girl to have sex (Sorensen, 1973).

Modern teen-agers express strong opinions against exploitation, as for example, against a boy's telling a girl he loves her just to get her to have sex with him. As one nineteen-year-old boy said, "Girls are people. They enjoy things and love and hate like everyone else. It's sickening to see a male using a woman [Sorensen, 1973, p. 85]."

Most sexually active young people do not engage in "recreational" sex, but instead perceive sex as part of a relationship, which may involve love, affection, or friendship. More often than not, they associate sex with love and are usually quite faithful to their current lovers.

SEX DIFFERENCES AND THE DOUBLE STANDARD

While most adolescents feel that moral standards apply equally to boys and to girls (Sorensen, 1973), the sexes still show some differences. Boys are still more active sexually: they start earlier, have sex with more partners, are less likely to be constrained by societal standards, and are less likely to insist on love as a prerequisite for sex.

Adolescent boys and girls have traditionally differed in the nature of their sex drives and in their sexual behavior. As a rule, boys are much more easily aroused. They are likely to have an erection when they inadvertently touch a girl or see one, when they read or hear about sexual activities, when they look at sexual pictures, when they think about sex, and when they become involved in necking or petting. They are often embarrassed by these erections but are rarely able to control them. Once aroused, they feel an intense urgency toward sexual release, an urgency concentrated specifically in the genital area. By the age of fifteen, most boys are having orgasms two or three times a week—mostly from masturbation, sexual dreams, and petting (Pomeroy, 1969). They reach their sexual peak in their late teens and, while they may remain sexually active well into old age, the rate of activity gradually decreases.

For most adolescent girls, sex is not so much a part of daily life. At fifteen, most girls are not having any orgasms at all. By and large, females don't reach their sexual peak until their thirties or forties. Teen-age girls are more likely to want romance and affection in a relationship rather than sexual satisfaction. Their sexual feelings tend to revolve more around the person they are with, and less on specific physical pressures.

A small minority of adolescent girls, though, become aroused as easily as most boys. These girls are aroused by seeing, reading, and thinking of sexual things. They have orgasm frequently, quickly and easily, and often undergo a real struggle to keep out of trouble in a society which does not approve of such behavior. They may also have difficulty in their own teen-age society, if most of the other girls are not so uninhibited, which is usually the case (Pomeroy, 1969, p. 31).

It is hard to say whether the differences in sexual response between the sexes is culturally or biologically based. Because of the woman's more vulnerable position in being the one who becomes impregnated and because of the man's need to be reassured that he is indeed the father of the children borne by his wife, girls are sex-socialized quite differently from boys all around the world. On the other hand, there is no denying the biological differences between the sexes. Mead (1949) hypothesizes differences based on structural anatomical differences: males masturbate earlier and more frequently, and are more responsive to sexual stimulation, because their sexual organs are more accessible. Other writers suggest that the greater intensity of the adolescent boy's sex drive is strictly hormonal. According to this theory, sexuality is different for boys and girls because biology is different for boys and girls. This would explain why the more urgent sexual needs of boys require release that is more physical than emotional, and why the more diffused sexual yearnings of girls find fulfillment in relationships that are more emotional than physical.

There is no doubt that the recent sexual revolution has affected girls and women much more than boys and men. It will be interesting to see whether, in this freer climate, female sexuality will become identical to male sexuality, or whether there will always be a difference between the sexes in sexual attitudes, expression, and needs.

HOMOSEXUALITY

Homosexuality is coming out of the closet in American society. While the rate of homosexual activity may not be on the rise, it is becoming a more visible phenomenon. More people are openly asserting their sexual preference for others of their own sex and demanding that they not be penalized for this preference. "Gay liberation" protests and marches demand an end to discrimination against homosexuals. And the American Psychiatric Association finally voted to remove homosexuality from its official list of mental disorders. No longer classifying it as an illness, the APA now designates it a "sexual orientation disturbance"—and that definition is really relevant only for homosexuals who "are either disturbed by, in conflict with, or wish to change, their sexual orientation [Gould, 1974]."

Despite the increased talk about homosexuality today, "homosexual behavior on a continuous basis and self-acknowledgment of one's own homosexuality are generally an adult rather than an adolescent phenomenon in contemporary American society [Sorensen, 1973, p. 285]." Only 9 percent of all adolescents (11 percent of the boys and 6 percent of the girls) reported having had any homosexual experiences, and only 2 percent of the boys and almost no girls reported having had any homosexual experiences during the preceding month [Sorensen, 1973].

Most boys and girls feel that homosexuality is abnormal and few say they would participate in it themselves. More than half support laws against homosexuality, and only about 40 percent feel that "if two boys/girls want to have sex together, it's all right so long as they both want to do it [Sorensen, 1973, p. 289]."

While theories abound about the nature and the causes of homosexuality, there is very little concrete knowledge about the phenomenon. All observers agree that male homosexuality is more common in our society than female homosexuality, but no one really knows why this should be. Either kind is thought to be a pathological dysfunction by some, or merely a variant of normal sexuality by others; at least one psychiatrist feels that "if there were no social restrictions on sexual object choice, most humans would be functioning bisexuals [Gould, 1974]."

Vocational Aspirations

Just as it is virtually impossible to separate the search for identity from sexuality, so also is identity closely linked with vocational choice. The question, "Who shall I be?" is very close to "What shall I do?"—especially in contemporary American life. And adolescents here often have a harder time solving their vocational dilemmas than their sexual ones. This is partly because of the extended adolescence so many young people go through, especially those who go on to college.

A 1949 study by Hollingshead found that upper- and middle-class high school students had more of an idea of what they wanted to do with their lives than did youths from working-class homes. In today's generation, the proportions might well be reversed. Many first-year college students have only the haziest notion of the type of work they want to pursue, and some are still at sea after they receive their diplomas. Turned off by what they see as a hypocritical, materialistic society, such students sometimes take low-level jobs as vehicles for their real lives, a hedonistic search for pleasure, while others volunteer for such service projects as the Peace Corps until they come to grips with what they want to do with their lives. In any case, many factors affect a young person's search for meaningful work. Socioeconomic status, race, sex, individual ability, personality, parental ambitions and encouragement, schooling, societal values, and the accident of particular life experiences all play their parts.

As an example, the decision of a late adolescent boy to become a physician may have many roots. His relationship with his father included the father's lengthy illness during which the doctor was the one whom the father turned to and obeyed; in becoming a doctor the young man thus becomes someone whom the father listens to and respects. Due to her husband's illness, the mother also had leaned heavily on the doctor; so in becoming a doctor the boy would fulfill unconscious oedipal wishes for closeness with his mother. To him, being a doctor also means activity rather than passivity, and masculine accomplishment, a kind of socially recognized potency. His desire to use his good intellect would be met in this highly professional occupation. The fact that there are substantial social and economic rewards in this profession is also important. And finally, beneath all of this lie forgotten childhood wishes that were never adequately resolved: to see the naked human body and to learn all about it; to hear intimate secrets; to encounter and deal with pain and bleeding [GAP, 1968, pp. 90–91].

SOCIOECONOMIC STATUS

At the age of five, Jason was used to hearing that ever-recurring question, "What do you want to be when you grow up?" One day he would say, "fireman," the next, "policeman." Ten years later, his chances of still wanting either of these occupations are lower if he is the son of a doctor, higher if he is the son of a laborer. The social class of Jason's parents is a major factor in his thinking about his future. Most of us are greatly influenced in our vocational aspirations by the kinds of homes we grow up in. Generally, the lower the social class, the lower the occupational goal.

Why is this so? There are undoubtedly many reasons. Most people are more comfortable in familiar situations, for one thing. And most people are more familiar with people of similar social class. Children who grow up in working-class neighborhoods are more likely to know, as individuals and in social situations, adults who work as secretaries, plumbers, postal workers, and hairdressers rather than doctors, lawyers, professors, and psychologists. They thus become more familiar with both the jobholders and the jobs themselves, which then appear more attainable. While young people often aim to reach higher socioeconomic levels than those of their parents, generally they aspire only to the next rung, rather than to the top of the vocational ladder.

We see dramatic evidence of this in one study that asked teen-agers of different social classes what kinds of jobs they aspired to. Only 7 percent from the lowest social class aimed for business and professional careers, while 77 percent from the two highest classes had such goals. Conversely, only 1 percent from the two highest classes expected to go to work in service or trade occupations, while 25 percent of those from the lowest class did (Hollingshead, 1949). An interesting sidelight on the vocational preparation of these young people can be seen in the degree to which they had made up their minds about their futures. Only 3 percent from the top two classes had no idea what they wanted to do with their lives, while 41 percent from the bottom class were undecided.

SEX

Traditionally in our society, boys have asked, "What shall I be?" while girls have asked, "Whom shall I marry?" Vocational counseling in the schools has reinforced this duality, generally channeling girls into less demanding occupations in the expectation that they will work sporadically during their lifetime and will, for the most part, be supported by an employed husband.

In line with these attitudes, male and female adolescents have held different definitions of success (Zazzo, 1962). Boys have felt that work would bring them wealth and prestige, while girls have looked for success in love and friendship. No wonder males have pursued vocational goals before emotional ones, while girls have given more thought to finding a husband than finding a career.

Problems of Girls

The limitations such thinking places on girls is twofold. First, there are those vast numbers of girls who do not give any thought to their future. Ignorant or oblivious to the fact that 9 out of 10 of them will work at some time during their lives, these girls set limited or unrealistic career sights. They either take low-level jobs right out of high school, expecting to work at them until—and only until—they get married. Or they go to college to find a husband instead of a profession. When financial need or a latent desire for self-fulfillment sends them, as more mature women, into the job arena, they find themselves unprepared, underemployed, and underpaid.

Other girls are hampered in a different way. These are capable students who want to achieve, but who feel that vocational success is not compatible with femininity. These women, while ostensibly striving for career success, are in fact hampered by a "fear of success [Horner, 1970]." As students they may refuse to divulge their good marks, preferring to talk about their failures. They often change their career plans toward goals that they consider to be more traditional, more feminine, and less ambitious. Middle- and upper-middle-class white girls whose fathers are successful professional or businessmen are more likely to fear success than are black girls or girls from lower- or lower-middle-class homes whose fathers have not been successful (Horner, 1970).

Problems of Boys

Teen-age boys often get a panicky feeling, burdened by their need to find a profession and prove their manhood by succeeding in it and supporting a family. This concentration on their job futures often makes them neglect their emotional development.

Changing Attitudes

In recent years, though, these attitudes have been changing. Teen- age girls are now more interested in preparing themselves to earn a good living, and most expect to make work a larger part of their lives than was once the case. Furthermore, when they do consider career possibilities, they are diverging from the traditionally female occupations, which have been thought to reflect innate, sex-based differences in abilities.

While preschool boys don't show any major differences from preschool girls in verbal or math abilities, the picture is quite different by adolescence.

There is no difference between the sexes in IQ, but by the secondary school years, boys do better in science and math, and girls in English and foreign languages. Is this an innate difference that becomes noticeable in adolescence—or is it the result of different interests and different encouragement? Studies such as those of Bing (1963) indicate that cultural factors may be at the root of these differences.

PARENTS

Not surprisingly, parents exert a great influence on their children's future careers. If parents do not encourage their children to pursue higher education and are not willing to help them through college, it is that much harder for the young people to prepare themselves. Some students do, of course, work their way through school, take out loans, or win scholarships, even though their parents are not able to or interested in helping them. But by and large, parental encouragement and financial support influence aspiration, as well as achievement.

The expectations that parents have of their children and their willingness to help them achieve their career goals will influence the vocations that students aspire to. When parents are ambitious for their children and reward them for good school work, the children aspire to occupations that are higher than those their parents presently hold (Bell, 1963). In studying high-IQ high school boys, Bell (1963) found that parental encouragement was a better predictor of high ambition than was the boys' social class.

Parents influence their children as models, too. This holds true especially for fathers and sons, and can be seen in the disproportionately high numbers of boys who follow the same line of work as their fathers.

On the other hand, girls are influenced less by the jobs their mothers and fathers hold. This is probably because the roles of women have changed much more over the past twenty-five years than the roles of men. In a time of flux, the old models lose some of their potency.

Some studies have shown that daughters of working women have higher career aspirations and are more likely to choose careers in male-dominated fields than are the daughters of housewives (Etaugh, 1973). But an intriguing recent study of 1,012 college-educated wives of graduate students (Lipman-Blumen, 1972) found that whether or not the mothers of these women had worked had no perceptible impact on whether the women lived traditional lives as housewives or whether they sought careers of their own. What was highly influential, though, was the mothers' feelings about their own lives. Dissatisfied mothers were more likely than satisfied ones to rear career-oriented daughters, while satisfied mothers were more likely to have daughters with the traditional orientation. The career-oriented women were also more likely to come from families in which neither parent was dominant, or in which the mother was dominant, than from families with dominant fathers.

As adolescents, the career-oriented women were less close to their parents, lonelier in general, and farther along on the way to finding their own identities. "A sense of loneliness in adolescence may be considered one kind of short-term psychological price paid for developing new patterns of behavior [p. 41]." Both the career women and the housewives seemed equally satisfied with their lives.

SCHOOL

According to a *Life* magazine poll (1969), which surveyed about 2,500 parents, high school students, teachers, and principals in 100 schools across the country, most people agree that the major function of a high school education today is to prepare young people for college. But they disagree on what the schools *should* be doing. Almost half the students and more than half the teachers felt that the high schools should be teaching the skills to live in a rapidly changing world. Only one-third of the parents felt this way. Parents are more likely to see the schools as prevocational training grounds, instead of as preparation for life itself.

In line with their beliefs, most high school students feel they don't have enough of a say in making school policy, and are especially interested in helping to make rules and decide curriculum. If given the opportunity, they would provide more in-school chances to discuss the use of drugs, the rights of black students, and sex hygiene. They would, though, retain many of their present courses—seeing the most useful ones as English, math, science, business, and history (especially black history). But despite their burning desire for more active involvement in their schools, most of these 1969 urban, suburban, small town, and rural students liked their schools. They liked their teachers, their principals, their class schedules, and the school facilities. They even felt the grade system was fair.

The particular school a student attends can affect his or her choice of occupation. Studies of high school students have shown, for example, that the sons of manual workers have higher educational and career aspirations when they attend largely middle-class schools than when they go to school mostly with other children of the working class. Similarly, sons of professionals have higher goals when they go to school with other upper- and middle-class youths than when they attend schools that have a high proportion of students from lower-class families (Wilson, 1959; Boyle, 1966). This effect is more pronounced in large, heterogeneous communities.

There are many possible explanations for this finding, and it is hard to know which one factor, or which combination of factors, is most responsible. Are the students influenced by their friends? Probably, to some extent. Do the teachers in middle-class schools have different expectations of their students than do teachers in working-class schools? Probably, and teachers' expectations often constitute a self-fulfilling prophecy (Rosenthal

& Jacobson, 1968). Is the quality of education better at middle-class schools? Probably, and higher aspirations are realistic for better-educated students. And finally, are the parents of students in a social class minority different from other parents of the same socioeconomic status? It is quite possible that working-class parents whose children go to middle-class schools are more ambitious for their children. They move into middle-class neighborhoods because they are willing to make sacrifices to give their children educational opportunities. Conversely, middle-class parents who are content to have their children attend schools heavily populated with children of lower social classes may not feel that occupational success is terribly important.

Dropping Out

The student who leaves school before getting a diploma is likely to have serious vocational and social problems. In our highly technological society, the number of jobs for unskilled workers are shrinking, day by day. The "school of hard knocks" doesn't have much to teach anymore. Many

(Charles Gatewood)

The drop-out: 800,000 annually swell the ranks of the minimally educated, minimally trained, and minimally employable.

employers will not consider hiring anyone who is not a high school graduate, even for jobs that do not require academic abilities. The high school diploma today is comparable to the certificate of eighth-grade graduation of fifty years ago.

Most adolescents realize the importance of staying in school, and fewer drop out these days. While 58 percent of all students graduated from high school in 1955, 70 percent finished in 1970, and this rate has appeared to be steadily on the rise (Silberman, 1970). In 1960, we had a million school dropouts, compared with "only" 800,000 in 1971. But 800,000 young people still represent a huge annual swelling of the ranks of the minimally educated, minimally trained, and minimally employable. These youths are more likely to be delinquent, more likely to go on drugs, and more likely to suffer from chronic unemployment (Cervantes, 1965a).

Who are the dropouts?   Poor black students are the ones most likely to drop out of school, although 4 out of 5 dropouts are white, and financial need is very rarely the primary reason for leaving school (Cervantes, 1965a). While we usually think of the typical dropout as male, girls drop out just as often as boys (Combs & Cooley, 1968). Dropouts are likely to have been left back one or more grades, to score lower than graduates on intelligence tests, and to have problems with reading (Combs & Cooley, 1968). But most dropouts are of at least normal intelligence, and some have IQs of 110 or more (Cervantes, 1965a; Combs & Cooley, 1968). At least half and maybe three-fourths of all those students who drop by the wayside before graduation day have the ability to graduate from high school. Why, then, don't they?

Why they drop out.   High school dropouts are not a homogeneous group, and their reasons for leaving school are many. Voss, Wendling, and Elliott (1966) have classified them into three subgroups: the *involuntary dropout,* who must leave school either because of some physical disability or because of emergency family circumstances; the *retarded dropout,* whose low intelligence or poor reading ability renders him incapable of doing high school work, and the *capable dropout,* who does have the ability to graduate. Those in the first category are relatively rare and those in the second can be easily explained. "Retarded dropouts" usually leave school fairly early. In one study, three-fourths of those who dropped out in seventh grade had IQ scores below 85, compared to only one-third of those who left between the seventh and twelfth grades (Voss et al., 1966). Another report showed that 45 percent of eleventh- and twelfth-grade dropouts were doing passing work (Dillon, in Voss, p. 365).

Those "capable dropouts" present the greatest challenge to society. For by dropping out of school, these young people sharply limit their own futures, as well as their potential contributions to society.

One longitudinal study that tested a large and diverse number of ninth-grade students in 1960 went back to these students four years later, to compare those who had dropped out of school with those who had graduated from high school but had not gone on to college (Combs and Cooley, 1968). In 1964, the graduates had been out of school one year and some of the dropouts had been out for four.

As ninth-graders, the dropouts had generally scored lower in tests of general academic ability, but some had scored in the highest quarter. Some differences in interest patterns showed up between the two groups, with the dropouts showing more interest in labor and skilled trades than the graduates. Dropout boys also showed more interest in music, and dropout girls in mechanical-technical areas. Some of these students may have felt, then, that further academic schooling would be neither relevant nor helpful for what they wanted to do in life.

Personality and school activity differences showed up, too. Both male and female graduates saw themselves as tidier, calmer, more vigorous, more cultured, and more mature, more sociable, and more self-confident than did the dropouts. The dropout boys considered themselves leaders more often than did the male graduates, but they also viewed themselves as more impulsive. It appears, then, that the dropouts had a lower sense of self-esteem than did the students who finished school.

The dropout boys dated more than the control boys and admitted to more trouble studying and concentrating on their schoolwork. While the girls who dropped out of school were more likely to come from lower socioeconomic circumstances than the girls who stayed to graduate, there was no such difference for the boys. This seems to indicate that financial need was not the spur for the boys to leave school. It may not have been the determining factor for the girls, either, since most of them got married and (presumably) moved away from home, rather than contributing to family income.

It is almost impossible to pin down the precise reasons why young people leave school. Three-fourths of the girls said they left to get married. But did they want to get married because they weren't doing well in school, because they couldn't see any value to remaining in school, because they became pregnant, because they wanted to get away from home? We don't know. The boys gave a variety of reasons for leaving—"needed at home, didn't like school, failing, got married, felt too old to stay in school [Combs & Cooley, 1968, p. 351]." But most of these explanations tell us very little about the underlying reasons. Similarly, in another survey, "lack of interest" and "lack of scholastic success" headed the list of reasons for leaving school (Huffington, 1962), but as Combs and Cooley (1968) say, these "are only symptoms, not the problems [p. 352]." Whatever their reasons, more than half of the dropouts interviewed by Combs and Cooley regretted having left school without graduating.

One researcher paired 150 white lower-class high school graduating seniors with 150 white dropouts, and concluded that a major difference between the two groups lay in family relationships (Cervantes, 1965b).

The homes of the youths interviewed were either in similar or identical neighborhoods. Externally, the homes appeared identical. Internally, there were on an average the same number of children, and by matched pairs the respondents were of the same age, the same sex, the same native ability, and had attended the same high schools. Yet the different climate of happiness in the homes of the dropouts as contrasted with the graduates is startling. Unhappiness is the characteristic of the one group, happiness that of the other [p. 222].

Four out of five of the dropouts did not feel that their families understood or accepted them nor that they understood and accepted their families, while four out of five graduates felt mutual understanding and acceptance within the family. The graduates' families communicated with each other better than the dropouts' families and enjoyed each other's company more. Said Vivian, a dropout girl:

We were all never together at one time. . . . My parents left at six in the morning and didn't get home until four. I just played hookey. . . . When I finally told them, they were sick about it but I had already signed myself out [Cervantes, 1965b, p. 221].

These differences in family relationships may not apply to youthful members of minority groups, whose reasons for dropping out of school may have more to do with alienation from the educational structure and society at large than from their immediate families. In an attempt to reach many of these young people, some school systems have established special job training or counseling programs, or special "schools without walls," which combine academic work with work in the community. To reach these youths effectively, though, it is necessary to change not only their schools, but many other elements in their communities.

SOCIETY

A major problem in our society is the scarcity of on-the-job training for young people. Apprentice programs for teen-agers no longer exist. As society becomes more complex, it becomes increasingly difficult to conceptualize what many jobs involve. Few adolescents have the opportunity to see adults at work in any jobs that don't touch their lives directly. It becomes harder and harder for teen-agers to find summer employment, by which they can get a taste of what a particular job involves. It is often hard for young teen-agers even to find meaningful volunteer work.

PERSONALITY

Huey Long, the controversial United States Senator and Governor of Louisiana, was brash and egotistical all his life. He craved attention and would go to almost any length to get it, used audacity and laughter to manipulate people for his own ends, and made up his own rules when he didn't like the ones in force. Commented his biographer, "These are qualities that make an ordinary person the opposite of endearing—but in a politician they are called genius [Williams, 1969, p. 37]."

Not every politician is a Huey Long, of course. But it is fairly safe to say that the typical successful politician has a very different personality from the typical successful nuclear physicist. A restless, energetic, outgoing person is more likely to succeed in politics—or in sales or military life—than in accounting or scientific research. And a shy, thoughtful, intellectual person would be happier working as a librarian than as a trial lawyer.

While most jobs require particular talents or training for specific skills, they also require certain personality traits. Those people who know themselves well enough to go into the kind of work that suits them temperamentally are more likely to achieve success in their chosen careers. A study of 638 bright, college-bound high school seniors found that the students had formed definite ideas of the personality types common to various occupations, and when asked to describe their own personalities and to indicate their vocational preferences, they tended to see themselves in line with the vocational stereotypes they had formed (Holland, 1963 I, 1963 II).

These students saw engineers as practical and useful builders, physicists as dedicated intellectuals, teachers as patient and helpful, accountants as precise but dull, artists as creative and temperamental, and business executives as smart, busy, and ambitious (Holland, 1963 I). Girls who expressed interest in scientific vocations tended to see themselves as analytical, curious, precise, and thorough, while girls who were interested in going into social work or related fields thought of themselves as easygoing, accepting of others, friendly, and understanding. Boys who looked ahead to business careers considered themselves aggressive, dominant, energetic, aggressive, and *not* artistic, idealistic, quiet, or scientific, while boys with artistic leanings saw themselves as dreamy, idealistic, impractical, and sensitive (Holland, 1963 II).

Not surprisingly, people also tend to go into occupations that match what they have to do on the job with what they are good at doing. Thus, boys who expressed interest in taking up skilled trades said that they most enjoyed working with their hands, tools, equipment, or apparatus; and girls who were attracted to accounting jobs said that they were most competent in solving numerical or mathematical problems, and that they most enjoyed keeping records and doing computations (Holland, 1963 III).

We also go into certain careers to fill basic personality needs. A woman may become a psychiatrist to clear up her questions about her own personality, or a man may become a business executive because he feels the need for the kind of power that comes from telling others what to do. When high school seniors were asked to rate a variety of jobs according to the personality needs they fulfill, they showed that they viewed the jobs and the jobholders write differently. Boys and girls thought very much alike in this regard.

The students considered scientists and engineers to be motivated by needs for achievement, but not by those for affection. Physicians and nurses emerged as much warmer people, with needs involving close human relationships (Dipboye & Anderson, 1961). So our own needs and the way we perceive various occupations as capable of meeting our needs tend to be a major factor in career choice.

The extent to which an individual fears success also affects career choice. A study of first- and second-year male college students found that those who fear success tend to respond to this fear in one of two ways. Either they aspire to a job so far below their ability that they are absolutely certain of getting it and doing it well, or they aspire to a job so difficult to get that they are virtually certain to fail.

> Both underaspiring and overaspiring allow the person to avoid a real test of competence. In the former case, success is a relatively sure thing; in the latter, success is not to be expected and failure is neither meaningful nor threatening [Burnstein, 1963, p. 192].

Bright college women who fear success tend to choose more traditionally feminine, less ambitious vocations than do those free of such fears (Horner, 1972). Black college men seem to be more afraid of success than white college men, and white college women more than black college women (Weston & Mednick, 1972). The relative freedom of fear of success among black women is undoubtedly related to different sex-role expectations between the races. Black parents have higher aspirations for their daughters than their sons. This may be partly an attempt to protect their sons, since the successful black man is seen as more of a threat by whites than is the successful black woman. The successful black man will have to defend himself from the hostility of white men; the successful black woman has no such fear. Nor is the black woman afraid that success will make her unfeminine, because a woman's success tends to be better accepted within the black community than within the white.

The Minority-group Adolescent

Teen-agers from a cultural or racial minority group are thrust into a particularly intense identity crisis. Not only do these young people have to

(Virginia Hamilton)

Raised by adults who generally do not share the value system of the dominant culture, and who rarely achieve positions of importance within it, minority group teen-agers are thrust into a particularly intense identity crisis.

deal with the same life changes as other teen-agers, but they also have a host of other problems attributable to their minority status. Raised by adults who generally do not share the value system of the dominant culture, and who rarely achieve positions of importance within it, minority-group adolescents often have trouble finding role models to identify with.

Some of the problems faced by black, Puerto Rican, and Mexican-American teen-agers illustrate this special difficulty of any minority-group adolescent.

THE BLACK ADOLESCENT
Black teen-agers often have to make the transition from a childhood spent entirely in a black world, where schoolmates, neighbors, and almost all adults were black, to an adulthood that will be lived to a great extent in the outside, white-dominated world. They have to deal with the racism that affects all black people, no matter what their personal accomplishments. Adolescents' tendencies to exclude those who are different often wreak particular hardships on black youths.

While the black middle class is constantly growing, the great majority of black Americans suffer a host of ills besides racial prejudice. The most basic of these is poverty. Growing up in an overcrowded urban slum apartment or in a ramshackle rural shack leaves its mark on a youth. So does growing up without a father, as do many black children. Poor nutrition, overcrowding, and the alienation of despair help to mold the personalities of many poor black children.

When they reach school, their problems are compounded. They arrive less well prepared for academic pursuits and steadily fall farther and farther behind their white classmates. By the time they reach secondary school, they are typically retarded some $3^1/2$ years in reading, and to various degrees in the abilities to think abstractly and to solve problems (Mussen, Conger & Kagan, 1969, p. 726). They are more likely to drop out of school—and then, because they are poorly prepared for jobs in a skilled-labor economy, to become unemployed or underemployed.

Black youths' problems lead to their alienation from the larger society, which in turn makes them ready prey for drug addiction, for the bearing of illegitimate children while they are barely more than children themselves, and for participating in rioting and street crime. Black adolescents have the highest crime rate of any group in our society. This is caused not only by their alienation, but by discrimination against them. Black youths are more likely to be arrested for something that might be dismissed as a prank when committed by an upper-class white boy. Once arrested, they are more likely to be brought to trial, and once tried, more likely to be convicted and institutionalized.

The civil rights movement and the legislation of the 1960s, the greater awareness of the needs of minority groups, and the slow but steady responsiveness of the media in showing positive black models have all made some impact on American life. The term "black" is turning from a mark of shame into a badge of honor, so that adolescents are now proud to refer to themselves as "black and beautiful" (Sheikh & Beglis, 1973). But things are not changing fast enough.

As many black people are forging ahead to take part in the better life, many others are falling further and further behind, to perpetuate the vicious cycle of poverty, poor education, unemployment, and more poverty. One recent study showed that while 45 percent of white high school graduates in one northern city were going on to college, only 15 percent of the black graduates would continue their education (Jones, 1969). Since the dropout rate among blacks is twice the rate among whites (Cervantes, 1965), the actual discrepancy is even higher.

Nothing will help the young black people of our country fulfill their true potential except total reform of their communities. When black children can get an education that will fit them for good jobs, when they recognize that these jobs will be available to them, when tax monies are allocated to improving the quality of life for minority-group citizens, then and only then will these young people be able to find the identity that is their birthright.

THE PUERTO RICAN ADOLESCENT[1]

Teen-agers with a Puerto Rican background have many of the same problems as black teens, with the added handicap of a language deficit. They tend to be poor, to live in deteriorating neighborhoods of big cities, and to have high rates of unemployment, public welfare assistance, juvenile delinquency, substandard housing, and poor education. Those who come to this country during the teen years suffer especially because of their inability to speak English. This handicaps them in school, often leading them to drop out—only to have problems finding a job and a place in society.

One of the greatest obstacles for Puerto Rican adolescents in America is the culture shock they encounter. They come from a semitropical island whose traditions include "the Spanish language, Catholic religion, extended family cohesion, male dominance, double standard, pre-marital family chastity, dignity, and hospitality [Preble, 1968, pp. 50–51]." They come to a country dominated by the English language, the Protestant religion, the individual nuclear family, equality between the sexes (at least

[1]The authors are indebted to the work of Preble (1968) for the information in this section.

(Hugh Rogers, Monkmeyer)

In addition to other minority-group problems, Puerto Rican adolescents in America face the obstacle of culture shock.

in theory), premarital sexual activity, and mistrust of strangers. Even the climate is their enemy, since many come to large northern cities, where they suffer from the cold.

The breakdown of traditional Puerto Rican family patterns is often aggravated by our system of public welfare assistance, which is more prone to aid mothers and children than intact families. As a result, an unemployed husband and father will often leave his family—or pretend to leave—so that they may be eligible for welfare assistance. Either way, he loses his position as head of the household, loses his dignity in the community, and loses his self-respect. His children end up growing up in a home with either no father or a bitter, passive, dependent one.

Such a situation is particularly hard on sons, who no longer have a strong masculine role model. They may become passive and dependent them- selves, or they may go out on the streets, find their role models among the local criminals, and end up as criminals themselves. Gang fighting used to provide the means for such youths to feel and act "masculine," but this has gradually given way to narcotics addiction, which is endemic among Puerto Rican youths in New York City. As many Puerto Rican teen-agers follow the black styles in dress, dance, and language, so too do many of them have the same kind of problems with drugs.

Puerto Rican girls have different problems, especially in those families that adhere strictly to the old ways. These girls are raised very strictly and get caught in a clash of two cultures. They see their girl friends free to go out with boys, while they have virtually no male-female social life. Many of them rebel against their parents, go overboard in their efforts to be free, and get into some kind of trouble. Said one girl from a liberal family (Preble, 1968):

> These are the ones that always get out of line. You know, they drink and if you would give them a pill they would take it just so they could show you they ain't scared or anything like that. They want to be big shots and they always turn out the wrong way. You know, like they will take anything that a guy will give them [p. 65].

Other girls get married very early to escape the tight rein of their families and often end up in unhappy marriages.

Not all Puerto Rican young people, though, are caught in such self- defeating traps. In fact, the vast majority of them do quite well in this country. They quickly become bilingual, they finish school, and their rates for college attendance and successful working lives compare very favorably with those of earlier European immigrants.

THE MEXICAN-AMERICAN ADOLESCENT
American teen-agers of Mexican ancestry have many of the same problems as Puerto Rican teens. They look different, they speak a different language,

they come from a very different culture, and they have the same kinds of social problems associated with poverty and minority status. To participate fully in American life, many leave their communities, change their names to more "American" ones, and deny their cultural background. Others tend to accept the dominant negative stereotypes toward their people and to develop a cultural inferiority complex.

When eighty-nine Mexican-American boys and girls, aged thirteen to nineteen, anonymously answered a 34-page questionnaire related to personal identity concepts, Derbyshire (1968) concluded that those adolescents who rejected their Mexican-American culture had greater problems resolving their identity crisis than those who identified with Mexican values. This study, then, carries important implications as to the need for exploring ways in which minority-group adolescents can be helped to respect the values of their families, while still incorporating enough of the values of the dominant society to succeed in that society.

Problems of Adolescence

Most discussions of adolescents are heavily problem-oriented, even though the great majority of the problems that most teen-agers have are just normal developmental hurdles. Most teens do not drop out of school, do not run away from home, do not abuse drugs, do not get into trouble with the law, do not contract venereal disease, do not bear or father illegitimate children, and do not commit suicide. Most people weather the crises of adolescence quite well, especially considering the complexity of the society in which they grow up. And yet, with this perspective, we still have to recognize that substantial numbers of young people do have serious problems, problems that affect their own future and, often, society at large.

DRUG ABUSE

From the very beginnings of recorded history, humankind has sought to relieve the variety of ills that flesh and spirit are heir to by developing a medicinal arsenal. People have always relied on drugs to alleviate their unhappiness, as well as their physical ailments, and to give a lift to their lives. The ancient Greeks got drunk on alcohol, marijuana was used in China and in India well before the birth of Christ, and cocaine, obtained by chewing coca leaves, was a staple among the sixteenth-century Incas. American Indians used to be so addicted to tobacco that they would not undertake a long journey without bringing along a supply, and untold numbers of nineteenth-century American women freely drank and gave their babies syrups heavily laced with opium (Brecher, 1972).

If drugs are such a constant in human society, why, then, are we so concerned about contemporary drug use? For one reason, because so many young people today are using drugs. They have both the money and the opportunity to buy what they want. And while certain drugs taken in moderation may not be excessively harmful, adolescents are not known for their moderation. In these years of identity crisis, they often turn to drugs to solve many social and psychological problems. As a result, many youths are "messing up their lives" with drugs, endangering their physical and psychological health. While some observers feel that drug use among students is on the downswing since its peak during the 1960s, it is nevertheless true that many young people are still ingesting a wide variety of drugs, ranging from legal ones like caffeine, nicotine, and alcohol, to illegal ones like marijuana, LSD, cocaine, amphetamines, barbiturates, and heroin.

Young people often protest vigorously their disaffection with the Establishment. Yet their drug-taking patterns closely follow those of the adult society around them (Lennard, 1971). Just as adults in our culture take barbiturates and stimulants to alleviate unhappiness, depression, and day-to-day pressures, so youths take some of the very same medications. The adults, though, buy their drugs at neighborhood pharmacies on the basis of medical prescriptions, while the adolescents buy theirs from underground suppliers on the basis of peer recommendations. Just as pharmaceutical companies extol the use of drugs in virtually every human situation, so do drug-oriented adolescents. The danger in this attitude (Lennard, 1971) is that opting for a chemical solution obscures the nature of the real problems facing young people and can impede recognition that social systems need to be altered or that new social arrangements need to be created (p. 48).

The most popular drugs among young people are tobacco, alcohol, and marijuana.

Tobacco

Sneaking a cigarette behind the barn or in the high school bathroom has become a humorous staple of adolescent lore. But the amused, indulgent smiles accepting youths' initial forays into regular use of tobacco have turned to concern, with the awareness of the dangers to health that tobacco represents. The publication of the U. S. Surgeon General's report in 1964 brought out clearly the relationships between smoking and lung cancer, heart attack, emphysema, and other diseases. Its message was brought to the public in magazine articles, antismoking TV messages, and school educational campaigns.

Adolescents got the message. A large majority of thirteen- to eighteen-year-olds feel that smoking causes cancer and increases the chance of heart attack (Lieberman, 1970). Yet one out of every four teen-agers smokes, and many who hold these opinions are regular smokers themselves. Most young smokers seem to feel that they will stop smoking in five years or less, apparently unaware of the tremendous difficulty many people experience in giving up this habit. In fact, many scientists feel that smoking is more than a habit and is an actual physiological addiction (Brecher, 1972).

Furthermore, many teen-agers are still taking up smoking. According to the National Clearinghouse for Smoking and Health (1972), teen-age boys were less likely to smoke in 1972 than they had been in 1970, but teen-age girls were filling the smoky vacuum by showing an increasing predilection toward smoking. In 1968, girls were half as likely to smoke as boys; by 1970, two-thirds as likely; and by 1972, smoking rates for the sexes were about the same. If this trend continues, one type of equality women will achieve will be the equal chance of contracting such smoking-related diseases as lung cancer and heart attack, as preliminary reports are already indicating (Brody, 1973).

Why do teen-agers start to smoke? It seems that most do not consciously decide to become regular smokers, but drift into it. They are more likely to smoke if their friends and parents do—and if they are doing poorly in school (Williams, 1971). A major factor in adolescent smoking seems to be the desire to seem older, as indicated by one study that found that late-maturing adolescents smoked more than early maturers (Clausen, 1968). Looking young, these teens tried to seem more mature by smoking. It is ironic that adolescents, who tend to rebel against adult values, see smoking as an adult activity and yet take it up eagerly. Thus, they copy the very persons they are rebelling against.

Alcohol

Many of the same people who are deeply worried about illegal youthful marijuana use are brought up short when reminded that alcohol is also illegal for most high school and college students—and is a much more serious problem. Alcohol is probably the most heavily abused drug in the United States today. It is certainly the most frequently used—with some 80

Figure 14-1   Teen-age Drinkers by Grade and Setting, 1974
(Department of Health, Education, and Welfare)

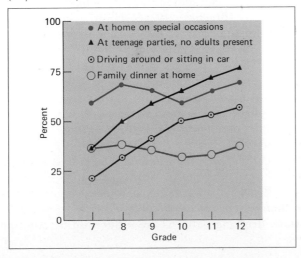

(Charles Gatewood)

Most teen-agers start to drink because it seems a grown-up thing to do, and they continue to do so for the same reasons adults do—to build up courage in difficult situations, to reduce anxiety, and to put a pleasant glow on social situations.

million drinkers in this country, many of whom are young people. Three men out of four and six women out of ten drink alcohol to some extent. About 20 percent of males and 5 percent of females are frequent or heavy drinkers, and 6 percent of all drinkers are alcoholics (Akers, 1970).

High school and college students are more likely to pick up a glass than to puff on a "joint" (Brecher, 1972). High school seniors from eleven Michigan schools ranging from public schools in urban slums and remote rural areas to a private academy were surveyed about their use of alcohol and marijuana. In two schools none of the students had ever smoked marijuana even once, and in only one (the private prep school) had as many as a third of the students tried it. But in only one school did less than half the students report drinking (and that was 49 percent), and in the private prep school, eight out of ten students drank (Boggs, Smith, & Russell, 1969; cited in Brecher, 1972).

Most high school students have had at least one drink in their lives, and about half the boys and a quarter of the girls drink on at least an occasional basis (Akers, 1970). A great many of these teens had their first drink at home with their parents or other adult relatives. As with cigarette smoking, then, teen-age drinking patterns are influenced by adult patterns.

The abstainer is most likely to come from an abstaining home; the moderate drinker from a home in which the parents drink moderately; and the heavy drinker from homes in which heavy drinking has been the pattern [Akers, 1970, p. 277].

Most teen-agers start to drink because it seems a grown-up thing to do, and they continue to do so for the same reasons adults do—to build up courage in difficult situations, to reduce anxiety, and to put a pleasant glow on social situations. The exceptions to this imitative pattern are drinking teen-agers from teetotaling families and heavily drinking youths from social-drinking families. Drinking teen-agers whose family and friends do not drink are often influenced by psychological pressures; in some cases, boys who feel rejected by their fathers choose this way of reacting against them (Alexander, 1966).

Aside from the illegality of alcohol below the legal drinking age, teen-age drinking causes problems because it is closely linked with other delinquent behavior. Youths who get into trouble with the law are more likely to have come from a drinking milieu. Their parents drink, their friends drink, and they themselves started to drink at an early age (Akers, 1970).

Marijuana

Of the three drugs most heavily used by teen-agers, marijuana represents the greatest intergenerational conflict. While many teens use marijuana in precisely the same way that their parents use alcohol, the fact that they are using a drug outside the ken of their parents' generation both enhances the appeal for youth and the anxiety for adults. Marijuana has been known all over the world for centuries, but its use among Western middle-class youth is a recent phenomenon.

As of October 1969, 10 million Americans, half of them under twenty-one, had smoked marijuana at least once (Brecher, 1972). In 1974, the Gallup Poll found an 11 percent jump since 1967 in the number of college students who said they had tried marijuana at least once (*Wisconsin State Journal*, 1974). In 1967, 5 percent said they had tried it; in 1969, the figure had risen to 22 percent; by 1970 it had gone up to 42 percent; and in 1974, 55 percent of 1,100 students surveyed answered "yes" to the question, "Have you yourself ever happened to have tried marijuana?" Students and nonstudents the same age are just as likely to smoke (Brecher, 1972), and even those who don't use it themselves generally accept its use by others (Tec, 1970).

Despite the usual classification of marijuana as a "dangerous drug," reports from several eminent investigative bodies indicate otherwise. Since 1894, at least five major governmental investigations of marijuana have yielded reports that have been "in substantial agreement on substantially all major points of fact [Brecher, 1972, p. 451]."

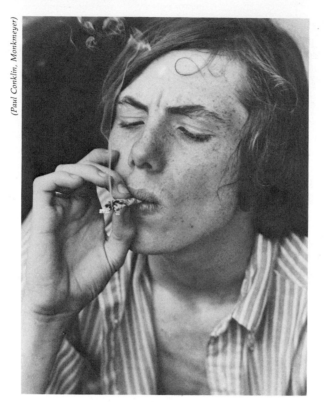

(Paul Conklin, Monkmeyer)

While many teens use marijuana in precisely the same way that their parents use alcohol, the fact that they are using a drug outside the ken of their parents' generation both enhances the appeal for youth and the anxiety for adults.

Marijuana is not physically addicting, but as with any psychoactive substance, some people apparently become psychologically dependent on it. While all the evidence is not in, it is possible that smoking marijuana may lead to some of the same respiratory problems as those caused by the smoking of tobacco (Rubin & Comitas, 1972). The general feeling among contemporary authorities is that marijuana will probably turn out to be no more injurious than cigarettes or alcohol. This conclusion gives support both to those forces that seek to legalize marijuana and to those who want to block legalization. Supporters of legalizing the substance say that keeping marijuana illegal is analogous to the ill-fated prohibition of alcohol in our country, and that only by legalizing it will we be able to control its purity and strength, take it out of the profitable underworld market, and keep young people from using other stronger, more dangerous drugs. The opponents of legalization argue that we should not sanction the use of a third possibly harmful drug, especially since we already have major health and social problems from the two that are now legitimate. According to many reports, people smoke marijuana not so much for complex psychological or sociological reasons, but just because it feels good. Says the Le Dain Commission, a Canadian body:

A major factor appears to be the simple pleasure of the experience. Time after time, witnesses have said to us in effect: "We do it for fun. Do not try to find a complicated explanation for it. We do it for pleasure [Cited in Brecher, 1972, p. 456]."

Adolescents probably start to smoke marijuana for many of the same reasons that they start to smoke cigarettes or to drink: they're curious, they want to do what their friends are doing, and they want to hurtle into adulthood by acting in "grown-up" ways. But marijuana also has something else going for it, as far as adolescents are concerned. Since it is not identified with the parental generation, its usage provides an easily available way to flout adult values and demonstrate independence from the Establishment. Some observers do, in fact, feel that marijuana smokers are more anti-Establishment than nonsmokers, more alienated, more artistic, and more politically oriented. But many others feel there is no one type of person who uses marijuana—that its usage cuts across class, racial, religious, political, and personality differences. One group of students who seem to stay away from it consistently, though, are high school athletes (Tec, 1970). This may reflect a "jock" personality—or, more likely, such a strong desire to excel in athletics that team members hew closely to the sanctions laid down by strict athletic coaches.

Not everyone smokes marijuana, though. The signs are that those students who are most strongly oriented toward achievement, who view school as a vehicle to success in life and who are satisfied with school, are less likely to smoke (Tec, 1970).

JUVENILE DELINQUENCY
At the age of fifteen, Vicky went to her father's liquor cabinet, took out a bottle of bourbon, and smuggled it out of the house. That evening, she and two girl friends went out. As they walked along the quiet, tree-shaded streets of their small town, they kept taking swigs from the bottle until one of the girls passed out. Since none of their parents were home, Vicky called the police, who took the unconscious girl to the hospital and kept the other two at the police station until their parents could come to pick them up.

Are Vicky and her friends juvenile delinquents? In a sense, yes. They have broken laws relating to public drunkenness and to the age of legal drinking. Will they be legally classified as juvenile delinquents? Not if their transgressions go no further than this. For delinquency is defined sociologically as much as legally. The local police know that Vicky and her friends come from "good" families, who are concerned about their children; the girls have never been in any other trouble; and in this case all the miscreants are white and middle class. In cases like this, young people are usually sent home after a good talking-to, and nothing further comes of the incident—except that Vicky's father may decide to lock up his liquor.

Had these same youngsters come from a low-income ghetto neighborhood, the outcome might be quite different. Studies of adults have shown that many young people commit offenses that are officially classifiable as delinquent but that few receive the kind of handling by the police that would label them as young criminals (Perlman, 1964). It is likely that youths from socially and economically deprived backgrounds do commit more crime than upper- and middle-class youth—but also that they are *much* more likely to get police records for minor offenses.

What constitutes juvenile delinquency? Generally, a delinquent is a young person under the age of sixteen or eighteen (the ages vary from state to state) who does anything that would be considered a crime if an adult had done it. Also, some types of juvenile misbehavior are considered delinquent. Truancy, running away, failure to abide by parental rules, and sexual activity are examples of behavior that is considered criminal only when committed by children. Since much delinquent behavior among middle- and upper-class adolescents never comes to the attention of authorities, it is impossible to estimate its real prevalence. We can, though, get some picture—albeit a skewed one—by looking at data on juvenile delinquency collected by the Federal Bureau of Investigation.

In 1972 about $1^1/_2$ million youths under eighteen were arrested for various offenses (FBI, 1973). Just under half the arrests were for crimes against property. Larceny and burglary headed the list in this category, followed by vandalism, car theft, and handling stolen property. Disorderly conduct and misuse of drugs and alcohol accounted for about 20 percent of all arrests. Only about 5 percent were for crimes involving injury to other persons. Many of the arrests involved juvenile misbehavior rather than actual crime.

In 1962, boys were arrested 5 times as often as girls (Perlman, 1964), but by 1972, the rising crime rate among girls had lowered the ratio to 3 to 1 (FBI, 1973). Both boys and girls are *most* likely to be arrested for larceny, and arrests for drug and liquor use and disorderly conduct rate fairly high for both sexes. For the most part, though, their crimes tend to be quite different. The boys are more likely to be picked up by police for burglary and car theft, while the girls are more often brought to court by their mothers for running away, ungovernable behavior, and sex offenses. More than half the girls referred to juvenile court in 1965 were referred for behavior that would not be criminal if it had been committed by an adult (President's Commission, 1967).

Who Is the Delinquent Youth?
The typical delinquent is a boy of about fifteen,, who is living with one parent and several brothers and sisters. The family lives in an overcrowded apartment in a deteriorating neighborhood in a big city. The boy has done poorly in school for years: He's gotten low grades, he was left back once or twice, and he is now about to drop out (President's Commission, 1967).

The neighborhood plays a large part in forming a delinquent, since a

(Hugh Rogers, Monkmeyer)

The typical delinquent is a boy of about fifteen, who is living with one parent and several brothers and sisters in an overcrowded apartment in a deteriorating neighborhood in a big city.

child from a poor family who lives in an upper-class area is less likely to become delinquent than the one who is surrounded by other deprived families (President's Commission, 1967). Studies of many ethnic groups—Germans, Irish, Poles, Italians, and blacks—show that crime is heaviest in the inner city and lowest as families are able to move out to the suburbs (President's Commission, 1967). The persistently high crime statistics for black youths reflects in part their families' greater difficulty in getting away from the high-crime urban core.

Drifting into delinquency in an urban slum, where being "in" requires belonging to a fighting gang, is not personally pathological in the same sense that delinquency would be for a suburban middle-class youngster. Johnson (1959) makes a distinction between the "sociologic" and the "individual" delinquent. The first youth is going along with subcultural norms, whereas the second is flouting them. This does not mean, of course, that all children from deprived neighborhoods are destined for a life of crime, nor that all delinquents from such backgrounds are well adjusted. What makes one child from a poor neighborhood get into trouble, while another manages to stay respectable and law-abiding? What makes a middle-class youth from a "nice" family in a "nice" neighborhood go out stealing cars? We don't have all the answers to this question, but we do know that family and personality factors are important, and that some aspects of the delinquent personality show up in early childhood.

The Delinquent's Family

The picture of the family of delinquent youths that emerges from study after study (Glueck & Glueck, 1950; Bandura & Walters, 1959) is one of parents who may be hostile or indifferent, but are rarely affectionate; of parents who either beat their children or neglect them, but rarely exercise consistent, firm guidance; and of parents who are unhappy, insecure, and inadequate at coping with life themselves. These parents tend to be separated or unhappily married. They are often so burdened with their own emotional or social problems that they have little time, energy, or sensitivity for those of their children.

In permissive homes, the children often get "premature autonomy." They come and go as they wish, eat when they feel like it (often having to get their own meals at the age of eight or nine), and act and feel like solitary people living in the same place as a bunch of other people, rather than members of a close family. They are inappropriately independent at an age when they should still be able to count on some measure of adult guidance and support. In strict families, discipline tends to be harsh. There is little trust between parent and child, and when the child transgresses, he is beaten. These children are not permitted the independence that would be appropriate for them, and they see their parents' overbearing control not as evidence of caring and concern, but as hostility and rejection.

In inconsistent homes, a child does not know from one time to the next what sort of reaction she will get. Coming home late one day may result in a beating from a drunken father; coming home late the next may be overlooked, since her lateness coincides with her father's wish not to be bothered. The inconsistency of discipline may be less important than the inconsistency of affection these young people feel. Many of them feel unloved and unwanted by their parents, and most especially by their fathers.

Personality

Why does one child become delinquent, while his brothers and sisters do not? We have to recognize that each child experiences a different family environment. The child whose conception forces her parents into an early marriage, the child who is born after her father has walked out on her mother, the child whose mother has to quit her job to look after her—the circumstances of all these children alter their home environments and the ways in which they will perceive the world. Furthermore, the children's own temperaments will affect their relationships with their parents and others close to them: The colicky baby who keeps his parents up all night with his crying will elicit different feelings than will the "good" baby who eats well, sleeps well, and rewards every little attention with a smile.

For whatever the reason, the personalities of delinquent youths do seem to be different from those of their nondelinquent brothers and sisters. Healy and Bronner (1936) found striking personality differences between delinquents and their siblings. The delinquents were a much unhappier group. They felt inadequate and inferior at home and in school. They felt unloved, unpopular, and not understood by anyone. They did more poorly in their school work, and in general presented a picture of unhappy, poorly adjusted youngsters.

Predicting Delinquency

The personality differences between delinquent and nondelinquent youths show up early in life. Conger, Miller, and Walsmith (1965) compared 86 tenth-grade delinquent boys with a control group of 86 nondelinquents, matched for age, IQ, socioeconomic status, school history, ethnic group, and neighborhood. When they examined early teacher ratings of "personal-social behavior," which had been kept for all the boys, they found that as early as the third grade teachers had seen the two groups of boys differently.

From kindergarten to third grade, the delinquent boys had more trouble getting along with other children. They had less regard for other children's rights and feelings; were aggressive, tactless, rude, and unfair in their dealings with them; and, not surprisingly, were not well liked by their peers. They had their problems with adults, too. They already had trouble accepting authority, and neither understood the need for nor abided by school regulations. They were more distractible and prone to daydreaming, and had more trouble doing their school work. Their teachers rarely noticed any special ability or interest. Their teachers noted that many of them came from disturbed home environments and felt that their problems often reflected underlying emotional problems.

In analyzing the data from this study, these investigators found not one clear-cut differentiation between delinquents and nondelinquents, but rather a complex series of relationships on various traits that differed when the boys were divided according to social class and IQ status.

If we can help parents to break out of the prison of poverty, unemployment, and despair; if we can help them to break the cycle of treating their children in the same harsh or indifferent ways they themselves were treated; and if we can help children learn that they can make it within the system, perhaps we will have a chance at stemming the tide of juvenile delinquency that blights so many young lives.

VENEREAL DISEASE

During 1972, more than 500,000 victims of the venereal diseases *syphilis* and *gonorrhea* were under twenty-one years of age, and a substantial number were under fifteen (Gordon, 1973). The VD rates for all ages have soared since the late 1950s, until public health experts consider us to be in the middle of a VD epidemic. Eleven percent of all nonvirgin boys and 10 percent of all nonvirgin girls who responded to the Sorensen (1973) survey have had VD themselves, and almost all adolescents over fifteen know at least one friend who has had it.

> After the common cold, syphilis and gonorrhea are the most common infectious diseases among young people, outranking all cases of hepatitis, measles, mumps, scarlet fever, strep throat and tuberculosis put together [*Time*, 1972].

The reasons for this rise among young people are manifold: increased sexual activity among all age groups; the advent of the oral contraceptive, which does *not* protect against venereal disease, replacing the condom, which does; the complacence among many people that VD can be easily cured; the *personal fable* attitude, which makes young people think that they and their lovers are immune to VD; and, finally, the willingness of many people to take the risk of contracting disease because they want sexual intercourse more than they don't want VD.

Most teen-agers are not ignorant of the basic facts about VD. They know that it is transmitted through sexual contact, that anyone can get it, and that it is serious (Sorensen, 1973). But they are often reluctant to seek help if they suspect they may have it, because they are afraid their parents will find out. Or they are ashamed and embarrassed to alert their sexual partners. Most of the educational campaigns aimed at eradicating venereal disease focus on catching and treating the disease early. But not until at least equal prominence is given to preventing it and to the moral obligation to avoid passing it on (as in Gordon's (1973) slogan, "Protect your lover, wear a rubber") will some headway be made in stopping this epidemic.

ADOLESCENT PREGNANCY

With what appears to be a trend toward sexual activity at an earlier age, it is not surprising that teen-age motherhood is on the rise. One out of ten teen-age girls in the general population, four out of ten black girls, and two out of ten nonvirgins have been pregnant at least once (Sorensen, 1973; Zelnik & Kantner, 1972). From 1961 to 1968, pregnancies among fifteen- to nineteen-year-old unmarried girls rose by almost 25 percent, although illegitimate births dropped in all other age groups (Gordon, 1973).

What happens to these pregnant girls? If they are from the lower classes, as two-thirds of all pregnant adolescents are, nine out of ten keep their babies (Gordon, 1973). Sometimes they bring them up themselves (whether or not they marry the father); often they turn them over to their own mothers to be raised. Middle- or upper-class girls usually have an abortion, put the baby up for adoption, or get married. From one-half to three-quarters of all teen-age marriages are "shotgun weddings" (Wagner, 1970), and about half of all teen marriages end in divorce (Gordon, 1973). These marriages of young people are two to four times as likely to split up as those of older persons (Gordon, 1973). Girls who carry their babies to term usually drop out of school, often never to return, and thereby cut off their chances for vocational training. Overwhelmed by the social, psychological, and physical pressures of pregnancy, too many of these girls try to kill themselves, making the suicide attempt rate for teen-age mothers some ten times higher than that of the general population (Gordon, 1973).

Becoming pregnant can change a girl's entire life, often with disastrous consequences. Why, then, in an age of improved contraception, are so many still getting pregnant? Few sexually active girls openly express a desire to have a baby outside of marriage, but some theorists believe that many a teen-ager gets pregnant to satisfy underlying psychological needs. She is thought to be acting out Oedipal fantasies in which she substitutes her boyfriend for her father, is trying to prove her maturity to her parents, trying to place herself on an equal footing with her mother, sees the baby as the one person who will give her the unconditional love that is missing from her life, has the baby to overcome her "penis envy," or has any number of other personality problems. Many other observers, however, feel that these conclusions are unwarranted, and that pregnant teen-agers are not different in important psychological ways from nonpregnant sexually active girls.

After comparing psychological profiles of pregnant and never-pregnant girls, Vincent (1961) concluded that "unwed motherhood is not the result of any one personality type, intrafamilial relationships, or social situations [quoted in Gordon, 1973, p. 39]." Based on this and other studies, Gordon (1973) concludes:

> The great majority of unwed pregnant teenagers are probably different from all other sexually active girls only in the specific circumstance of being pregnant. Differences in their behavior and motivation are not likely to be significant [p. 41].

There may be some physical differences between pregnant and non-pregnant teen-agers. Girls who conceive babies while still in their teens— whether they are married or not—have often started to be sexually active at an early age. Many of them have started to go with boys before the age of thirteen, which may suggest earlier sexual maturation and more precocious fertility (Kinch, 1970).

Most pregnant teen-agers are not promiscuous, and most have had intercourse with only one boy, the father of their child (Kinch, 1970; Gordon, 1973).

Why Many Girls Do Not Use Birth Control

Pregnancy among teen-agers is usually the result of using no contraception at all, or very unreliable, inefficient methods. While almost all the 150 pregnant girls in Kinch's (1970) study had some knowledge of contraception, none had ever used it. The Sorensen (1973) survey showed that almost half of all young people who had had sexual intercourse during the preceding month had taken no contraceptive measures, and Zelnik and Kantner (1972) found that more than three-quarters of their interviewees practiced birth control rarely or never.

Girls do not use contraception for many different reasons. They may be ignorant of some of the most effective methods, especially the diaphragm or the intrauterine device. If they do know what the devices are, they may not know where they can obtain them or are afraid their parents will find them. They are reluctant to disturb the spontaneity of the sex act by appearing too well prepared ahead of time. They may feel that contraception is too much trouble or they may forget to take the proper measures. They may feel that it is their boyfriends' responsibility. As abortions are legalized and become easier to get, they feel they can always turn to this as a last resort (Kinch, 1970; Sorensen, 1973).

The phrase, "I am not that kind of girl," sums up a major reason why many girls do not use birth control (Wagner, 1970). These girls feel that sexual intercourse is wrong and that they should not be indulging in it. They either deny to themselves that they are sexually active, or they keep making resolutions that this night is going to be different. They avoid the appearance, even to themselves, of planning to "go all the way." Thus, they save their self-respect by considering themselves as having been so swept away by love that they could not help themselves. Unpremeditated sex is acceptable, while carefully planned sex is something "bad" girls engage in.

Then there is the *personal fable* (see p. 566). One girl out of three believes that a girl who does not want a baby will not have one (Sorensen, 1973). Said one eighteen-year-old:

> Like when I'm having sex, I don't really connect it with getting pregnant 'cause I've never been pregnant, you know, and a lot of my friends have but I just can't picture it happening to me. And like you really don't connect it, you know, until once you've been pregnant. Because when it's never happened you say, "Why should it happen?" or, "It's never happened yet," you know. You always look at the other person and say, "It happened to them, but it'll never happen to me [p. 324]."

Why Many Boys Do Not Use Birth Control

One effect of the technological advances in contraception has been to shift the responsibility for birth control from the male partner to the female. Since the most common method of teen-age birth control today is "The Pill," many boys automatically assume that their girl friends have "taken care of things." More than 60 percent of all boys who had had intercourse during the preceding month never used a condom (Sorensen, 1973), once the most common birth control device for young people. At times, boys are reluctant to bring up the possibility of pregnancy, afraid that their partners will change their mind about wanting sexual intercourse. There is no basis for believing that unmarried fathers have any deep psychological motivations for fathering children. When they have been compared to nonfathers, teen-age boys who have fathered children turn out to be quite similar in personality and intellectual functioning (Pauker, 1971).

Needs of Pregnant Teen-agers

While pregnant girls may not be different from other sexually active girls *before* they conceive, they do have special needs afterward. Any pregnant woman needs reassurance of her ability to bear and care for a child and of her continued attractiveness. She needs to communicate her anxieties to someone, and to receive sympathy and reassurance. The unmarried teenage woman is especially vulnerable. Thrust into reproductive maturity, she realizes with a start that emotionally and intellectually she is far less mature than she had thought she was. And whatever she decides to do about the baby, she is bound to have conflicting feelings.

At the time a pregnant girl needs the most emotional support, she usually gets the least. Her boyfriend may turn away from her. Her family may be angry with her. She may be isolated from her friends by not being able to attend school with them. This emotional isolation in a time of great tension can disrupt the adolescent search for identity. To alleviate these pressures, the pregnant teen-ager should be able to discuss her problems with an interested, sympathetic, and knowledgeable counselor.

SUICIDE

Few things are so tragic as an adolescent suicide. The realization that someone whose life has barely begun has deemed it an affliction to be rid of saddens all who have come into contact with that young person. Suicide is the fourth most frequent cause of death for fifteen- to nineteen-year-olds, only after accidents, cancer, and homicide (Teicher & Jacobs, 1966). What has made life so intolerable for these young people?

Erik Erikson (1960) feels that adolescents who fail to resolve their identity crisis may suffer "so seriously from a feeling of being (or, indeed, wanting to be) nobody that they were withdrawing from reality, and in some cases even attempting to withdraw from life itself [p. 258]."

According to Jacobs and Teicher (1967), adolescents who commit, or try to commit, suicide do so because they feel completely isolated from any meaningful social relationships. These researchers interviewed 50 fourteen- to eighteen-year-olds who had attempted suicide, and a control group of adolescents, matched for age, race, sex, and family income. They also interviewed one parent of each young person. Those adolescents who had tried to kill themselves had experienced very different patterns of life from the control teens. The suicide attempters had had problems in childhood, an escalation of these problems during adolescence, and a final phase in the weeks and days just before the suicide attempt, when they suffered the loss of meaningful social relationships.

What were some of their problems? While many children in both groups experienced the break-up of their parents' marriages (72 percent of the suicide attempters and 53 percent of the controls), the home lives of the controls had been fairly stable over the preceding five years, while the would-be suicides' had not. The suicide attempters' parents were more likely to remarry during the youths' adolescence, to step-parents the young people didn't like, or to have been remarried and divorced several times during their children's lives.

The suicide attempters were more alienated from their parents, and more likely to have been depressed during the five years before they tried to take their lives. Seeking to establish an alternate intimate relationship, they often became involved in intense romances. Involved with their loves, they ignored or broke off ties with their other friends, and if the romance failed, they were left alone, with no one to turn to. Of those teens involved with sweethearts, 58 percent of the suicide attempters' romances were breaking up at the time of the attempt, compared to none of the control adolescents'.

Three-fourths of the suicide attempters were girls, and of these, five were either pregnant or worried that they might be pregnant, compared to none of the controls. When they told their boyfriends or their parents about their pregnancies, they were often rebuffed by both. Jacobs and Teicher (1967) conclude:

> The state of depression characteristic of adolescents who attempt suicide stems from a series of real life experiences. Although most people accept as a truism that 'we all have our ups and downs', the perspective of the suicide attempter at the time of his interview was that his life was not characterized by ups and downs, but only 'downs'. We feel it is unwarranted to attribute this belief to a restricted view of reality stemming from a 'state of depression'. By comparing the life histories of the experimental and control adolescents, there is good evidence to show that this *Weltanschauung* is justified by the suicide attempters' real life experiences [pp. 147–148].

Among older adolescents, college students are more likely to commit suicide than nonstudents (Seiden, 1966). Based on a study of twenty-three University of California students who killed themselves between 1952 and 1961, Seiden found that students are likely to commit suicide not toward the end of the semester at "finals" time, but in October or February, at the beginning of the term. Precipitating crises are often concern over studies (even though the students often have high grades), usually physical complaints (like an inability to eat or sleep), and difficulties with interpersonal relationships—sometimes due to stormy love affairs and at other times due to social isolation. (A particularly tragic case of the latter was the student who had been dead for eighteen days, unmissed and unnoticed before he was found in his room.)

Ego Strengths of Adolescents

With all the serious problems that we have just been discussing, let us not overlook the positive aspects of this time of life. And there are many. Normal adolescence is an exciting time of life. It is a time when all things appear possible, when one is on the threshold of love and life's work and participation in the broader society, when one is getting to know the most interesting person in the whole world, oneself. Yet few adolescents recognize and value their positive attributes.

Researchers who gave blank sheets of paper to 100 high school students and asked them to list what they saw as their strengths found that out of a total of nineteen categories (see Chart 14-1), the average student listed only seven strengths (Otto & Healy, 1966). Say the authors,

Chart 14-1   **Strength Categories** *(Otto & Healy, 1966)*

1   *Health*—this includes being in general good health, promoting and maintaining health, and having energy and vitality.

2   *Aesthetic strengths*—included here are the ability to enjoy and recognize beauty in nature, objects, or people.

3   *Special aptitudes or resources*—this includes special abilities or capacities such as having special skills to repair things, ability to make things grow, or "green thumb," having ability in mathematics or music, etc.

4   *Employment satisfaction*—enjoyment of work or duties, ability to get along with co-workers, pride in work, superior satisfaction with work.

5   *Social strengths*—having sufficient friends of both sexes, use of humor in social relations, and the ability to entertain others were included here.

6   *Spectator sports*—attendance or interest in football, baseball games, the reading of books, fiction, plays, etc., were listed under this category.

7   *Strengths through family and others*—included here were getting along with brothers and sisters and parents, ability to talk over problems with father or mother, feelings of closeness or loyalty to family, etc.

8   *Imaginative and creative strengths*—use of creativity and imagination in relation to school, home or family, expression of creative capacity through writing, etc.

9   *Dependability and responsibility strengths*—listed here were ability to keep appointments, trust placed in respondent by other people, keeping promises, and perseverance in bringing a task to conclusion.

(Continued)

> *Chart 14-1 (Continued)*
>
> 10 *Spiritual strengths*—attendance at church activities and meetings, church membership, reliance on religious beliefs, feeling close to God, using prayer, meditation, etc.
>
> 11 *Organizational strengths*—ability to lead clubs, teams, or organizations, capacity to give or carry out orders, having long- or short-range plans, etc.
>
> 12 *Intellectual strengths*—included here were an interest in new ideas from people, books or other sources, enjoyment of learning, interest in the continuing development of the mind, etc.
>
> 13 *Other strengths*—listed here were such items as ability to risk oneself, liking to adventure or pioneer, the ability to grow through defeat or crisis, etc.
>
> 14 *Emotional strengths*—ability to give and receive warmth, affection, or love, capacity to "take" anger from others, being aware of the feelings of others, etc., capacity for empathy, etc.
>
> 15 *Expressive arts*—included here were participation in dramatic plays, ballroom and other types of dancing, sculpting, playing a musical instrument, etc.
>
> 16 *Relationship strengths*—this category includes such items as getting along well with most of the teachers, being patient and understanding with people, helping others, accepting people as individuals regardless of sex, beliefs, or race; other people confiding in respondent, etc.
>
> 17 *Education, training, and related areas*—this included good grades received, the acquisition of special skills, such as typing, selling, or mechanical drawing, etc.
>
> 18 *Hobbies, crafts, etc.*—listing of any hobbies or interests such as stamp or coin collecting, sewing or knitting, hairstyling, etc.
>
> 19 *Sports and activities*—participation in swimming, football, tennis, basketball, etc., and enjoyment or skill in the foregoing activities or outdoor activities such as camping, hiking, etc., were listed here.

This indicates a limited self-perception of personality strengths not too markedly different from that of adults. In similar studies which have been conducted, adults have listed an average of six strengths but at the same time were able to fill one or more pages with listings of their "problems" or "weaknesses" [p. 293].

Most of the young people listed relationship, intellectual, or emotional strengths; more girls listed social and dependability strengths, while more boys listed sports and activities. While the listings of boys and girls differed somewhat, they were more alike than dissimilar. (See Tables 14-2 and 14-3.)

Table 14-2 Number and Percentage of Male Adolescents Listing Strengths as Grouped in Strength Categories (Otto & Healy, 1966).

Strength Category	Number of Males Responding	Percent
Relationship	37	74
Intellectual	25	50
Emotional	25	50
Hobbies, Crafts, etc.	15	30
Sports and Activities	15	30
Social	15	30
Health	15	30
Expressive Arts	12	24
Dependability	12	24
Education, Training, etc.	10	20
Spiritual	9	18
Organizational	8	16
Spectator Sports	7	14
Imaginative and Creative	6	12
Other	5	10
Special Aptitudes	5	10
Aesthetic	3	6
Employment Satisfaction	0	0
Family and Others	0	0

Table 14-3 Number and Percentage of Female Adolescents Listing Strengths as Grouped in Strength Categories (Otto & Healy, 1966)

Strength Category	Number of Females Responding	Percent
Relationship	48	94
Emotional	38	74
Intellectual	28	55
Social	25	49
Dependability	19	37
Hobbies, Crafts, etc.	16	31
Spiritual	13	25
Other	15	29
Organizational	15	29
Health	14	27
Expressive Arts	14	27
Sports and Activities	10	20
Education, Training, etc.	7	14
Imaginative and Creative	6	12
Family and Others	6	12
Aesthetic	4	8
Special Aptitudes	4	8
Spectator Sports	3	6
Employment Satisfaction	1	2

The authors of this report gave adolescents more credit for personality strengths than the young people did themselves, listing the following as "personality resources or strengths" of adolescents, "which differ qualitatively from those of adults" and appear in "unique and distinctive" distributions or patterns:

1 Considerable energy or drive and vitality.
2 Idealistic, and have a real concern for the future of this country and the world.
3 More often exercise their ability to question contemporary values, philosophies, theologies, and institutions.
4 Have heightened sensory awareness and perceptivity.
5 Courageous, able to risk themselves or stick their necks out.
6 Have a feeling of independence.
7 Possess a strong sense of fairness and dislike intolerance.
8 More often than not they are responsible and can be relied on.
9 Flexible and adapt to change more readily.
10 Usually open, frank, and honest.
11 An above average sense of loyalty to organizations, causes, etc.
12 Have a sense of humor which (more) often finds expression.
13 Have an optimistic and positive outlook on life more often than not.
14 Often think seriously and deeply.
15 Greater sensitivity and awareness of other person's feelings.
16 They are engaged in a sincere and on-going research for identity [p. 296].

If we can help more young people to recognize and build upon their very real strengths as they are about to enter adult life, the adolescent search for identity can be a fruitful one.

Summary

1 Probably the most important task for the adolescent is the search for identity, which can occur in many ways: by developing one's values, by developing pride in one's achievements, and by developing close relationships with peers.

2 The relationship between teen-agers and parents is not always smooth. Adolescents often feel conflict between wanting independence from parents and realizing how dependent they are. Many adolescents have trouble talking freely with parents—especially about sexual matters.

3 Teen-agers are highly influenced by their peer group. They strongly identify with others in this group and tend to do what their crowd does. Teen-agers identify with other teen-agers rather than with other people of

their own race, religion, community, or sex. And they consider themselves more idealistic, less materialistic, healthier in their sexuality, and better able to understand friendship and the important things in life than are members of the older generation.

4   Adolescent sexual experiences have repercussions on budding identity. Many conflicts between parents and adolescent children focus on sexuality.

5   About half of all nineteen-year-old girls and almost half of nineteen-year-old boys are virgins. It is difficult to compare these data with information from past generations. Teen-agers tend to enter into meaningful, monogomous sexual relationships, rather than promiscuous ones.

6   Current sexual attitudes are more liberal than in the past. Most males do not lose respect for females who have intercourse before marriage, and most members of both sexes approve of living together before marriage. Still, males tend to be more active sexually.

7   The search for identity is closely linked to vocational choice, which is related to and influenced by socioeconomic status, sex, parental attitudes, schooling, and personality.

8   Poor black students are most likely to drop out of school, although four of five dropouts are white, and financial need is rarely the cause for dropping out. Females leave school as often as males.

9   Minority-group teens have particularly difficult identity crises with special problems attributable to their minority status.

10   Adolescent problems include drug abuse, juvenile delinquency, suicide, and sexual problems such as venereal disease and unwanted pregnancy.

11   Even with all the difficulties of establishing a personal, sexual, social, and vocational identity, adolescence is typically an interesting, exciting, positive threshold to adulthood.

Suggested Readings

Ahlstrom, W. M., & Havighurst, R. J. *400 Losers: Delinquent Boys in High School.* Jossey-Bass, 1971. *The authors examine a broad range of factors related to delinquent boys' community, family, and school backgrounds. The 400 boys were followed closely for six or seven years.*

Ambrosino, L. *Runaways.* Boston: Beacon, 1971. *A practical guide for the runaway youth, his or her parents, teachers, and counselors.*

Brody, E. B. *Minority Group Adolescents in the United States.* Philadelphia: Williams and Wilkins, 1968. *A collection of essays on problems of the American Negro, the Puerto Rican American, Mexican-American, Chinese, Japanese, and Indian-American youth.*

Feshback, S. Singer, D. *Television and Aggression.* Jossey-Bass, 1971. *A report on an experimental field study of the effects of aggressive and nonaggressive television content on adolescent and preadolescent boys in seven residential schools.*

Freud, A. *The Writings of Anna Freud, Volume VII (1966-1970): Problems of Psychoanalytic Training, Diagnosis and the Technique of Therapy.* International Universities Press, 1971. *A beautifully illustrated collection of Anna Freud's writings. The clear and lucid text deals with present psychoanalytic training issues and child analysis.*

Mead, M. *Culture and Commitment: A Study of the Generation Gap.* Garden City, N.Y.: Natural History Press/Doubleday, 1970. *Mead examines our present knowledge of culture, with its basis in the model she derives from primitive society. She explores living cultures of different degrees of complexity, all existing at the same time, and emphasizes the differences between primitive, historic, and comtemporary post-World War II cultures.*

Muuss, E. *Theories of Adolescence.* New York: Random House, 1968. *A systematic and comprehensive picture of different theoretical positions on adolescent development that shows the relationships among them.*

(Charles Harbutt, Magnum)

With all its serious problems, normal adolescence is an exciting time of life when all things appear possible when one is on the threshold of love and life's work and participation in the broader society.

Bibliography

Abbot, W. L., & Bruning, J. L. Given names: A neglected social variable. *Psychological Record*, 1970, **20**, 527–533.

Ainsworth, M. The affects of maternal deprivation: A review of findings and controversy in the context of research strategy in deprivation of maternal care. Geneva: World Health Organization, 1962, 97–165.

Ainsworth, M. D. Patterns of attachment behavior shown by the infant in interaction with his mother. *The Merrill-Palmer Quarterly of Behavior and Development*, 1964, **10**, 51–58.

Ainsworth, M. D. S. Object relations, dependency, and attachment: A theoretical review of the infant-mother relationship. *Child Development*, 1969, **40**, 969–1025.

Ainsworth, M. D. S., & Bell, S. M. Some contemporary patterns of mother-infant interaction in the feeding situation. In A. Ambrose (Ed.), *Stimulation in early infancy*. London: Academic Press, 1969. Pp. 133–170.

Ainsworth, M. D. S., & Bell, S. M. Attachment, exploration, and separation: Illustration by the behavior of one-year-olds in a strange situation. *Child Development*, 1970, **41**, 49–67.

Akers, R. L. Teenage drinking and drug use. In E. D. Evans (Ed.), *Adolescents: Readings in behavior and development*. Hinsdale, Ill.: Dryden Press, 1970. Pp. 267–288.

Almy, M., Chittenden, E., & Miller, P. *Young children's thinking*. New York: Teachers College Press, 1966.

Altus, W. D. Birth order and its sequalae. *Science*, 1966, **151**, 44–48.

American Academy of Pediatrics Committee Statement. The ten-state nutrition survey: A pediatric perspective. *Pediatrics*, 1973, **51**(6), 1095–1099.

American Dental Association. *Dental health facts for teachers*. Chicago, 1966.

American Heritage Dictionary of the English Language (Morris, W., Ed.). Boston: Houghton Mifflin, 1971.

Ames, L. B., & Learned, J. Imaginary companions and related phenomena. *Journal of Genetic Psychology*, 1946, **69**, 147–167.

Anandalakshmy, S., & Grinder, R. Conceptual emphasis in the history of developmental psychology. *Child Development*, 1970, **41**, 1113–1123.

Anastasi, A. Heredity, environment, and the question "how"? *Psychological Review*, 1958, **65**(4), 197–208.

Anastasi, A. *Psychological testing*. New York: Macmillan, 1968.

Anastasiow, N. J. Success in school and boys' sex-role patterns. *Child Development*, 1965, **36**, 1053–1066.

Anderson, L. D. The predictive value of infant tests in relation to intelligence at five years. *Child Development*, 1939, **10**, 202–212.

Andre-Thomas, Chesni, Y., & Saint-Anne Dargassies, S. *The neurological examination of the infant*. London: Medical Advisory Committee of the National Spastics Society, 1960.

Anthony, S. *The child's discovery of death*. London: Routledge & Kegan Paul, 1940.

Anthony, S. The child's idea of death. In T. Talbot (Ed.), *The world of the child*. New York: Anchor Books, 1968.

Apgar, V., & Beck, J. *Is my baby all right?* New York: Trident Press, 1973.

Arena, J. Contamination of the ideal food. *Nutrition Today*, winter 1970, pp. 2–8.

Aries, P. *Centuries of childhood: A social history of family life*. (Translated by Robert Baldick.) New York: Vintage Books, 1962.

Ausubel, D. *Theory and problems of adolescent development*. New York: Grune & Stratton, 1954.

Ausubel, D. Historical overview of theoretical trends. In D. Ausubel (Ed.), *Theory and problems of child development*. New York: Grune & Stratton, 1957. Pp. 27–49.

Avedon, E. M., & Sutton-Smith, B. *The study of games*. New York: Wiley, 1971.

Bakan, D. *Slaughter of the innocents: A study of the battered child phenomenon*. San Francisco: Jassey-Bass, 1971.

Bakwin, H. Thumbsucking and fingersucking in children. *Journal of Pediatrics*, 1948, **32**, 99.

Bakwin, H. Sleep-walking in twins. *The Lancet*, Aug. 29, 1970, pp. 446–447.

Bakwin, H. Car-sickness in twins. *Develop. Med. Child Neurol.* 1971*a*, **13**, 310–312.

Bakwin, H. Constipation in twins. *Journal of Diseases of Children*, 1971*b*, **121**, 179–181.

Bakwin, H. Nail-biting in twins. *Develop. Med. Child. Neurol.* 1971*c*, **13**, 304–307.

Bakwin, H. Onuresis in twins. *American Journal of Diseases of Children*, 1971*d*, **121**, 222–225.

Bakwin, H., & McLaughlin, S. M. Secular increase in height: Is the end in sight? *The Lancet*, Dec. 5, 1964, pp. 1195–1196.

Baldwin, A. *Theories of child development.* New York: Wiley, 1968.

Bandura, A. Transmission of aggression through imitation of aggressive models. *Journal of Abnormal and Social Psychology*, 1961, **63**, 575–582.

Bandura, A. The stormy decade: Fact or fiction? *Psychology in the School*, 1964, **1**, 224–231.

Bandura, A., Grusec, J. E., & Menlove, F. L. Vicarious extinction of avoidance behavior. *Journal of Personality and Social Psychology*, 1967, **5**, 16–23

Bandura, A., & McDonald, F. J. Influence of social reinforcement and the behavior of models in shaping children's moral judgments. 1963, **67**, 274–281.

Bandura, A., Ross, D., & Ross, S. A. Imitation of film-mediated aggressive models. *Journal of Abnormal and Social Psychology*, 1963, **66**(1), 3–11.

Bandura, A., & Walters, R. H. *Adolescent aggression.* New York: Ronald Press, 1959.

Bandura, A., & Walters, R. H. Aggression. In H. Stevenson (Ed.), *Child psychology: The sixty-second yearbook of the National Society for the Study of Education, part I.* University of Chicago Press, 1963. Pp. 364–415.

Banikiotes, F. G., Montgomery, A. A., & Banikiotes, P. G. Male and female auditory reinforcement of infant vocalization. *Developmental Psychology*, 1972, **6**(3), 476–481.

Barglow, P., Bornstein, M. B., Exum, D. B., Wright, M. K., & Visotsky, H. M. Some psychiatric aspects of illegitimate pregnancy during early adolescence. *American Journal of Orthopsychiatry*, 1967, **37**, 266–267.

Barnes, K. E. Preschool play norms: A replication. *Developmental Psychology*, 1971, **5**(1), 99–103.

Barnett, C. R., Leiderman, P. H., Grobstein, R., & Klaus, M. Neonatal separation: The maternal side of interactional deprivation. *Pediatrics*, 1970, **45**(2), pp. 197–205.

Barry, H., Bacon, M. K., & Child, I. L. A cross-cultural survey of some sex differences in socialization. *Journal of Abnormal and Social Psychology*, 1957, **55**, 327–332.

Barth, R. S. *Open education and the American school.* New York: Agathon Press, 1973.

Battle, H. Relations between personal values and scholastic achievement. *Journal of Experimental Education*, 1957, **26**, 27–41.

Baughman, E. E. *Black Americans.* New York: Academic Press, 1971.

Baum, J. Nutritional value of human milk. *Obstetrics and Gynecology*, 1971, **37**, 126–130.

Baumgartner, L., Pessin, V., Wegmen, M., & Parker, S. Weight in relation to fetal and newborn mortality: Influence of sex and color. *Pediatrics*, 1950, **6**, 329–342.

Baumrind, D. Child care practices anteceding three patterns of preschool behavior. *Genetic Psychological Monographs*, 1967, **75**, 43–88.

Baumrind, D. Harmonious parents and their preschool children. *Developmental Psychology*, 1971, **4**(1) 99–102.

Baumrind, D., & Black, A. E. Socialization practices associated with dimensions of competence in preschool boys and girls. *Child Development*, 1967, **38**(2), 291–327.

Bayer, L. M. & Snyder, M. M. Illness experience of a group of normal children. *Child Development*, 1950, **21**(93), 120.

Bayley, N. Comparisons of mental and motor test scores for age 1–15 months by sex, birth order, race, geographic location, and education of parents. *Child Development*, 1965, **36**, 379–411.

Bayley, N. Research in child development: A longitudinal perspective. *Merrill-Palmer Quarterly of Behavior and Development*, 1965, **11**, 184–190.

Bayley, N., & Schaefer, E. Correlations of maternal and child behaviors with the development of mental abilities: Data from the Berkeley growth study. *Monographs of the Society for the Research in Child Development*, 1964, **29**(6), 1–80.

Bealer, R., Willits, F., & Maida, P. The rebellious youth subculture: A myth. *Children*, 1964, **11**, 43–48.

Beard, R. M. *An outline of Piaget's developmental psychology for students and teachers.* New York: Basic Books, 1969.

Becker, R. F., King, J. E., & Little, C. R. D. Experimental studies in nicotine absorption during pregnancy, IV: The postmature neonate. *American Journal of Obstetrics and Gynecology*, 1968, **101**, 1109–1119.

Beckwith, L. Relationships between attributes of mothers and their infants I.Q. scores. *Child Development*, 1971, **42**, 1083–1097.

Beckwith, L. Relationships between infants social behaviors and their mothers' behavior. *Child Development*, 1972, **43**(2), 397–411.

Bee, H. L., Van Egeren, L., Streissguth, A. P., Nyman, B. A., & Leckie, M. S. Social class differences in maternal teaching strategies and speech patterns. *Developmental Psychology*, 1969, **1**(6), 726–734.

Bell, G. D. Processes in the formation of adolescents' aspirations. *Social Forces*, 1963, **42**, 179–195.

Bell, R. R. *Premarital sex in a changing society.* Englewood Cliffs, N.J.: Prentice-Hall, 1966.

Bell, R. R. Parent-child conflict in sexual values. *Journal of Social Issues*, 1966, **22**, 34–44.

Belmont, L., & Birch, H. G. Lateral dominance and right-left awareness in normal children. *Child Development*, 1963, **34**, 257–270.

Belmont, L., & Marolla, A. F. Birth order, family size, and intelligence. *Science*, 1973, **182**, 1096–1101.

Benech, A. Variations paisonnieres du poids de naissance. *Biométrie Humaine*, 1971, **5**, 63–74.

Berenda, R. W. *The influence of the group on the*

judgments of children. New York: King's Crown Press, 1950.

Berg, A. The economics of breast-feeding. *Saturday Review of the Sciences,* 1973, **1**(4), 29–32.

Berger, B. Child-rearing practices of the communal family. In A. Skolnick & J. Skolnick (Eds.), *Family in transaction.* Boston: Little, Brown, 1971.

Bergman, J. Are little girls being harmed by "Sesame Street"? *New York Times,* Jan. 2, 1972, 13D.

Berlin, C. M. Effects of LSD taken by pregnant women on chromosomal abnormalities of offf spring. *Pediatric Herald,* January–February 1969, 1.

Bernard, J., & Sontag, L. W. Fetal reactivity to sound. *Journal of Genetic Psychology,* 1947, **70**, 205–210.

Berstein, B. Social class and linguistic development: A theory of social learning. In A. H. Halsey, J. Floud, & C. A. Anderson (Eds.), *Education, economy, and society.* New York: Free Press, 1961.

Berscheid, E., Walster, E., & Bohrnstedt, G. The happy American body, a survey report. *Psychology Today,* 1973, **7**(6), 119–131.

Bettelheim, B. *The children of the dream.* New York: Macmillan, 1969.

Biber, B. The role of play. In R. H. Anderson & H. G. Shane (Eds.), *As the twig is bent: Readings in early childhood education.* Boston: Houghton Mifflin, 1971. Pp. 98–107.

Biber, H., Miller, L. B., & Dyer, J. L. Feminization in preschool. *Developmental Psychology,* 1972, **7**(1), 86.

Biller, H. B. Father absence, maternal encouragement, and sex role development in kindergarten-age boys. *Child Development,* 1960, **40**, 539–546.

Biller, H. B. Father absence and the personality development of the male child. *Developmental Psychology,* 1970, **2**, 181–201.

Biller, H., & Bahm, R. Father absences, perceived maternal behavior, and masculinity of self-concept among junior high school boys. *Developmental Psychology,* 1971, **4**, 178–181.

Biller, H. B., & Weiss, S. D. The father-daughter relationship and the personality development of the female. *The Journal of Genetic Psychology,* 1970, **116**, 79–93.

Bing, E. Effects of child-rearing practices on development of differential cognitive abilities. *Child Development,* 1963, **34**, 631–648.

Birch, H. G., & Gussow, J. D. *Disadvantaged children: Health, nutrition and school failure.* New York: Grune & Stratton, 1970.

Birns, B. Individual differences in human neonates' responses to stimulation. *Child Development,* 1965, **36**(1), 249–256.

Birns, B., & Blank, M. The effectiveness of various soothing techniques on human neonates. Paper presented at the meeting of the Society for Research in Child Development. Minneapolis, April 1965.

Bishop, E. H., Israel, S. L., & Briscoe, C. C. Obstetric influences on premature infant's first year of development: A report from the collaborative study of cerebral palsy. *Obstetrics and Gynecology,* 1965, **26**, 628–635.

Blackwood, B. *Both sides of Buka Passage.* Oxford: Clarendon Press, 1935.

Blanchard, R., & Biller, H. Father availability and academic performance among third-grade boys. *Developmental Psychology,* 1971, **4**(3), 301–305.

Blank, M., & Solomon, F. A tutorial language program to develop abstract thinking in socially disadvantaged preschool children. *Child Development,* 1968, **39** 379–389.

Blauvelt, H. Dynamics of the mother-newborn relationship in goats. In B. Schaffner (Ed.), *Group processes.* New York: Macy Foundation, 1955.

Bledsoe, J. C. Self-concepts of children and their intelligence, achievement, interests, and anxiety. *Journal of Individual Psychology,* 1964, **20**, 55–58.

Blum, G. S. *Psychoanalytic theories of personality.* New York: McGraw-Hill, 1953.

Blumer, H. et al. The world of youthful drug use. Center Final Report. University of California. HEW Grants No. 65029 and 66022.

Boehm, L., & Nass, M. L. Social class differences in conscience development. *Child Development,* 1962, **33**, 565–574.

Bongiovanni, A. M., DeGeorge, A. M., & Grumbach, M. M. Masculinization of the female infant associated with estrogenic therapy alone during gestation. *Journal of Clinical Endocrinology and Metabolism,* 1959, **19**, 1004–1011.

Bonica, J. J. *Principles and practice of obstetric analgesia and anesthesia.* Vol. 1. Philadelphia: Davis, 1967.

Bowes, W. A. Obstetrical medication and infant outcome: A review of the literature. *Monographs of the Society for Research in Child Development,* 1970, **35**(4), 137, 3–23.

Bowlby, J. The nature of the child's tie to his mother. *International Journal of Psychoanalysis,* 1958, **39**, 350–373.

Bowlby, J. Separation anxiety. *International Journal of Psycho-Analysis,* 1960, **41**, 89–113.

Bowlby, J. *Attachment and loss,* vol. 1 (attachment). London: Hogarth Press and Institute of Psychoanalysis, 1969.

Boyle, R. P. The effects of the high school of students aspirations. *American Journal of Sociology,* 1966, **71**, 628–639.

Brackbill, Y. Extinction of the smiling response in infants as a function of reinforcement schedule. *Child Development,* 1958, **29**, 115–124.

Brackbill, Y. Cumulative effects of continuous stimulation on arousal level in infants. *Child Development,* 1971, **42**, 17–26.

Brackbill, Y. The role of the cortex in orienting:

Orienting reflex in an anencephalic human infant. *Developmental Psychology*, 1971, **5**, 195–201.

Brackbill, Y., Adams, G., Crowell, D. H., & Gray, M. L. Arousal level in neonates and preschool children, under continuous auditory stimulation. *Journal of Experimental Child Psychology*, 1966, **4**(2), 178–188.

Brackbill, Y., & Thompson, G. (Eds.) *Behavior in infancy and early childhood.* New York: Free Press, 1967.

Braine, M. D. S. On learning the grammatical order of words. *Psychological Review*, 1963, **70**, 323–348.

Braine, M. D. S., Heimer, C. B., Wortis, H., & Freedman, A. M. Factors associated with impairment of the early development of prematures. *Monographs of the Society of Research in Child Development*, 1966, Whole No. 3.

Brazelton, T. B. Sucking in infancy. *Pediatrics*, 1956, **17**, 400–404.

Brazelton, T. B. Effects of prenatal drugs on the behavior of the neonate. *American Journal of Psychiatry*, 1970, **126**(9), 95–100.

Brazelton, T. B. Implications of infant development among Mayan Indians of Mexico. *Human Development*, 1972, **15**(2), 90–111.

Brazelton, T. B., Robey, J. S., & Collier, G. A. Infant development in the Zinacanteco Indians of Southern Mexico. *Pediatrics*, 1969, **44**(2), 274–290.

Brecher, E., & the Editors of *Consumer Reports. Licit & illicit drugs.* Mount Vernon, N.Y.: Consumers Union, 1972.

Brewster, P. G. The importance of the collecting and study of games. *Eastern Anthropologist*, 1956, **10**(1), 5–12.

Bridges, K. M. B. Emotional development in early infancy. *Child Development*, 1932, **3**, 324–341.

Brim, O. G. Family structure and sex role learning by children: A further analysis of Helen Koch's data. *Sociometry*, 1958, **21**, 1–16.

Brittain, C. Adolescent choices and parent-peer cross-pressures. *American Sociological Review*, 1963, **28**, 385–391.

Brockman, L. M., & Riccuiti, H. N. Severe protein-calorie malnutrition and cognitive development in infancy and early childhood. *Developmental Psychology*, 1971, **4**(3), 312–319.

Brodbeck, A. J., & Irwin, O. C. The speech behavior of infants without families. *Child Development*, 1946, **17**, 145–156.

Brody, E. B. (Ed.) *Minority group adolescents in the United States.* Baltimore: Williams & Williams, 1968.

Brody, J. E. Deaths of women linked to smoking. *New York Times*, May 20, 1973.

Brody, J. E. Most pregnant women found taking excess drugs. *New York Times*, Mar. 18, 1973.

Bronfenbrenner, U. Freudian theories of identification and their derivatives. *Child Development*, 1960, **31**, 15–40.

Bronfenbrenner, U. Soviet methods of character education: Some implications for research. *Religious Education*, July–August 1962, 845–861.

Bronfenbrenner, U. Response to pressure from peers versus adults among Soviet and American schoolchildren. *International Journal of Psychology*, 1967, **2**, 199–207.

Bronshtein, A. I., Antonova, T. G., Kamenetskaya, N. H., Luppova, V. A., & Sytova, V. A. On the development of the functions of analyzers in infants and some animals at the early stage of ontogenesis. In problems of evolution of physiological functions. Academy of Science, U.S.S.R., 1958.

Bronshtein, A. I., & Petrova, E. P. The auditory analyzer in young infants. In Y. Brackbill & G. Thompson (Eds.), *Behavior in infancy and early childhood.* New York: MacMillan, 1967. Pp. 163–172.

Bronson, F. H., & Desjardins, C. Aggressive behavior and seminal vesicle function in mice: Differential sensitivity to androgen given neonatally. *Endocrinology*, 1969, **85**, 871–975.

Brophy, J. E., & Good, T. L. Feminization of American elementary schools. *Phi Delta Kappan*, 1973, **54**, 564–566.

Brophy, J. E., & Good, T. L. *Teacher-student relationships.* New York: Holt, Rinehart, & Winston, 1974.

Brown, A. M., & Mathery, A. P., Jr. Feeding problems and preschool intelligence scores: A study using the co-twin method. *American Journal of Cunical Nutrition*, 1971, **24**, 1207–1209.

Brown, D. G. Sex-role development in a changing culture. *Psychological Bulletin*, 1958, **55**, 232–242.

Brown, P., & Elliott, R. Control of aggression in a nursery school class. *Journal of Experimental Child Psychology*, 1965, **2**, 103–107.

Brown, R. How shall a thing be called? *Psychological Review*, 1958, **65**(1), 14–21.

Brutten, M., Richardson, S. O., & Mangel, C. *Something's wrong with my child: A parents' book about children with learning disabilities.* New York: Harcourt Brace Jovanovich, 1973.

Burke, B. S., Beal, V. A., Kirkwood, S. B., & Stuart, H. C. Nutrition studies during pregnancy. *American Journal of Obstetrics and Gynecology*, 1943, **46**, 38–52.

Burnett, A. Assessment of intelligence in a restricted environment. Unpublished doctoral dissertation, McGill University, 1955.

Burke-Merkle, A., & Hooper, F. Logical task performance in the preschool: The effects of classification and seriation instruction. Paper presented at the biennial meeting of the Society for Research in Child Development, Philadelphia, 1973.

Burnstein, E. Fear of failure, achievement motivation, and aspiring to prestigeful occupations. *Journal of Abnormal and Social Psychology*, 1963, **67**, 189–193.

Burrell, R. J. W., Healy, M. J. R., & Tanner, J. M.

Age at menarche in South African Bantu schoolgirls living in Transkei reserve. *Human Biology*, 1961, **33**, 250–261.

Burt, C. The genetic determination of differences in intelligence: A study of monozygotic twins reared together and apart. *British Journal of Psychology*, 1966, **57**(1&2), 137–153.

Burton, B., & Whiting, J. The absent father and cross-sex identity. *Merrill-Palmer Quarterly*, 1961, **7**, 85–95.

Butler, F. "Over the garden wall/I let the baby fall." *New York Times Magazine*, Dec. 16, 1973, pp. 90–95.

Butler, R. N., Goldstein, H., Ross, E. M. Cigarette smoking in pregnancy: Its influence on birth weight and perinatal mortality. *British Medical Journal*, 1972, **2**, 127–130.

Byrne, P., & Carey, M. *The parent's friend, vol. I.* Philadelphia: Printed by Jane Aitken, 1803. Cited in *Pediatrics*, 1972, **49**(6), 915.

Caldwell, B. M. The effects of psychosocial deprivation on human development in infancy. *Merrill-Palmer Quarterly of Behavior and Development*, 1970, **16**(3).

Caldwell, B. M., & Richmond, J. B. Social class level and stimulation potential of the home. In J. Hellmuth (Ed.), *Exceptional infant*, vol. 1. New York: Brunner/Mazel, 1967. Pp. 455–466.

Campbell, J. D. Peer relations in childhood. In M. Hoffman & L. Hoffman (eds.), *Review of child development research.* New York: Russell-Sage Foundation, 1964.

Campbell, S. B. Mother-child interaction in reflective, impulsive, and hyperactive children. *Developmental Psychology*, 1973, **8**(3), 341–349.

Campos, J. J., Langer, A., & Krowitz, A. Cardiac responses on the visual cliff in prelocomotor human infants. *Science*, 1970, **170**, 196–197.

Caplan, F., (Ed.). *The first twelve months of life: Your baby's growth month by month.* New York: Grossett & Dunlap, 1973.

Caputo, D. V., & Mandell, W. Consequences of low birth weight. *Developmental Psychology*, 1970, **3**, 363–383.

Cazden, C. B. Suggestions from studies of early language acquisition. In R. H. Anderson & H. G. Shane (Eds.). *As the twig is bent: Readings in early childhood education.* Boston: Houghton Mifflin, 1971.

Carlson, C. S., Arnold, C. R., Becker, W. C., & Madsen, C. H. The elimination of tantrum behavior of a child in an elementary classroom. *Behav. Res. & Therapy* 1968, 6, 117–119.

Carlson, P., & Anisfeld, M. Some observations of the linguistic competence of a two-year-old child. *Child Development*, 1969, **40**(2), 569–575.

Carr, D. H. Chromosome studies in selected spontaneous abortions: 1, conception after oral contraceptives. *Canadian Medical Association Journal*, 1970, **103**, 343–348.

Carson, A. S., & Raybin, A. I. Verbal comprehension and communication in negro and white children. *Journal of Educational Psychology*, 1960, **51**, 47–51.

Cattell, P. *The measurement of intelligence of infants and young children.* New York: The Psychological Corporation, 1960.

Cattell, R. B. *The scientific analysis of personality.* Baltimore: Penguin Books, 1965.

Catz, C. S. Drugs and breast milk. *Pediatric Clinics of North America*, February 1972.

Cazden, C. B. Three sociolinguistic views of the language and speech of lower-class children—with special attention to the work of Basil Bernstein. *Develop. Med. Child Neurol.* 1968, **10**, 600–612.

Cervantes, L. F. Family background, primary relationships, and the high school dropout. *Journal of Marriage and the Family*, 1965, **5**, 218–223.

Chapel, J. L., & Taylor, D. W. Drugs for kicks. *Crime and Delinquency*, 1970, **16**(1), 2–32.

Charlesworth, W. R. Cognition in infancy: Where do we stand in the mid-sixties? *Merrill-Palmer Quarterly of Behavior and Development*, 1968, **14**(1), 25–46.

Cherry, R., & Cherry, L. The Horney heresy. New York Times Magazine, Aug. 26, 1973, p. 12+.

Chess, S. Temperament and learning ability of school children. *American Journal of Public Health*, 1968, **58**(12), 2231–2239.

Chess, S., Thomas, A., & Birch, H. G. *Your child is a person.* New York: Viking, 1965.

Child, I., Potter, E., & Levine, E. Children's textbooks and personality development: An exploration in the social psychology of education. *Psychological Monographs*, 1946, **60**, 3.

Childs, B. Genetic origin of some sex differences among human beings. *Pediatrics*, 1963, **35**, 798–812.

Chomsky, C. Language development after age six. In C. S. Lavatelli & F. Stendler (Eds.), *Readings in child behavior and development* (3d ed.). New York: Harcourt Brace Jovanovich, 1972.

Church, J. *Three babies.* New York: Random House, 1966.

Clark, J. P., & Haurek, E. W. Age and sex roles of adolescents and their involvement in misconduct: A reappraisal. *Sociology and Social Research*, 1966, **50**(4), 495–503.

Clausen, J. A. Adolescent antecedents of cigarette smoking: Data from the Oakland growth study. *Social Science and Medicine*, 1968, **1**, 357–382.

Clifton, C. Language acquisition. In T. D. Spencer & N. Kass (Eds.), *Perspectives in child psychology.* New York: McGraw-Hill, 1970.

Cobrinik, P. W., Hood, R. T., & Chused, E. Effects of maternal narcotic addiction on the newborn infant. *Pediatrics*, 1959, **24**, 288–290.

Cole, M., & Cole, C. Russian nursery schools. In P. Cramer (Ed.), *Reading in developmental psychology today*. Del Mar, Calif.: CRM Books, 1970. Pp. 43–49.

Combs, J., & Coley, W. Dropouts: In high school and after school. *Americal Educational Research Journal*, 1968, **5**, 343–363.

Condry, J. C., Jr., Siman, M. L., & Bronfenbrenner, U. "Characteristics of peer- and adult-oriented children. Unpublished manuscript, Dept. of Child Development, Cornell University, 1968

Conger, J. J. *Adolescence and youth: Psychological development in a changing world*. New York: Harper & Row, 1973.

Conger, J. J., Miller, W. C., & Walsmith, C. R. Antecedents of delinquency: Personality, social class, and intelligence. In P. H. Mussen, J. J. Conger, & J. Kagan (Eds.), *Readings in child development and personality*. New York: Harper & Row, 1965.

Conklin, E. S. *Principles of adolescent psychology*. New York: Holt, Rinehart, & Winston, 1933.

Cook, J. Jersey bids Little League let girls play on teams. *New York Times*, Nov. 8, 1973.

Conway, E., & Brackbill, Y. Delivery medication and infant outcome: An empirical study. *Monographs of the Society for Research in Child Development*, 1970, **35**(4), 24–34.

Coopersmith, S. *The antecedents of self-esteem*. San Francisco: W. H. Freeman, 1967.

Copans, S. A. Clinical impressions of communal child rearing. Paper presented at the meeting of the American Psychological Association, Honolulu, 1972.

Corah, N. L., Anthony, E. J., Painter, P., Stern, J. A., & Thurstan, D. Effects of prenatal anoxia after seven years. *Psychological Monographs*, 1965, **79** (Whole No. 596).

Corman, H. H., & Escalona, S. K. Stages of sensorimotor development: A replication. *Merrill-Palmer Quarterly*, 1969, **15**, 351–361.

Cosler, L. Maternal deprivation: A critical review of the literature. *Monographs of the Society for Research in Child Development*, 1961, **26**, 1–64.

Costanzo, P. R., & Shaw, M. E. Conformity as a function of age level. *Child Development*, 1966, **37**, 967–975.

Cox, C. M. Genetic studies of geniuses, vol. II. The early mental traits of three hundred geniuses. California: Stanford University Press, 1926.

Crandall, V. J., Preston, A., & Rabson, A. Maternal reactions and the development of independence and achievement behavior in young children. *Child Development*, 1960, **31**, 243–251.

Cravioto, J. Nutritional deficiencies and mental performance in childhood. In D. C. Glass (Ed.), *Environmental Influences*. New York: The Rockefeller University Press and Russell Sage Foundation, 1968.

Croake, J. W. Fears of children. *Human Development*, 1969, **12**, 239–247.

Croake, J. W. The changing nature of children's fears. *Child Study Journal*, 1973, **3**(2), 91–105.

Crow, L. D., Murray, W. I., Smythe, H. H. *Educating the culturally disadvantaged child*. New York: David McKay, 1966.

Damon, A., Damon, S. T., Reed, R. B., & Valadran, I. Age at menarche of mothers and daughters with a note on accuracy of recall. *Human Biology*, 1969, **41**, 161–175.

Daniel, W. G. Some essential ingredients in educational programs for the socially disadvantaged. In J. Hellmuth (Ed.), *Disadvantaged child*, vol. 1. New York: Brunner/Mazel, 1967. Pp. 207–221.

Daniels, N. The smart white man's burden. *Harper's*, 1973, **247**(1481), 24–40.

Dann, M., Levine, S. Z., & New, D. The development of prematurely born children with birth weights or minimal postnatal weight of 1000 grams or less. *Pediatrics*, 1958, **22**, 1037–1053.

Davids, A., DeVault, S., & Talmadge, M. Anxiety, pregnancy and childbirth abnormalities. *Journal of Consulting Psychology*, 1961, **25**, 74–77.

Davids, A., Holden, R. H., & Gray, G. Maternal anxiety during pregnancy and adequacy of mother and child adjustment eight months following childbirth. *Child Development*, 1963, **34**, 993–1002.

Davidson, K. S., Gibby, R. G., McNeil, E. B., Segal, S. J., & Silverman, H. A preliminary study of Negro and White differences on Form 1 of the Wessler-Bellevue Scale. *Journal of Consulting Psychology*, 1950, **14**, 489–492.

Davis, J. A., & Tizard, J. P. M. Practical problems of neonatal paediatrics considered in relation to animal physiology. *British Medical Bulletin*, 1961, **17**, 168–172.

Davson, H. (Ed.) *The eye*. New York: Academic Press, 1962.

Dayton, D. H. Early malnutrition and human development. *Children*, 1969, **16**(6), 210–217.

Decarie, T. G. *Intelligence and affectivity in early childhood*. New York: International University Press, 1965.

Demos, J. Developmental perspectives on the history of childhood. *Journal of Interdisciplinary History*, 1971, **2**, 315–327.

Dennis, W. A bibliography of baby biographies. *Child Development*, 1936, **7**, 71–73.

Dennis, W. Causes of retardation among institutional children: Iran. *Journal of Genetic Psychology*, 1960, **96**, 47–59.

Dennis, W., & Dennis, M. G. The effect of cradling practice upon the onset of walking in Hopi children.

Journal of Genetic Psychology, 1940, **56**, 77–86.

Derbyshire R. L. Adolescent identity crisis in urban Mexican Americans in East Los Angeles. In E. B. Brody (Ed.), *Minority group adolescents in the United States.* Baltimore: Williams & Wilkins, 1968. Pp. 73–110.

Deutsch, C. P. Auditory discrimination and learning: Social factors. *Merrill-Palmer Quarterly of Behavior and Development,* 1964, **10**, 277–296.

Dewey, J. (Ed.) *Elementary school record,* vol. 1, no. 5. Chicago: University of Chicago Press, 1900.

Dipboye, W. J., & Anderson, W. F. Occupational stereotypes and manifest needs of high school students. *Journal of Counseling Psychology,* 1961, **8**, 296–304.

Dippel, A. L. The relationship of congenital syphilis to abortion and miscarriage and the mechanism of interuterine protection. *American Journal of Obstetrics and Gynecology,* 1945, **47**, 369–379.

Dishotsky, N. I., Loughman, W. D., Mogar, R. E., & Lipscomb, W. R. LSD and genetic damage. *Science,* 1971, **172**(3982), 431–440.

Distressed parents get help to keep them from child abuse. *Wisconsin State Journal,* Feb. 4, 1973.

Dodge, J. A. Psychosomatic aspects of infantile pyloric stenosis. *Journal of Psychosomatic Research,* 1972, **16**, 1–5.

Doris, J., Cooper, & Poresky, R. Differential brightness thresholds in infancy. *Journal of Experimental Child Psychology,* 1967, **5**, 52–535.

Drage, J. S., Kennedy, C., Berendes, H., Schwartz, B. K., & Weiss, W. Apgar score as index of infant morbidity: A report from collaborative study of cerebral palsy. *Developmental Medicine and Child Neurology,* 1966, **8**, 141–148.

Drillien, C. M. The incidence of mental and physical handicaps in school-age children of very low birth weights. *Pediatrics,* 1961, **27**, 452–464.

Drillien, C. M. *The growth and development of the prematurely born infant.* Edinburgh: E. & S. Livingstone, 1964.

Dumars, K. W., Jr. Parental drug usage: Effect upon chromosomes of progeny. *Pediatrics,* 1971, **47**(6), 1037–1041.

Dunn, P. M. Some perinatal observations on twins. *Develop. Med. Child Neurol.* 1965, **7**, 121.

Dwyer, J., & Mayer, J. Psychological effects of variations in physical appearance during adolescence. *Adolescence,* 1968–69, **3**, 353–380.

Edwards, C., & Williams, J. Generalization between evaluative words associated with racial figures in preschool children. *Journal of Experimental Research in Personality,* 1970, **4**, 144–155.

Edwards, D. A. Early androgen stimulation and aggressive behavior in male and female mice. *Physiology and Behavior,* 1969, **4**, 333–338.

Ehrhardt, A. A., & Money, J. Progestin-induced hermaphroditism: I.Q. and psychosocial identity. *Journal of Sexual Research,* 1967, **3**, 83–100.

Eisenson, J., Auer, J. J., & Irwin, J. V. *The psychology of communication.* New York: Appleton-Century-Croft, 1963.

Elkind, D. Cognition in infancy and early childhood. In Y. Brackbill (Ed.), *Infancy and early childhood.* New York: Free Press, 1967.

Elkind, D. Egocentrism in adolescence. *Child Development,* 1967, **38**, 1025–1034.

Ellis, H. *A study of British genius.* Boston: Houghton Mifflin, 1926.

Elmer, E., & Gregg, G. Developmental characteristics of abused children. *Pediatrics,* 1967, **40**, 596–602.

Engen, T., & Lipsitt, L. P. Decrement and recovery of responses to olfactory stimuli in the human neonate. *Journal of Comparative and Physiological Psychology,* 1965, **59**, 312–316.

Engen, T., Lipsitt, L. P., & Kaye, H. Olfactory responses and adaptation in the human neonate. *Journal of Comparative and Physiological Psychology,* 1963, **56**, 73–77.

English, H. B., & English, A. C. *A comprehensive dictionary of psychological and psychoanalytical terms.* New York: David McKay, 1958.

Erikson, E. H. *Childhood and society.* New York: Norton, 1950.

Erikson, E. H. In B. Schaffner (Ed.), *Group Process.* New York: Josiah Macy, Jr., Foundation, 1956.

Erikson, E. H. Growth and crises of the healthy personality. *Psychological Issues,* 1959, **1**, 50–100.

Escalona, S., & Heider. *Prediction of outcome.* New York: Basic Books, 1959.

Espenschade, A. Motor development. In W. R. Johnson (Ed.), *Science and Medicine of Exercise and Sports.* New York: Harper & Row, 1960.

Etaugh, C. Effects of maternal employment upon children: A review of recent research. Paper presented at the biennial meeting of the Society for Research in Child Development, Philadelphia, 1973.

Etaugh, C., & Harlow, H. School attitudes and performances of elementary school children as related to teacher's sex and behavior. Paper presented at the annual meeting of the Society for Research in Child Development, Philadelphia, March 1973.

Evans, E. D. *Contemporary influences in early childhood education.* New York: Holt, Rinehart & Winston, 1971.

Eysenck, H. J., & Prell, D. B. The inheritance of neuroticism: An experimental study. *Journal of Mental Science,* 1951, **97**, 441–465.

Fagen, J. F., Fantz, R. L., Miranda, S. B. Infants attention to novel stimuli as a function of post-natal and conceptual age. Paper presented at the meeting of the Society for Research in Child Development, Minneapolis, 1971.

Fantz, R. L. Pattern vision in young infants. *Psychological Record*, 1958, **8**, 43–47.

Fantz, R. Pattern vision in newborn infants. *Science*, 1963, **140**, 246–297.

Fantz, R. Visual perception from birth as shown by pattern selectivity. In H. E. Whipple (Ed.), *New issues in infant development.* Annals of the New York Academy of Sciences, 1965, **118**, 793–814.

Farquhar, J. W. Prognosis for babies born to diabetic mothers in Edinburgh. *Archives of Diseases in Childhood*, 1969, **44**, 36.

Faust, M. S. Developmental maturity as a determinant in prestige of adolescent girls. *Child Development*, 1960, **31**, 173–184.

Feffer, M. H. The cognitive implications of role taking behavior. *Journal of Personality*, 1959, **27**, 152–168.

Feffer, M. H., & Gourevitch, V. Cognitive aspects of role-taking in children. *Journal of Personality*, 1960, **28**, 383–396.

Feinberg, M. R., Smita, M., & Schmidt, R. An analysis of expressions used by adolescents at varying economic levels to describe accepted and rejected peers. *Journal of Genetic Psychology*, 1958, **93**, 133–148.

Ferguson, G. A. On learning and human ability. *Canadian Journal of Psychology*, 1954, **8**, 95–112.

Ferguson, G. A. On transfer and the abilities of man. *Canadian Journal of Psychology*, 1956, **10**, 121–131.

Ferreira, A. J. The pregnant woman's emotional attitude and its reflection on the newborn. *American Journal of Orthopsychiatry*, 1960, **30**, 553–561.

Ferretti, F. *The great American marble book.* New York: Workman Publishing, 1973.

Field, M. S., & Flynn, K. L. Worker, mother, housewife: Soviet women today. In D. R. Brown (Ed.), *Role and status of women in the Soviet Union.* New York: Teachers College Press, 1968. Pp. 7–56.

Fiske, E. B. Can fear be a substitute for ethical insight? *New York Times*, Nov. 18, 1973.

Flanagan, G. L. *The first nine months of life.* New York: Simon & Schuster, 1962.

Flanders, N. A., & Havumaki, S. The effect of teacher-pupil contacts involving praise on the sociometric choices of students. *Journal of Educational Psychology*, 1960, **51**, 65–68.

Flaste, R. Helping handicapped into education's mainstream. *New York Times*, May 19, 1974, p. E7.

Flavell J. *The developmental psychology of Jean Piaget.* New York: Van Nostrand, 1963.

Flavell, J. H. Role-taking and communication skills in children. *Young Children*, 1966, **21**(3), 164–177.

Fleming, T. J., & Fleming, A. *Develop your child's creativity.* Associated Press, 1970.

Fomon, S. A pediatrician looks at early nutrition. *Bulletin of the New York Academy of Medicine*, 1971, **47**, 569–578.

Frank, A. *The diary of a young girl.* New York: Doubleday, 1952.

Frasier, S. D., & Rallison, M. L. Growth retardation and emotional deprivation: Relative resistance to treatment with human growth hormone. *Journal of Pediatrics*, 1972, **80**, 603.

Freedman, D. G. Genetic influences on development of behavior. In G. B. S. Storring & J. J. Nander Werfften Bosch (Eds.), *Normal and abnormal development of behavior.* Leiden, The Netherlands: Luden University Press, 1971.

Freud, A. *The ego and the mechanism of defense.* New York: International Universities Press, 1946.

Freud, S. Infantile feeding disturbances, vol. II., *Psychoanalytic Study of the Child*, 1946, **2**, 120.

Freud, S. *The ego and the id.* London: Hogarth Press, 1947.

Freud, S. Some psychological consequences of the anatomical distinction between the sexes. In *Collected papers*, vol. V. London: Hogarth, 1950. Pp. 186–197.

Freud, S. *Inhibitions, symptoms, and anxiety.* London: Hogarth, 1959. Pp. 77–178.

Freud, S. *A general introduction to psychoanalysis.* New York: Washington Square Press, 1960.

Friedman, C. J., Sibinga, M. S., Stersel, I. M., & Baker, E. C. An objective approach to measurement of interpersonal behavior in phenylketonuria. *Journal of Consulting and Clinical Psychology*, 1971, **37**, 224–227.

Friedman, S. B. The need for intensive follow-up of abused children. In C. H. Kempe & R. E. Helfer (Ed.), *Helping the battered child and his family.* Philadelphia: Lippincott, 1972.

Friedrick, D. *A primer for developmental methodology.* Minneapolis: Burgess Publishing, 1972.

Frisch, R. E. Weight at menarche: Similarity for well-nourished and undernourished girls at differing ages, and evidence for historical constancy. *Pediatrics*, 1972, **50**(3), 445–450.

Frisk, M., Tenhunen, T., Widholm, O., & Hortling, H. Psychological problems in adolescents showing advanced or delayed physical maturation. *Adolescence*, 1966, **1**(2), 126–140.

Gaer, E. P. Children's understanding and production of sentences. *Journal of Verbal Learning and Verbal Behavior*, 1969, **8**, 289–294.

Galton, F. *Hereditary genius.* Macmillan, London, & Appleton, 1869.

Garbarino, J. A note on the effects of television viewing. In U. Bronfenbrenner (Ed.), *Influences on human development.* Hinsdale, Ill. Dryden Press, 1972.

Gardner, H. *The quest for mind.* New York: Knopf, 1973.

Garai, J. E., & Scheinfeld, A. Sex differences in mental and behavioral traits. *Genetic Psychology Monographs*, 1968, **77**, 169–299.

Garn, S. Growth and development. In E. Ginzberg (Ed.), *The nation's children.* New York: Columbia University Press, 1966. Pp. 24–42.

Garn, S. M. Body size and its implications. In L. W. Hoffman & M. L. Hoffman (Eds.), *Review of child development research*, vol. II. New York: Russell Sage Foundation, 1966.

Geber, M. Development psychomoteur de l'enfant Africain. *Courier*, 1956, **6**, 17–29.

Geber, M. Longitudinal study and psychomotor development among Baganda children. *Proceedings of the XIV International Congress of Applied Psychology*, 1962, **3**, 50–60.

Geber, M., & Dean, R. F. A. The state of development of newborn African children. *Lancet*, 1957, **1**, 1216–1219.

Gedda, L. *Twins in history and science.* Springfield, Ill.: Thomas, 1961.

Geiger, K. *The family in Soviet Russia.* Cambridge: Harvard University Press, 1968.

Gentry, E. F., & Aldrich, C. A. Rooting reflex in the newborn infant: Incidence and effect on it of sleep. *American Journal of Diseases of Children*, 1948. **75**, 528–539.

Gesell, A. Maturation and infant behavior patterns. *Psychological Review*, 1929, **36**, 307–319.

Gesell, A. The genesis of behavior form in fetus and infant: The growth of the mind from the standpoint of developmental morphology. *Proceedings of the American Philosophical Society*, 1941, **84**, 471–488.

Gesell, A., & Amatruda, C. S. *Developmental diagnosis.* (2d ed.) New York: Hoeber-Harper, 1947.

Gesell, A., & Ames, L. The development of handedness. *Journal of Genetic Psychology*, 1947, **70**, 155–175.

Getzels, J. W. Preschool education. *Teacher's College Record*, 1966, **68**(3), 219–228.

Gewirtz, H. B., & Gewirtz, J. L. Caretaking settings, background events, and behavior differences in four Israeli child-rearing environments: Some preliminary trends. In B. M. Foss (Ed.), *Determinants of infant behavior, IV.* London: Methuen, 1968.

Gil, D. *Violence against children.* Cambridge, Mass.: Harvard University Press, 1970.

Gilmore, J. B. The role of anxiety and cognitive factors in children's play behavior. *Child Development*, 1966, **37**, 397–416.

Ginsberg, H., & Opper, S. *Piaget's theory of intellectual development.* Englewood Cliffs, N.J.: Prentice-Hall, 1969.

Glueck, S., & Glueck, E. *Unraveling juvenile delinquency.* New York: Commonwealth Fund, 1950.

Goertzel, V., & Goertzel, M. G. *Cradles of eminence.* Boston: Little, Brown, 1962.

Gohesman, I. I. Heritability of personality: A demonstration. *Psychological Monographs*, 1963, **77**(9), 572.

Goldberg, S., & Lewis, M. Play behavior in the year-old infant: Early sex differences. In J. Bardwick (Ed.), *Readings on the psychology of women.* New York: Harper & Row, 1972.

Golden, M., & Birns, B. Social class and cognitive development in infancy. *Merrill-Palmer Quarterly of Behavior and Development*, 1968, **14**, 139–149.

Goldman, R. K. Psychosocial development in cross-cultural perspective: A new look at an old issue. *Developmental Psychology*, 1971, **5**(3), 211–419.

Goldschmid, M. L., & Bentler, P. M. The dimensions and measurement of conservation. *Child Development*, 1968, **39**, 787–815.

Goldstein, I., & Wexler, D. Rosette formation in the eyes of irradiated human embryos. *Archives of Opthomology*, 1931, **5**, 591.

Goode, W. J. Postdivorce economic activities. *After divorce.* New York: Free Press, 1956.

Goodpasture, E. W. Virus infection of the mammalian fetus. *Science*, 1942, **99**, 391–396.

Gordon, S. *The sexual adolescent.* North Scituate, Mass.: Duxbury Press, 1973.

Gorer, J. *Himalayan Village: An account of the Lepchas of Sikkim.* London: Michael Joseph, 1938.

Gottesman, I. I. Differential inheritance of the psychoneuroses. *Eugenics Quarterly*, 1962, **9**, 223–227.

Gottesman, I. I. Personality and natural selection. In S. G. Vandenberg (Ed.), *Methods and goals in human behavior genetics.* New York: Academic Press, 1965, Pp. 63–80.

Gottesman, I. I., & Shields, J. Schizophrenia in twins: 16 years consecutive admission to a psychiatric clinic. *British Journal of Psychiatry*, 1966, **112**, 809–818.

Gould, R. E. What we don't know about homosexuality. *New York Times Magazine*, Feb. 24, 1974.

Govatos, L. A. Relationships and age differences in growth measures and motor skills. *Child Development*, 1959, **30**, 333–340.

Government of Israel, Central Bureau of Statistics. *Statistical Abstract of Israel*, 1973, no. 24.

Graham, L., Ernhard, C. B., Thurston, D., & Craft, M. Development three years after perinatal anoxia and other potentially damaging newborn experiences. *Psychological Monographs*, 1962, **76**(3) (Whole No. 522), 1–51.

Graham, F. G., Matarazzo, R. G., & Caldwell, B. G. Behavioral differences between normal and traumatized newborns. *Psychological Monograph*, 1956, **70**(5), 427–438.

Gratch, G., & Landers, W. F. Stage IV of Piaget's theory of infants' object concepts: A longitudinal study. *Child Development*, 1971, **42**, 359–372.

Greenberg, D. J., Hillman, D., & Grice, D. Infant and stranger variables related to stranger anxiety in the first year of life. *Developmental Psychology*, 1973, **9**(2), 207–212.

Greenberg, S. B. Attitudes toward increased social, economic and political participation by women as reported by elementary and secondary students. Paper presented to AERA Convention Chicago, 1972.

Greenfield, P. On culture and conservation. In J. S.

Bruner et al. (Eds.), *Studies in cognitive growth.* New York: Wiley, 1966.

Greenstein, J. Father characteristics and sex-typing. *Journal of Personality and Social Psychology*, 1966, **3**, 271–277.

Gregg, N. M. A. Congenital cataract following German measles. *Treanse of Ophthalmic Society of Australia*, 1941, **3**, 35.

Gregory, D. *nigger.* Dutton, New York: 1964.

Griffiths, R. *The abilities of babies.* New York: Exposition, 1954.

Grimwade, J. C., Walker, D. W., & Word, C. Sensory stimulation of the human fetus. *Australian Journal of Mental Retardation*, 1970, **1**, 63–64.

Grinder, R. & Spector, J. C. Sex differences in adolescents' perceptions of parental resource control. *Journal of Genetic Psychology*, 1965, **106**, 337–344.

Grossmann, B., & Wrighter, J. The relationship between selection-rejection and intelligence, social status, and personality amongst sixth grade children. *Sociometry*, 1948, **11**, 346–355.

Group for the Advancement of Psychiatry. *Normal Adolescence.* New York: Scribner's 1968.

Grumbach, M. M., & Ducharme, J. R. The effects of androgens of fetal sexual development. *Fertility and Sterility*, 1960, **11**, 157–180.

Guilford, J. P. Three faces of intellect. *American Psychologist*, 1959, **14**, 469–479.

Gutteridge, M. A study of motor achievement of young children. *Archives of Psychology*, 1939, 244.

Guttmacher, A. F. *Pregnancy and Birth.* New York: Signet, 1956.

Hagman, R. R. A study of fears of children of preschool age. *Journal of Experimental Education*, 1932, **1**, 110–130.

Haimowitz, N. R. Developmental patterns: Birth to five years. In H. L. Haimowitz & N. R. Haimowitz (Eds.), *Human development: Selected readings.* New York: Crowell, 1973.

Haire, D. The cultural warping of childbirth. *International Childbirth Education Association News*, 1972, 35.

Hall, J. S. *Adolescence.* New York: Appleton, 1901.

Halverson, H. M. An experimental study of prehension in infants by means of systematic cinema record. *Genetic Psychology Monographs*, 1931, **10**, 107–286.

Harlow, H. F. The nature of love. *American Psychologist*, 1958, **13**, 673–685.

Harlow, H. F. Primary affectional patterns in primates. *American Journal of Orthopsychiatry*, 1960, **30**, 676–684.

Harlow, H. F. The development of affectional patterns in infant monkeys. In B. M. Foss (Ed.), *Determinants of infant behavior*, vol. 1. London: Methuen & Co., 1961. Pp. 75–88.

Harlow, H. F. Effects of early experiences on personal-social, sexual, and maternal behavior. Paper presented at the biennial meeting of the Society for Research in Child Development, Berkeley, Calif., April 1963.

Harlow, H. F., & Harlow, M. K. A study of animal affection. *Natural History*, 1961, **70**, 48–55.

Harlow, H. F., & Harlow, M. K. The effect of rearing conditions on behavior. *Bulletin of the Menninger Clinic*, 1962, **26**, 213–224.

Harlow, H. F., & Zimmerman, R. R. Affectional responses in the infant monkey. *Science*, 1959, **130**, 421–432.

Harmin, M., & Simon, S. B. Values. In Simon, S. B., & Kirschenbaum, H. (Eds.), *Readings in values clarification.* Minneapolis, Minn: Winston, 1973.

Harrell, R. F., Woodyard, E., & Gates, A. The effect of mothers' diets on the intelligence of the offspring. New York: Bureau of Publications, Teacher's College, 1955.

Harris, L. Survey: What people think of their high schools. *Life*, 1969, **66**, 22–23.

Harrison, A., & Nadelman, L. Conceptual tempo and inhibition of movement in black preschool children. *Child Development*, 1972, **43**, 657–668.

Hartley, R. E. Sex-role pressures and the socialization of the male child. *Psychological Reports*, 1959, **5**, 457–468.

Hartup, W. H. Peer relations. In T. D. Spencer & N. Kass (Eds.), *Perspectives in child psychology: Research and review.* New York: McGraw-Hill, 1970.

Hartup, W. W., & Coates, B. Imitation of a peer as a function of reinforcement from the peer group and rewardingness of the model. *Child Development*, 1967, **38**, 1003–1016.

Hartshorne, H., & May, M. A. *Studies in the nature of character: Vol. I, Studies in deceit; Vol. II, Studies in self-control; Vol. III, Studies in the organization of character.* New York: Macmillan, 1928–1930.

Hartshorne, J., & May, M. A. *Studies in service and self-control.* New York: Macmillan, 1928–1930.

Hauck, B. B. Differences between the sexes at puberty. In E. D. Evans (Ed.), *Adolescents: Reading in behavior and development.* Hinsdale, Illinois: Dryden Press, 1970.

Haynes, H., Whites, B. L., & Held, R. Visual accommodation in human infants. *Science*, 1965, **148**, 528–530.

Healy, W., & Bronner, A. *New light on delinquency and its treatment.* New Haven: Yale University Press, 1936.

Hebb, D. O. A neuropsychological theory. In S. Koch (Ed.), *Psychology: A study of a science*, vol. 1. New York: McGraw-Hill, 1959. Pp. 622–643.

Heckel, R. V. The effects of fatherlessness on the preadolescent female. *Mental Hygiene*, 1963, **47**, 69–73.

Helfer, R. M. The etiology of child abuse. *Pediatrics*, 1973, **51**(4), 777–779.

Helmreich, R. Birth order effects. *Naval Research Reviews*, 1968, **21**.

Henly, W. L., & Fitch, B. R. Newborn narcotic withdrawal associated with regional enteritis in pregnancy. *New York Journal of Medicine*, 1966, **66**, 2565–2567.

Hennessee, J. A. & Nicholson, J. NOW says: TV commercials insult women. *New York Times Magazine*, May 28, 1972.

Herbst, A. L., Kurman, R. J., Scully, R. E., & Poskanzer, D. C. Clear-cell adenocarcinoma of the genital tract in young females. *The New England Journal of Medicine*, December 21, 1972, **287**(25), 1259–1264.

Herbst, A. L., Ulfelder, H., & Poskanzer, D. C. Adenocarcinoma of the vagina. *The New England Journal of Medicine*, 1971, **284**(16), 878–881.

Herndon, J. *The way it spozed to be.* New York: Simon & Schuster, 1968.

Herzog, E., & Sudia, C. E. Fatherless homes: A review of research. *Children*, 1968, **15**, 177–182.

Hess, R. D., & Shipman, V. C. Early experiences and the socialization of cognitive modes in children. *Child Development*, 1965, **36**, 869–886.

Heston, L. L. Psychiatric disorders in foster-home-reared children of schizophrenic mothers. *British Journal of Psychiatry*, 1966, **112**, 819–825.

Hetherington, E. M. Effects of paternal absence on sex-typed behaviors in Negro and White preadolescent males. *Journal of Personality and Social Psychology*, 1966, **4**(1), 87–91.

Hetherington, E. M. Sex typing, dependency, and aggression. In T. D. Spencer & N. Kass (Eds.), *Perspectives in child psychology: Research review.* New York: McGraw-Hill, 1970.

Hetherington, E. M. Effects of father absence on personality development in adolescent daughters. *Developmental Psychology*, 1972, **7**(3), 313–326.

Hiernaux, J. Ethnic differences in growth and development. *Eugenics Quarterly*, 1968, **15**, 12–21.

Hillman, D., & Bruner, J. S. Infant sucking in response to variations in schedules of feeding reinforcement. *Journal of Experimental Child Psychology*, in press February 1971.

Hirsch, J. Can we modify the number of adipose cells? *Postgraduate Medicine*, 1972, **51**(5), 83–86.

Hodes, H. Colostrum: A valuable source of antibodies. *Obstetrics-Gynecology Observer*, 1964, **3**, 7.

Hoehn, A. J. A study of social class differentiation in the classroom behavior of nineteen third grade teachers. *Journal of Social Psychology*, 1954, **39**, 269–292.

Hoffman, M. L. Identification and conscience development. *Child Development*, 1971, **42**, 1071–1082.

Hoffman, L. W. Effects of maternal employment on the child. *Child Development*, 1961, **32**, 187–197.

Hoffman, M. L. Moral development. In P. H. Mussen (Ed.), *Carmichael's manual of child psychology.* New York: Wiley, 1970.

Hoffman, M. L. Father absence and conscience development. *Developmental Psychology*, 1971, **4**(3), 400–406.

Holden, C. TV violence: Government study yields more evidence, no verdict. *Science*, 1972, **175**, 608–611.

Holland, J. L. Explorations of a theory of vocational choice: Part 1. Vocational images and choice. *Vocational Guidance Quarterly*, 1963, **11**, 232–239.

Holland, J. L. Explorations of a theory of vocational choice: Part II. Self-descriptions and vocational preferences. *Vocational Guidance Quarterly*, 1963, **12**, 17–24.

Hollingshead, A. *Elmstown's youth: The impact of social classes on youth.* New York: Wiley, 1949.

Holmes, F. An experimental investigation of a method of overcoming children's fears. *Child Development*, 1936, **7**, 6–30.

Homosexuality dropped as mental disorders. *American Psychological Association Monitor*, February 1974, **5**(2), 1–9.

Honzik, M. P., Macfarlane, J. W., & Allen, L. The stability of mental test performance between two and 18 years. *Journal of Experimental Education*, 1948, **17**, 309–323.

Hooker, D. *The prenatal origin of behavior.* University of Kansas Press, 1953.

Horn, J. L. Intelligence—why it grows, why it declines. *Transaction*, 1967, **5**(1), 23–31.

Horn, J. L. Organization of abilities and the development of intelligence. *Psychological Review*, 1968, **75**, 242–259.

Horn, J. L. Organization of data on lifespan development of human abilities. In L. R. Goulet & P. B. Baltes (Eds.), *Life-span developmental psychology: Theory and research.* New York: Academic Press, 1970.

Horner, M. The motive to avoid success and changing aspirations of college women. *Women on campus: 1970 a Symposium*, Ann Arbor, Mich.: Center for the continuing education of women, 1970.

Horowitz, S. L., & Hixon, E. H. *The nature of orthodontic diagnosis.* St. Louis: C. V. Mosby, 1966.

Houston, S. H. The study of language: Trends and positions. In J. Eliot (Ed.), *Human development and cognitive processes.* New York: Holt, Rinehart, & Winston, 1971.

Howard, R. G., & Brown, A. M. Twinning: A marker for biological insults. *Child Development*, 1970, **41**(2), 519–530.

Howe, F. Sexism and the aspirations of women. *Phi Delta Kappan*, October 1973, **55**(2), 99–104.

Howell, M. C. Employed mothers and their families. *Pediatrics*, 1973, **52**(2), 252–263.

Howell, M. C. Effects of maternal employment on the child. *Pediatrics*, 1973, **52**(3), 327–343.

Huang, L. J. A re-evaluation of the primary role of the Communist Chinese woman: The homemaker or the worker. *Marriage and Family Living*, May 1963, 162–168.

Hunt, J. McV. *Intelligence and experience.* New York: Ronald Press, 1951.

Hunt, J. McV. *Intelligence and experience.* New York: Ronald Press, 1961.

Hunt, W. A., Clarke, F. M., & Hunt, E. B. From the moro reflex to the nature startle pattern. In Y. Brackbill & G. Thompson (Eds.), *Behavior in infancy and early childhood.* New York: Free Press, 1967, Pp. 134–140.

Hutt, C. *Males and females.* Middlesex, England: Penguin Books, 1972.

Hutt, S. J., Lenard, H. G., & Prechtl, H. F. R. Psychophysiology of the newborn. In L. P. Lipsitt & H. W. Reese (Eds.), *Advances in child development and behavior.* New York: Academic Press, 1969.

Illsley, R. Significance of class differences to child-bearing. In S. A. Richardson & A. F. Guttmacher (Eds.), *Childbearing—Its social and psychological aspects.* Baltimore: Williams and Wilkins, 1967. Pp. 82–86, 105–106.

Infants walks alone earlier if reflex is stimulated by exercise. *Pediatric News*, 1972, 6(10), 25–26.

Ingelman-Sundberg, A., & Wersen, C. *A child is born.* New York: Dell, 1965.

Inhelder, B., & Piaget, J. *The growth of logical thinking from childhood to adolescence.* New York: Basic Books, 1958.

Inouye, E. Similar and dissimilar manifestations of obsessive-compulsive neuroses in monozygotic twins. *American Journal of Psychology*, 1965, 121, 1171–1175.

Iriwin, D. M., & Moore, S. G. The young child's understanding of social justice. *Developmental Psychology*, 1971, 5(3), 406–410.

Irwin, O. C. Effect of strong light on the body activity of newborns. *American Journal of Physiology*, 1941, 32, 233–236.

Irwin, O. C., & Weiss, L. A. Differential variations in the activity and crying of the newborn infant under different intensities of light: A comparison of observational with polygraph findings. *University of Iowa Studies of Child Welfare*, 1934a, 9, 139–147.

Irwin, O. C., & Weiss, L. A. The effects of clothing on the general and vocal activity of the newborn infant. *University of Iowa Studies of Child Welfare.* 1934b, 9, 151–162.

Irwin, O. C., & Weiss, L. A. The effect of darkness on the activity of newborn infants. *University of Iowa Studies of Child Welfare*, 1934c, 9, 165–175.

Irwin, T. First child? Second child? Middle child? Last child? Only child? What's the Difference? *Today's Health*, October 1969, p. 26.

Iscoe, I., Williams, M., & Harvey, J. Age, intelligence, and sex as variables in the conformity behavior of Negro and white children. *Child Development*, 1964, 35, 451–460.

Jacobs, J., & Teicher, J. D. Broken homes and social isolation in attempted suicides of adolescence. *International Journal of Social Psychiatry*, 1967, 13, 139–149.

Jacobson, C. Association between LSD in pregnancy and fetal defects. Personal communication to T. B. Brazelton from C. S. Jacobson, 1969.

Jacobson, C. B., & Berlin, C. M. Possible reproductive detriment in LSD users. J.A.M.A., Dec. 11, 1972, 222(11), 1367–1373.

Jarvik, L. F., Kallman, F. J., & Klaber, N. M. Changing intellectual functions in senescent twins. *Acta Genetic Statistica Medica*, 1957, 7, 421–430.

Jelliffe, D., & Jelliffe, E. The uniqueness of human milk: An overview. *American Journal of Clinical Nutrition*, 1971, 24, 1013–1024.

Jelliffe, D. B., & Jelliffe, E. F. P. *Fat babies: Prevalence, perils and prevention.* London, Incentive Press, 1974.

Jersild, A. T. Characteristics of teachers who are "liked best" and "disliked most." *Journal of Experimental Education*, 1940, 9, 139–151.

Jersild, A. T. Emotional development. In L. Carmichael (Ed.), *Manual of Child Psychology.* New York: Wiley, 1946.

Jersild, A. T. *In search of self.* New York: Columbia University Press, 1952.

Jersild, A. T. *Child psychology* (6th ed.). Englewood Cliffs, N.J.: Prentice-Hall, 1968.

Jersild, A., & Holmes, F. Children's fears. *Child Development Monograph*, 1935, 20.

Jersild, A., & Holmes, F. Children's fears. *Child Development Monograph*, 1935, 29.

Jersild, A. T., Markey, F. V., & Jersild, C. L. Children's fears, dreams, wishes, daydreams, likes, dislikes, pleasant and unpleasant memories. *Child Development Monograph*, 1933, 12.

Johnson, A. Juvenile delinquency. In S. Arieti (Ed.), *American handbook of psychiatry.* New York: Basic Books, 1959.

Johnson, D. L. The influence of social class and race on language test performance and spontaneous speech of preschool children. Paper presented at the biennial meeting of the Society for Research in Child Development, Philadelphia, 1973.

Johnson, H. R., Myhre, S. A., Ruvalcaba, R. H. A., Thuline, H. C., & Kelley, V. C. Effects of testosterone on body image and behavior in Klinefelter's syndrome: A pilot study. *Developmental Medicine and Child Neurology*, 1970, 12, 454–460.

Johnston, C. Berkeley group offers pressure valve for troubled parents. *Healthnews*, Dec. 1973, 1(6), 9.

Johnston, C. M., & Deisher, R. W. Contemporary communal child rearing: A first analysis. *Pediatrics*, 1973, 52(3), 319–326.

Jones, E. T. Needs of Negro youth. In G. D. Winter &

E. M. Nuss (Eds.), *The young adult: Identity and awareness.* Glenview, Ill.: Scott, Foresman, 1969.

Jones, K. L., & Smith, D. W. Recognition of the fetal alcohol syndrome in early infancy. *Lancet*, 1973, 11, 999.

Jones, K. L., Smith, D. W., Ulleland, C. N., & Streissguth, A. P. Pattern of malformation in offspring of chronic alcoholic mothers. *Lancet*, 1973, 1(7815), 1267–1271.

Jones, M. C. The later careers of boys who were early or late maturing. *Child Development*, 1957, 28, 113–128.

Jones, M. C., & Mussen, P. H. Self-conceptions, motivations, and interpersonal attitudes of early- and late-maturing girls. *Child Development*, 1958, 29, 491–501.

Jost, H., & Sontag, L. The genetic factor in autonomic nervous system function. *Psychosomatic Medicine*, 1944, 6, 308–310.

Kagan, J. The child's perception of the parent. *Journal of Abnormal and Social Psychology*, 1956, 53, 257–258.

Kagan, J. The concept of identification. *Psychological Review*, 1958, 65(5), 296–305.

Kagan, J. Acquisition and significance of sex typing and sex role identity. In M. L. Hoffman & L. W. Hoffman (Eds.), *Review of child development research*, vol. 1. New York: Russell Sage Foundation, 1964.

Kagan, J. Impulsive and reflective children: Significance of conceptual tempo. In J. D. Krumboltz (Ed.), *Learning and the educational process.* Chicago: Rand McNally, 1965.

Kagan, J. Personality development. In I. L. Janis (Ed.), *Personality dynamics, development, and assessment.* New York: Harcourt, Brace & World, 1969.

Kagan, J., Hoskin, B., & Watson, S. Child's symbolic conceptualization of parents. *Child Development*, 1961, 32, 625–636.

Kagan, J., & Kogan, N. Individual variation in cognitive processes. In P. H. Mussen (Ed), *Carmichael's manual of child psychology.* New York: Wiley, 1970.

Kagan, J., & Lemkin, I. The child's differential perception of parental attributes. *Journal of Abnormal and Social Psychology*, 1960, 61, 440–447.

Kagan, J., & Moss, H. A. The stability of passive and dependent behavior from childhood through adulthood. *Child Development*, 1960, 31, 577–591.

Kagan, J., Moss, H. A., & Sigel, I. E. Psychological significance of styles of conceptualization. In J. C. Wright & J. Kagan (Eds.), *Basic cognitive processes in children: Monographs of the Society for Research in Child Development*, 1963, 28(2), 82, 73–112.

Kagan, J., Rosman, B. L., Day, D., Albert, J., & Phillips, W. Information processing in the child: Significance of analytic and reflective attitudes.

Psychological Monographs, 1964, 78(1, Whole No. 578), 1–37.

Kallman, F. J. *Heredity in health and mental disorder.* New York: Norton, 1953.

Kalnins, J. V. & Bruner, J. S. The coordination of visual observation and instrumental behavior in early infancy. *Perception*, 1974.

Kaplan, E., & Kaplan, G. The prelinguistic child. In J. Eliot (Ed.), *Human Development and Cognitive Processes.* New York: Holt, Rinehart, & Winston, 1971.

Karmel, B. Z. The effects of age, complexity and amount of contour on pattern preferences in human infants. *Journal of Experimental Child Psychology*, 1972, 4.

Karnes, M. B., Teska, J. A., Hodgins, A. S., & Badger, E. D. Educational intervention at home by mothers of disadvantaged infants. *Child Development*, 1970, 41, 925–935.

Katz, L. Research on open education: Problems and issues. In D. D. Hearn, J. Burdin, & L. Katz (Eds.), *Current research and perspectives in open education.* Washington: E/K/N/E, 1972.

Kawi, A., & Pasamanick, B. The association of factors of pregnancy with the development of reading disorders in childhood. *Journal of the American Medical Association*, 1958, 166, 1420–1423.

Kaye, H. The conditioned Babkin reflex in human newborns. *Psychonomic Science*, 1965, 2, 287–288.

Kaye, H. E. Lesbian relationships. *Sexual Behavior*, April 1971, 80–87.

Kempe, C. H. A practical approach to the protection of the abused child and rehabilitation of the abusing parent. *Pediatrics*, 1973, 51(4), 804–808.

Keniston, K. Heads and seekers: Drugs on campus, counter-cultures, and American Society. *The American Scholar*, Winter 1968–69, 38(1).

Kennedy, W. A. School phobia: Rapid treatment of fifty cases. *Journal of Abnormal Psychology*, 1965, 70, 285–289.

Kennedy, W. A. *Child psychology.* Englewood Cliffs, N.J.: Prentice-Hall, 1971.

Kephart, W. M. *The Oneida community.* Boston: Houghton Mifflin, 1966.

Kessen, W. Research in the psychological development of infants: An overview. *Merrill-Palmer Quarterly of Behavior and Development*, 1963, 9, 83–94.

Kessen, W., Haith, M. M., Salapatek, P. H. Human infancy: A bibliography and guide. In P. H. Mussen (Ed.), *Carmichael's Manual of Child Psychology*, vol. I. New York: Wiley, 1970. Pp. 287–445.

Kessen, W., & Leutzendorff, A. M. The effect of non-nutritive sucking in movement in the human newborn. *Journal of Comparative and Physiological Psychology*, 1963, 56, 69–72.

Keyserling, M. D. *Windows on day care.* New York: National Council of Jewish Women, 1972.

Kimble, G. A. Hilgard and Marques' conditioning

and learning. (2d ed.) New York: Appleton-Century-Crofts, 1961.

Kinch, R. A. H. Some sociomedical aspects of the adolescent pregnancy. Paper presented to the Sixth World Congress of Gynecology & Obstetrics, New York, Apr. 14, 1970.

Kinnie, E. J., & Sternlof, R. E. The influence of nonintellectual factors on the I.Q. scores of middle- and lower-class children. *Child Development*, 1971, **42**, 1989–1995.

Kinsey, A. C., Pomeroy, W. B., & Martin, C. E. *Sexual behavior in the human male*. Philadelphia: Saunders, 1948.

Kirchner, E. P., & Vondracek, S. I. What do you want to be when you grow up? Vocational choice in children aged three to six. Paper presented at the biennial meeting of the Society for Research in Child Development, 1973.

Klaus, M. H., Kennell, J. H., Plumo, N., & Zuehlke, S. Human maternal behavior at the first contact with her young. *Pediatrics*, 1970, **46**(2), 187–192.

Klein, C. *The single parent experience*. New York: Walker, 1973.

Knobloch, H., & Pasamanick, B. Predicting intellectual potential in infancy. *American Journal of the Diseases of Children*, 1963, **107**(1), 43–51.

Koch, H. L. Sissiness and tomboyishness in relation to sibling characteristics. *Journal of Genetic Psychology*, 1956, **88**, 231–244.

Kohen-Raz, R. Mental and motor development of kibbutz, institutionalized, and home-reared infants in Israel. *Child Development*, 1968, **39**, 489–504.

Kohlberg, L. Moral development and identification. In H. W. Stevenson (Ed.), *Child Psychology*. University of Chicago Press, 1963. Pp. 277–332.

Kohlberg, L. Development of moral character and moral ideology. In M. Hoffman & L. Hoffman (Eds.), *Review of child development research*. New York: Russell Sage Foundation, 1964.

Kohlberg, L. A cognitive-developmental analysis of children's sex-role concepts and attitudes. In E. E. Maccoby (Ed.) *The development of sex differences*. Stanford, Calif.: Stanford University Press, 1966. Pp. 82–173.

Kohlberg, L. The child as a moral philosopher. *Psychology Today*, 1968, **2**(4), 25–30.

Kohlberg, L., Yeager, J., & Hjertholm, E. Private speech: Four studies and a review of theories. *Child Development*, 1968, **39**, 691–736.

Kon, S. K., & Cowie, A. T. (Eds.) *Milk: The mammary gland and its secretion*. New York, Academic Press, 1961.

Konner, M. J. Newborn walking: Additional data. *Science*, 1973, **179**, 307.

Korner, A. Neonatal startles, smiles, erections and reflexes as related to state, sex and individuality. *Child Development*, 1969, **40**, 1039–1053.

Kotelchuck, M. The nature of the infant's tie to his father. Paper presented at the meeting of the Society for Research in Child Development, Philadelphia, March 29–April 1, 1973.

Kraft, I. Child rearing in the Soviet Union. *Children*, 1966, **12**(5), 235–238.

Kraft, I. Some observations of Kibbutz children. *Children*, 1965, **13**(5), 195–197.

Kratochwill, T., & Goldman, J. Developmental changes in children's judgments of age. *Developmental Psychology*, 1973, **9**, 358–362.

Kretschmer, E. *Physique and character*. New York: Harcourt, 1925.

Kreutzer, M., & Charlesworth, W. R. Infant recognition of emotions. Paper presented at the biennial meeting of The Society for Research in Child Development, Philadelphia, 1973.

Kron, R. E., Stern, M., & Goddard, K. E. Newborn sucking behavior affected by obstetric sedation. *Pediatrics*, 1966, **37**, 1012–1016.

Kuffler, P. *It is time to learn: A survey of children's learning from birth to 6 years*. American Toy Institute, New York, 1969.

Lacey, J., & Lacey, I. The relationship of resting autonomic activity to motor impulsivity. *Research Publication of the Association for Research on Nervous and Mental Diseases*, 1958, **36**, 144–209.

Lamper, C., & Eisdorfer, C. Prestimulus activity level and responsivity in the neonate. *Child Development*, 1971, **42**, 465–471.

Lang, C. The real difference between the sexes: An interview by Cynthia Lang with Jerome Kagan, Ph.D. *Parents' Magazine*, 1973, **XLVIII**(9).

Langer, J. *Theories of development*. New York: Holt, Rinehart, & Winston, 1969.

Laycock, F., & Caylor, J. S. Physiques of gifted children and their less gifted siblings. *Child Development*, 1964, **35**, 63–74.

Lederberg, J. Humanics and genetic engineering. *Britannica Yearbook of Science and the Future*, 1970.

Lee, R. V. What about the right to say "no"? *New York Times Magazine*, Sept. 16, 1973.

Lehtovaara, A., Saarinen, P., & Jarvinen, J. *Psychological studies of twins: I. GSR reactions*. Psychological Institute, University of Helsinki, 1965.

Leichty, M. M. Family attitudes and self-concept in Vietnamese and U.S. children. *American Journal of Orthopsychiatry*, 1963, **33**, 38–50.

Leifer, A. D. Television and the development of social behavior. Paper presented at the meeting of the International Society for the Study of Behavior Development, Ann Arbor, Mich., August 1973.

Leifer, A. D., Leiderman, P. H., Barnett, C. R., & Williams, J. A. Effects of mother-infant separation on maternal attachment behavior. *Child Development*, 1972, **43**, 1203–1218.

LeMasters, E. E. Parents without partners. In *Parents in modern America*. Homewood, Ill.: Dorsey, 1970. Pp. 157–174.

Lenard, H. G., von Bernuth, H., & Prechtl, H. F. R. Reflexes and their relationship to behavioral state in the newborn. *Acta Paediatrica*, 1968, **57**, 177–185.

Lennard, H. L. and Associates. *Mystification and drug misuse.* New York: Jossey-Bass, 1971.

Lenneberg, E. H. *Biological functions of language.* New York: Wiley, 1967.

Lenz, W. Malformations caused by drugs in pregnancy. *American Journal of Diseases of Children*, 1966, **112**, 99–106.

Lesser, G. S., Fifer, G., & Clark, D. H. Mental abilities of children from different social-class and cultural groups. *Monographs of the Society for Research in Child Development*, 1965, **30**(12), 1–115.

Levenstein, P. Cognitive growth in preschoolers through verbal interaction with mothers. *American Journal of Orthopsychiatry*, 1970, **40**(3), 426–432.

Levy, B., & Stacey, J. Sexism in the elementary school: A backward and forward look. *Phi Delta Kappan*, October 1973, **55**(2), 105–109.

Levy, D. M. *Maternal overprotection.* New York: Norton, 1966.

Lewin, K., Lippitt, R., & White, R. K. Patterns of aggressive behavior in experimentally created "social climates." *Journal of Social Psychology*, 1939, **10**, 271–299.

Lewis, M. Sex typing within the opening months of life: Mother-infant interaction. Washington, 1972.

Lickona, T. An experimental test of Piaget's theory of moral development. Paper presented at the meeting of the Society for Research in Child Development, 1973.

Lidz, T. *The person: His development throughout the life cycle.* New York: Basic Books, 1968.

Lieberman Research, Inc. The teenager looks at cigarette smoking. American Cancer Society, September 1969.

Liebert, R. M., & Baron, R. A. Some immediate effects of televised violence on children's behavior, *Developmental Psychology*, 1972, **6**(3), 469–475.

Liebert, R. M., Poulos, R. W., & Strauss, G. *Developmental psychology.* Englewood Cliffs, N.J.: Prentice-Hall, 1974.

Life. The new fathers. July 14, 1972, **73**(2), 68.

Lilienfeld, A. M., & Parkhurst, E. A study of the association of the factors of pregnancy and partrution with the development of cerebral palsey. *American Journal of Hygiene*, 1951, **53**, 262.

Lilienfeld, A. M., & Pasamanick, B. Association of maternal and fetal factors with the development of epilepsy. I. Abnormalities in the prenatal and paranatal periods. *Journal of the American Medical Association*, 1954, **155**, 719.

Lilienfeld, A. M., & Pasamanick, B. The Association of prenatal and paranatal factors with the development of cerebral palsy and epilepsy. *American Journal of Obstetrics and Gynecology*, 1955, **70**, 93.

Lindeman, B. *The twins who found each other.* New York: Morrow, 1969.

Ling, B. C. I. A genetic study of sustained visual fixation and associated behavior in the human infant from birth to six months. *Journal of Genetic Psychology*, 1942, **61**, 227–277.

Lipman-Blumen, J. How ideology shapes women's lives. *Scientific American*, 1972, pp. 34–42.

Lipsitt, L. P., Engen, T., & Kaye, H. Developmental changes in the olfactory threshold of the neonate. *Child Development*, 1963, **34**, 371–376.

Lipsitt, L. P., & Levy, N. Electrotactual threshold in the neonate. *Child Development*, 1959, **30**, 547–554.

Lipton, E. L., & Steinschneider, A. Studies on the psychophysiology of infancy. *Merrill-Palmer Quarterly*, 1964, **10**, 102–117.

Lipton, E. L., Steinschneider, A., & Richmond, J. B. A study of the sensitivity of newborn infants to stimulation: Evaluation by means of autonomic and somatic responses. *American Journal of Diseases of Children*, 1961, **102**, 537.

Lipton, E. L., Steinschneider, A., & Richmond, J. B. Auditory discrimination in the newborn infant. *Psychosomatic Medicine*, 1963, **25**, 490.

Lipton, E., & Steinschneider, A. Studies on the psychophysiology of infancy. *Merrill-Palmer Quarterly*, 1964, **10**, 102–117.

Lipton, E. L., Steinschneider, A., & Richmond, J. B. The autonomic nervous system in early life. *New England Journal of Medicine*, 1965, **273**, 201–208.

Long, B. H., Henderson, E. H., & Ziller, R. C. Developmental changes in the self-concept during middle childhood. *Merrill-Palmer Quarterly*, 1967, **13**, 201–215.

Looft, W. R. Children's judgment of age. *Child Development*, 1971, **42**, 1282–1284.

Looft, W. R. Toward a history of life-span developmental psychology. Unpublished manuscript, University of Wisconsin, 1971.

Looft, W. R., Rayman, J. R., & Rayman, B. Children's judgments of age in Sarawak. *Journal of Social Psychology*, 1972, **86**, 181–185.

Lorenz, K. Comparative study of behavior. In C. H. Schiller (Ed.), *Instinctive behavior.* New York: International University Press, 1957.

Louria, D. B. *The drug scene.* New York: McGraw-Hill, 1968.

Lovell, K. Some recent studies in cognitive and language development. *Merrill-Palmer Quarterly*, 1968, **14**, 123–127.

Lubchenco, L. O. et al. Sequelae of premature birth. *American Journal of Diseases of Children*, 1963, **106**, 101–115.

Luckey, E., & Nass, G. A comparison of sexual attitudes and behavior in an international sample. *Journal of Marriage and the Family*, 1969, **31**, 364–379.

Luria, A. *The role of speech in the regulation of normal* *and abnormal behavior.* New York: Pergamon, 1961.

Lyle, J. G. Certain antenatal, perinatal, and developmental variables and reading retardation in middle-class boys. *Child Development*, 1970, **41**, 481–491.

Lynn, D. B., & Sawrey, W. L. The effects of father-absence on Norwegian boys and girls. *Journal of Abnormal and Social Psychology*, 1959, **59**, 258–262.

Maccoby, E. *The development of sex differences.* Stanford, Calif.: Stanford University Press, 1966.

Maccoby, E., & Master, J. Attachment and dependency. In P. H. Mussen (Ed.), *Carmichael's Manual of Child Psychology.* New York: Wiley, 1971.

Maier, H. W. *Three theories of child development.* New York: Harper and Row, 1969.

Mann, I. *The development of the human eye.* (3d ed.) New York: Grune & Stratton, 1964.

Manosevitz, M., Prentice, N. M., & Wilson, F. Individual and family correlates of imaginary companions in preschool children. *Developmental Psychology*, 1973, **8**(1), 72–79.

Marijuana and health: Latest government findings. *U.S. News and World Report.* Feb. 21, 1972, **72**(8), 75.

March of Dimes. *Leaders alert.* Bulletin no. 26–A.

Marquis, D. P. Can conditioned responses be established in the newborn infant? *Journal of Genetic Psychology*, 1931, **39**(4), 479–492.

Marshall, H. R., & McCandless, B. R. Relationship between dependence on adults and social acceptance by peers. *Child Development*, 1957, **28**(4), 413–419.

Mason, S. Ross Laboratories, Columbus, Ohio, Mar. 28, 1973. Personal communication.

Masters, W. H., & Johnson, V. E. *Human sexual response.* Boston: Little, Brown, 1966.

Matheny, A. P. Genetic determinants of the Ponzo illusion. *Psychonomic Science*, 1971, **24**, 155–156.

Maw, W. H., & Maw, E. W. Self-concepts of high- and low-curiosity boys. *Child Development*, 1970, **41**, 123–129.

Mayer, F. A. *History of educational thought.* Columbus: Merrill, 1960.

Mayer, J. Fat babies grow into fat people. *Family Health*, 1973, **5**(3), 24–26.

Maynard, J. *Looking back: A chronicle of growing up old in the sixties.* Garden City, N.Y.: Doubleday, 1973.

McCallon, E. L. Self-ideal discrepancy and the correlates sex and academic achievement. *Journal of Experimental Education*, 1967, **35**, 45–49.

McCaskill, C. L., & Wellman, B. A study of common motor achievements at the preschool ages. *Child Development*, 1938, **9**, 141–150.

McClearn, G. E. Genetics and behavior development. In M. Hoffman & L. Hoffman (Eds.), *Review of child development research*, vol. 1. New York: Russell Sage Foundation, 1964.

McDermott, J. F. Divorce and its psychiatric sequelae in children. *Archives of General Psychiatry*, 1970, **23**(5), 421–427.

McDonald, R. L., & Christakos, A. C. Relationship of emotional adjustment during pregnancy in obstetrical complications. *American Journal of Obstetrics and Gynecology*, 1963, **86**, 341–348.

McGlothlin, W. H., & West, L. J. The marijuana problem: An overview. *American Journal of Psychiatry*, 1968, **125**, 126–134.

McGraw, M. B. Swimming behavior of the human infant. *Journal of Pediatrics*, 1939, **15**, 485–490.

McGraw, M. B. Suspension grasp behavior of the human infant. *American Journal of the Diseases of Children*, 1940, **60**, 799–811.

McGraw, M. B. Neural maturation as exemplified in achievement of bladder control. *Journal of Pediatrics*, 1940, **16**, 580–589.

McKennon, C., Koyske, J. E., & Apland, R. The effect of social reinforcement on the performance of one-year-old children. *Psychonomic Science*, 1971, **23**(4), 313–315.

McNeill, D. The creation of language. *Discovery*, 1966, **27**, 34–35.

McPhee, R. Personal Communication, Nov. 15, 1966.

Mead, M. *Sex and temperament in three primitive societies.* New York: Morrow, 1935.

Mead, M. *Growing Up in New Guinea.* New York, Mentor, 1953.

Mead, M. *Coming of age in Samoa.* New York: Morrow, 1961.

Mead, M., & Newton, N. Fatherhood. In S. A. Richardson & A. F. Guttmacher (Eds.), *Childbearing—Its social and psychological aspects.* Baltimore: Williams and Wilkins, 1967. Pp. 189–192.

Mednick, S. A., & Schulsinger, F., Children of schizophrenic mothers. *Bulletin de l'Association Internatione de Psychologie Appliquee*, 1965, **14**, 11–27.

Meredith, H. V. Body size of contemporary groups of eight-year-old children studies in different parts of the world. *Monograph of the Society for Research in Child Development*, 1969, **34**(1).

Mestyan, G., & Varga, F. Chemical thermoregulation of full-term and premature newborn infants. *Journal of Pediatrics*, 1960, **56**, 623–629.

Metraux, A. Ethnology of Easter Island. *Bernice P. Bishop Museum Bulletin*, 1971, 160, 1–432.

Meyer, W. J., & Thompson, G. G. Sex differences in the distribution of teacher approval and disapproval among sixth grade children. *Journal of Educational Psychology*, 1956, **47**, 385–396.

Millar, T. P. The child who refuses to attend school. *The American Journal of Psychiatry*, 1961, **118**(5), 398–404.

Miller, G. A. *Language and communication.* New York: McGraw-Hill, 1951.

Miller, N., & Zimbordo, P. G. Motives for fear-induced affiliation: Emotional comparison or interpersonal similarity. *Journal of Psychology*, 1966, **34**, 481–503.

Minuchin, P. Sex-role concepts and sex typing in childhood as a function of school and home environments. *Child Development*, 1965, **36**, 1033–1048.

Mittler, P. Psycholinguistic skills in four-year-old twins and singletons. PhD. thesis, University of London, 1969.

Mittler, P. Biological and social aspects of language development in twins. *Developmental Medicine and Child Neurology*, 1970, **12**, 741–757.

Mittler, P. *The study of twins.* Baltimore: Penguin, 1971.

Mizner, G. L., Barter, J. T., & Werme, P. H. Patterns of drug use among college students. *American Journal of Psychiatry*, 1970, **127**, 15–24.

Mock, R., & Tuddenham, R. Race and conformity among children. *Developmental Psychology*, 1971, **4**, 349–365.

Money, J. Cytogenetic and psychosexual incongruities with a note on space-form blindness. *American Journal of Psychiatry*, 1963, **1A**, 820–827.

Money, J. Cognitive defects in Turner's syndrome. Second invitational conference on human behavior genetics. Louisville, Ky., 1966.

Money, J., Ehrhard, A., & Masica, D. N. Fetal feminization induced by androgen insensitivity in the testicular feminizing syndrome: Effect on marriage and maternalism. *Johns Hopkins Medical Journal*, 1968, **123**, 105–114.

Money, J., Hampson, J. G., & Hampson, J. L. An examination of some basic sexual concepts: The evidence of human hermophroditism. *Bulletin of Johns Hopkins Hospital*, 1955, **97**, 301–319.

Money, J., & Pollitt, E. Cytogenetic and psychosexual ambiguity: Kleinfelters' Syndrome and transvestism compared. *Archives of General Psychiatry*, 1964, **11**, 589–595.

Montagu, A. Life before birth. New York: New American Library, 1964.

Montagu, A. Chromosomes and crime. *Psychology Today*, 1968, **2**(5), 43–49.

Montagu, A. *Touching: The human significance of the skin.* New York: Columbia University Press, 1971.

Montagu, M. F. A. Constitutional and prenatal factors in infant and child health. M. J. Senn (Ed.), *Symposium of the healthy personality*. New York: Josiah Macy Jr. Foundation, 1950. Pp. 148–169.

Morgan, G. A., Ricciuti, H. N. Infants' response to strangers during the first year. In B. M. Foss (Ed.), *Determinants of infant behavior*, vol. IV. London: Methuen, 1968.

Morgan, T. *Remembering Rene.* New York Times Magazine, Nov. 11, 1973, pp. 34–36.

Morland, J. A comparison of race awareness in northern and southern children. *American Journal of Orthopsychiatry*, 1966, **36**, 22–31.

Moore, A. U. Studies on the formation of the

mother-neonate bond in sheep and goats. Paper presented at the annual meeting of the American Psychological Association, 1960.

Morris, J. *Living with Lepchas: A book about the Sekkin Himalayas.* London: William Heinemann, 1938.

Morrison, J. R. & Stewart, M. A. The psychiatric status of the legal families of adopted hyperactive children. *Arch Gen Psychiatry*, 1973, **28**, 888–891.

Moss, H. A. Sex, age, and state as determinants of mother-infant interaction. *Merrill-Palmer Quarterly of Behavior and Development*, 1967, **13**(1), 19–36.

Moss, H. A., & Kagan, J. Maternal influences on early IQ score. *Psychological Reports*, 1958, **4**, 655–661.

Moss, H. A., Robson, K. S., & Pederson, F. Determinants of maternal stimulation of infants and consequences of treatment of later reactions to strangers. *Developmental Psychology*, 1969, **1**(3), 239–246.

Mowrer, O. H. *Learning theory and the symbolic processes.* New York: Wiley, 1960.

Moya, F., & Thorndike, V. Passage of drugs across the placenta. *American Journal of Obstetrics and Gynecology*, 1962, **84**, 1778–1798.

Mukerji, R. Roots in early childhood for continuous learning. *Young Children*, 1965, **20**(6).

Mulford, R. M., & Cohen, M. I. Psychosocial characteristics of neglecting parents. In *Neglecting parents: A study of psychosocial characteristics*. Material presented at the meeting of the American Humane Association Children's Division. Dallas, May 25, 1967.

Mull, M. M. The tetracyclines. *American Journal of Diseases of Children*, 1966, **112**, 483–493.

Murchison, C., & Langer, S. Tiedemann's observations on the development of the mental facilities of children. *Journal of Genetic Psychology*, 1927, **34**, 205–230.

Murdock, G. Comparative data on the division of labor by sex. *Social Forces*, 1937, **15**, 551–553.

Murphy, C. M., & Bootzin, R. R. Active and passive participation in the contact desensitization of snake fear in children. *Behavior Therapy*, 1973, **4**, 203–211.

Murphy, D. P. The outcome of 625 pregnancies in women subjected to pelvic radium reontgen irradiation. *American Journal of Obstetrics and Gynecology*, 1929, **18**, 179–187.

Murphy, D. P. *Congenital malformation.* (2d ed.) Philadelphia: University of Pennsylvania Press, 1947.

Mussen, P., and Disteer, L. Masculinity, identification and father-son relationships. *Journal of Abnormal and Social Psychology*, 1959, **59**, 350–356.

Mussen, P. H. Early sex-role development. In D. A. Goslin (Ed.), *Handbook of socialization theory and research*. Chicago: Rand McNally, 1969.

Mussen, P. H., Conger, J. J., & Kagen, J. *Child*

development and personality. New York: Harper & Row, 1969.

Mussen, P. H., & Jones, M. C. Self-conceptions, motivations, and interpersonal attitudes of late- and early-maturing boys. *Child Development*, 1957, **28**, 243–256.

Muuss, R. E. *Theories of adolescence.* New York: Random House, 1968.

Muuss, R. E. Puberty rites in primitive and modern societies. *Adolescence*, 1970, **5**, 109–128.

Muuss, R. E. Adolescent development and the secular trend. *Adolescent*, 1970, **5**, 267–284.

Naeye, R. L., Blanc, W., & Paul, C. Effects of maternal nutrition on the human fetus. *Pediatrics*, 1973, **52**(4), 494–503.

National Center for Educational Statistics. *Preprimary enrollment.* October 1972.

National Clearinghouse for Smoking & Health. Patterns and prevalence of teen-age cigarette smoking: 1968, 1970, and 1972. U.S. Dept. of Health, Education, & Welfare, Aug. 6, 1972, publication No. (HSM) 73-8701.

National Foundation/March of Dimes. *Science News*, January 1972, unpaged.

National Foundation/March of Dimes. Alcoholism and birth defects. *Science News*, August 1973, unpaged.

National Foundation/March of Dimes *Genetic counseling.* New York, 1973.

Nemy, E. Where disturbed parents find help. New York Times, Mar. 15, 1972.

Newman, H. H., Freeman, F. H., & Holzinger, K. J. *Twins: A study of heredity and environment.* Chicago: University of Chicago Press, 1937.

Newsweek. The teen-agers. Mar. 21, 1966, pp. 57–72.

Newsweek. The drug generation: Growing up younger. Apr. 21, 1969, 107–108.

Newton, N. *Maternal Emotions,* New York: Paul B. Hoeber, Inc., Medical Book Department of Harper & Row, 1955.

Newton, N. *The family book of child care.* New York: Harper & Row, 1957.

Newton, N. Childbirth and culture. *Psychology Today*, 1970, **4**(6), 74–75.

Nichols, W. W., Levan, A., Hall, B., Ostergren, G. Measles—associated chromosomal breakage: Preliminary communication. *Hereditas*, 1962, **48**, 367–370.

Nine out of ten "DES babies" have vaginal adenosis. *Medical World News*, 1973, **11**(9), 17–19.

Northway, M. L. Outsiders: A study of the personality patterns of children least acceptable to their age mates. *Sociometry*, 1944, **7**, 10–25.

Nunnally, J. C. *Psychometric theory.* New York: McGraw-Hill, 1967.

Nyquist, E. B., & Hawes, G. R. (Eds.) *Open education: A sourcebook for parents and teachers.* New York: Bantam, 1972.

O'Grady, D. R., Berry, H. K., & Sutherland, B. S.
Phenylketonuria: Intellectual development and early treatment. *Developmental Medicine and Child Neurology*, 1970, **12**, 343–347.

Olds, S. What we do—and don't—know about miscarriage. *Today's Health*, February, 1971, pp. 42–45.

Olds, S. W. & Eiger, M. S. *The complete book of breastfeeding.* New York: Bantam Books, 1973.

Olds, S., & Witt, L. Fathers in the delivery room. *Today's Health*, October 1970, pp. 52–56.

Ontogeny of perception. In A. M. Schrier, H. F. Harlow, & F. Stollnitz (Eds.), *Behavior of nonhuman primates*, vol. II. New York: Academic Press, 1965. Pp. 365–403.

Oppel, W. C., Harper, P. A., & Rider, R. V. The age of attaining bladder control *Pediatrics*, October 1968, **42**(4), 614–626.

Oppie, I., & Oppie, P. *The lore and language of the school child.* Oxford: Clarendon, 1959.

Ottinger, D. R., & Simmons, J. E. Behavior of human neonates and prenatal maternal emotions. *Psychological Reports*, 1964, **14**, 391–394.

Otto, H., & Healy, S. Adolescents' self-perception of personality strengths. *Journal of Human Relations*, 1966, **14**(3), 483–490.

Palmer, R. H., Ouellette, M. D., Warner, L., & Leichtman, S. R. Congenital malformations in offspring of a chronic alcoholic mother. *Pediatrics*, 1974, **53**(4), 490–494.

Palmisano, P., & Cassidy, G. Aspirin linked to diminished binding capacity in neonates. *Psychiatric Herald*, Jan. 10, 1969, 1–7.

Papousek, H. A method of studying conditioned food reflexes in young children up to age six months. *Pavlovian Journal of Higher Nervous Activity*, 1959, **9**, 136–140.

Papousek, H. Conditioned motor alimentary reflexes in infts: I. Experimental conditioned sucking reflex. *Cesk. Pediatr.*, 1960a, **15**, 861–872.

Papousek, H. Conditioned motor alimentary reflexes in infants: II. A new experimental method of investigation. *Cesk. Pediatr.*, 1960b, **15**, 981–988.

Papousek, H. Conditioned head rotation reflexes in infants in the first month of life. *Acta Pediatrica*, 1961, **50**, 565–576.

Parmelee, A. H., Jr., Brück, K., & Bruck, M. Activity and inactivity cycles during sleep of premature infants exposed to neutral temperature. *Biologia Neonatorum*, 1962, **4**, 317–339.

Parten, M. Social play among preschool children. *Journal of Abnormal and Social Psychology*, 1932, **27**, 243–269.

Pasamanick, B., & Knobloch, H. Early feeding and birth difficulties in childhood schizophrenia: An explanatory note. *Journal of Psychology*, 1963, **56**, 73–77.

Pasamanick, B., & Knobloch, H. Epidemiological studies of the complications of pregnancy and the birth process. In G. Caplan (Ed.), *Prevention of* *mental disorders in childhood.* New York: Basic Books, 1961.

Pasamanick, B., & Knobloch, H. Retrospective studies on the epidemeology of reproductive casualty: Old and new. *Merrill-Palmer Quarterly of Behavior and Development,* 1966, **12**(1), 7–26.

Pasamanick, B., & Lilienfeld, A. M. Association of maternal and fetal factors with the development of mental deficiency. I. Abnormalities in the prenatal and paranatal periods. *Journal of the American Medical Association,* 1955, **159**, 155.

Pasamanick, B., Rogers, M., & Lilienfeld, A. Pregnancy experience and the development of behavior disorders in children. *American Journal of Psychiatry,* 1956, **112**, 613–618.

Passow, A. H. Education of the culturally deprived child. In J. Hellmuth (Ed.), *Disadvantaged child,* vol. 1. New York: Brunner/Mazel, 1967. Pp. 149–159.

Pauker, J. D. Fathers of children conceived out of wedlock: Prepregnancy, high school, psychological test results. *Developmental Psychology,* 1971, **4**(2), 215–218.

Pavlov, I. P. *Conditioned reflexes.* New York: Liveright, 1927.

Pedersen, F., & Robson, K. Father participation in infancy. *American Journal of Orthopsychiatry,* 1969, **39**, 466–472.

Pedersen, F. A., Rubenstein, J., & Yarrow, L. J. Father absence in infancy. Paper presented at the meeting of the Society for Research in Child Development, Philadelphia, March 29–April 1, 1973.

Pedersen, F. A., & Wender, P. H. Early social correlates of cognitive functioning in six-year-old boys. *Child Development,* 1968, **39**, 185–194.

Peiper, A. *Cerebral function in infancy and childhood.* Translated by B. Nagler & H. Nagler from the 3d German edition original publication, 1961. New York: Consultant Bureau, 1963.

Perkins, H. V. Factors influencing change in children's self-concepts. *Child Development,* 1958, **29**, 221–230.

Perlman, R. Antisocial behavior of the minor in the United States. *Federal Probation,* 1964, **28**(4), 23–27.

Peters, D. L., Hendrikson, J., Marcus, R., & Redley, P. Defining day care goals: A preliminary study. The Pennsylvania Day Care Study Project. Technical Report No. 5. June 1, 1972.

Peterson, D. R., Quay, H. C., & Tiffany, T. L. Personality factors related to juvenile delinquency. *Child Development,* 1961, **32**, 355–372.

Petri, E. Untersuchungen zur erbedingtheit der menarche. *Z. Morph. Anthr.,* 1934, **33**, 43–48.

Pettigrew, T. F. Negro American intelligence. In T. F. Pettigrew (Ed.), *Profile of the Negro American.* Princeton, N.J.: D. Van Nostrand, 1964. Pp. 100–135.

Phillips, B. N. Age changes in accuracy of self-perceptions. *Child Development,* 1963, **34**, 1041–1046.

Piaget, J. *Judgment and reasoning in the child.* New York: Harcourt Brace, 1926.

Piaget, J. *Judgment and reasoning in the child.* New York: Harcourt, Brace, 1928.

Piaget, J. *The child's conception of the world.* New York: Harcourt, Brace, 1929.

Piaget, J. *The child's conception of physical causality.* London: Kegan Paul, 1930.

Piaget, J. *Play, dreams, and imitation.* (Translated by C. Gattegno and F. M. Hodgson.) New York: Norton, 1951.

Piaget, J. *The child's conception of number.* London: Routledge & Kegan Paul, 1952.

Piaget, J. *The origins of intelligence in children.* New York: International Universities Press, 1952.

Piaget, J. *The child's construction of reality.* London: Routledge & Kegan Paul, 1955.

Piaget, J. *The moral judgment of the child.* New York: Macmillan, 1955.

Piaget, J. *Logic and psychology.* New York: Basic Books, 1957.

Piaget, J., & Inhelder, B. *La Genèse des structures logiques elementaires: Classifications et seriations.* Neuchâtel: Delachaux et Niestlé, 1959.

Piaget, J., & Inhelder, B. *The psychology of the child.* New York: Basic Books, 1969.

Pine, G. The affluent delinquent. *Phi Delta Kappan,* 1966, **48**(4), 138–143.

Pineau, M. Poids de naissance: Variations paisonnieres, ordre de naissance, puberté, characterès physiques et tests psychologique chez des filles agies de 13 ans. *Brométrie Humaine,* 1970, **5**, 47–62.

Pines, M. Why some three-year-olds get A's—and some get C's. *The New York Times Magazine,* July 6, 1969.

Pomeroy, W. *Girls & sex.* New York: Dell, 1969.

Powell, G. F., Brasel, J. A., Beizzard, R. M. Emotional deprivation and growth retardation simulating idiopathic hypopituitarism. *New England Journal of Medicine,* 1967, **276**, 1271–1278.

Pratt, K. C. The Neonate. In L. Carmichael (Ed.), *Manual of child psychology.* (2d ed.) New York: Wiley, 1954. Pp. 215–291.

Pratt, K. C., Nelson, A. K., & Sun, K. H. *The behavior of the newborn infant.* Columbus, Ohio: Ohio State University Press, 1930.

Preble, E. The Puerto-Rican American teen-ager in New York City. In E. B. Brody (Ed.), *Minority group adolescents in the United States.* Baltimore: Williams & Wilkins, 1968. Pp. 48–72.

Prechtl, H. F. R. Problems of behavioral studies in the newborn infant. In D. S. Lehrmann, R. A. Hinde, & E. Shaw (Eds.), *Advances in the study of behavior,* vol. I. New York: Academic Press, 1965, Pp. 75–98.

Prechtl, H. F. R., & Beintema, D. J. *The neurological examination of the full-term newborn infant: Clinics in developmental medicine*, no. 12. London: Heinemann, 1964.

Prechtl, H. F. R., Theorell, K., Gramsbergen, A., & Lind, J. A statistical analysis of cry patterns in normal and abnormal newborn infants. *Developmental Medicine and Child Neurology*, 1969, **11**, 142–152.

Prescott, E., & Jones, E. (with S. Kritchevsky). *Day care as a child-rearing environment.* Washington: National Association for the Education of Young Children, 1972.

Prescott, E., Milich, C., & Jones, E. The "politics" of day care. Washington: National Association for the Education of Young Children, 1972.

The President's Commission on Law Enforcement and Administration of Justice. The challenge of crime in a free society. Washington: Government Printing Office, 1967.

Pulaski, M. A. S. *Understanding Piaget: An introduction to children's cognitive development.* New York, Harper & Row, 1971.

Rabban, M. Sex role identification in young children in two diverse social groups. *Genetic Psychology Monographs*, 1950, **42**, 81–158.

Rabin, A. I. *Growing up in the kibbutz.* New York: Springer, 1965.

Radin, N. Maternal warmth, achievement motivation, and cognitive functioning in lower-class preschool children. *Child Development*, 1971, **42**, 1560–1565.

Radin, N. Father-child interaction and the intellectual functioning of four-year-old boys. *Developmental Psychology*, 1972, 6(2), 353–361.

Radin, N. Observed paternal behaviors as antecedents of intellectual functioning in young boys. *Developmental Psychology*, 1973, 8(3), 369–376.

Raths, L. E., Harmin, M., & Simon, S. B. *Values and teaching.* Columbus, Ohio: Merrill, 1966.

Rawlings, G., Reynolds, E. O. R., Stewart, A., & Strang, L. B. Changing prognosis for infants of very low birth weight. *The Lancet*, 1971, **1**, 516–519.

Read, M. S., Habicht, J-P, Lechtig, A., & Klein, R. E. Maternal malnutrition, birth weight, and child development. Paper presented before the International Symposium on Nutrition, Growth and Development, May 21–25, 1973, Valencia, Spain.

Rebelsky, F., & Block, R. Crying in infancy. *Journal of Genetic Psychology*, 1972, 121(1), 49–57.

Rebelsky, F., & Hanks, C. Fathers' verbal interaction with infants in the first three months of life. *Child Development*, 1972, **42**, 63–68.

Reese, H. W. Relationships between self-acceptance and sociometric choices. *Journal of Abnormal and Social Psychology*, 1961, **62**, 472–474.

Reese, H. W., & Lipsitt, L. P. *Experimental Child Psychology.* New York: Academic Press, 1970.

Reinhold, R. The early years are crucial. *New York Times*, Oct. 21, 1973.

Report to the Surgeon General. *Television and growing up: The impact of televised violence.* Washington: Government Printing Office, 1972.

Reymert, M. L. Relationships between menarcheal age, behavior disorders, and intelligence. *Character and Personality*, 1940, **8**, 292–300.

Rheingold, H. L. The modification of social responsiveness in institutionalized babies. *Monograph of the Society for Research in Child Development*, 1956, **21** (Whole No. 63), 5–48.

Rheingold, H. L. The effect of environmental stimulation upon social and exploratory behavior in the human infant. In B. M. Foss (Ed.), *Determinants of infant behavior*, vol. III. New York: Wiley, 1961. Pp. 143–177.

Rheingold, H. L. The development of social behavior in the human infant. In H. W. Stevenson (Ed.), *Concept of development*, Monographs of the Society for Research in Child Development, 1966, 31(107). Pp. 1–17.

Rheingold, H. L., & Bayley, N. The later effects of an experimental modification of mothering. *Child Development*, 1959, **30**, 363–372.

Rheingold, H. L., Gewirtz, J. L., & Ross, H. W. Social conditioning of vocalization in the infant. *Journal of Comparative and Physiological Psychology*, 1959, **52**, 68–73.

Rheingold, H. R., & Eckerman, C. O. The infant separates himself from his mother. *Science*, 1970, **168**, 78–83.

Rhodes, P. Sex of the fetus in ante partum hemorrhage. *The Lancet*, 1965, **2**, 718–719.

Richards, M. P. M. Social interaction in the first week of human life. *Psychiatria, Neurologia, Neurochirugia*, 1971, **74**, 35–42.

Richards, T. W., & Nelson, V. L. Studies in mental development: II. Analyses of abilities tested at six months by the Gesell schedule. *Journal of Genetic Psychology*, 1938, **52**, 327–331.

Ritter, B. The group desensitization of children's snake phobias using vicarious and contact desensitization procedures. *Behavioral Research and Therapy*, 1968, **6**, 1–6.

Roberts, J., & Sutton-Smith, B. Child training and game involvement. *Ethnology*, 1962, **1**, 166–185.

Robson, K. S. The role of eye-to-eye contact in maternal-infant attachment. *Journal of Child Psychology and Psychiatry*, 1967, **8**, 13–25.

Roche, A. F. & Davila, G. H. Late adolescent growth in stature. *Pediatrics*, 1972, 50(6), 874–880.

Rodgers, R. R., Bronfenbrenner, U., & Devereux, E. C., Jr. Standards of social behavior among children in four cultures. *International Journal of Psychology*, 1968, III(1), 31–41.

Roff, M., & Sells, S. B. Relations between intelligence and sociometric status in groups differing in sex and socio-economic background. *Psychological Reports*, 1965, **16**, 511–516.

Rose, R. M., Gordon, T. P., & Bernstein, I. S. Plasma testosterone levels in the male rhesus: Influences of sexual and social stimuli. *Science*, 1972, **178**(4061), 643–645.

Rosefsky, J., & Petersiel, M. Perinatal deaths associated with one pivacaine paracervical block anasthesia in labor. *N.E.J. Medicine,* 1968, **278**, 530–533.

Rosen, B. C. Social class and the child's perception of the parent. *Child Development*, 1964, **35**, 1147–1153.

Rosenberg, B. G., & Sutton-Smith, B. A revised conception of masculine-feminine differences in play activities. *The Journal of Genetic Psychology*, 1960, **96**, 165–170.

Rosenblith, J. E. The modified Graham behavior test for neonates, test-retest reliability, normative data and hypotheses for future work. *Biologia Neonatorum*, 1961, **3**, 174–192.

Rosenhan, D. The kindnesses of children. *Young Children*, 1969, **25**(1).

Rosenthal, R. Self-fulfilling prophecy. In P. Cramer (Ed.), *Reading in developmental psychology today.* Del Mar, Calif.: CRM Books, 1970. Pp. 43–49

Rosenthal, R., & Jacobson, L. *Pygmalion in the classroom.* New York: Holt, Rinehart & Winston, 1968.

Rosenthal, R., & Jacobson, L. Teacher expectations for the disadvantaged. *Scientific American*, 1968, **218**(4), 19–23.

Rosner, M. Women in the kibbutz: Changing status and concepts. *Asian and African Studies*, 1967, **3**, 35–68.

Ross, A. *Psychological disorders of children.* New York: McGraw-Hill, 1974.

Ross, J. B., McLaughlin, (Eds.) *A portable medieval reader.* New York: Viking, 1949.

Rothbart, M. K., & Maccoby, E. E. Parents' differential reactions to sons and daughters. *Journal of Personality and Social Psychology*, 1966, **4**(3), 237–243.

Rubin, V., & Comitas, L. *Effects of chronic smoking of cannabis in Jamaica.* Unpublished report by the Research Institute for the Study of Man to the Center for Studies of Narcotic and Drug Abuse, National Institute of Mental Health, contract no. HSM-42-70-97.

Rugh, R., & Shettles, L. B., with Einhorn, R. N. *From conception to birth: The drama of life's beginnings.* New York: Harper & Row, 1971.

Russell, A. Progesterone is harmful to male fetus. *Pediatrics News*, January 1969.

Russell, L. B., & Russell, W. L. Radiation hazards to the embryo and fetus. *Radiology*, 1952, **58**(3), 369–376.

Rutter, M. Parent-child separation: Psychological effects on the children. *Journal of Child Psychology and Psychiatry*, 1971, **12**, 233–260.

Saint-Anne Dargassies, S. Neurological development of the infant: The contributions of André Thomas. *World Neurology*, 1960, **1**, 71–77.

Salber, E., & Feinlib, M. Breast-feeding in Boston. *Pediatrics*, 1966, **37**, 299–303.

Salk, L. The effects of the normal heartbeat sound on the behavior of the newborn infant; implications for mental health. *World Mental Health*, 1960, **12**, 168–175.

Salk, L. *Proceedings of the third world congress of psychiatry.* Canada: University of Toronto Press, 1961.

Salk, L. The role of the heartbeat in the relations between mother and infant. *Scientific American*, May 1973, pp. 24–29.

Saltz, R. Effects of part-time mothering on I.Q. and S.Q. of young institutionalized children. *Child Development*, 1973, **44**, 166–170.

Sapir, E. *Language.* New York: Harcourt, 1921.

Scarr-Salapatek, S., & Williams, M. L. The effects of early stimulation on low-birth-weight infants. *Child Development*, 1973, **44**, 94–101.

Schachter, F. F. Everyday preschool interpersonal speech usage: Developmental and sociolinguistic studies. Paper presented at the biennial meetings of the Society for Research in Child Development, Philadelphia, 1973.

Schachter, S. *The Psychology of Affiliation.* Stanford, Calif: Stanford University Press, 1959.

Schaefer, C. E. Imaginary companions and creative adolescents. *Developmental Psychology*, 1969, **1**, 747–749.

Schaefer, E. S., & Bayley, N. Maternal behavior, child behavior, and their intercorrelations from infancy through adolescence. *Monographs of the Society for Research in Child Development*, 1963, **28**(3), 1–127.

Schaeffer, D. L. *Sex differences in personality: Readings.* Belmont, Calif.: Brooks/Cole, 1971.

Schaffer, H. R., & Callender, W. M. Psychological effects of hospitalization in infancy. *Monographs of the Society for Research in Child Development*, 1964, **29**, 1–77.

Schaffer, H. R., & Emerson, P. The development of social attachments in infancy. *Monographs of the Society for Research in Child Development*, 1964, **29**(3).

Schaffer, H. R., & Emerson, P. E. Patterns of response to physical contact in early human development. *Journal of Child Psychology and Psychiatry*, 1964, **5**, 1–13.

Scheinfeld, A. *Your heredity and environment.* Philadelphia: Lippincott, 1965.

Scheinfeld, A. *Twins and supertwins.* New York: Lippincott, 1967.

Scherman, A. Cognitive goals in the nursery school. *Child Study*, 1966, **28**(2), 109.

Schifrin, B. S., & Dame, Y. Fetal heart rate patterns:

Predictions of Apgar score. *Journal of the American Medical Association*, 1972, **219**(10), 1322–1355.

Schindler-Rainman, E. Communicating with today's teenagers: An exercise between generations. *Children*, November–December 1969.

Schmitt, M. H. Superiority of breast-feeding: Fact or fancy? *American Journal of Nursing*, July 1970, pp. 1488–1493.

Schulman, C. A. Effects of auditory stimulation on heart rates in premature infants as a function of level of arousal, probability of CNS damage, and conceptional age. *Developmental Psychobiology*, 1969, **2**(3), 172–183.

Scott, J. P. *Animal behavior*. University of Chicago Press, 1958.

Scrimshaw, N. S. Malnutrition, learning and behavior. *American Journal of Clinical Nutrition*. 1967, **20**, 493–502.

Sears, R. R. Relation of early socialization experiences to self-concepts and gender role in middle childhood. *Child Development*, 1970, **41**, 267–289.

Sears, R. R., Maccoby, E. E., & Levin, H. *Patterns of child rearing*. New York: Harper & Row, 1957.

Seiden, R. H. Campus tragedy: A study of student suicide. *Journal of Abnormal Psychology*, 1966, **71**, 389–399.

Selman, R. L. A structural analysis of the ability to take another's social perspective: Stages in the development of role-taking ability. Paper presented at the meeting of the Society for Research in Child Development, 1973.

Shainess, N. "A re-evaluation of some aspects of femininity through a study of menstruation: A preliminary report. *Comprehensive Psychiatry*, 1961, **2**(1), 20–26.

Shantz, C. U., & Watson, J. S. Spatial abilities and spatial egocentrism in the young child. *Child Development*, 1971, **42**, 171–181.

Shapira, A., & Madsen, M. Between- and within-group cooperation and competition among kibbutz and nonkibbutz children. *Developmental Psychology*, 1974, **10**(1), 140–145.

Sheikh, A. A., & Beglis, J. F. Development of the self-concept in Negro and White children. Paper presented at the biennial meeting of the Society for Research in Child Development, Philadelphia, March 29–April 1, 1973.

Shenker, I. How do parents talk to their children? Two psychologists listened in. . . . *New York Times*, Oct. 10, 1971.

Shepher, J. The child and the parent-child relationship in kibbutz communities in Israel. *Assignment children*, United Nations Children's Fund, 1969, **10**, 47–71.

Sherman, M. The differentiation of emotional responses in infants. I. Judgments of emotional responses from motion picture views and from actual observations. *Journal of Comparative Psychology*, 1927, **7**, 265–284.

Sherman, M., Sherman, I., Flory, C. D. Infant behavior. *Comparative Psychology Monographs*, 1936, **12**, 1–107.

Shettles, L. B. Conception and birth sex ratios. *Obstetrics and Gynecology*, 1961, **18**, 123–127.

Shields, J. Twins brought up apart. *Eugenics Review*, 1958, **50**, 115–123.

Shipman, G. The psychodynamics of sex education. *Family Coordinator*, 1968, **17**, 3–12.

Shirley, M. M. The first two years: A study of twenty-five babies. Vol. II, *Intellectual development*. Minneapolis: University of Minnesota, 1933.

Shore, M. F. Drugs can be dangerous during pregnancy and lactation. *Canadian Pharmaceutical Journal*, December 1970.

Shuster, A. Better as is than not at all. *New York Times Magazine*, Apr. 29, 1973, p. 14ff.

Silberman, C. E. *Crisis in the classroom: The remaking of American education*. New York: Random House, 1970.

Silberman, C. E. *The open classroom reader*. New York: Random House, 1973.

Simner, M. L. Newborn's response to the cry of another infant. *Developmental Psychology*, 1971, **5**(1), 136–150.

Simon, S. B., Howe, L. W., & Kirschenbaum, H. *Values clarification*. New York: Hart, 1972.

Singer, J. E., Westphal, M., & Niswander, K. R. Sex differences in the incidence of neonatal abnormalities and abnormal performance in early childhood. *Child Development*, 1968, **39**, 103–222.

Siqueland, E. R. The development of instrumental eapeoratory behavior during the first year of human life. Paper presented at the meeting of the Society for Research in Child Development, Santa Monica, Calif., March 1969.

Siqueland, E., & Lipsitt, L. P. Conditioned head-turning behavior in the newborn. *Journal of Experimental Child Psychology*, 1966, **3**, 356–376.

Skard, A. G. Maternal deprivation: The research and its implications. *Journal of Marriage and the Family*, 1965, **27**, 333–343.

Skeels, H. M. Adult status of children with contrasting early life experiences. *Monograph of the Society for Research in Child Development*, 1966, **31** (Whole No. 3), 1–65.

Skeels, H. M., & Dye, H. B. A study of the effects of differential stimulation on mentally retarded children. *Program of the American Association of Mental Deficiency*, 1939, **44**, 114–136.

Skinner, B. F. *The behavior of organisms: An experimental approach*. New York: Appleton-Century, 1938.

Slater, E. (with Shields, J.). Psychotic and neurotic illnesses in twins. *Medical Research Council Special Report*. Series No. 278. London: HMSO, 1953.

Slater, P. Parental role differentiation. In Rose L. Coser (Ed.), *The Family: Its structure and functions*. New York: St. Martin's.

Slayton, D. J., & Ainsworth, M. D. Individual differences in infant response to brief, everyday separations as related to other infant and maternal behaviors. *Developmental Psychology*, 1973, *9*(2), 226–235.

Slovut, G. Genes called not sole schizophrenia cause. *Minneapolis Star*, Nov. 23, 1973.

Slovut, G. Mayo tests don't support "cancer-causing drug" scare. *Minneapolis Star*, Nov. 24, 1973.

Smedslund, J. Development of concrete transitivity of length in children. *Child Development*, 1963, *34*, 389–405.

Smith, B. Socialization for competence. *Social Science Research Council*, 1965, *19*, 17–25.

Smith, D. E., & Sternfield, J. C. The hippie communal movement: Effects on child birth and development. *American Journal of Orthopsychiatry*, 1970, *40*, 527–530.

Smith, D. W., & Wilson, A. A. *The child with Down's Syndrome (mongolism)*. Philadelphia: Saunders, 1973.

Smith, G. H. Sociometric study of best-liked and least-liked children. *Elementary School Journal*, 1950, *51*, 77–85.

Smith, M. B. Conflicting values affecting behavioral research with children. *Children*, 1967, *4*(5), 377–382.

Smith, M. E. An investigation of the sentence and the extent of vocabulary in young children. *University of Iowa Studies in Child Welfare*, 1926, *3*(5).

Smith, M. S. An investigation of the development of the sentence and the extent of vocabulary in young children. University of Iowa Studies in Child Welfare, 1926, *3*(5).

Smith, R. P. *"Where did you go?" "Out." "What did you do?" "Nothing."* New York: Pocket Books, 1959.

Smith, S. "Out of the ivory playpen. *Ms.*, 1974, *2*(8), 90.

Soares, A. T., & Soares, L. M. Self-perceptions of culturally disadvantaged children. *American Educational Research Journal*, 1969, *6*, 31–45.

Solkoff, N., Yaffe, S., & Weintraub, D. The effects of handling on the development of premature infants. Paper presented at the meeting of the Eastern Psychological Association Convention, Boston, 1967.

Solomon, T. History and demography of child abuse. *Pediatrics*, 1973, *51*(4), 773–776.

Sontag, L. W. Implications of fetal behavior and environment for adult personality. *Annals of the New York Academy of Science*, 1966, *134*, 782–786.

Sontag, L. W., & Harris, L. M. Evidence of disturbed prenatal and neonatal growth in bones of infants aged one month. *American Journal of Diseases of Children*, 1938, *56*, 1248–1255.

Sontag, L. W., & Richards, T. W. Studies in fetal behavior: Fetal heart rate as a behavioral indicator. *Child Development Monographs*, 1938, *3*(4).

Sontag, L., & Wallace, R. I. Preliminary report of the Fels fund: A study of fetal activity. *American Journal of Diseases of Children*, 1934, *48*, 1050–1057.

Sontag, L. W., & Wallace, R. I. The effect of cigarette smoking during pregnancy upon the fetal heart rate. *American Journal of Obstetrics, and Gynecology*, 1935, *29*, 3–8.

Sontag, L. W., & Wallace, R. I. Changes in the heart rate of the human fetal heart in response to vibratory stimuli. *American Journal of Diseases of Children*, 1936, *51*, 583–589.

Sorenson, R. C. *Adolescent sexuality in contemporary America*. New York: World, 1973.

Soviet Methods of Character Education, *American Psychologist*, 1962, *17*, 550–564.

Spearman, C. *The abilities of man*. New York: Macmillan, 1927.

Spears, W. C., & Hohle, R. H. Sensory and perceptual processes in infants. In Y. Brackbill (Ed.), *Infancy and early childhood*. New York: Free Press, 1967. Pp. 51–121.

Spiro, M. E. *Children of the kibbutz*. Cambridge: Harvard University Press, 1958.

Spitz, R. A. Hospitalism: An inquiry into the genesis of psychiatric conditioning in early childhood. In D. Fenschel et al. (Eds.), *Psychoanalytic studies of the child*, vol. 1. New York: International University Press, 1945. Pp. 53–74.

Spitz, R. A. Hospitalism: A follow-up report. In D. Fenschel et al. (Eds.), *Psychoanalytic studies of the child*, vol. 2. New York: International Universities Press, 1946. Pp. 113–117.

Spitz, R. A. The smiling response: A contribution to the ontogenesis of social relations. *Genetic Psychology Monographs*, 1946, *34*, 57–125.

Staffieri, J. R. A study of social stereotype of body image in children. *Journal of Personality and Social Psychology*, 1967, *7*, 101–104.

Stayton, D. J., Ainsworth, M. D., & Main, M. B. Development of separation behavior in the first year of life: Protest, following, and greeting. *Developmental Psychology*, 1973, *9*(2), 213–225.

Stechler, G., Bradford, S., & Levy, H. Attention in the newborn: Effect on motility and skin potential. *Science*, 1966, *151*, 1246–1248.

Steele, B. F., & Pollack, C. B. A psychiatric study of parents who abuse infants and small children. In R. E. Helfer & C. H. Kempe (Eds.), *The battered child*. University of Chicago Press, 1968.

Stein, A. Imitation of resistance to temptation. *Child Development*, 1967, *38*, 157–169.

Stein, M. I., & Heinze, S. J. *Creativity and the individual*. New York: Free Press, 1960.

Stein, Z., & Polkes, A. V. The prevention of Down's Syndrome. *Annals of Clinical Research*, 1973, *5*, 66–67.

Stein, Z. A., Susser, M. W., & Wilson, A. E. Families of enuretic children. Part I: Family type and age. *Developmental Medicine and Child Neurology*, 1965, *7*, 658–663.

Stein, Z. A., Susser, M. W., & Wilson, A. E. Families of enuretic children. Part II: Family culture, structure, and organization. *Developmental Medicine and Child Neurology*, 1965, **7**, 663–676.

Stein, Z. Susser, M., Saenger, G., & Marolla, F. Nutrition and mental performance. *Science*, 1972, **178**, 708–712.

Steinschneider, A. Developmental psychophysiology. In Y. Brackbill (Ed.), *Infancy and early childhood: A handbook and guide to human development.* New York: Free Press, 1967.

Stendler, C. B., & Young, N. Impact of first grade entrance upon the socialization of the child: Changes after 8 months of school. *Child Development*, 1951, **22**(2), 113–122.

Sternglanz, S. H., & Serbin, L. An analysis of the sex roles presented on children's television programs. Paper presented at the meeting of the Society for Research in Child Development, 1973.

Stewart, M. A. Personal communication, Apr. 12, 1974.

Stewart, M. A. & Olds, S. W. *Raising a hyperactive child.* New York: Harper & Row, 1973.

Stewart, M. A., Pitts, F. N., Craig, A. G., & Dieruf, W. The hyperactive child syndrome. *American Journal of Orthopsychiatry*, 1966, **36**, 861–867.

Stock, M. B., & Smythe, P. M. Does undernutrition during infancy inhibit brain growth and subsequent intellectual development? *Archives of the Diseases of Children*, 1963, **38**, 546–552.

Stocker, J. *Early childhood education: Current trends in school policies and programs.* Arlington, Va.: National School Public Relations Association, 1973.

Stoll, L. H., & Ball, R. S. Infant and preschool mental tests: Review and evaluation. *Monographs of the Society for Research in Child Development*, 1965, **30**(3), 151.

Stolz, H. R., & Stolz, L. M. Adolescent related to somatic variation. In N. B. Henry (Ed.), *Adolescence: 43rd yearbook of the National Committee for the Study of Education.* University of Chicago Press, 1944. Pp. 80–99.

Stone, L. J., Smith, H. T., & Murphy, L. B. *The competent infant: Research and commentary.* New York: Basic Books, 1973.

Stott, L. Physical and mental handicaps following a disturbed pregnancy. *The Lancet*, 1957, **1**, 1006–1012.

Stott, L. H., & Ball, R. S. Infant and preschool mental tests: Review and evaluation. *Monographs of the Society for Research in Child Development*, 1965, **30**(3), 4–42.

Stourvie, R. J. Inconsistent verbal instructions and children's resistance-to-temptation behavior. *Child Development*, 1971, **42**, 1517–1531.

Stouwie, R. J. Inconsistent verbal instructions and children's resistance-to-temptation behavior. *Child Development*, 1971, **42**, 1517–1531.

Strack, A. E. Drug use and abuse among youth. *Journal of Health, Physical Education, and Recreation*, 1968, **39**, 26–28, 55–57.

Strean, L. P., & Peer, L. A. Stress as an etiological factor in the development of cleft palate. *Plastic and Reconstructive Surgery*, 1956, **18**(1), 1–8.

Suchman, E. A. The "hang-loose" ethic and the spirit of drug abuse. *Journal of Health and Social Behavior*, 1968, **9**, 146–155.

Sugar, M. Children of divorce. *Pediatrics*, 1970, **46**(4), 588–595.

Sullivan, W. Boys and girls are now maturing earlier. *New York Times*, Jan. 24, 1971, pp. 1, 36.

Swan, C. Rubella in pregnancy as an aetiological factor in congenital malformation, stillbirth, miscarriage, and abortion. *Journal of Obstetrics and Gynecology of British Empire*, 1948, **56**, 341–363, 591–605.

Talmon-Garber, Y. The modern family in Israel: The kibbutz. *Marriage and Family Living*, 1954, **16**(4), 346–349.

Tank, G. Relation of diet to variation of dental carries. *Journal of the American Dental Association*, 1965, **70**, 394–403.

Tanner, J. M. The adolescent growth-spurt and developmental age. In G. A. Harrison, J. S. Werner, J. M. Tannert, & N. A. Barnicot. *Human Biology: An introduction to human evolution, variation, and growth.* Oxford: Clarendon Press, 1964. Pp. 321–339.

Tanner, J. M. Earlier maturation in man. *Scientific American*, 1968, **218**, 21–27.

Tanner, J. M. Physical growth. In P. H. Mussen (Ed.), *Carmichael's manual of child psychology* (3d ed.), vol. 1. New York: Wiley 1970.

Tanner, J. M. Growing up. *Scientific American*, 1973, **229**(3), 35–43.

Tanzer, D. (with Block, J. L.). *Why natural childbirth?* Garden City, N. Y.: Doubleday, 1972.

Tautermannova, M. Smiling in infants. *Child Development*, 1973, **44**, 701–704.

Tec, N. Some aspects of high school status and differential involvement with marihuana. *Adolescence*, 1972, **6**, 1–28.

Teicher, J., & Jacobs, J. Adolescents who attempt suicide. *American Journal of Psychiatry*, 1966, **11**, 122.

Telfer, M. A., Baker, D., Clark, G. R., & Richardson, C. E. Incidence of gross chromosomal errors among tall, criminal American males. *Science*, 1968, **159**, 1249–1250.

Templin, M. Certain language skills in children, their development and inter-relationship. Institute of Child Welfare Monographs, Minneapolis: University of Minnesota Press, 1957.

Terman, L. *Genetic studies of genius.* vol. I. Palo Alto: Stanford University Press, 1926.

Terman, L. M. Psychological approaches to the study of genius. *Papers on Eugenics*, 1947, **4**, 3–20.

Terman, L. M., & Merrill, M. A. *Measuring intel-*

ligence: A guide to the administration of the new revised Stanford-Binet tests of intelligence. Cambridge: Houghton Mifflin, 1937.

Terman, L. M., & Oden, M. H. Genetic studies of genius, V. The gifted group at mid-life. Stanford, Calif.: Stanford University Press, 1959.

Thomas, A., Chess, S., & Birch, H. G. Temperament and behavior disorders in children. New York University Press, 1968.

Thomas, A., Chess, S., Birch, H. G., Hertzig, M. E., & Korn, S. Behavioral individuality in early childhood. New York University Press, 1963.

Thorndike, E. L. Man and his works. Cambridge, Mass.: Harvard University Press, 1943.

Thurstone, L. L., & Thurstone, T. G. Factorial studies of intelligence. Psychometric Monograph, 1941, 2.

Tidyman, E. Dummy. Boston: Little, Brown, 1974.

Time. Teen-age sex: Letting the pendulum swing. Aug. 21, 1972, pp. 34–40.

Time. Sexist texts. Nov. 5, 1973, p. 66.

Time. Lefty liberation. Jan. 7, 1974, p. 85.

Timirias, P. S. Developmental physiology and aging. New York: Macmillan, 1972.

Todd, G. A., & Palmer, B. Social reinforcement of infant babbling. Child Development, 1968, **39**(2), 591–596.

Travers, R. Analysis of the characteristic of children implicit in the Montessori method. In J. L. Frost (Ed.), Early childhood education rediscovered. New York: Rinehart & Winston, 1968.

Trecker, J. L. Sex stereotyping in the secondary school curriculum. Phi Delta Kappan, October 1973, **55**(2), 110–112.

Tronick, E., Koslowski, B., & Brazelton, T. B. Neonatal behavior among urban Zambians and Americans. Presented at the biennial meeting of the Society for Research in Child Development, Minneapolis, Minn., Apr. 4, 1971.

Trowbridge, H., & Trowbridge, L. Self-concept and socio-economic status. Child Study Journal, 1972, **2**(3), 123–139.

Tuddenham, R. D. Studies in reputation: III. Correlates of popularity among elementary school children. Journal of Educational Psychology, 1951, **42**, 257–276.

Tulkin, S. R., & Kagan, J. Mother-child interaction in the first year of life. Child Development, 1972, **43**, 31–41.

Tylor, E. B. The history of games. The Fortnightly Review. London: Chapman and Hall, January 1–June 1, 1879, **25**, 735–747.

Usdan, M. D. The preparation of teachers for the disadvantaged. In J. Hellmuth (Ed.), Disadvantaged child, vol. 1. New York: Brunner/Mazel, 1967. Pp. 225–251.

U.S. Department of Health, Education and Welfare. Vital Statistics of the U.S., Public Health Service, Washington, 1967, 1969.

U.S. Department of Health, Education and Welfare.

The health consequences of smoking. Washington, 1973.

U.S. Department of Labor. Employment Standards Administration, Women's Bureau. Expanding opportunities for girls: Their special counseling needs. Washington, 1971.

1973.

Utech, D. A. Modeling, praise, and logical explanations for influencing the moral judgments of objectives and subjective boys and girls. Paper presented at the annual meeting of the Midwestern Psychological Association, Cleveland, 1972.

Uzgiris, I. Patterns of vocal and gestural imitation in infants. Paper presented at the annual meeting of the International Society for the Study of Behavioral Development, University of Nijmegen, Netherlands, July 4–8, 1971.

Uzgiris, I. C. Patterns of cognitive development in infancy. Merrill-Palmer Institute Conference on Infant Development. Detroit, February 9–12, 1972.

Uzgiris, I., & Hunt, J. McV. Unpublished manuscript, University of Illinois Psychological Development Laboratory, Urbana, N.D.

Valadian, I., Stuart, H. C., & Reed, R. B. Studies of illnesses of children followed from birth to eighteen years. Monographs of the Society for Research in Child Development, 1961, **26**, 3.

Valenti, C. The child: His right to be normal. Saturday Review, Dec. 7, 1968, 75–78.

Valsik, J. A., Stukovsky, R., & Bernàtovà, L. Quelques facteurs geographiques et sociaux ayant une influence sur l'âge de la puberté. Biotypol., 1963, **24**, 109–123.

Vandenberg, S. G. The nature and nurture of intelligence. Paper presented at conference on Biology and Behavior. Rockefeller University, 1966.

Vandenberg, S. G. Hereditary factors in normal personality traits (as measured by inventories). In J. Wortis (Ed.), Recent advances in biological psychiatry, vol. 9. New York: Plenum Press, 1967. Pp. 65–104.

Van den Daele, L. D. Modification of infant state by treatment in a rockerbox. Journal of Psychology, 1970, **74**, 161–165.

Van Leewen, J., Guthrie, R., & Stange, F. Narcotic withdrawal reaction in a newborn infant due to codeine. Pediatrics, 1965, **36**, 635–736.

Vetter, H. J. The ontogenesis of language. In H. J. Vetter, Language behavior and communication. Itasca, Ill.: F. E. Peacock, 1969. Pp. 55–65.

Visual perception and experience in early infancy: A look at the hidden side of behavior development. In H. W. Stevenson, E. H. Hess, & H. L. Rheingold (Eds.), Early behavior: comparative and developmental approaches. New York: Wiley, 1967. Pp. 181–224.

Vore, D. H. Prenatal nutrition and post-natal intellectual development. Paper presented at the annual meeting of the Society for Research in Child Development, Minneapolis, April 1971.

Voss, H., Wendling, A., & Elliott, D. Some types of high-school dropouts. *Journal of Education Research*, 1966, **59**, 363–368.

Vygotsky, L. S. *Thought and Language.* Cambridge, Mass.: M.I.T. Press, 1962.

Wagner, N. N. Adolescent sexual behavior. In E. D. Evans (Ed.), *Adolescents: Readings in behavior and development.* Hinsdale, Ill.: Dryden Press, 1970. Pp. 44–51.

Waldfogel, S., Coolidge, J. C., & Hahn, D. B. The development, meaning, and management of school phobia. *American Journal of Orthopsychiatry*, 1957, **27**, 754–780.

Waldman, E., & Grover, K. R. Children of women in the labor force. *Monthly Labor Review*, July 1971, 19–25.

Walk, R. D., & Gibson, E. J. A comparative and analytical study of visual depth perception. *Psychological Monographs*, 1961, **75**(15), 170.

Walker, R. N. Body build and behavior in young children. Body build and parent's ratings. *Child Development*, 1963, **34**, 1–23.

Wallach, L., & Sprott, R. L. Inducing number conservation in children. *Child Development*, 1964, **35**, 1057–1071.

Wallach, M., & Kogan, N. *Modes of thinking in young children: A study of the creativity-intelligence distinction.* New York: Holt, Rinehart, & Winston, 1965.

Wallach, M. A., & Kogan, N. Creativity and intelligence in children's thinking. *Transaction*, 1967, **4**(1), 38–43.

Ward, S. Television advertising and children: Needed research. Paper presented at the meeting of the Society for Research in Child Development, 1973.

Watson, E. H., & Lowrey, G. H. *Growth and development of children* (5th ed.). Chicago: Year Book Medical Publishers, 1967.

Watson, J. B. *Psychology from the standpoint of a behaviorist.* Philadelphia: Lippincott, 1919.

Watson, J. B. *The psychological care of infant and child.* New York: Norton, 1928.

Watson, J. B. *Behaviorism.* Chicago: University of Chicago Press (rev. ed.), 1958.

Watson, J. B., & Rayner, R. Conditioned emotional reactions. *Journal of Experimental Psychology*, 1920, **3**, 1–14.

Watson, J. D. *The double helix.* New York: Atheneum, 1968.

Watson, J. S. Cognitive-perceptual development in infancy: Setting for the seventies. *Merrill-Palmer Quarterly*, 1971, **17**(2), 139–152.

Watson, J. S., & Ramey, C. T. Reactions to response-contingent stimulation in early infancy. *Merrill-Palmer Quarterly of Behavior and Development*, 1972, **18**(3), 219–227.

Weber, E. Early childhood education: perspectives on change. Worthington, Ohio: Charles A. Jones, 1970.

Wechsler, D. *The measurement of adult intelligence.* Baltimore: Williams & Wilkins, 1944.

Wechsler, D. The I.Q. is an intelligent test. *The New York Times Magazine*, June 26, 1966.

Weisberg, P. Social and nonsocial conditioning of infant vocalizations. *Child Development*, 1963, **34**, 377–388.

Weitzman, L., Eifler, D., Hokada, E., & Ross, C. Sex-role socialization in picture books for preschool children. *American Journal of Sociology*, 1972, **77**(6), 1125–1150.

Werner, E., Bierman, J., French, F. E., Simonian, K., Connor, A., Smith, R., & Campbell, M. Reproductive and environmental casualties: A report on the 10-year follow-up of the children of the Kauai pregnancy study. *Pediatrics*, 1968, **42**(1), 112–127.

Werner, E. E., Honzik, M. P., & Smith, R. S. Prediction of intelligence and achievement at ten years from twenty month pediatric and psychological examinations. *Child Development*, 1968, **39**, 1063–1075.

Werner, H. *Comparative psychology of mental development.* Chicago: Follet, 1948.

Westinghouse Learning Corporation. *The impact of Head Start.* Athens, Ohio: Ohio University Press, 1969.

Weston, P. J., & Mednick, M. T. Race, social class, and the motive to avoid success in women. *Journal of Cross-Cultural Psychology*, 1971, **1**(3), 284–291.

Whipple, D. V. *Dynamics of development: Euthenic pediatrics.* New York: McGraw-Hill, 1966.

White, B. L., & Castle, P. W. Visual exploratory behavior following post-natal handling of human infants. *Perceptual and Motor Skills*, 1964, **18**, 497–502.

White House Conference on Children. *Profiles of Children.* Washington: Government Printing Office, 1970.

White House Conference on Children. *Report to the President.* Washington: Government Printing Office, 1970.

Whorf, B. L. *Language, thought, and reality.* Cambridge, Mass.: MIT Press, 1956.

Wickelgren, L. W. The ocular response of human newborns to intermittent visual movements. *Journal of Experimental Child Psychology*, 1969, **8**, 469–482.

Widmer, E. L. In kindergarten. *Elementary School Journal*, 1967.

Wiener, G. The relationship of birth weight and length of gestation to intellectual development at ages 8 to 10 years. *Journal of Pediatrics*, 1970, **76**, 694.

Willerman, L. Activity level and hyperactivity in twins. *Child Development*, 1973, **44**, 288–293.

Williams, J., & Edwards, C. An exploratory study of the modification of color and racial concept attitudes in preschool children. *Child Development*, 1969, **40**, 737–750.

Williams, M. L., & Scarr, S. Effects of short term intervention on performance in low-birth-weight, disadvantaged children. *Pediatrics*, 1971, **47**, 289–298.

Williams, T. H. *Huey Long.* New York: Knopf, 1969.

Williams, T. M. *Summary and implications of review of literature related to adolescent smoking.* Bethesda, Md.: U.S. Dept. of Health, Education, & Welfare, 1971.

Wilson, A. B. Residential segregation of social classes and aspirations of high school boys. *American Sociological Review*, 1959, **24**, 836–845.

Wilson, R. S. Twins: Early mental development. *Science*, 1972, **175**(4024), 915–917.

Wilson, R. S., & Harpring, E. B. Mental and motor development in infant twins. *Developmental Psychology*, 1972, **7**(3), 277–287.

Wingerd, J., Solomon, I. L., & Schoen, E. J. "Parent-specific height standards for preadolescent children of three racial groups, with method for rapid determination" *Pediatrics* vol. 52, no. 4, Oct., 1973 pp. 555–560.

Winick, M. Nutrition and cell growth. *Nutrition Review*, 1968, **26**, 195–197.

Winick, M., & Rosso, P. Head circumference and cellular growth of the brain in normal and marasmic children. *Journal of Pediatrics*, 1969, **74**, 774–778.

Winnick, M., & Noble, A. Cellular response with increased feeding in neonatal rats. *Journal of Nutrition*, 1967, **91**, 179–182.

Wisconsin State Journal. Marijuana use shows increase. May 13, 1974, p. 10.

Wohlford, P., Sontrock, J. W., Berger, S. E., & Liberman, D. Older brothers' influence on sex-typed, aggressive, and dependent behavior in father-absent children. *Developmental Psychology*, 1971, **4**, 124–134.

Wolfenstein, M. *Children's humor.* New York: Free Press, 1954.

Wolff, P. The causes, controls, and organizations of behavior in the newborn. *Psychological Issues*, 1966, **5**(1) (Whole No. 17), 1–105.

Wolff, P. H. Observations on the early development of smiling. In B. M. Foss (Ed.), *Determinants of infant behavior, II.* London: Methuen, 1963.

Wolff, P. H. The serial organization of sucking in the young infant. *Pediatrics*, 1968, **42**, 943–956.

Wolff, P. H. The natural history of crying and other vocalizations in early infancy. In B. Foss (Ed.), *Determinants of infant behavior IV.* London: Methuen & Co., Ltd., 1969.

Wolf, K. M. Observations of individual tendencies in the first year of life. In M. J. E. Senn (Ed.), *Problem of infancy and childhood.* New York: Josiah Macy, Jr., Foundation, 1952.

Women on Words and Images. *Dick and Jane as Victims.* Princeton, N.J.: Central New Jersey NOW, 1972.

Women's Bureau, Workplace Standards Administration, U.S. Dept. of Labor. Background facts on women workers in the United States. Washington, 1970.

Woods, M. B. The unsupervised child of the working mother. *Developmental Psychology*, 1972, **6**(1), 14–25.

World Health Organization. Genetic Counselling Technical Report No. 416, 1969, 23.

Wortis, H. Social class and premature birth. *Social casework*, 1963, **45**, 541–543.

Wortis, R. The acceptance of the concept of the maternal role by behavioral scientists: Its effect on women. *American Journal of Orthopsychiatry*, 1971, **41**(5), 733–746.

Wouk, H. *Marjorie Morningstar.* Garden City: Doubleday, 1955.

Wylie, P. *An essay on morals.* New York: Holt, Rinehart, & Winston, 1947.

Yablonsky, L. *The hippie trip.* New York: Pegasus, 1968.

Yamamoto, K. The concept of self: Introduction. In K. Yamamoto (Ed.), *The child and his image: Self-concept in the early years.* Boston: Houghton Mifflin, 1972.

Yando, R. M., & Kagan, J. The effects of task complexity on reflection-impulsivity. *Cognitive Psychology*, 1970, **1**, 192–200.

Yarrow, L. J. Research in dimensions of early maternal care. *Merrill-Palmer Quarterly of Behavior and Development*, 1963, **9**, 101–114.

Yarrow, M., et al. Child-rearing in families of working and non-working mothers. *Sociometry*, 1962, **25**, 122–140.

Yarrow, M., Waxler, C., & Scott, P. M. Child effects on adult behavior. *Developmental Psychology*, 1971, **5**(2), 300–311.

Young, H. B., & Knapp, R. P. Personality characteristics of converted left-handers. *Perceptual and Motor Skills*, 1966, **23**, 35–40.

Young, L. *Wednesday's children.* New York: McGraw-Hill, 1964.

Yudkin, S., & Holme, A. *Working mothers and their children.* London: Sphere Books, 1969.

Zacharias, L., & Wurtman, R. J. Age at menarche. *New England Journal of Medicine*, 1969, **280**, 868–875.

Zander, A., & Van Egmond, E. Relationship of intelligence and social power to the interpersonal behavior of children. *Journal of Educational Psychology*, 1958, **49**(5), 257–267.

Zelazo, P. R., Zelazo, N. A., & Kolb, S. Walking

in the newborn. *Science,* 1972, **176**(4032), 314–315.

Zelazo, P. R. Psychological development. In J. Mayer (Ed.), *Health and the patterns of life.* New York: Van Nostrand-Reinhold, in press.

Ziegel, E., & Van Blarcom, C. *Obstetric Nursing.* New York: Macmillan, 1964.

Zelnik, M., & Kantner, J. Survey of female adolescent sexual behavior. Conducted for Commission of Population, Washington, D.C. 1972.

Zimmerman, D. R. RH: The intimate history of a disease and its conquest. New York: Macmillan, 1973.

Zimmerman, P., Clark, M., & Coleman, K. Marijuana: The pot problem. *Newsweek,* July 24, 1967, 46–52.

INDEX

664